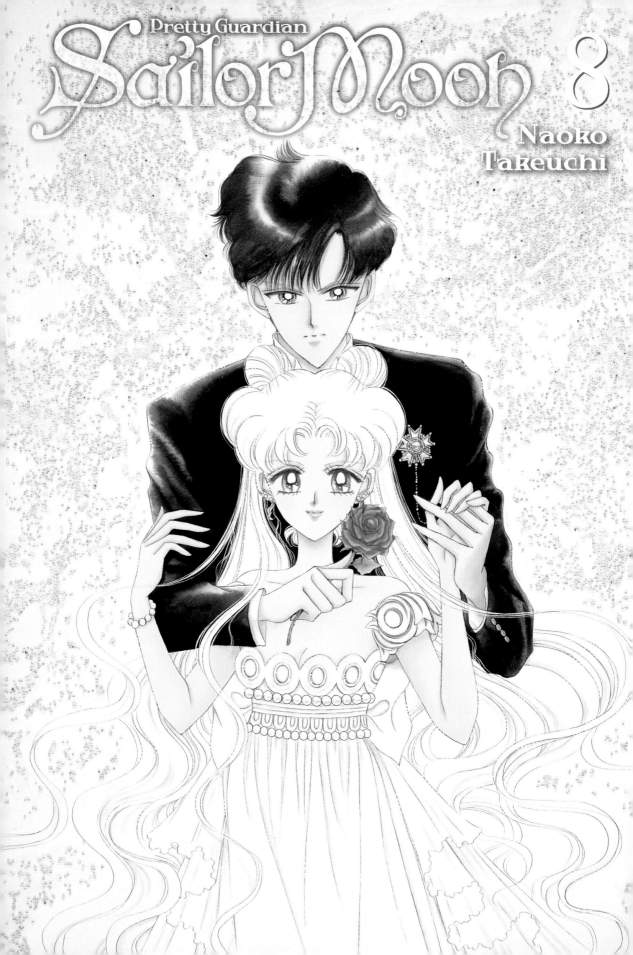

Pretty Guardian

Sailor Moon 8

Naoko Takeuchi

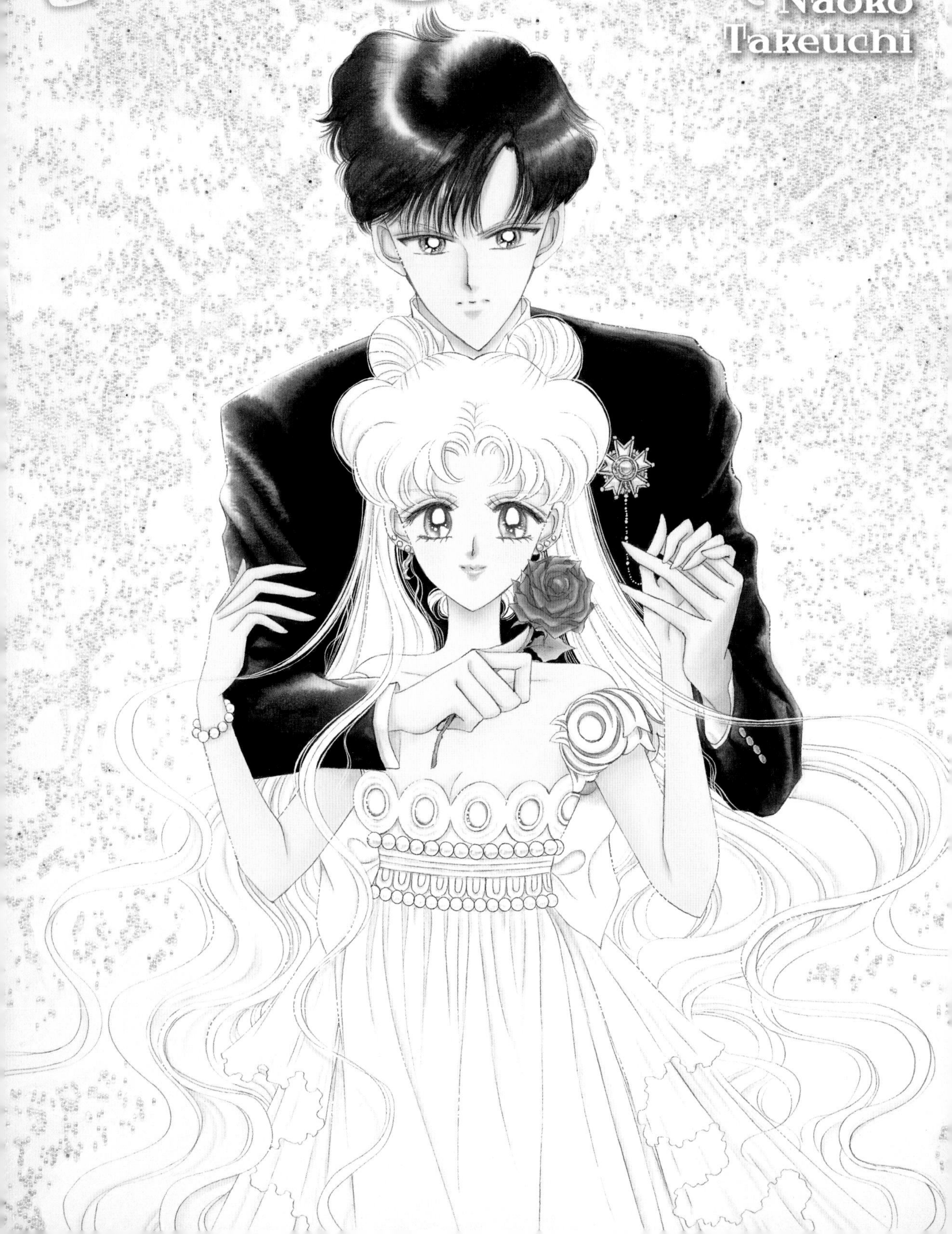

CONTENTS

Pretty Guardian Sailor Moon

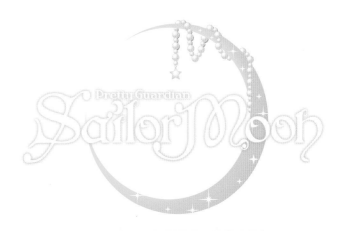

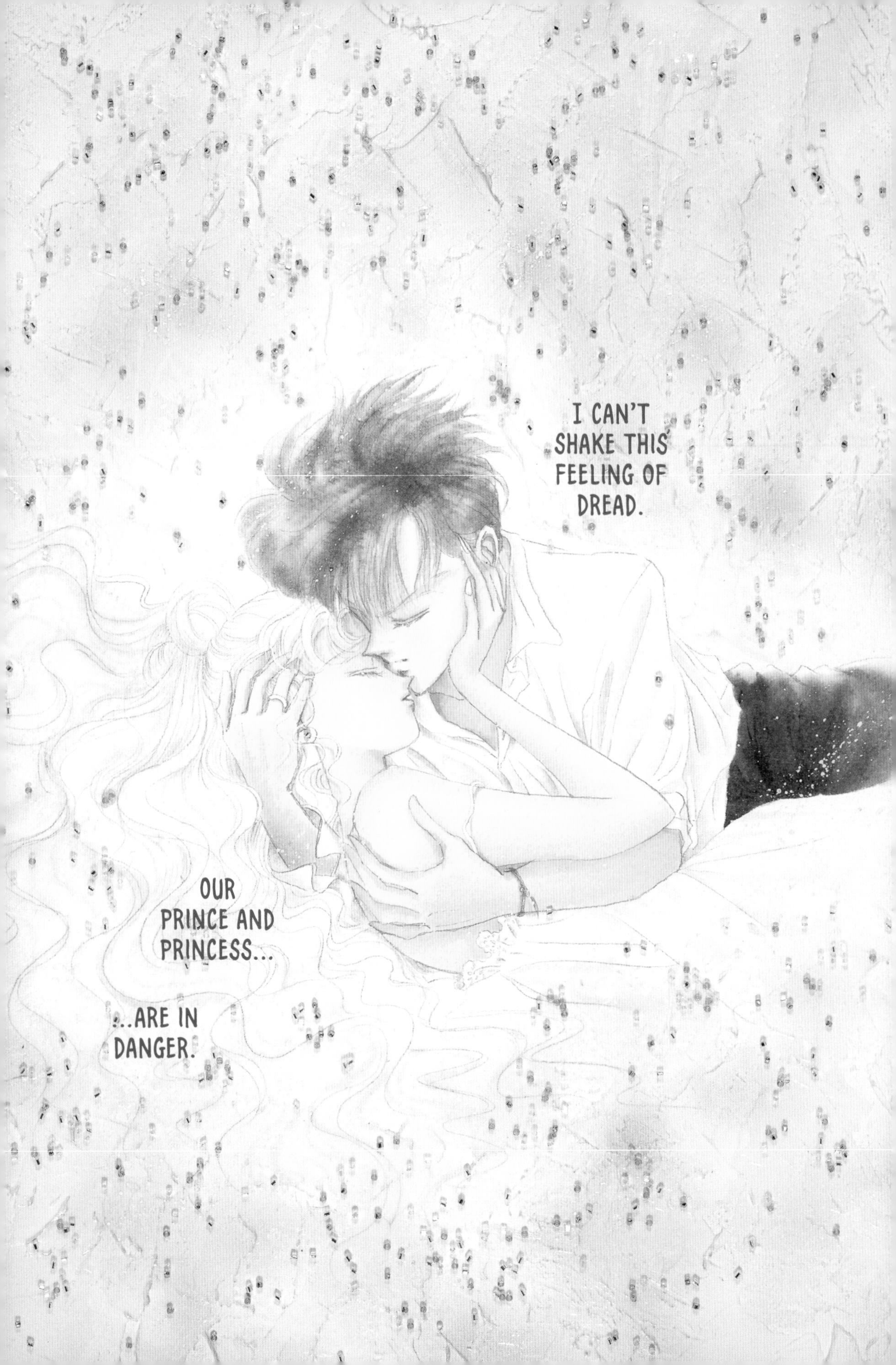
I CAN'T SHAKE THIS FEELING OF DREAD.
OUR PRINCE AND PRINCESS...
...ARE IN DANGER.

Act. 45 Dream 7: Mirror Dream

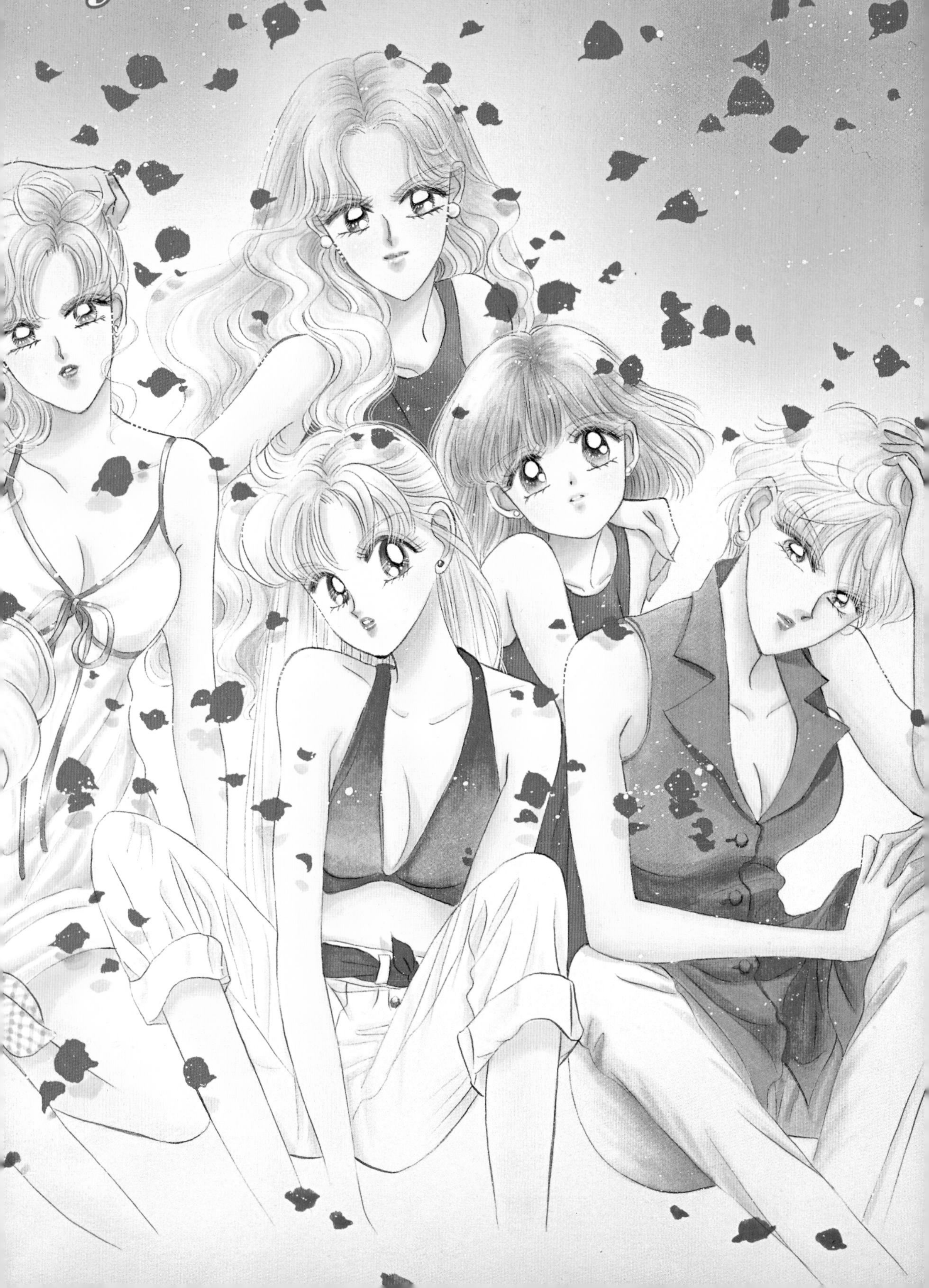

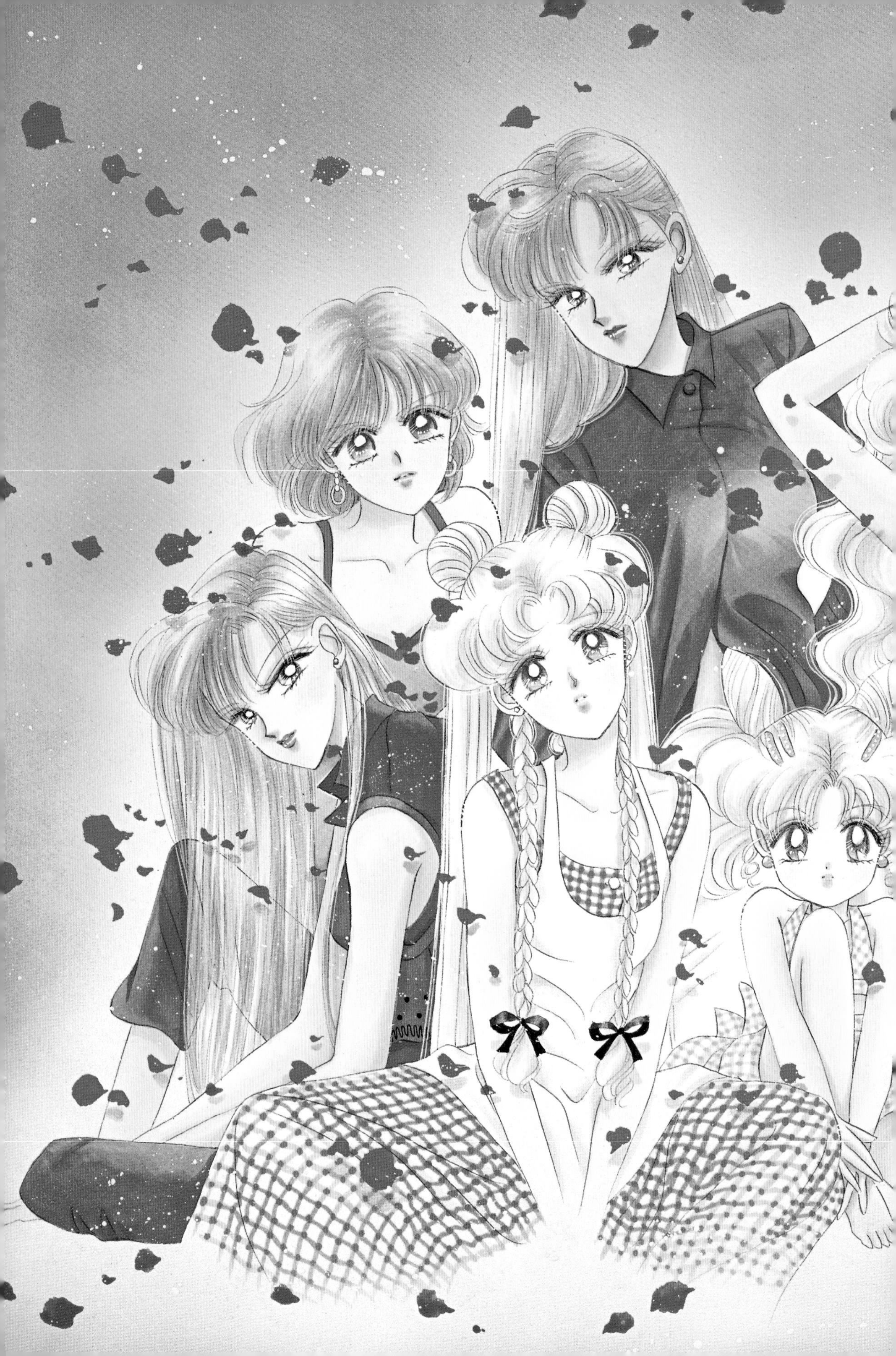

Pretty Guardian

Sailor Moon

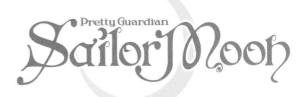

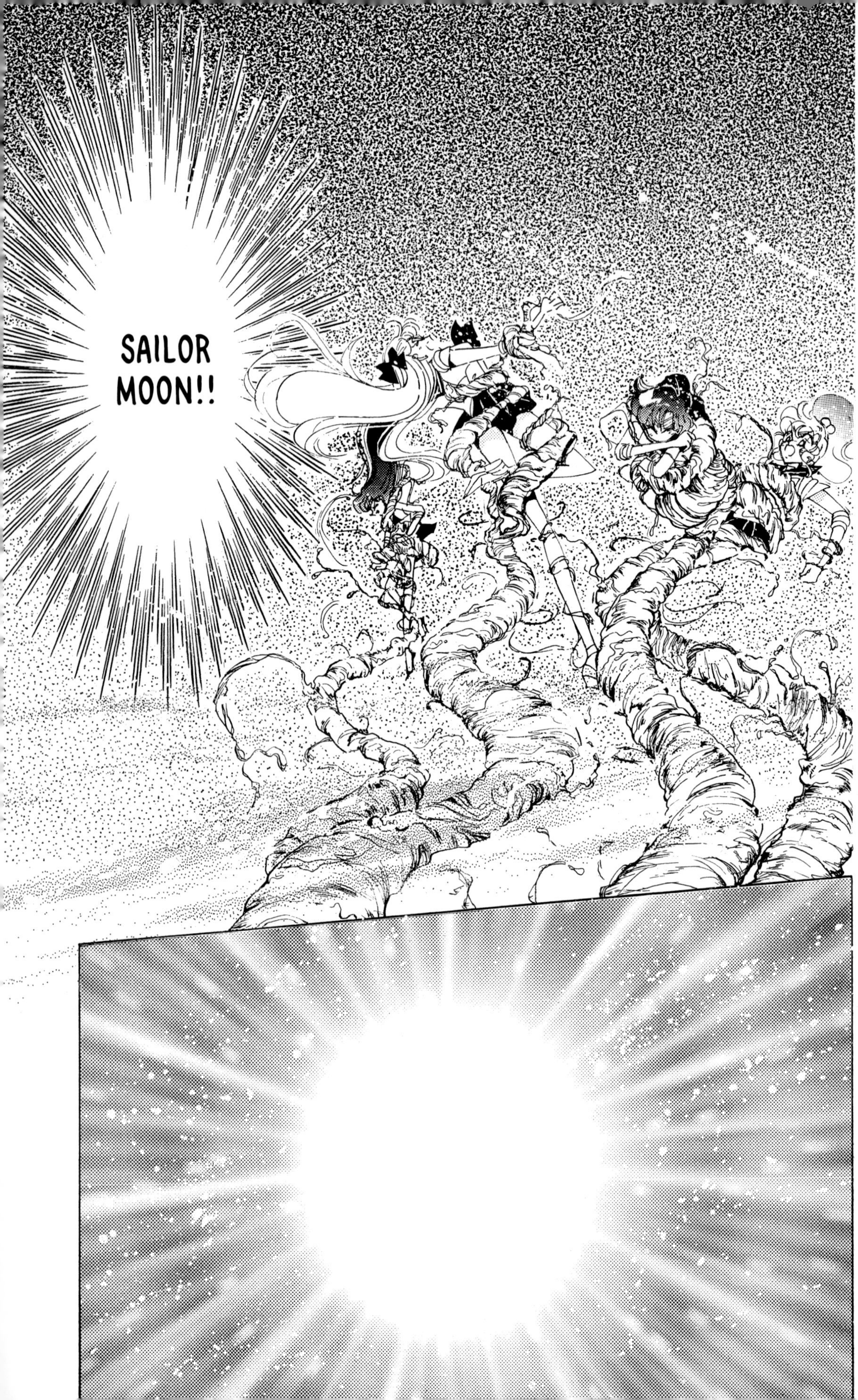
SAILOR MOON!!

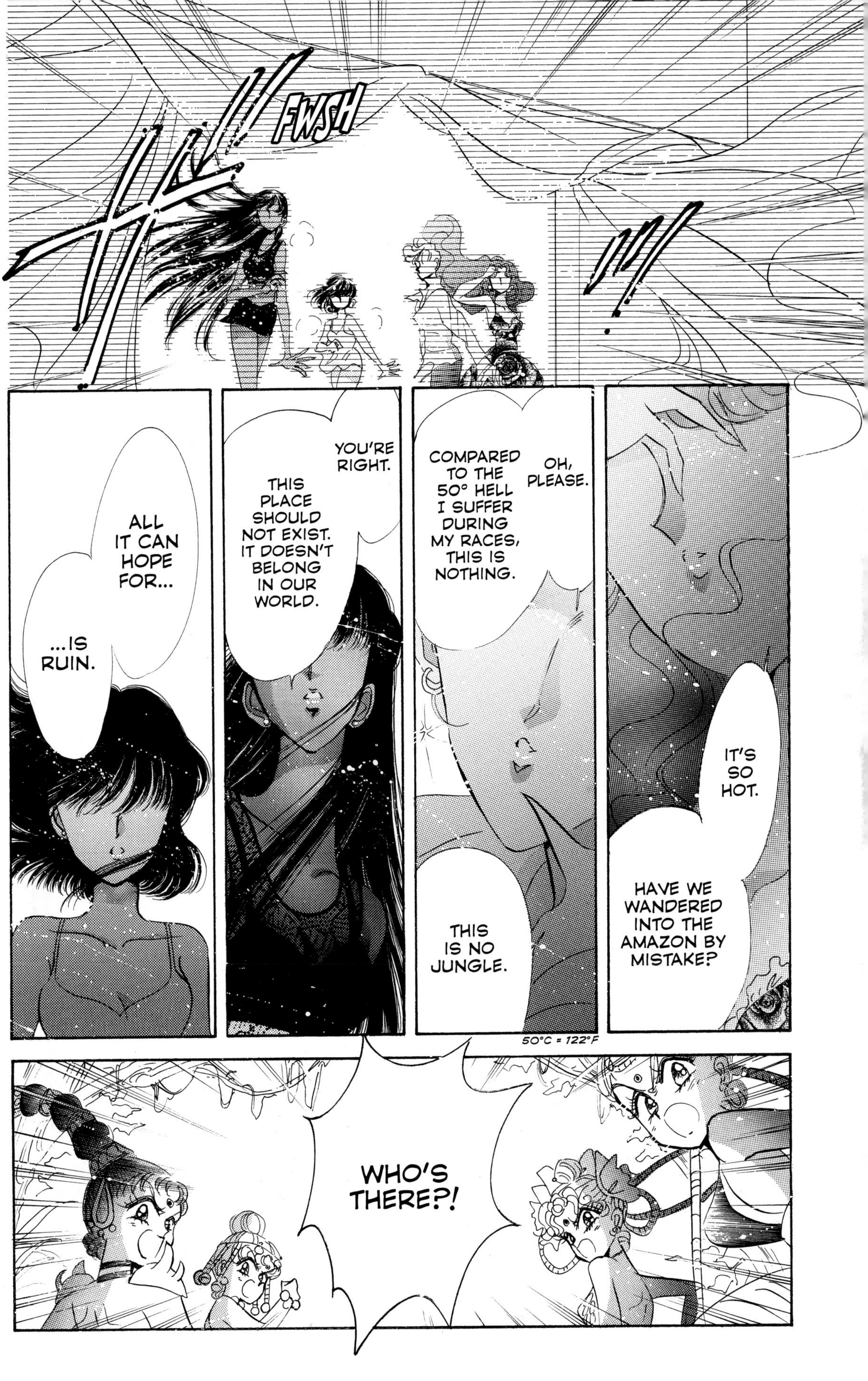
FWSH
IT'S SO HOT.
HAVE WE WANDERED INTO THE AMAZON BY MISTAKE?
OH, PLEASE.
COMPARED TO THE 50° HELL I SUFFER DURING MY RACES, THIS IS NOTHING.
THIS IS NO JUNGLE.
YOU'RE RIGHT.
THIS PLACE SHOULD NOT EXIST. IT DOESN'T BELONG IN OUR WORLD.
ALL IT CAN HOPE FOR...
...IS RUIN.
WHO'S THERE?!

50°C = 122°F

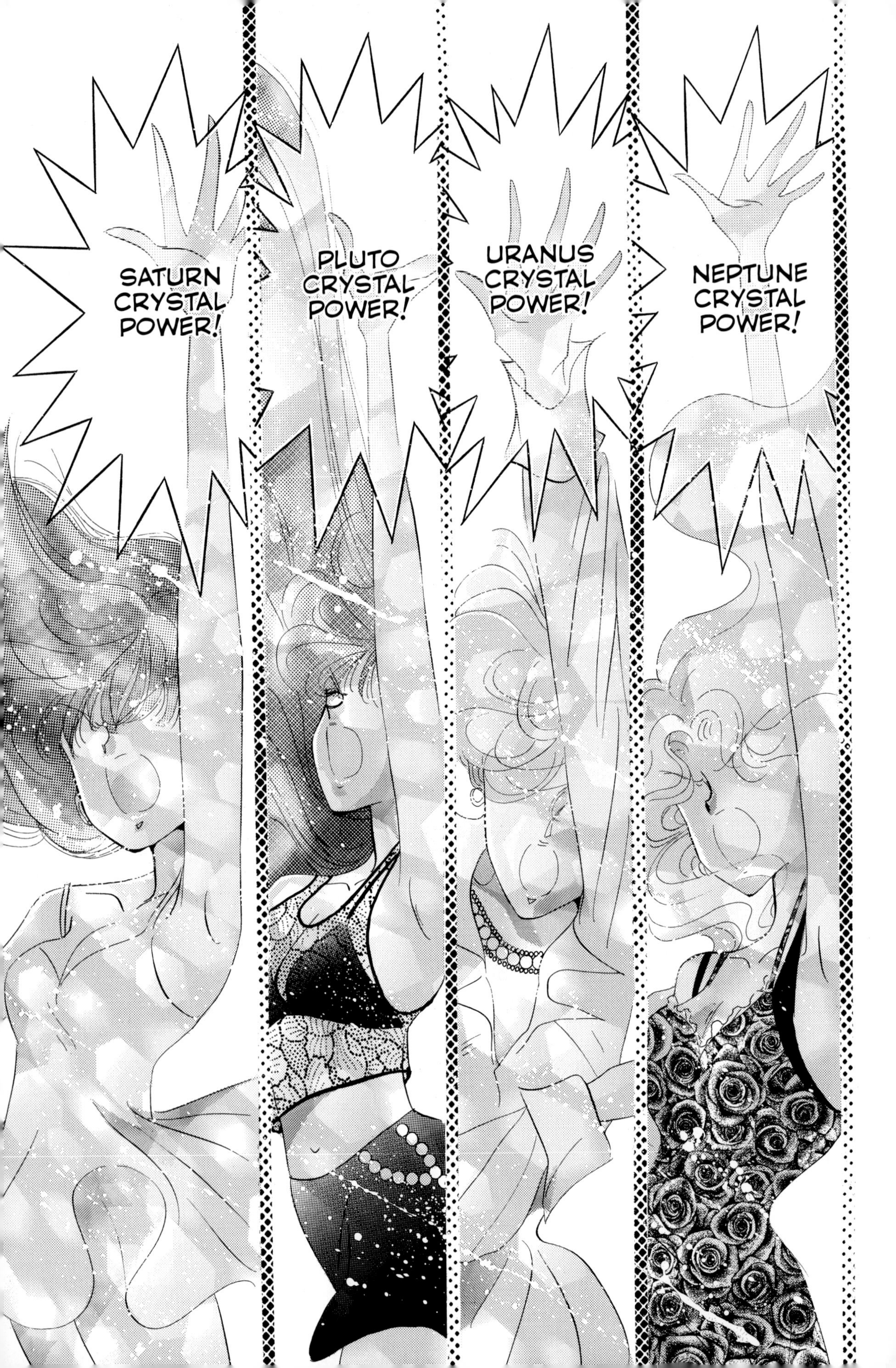
NEPTUNE CRYSTAL POWER!
URANUS CRYSTAL POWER!
PLUTO CRYSTAL POWER!
SATURN CRYSTAL POWER!

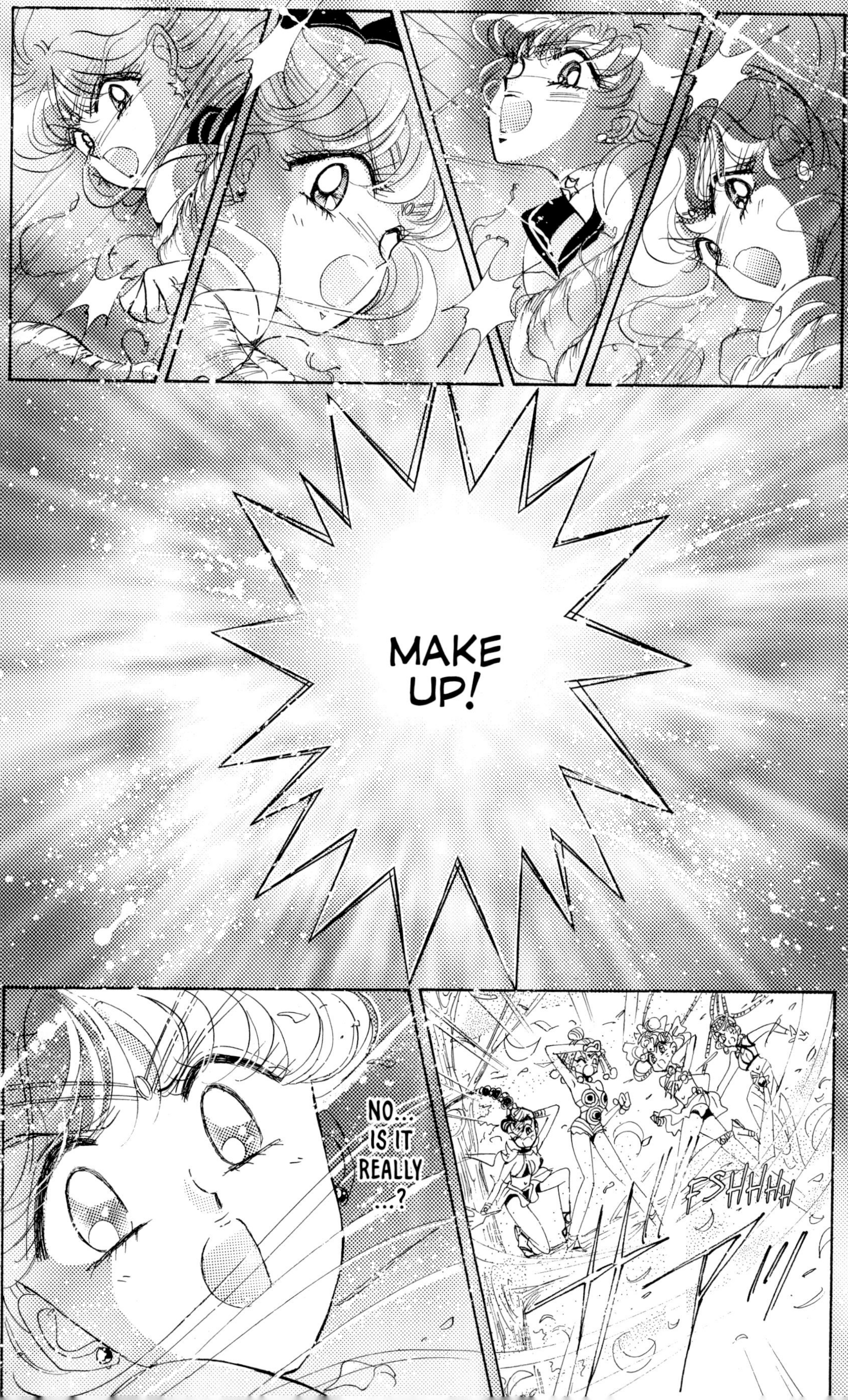
MAKE UP!
FSHHHH
NO... IS IT REALLY ...?

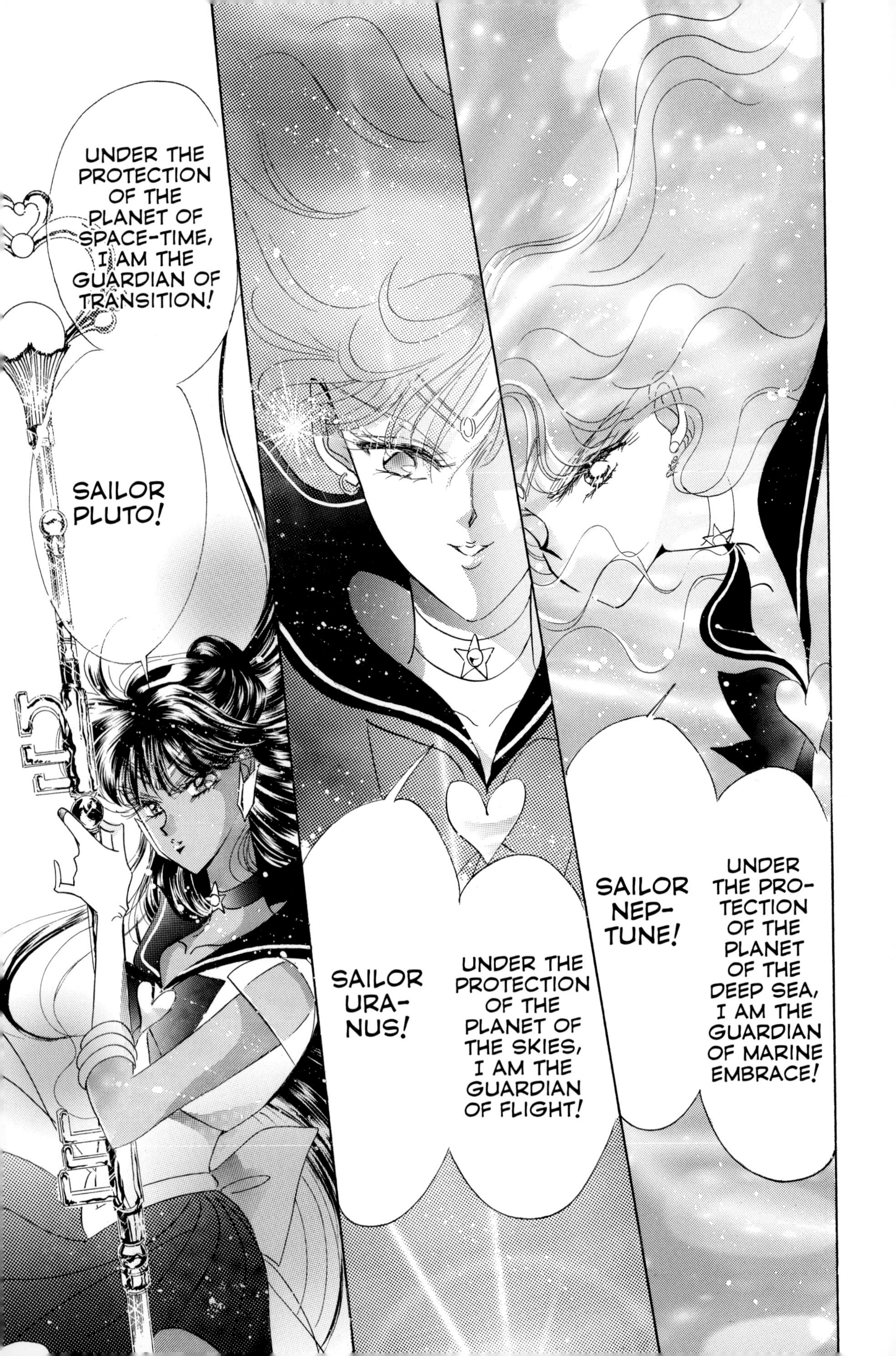
UNDER THE PROTECTION OF THE PLANET OF THE DEEP SEA, I AM THE GUARDIAN OF MARINE EMBRACE!
SAILOR NEPTUNE!
UNDER THE PROTECTION OF THE PLANET OF THE SKIES, I AM THE GUARDIAN OF FLIGHT!
SAILOR URANUS!
UNDER THE PROTECTION OF THE PLANET OF SPACE-TIME, I AM THE GUARDIAN OF TRANSITION!
SAILOR PLUTO!

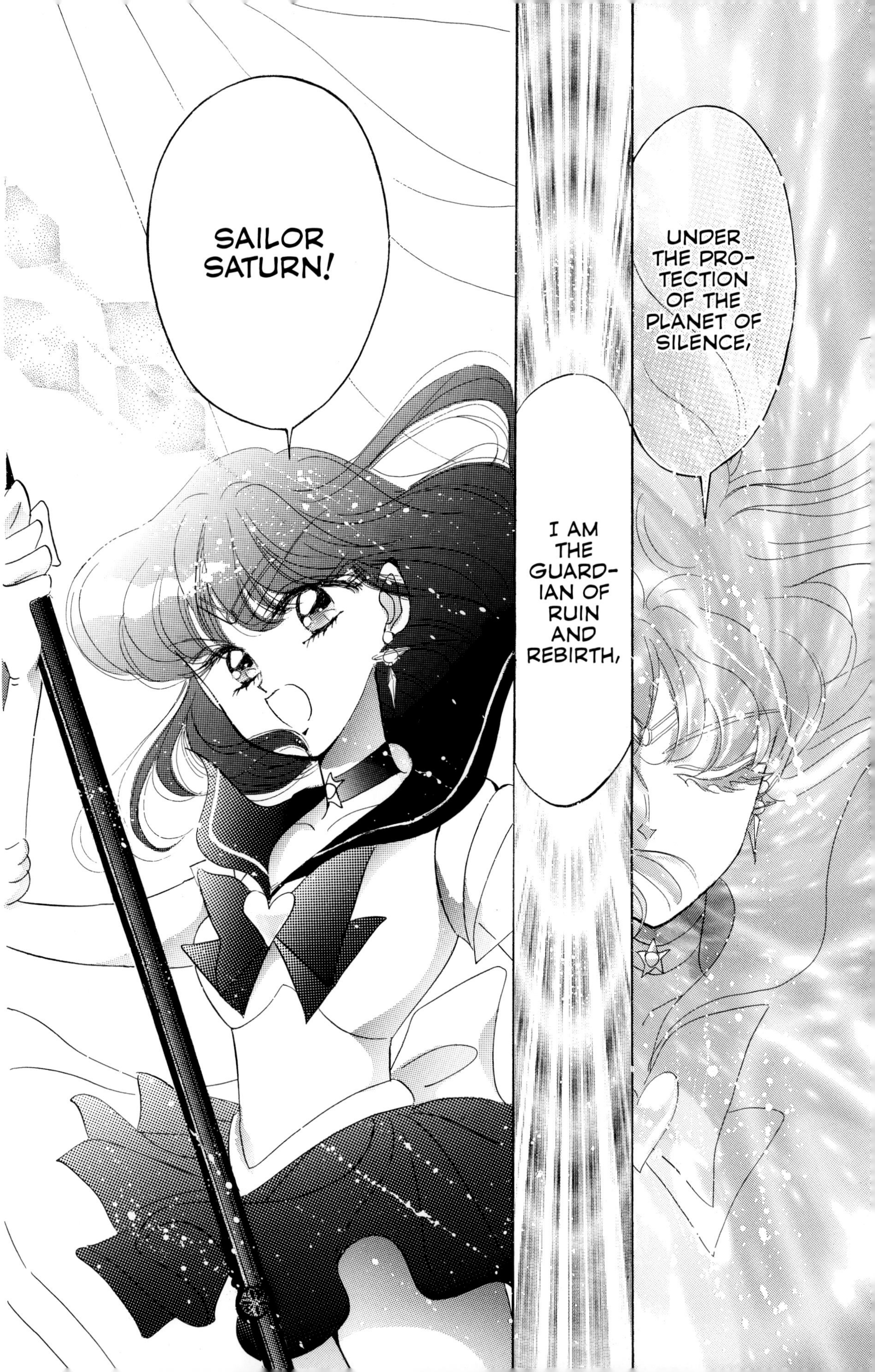
UNDER THE PROTECTION OF THE PLANET OF SILENCE,
I AM THE GUARDIAN OF RUIN AND REBIRTH,
SAILOR SATURN!

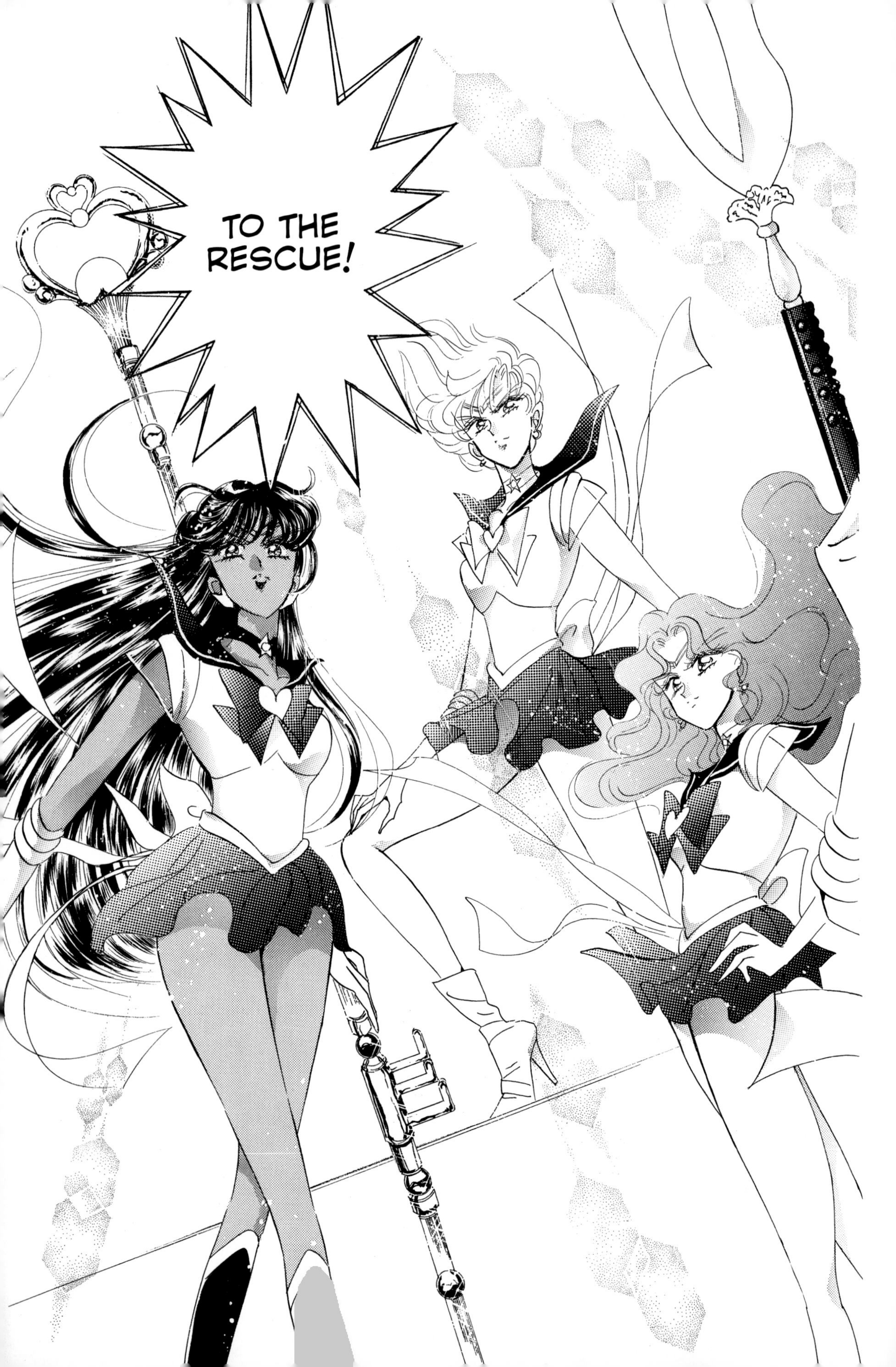
TO THE RESCUE!

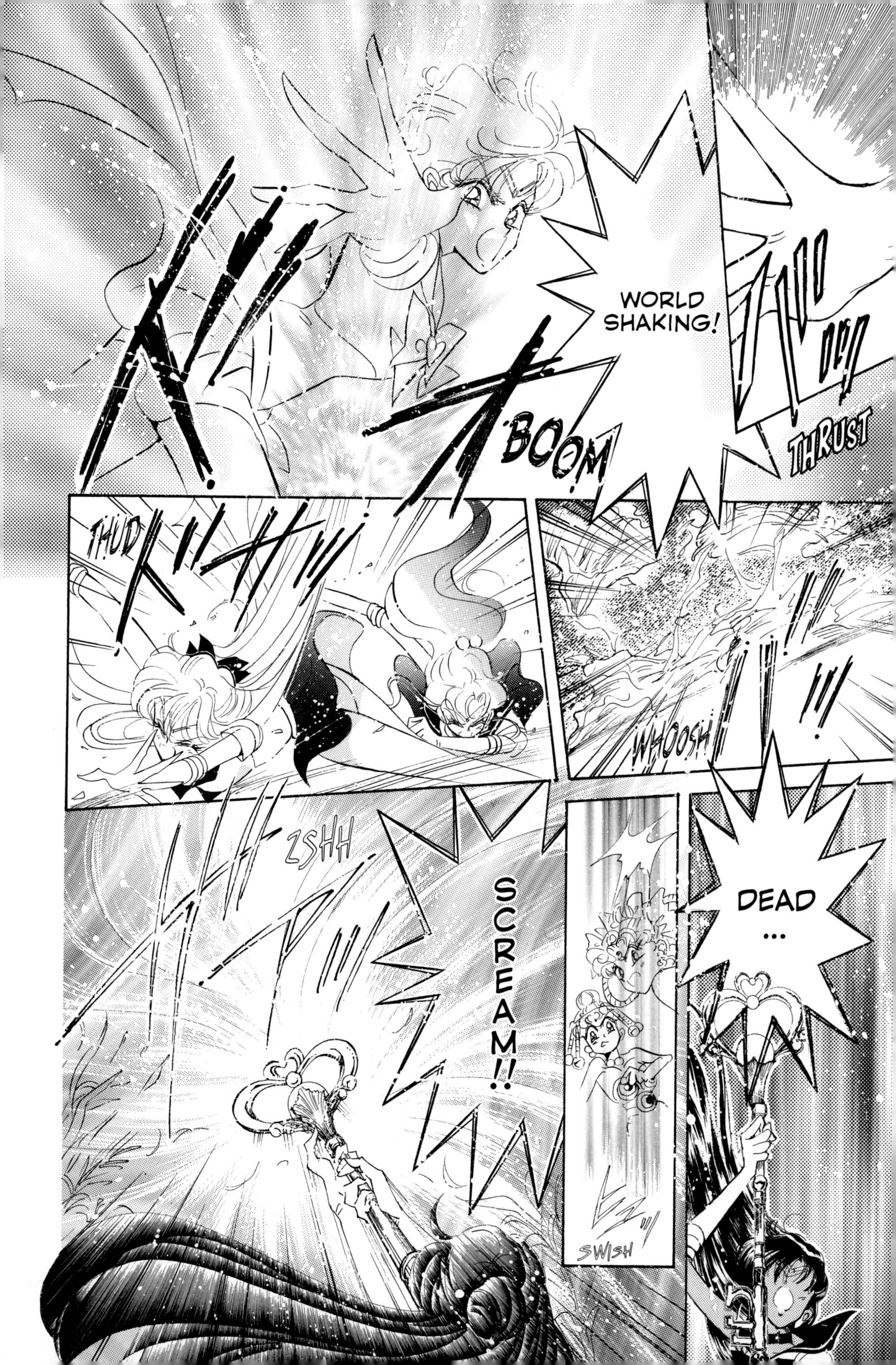
THRUST
WORLD SHAKING!
BOOM
WHOOSH
THUD
DEAD ...
SWISH
SCREAM!!
ZSHH

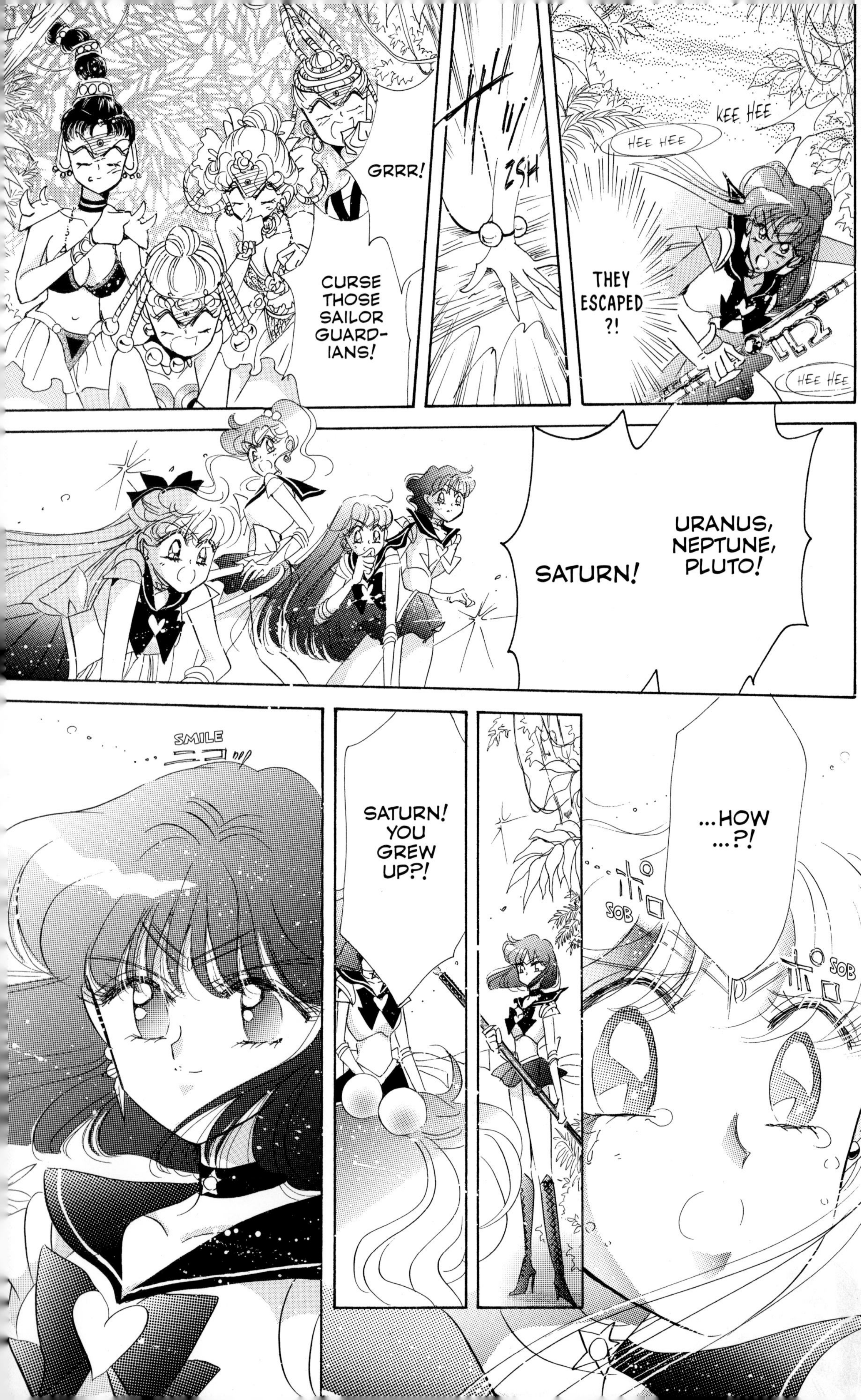
KEE HEE
HEE HEE
THEY ESCAPED ?!
HEE HEE
ZSH
GRRR!
CURSE THOSE SAILOR GUARDIANS!
URANUS, NEPTUNE, PLUTO!
SATURN!
...HOW ...?!
SOB
SOB
SATURN! YOU GREW UP?!
SMILE

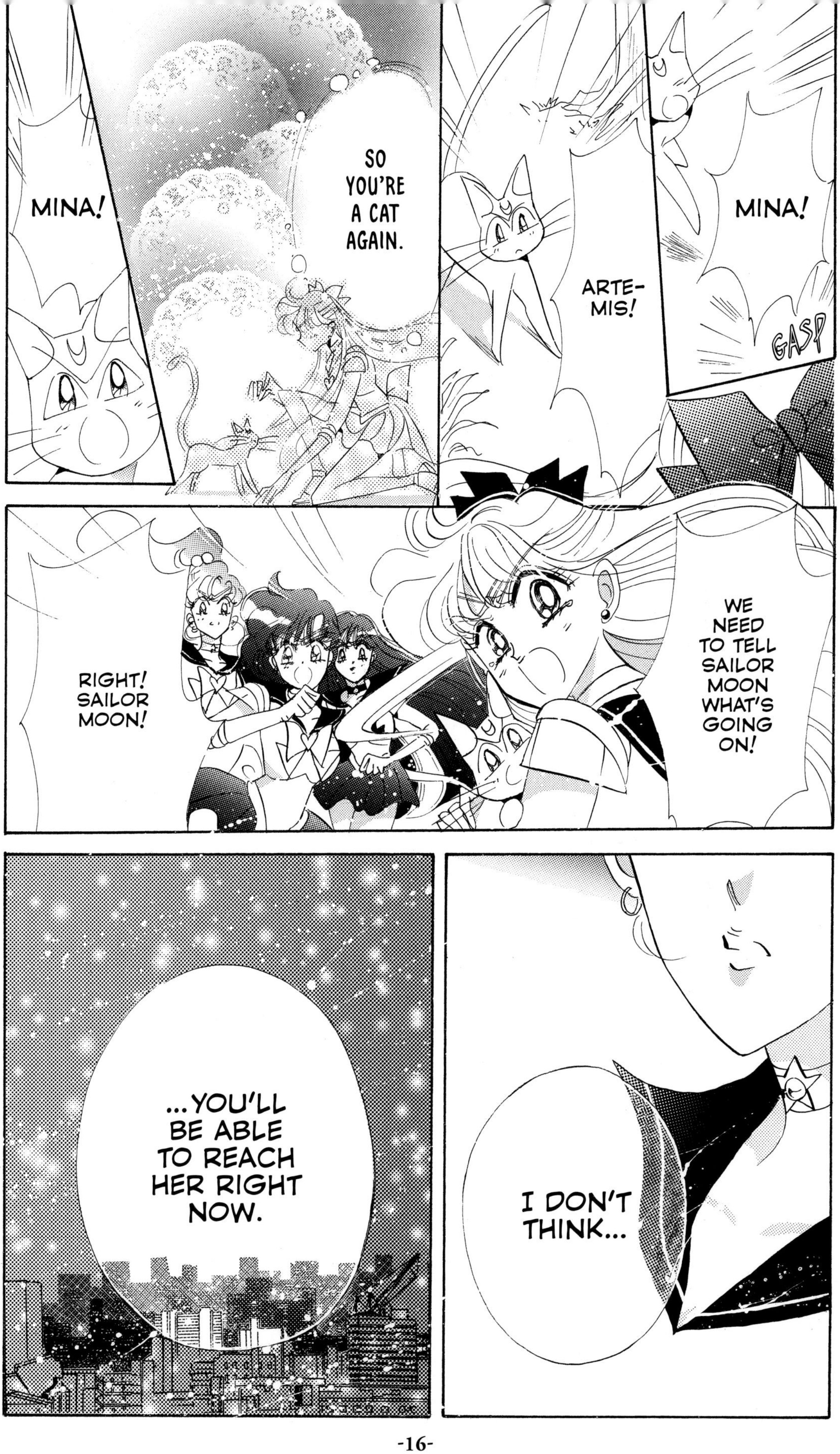
MINA!
GASP
ARTEMIS!
SO YOU'RE A CAT AGAIN.
MINA!
WE NEED TO TELL SAILOR MOON WHAT'S GOING ON!
RIGHT! SAILOR MOON!
I DON'T THINK...
...YOU'LL BE ABLE TO REACH HER RIGHT NOW.

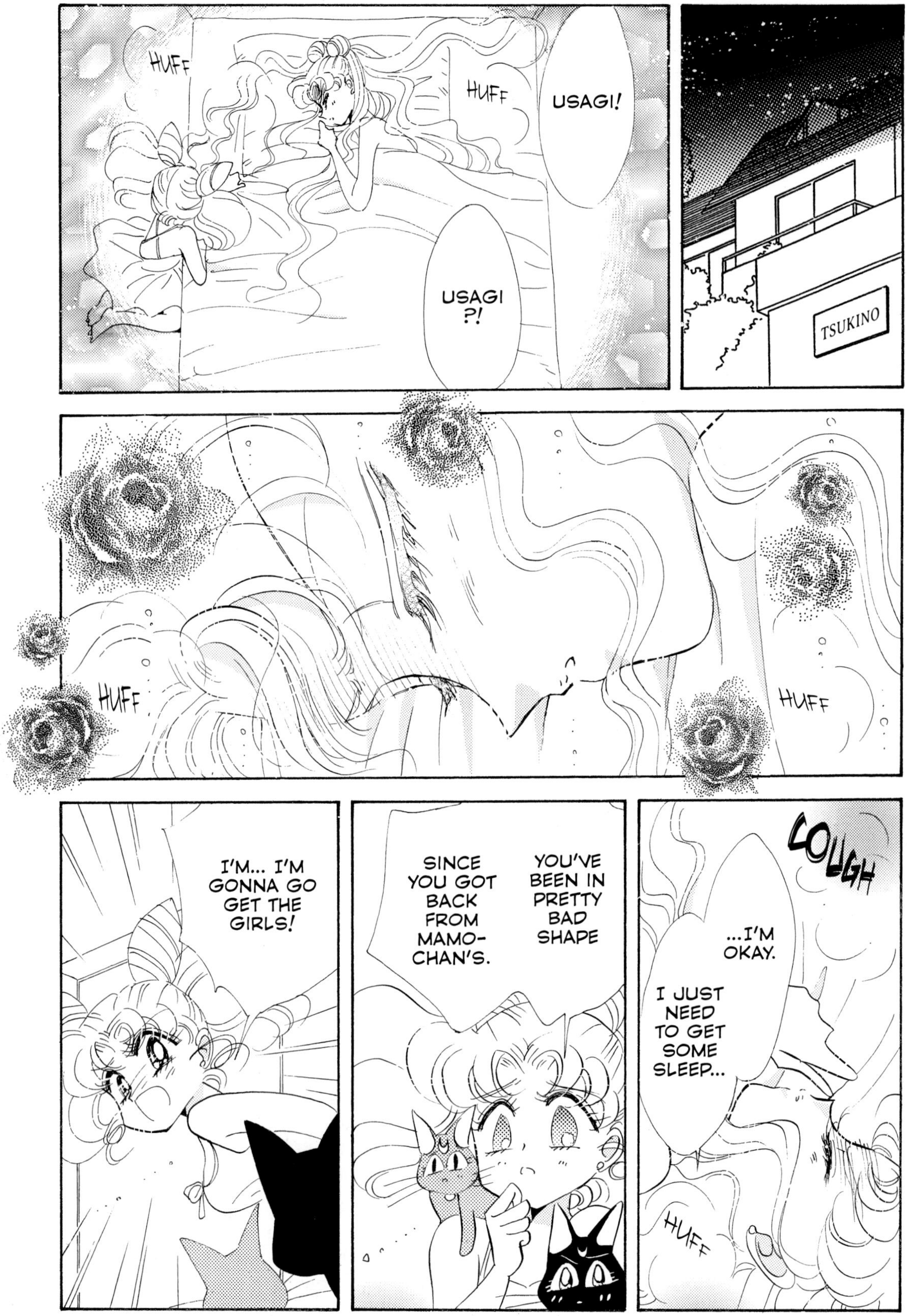
TSUKINO
USAGI!
HUFF
HUFF
USAGI ?!
HUFF
HUFF
COUGH
...I'M OKAY.
I JUST NEED TO GET SOME SLEEP...
HUFF
YOU'VE BEEN IN PRETTY BAD SHAPE
SINCE YOU GOT BACK FROM MAMO-CHAN'S.
I'M... I'M GONNA GO GET THE GIRLS!

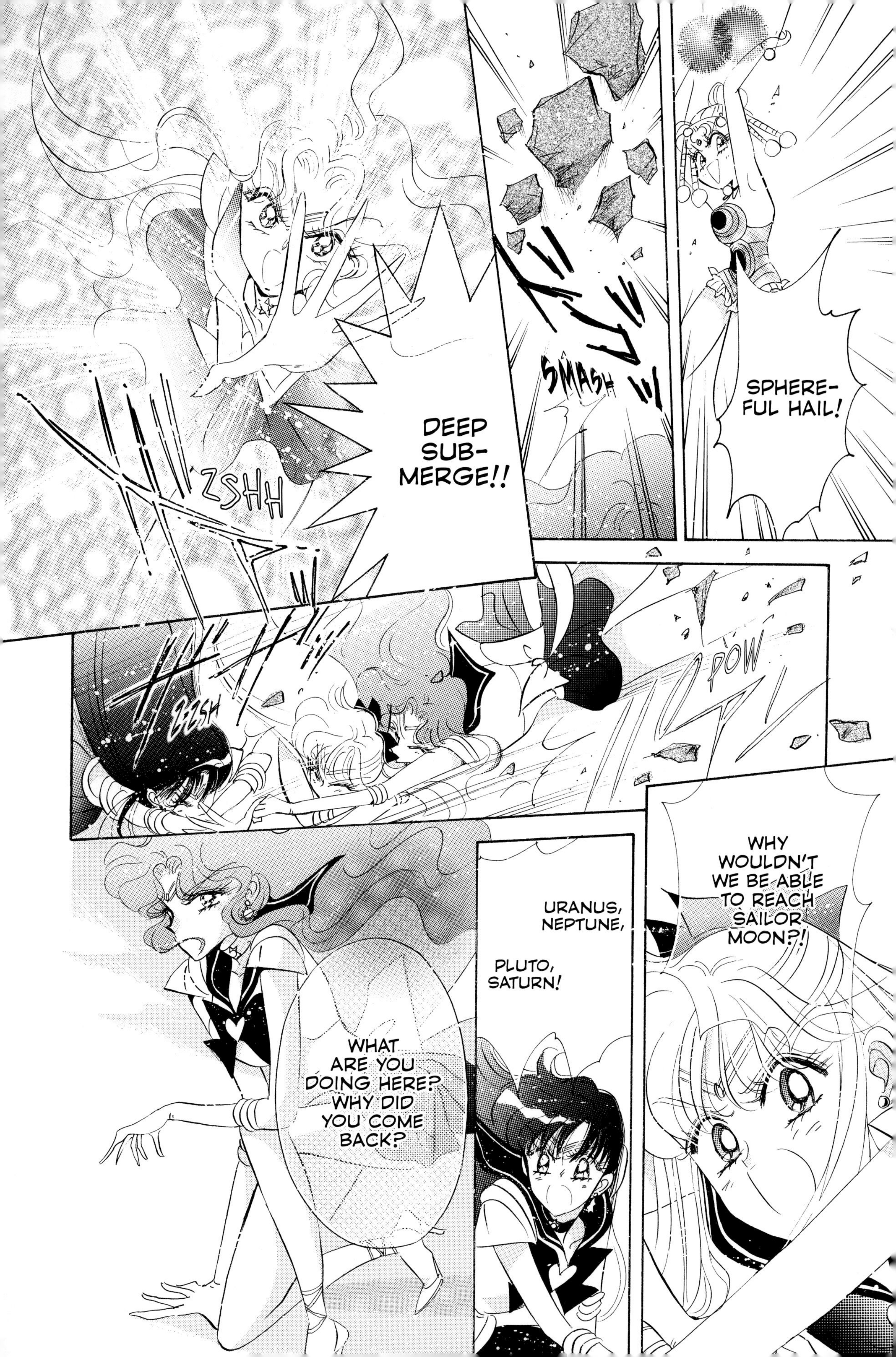
SPHERE-FUL HAIL!
SMASH
DEEP SUB-MERGE!!
ZSHH
POW
WHY WOULDN'T WE BE ABLE TO REACH SAILOR MOON?!
URANUS, NEPTUNE,
PLUTO, SATURN!
WHAT ARE YOU DOING HERE? WHY DID YOU COME BACK?

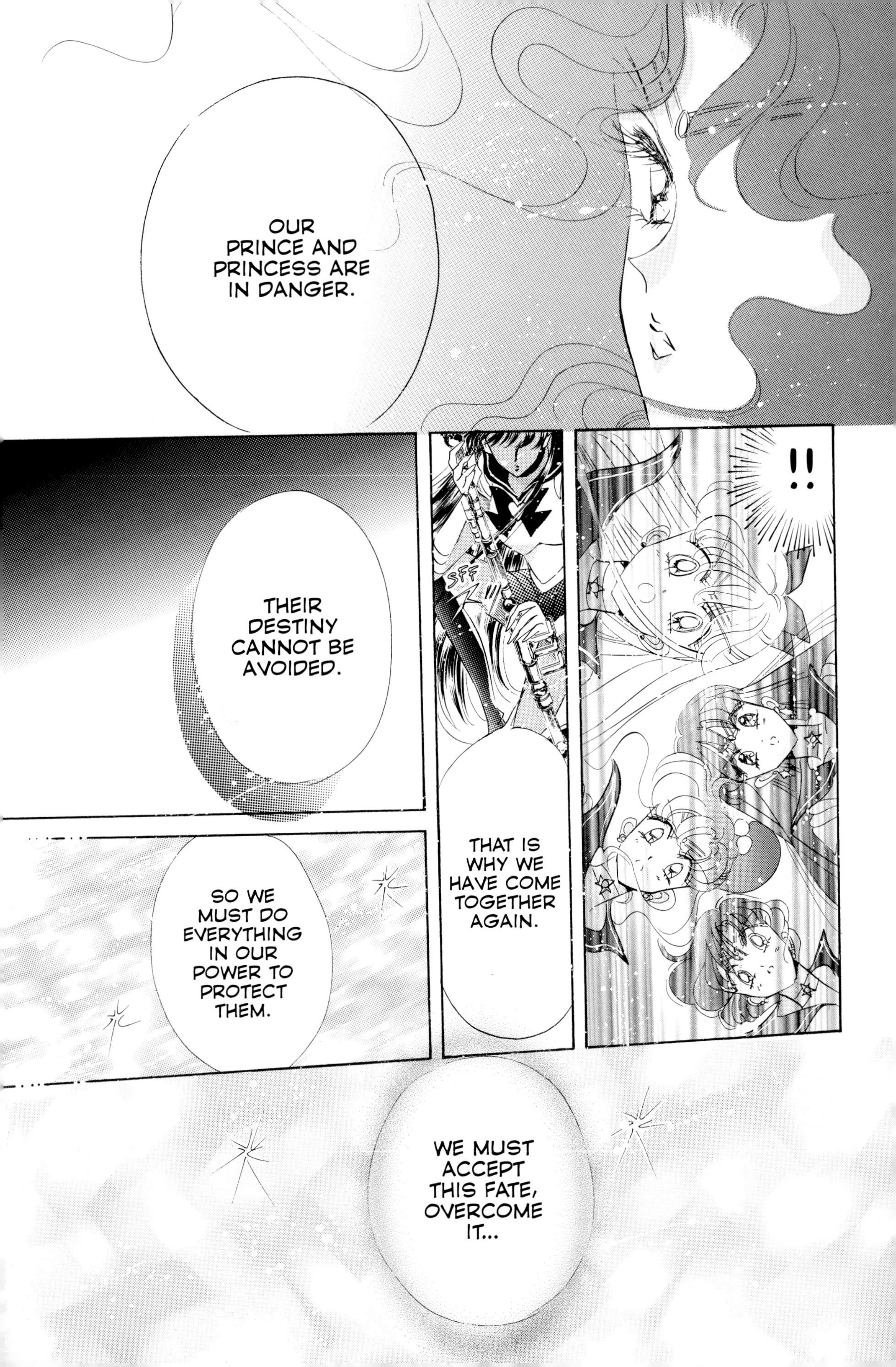
OUR PRINCE AND PRINCESS ARE IN DANGER.
!!
SFF
THAT IS WHY WE HAVE COME TOGETHER AGAIN.
THEIR DESTINY CANNOT BE AVOIDED.
SO WE MUST DO EVERYTHING IN OUR POWER TO PROTECT THEM.
WE MUST ACCEPT THIS FATE, OVERCOME IT...

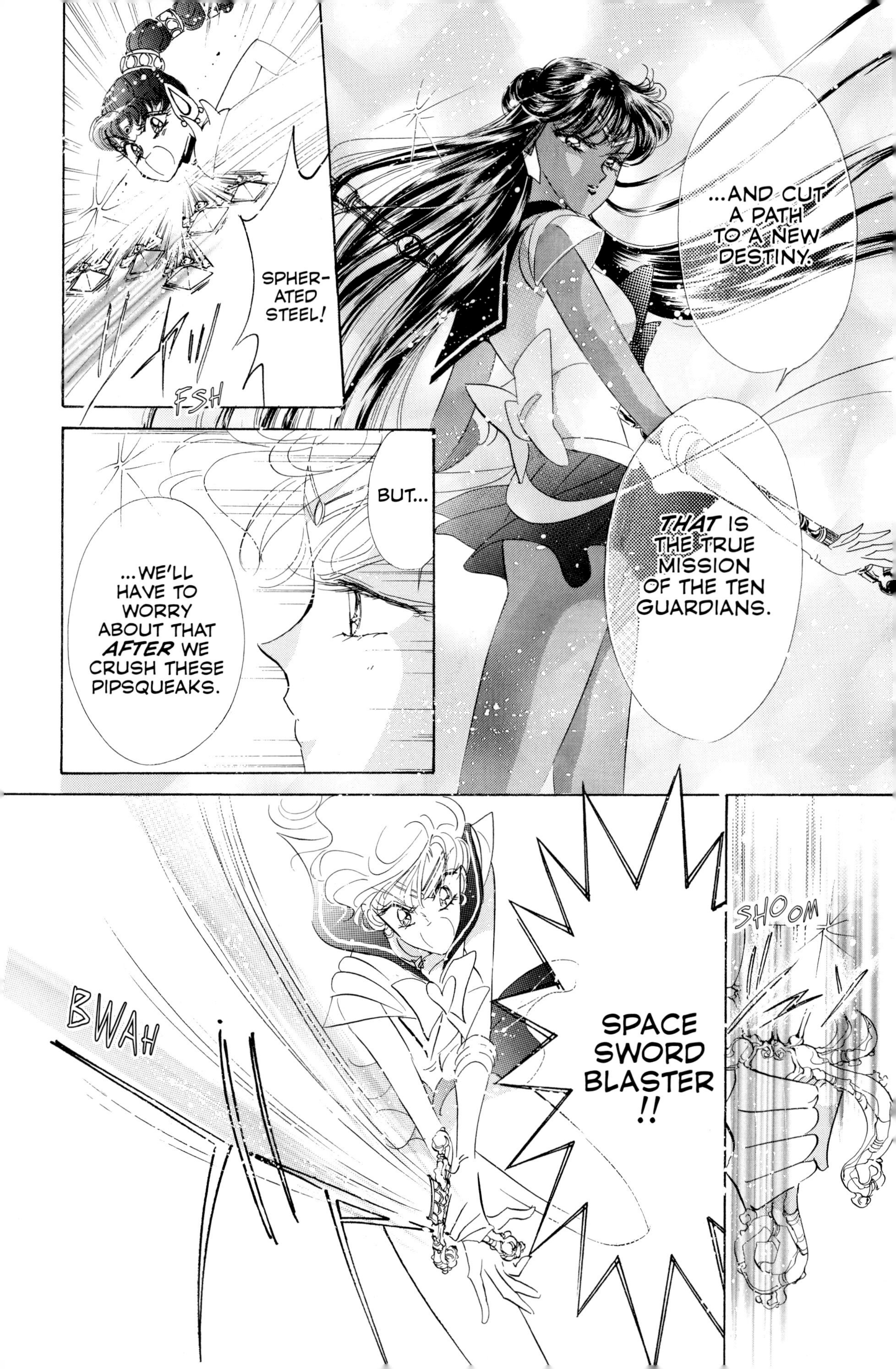
...AND CUT A PATH TO A NEW DESTINY.
THAT IS THE TRUE MISSION OF THE TEN GUARDIANS.
FSH
SPHER-ATED STEEL!
BUT...
...WE'LL HAVE TO WORRY ABOUT THAT AFTER WE CRUSH THESE PIPSQUEAKS.
SHOOM
SPACE SWORD BLASTER!!
BWAH

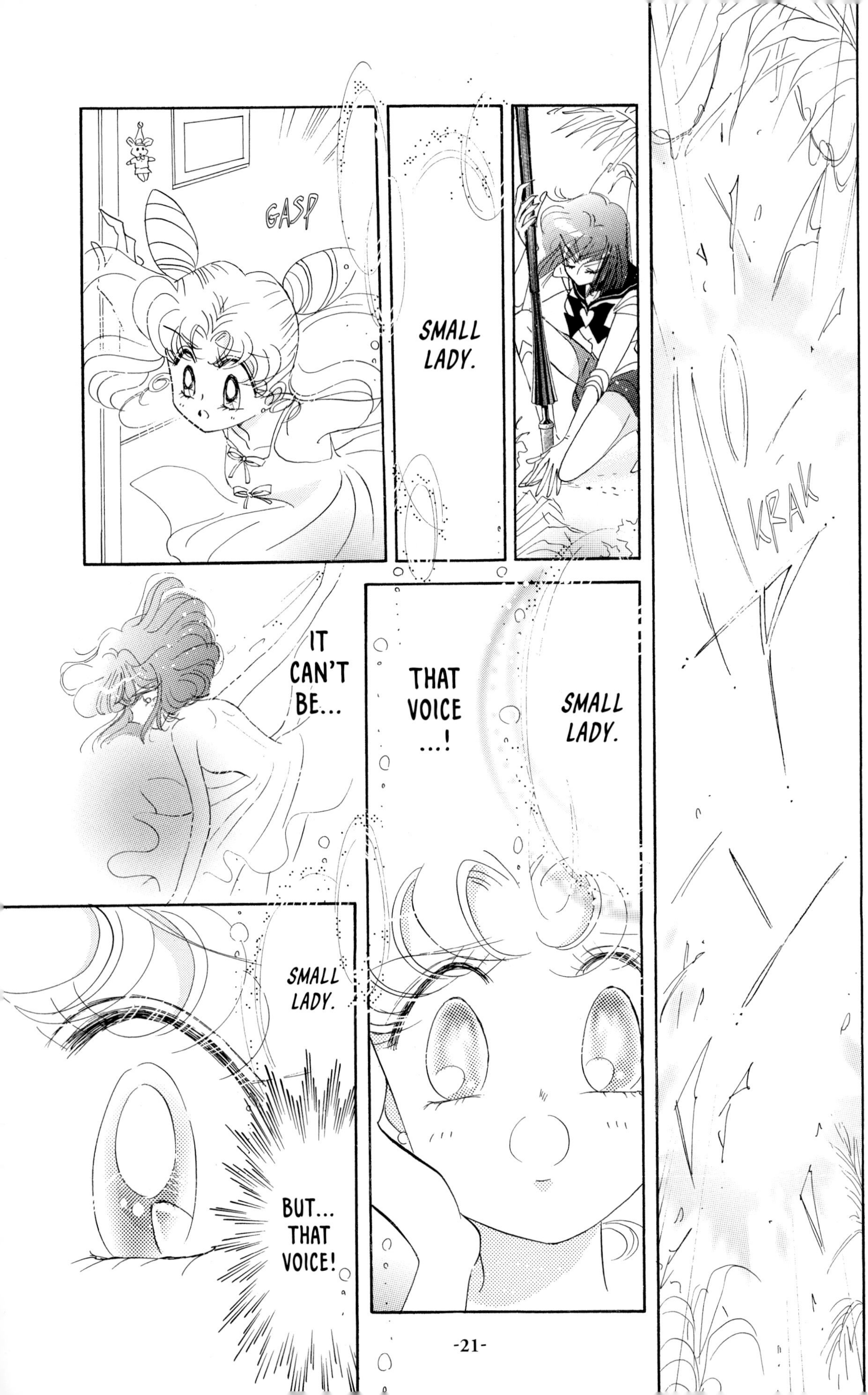
KRAK
SMALL LADY.
GASP
SMALL LADY.
THAT VOICE ...!
IT CAN'T BE...
SMALL LADY.
BUT... THAT VOICE!

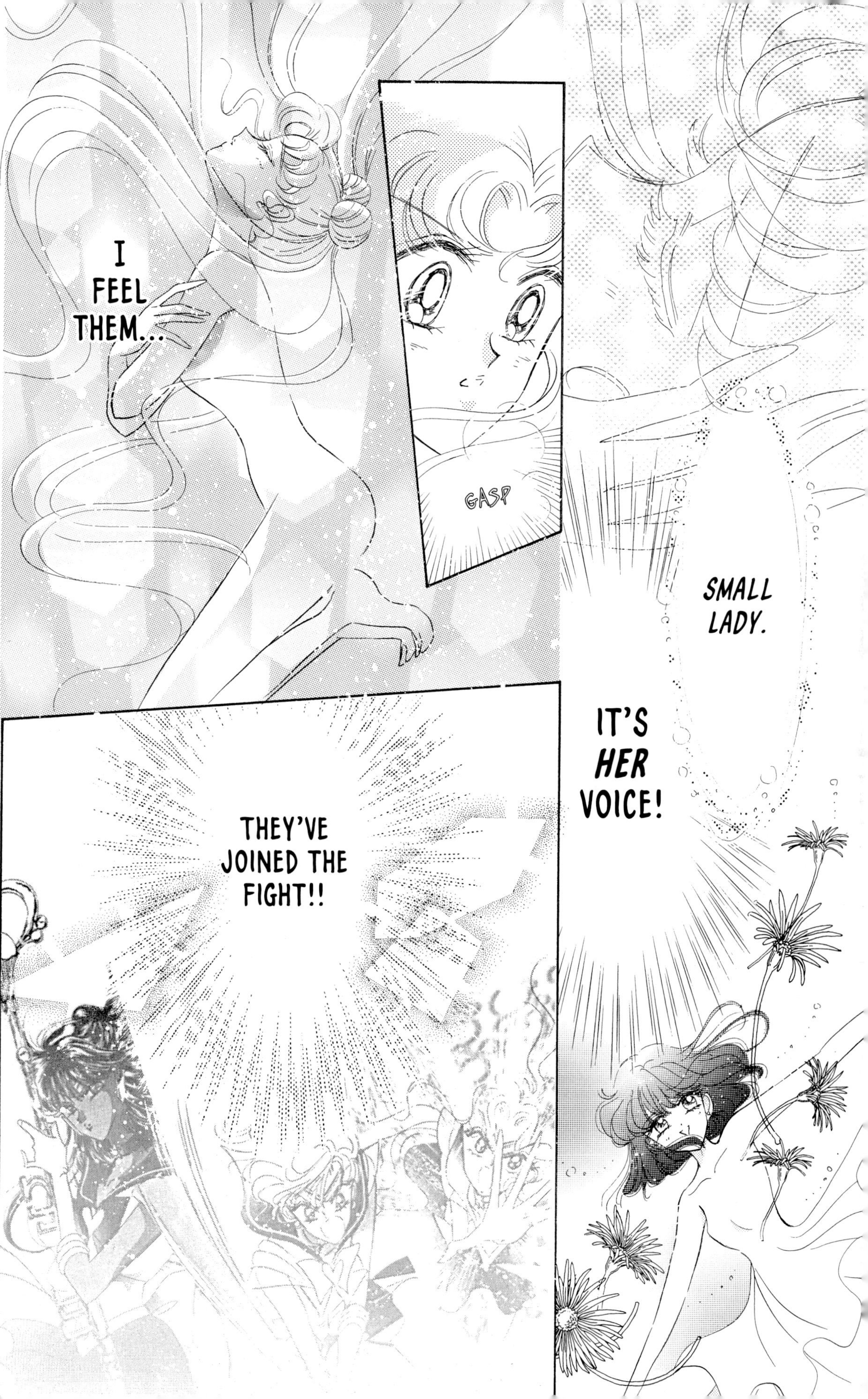
SMALL LADY.
IT'S *HER* VOICE!
GASP
I FEEL THEM...
THEY'VE JOINED THE FIGHT!!

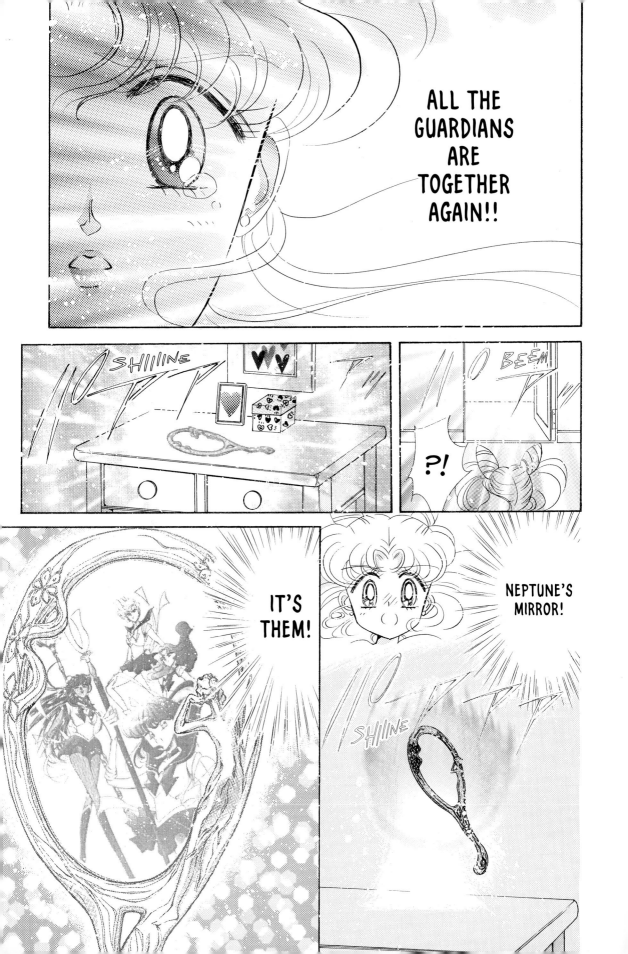

ALL THE GUARDIANS ARE TOGETHER AGAIN!!

SHIIINE

BEEM

?!

IT'S THEM!

NEPTUNE'S MIRROR!

SHIIINE

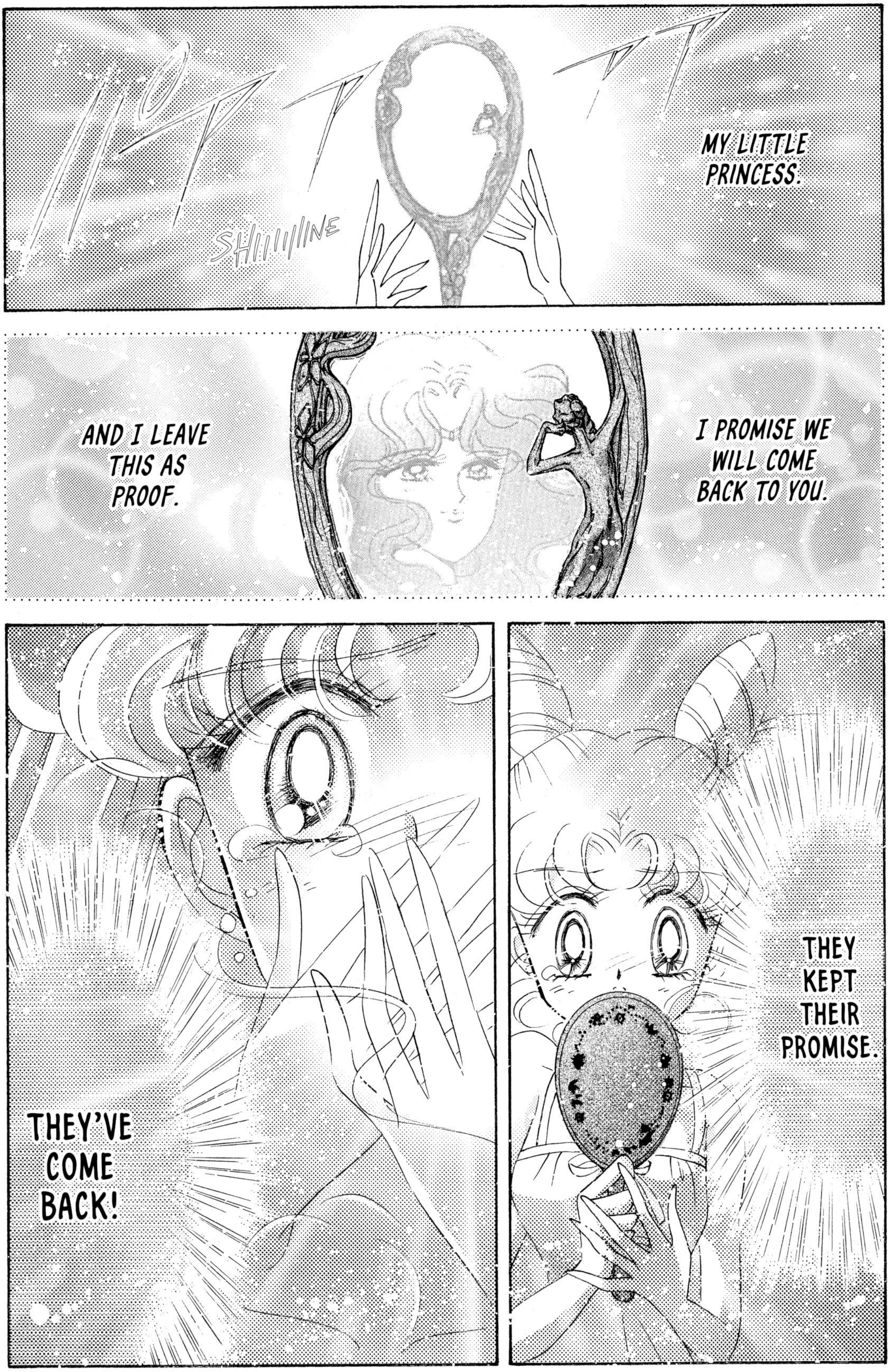
MY LITTLE PRINCESS.
SHIIIIIIINE
I PROMISE WE WILL COME BACK TO YOU.
AND I LEAVE THIS AS PROOF.
THEY KEPT THEIR PROMISE.
THEY'VE COME BACK!

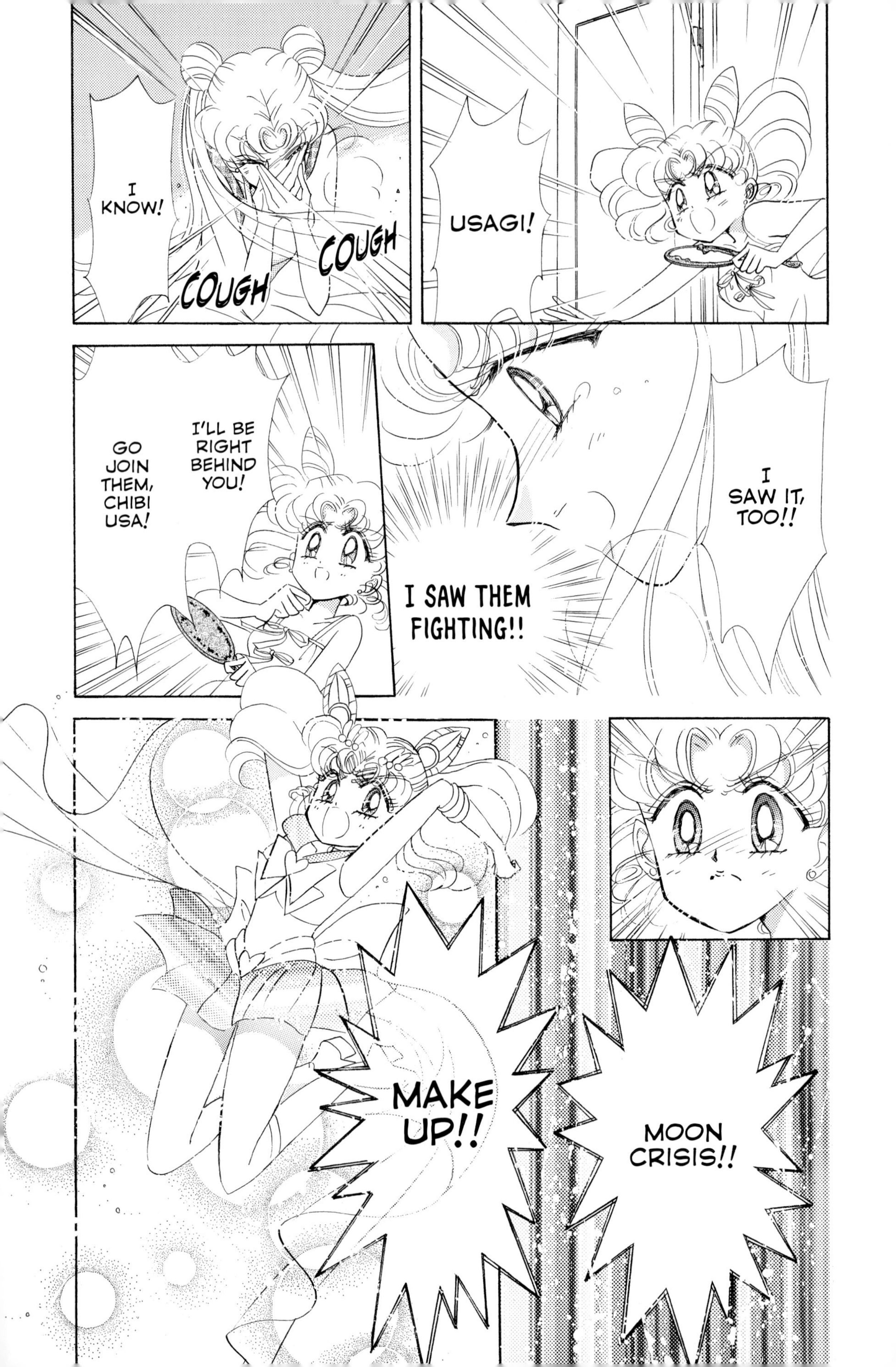
USAGI!
I KNOW!
COUGH
COUGH
I SAW IT, TOO!!
I SAW THEM FIGHTING!!
I'LL BE RIGHT BEHIND YOU!
GO JOIN THEM, CHIBI USA!
MOON CRISIS!!
MAKE UP!!

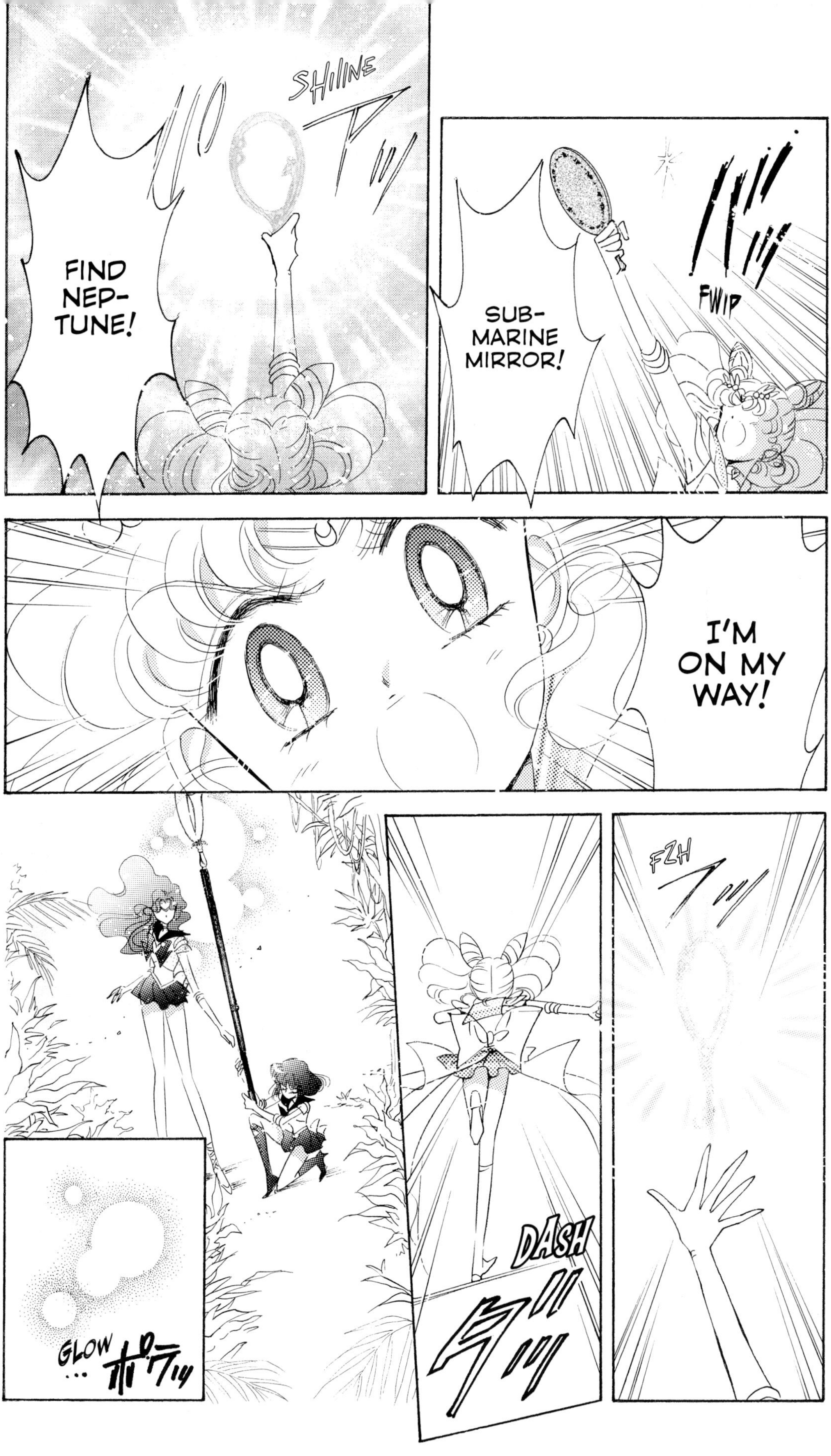
FWIP
SUB-MARINE MIRROR!
SHIIINE
FIND NEP-TUNE!
I'M ON MY WAY!
FZH
DASH
GLOW...

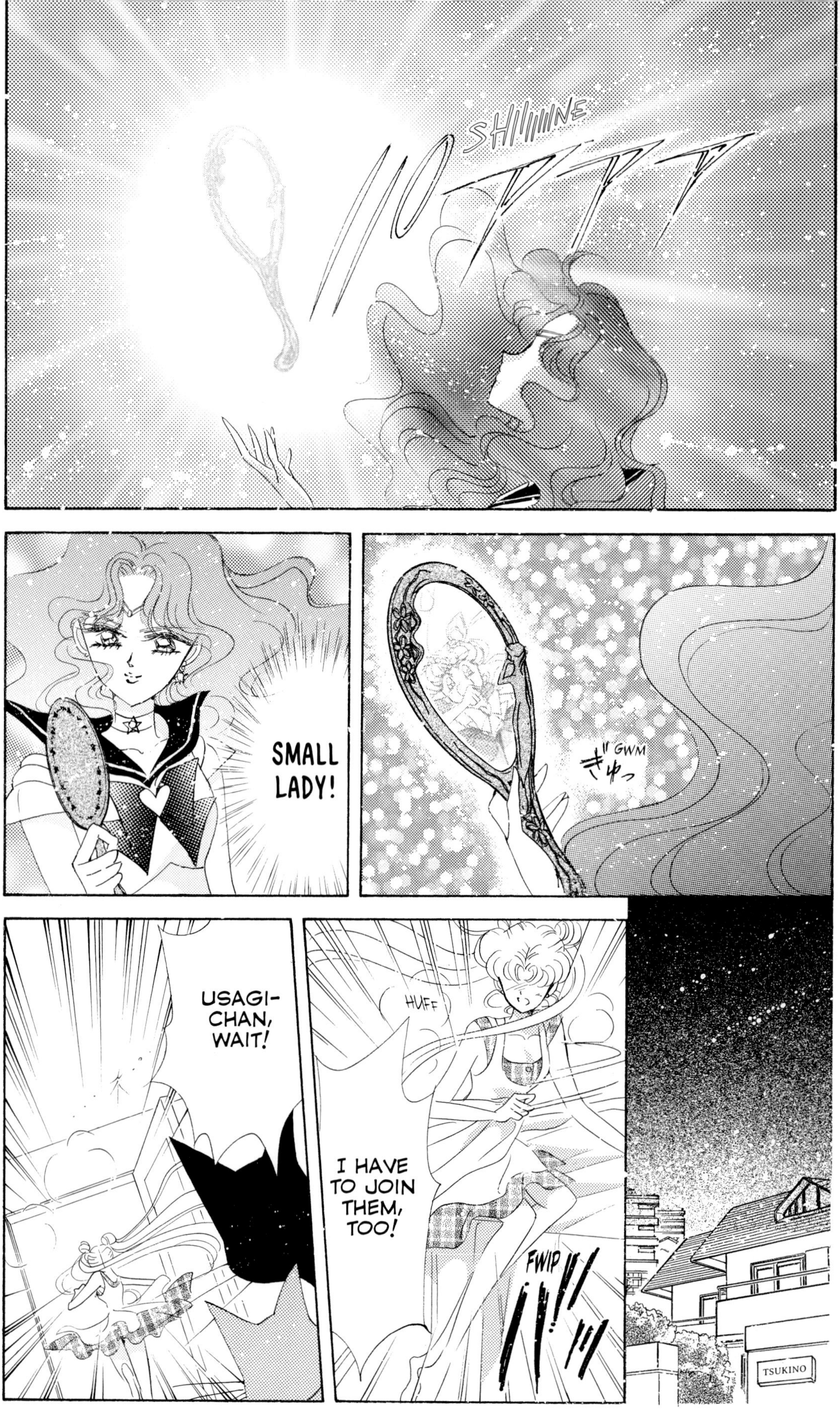
SHIIIIIINE
ぎゅっ
GWM
SMALL LADY!
TSUKINO
HUFF
I HAVE TO JOIN THEM, TOO!
FWIP
USAGI-CHAN, WAIT!

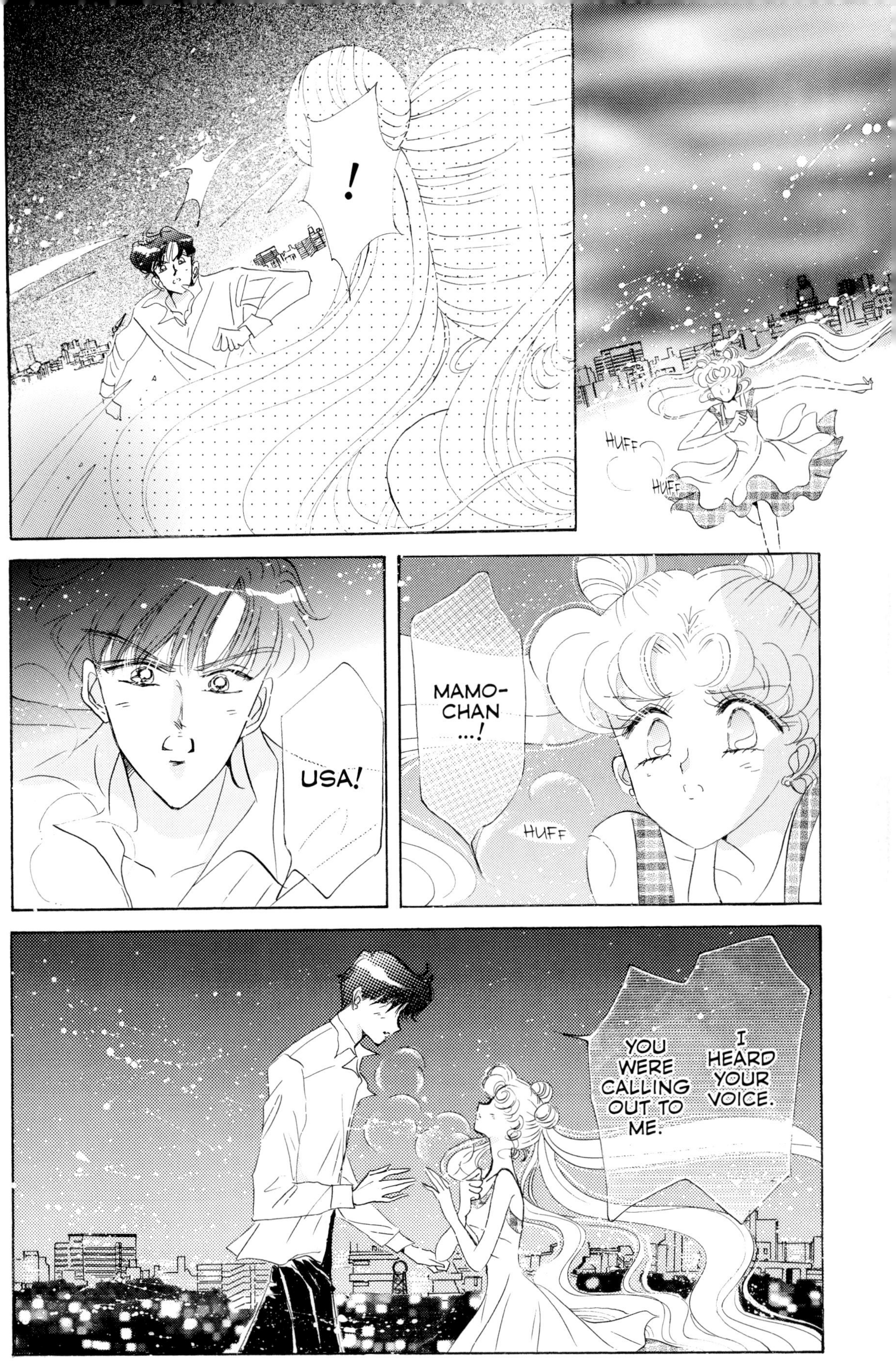
HUFF
HUFF
!
MAMO-CHAN ...!
HUFF
USA!
I HEARD YOUR VOICE.
YOU WERE CALLING OUT TO ME.

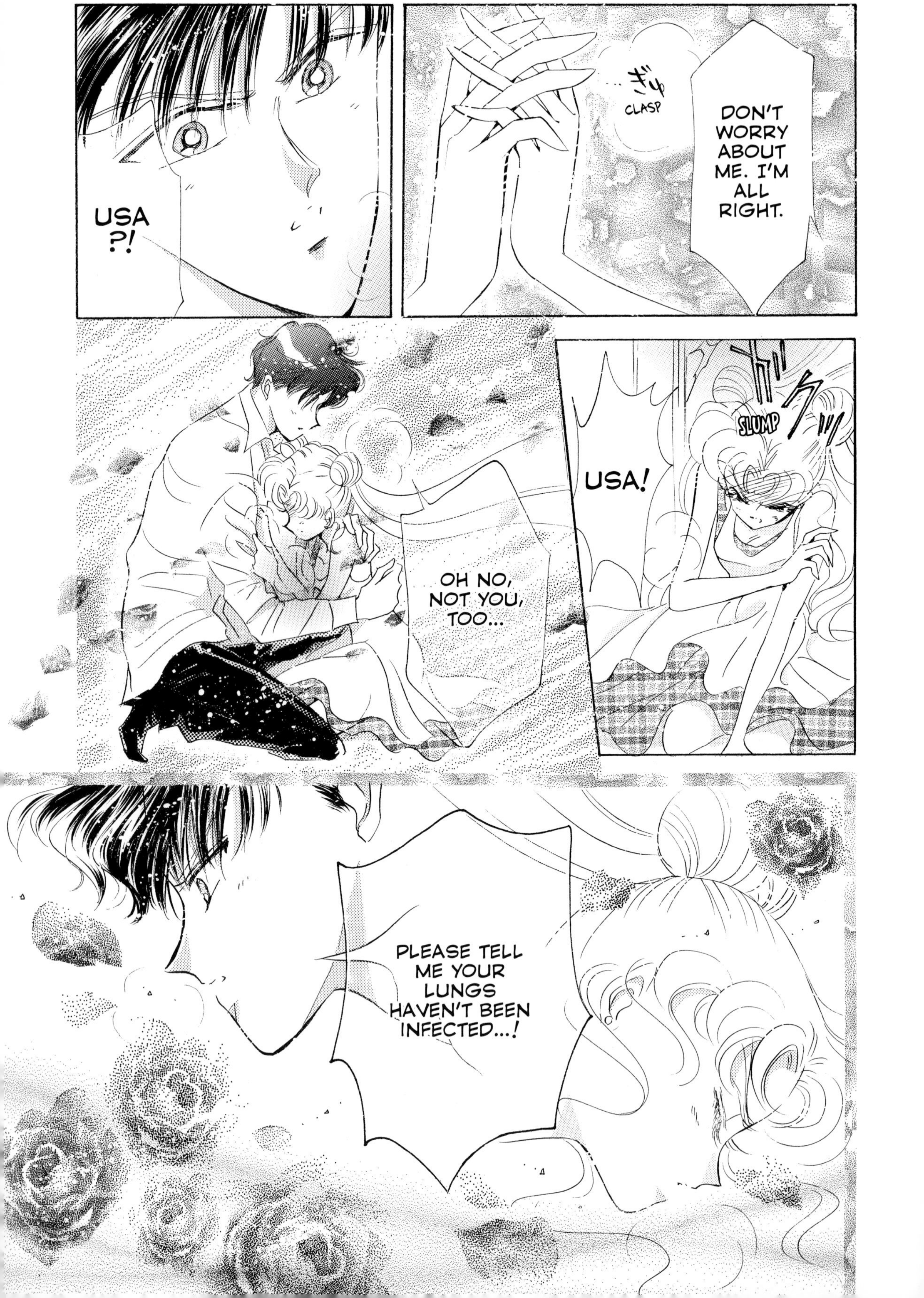
ぎゅ
CLASP
DON'T WORRY ABOUT ME. I'M ALL RIGHT.
USA?!
SLUMP
USA!
OH NO, NOT YOU, TOO...
PLEASE TELL ME YOUR LUNGS HAVEN'T BEEN INFECTED...!

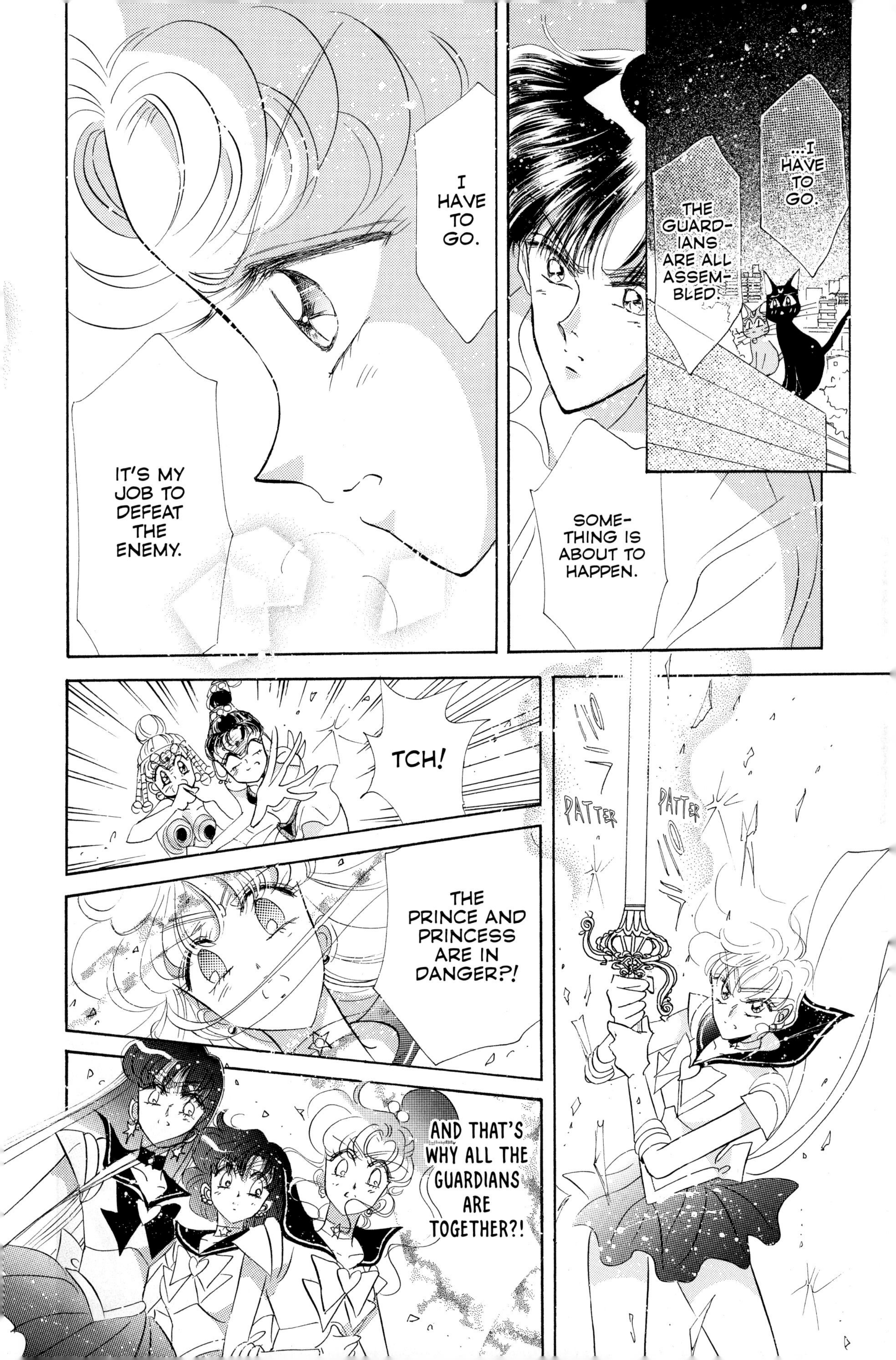
...I HAVE TO GO.
THE GUARDIANS ARE ALL ASSEMBLED.
SOMETHING IS ABOUT TO HAPPEN.
I HAVE TO GO.
IT'S MY JOB TO DEFEAT THE ENEMY.
PATTER
PATTER
TCH!
THE PRINCE AND PRINCESS ARE IN DANGER?!
AND THAT'S WHY ALL THE GUARDIANS ARE TOGETHER?!

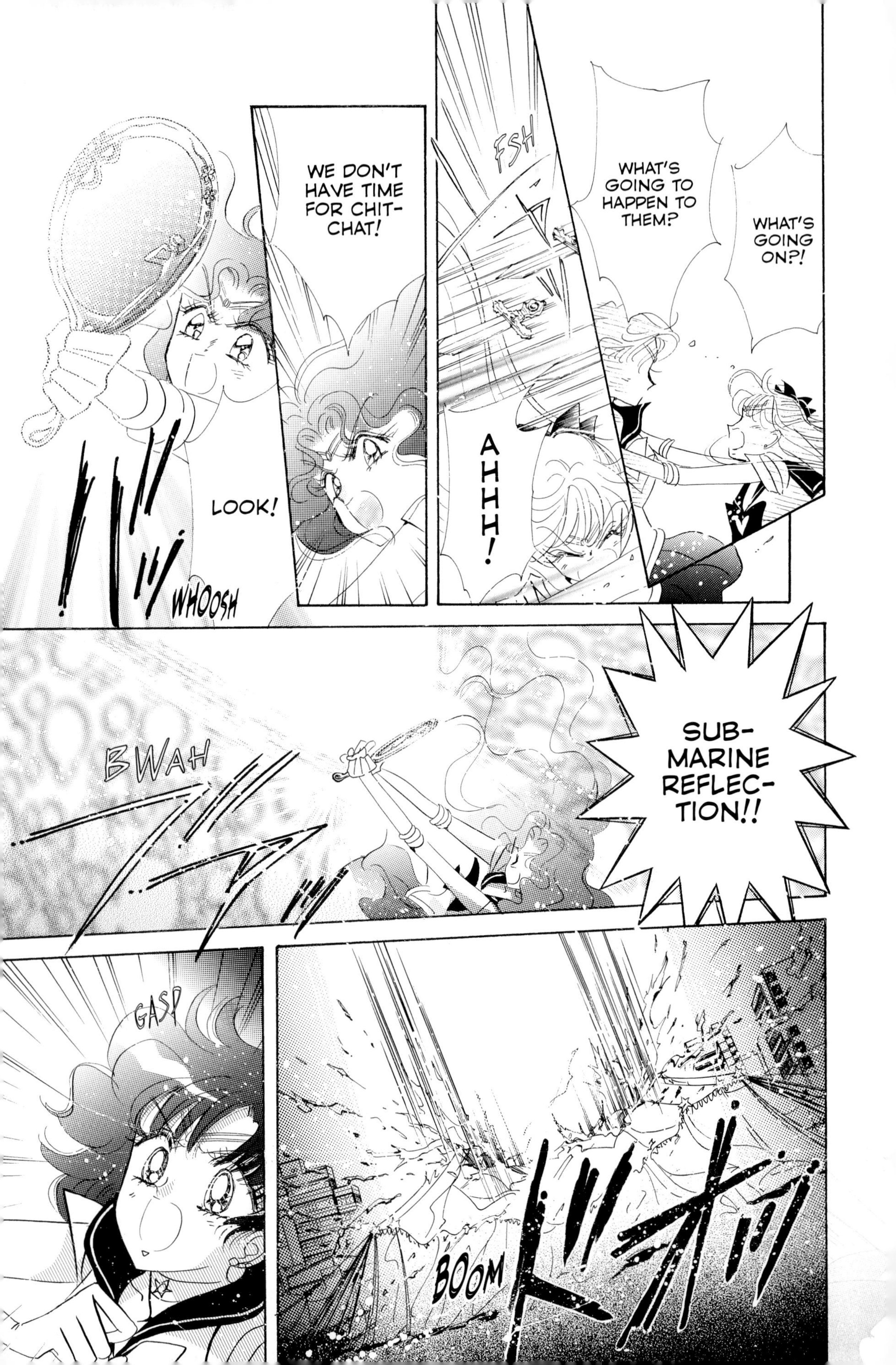
WHAT'S GOING ON?!
WHAT'S GOING TO HAPPEN TO THEM?
FSH
AHHH!
WE DON'T HAVE TIME FOR CHIT-CHAT!
LOOK!
WHOOSH
SUB-MARINE REFLECTION!!
BWAH
BOOM
GASP

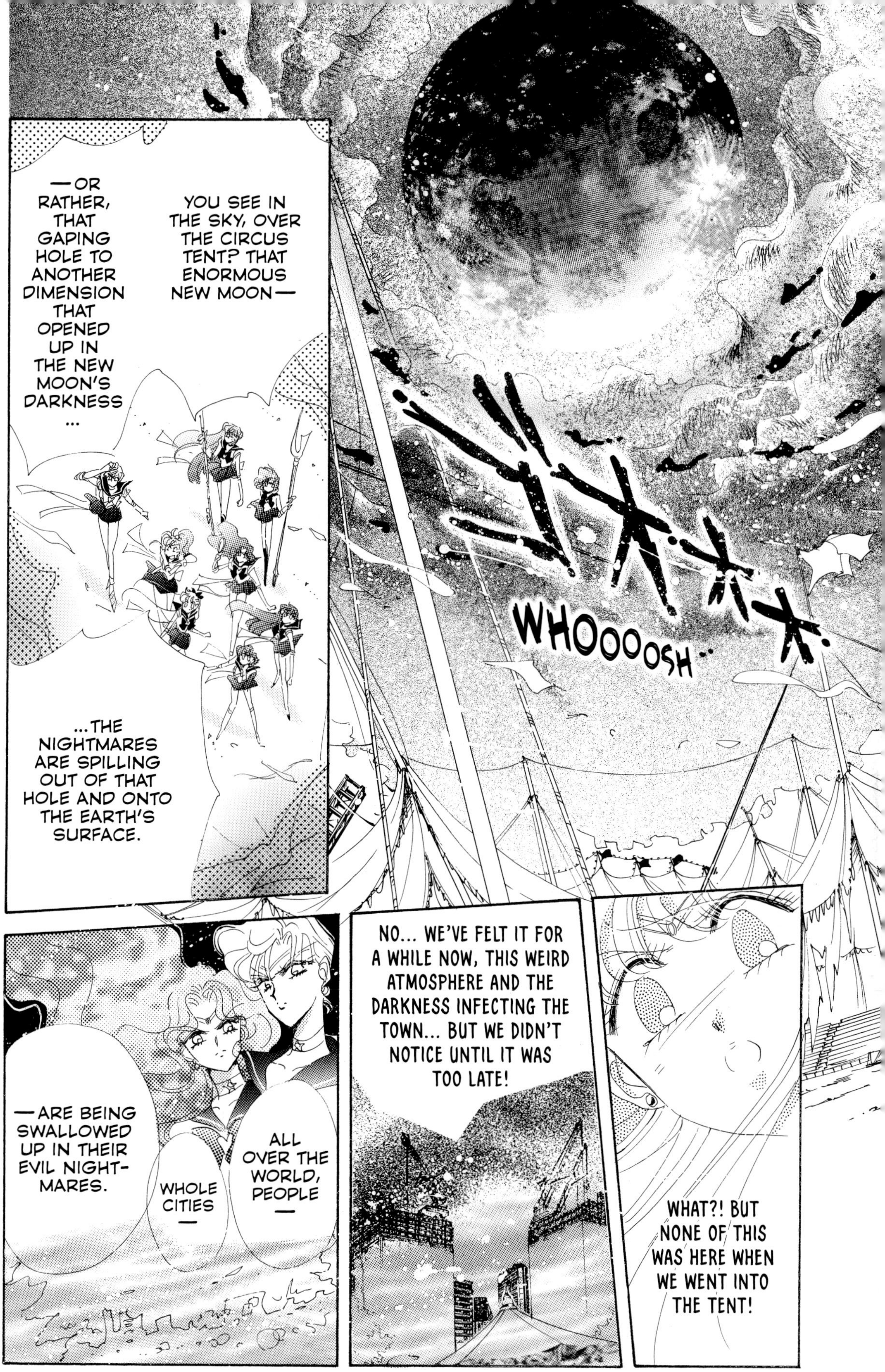
WHOOOOSH...
YOU SEE IN THE SKY, OVER THE CIRCUS TENT? THAT ENORMOUS NEW MOON—
—OR RATHER, THAT GAPING HOLE TO ANOTHER DIMENSION THAT OPENED UP IN THE NEW MOON'S DARKNESS...
...THE NIGHTMARES ARE SPILLING OUT OF THAT HOLE AND ONTO THE EARTH'S SURFACE.
WHAT?! BUT NONE OF THIS WAS HERE WHEN WE WENT INTO THE TENT!
NO... WE'VE FELT IT FOR A WHILE NOW, THIS WEIRD ATMOSPHERE AND THE DARKNESS INFECTING THE TOWN... BUT WE DIDN'T NOTICE UNTIL IT WAS TOO LATE!
ALL OVER THE WORLD, PEOPLE—
WHOLE CITIES—
—ARE BEING SWALLOWED UP IN THEIR EVIL NIGHT-MARES.

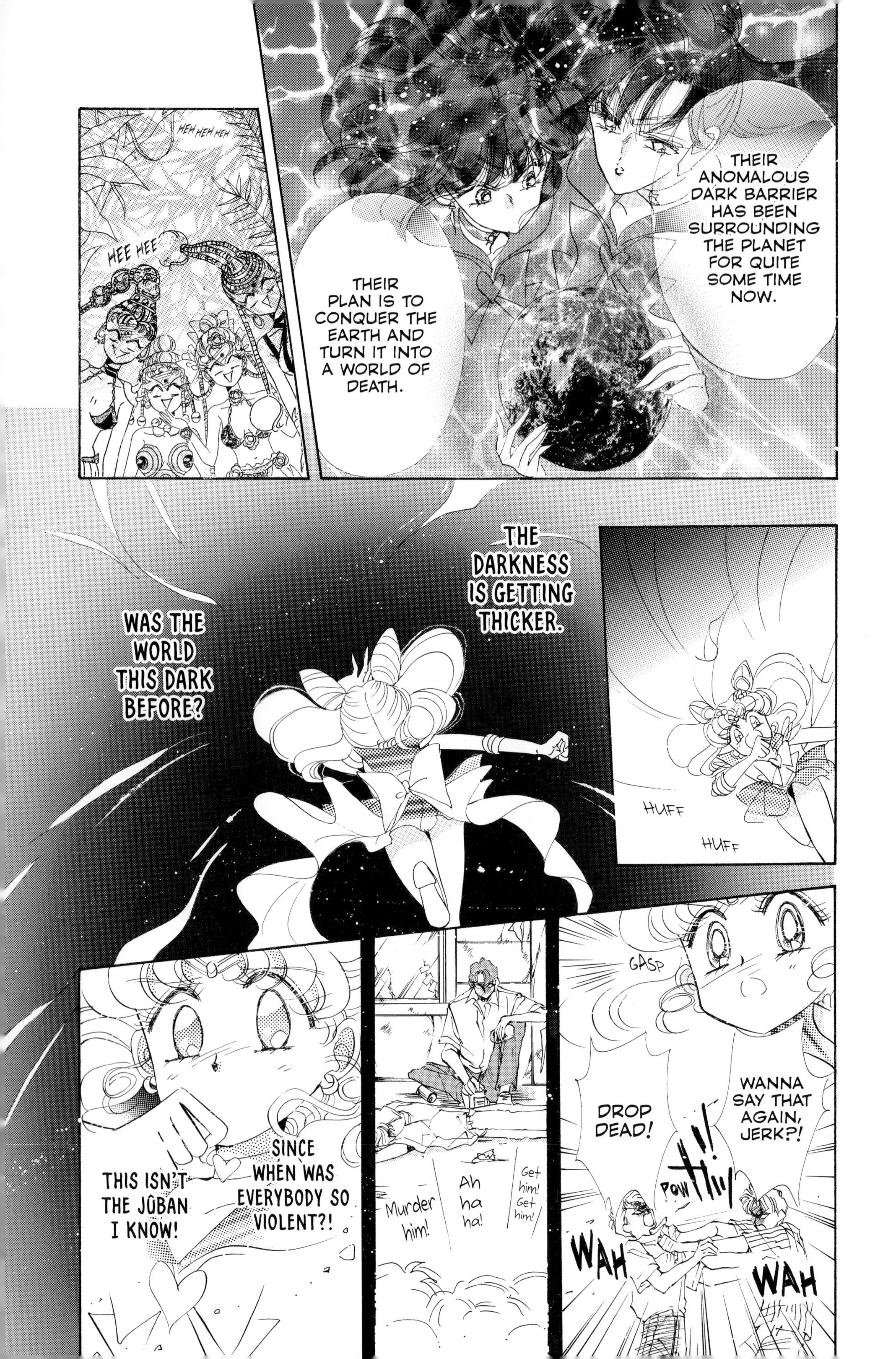
THEIR ANOMALOUS DARK BARRIER HAS BEEN SURROUNDING THE PLANET FOR QUITE SOME TIME NOW.
THEIR PLAN IS TO CONQUER THE EARTH AND TURN IT INTO A WORLD OF DEATH.
HEH HEH HEH
HEE HEE
HUFF
HUFF
THE DARKNESS IS GETTING THICKER.
WAS THE WORLD THIS DARK BEFORE?
GASP
WANNA SAY THAT AGAIN, JERK?!
DROP DEAD!
POW
WAH
WAH
Get him! Get him!
Ah ha ha!
Murder him!
SINCE WHEN WAS EVERYBODY SO VIOLENT?!
THIS ISN'T THE JÛBAN I KNOW!

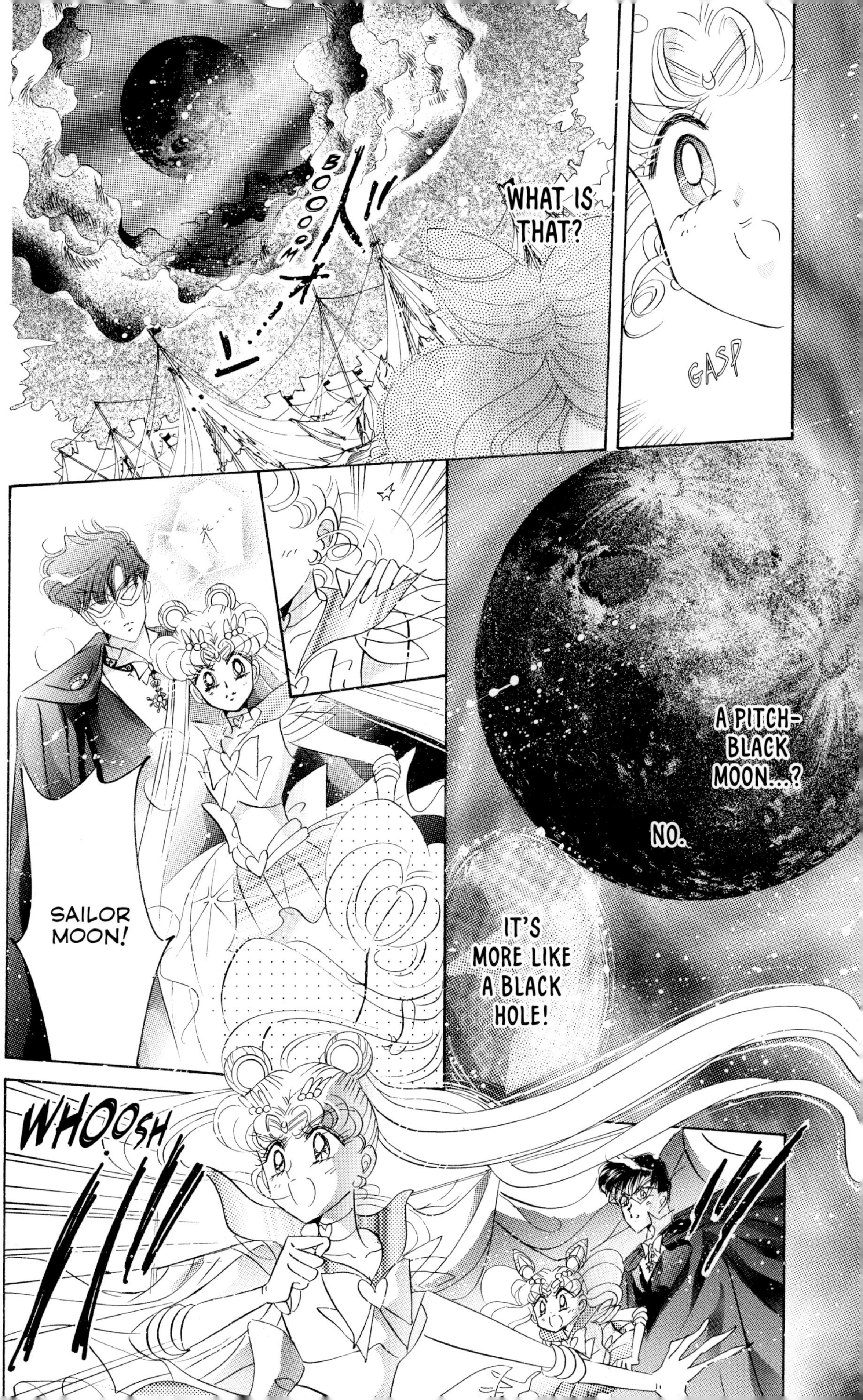
GASP
WHAT IS THAT?
BOOOOOM
A PITCH-BLACK MOON...?
NO.
IT'S MORE LIKE A BLACK HOLE!
SAILOR MOON!
WHOOSH

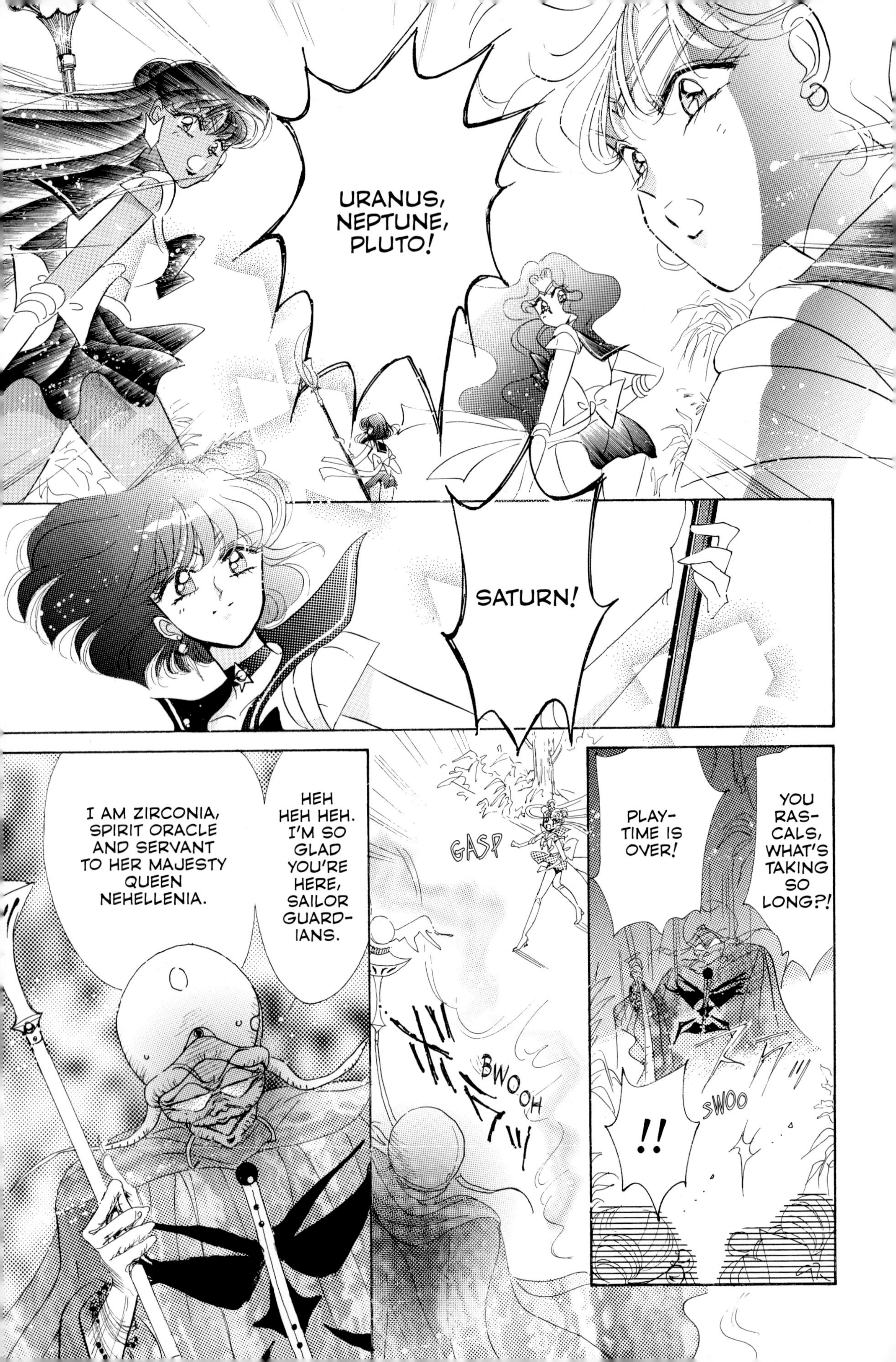
URANUS, NEPTUNE, PLUTO!
SATURN!
YOU RASCALS, WHAT'S TAKING SO LONG?!
PLAY-TIME IS OVER!
SWOO
!!
GASP
BWOOOH
HEH HEH HEH. I'M SO GLAD YOU'RE HERE, SAILOR GUARDIANS.
I AM ZIRCONIA, SPIRIT ORACLE AND SERVANT TO HER MAJESTY QUEEN NEHELLENIA.

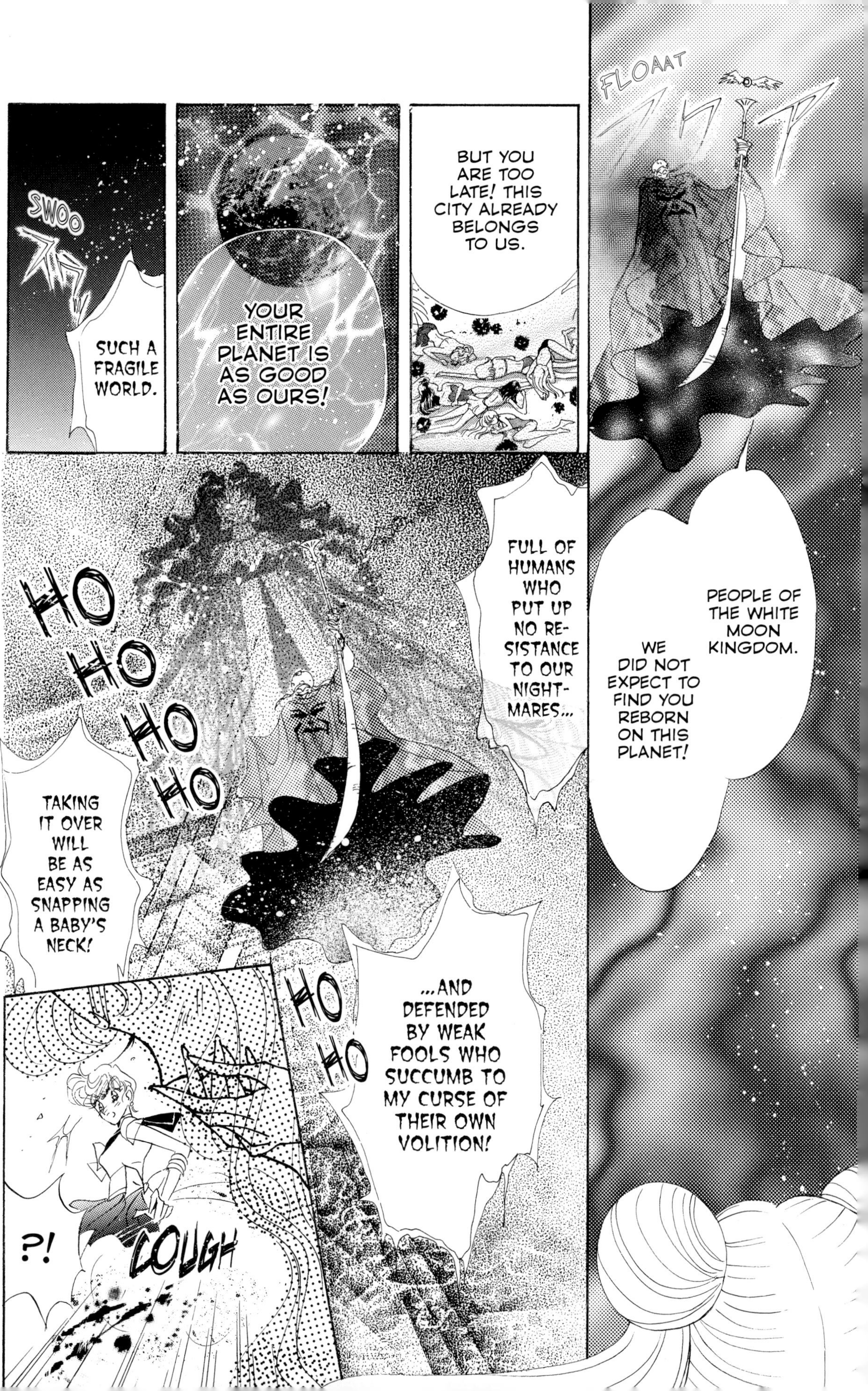
FLOAAT
PEOPLE OF THE WHITE MOON KINGDOM.
WE DID NOT EXPECT TO FIND YOU REBORN ON THIS PLANET!
BUT YOU ARE TOO LATE! THIS CITY ALREADY BELONGS TO US.
YOUR ENTIRE PLANET IS AS GOOD AS OURS!
SWOO
SUCH A FRAGILE WORLD.
FULL OF HUMANS WHO PUT UP NO RE-SISTANCE TO OUR NIGHT-MARES...
HO HO HO HO HO
TAKING IT OVER WILL BE AS EASY AS SNAPPING A BABY'S NECK!
HO HO
...AND DEFENDED BY WEAK FOOLS WHO SUCCUMB TO MY CURSE OF THEIR OWN VOLITION!
?!
COUGH

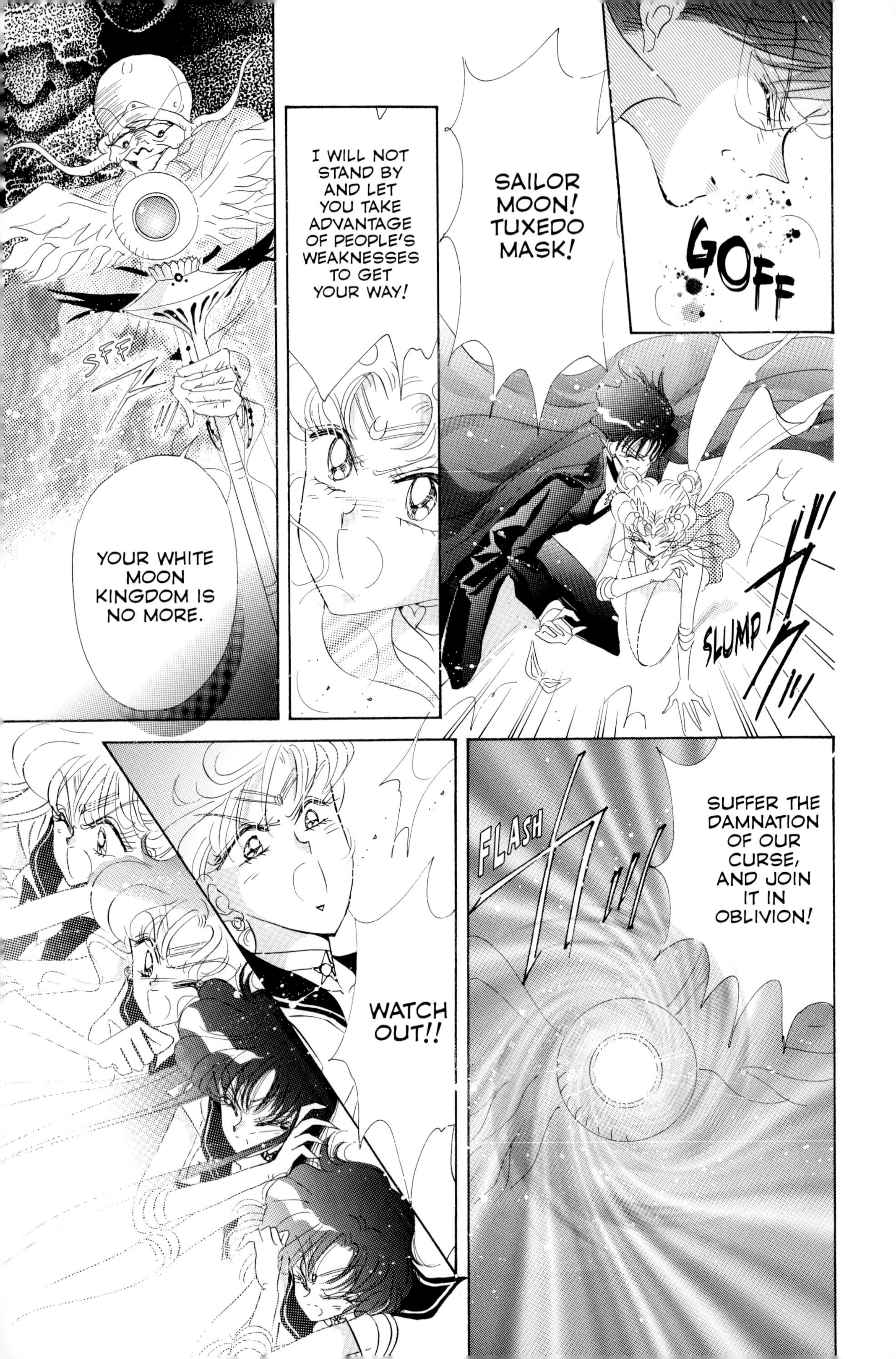
GOFF
SAILOR MOON! TUXEDO MASK!
SLUMP
I WILL NOT STAND BY AND LET YOU TAKE ADVANTAGE OF PEOPLE'S WEAKNESSES TO GET YOUR WAY!
YOUR WHITE MOON KINGDOM IS NO MORE.
SFF
SUFFER THE DAMNATION OF OUR CURSE, AND JOIN IT IN OBLIVION!
FLASH
WATCH OUT!!

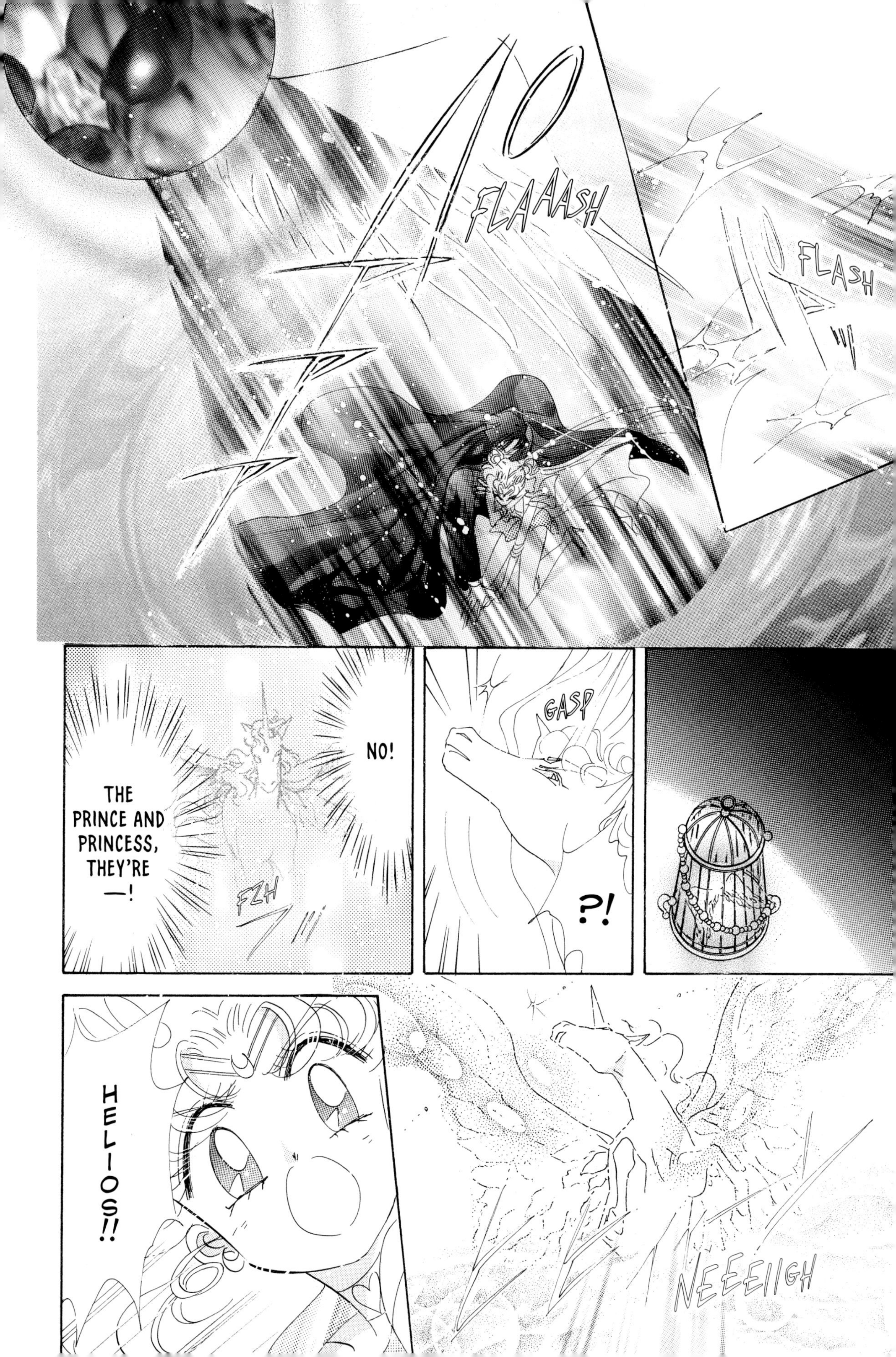
FLASH
FLAAASH
GASP
?!
NO!
THE PRINCE AND PRINCESS, THEY'RE—!
FZH
NEEEIIGH
HELIOS!!

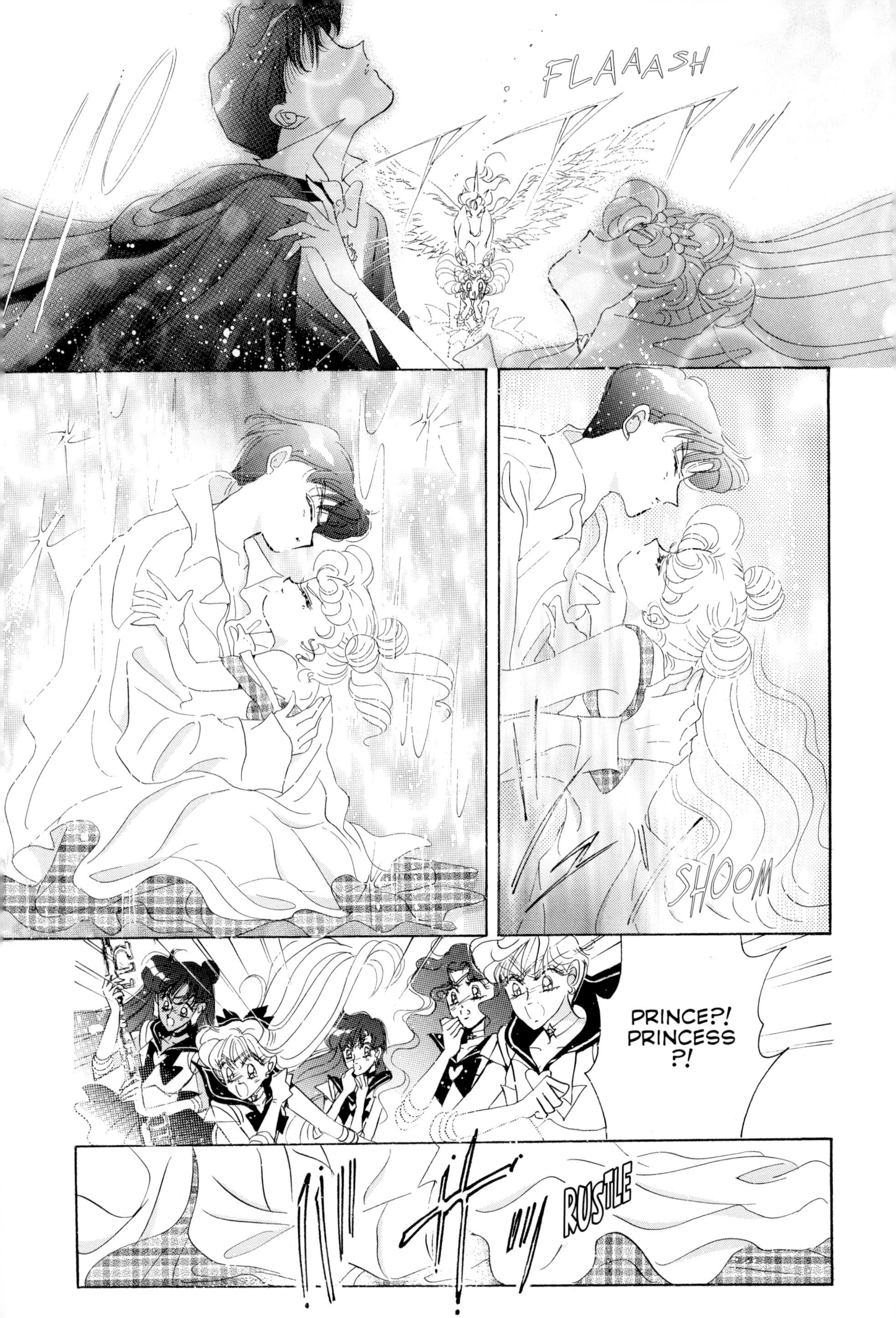
FLAAASH
SHOOM
PRINCE?! PRINCESS ?!
RUSTLE

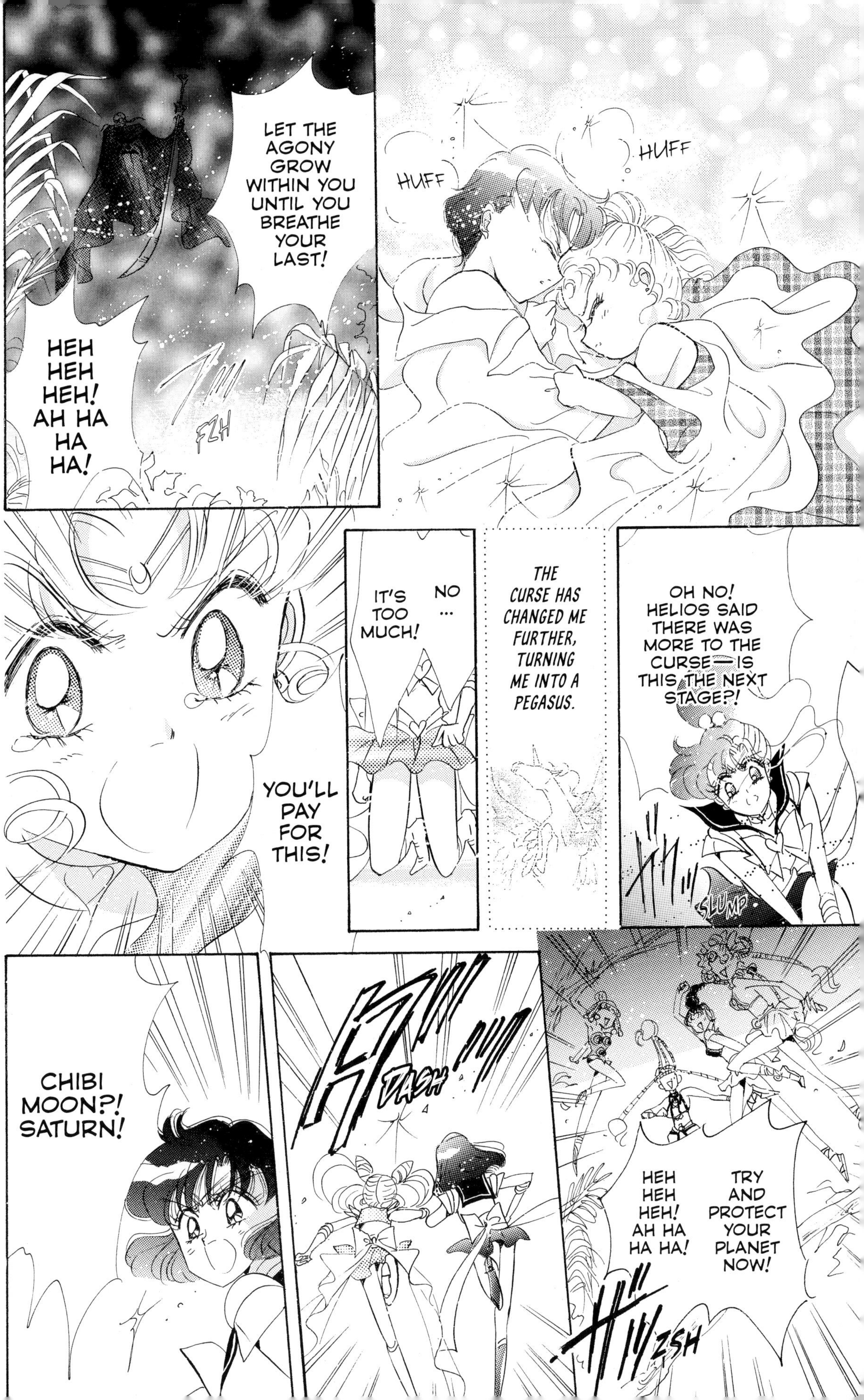
HUFF
HUFF
LET THE AGONY GROW WITHIN YOU UNTIL YOU BREATHE YOUR LAST!
HEH HEH HEH! AH HA HA HA!
FZH
OH NO! HELIOS SAID THERE WAS MORE TO THE CURSE—IS THIS THE NEXT STAGE?!
SLUMP
THE CURSE HAS CHANGED ME FURTHER, TURNING ME INTO A PEGASUS.
NO ...
IT'S TOO MUCH!
YOU'LL PAY FOR THIS!
TRY AND PROTECT YOUR PLANET NOW!
HEH HEH HEH! AH HA HA HA!
ZSH
DASH
CHIBI MOON?! SATURN!

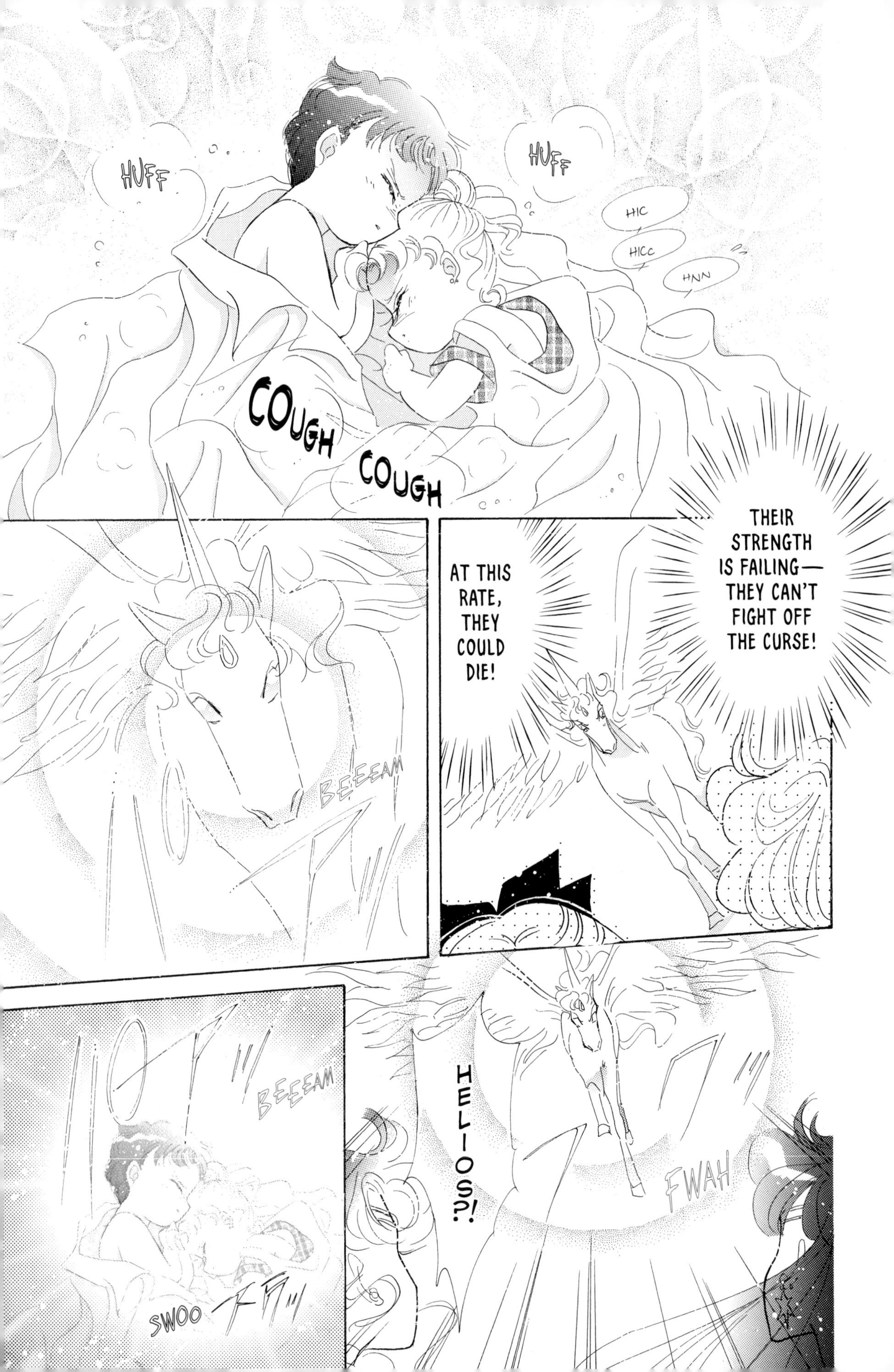
HUFF
HIC
HICC
HNN
HUFF
COUGH
COUGH
THEIR STRENGTH IS FAILING—THEY CAN'T FIGHT OFF THE CURSE!
AT THIS RATE, THEY COULD DIE!
BEEEAM
FWAH
HELIOS?!
BEEEAM
SWOO

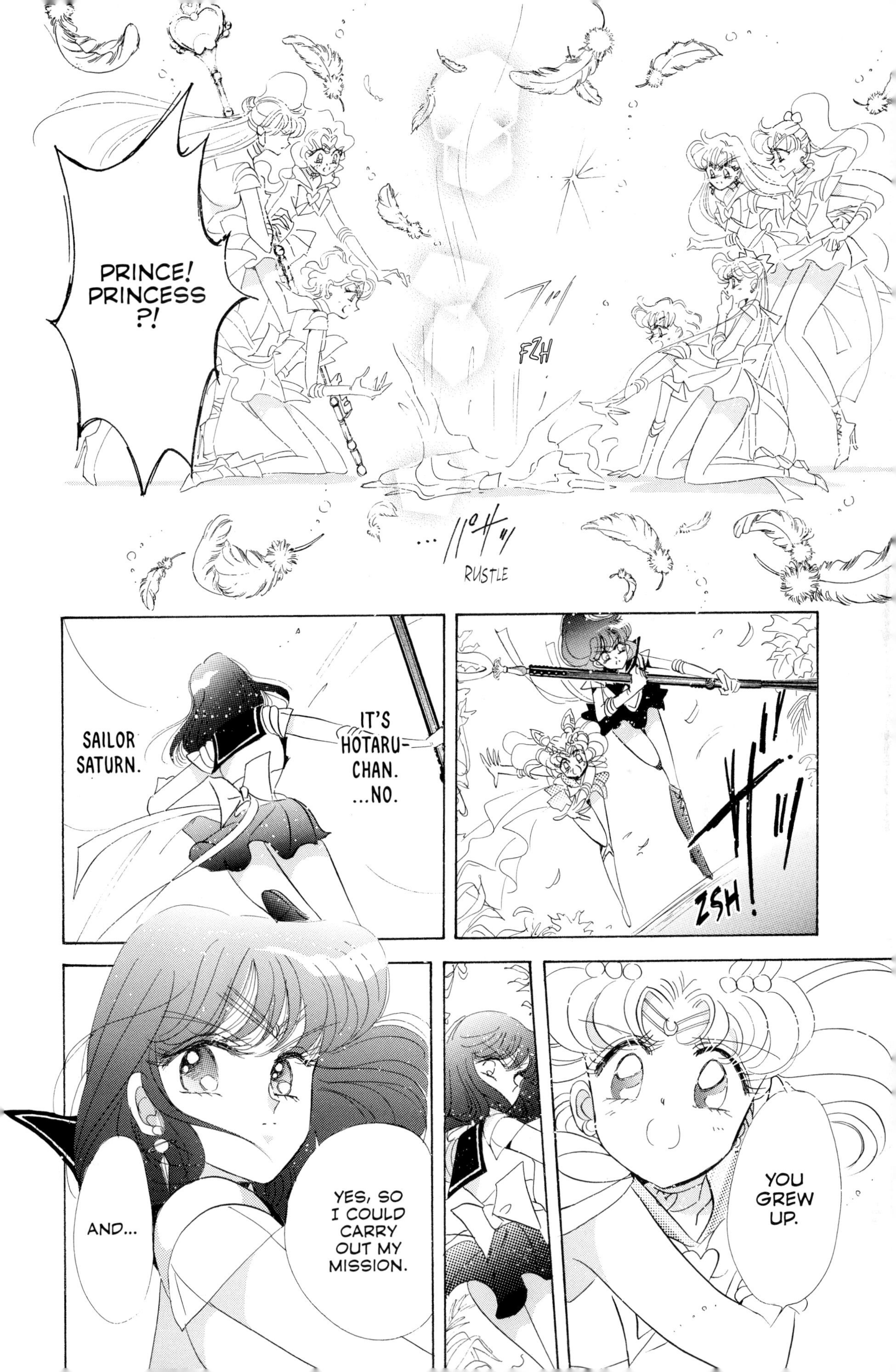
PRINCE! PRINCESS ?!
FZH
...
RUSTLE
ZSH!
IT'S HOTARU-CHAN. ...NO.
SAILOR SATURN.
YOU GREW UP.
YES, SO I COULD CARRY OUT MY MISSION.
AND...

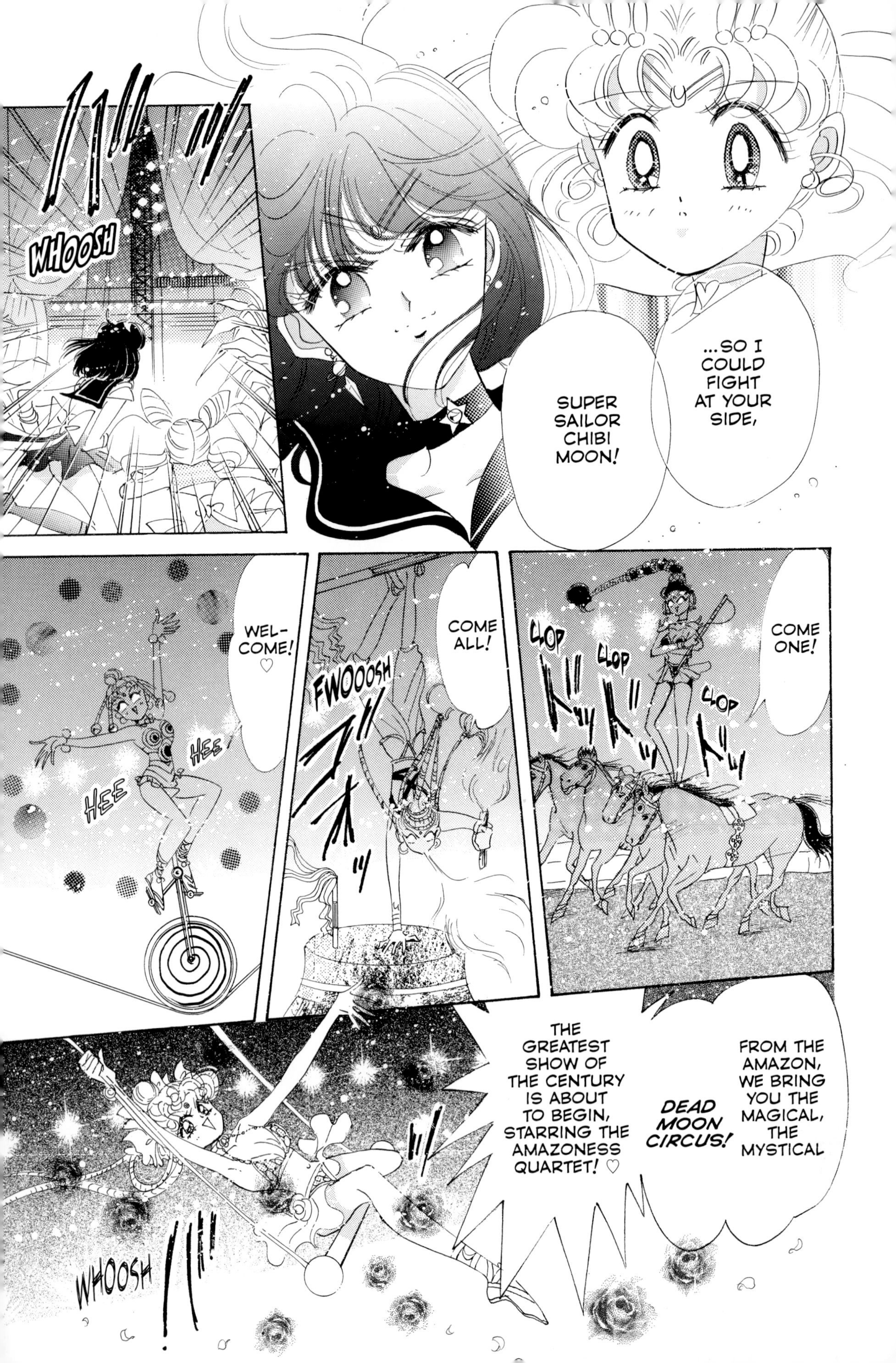
...SO I COULD FIGHT AT YOUR SIDE,
SUPER SAILOR CHIBI MOON!
WHOOSH
COME ONE!
CLOP
CLOP
CLOP
COME ALL!
FWOOOSH
WEL-COME! ♡
HEE
HEE
FROM THE AMAZON, WE BRING YOU THE MAGICAL, THE MYSTICAL
DEAD MOON CIRCUS!
THE GREATEST SHOW OF THE CENTURY IS ABOUT TO BEGIN, STARRING THE AMAZONESS QUARTET! ♡
WHOOSH

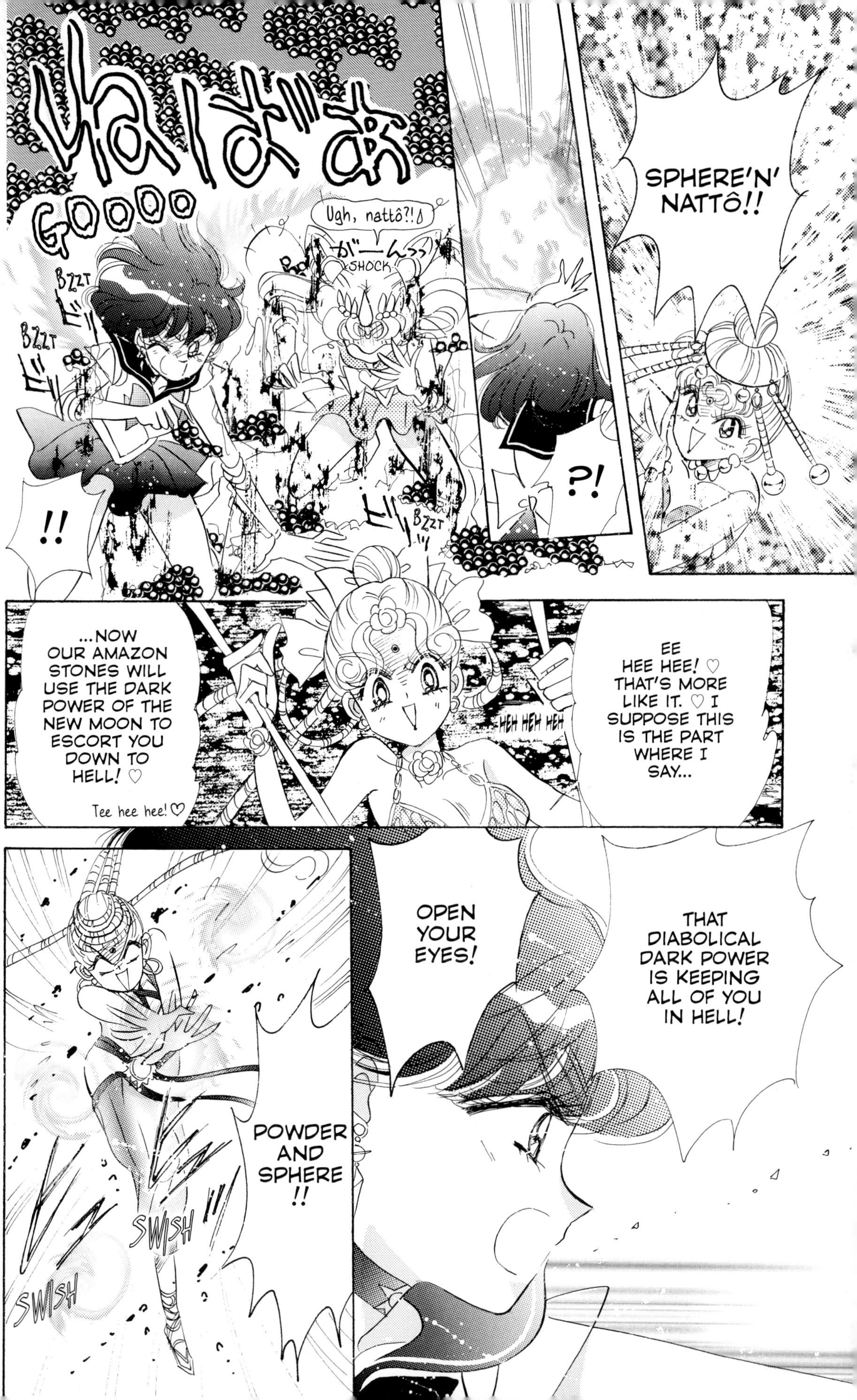
SPHERE'N' NATTÔ!!
?!
GOOOO
Ugh, nattô?!
がーん
SHOCK
BZZT
BZZT
BZZT
!!
EE HEE HEE! ♡ THAT'S MORE LIKE IT. ♡ I SUPPOSE THIS IS THE PART WHERE I SAY...
HEH HEH HEH
...NOW OUR AMAZON STONES WILL USE THE DARK POWER OF THE NEW MOON TO ESCORT YOU DOWN TO HELL! ♡
Tee hee hee! ♡
THAT DIABOLICAL DARK POWER IS KEEPING ALL OF YOU IN HELL!
OPEN YOUR EYES!
POWDER AND SPHERE!!
SWISH
SWISH

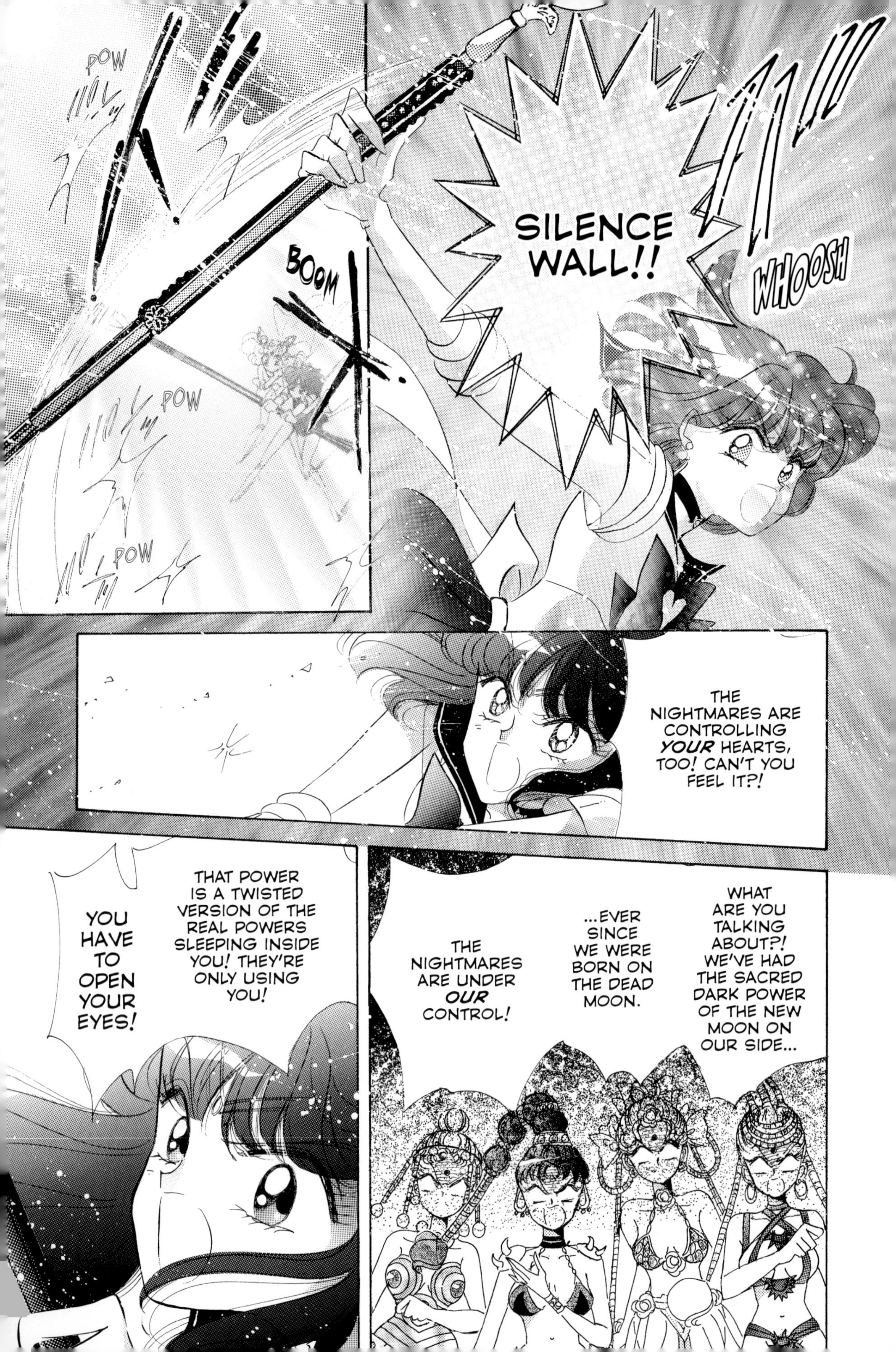

SILENCE WALL!!
WHOOSH
POW
BOOM
POW
POW
THE NIGHTMARES ARE CONTROLLING *YOUR* HEARTS, TOO! CAN'T YOU FEEL IT?!
WHAT ARE YOU TALKING ABOUT?! WE'VE HAD THE SACRED DARK POWER OF THE NEW MOON ON OUR SIDE...
...EVER SINCE WE WERE BORN ON THE DEAD MOON.
THE NIGHTMARES ARE UNDER *OUR* CONTROL!
THAT POWER IS A TWISTED VERSION OF THE REAL POWERS SLEEPING INSIDE YOU! THEY'RE ONLY USING YOU!
YOU HAVE TO OPEN YOUR EYES!

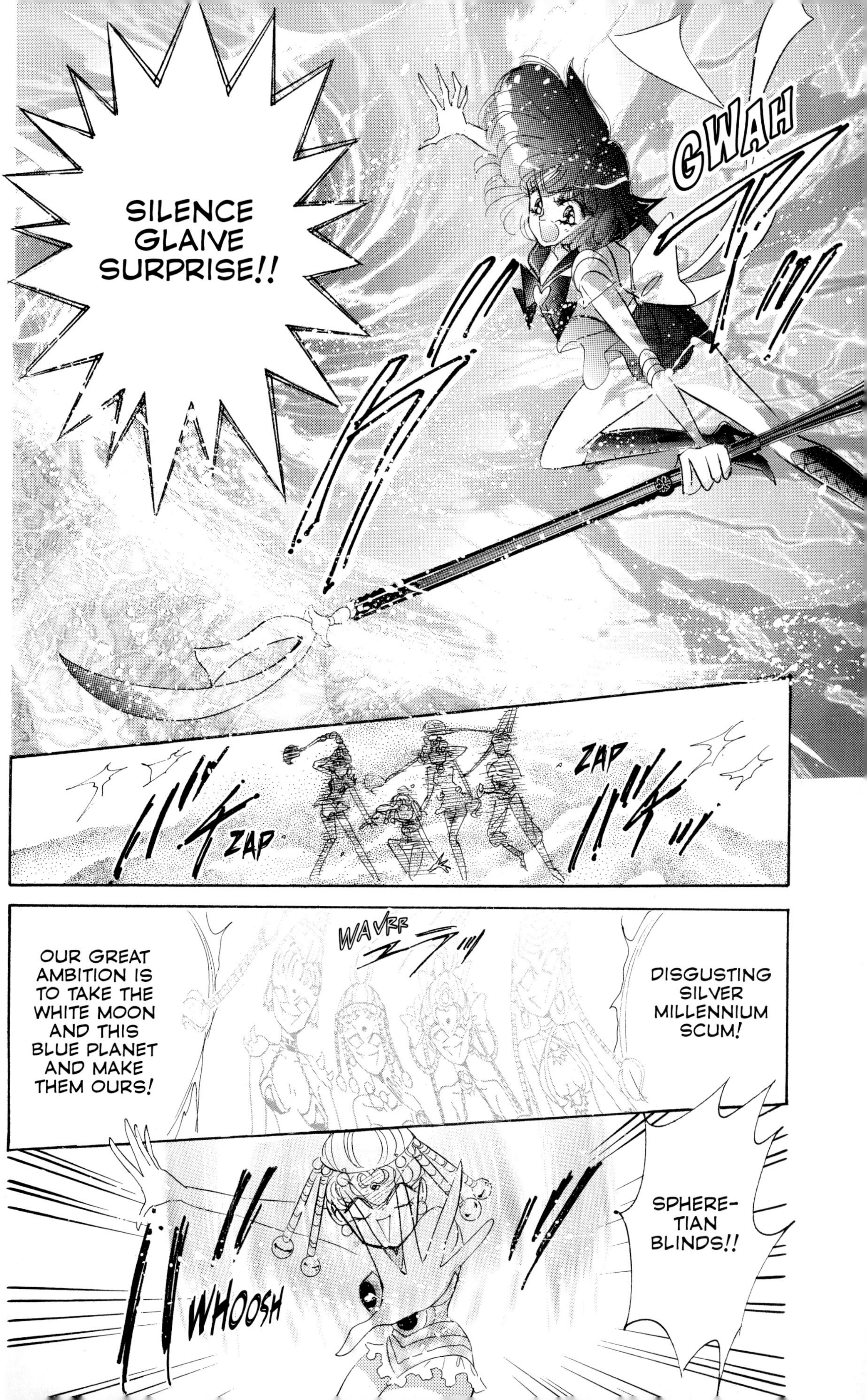
GWAH
SILENCE GLAIVE SURPRISE!!
ZAP
ZAP
WAVRR
DISGUSTING SILVER MILLENNIUM SCUM!
OUR GREAT AMBITION IS TO TAKE THE WHITE MOON AND THIS BLUE PLANET AND MAKE THEM OURS!
SPHERE-TIAN BLINDS!!
WHOOSH

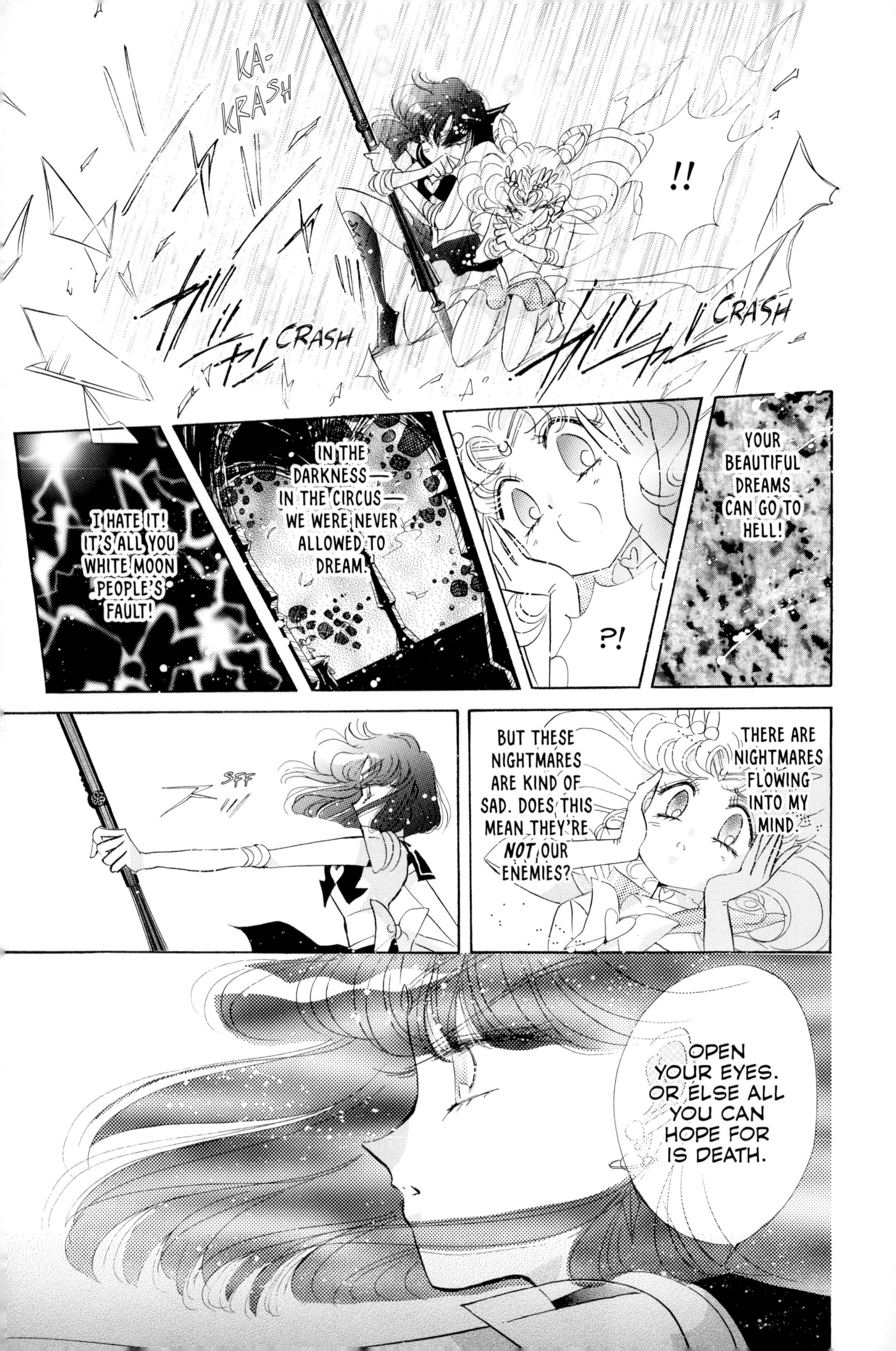
!!
CRASH
KA-KRASH
CRASH
YOUR BEAUTIFUL DREAMS CAN GO TO HELL!
?!
IN THE DARKNESS— IN THE CIRCUS— WE WERE NEVER ALLOWED TO DREAM.
I HATE IT! IT'S ALL YOU WHITE MOON PEOPLE'S FAULT!
THERE ARE NIGHTMARES FLOWING INTO MY MIND.
BUT THESE NIGHTMARES ARE KIND OF SAD. DOES THIS MEAN THEY'RE *NOT* OUR ENEMIES?
SFF
OPEN YOUR EYES. OR ELSE ALL YOU CAN HOPE FOR IS DEATH.

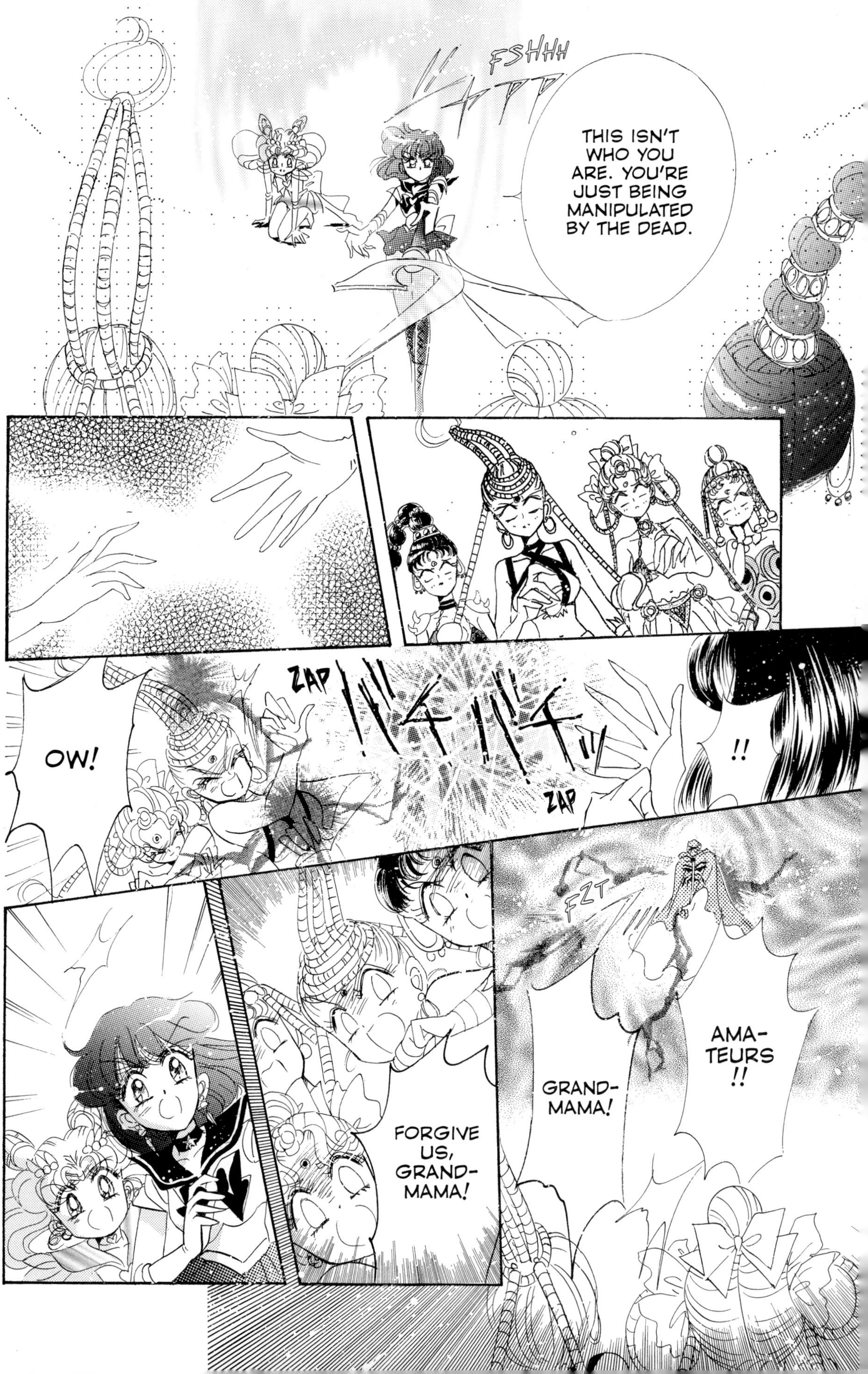
FSHHH
THIS ISN'T WHO YOU ARE. YOU'RE JUST BEING MANIPULATED BY THE DEAD.
!!
ZAP
ZAP
OW!
FZT
AMA-TEURS!!
GRAND-MAMA!
FORGIVE US, GRAND-MAMA!

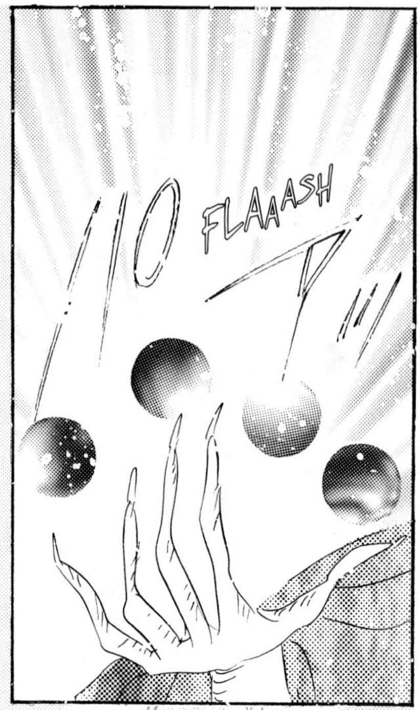
FLAAASH

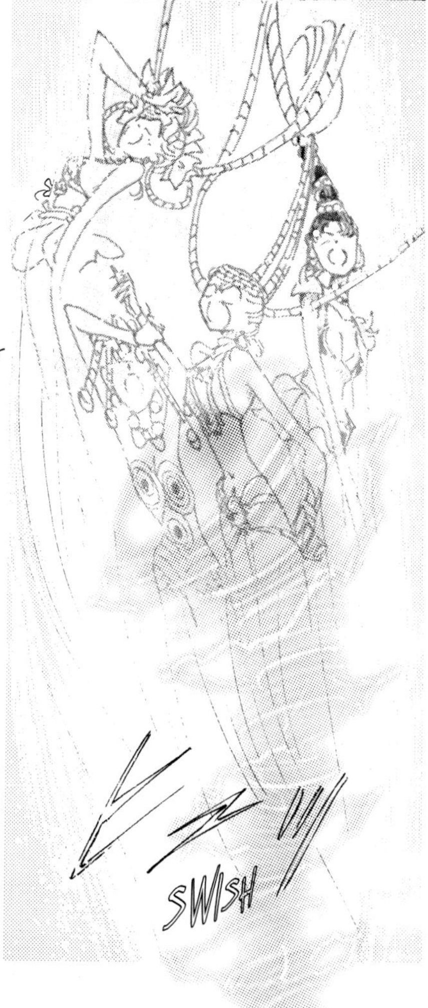
SWISH

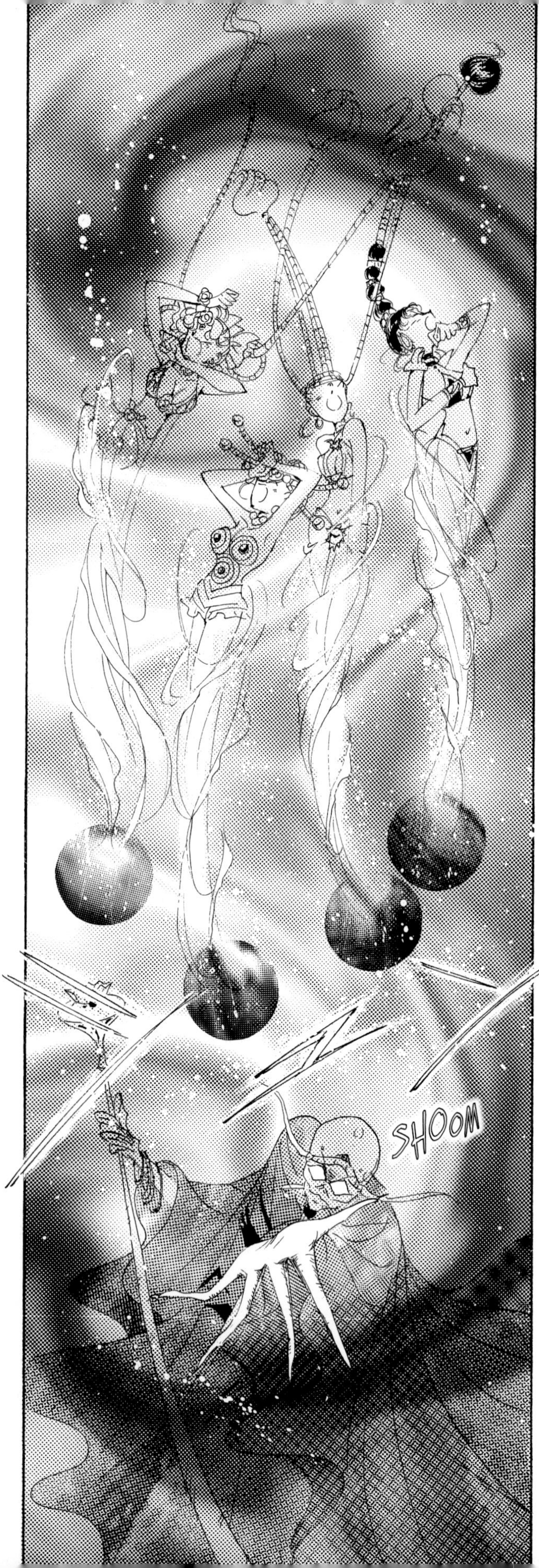
SHOOM

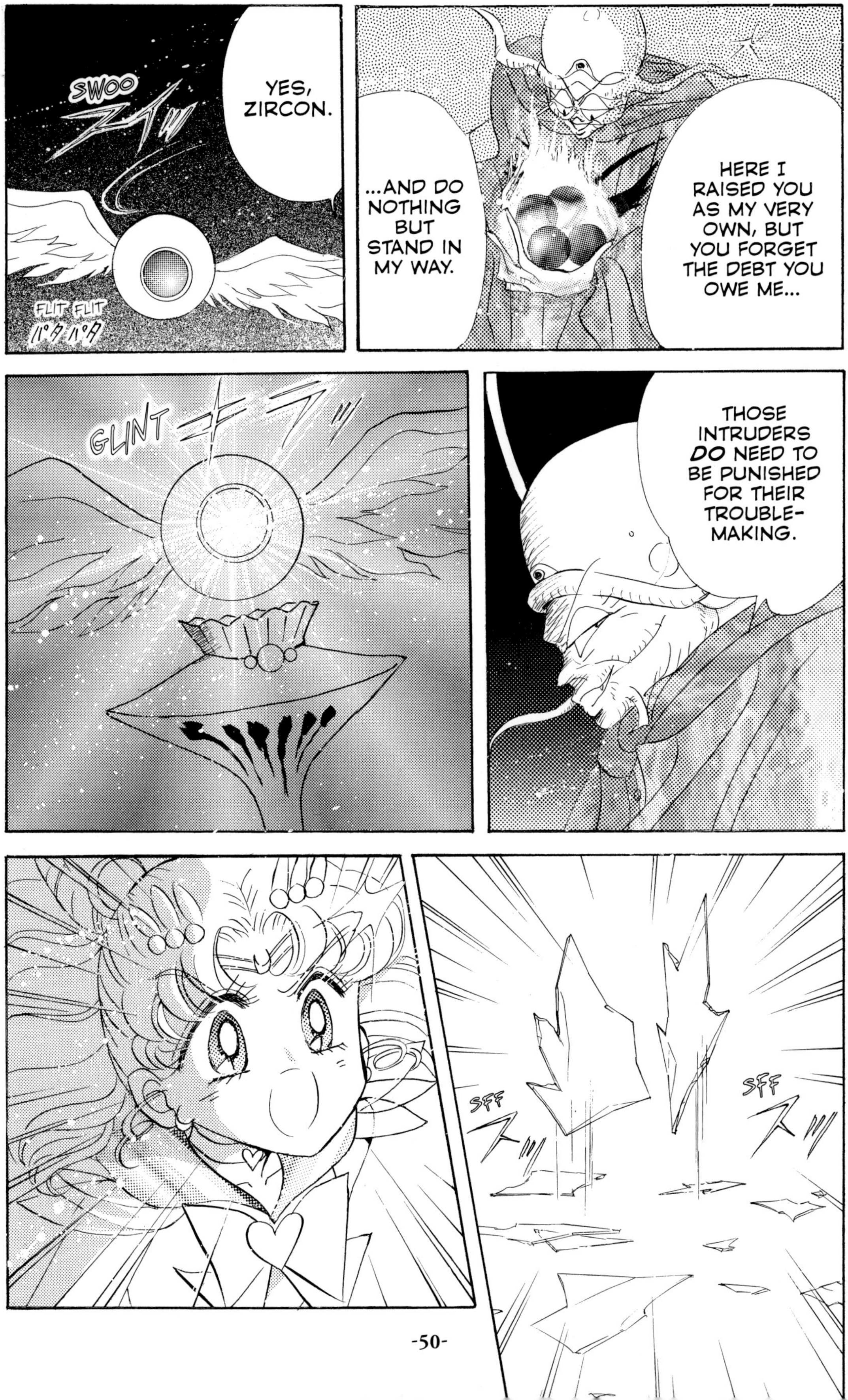
HERE I RAISED YOU AS MY VERY OWN, BUT YOU FORGET THE DEBT YOU OWE ME...
...AND DO NOTHING BUT STAND IN MY WAY.
YES, ZIRCON.
SWOO
スイッ
FLIT FLIT
パタパタ
THOSE INTRUDERS **DO** NEED TO BE PUNISHED FOR THEIR TROUBLE-MAKING.
GLINT
キラッ
SFF
スッ
SFF
スッ

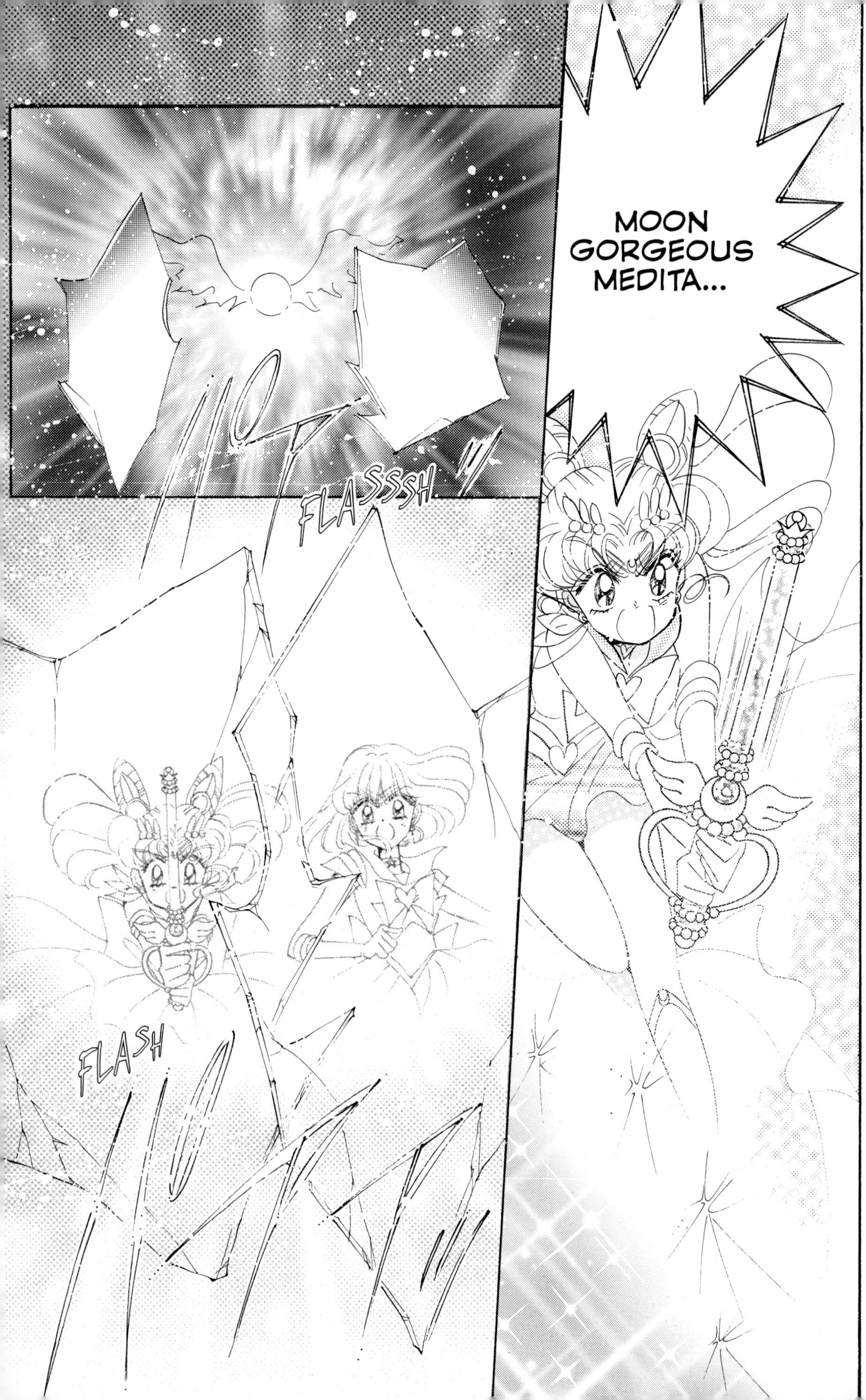
MOON GORGEOUS MEDITA...
FLASSSH
FLASH

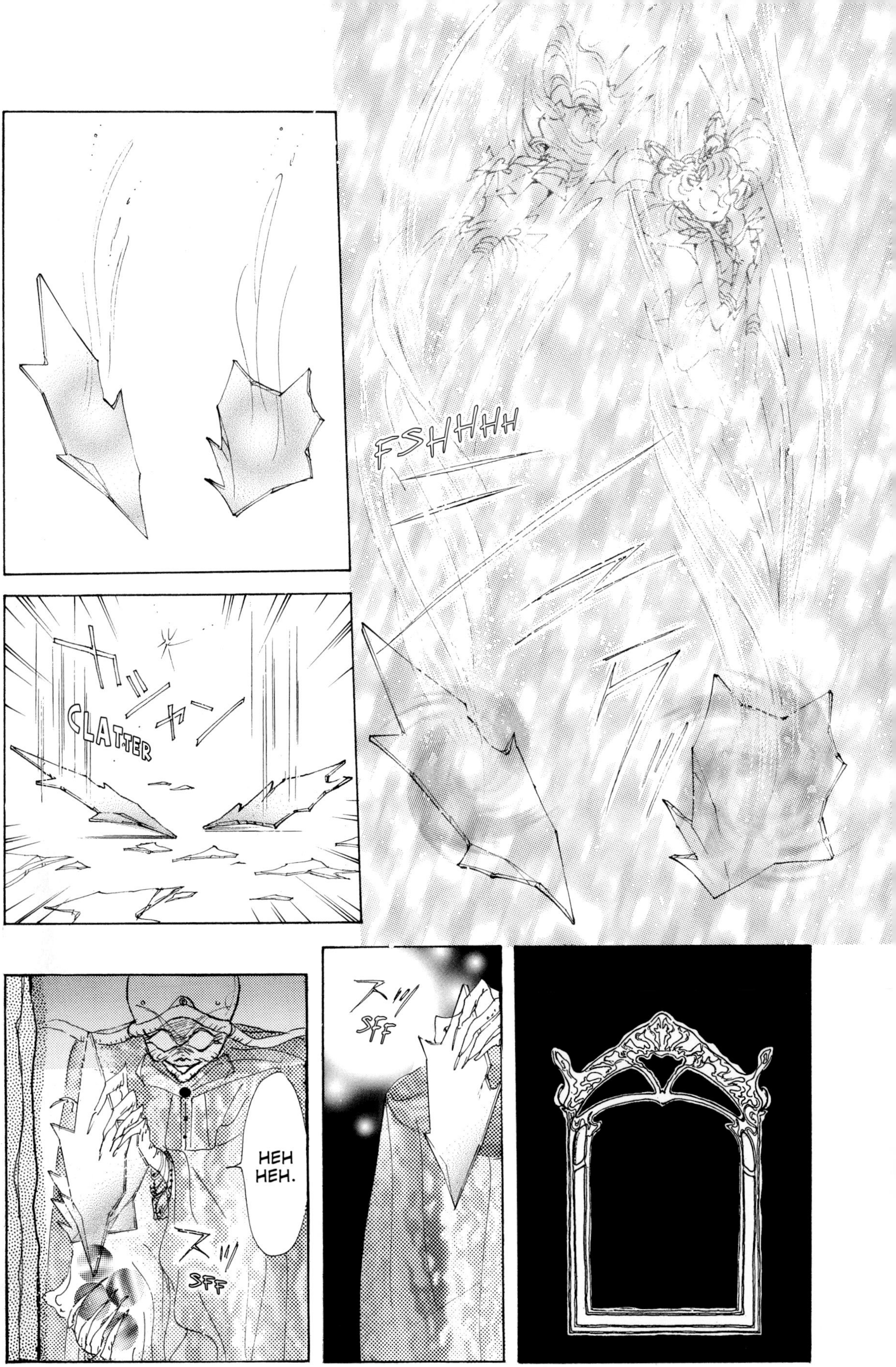
FSHHHH
CLATTER
SFF
HEH HEH.
SFF

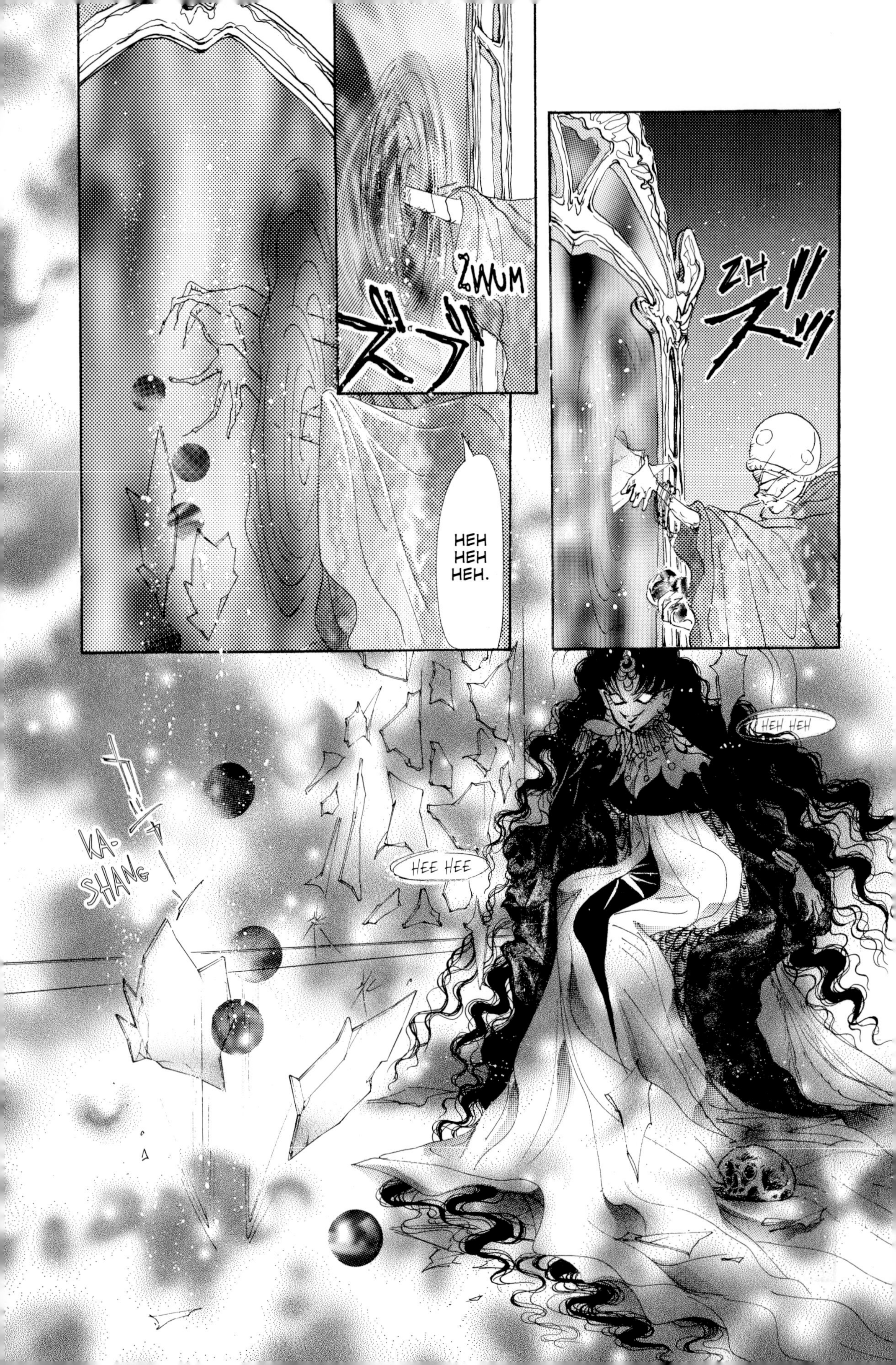
ZH
ZWUM
HEH HEH HEH.
HEH HEH
HEE HEE
KA-SHANG

Pretty Guardian Sailor Moon

Act. 46 Dream 8: Elysium Dream

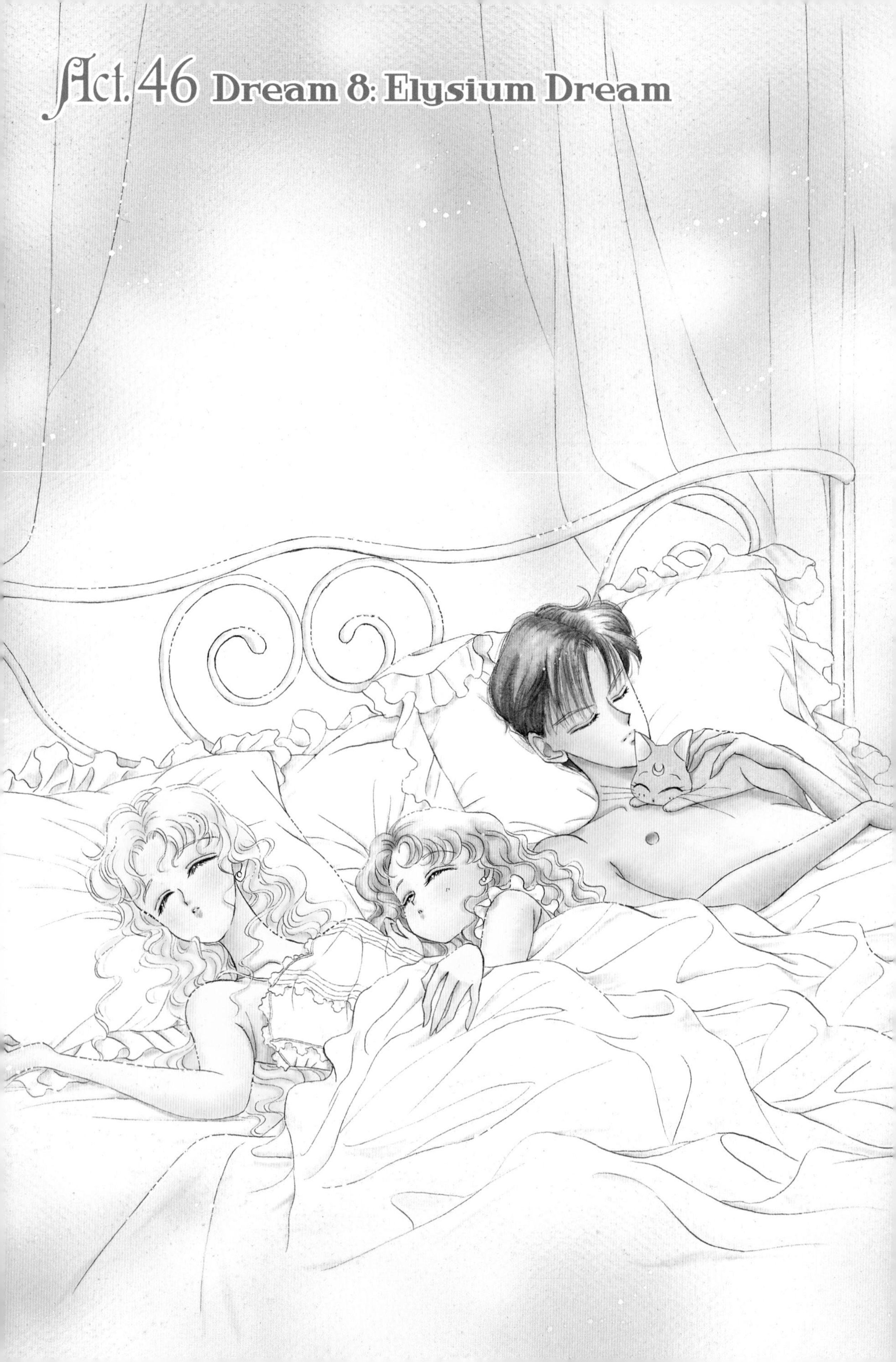

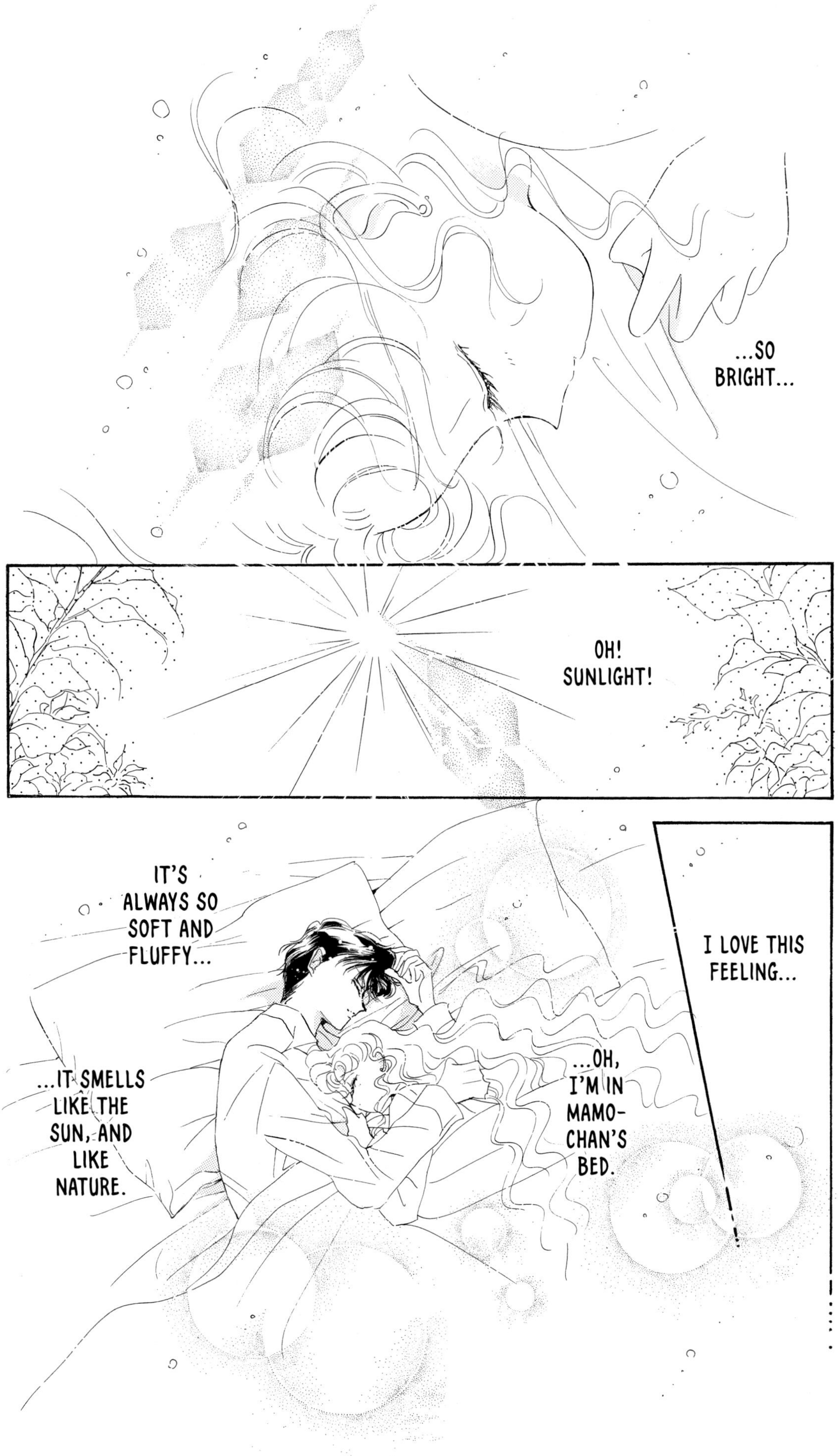
...SO BRIGHT...
OH! SUNLIGHT!
I LOVE THIS FEELING...
IT'S ALWAYS SO SOFT AND FLUFFY...
...IT SMELLS LIKE THE SUN, AND LIKE NATURE.
...OH, I'M IN MAMO-CHAN'S BED.

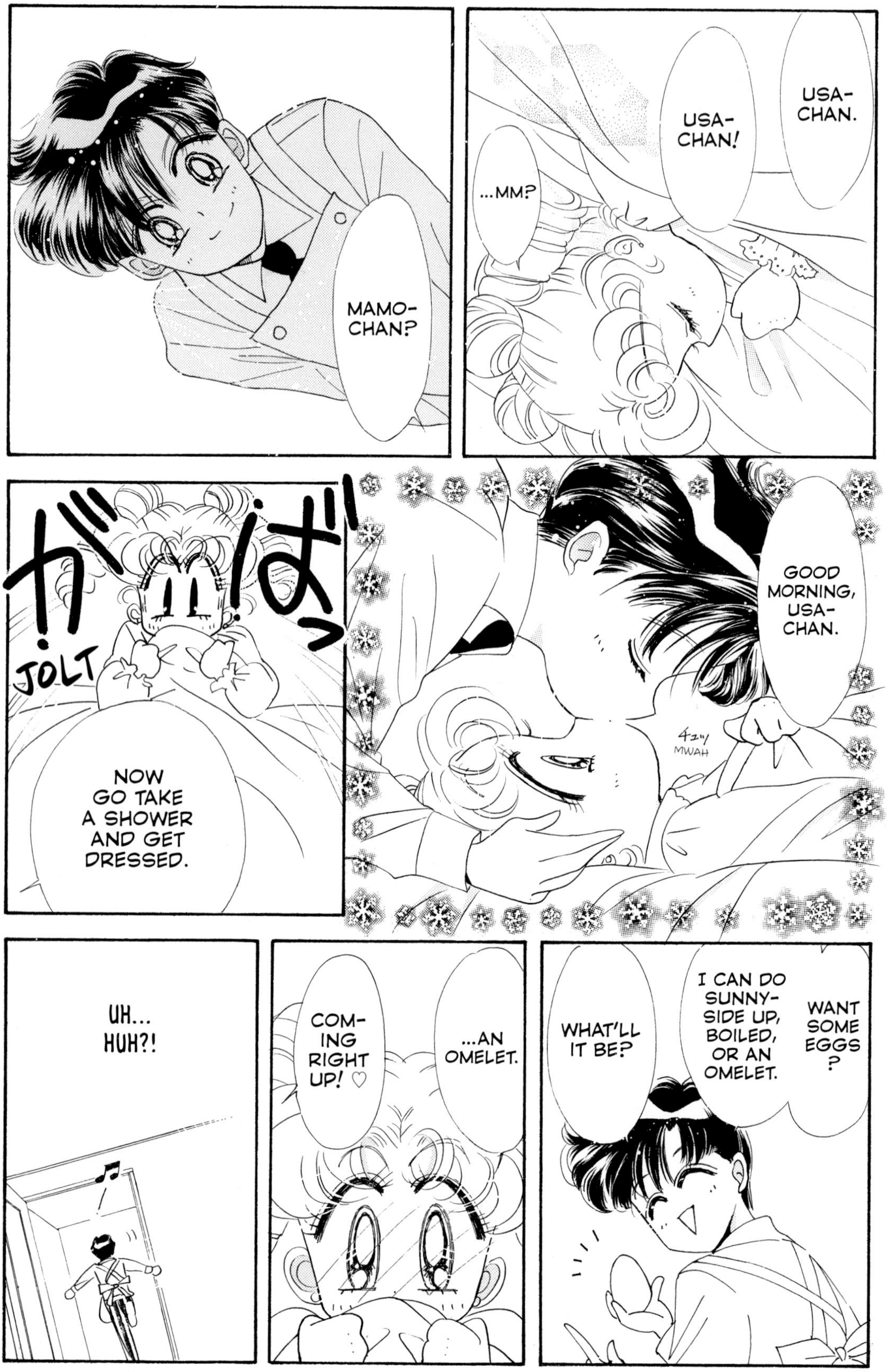
USA-CHAN.
USA-CHAN!
...MM?
MAMO-CHAN?
GOOD MORNING, USA-CHAN.
チュッ
MWAH
がばっ
JOLT
NOW GO TAKE A SHOWER AND GET DRESSED.
WANT SOME EGGS?
I CAN DO SUNNY-SIDE UP, BOILED, OR AN OMELET.
WHAT'LL IT BE?
...AN OMELET.
COM-ING RIGHT UP! ♡
UH... HUH?!

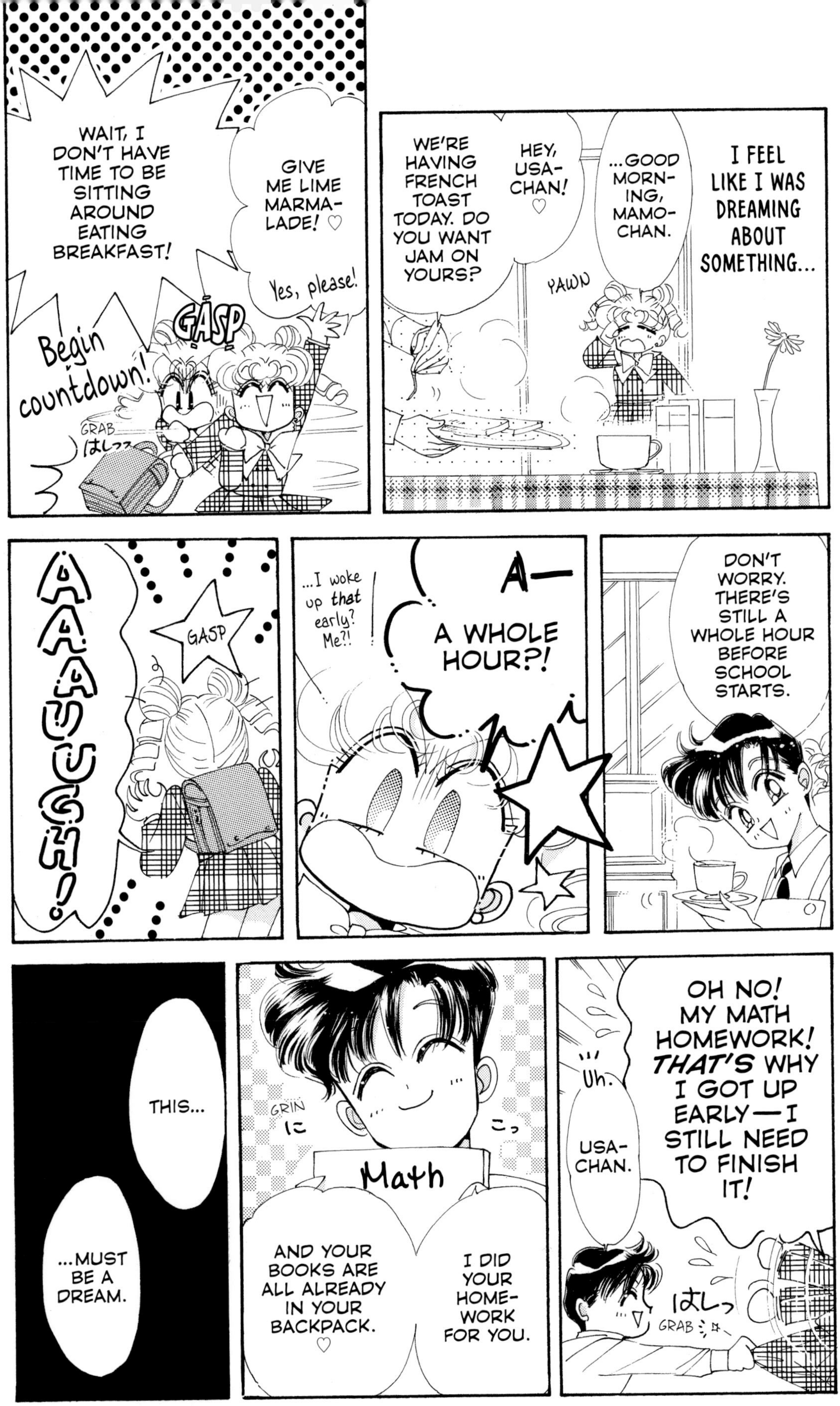
I FEEL LIKE I WAS DREAMING ABOUT SOMETHING...
...GOOD MORNING, MAMO-CHAN.
YAWN
HEY, USA-CHAN! ♡
WE'RE HAVING FRENCH TOAST TODAY. DO YOU WANT JAM ON YOURS?
GIVE ME LIME MARMALADE! ♡
Yes, please!
WAIT, I DON'T HAVE TIME TO BE SITTING AROUND EATING BREAKFAST!
GASP
Begin countdown!
GRAB
はしっ
DON'T WORRY. THERE'S STILL A WHOLE HOUR BEFORE SCHOOL STARTS.
A—
A WHOLE HOUR?!
...I woke up that early? Me?!
GASP
AAAUGH!!
OH NO! MY MATH HOMEWORK! THAT'S WHY I GOT UP EARLY—I STILL NEED TO FINISH IT!
Uh.
USA-CHAN.
はしっ
GRAB
Math
GRIN
にこっ
I DID YOUR HOMEWORK FOR YOU.
AND YOUR BOOKS ARE ALL ALREADY IN YOUR BACKPACK. ♡
THIS...
...MUST BE A DREAM.

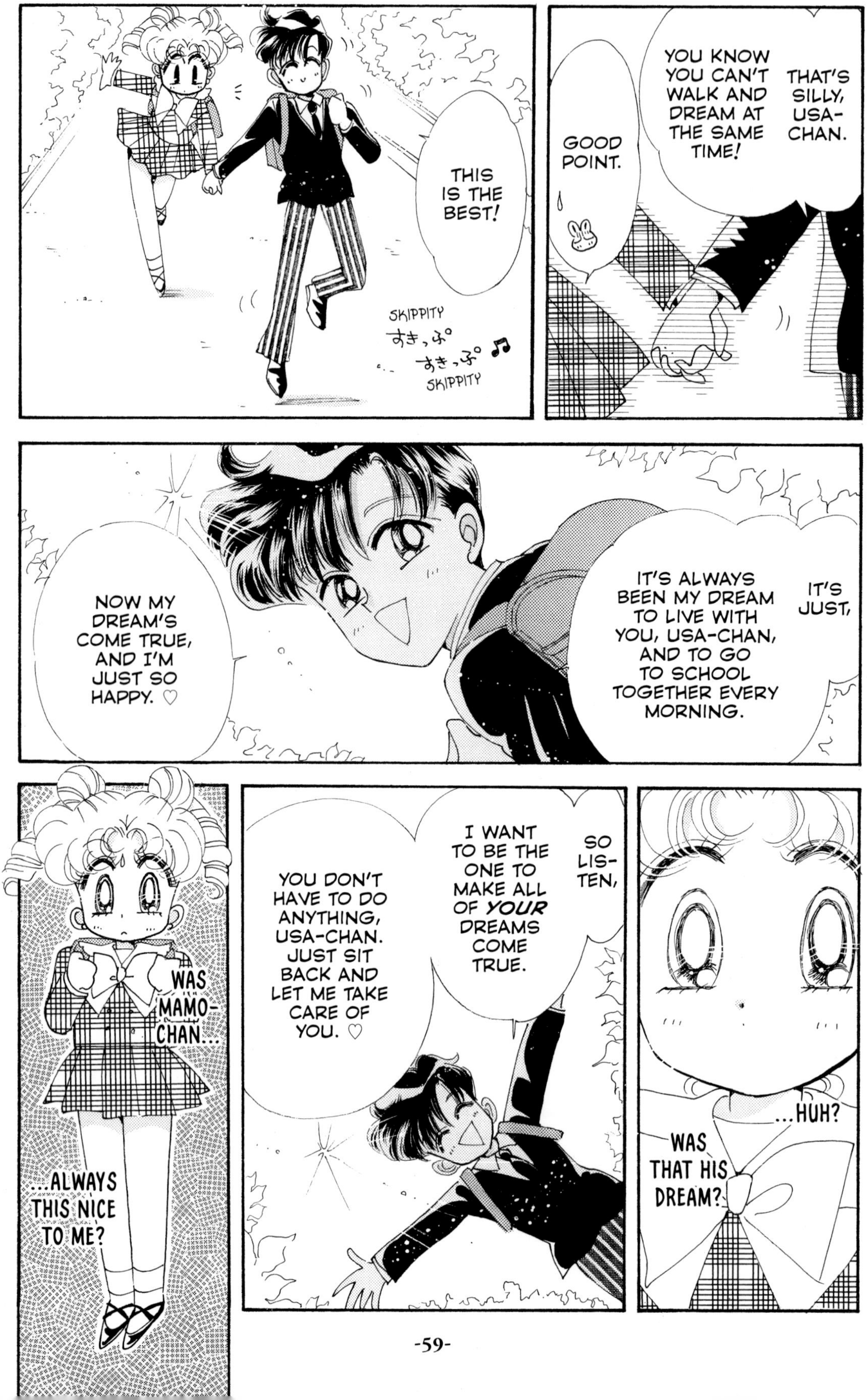
THAT'S SILLY, USA-CHAN.
YOU KNOW YOU CAN'T WALK AND DREAM AT THE SAME TIME!
GOOD POINT.
THIS IS THE BEST!
すきっぷ
SKIPPITY
すきっぷ
SKIPPITY
IT'S JUST,
IT'S ALWAYS BEEN MY DREAM TO LIVE WITH YOU, USA-CHAN, AND TO GO TO SCHOOL TOGETHER EVERY MORNING.
NOW MY DREAM'S COME TRUE, AND I'M JUST SO HAPPY. ♡
...HUH?
WAS THAT HIS DREAM?
SO LISTEN,
I WANT TO BE THE ONE TO MAKE ALL OF *YOUR* DREAMS COME TRUE.
YOU DON'T HAVE TO DO ANYTHING, USA-CHAN. JUST SIT BACK AND LET ME TAKE CARE OF YOU. ♡
WAS MAMO-CHAN...
...ALWAYS THIS NICE TO ME?

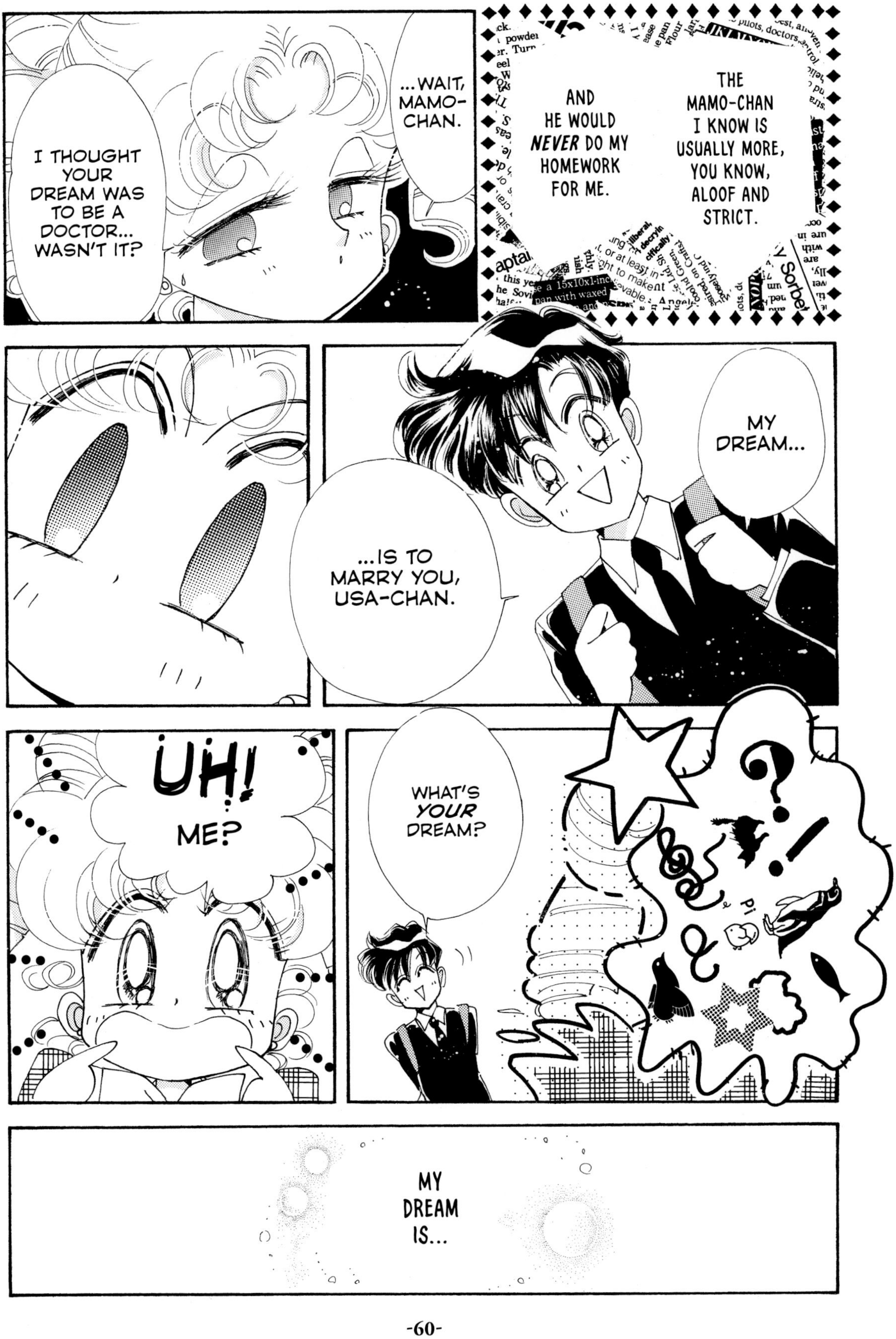
THE MAMO-CHAN I KNOW IS USUALLY MORE, YOU KNOW, ALOOF AND STRICT.
AND HE WOULD *NEVER* DO MY HOMEWORK FOR ME.
...WAIT, MAMO-CHAN.
I THOUGHT YOUR DREAM WAS TO BE A DOCTOR... WASN'T IT?
MY DREAM...
...IS TO MARRY YOU, USA-CHAN.
WHAT'S *YOUR* DREAM?
?!
Pi
UH!
ME?
MY DREAM IS...

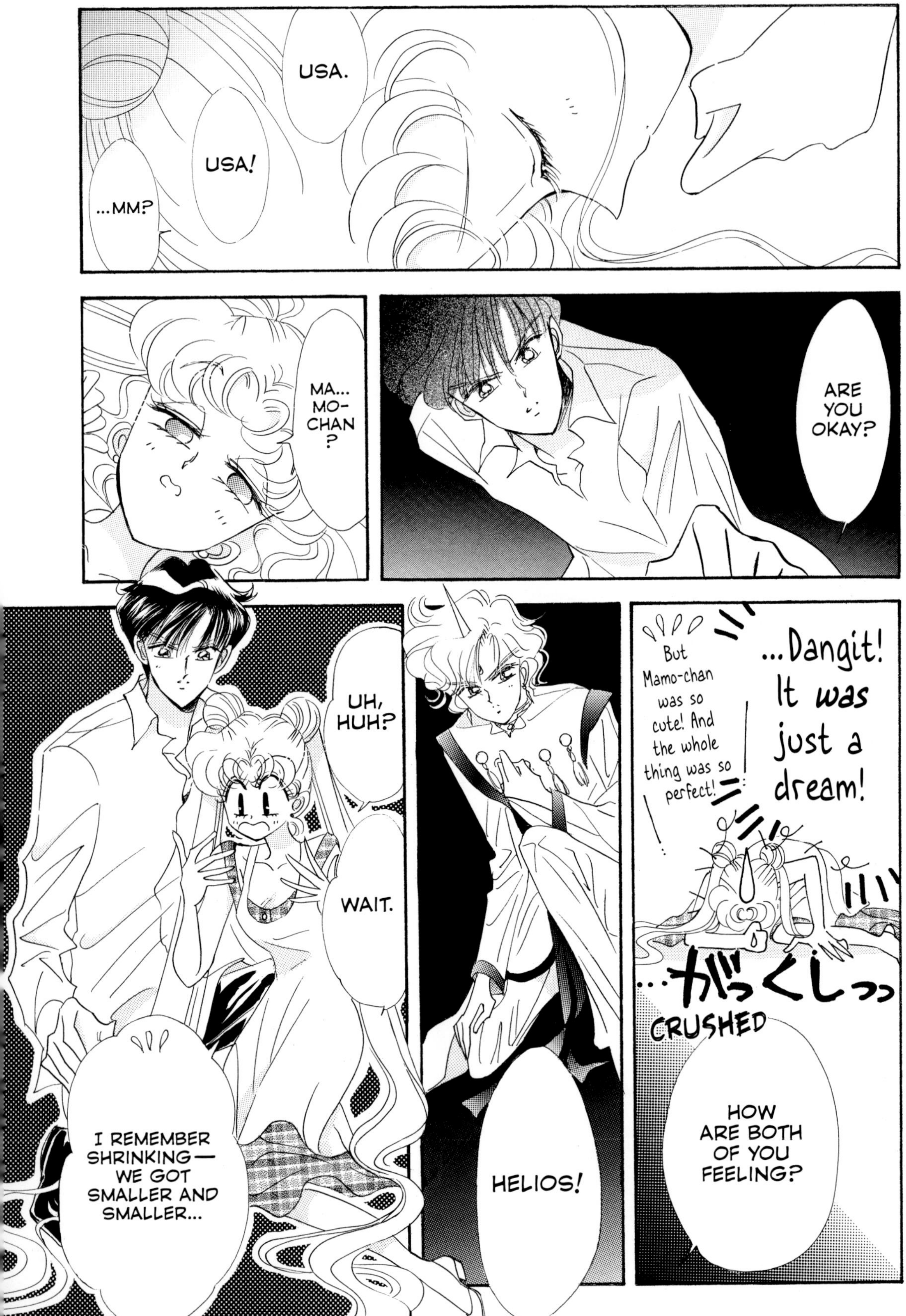
USA.
USA!
...MM?
ARE YOU OKAY?
MA... MO-CHAN?
...Dangit! It *was* just a dream!
But Mamo-chan was so cute! And the whole thing was so perfect!
...がっくしっっ
CRUSHED
HOW ARE BOTH OF YOU FEELING?
HELIOS!
UH, HUH?
WAIT.
I REMEMBER SHRINKING—WE GOT SMALLER AND SMALLER...

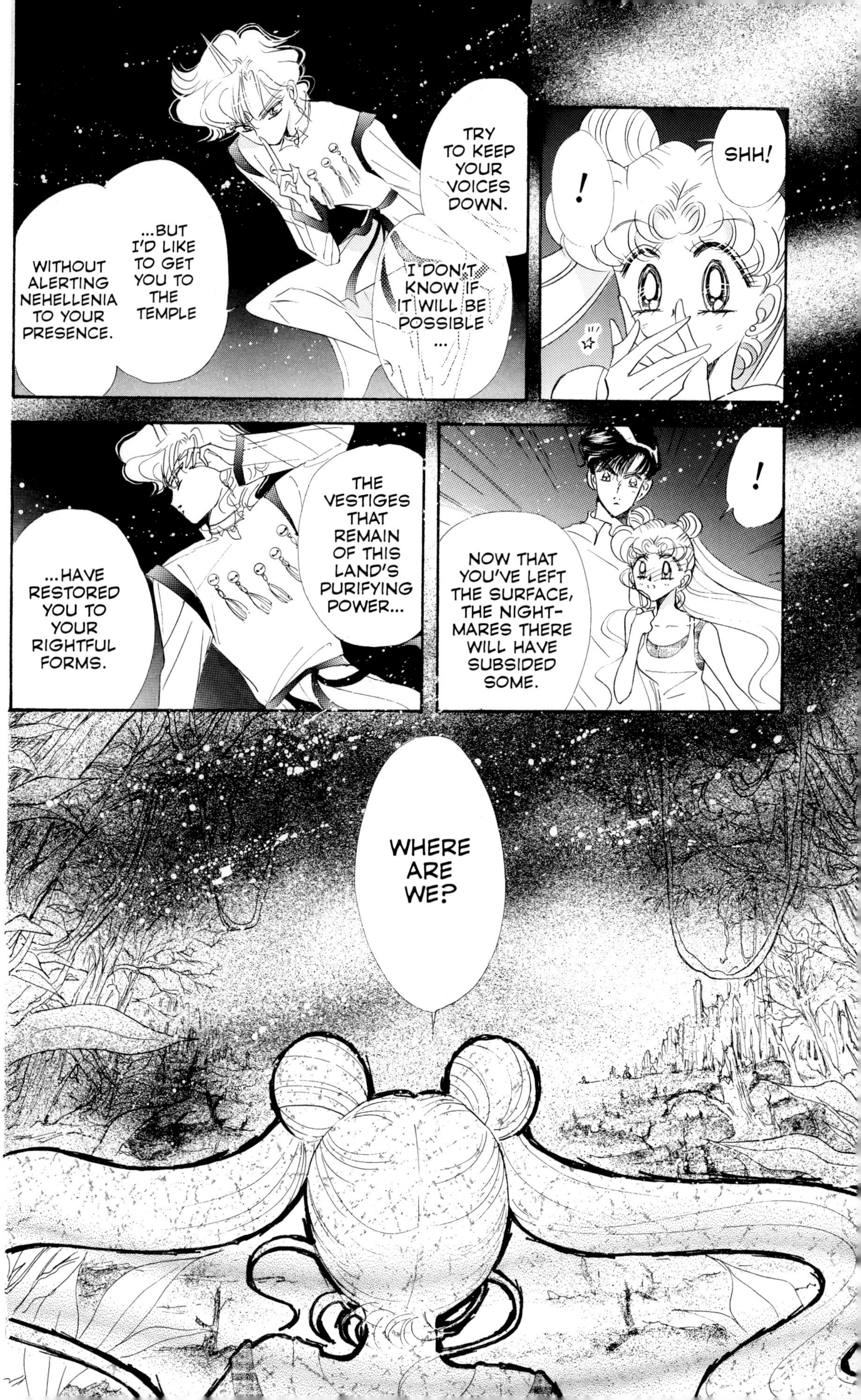
SHH!
!
TRY TO KEEP YOUR VOICES DOWN.
I DON'T KNOW IF IT WILL BE POSSIBLE ...
...BUT I'D LIKE TO GET YOU TO THE TEMPLE
WITHOUT ALERTING NEHELLENIA TO YOUR PRESENCE.
!
NOW THAT YOU'VE LEFT THE SURFACE, THE NIGHT-MARES THERE WILL HAVE SUBSIDED SOME.
THE VESTIGES THAT REMAIN OF THIS LAND'S PURIFYING POWER...
...HAVE RESTORED YOU TO YOUR RIGHTFUL FORMS.
WHERE ARE WE?

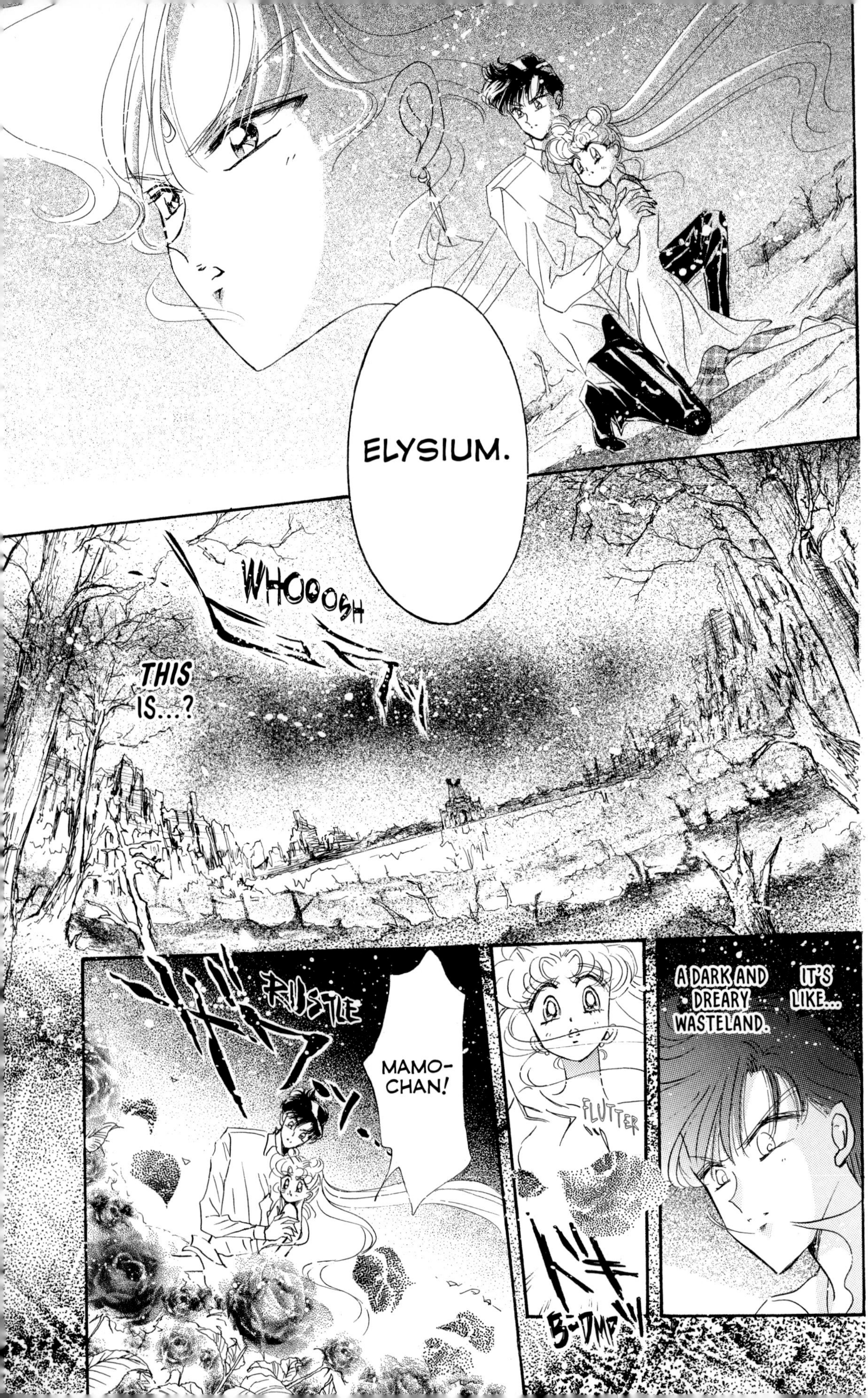
ELYSIUM.
WHOOOOSH
THIS IS...?
IT'S LIKE...
A DARK AND DREARY WASTELAND.
FLUTTER
B-DMP
RUSTLE
MAMO-CHAN!

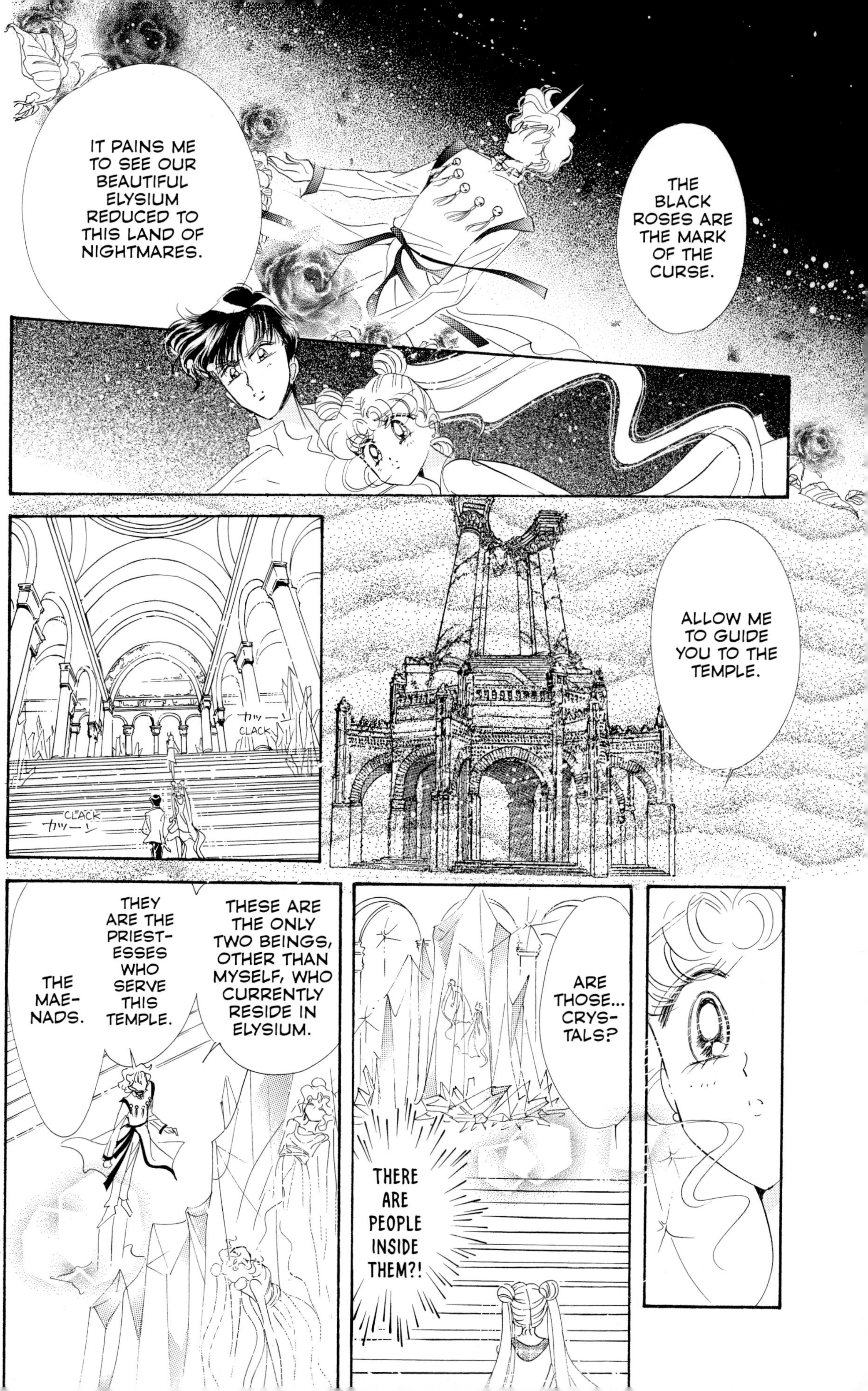
THE BLACK ROSES ARE THE MARK OF THE CURSE.
IT PAINS ME TO SEE OUR BEAUTIFUL ELYSIUM REDUCED TO THIS LAND OF NIGHTMARES.
ALLOW ME TO GUIDE YOU TO THE TEMPLE.
カッー! CLACK
CLACK カッー!
ARE THOSE... CRYS-TALS?
THERE ARE PEOPLE INSIDE THEM?!
THESE ARE THE ONLY TWO BEINGS, OTHER THAN MYSELF, WHO CURRENTLY RESIDE IN ELYSIUM.
THEY ARE THE PRIEST-ESSES WHO SERVE THIS TEMPLE.
THE MAE-NADS.

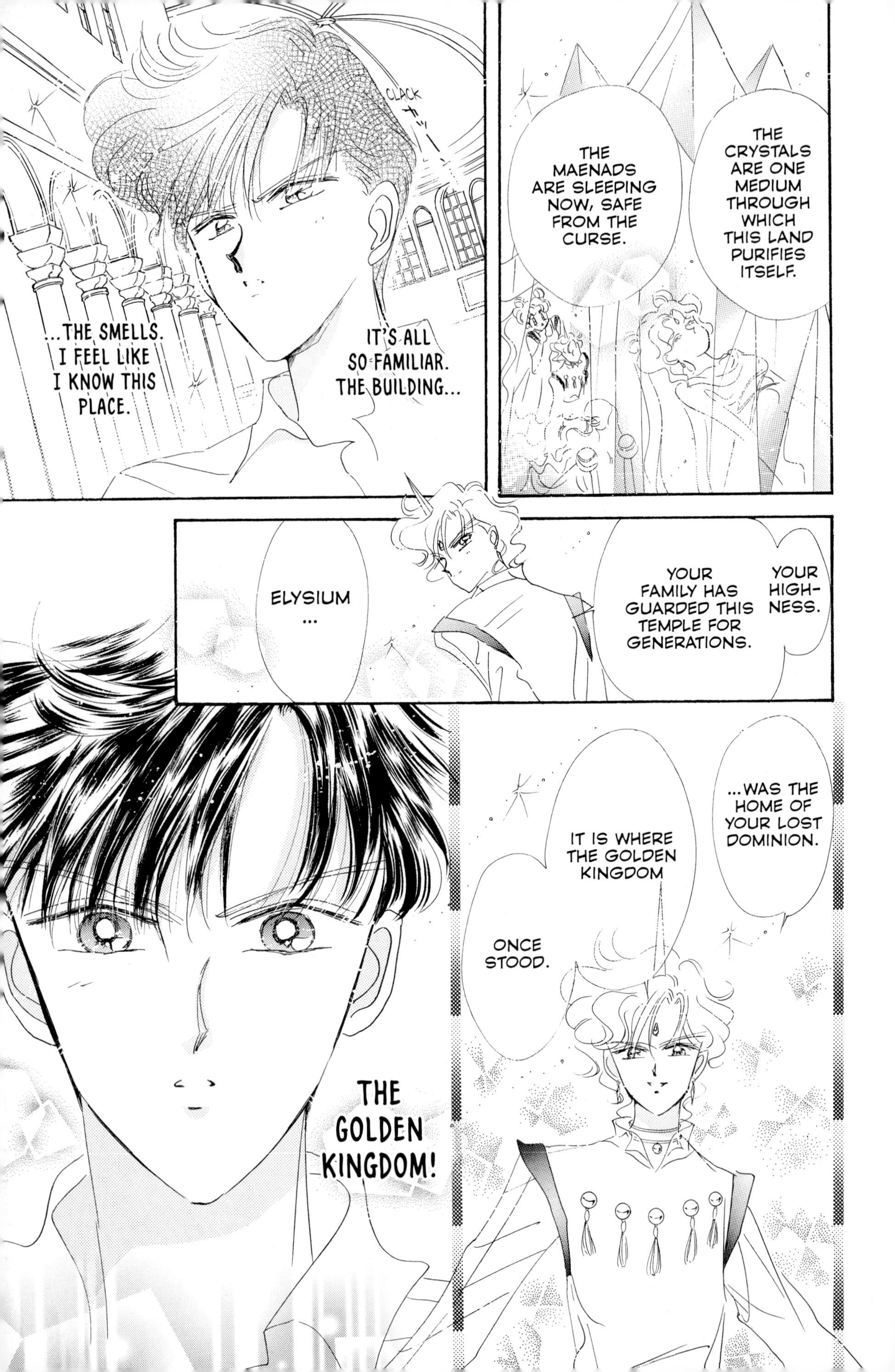
THE CRYSTALS ARE ONE MEDIUM THROUGH WHICH THIS LAND PURIFIES ITSELF.
THE MAENADS ARE SLEEPING NOW, SAFE FROM THE CURSE.
CLACK
IT'S ALL SO FAMILIAR. THE BUILDING...
...THE SMELLS. I FEEL LIKE I KNOW THIS PLACE.
YOUR HIGH-NESS.
YOUR FAMILY HAS GUARDED THIS TEMPLE FOR GENERATIONS.
ELYSIUM ...
...WAS THE HOME OF YOUR LOST DOMINION.
IT IS WHERE THE GOLDEN KINGDOM
ONCE STOOD.
THE GOLDEN KINGDOM!

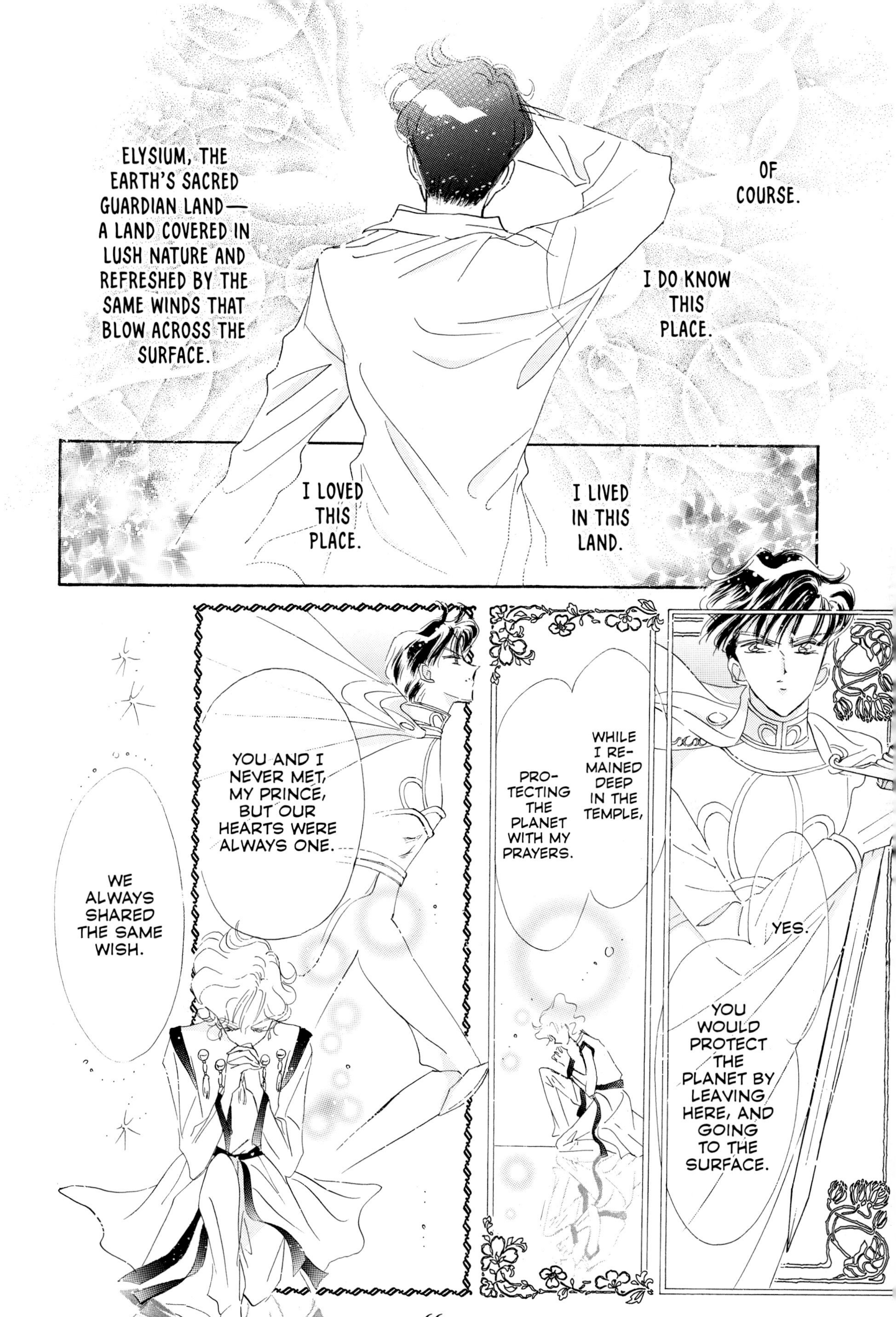
OF COURSE.
I DO KNOW THIS PLACE.
ELYSIUM, THE EARTH'S SACRED GUARDIAN LAND— A LAND COVERED IN LUSH NATURE AND REFRESHED BY THE SAME WINDS THAT BLOW ACROSS THE SURFACE.
I LIVED IN THIS LAND.
I LOVED THIS PLACE.
YES.
YOU WOULD PROTECT THE PLANET BY LEAVING HERE, AND GOING TO THE SURFACE.
WHILE I RE-MAINED DEEP IN THE TEMPLE,
PRO-TECTING THE PLANET WITH MY PRAYERS.
YOU AND I NEVER MET, MY PRINCE, BUT OUR HEARTS WERE ALWAYS ONE.
WE ALWAYS SHARED THE SAME WISH.

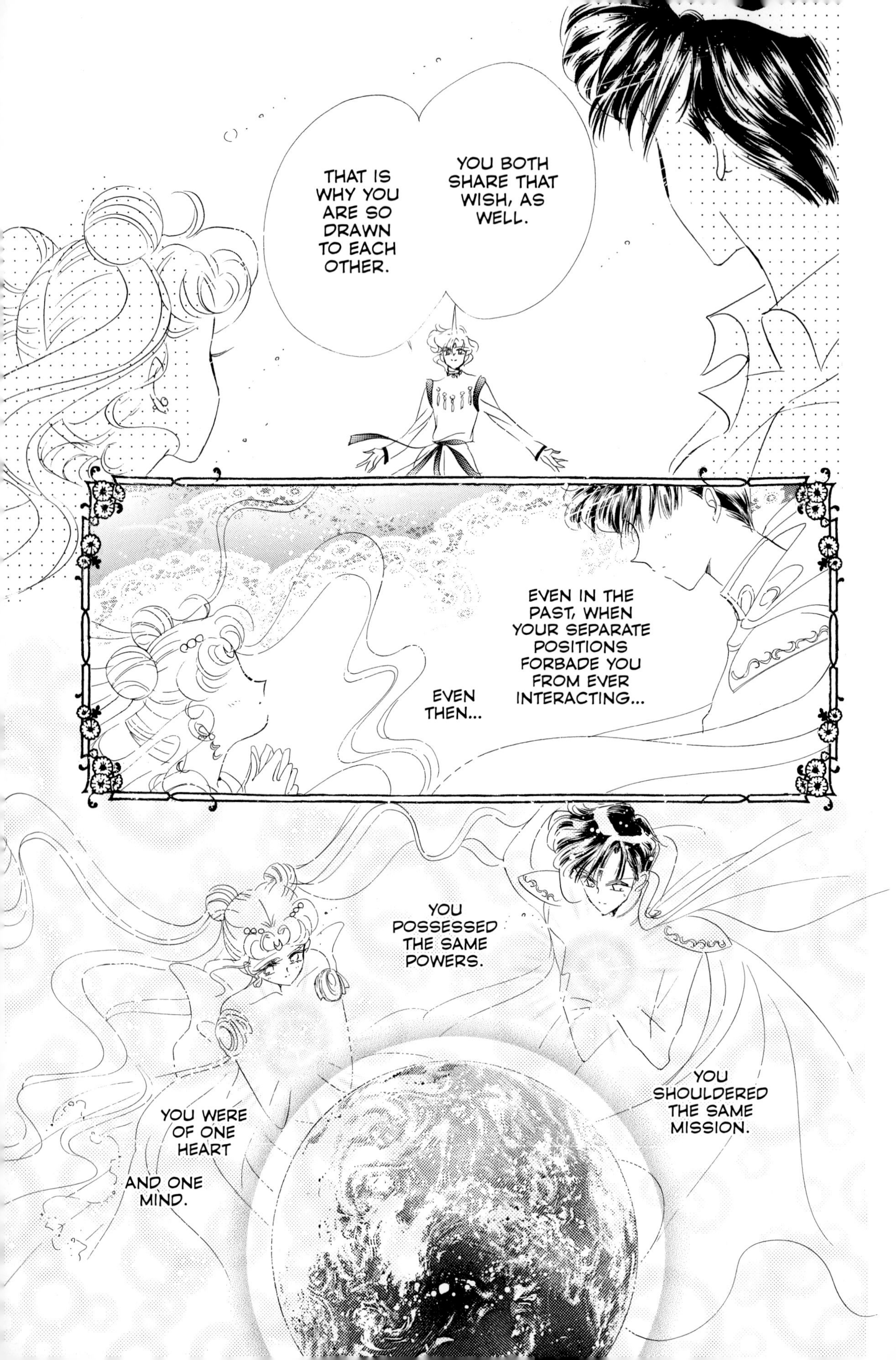
YOU BOTH SHARE THAT WISH, AS WELL.
THAT IS WHY YOU ARE SO DRAWN TO EACH OTHER.
EVEN IN THE PAST, WHEN YOUR SEPARATE POSITIONS FORBADE YOU FROM EVER INTERACTING...
EVEN THEN...
YOU POSSESSED THE SAME POWERS.
YOU SHOULDERED THE SAME MISSION.
YOU WERE OF ONE HEART
AND ONE MIND.

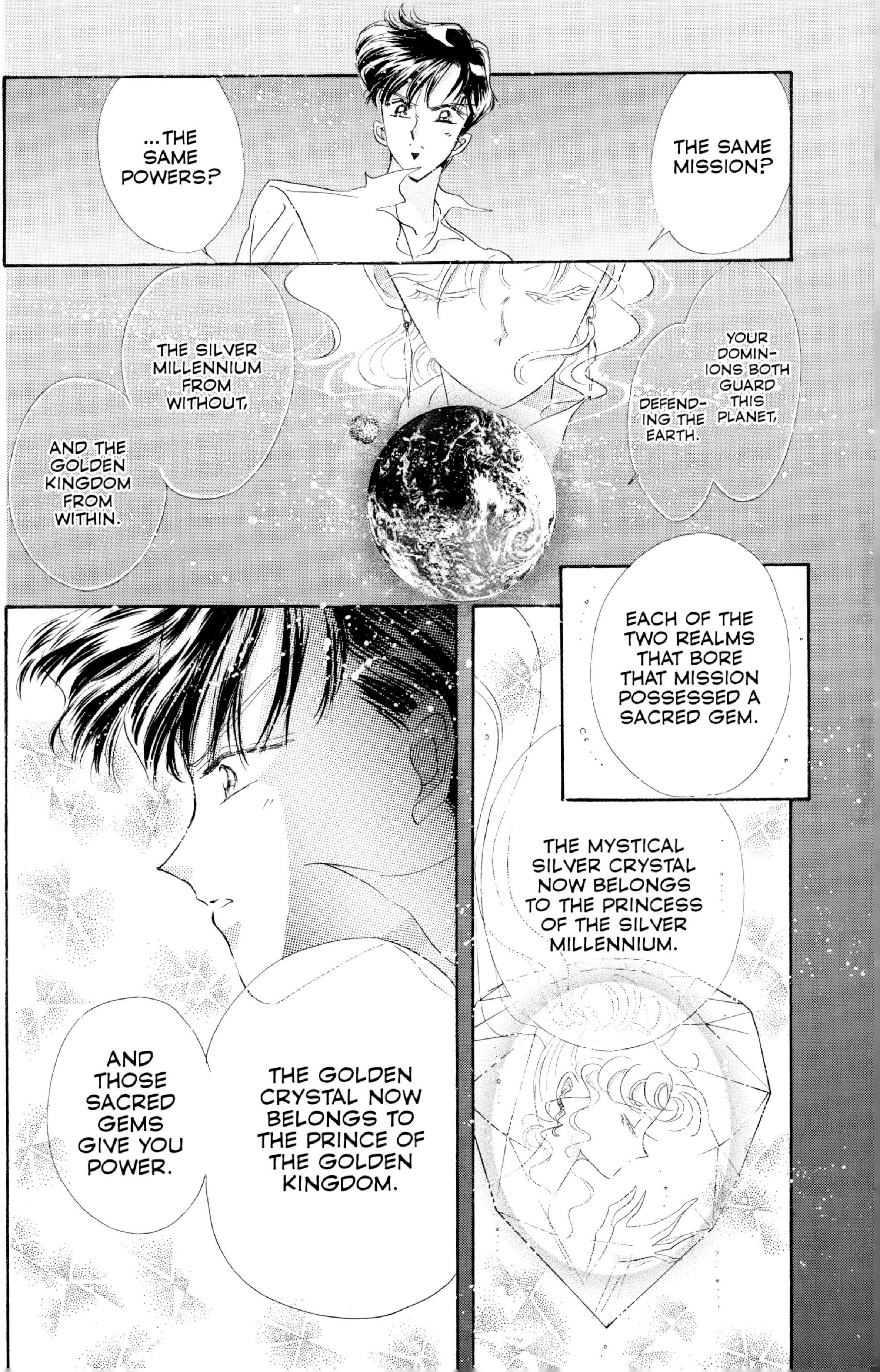
THE SAME MISSION?
...THE SAME POWERS?
YOUR DOMIN-IONS BOTH GUARD THIS PLANET,
DEFEND-ING THE EARTH.
THE SILVER MILLENNIUM FROM WITHOUT,
AND THE GOLDEN KINGDOM FROM WITHIN.
EACH OF THE TWO REALMS THAT BORE THAT MISSION POSSESSED A SACRED GEM.
THE MYSTICAL SILVER CRYSTAL NOW BELONGS TO THE PRINCESS OF THE SILVER MILLENNIUM.
THE GOLDEN CRYSTAL NOW BELONGS TO THE PRINCE OF THE GOLDEN KINGDOM.
AND THOSE SACRED GEMS GIVE YOU POWER.

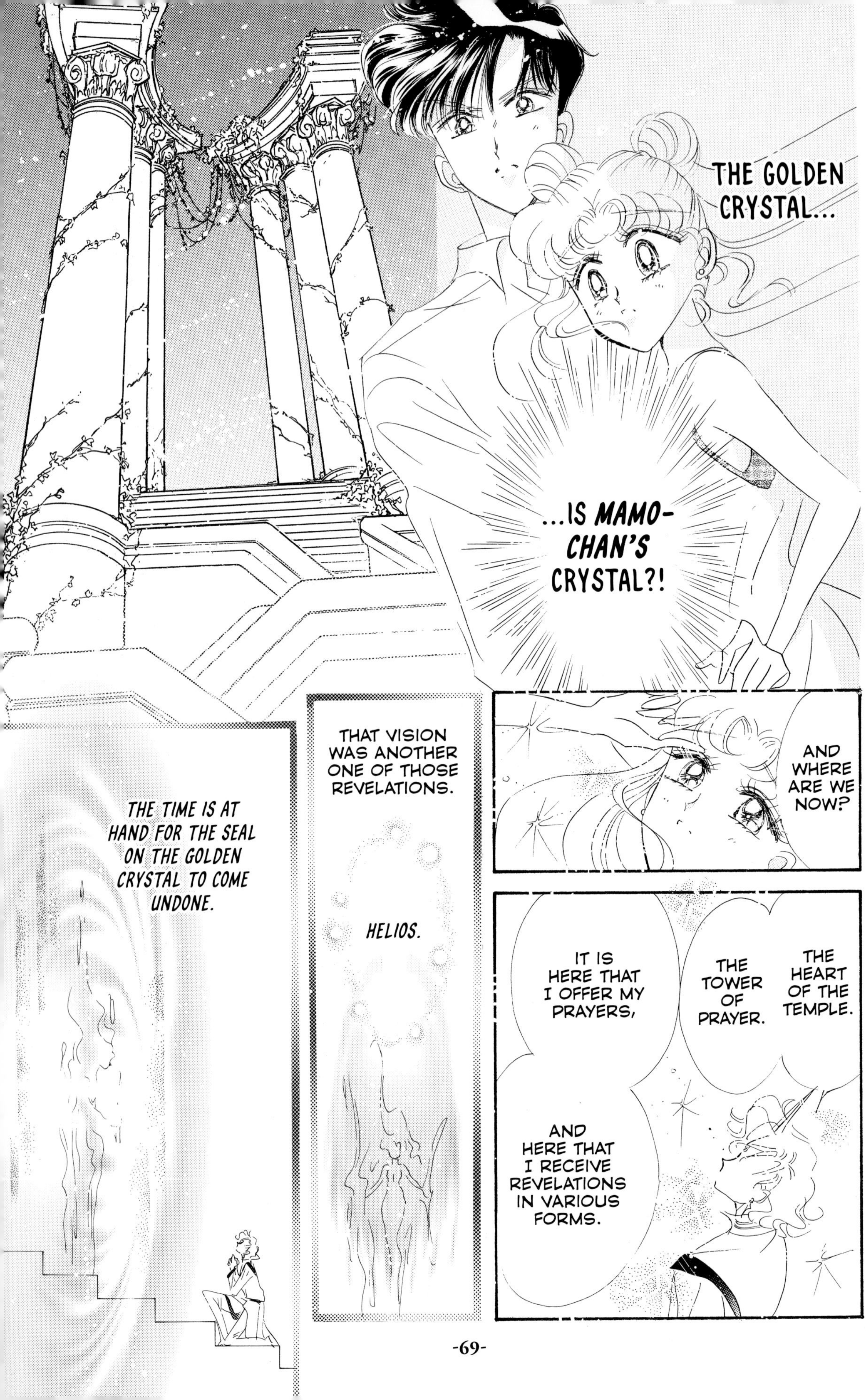
THE GOLDEN CRYSTAL...
...IS *MAMO-CHAN'S* CRYSTAL?!
AND WHERE ARE WE NOW?
THE HEART OF THE TEMPLE.
THE TOWER OF PRAYER.
IT IS HERE THAT I OFFER MY PRAYERS,
AND HERE THAT I RECEIVE REVELATIONS IN VARIOUS FORMS.
THAT VISION WAS ANOTHER ONE OF THOSE REVELATIONS.
HELIOS.
THE TIME IS AT HAND FOR THE SEAL ON THE GOLDEN CRYSTAL TO COME UNDONE.

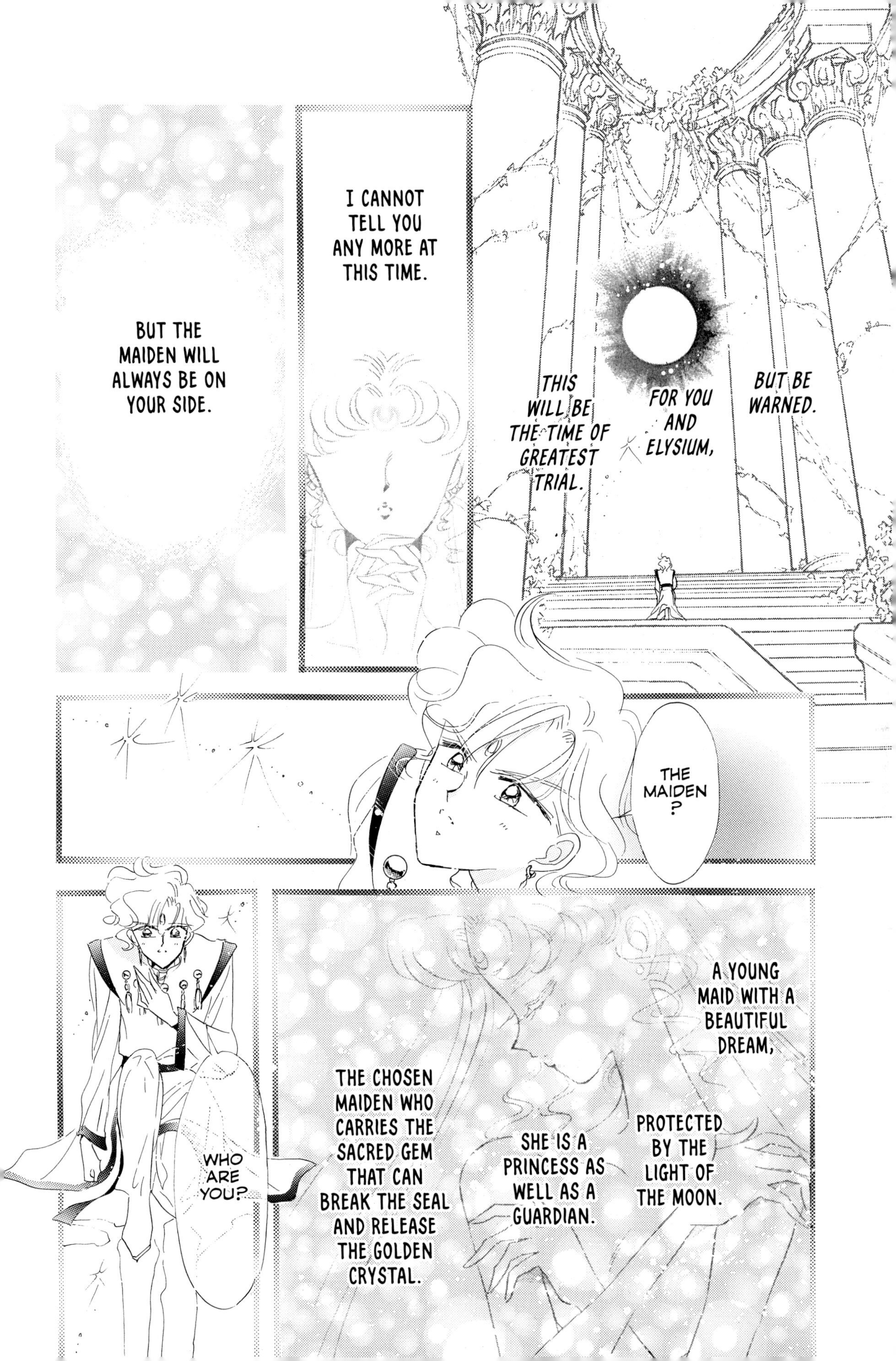
BUT BE WARNED.
FOR YOU AND ELYSIUM,
THIS WILL BE THE TIME OF GREATEST TRIAL.
I CANNOT TELL YOU ANY MORE AT THIS TIME.
BUT THE MAIDEN WILL ALWAYS BE ON YOUR SIDE.
THE MAIDEN?
A YOUNG MAID WITH A BEAUTIFUL DREAM,
PROTECTED BY THE LIGHT OF THE MOON.
SHE IS A PRINCESS AS WELL AS A GUARDIAN.
THE CHOSEN MAIDEN WHO CARRIES THE SACRED GEM THAT CAN BREAK THE SEAL AND RELEASE THE GOLDEN CRYSTAL.
WHO ARE YOU?

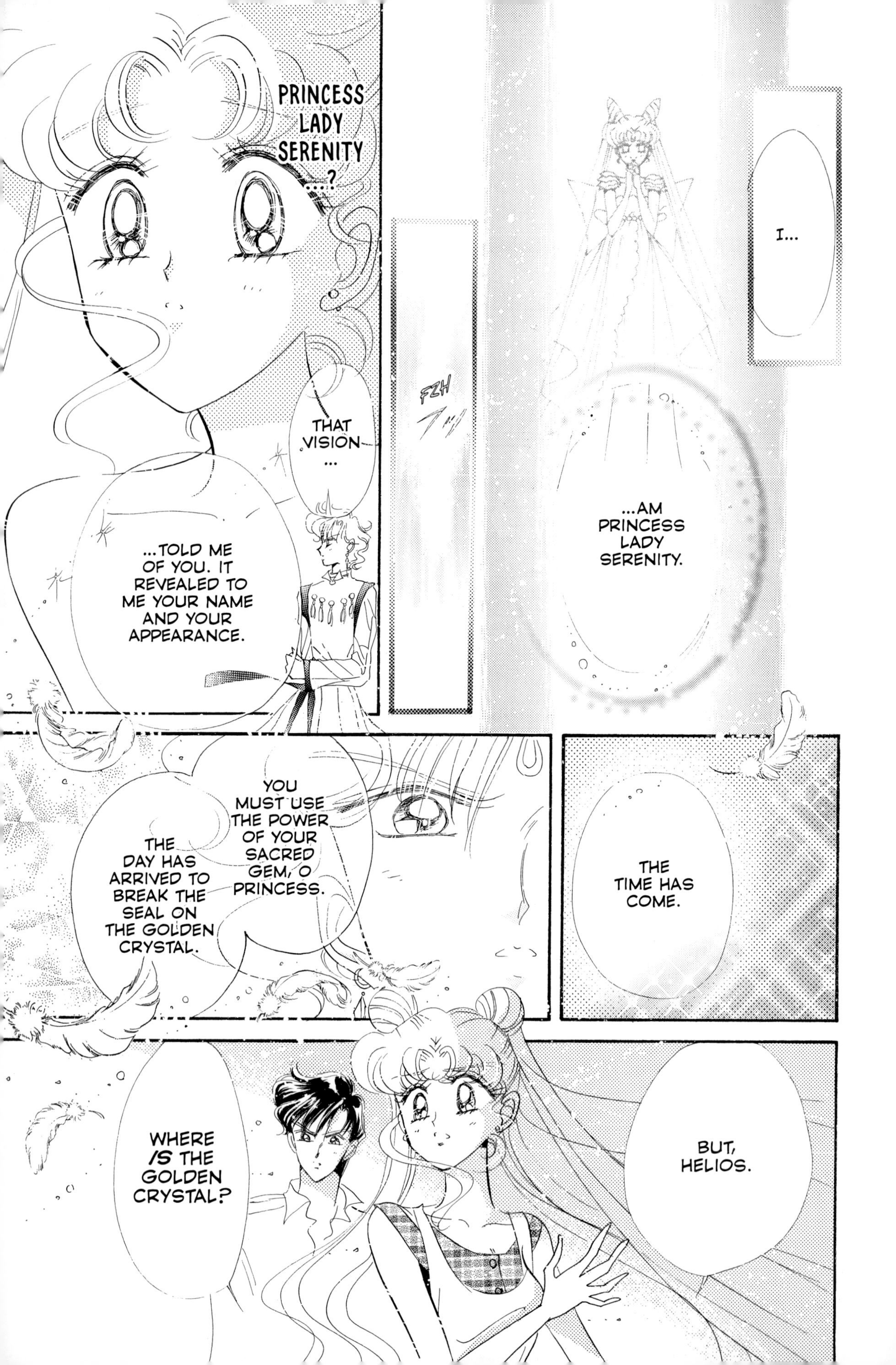
I...
...AM PRINCESS LADY SERENITY.
FZH
PRINCESS LADY SERENITY ...?
THAT VISION ...
...TOLD ME OF YOU. IT REVEALED TO ME YOUR NAME AND YOUR APPEARANCE.
THE TIME HAS COME.
YOU MUST USE THE POWER OF YOUR SACRED GEM, O PRINCESS.
THE DAY HAS ARRIVED TO BREAK THE SEAL ON THE GOLDEN CRYSTAL.
BUT, HELIOS.
WHERE *IS* THE GOLDEN CRYSTAL?

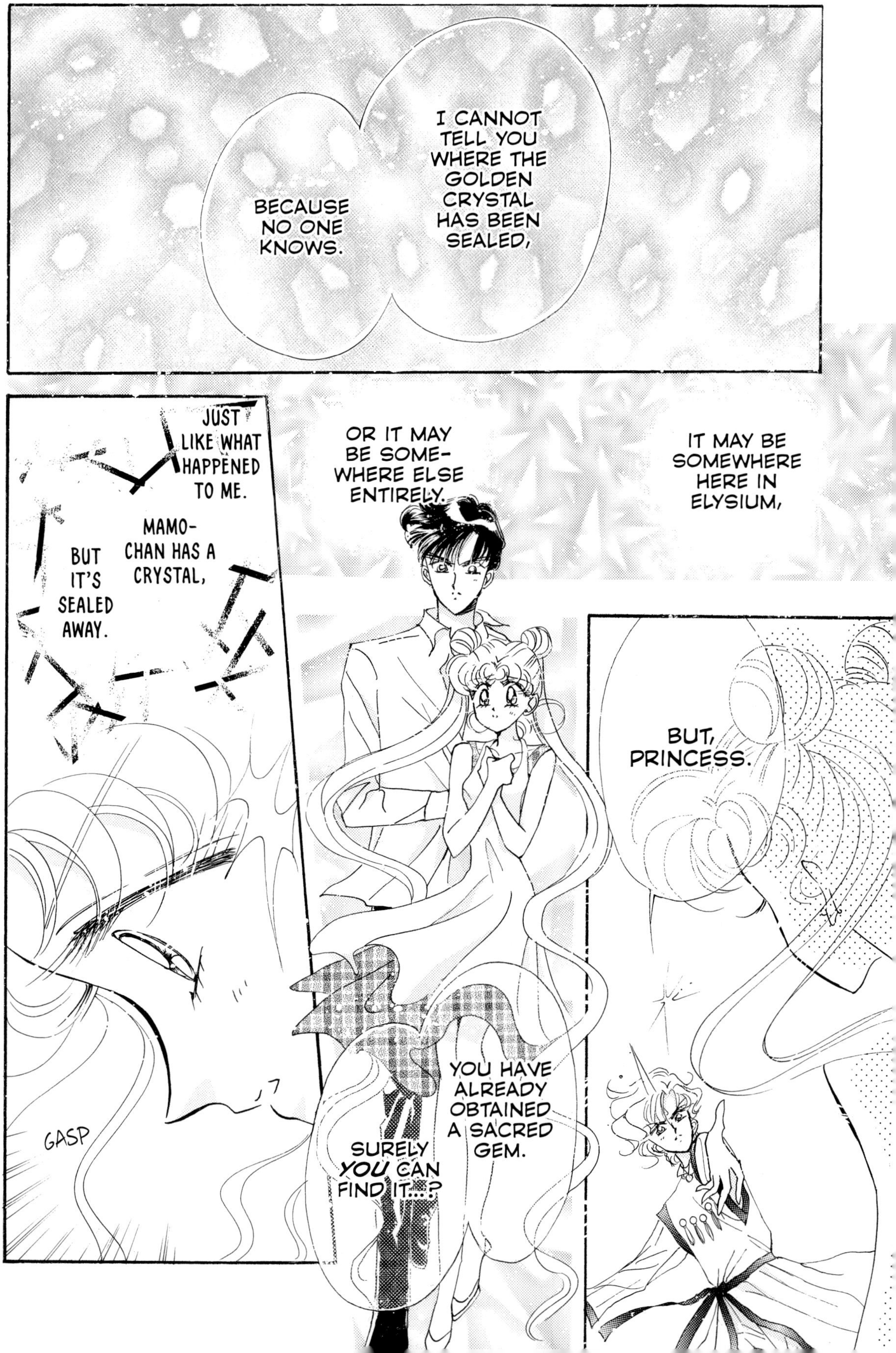
I CANNOT TELL YOU WHERE THE GOLDEN CRYSTAL HAS BEEN SEALED,
BECAUSE NO ONE KNOWS.
IT MAY BE SOMEWHERE HERE IN ELYSIUM,
OR IT MAY BE SOME-WHERE ELSE ENTIRELY.
BUT, PRINCESS.
YOU HAVE ALREADY OBTAINED A SACRED GEM.
SURELY *YOU* CAN FIND IT...?
MAMO-CHAN HAS A CRYSTAL,
BUT IT'S SEALED AWAY.
JUST LIKE WHAT HAPPENED TO ME.
GASP

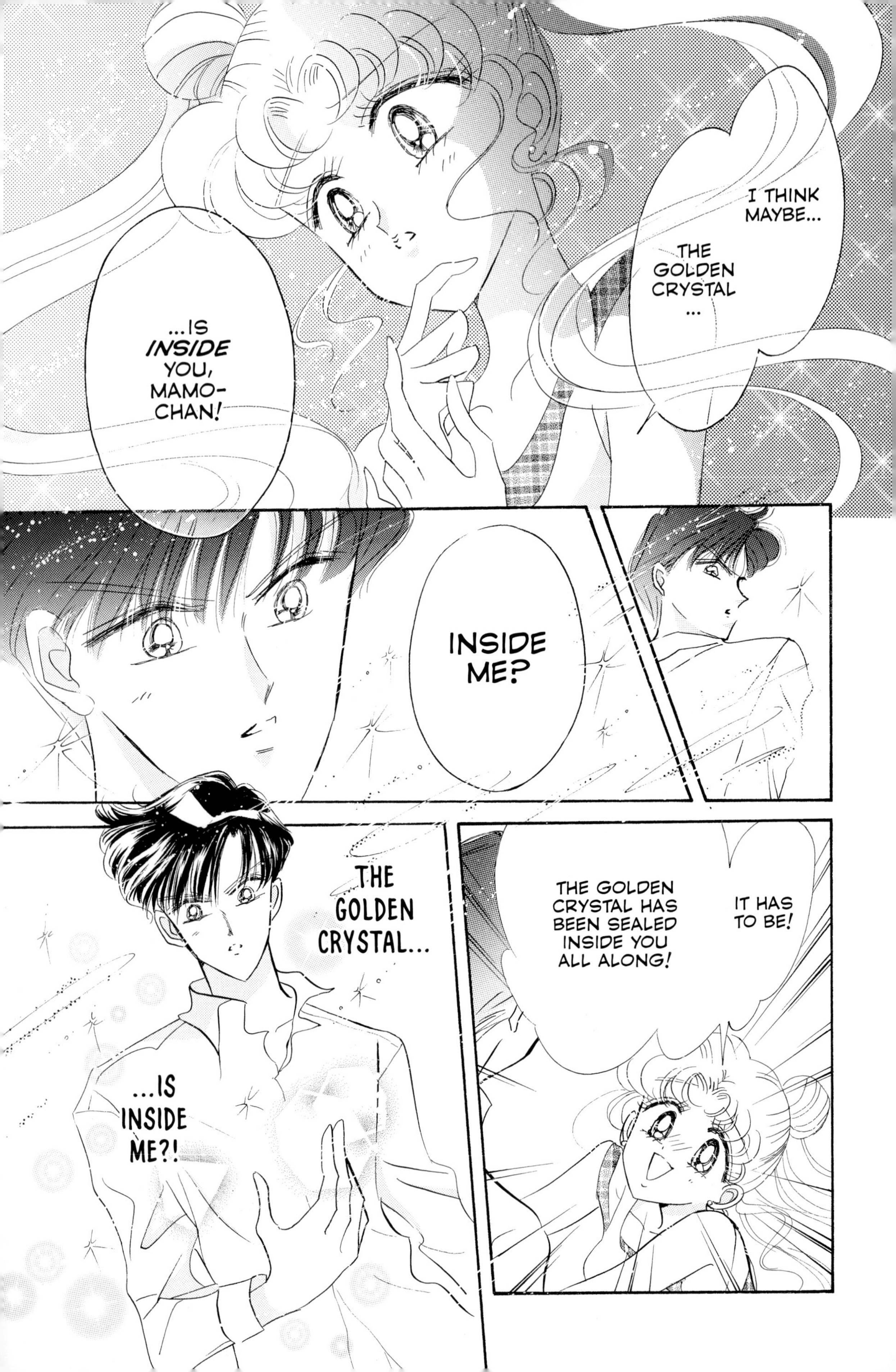
I THINK MAYBE...
THE GOLDEN CRYSTAL ...
...IS *INSIDE* YOU, MAMO-CHAN!
INSIDE ME?
IT HAS TO BE!
THE GOLDEN CRYSTAL HAS BEEN SEALED INSIDE YOU ALL ALONG!
THE GOLDEN CRYSTAL...
...IS INSIDE ME?!

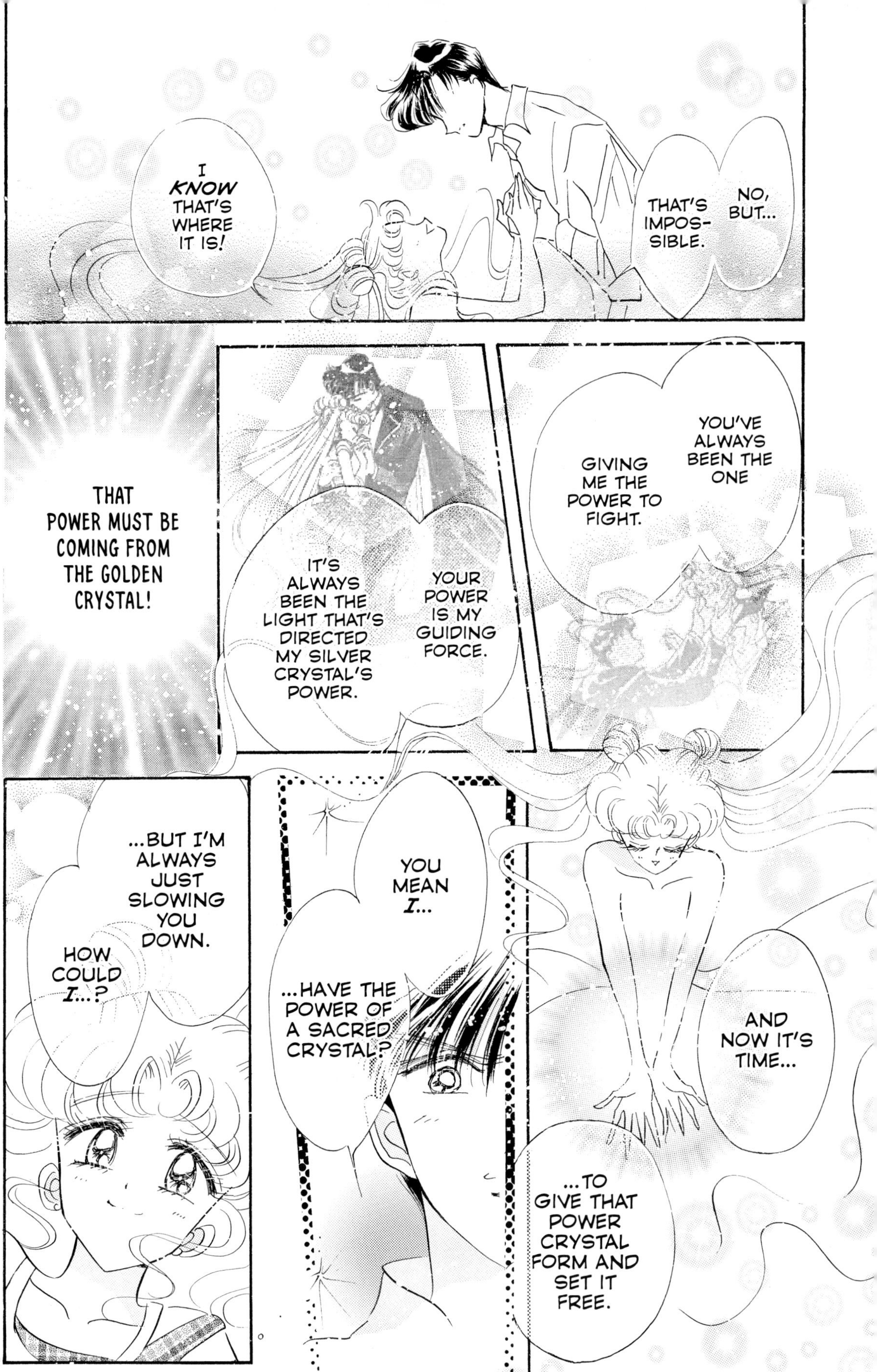
NO, BUT...
THAT'S IMPOSSIBLE.
I KNOW THAT'S WHERE IT IS!
YOU'VE ALWAYS BEEN THE ONE
GIVING ME THE POWER TO FIGHT.
YOUR POWER IS MY GUIDING FORCE.
IT'S ALWAYS BEEN THE LIGHT THAT'S DIRECTED MY SILVER CRYSTAL'S POWER.
THAT POWER MUST BE COMING FROM THE GOLDEN CRYSTAL!
AND NOW IT'S TIME...
...TO GIVE THAT POWER CRYSTAL FORM AND SET IT FREE.
YOU MEAN I...
...HAVE THE POWER OF A SACRED CRYSTAL?
...BUT I'M ALWAYS JUST SLOWING YOU DOWN.
HOW COULD I...?

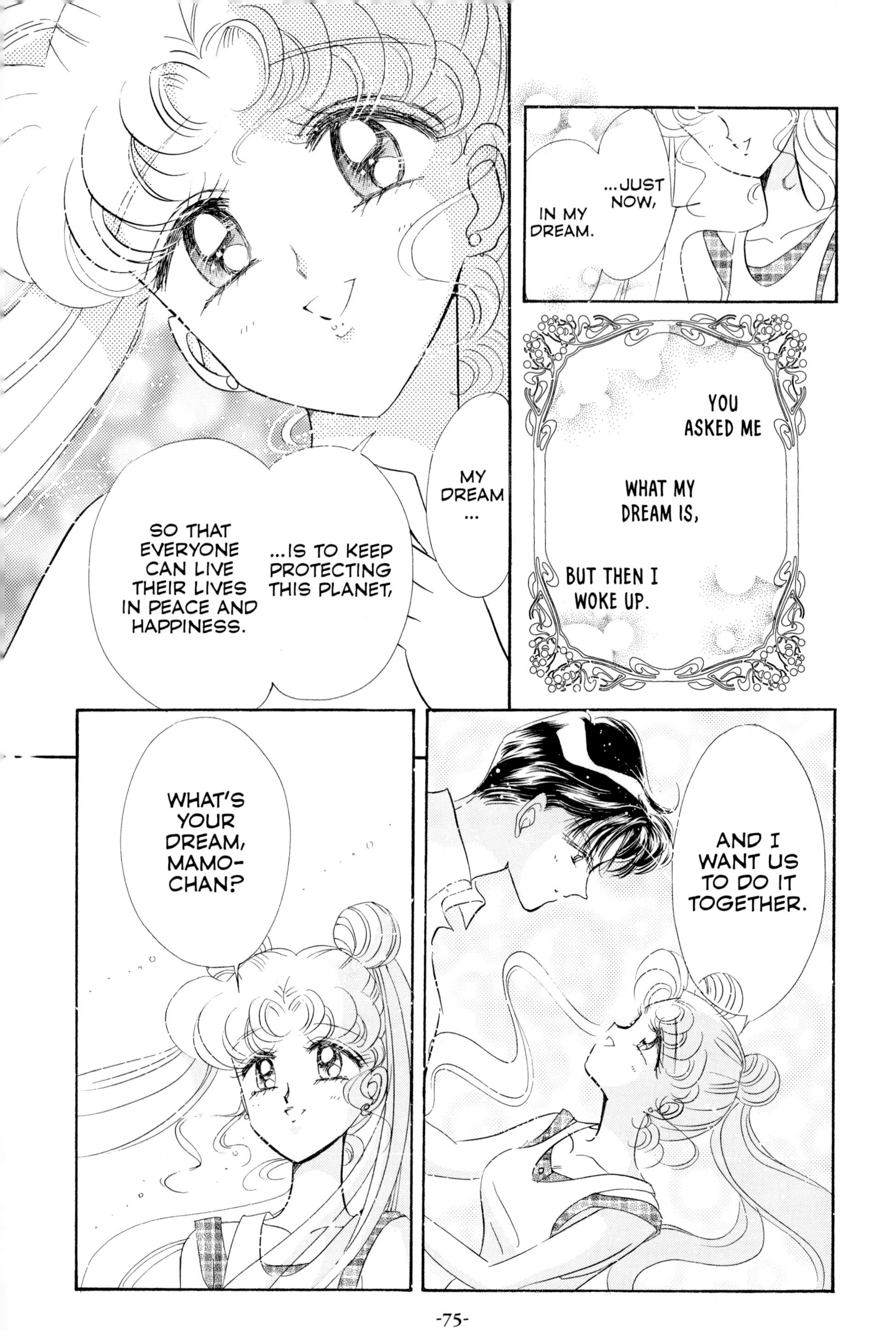
...JUST NOW,
IN MY DREAM.
YOU ASKED ME
WHAT MY DREAM IS,
BUT THEN I WOKE UP.
MY DREAM ...
...IS TO KEEP PROTECTING THIS PLANET,
SO THAT EVERYONE CAN LIVE THEIR LIVES IN PEACE AND HAPPINESS.
AND I WANT US TO DO IT TOGETHER.
WHAT'S YOUR DREAM, MAMO-CHAN?

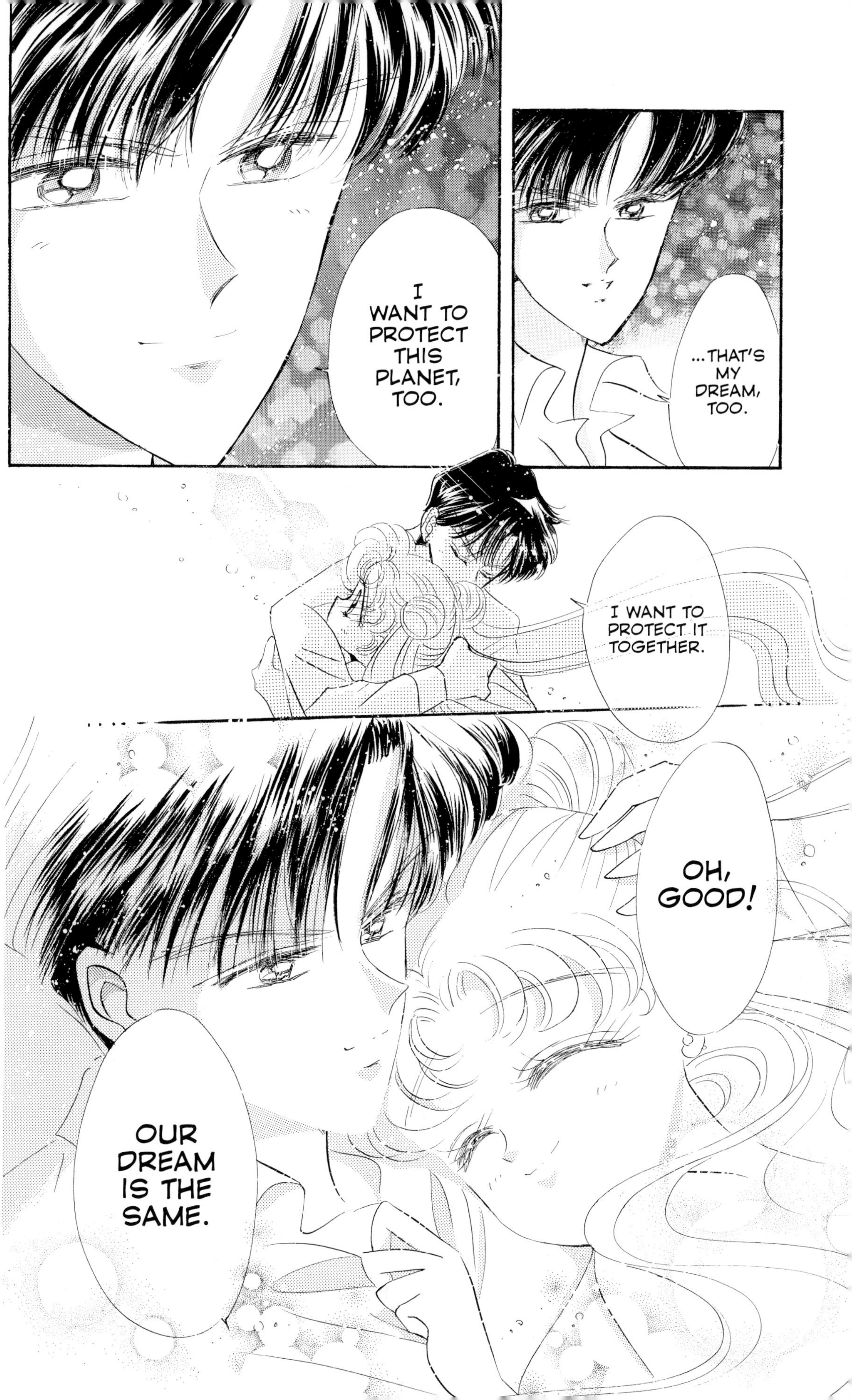
...THAT'S MY DREAM, TOO.
I WANT TO PROTECT THIS PLANET, TOO.
I WANT TO PROTECT IT TOGETHER.
OH, GOOD!
OUR DREAM IS THE SAME.

WE SHARE THE SAME DREAM,

AND WE ALWAYS WILL.

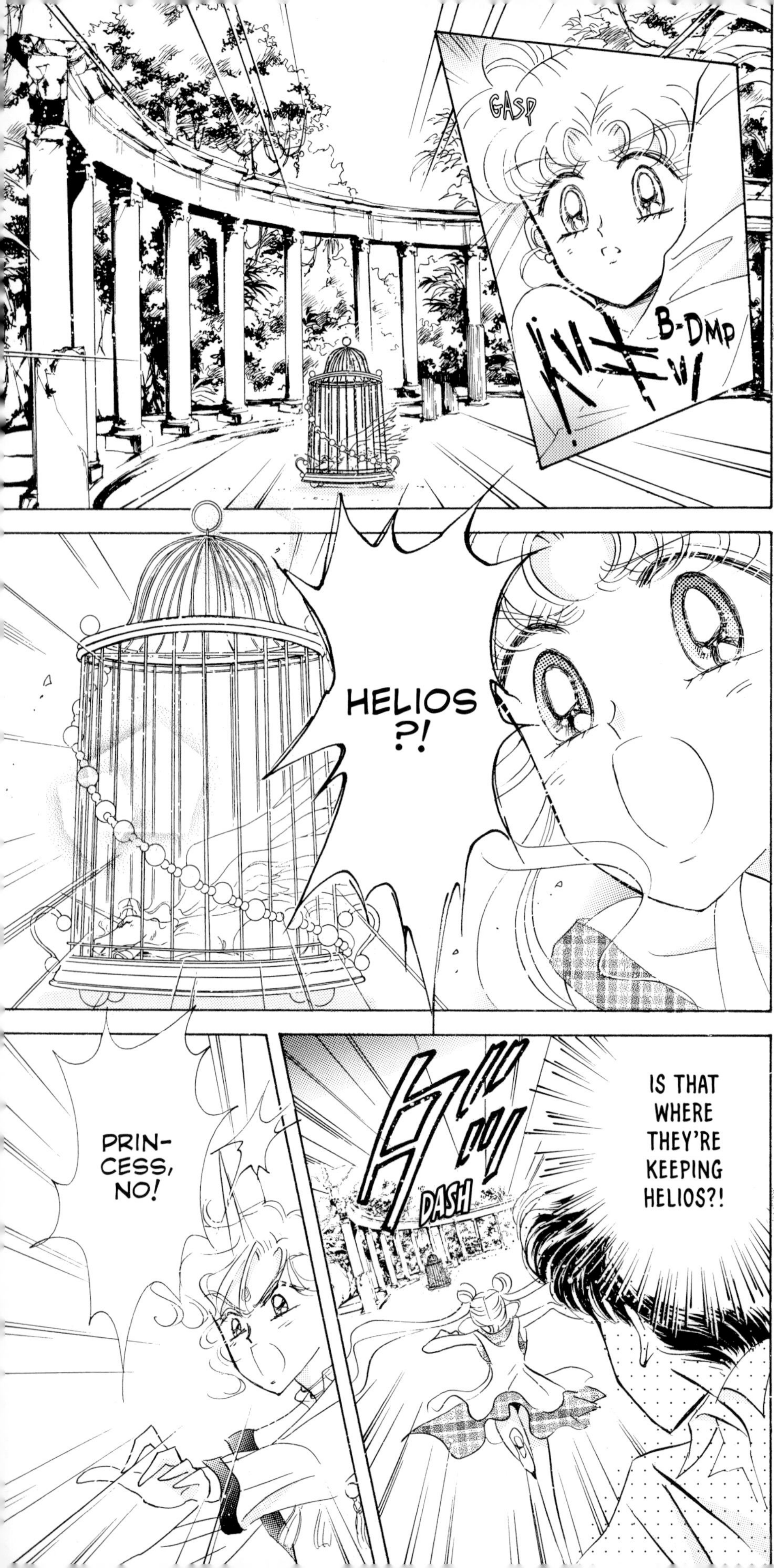
GASP
B-DMP
HELIOS ?!
IS THAT WHERE THEY'RE KEEPING HELIOS?!
DASH
PRINCESS, NO!

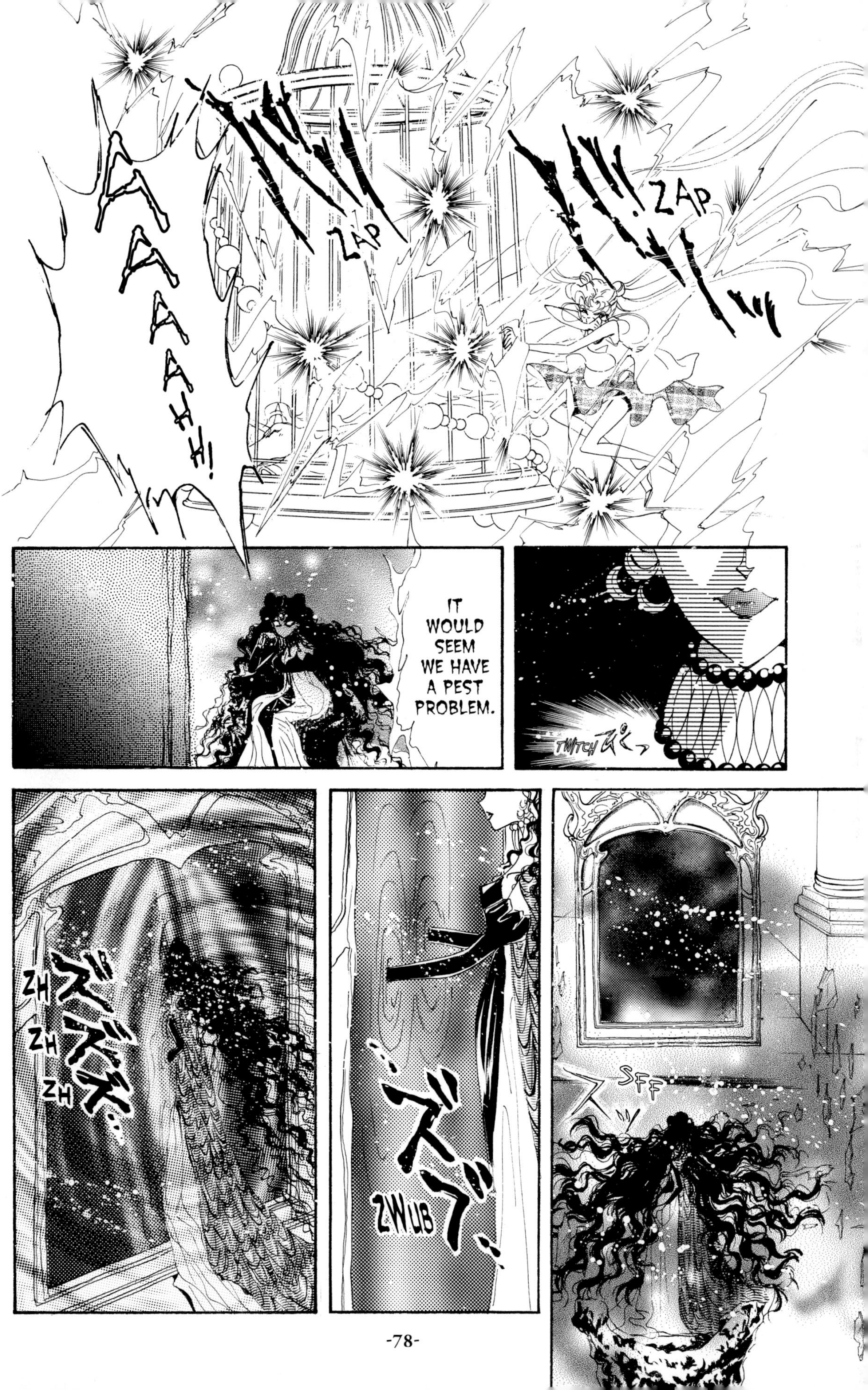

ZAP
ZAP
AAAAAHH!
TWITCH ぴくっ
IT WOULD SEEM WE HAVE A PEST PROBLEM.
SFF ズッ
ズズ… ZWUB
ズズズ… ZH ZH ZH

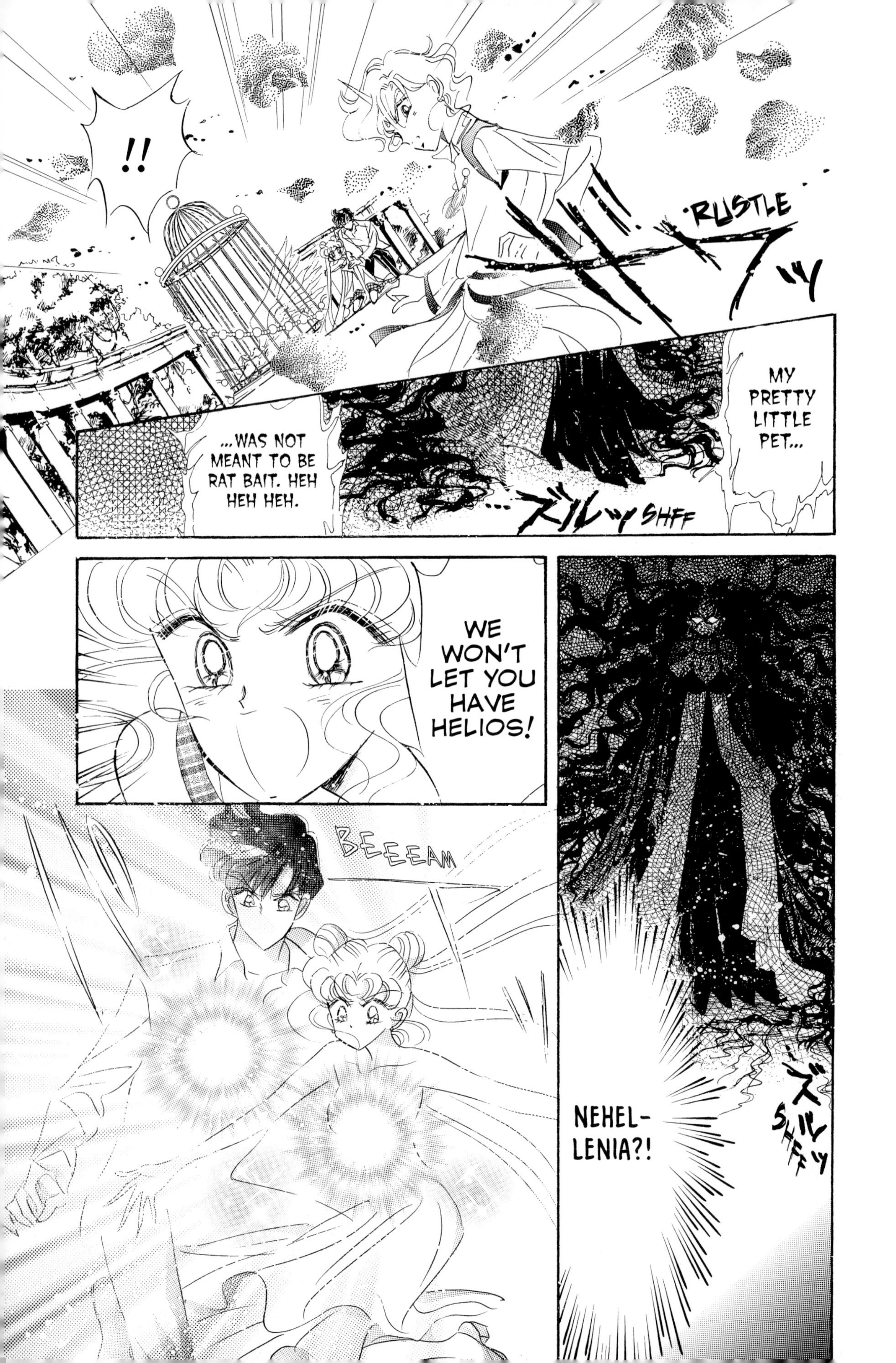
RUSTLE
!!
MY PRETTY LITTLE PET...
ズルッ SHFF
...WAS NOT MEANT TO BE RAT BAIT. HEH HEH HEH.
ズルッ SHFFF
WE WON'T LET YOU HAVE HELIOS!
BEEEAM
NEHEL-LENIA?!

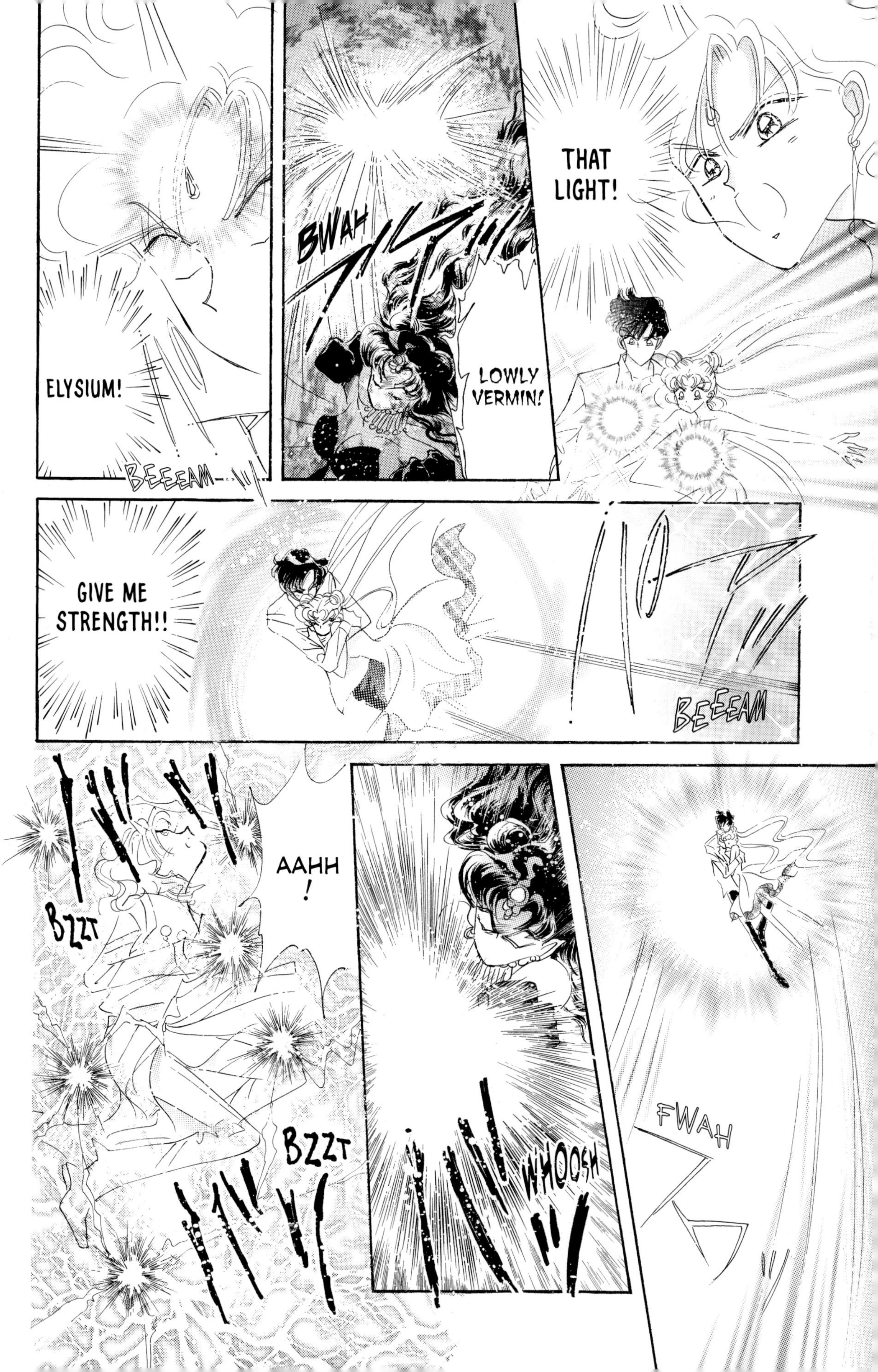

THAT LIGHT!
BWAH
LOWLY VERMIN!
ELYSIUM!
BEEEAM
GIVE ME STRENGTH!!
BEEEAM
FWAH
WHOOSH
AAHH!
BZZT
BZZT

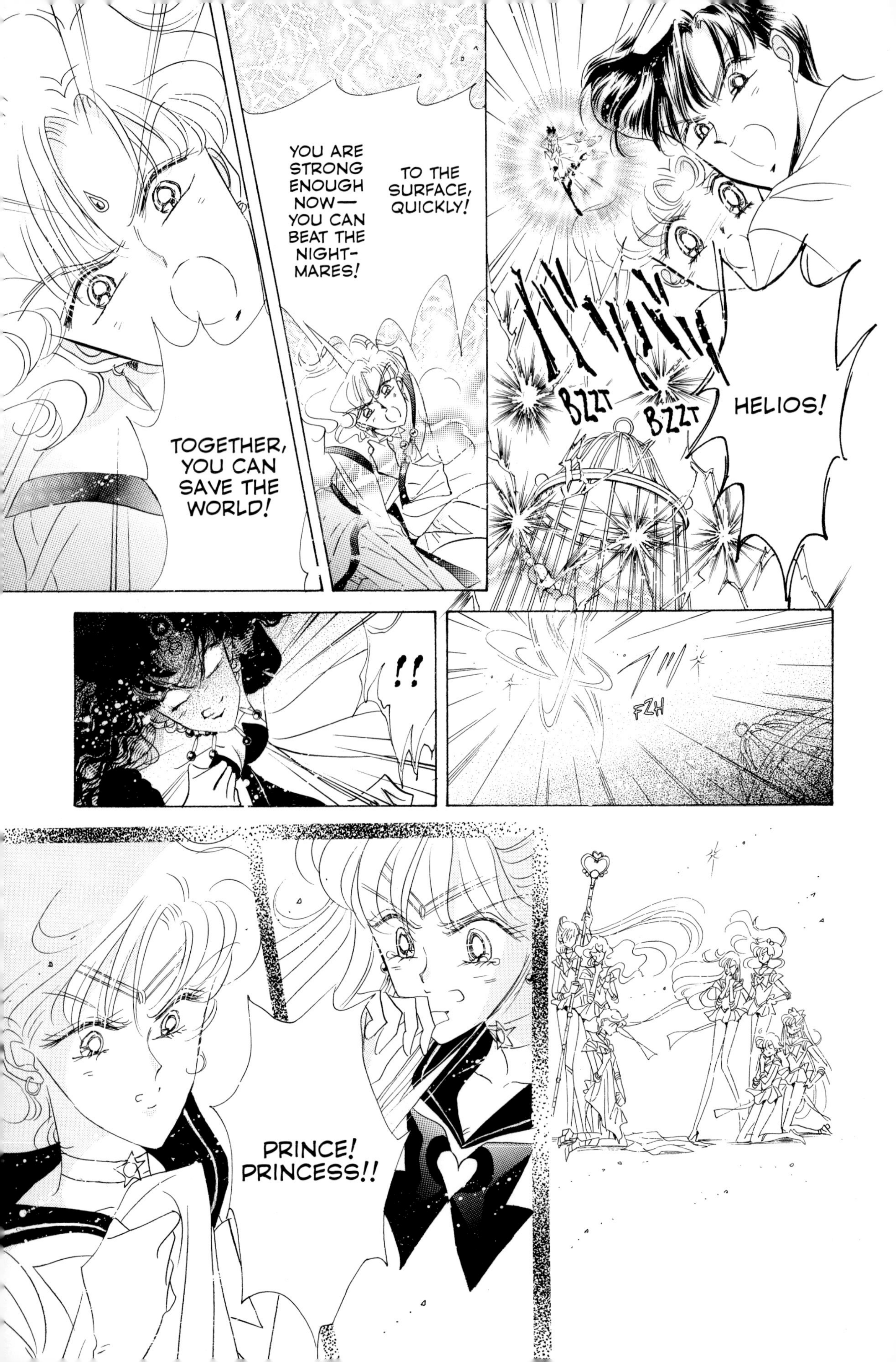
HELIOS!
BZZT
BZZT
TO THE SURFACE, QUICKLY!
YOU ARE STRONG ENOUGH NOW—YOU CAN BEAT THE NIGHT-MARES!
TOGETHER, YOU CAN SAVE THE WORLD!
FZH
!!
PRINCE! PRINCESS!!

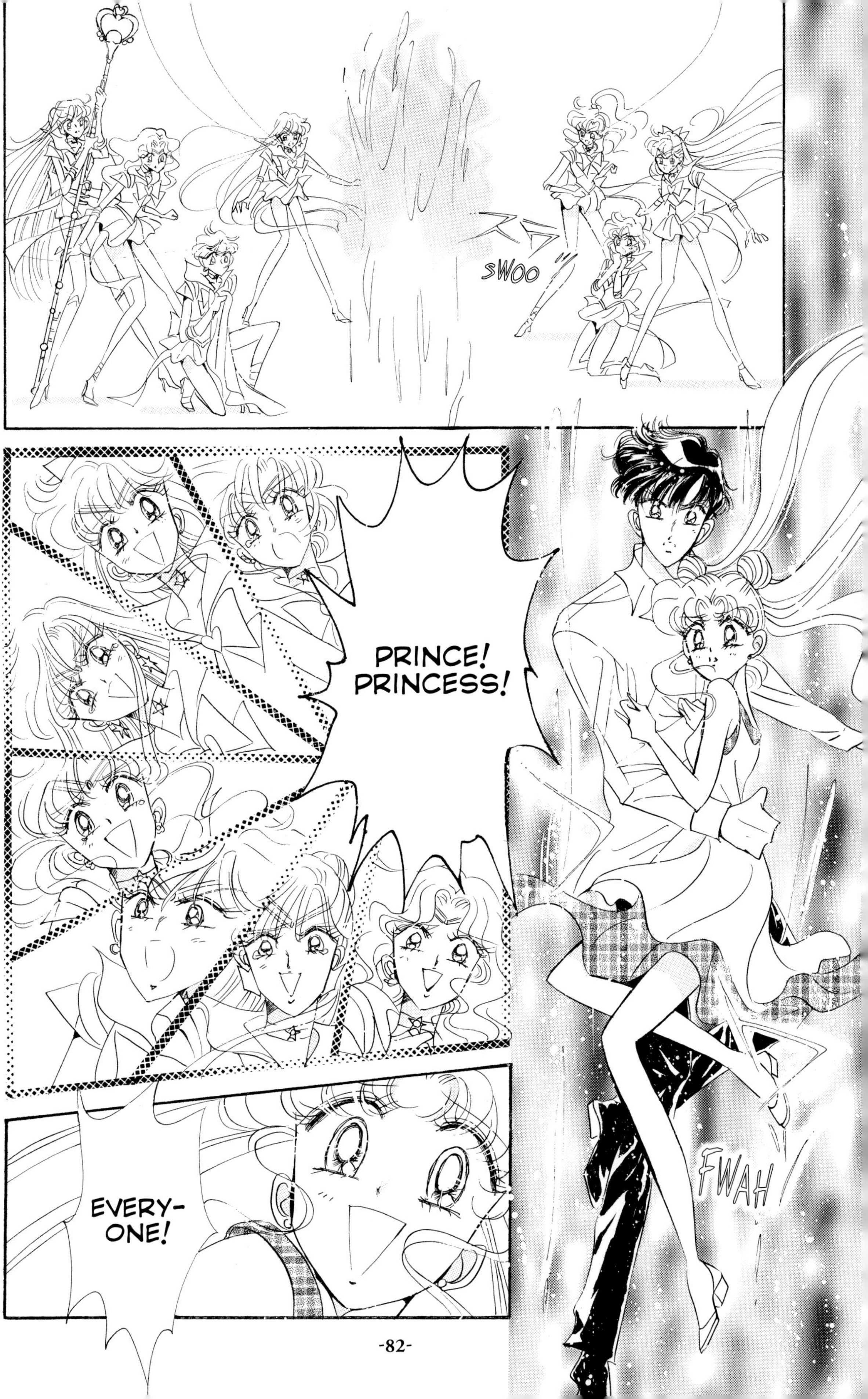

スワ
SWOO
FWAH
PRINCE! PRINCESS!
EVERY-ONE!

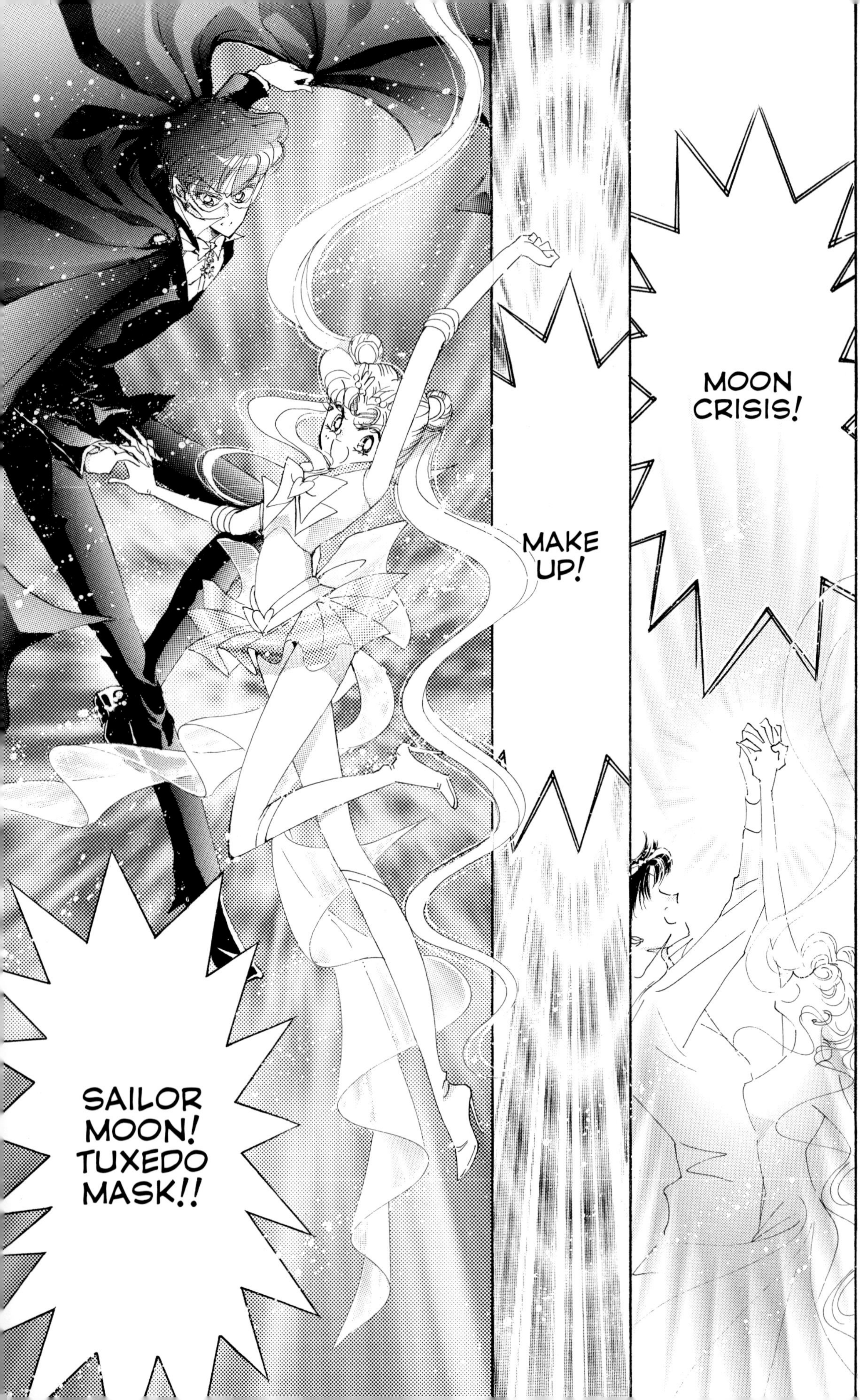
MOON CRISIS!
MAKE UP!
SAILOR MOON! TUXEDO MASK!!

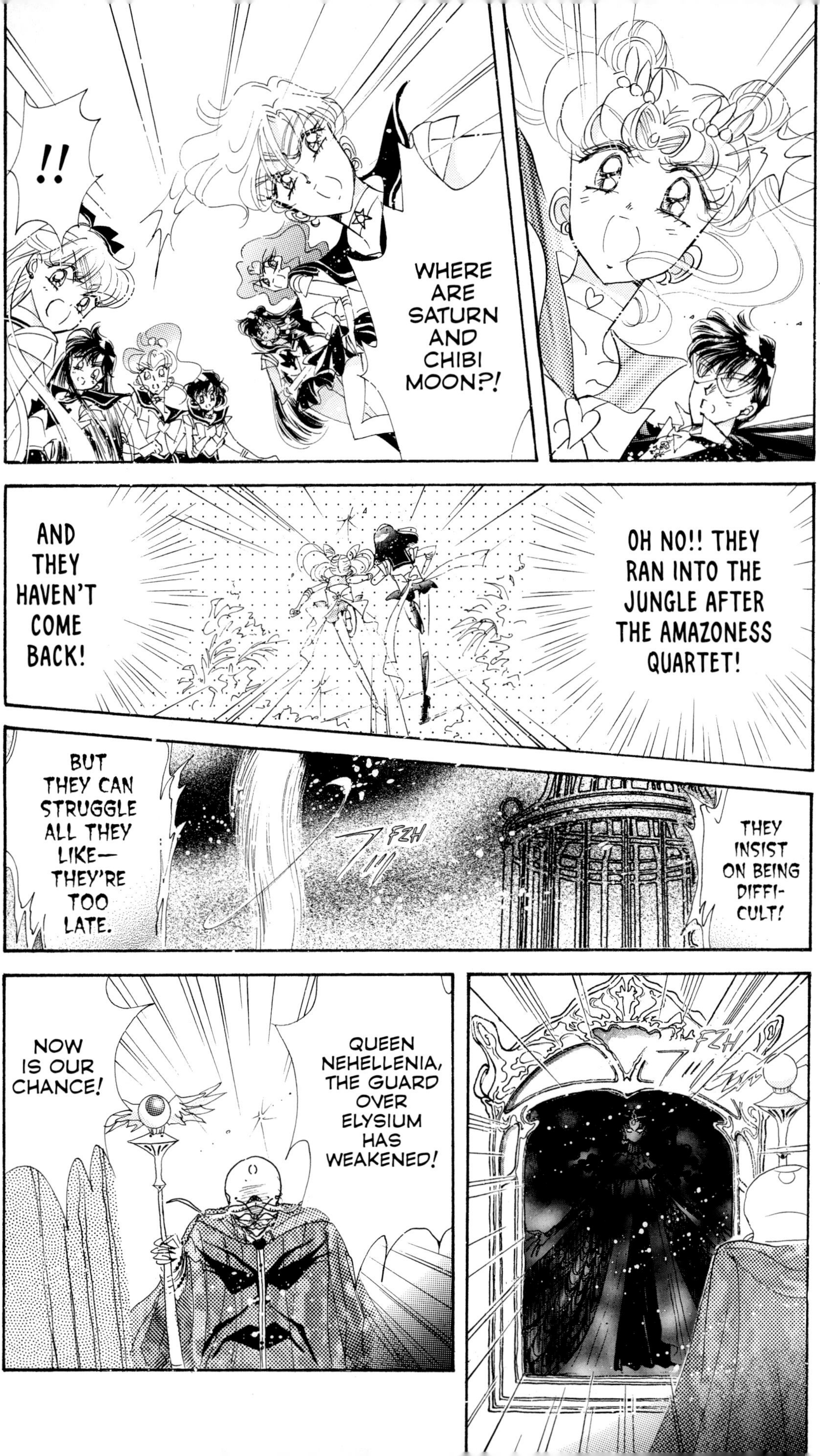
!!
WHERE ARE SATURN AND CHIBI MOON?!
OH NO!! THEY RAN INTO THE JUNGLE AFTER THE AMAZONESS QUARTET!
AND THEY HAVEN'T COME BACK!
THEY INSIST ON BEING DIFFI-CULT!
FZH
BUT THEY CAN STRUGGLE ALL THEY LIKE— THEY'RE TOO LATE.
FZH
QUEEN NEHELLENIA, THE GUARD OVER ELYSIUM HAS WEAKENED!
NOW IS OUR CHANCE!

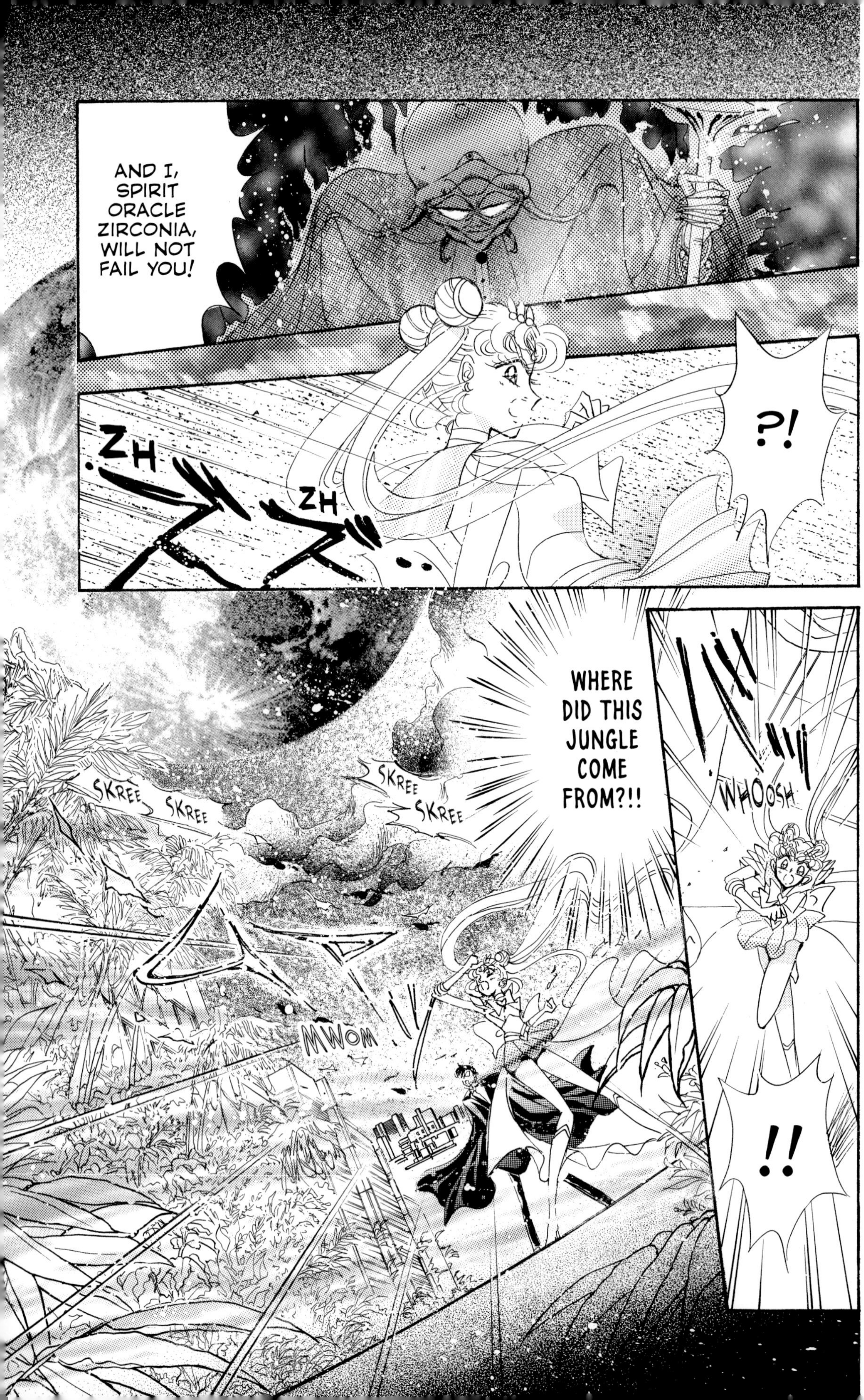
AND I, SPIRIT ORACLE ZIRCONIA, WILL NOT FAIL YOU!
?!
ZH
ZH
WHOOSH
!!
WHERE DID THIS JUNGLE COME FROM?!!
SKREE
SKREE
SKREE
SKREE
MWOM

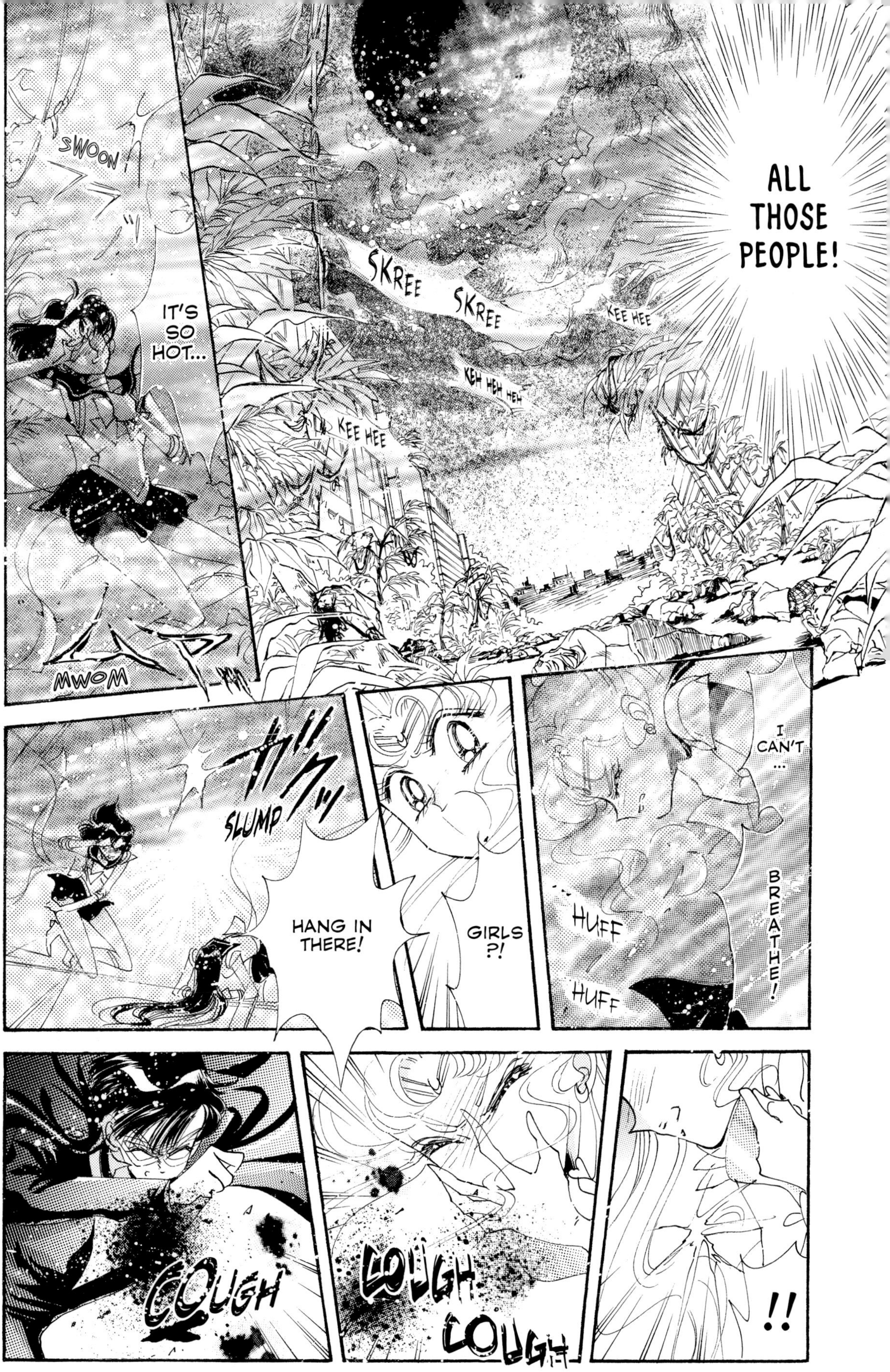
ALL THOSE PEOPLE!
SKREE
SKREE
KEE HEE
KEH HEH HEH
KEE HEE
SWOON
IT'S SO HOT...
MWOM
I CAN'T ...
BREATHE!
HUFF
HUFF
GIRLS?!
SLUMP
HANG IN THERE!
!!
COUGH
COUGH
COUGH

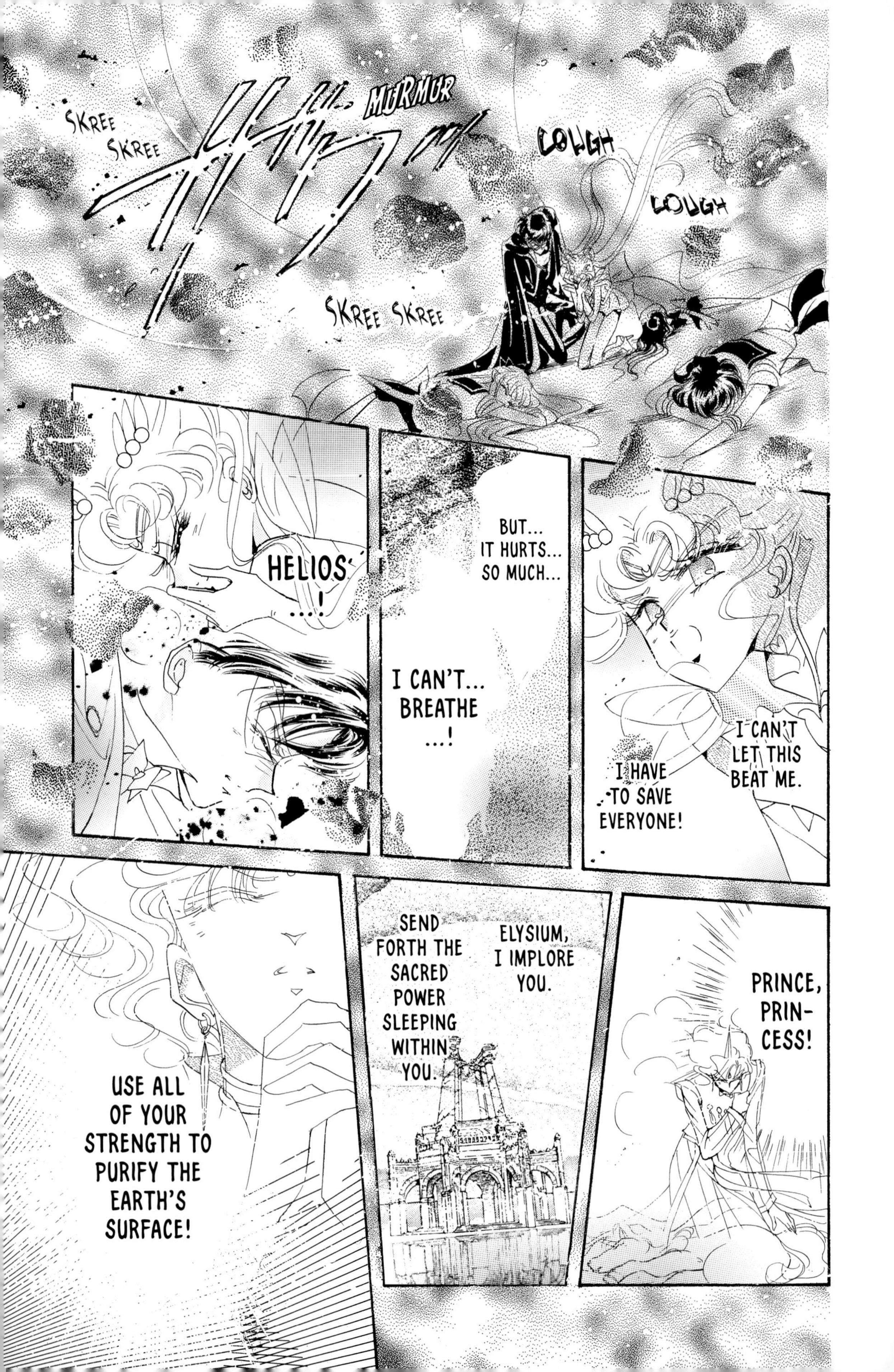
COUGH
COUGH
MURMUR
SKREE SKREE
SKREE SKREE
I CAN'T LET THIS BEAT ME.
I HAVE TO SAVE EVERYONE!
BUT... IT HURTS... SO MUCH...
I CAN'T... BREATHE ...!
HELIOS ...!
PRINCE, PRIN-CESS!
ELYSIUM, I IMPLORE YOU.
SEND FORTH THE SACRED POWER SLEEPING WITHIN YOU.
USE ALL OF YOUR STRENGTH TO PURIFY THE EARTH'S SURFACE!

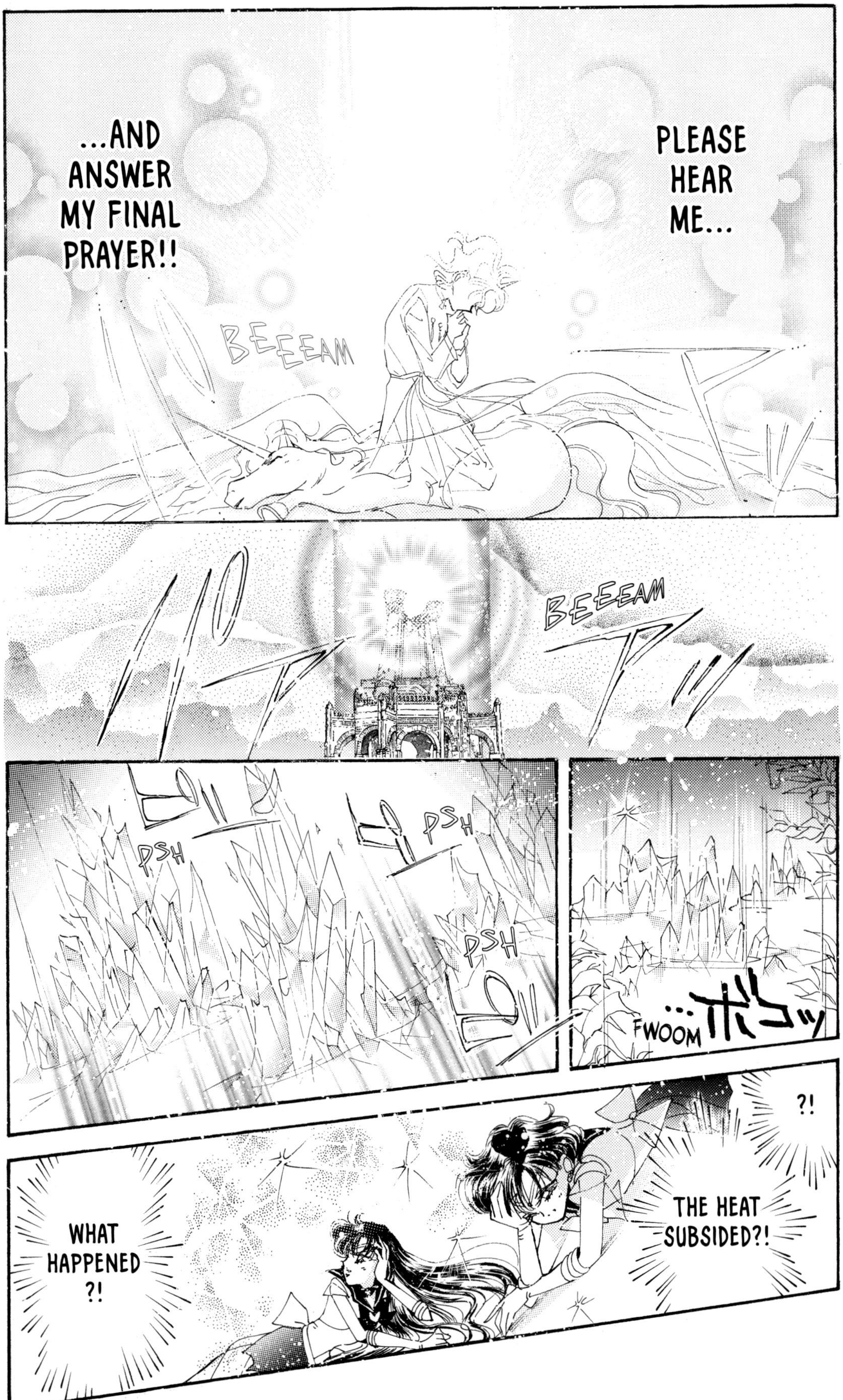
PLEASE HEAR ME...
...AND ANSWER MY FINAL PRAYER!!
BEEEAM
BEEEAM
...FWOOM
PSH
PSH
PSH
?!
THE HEAT SUBSIDED?!
WHAT HAPPENED ?!

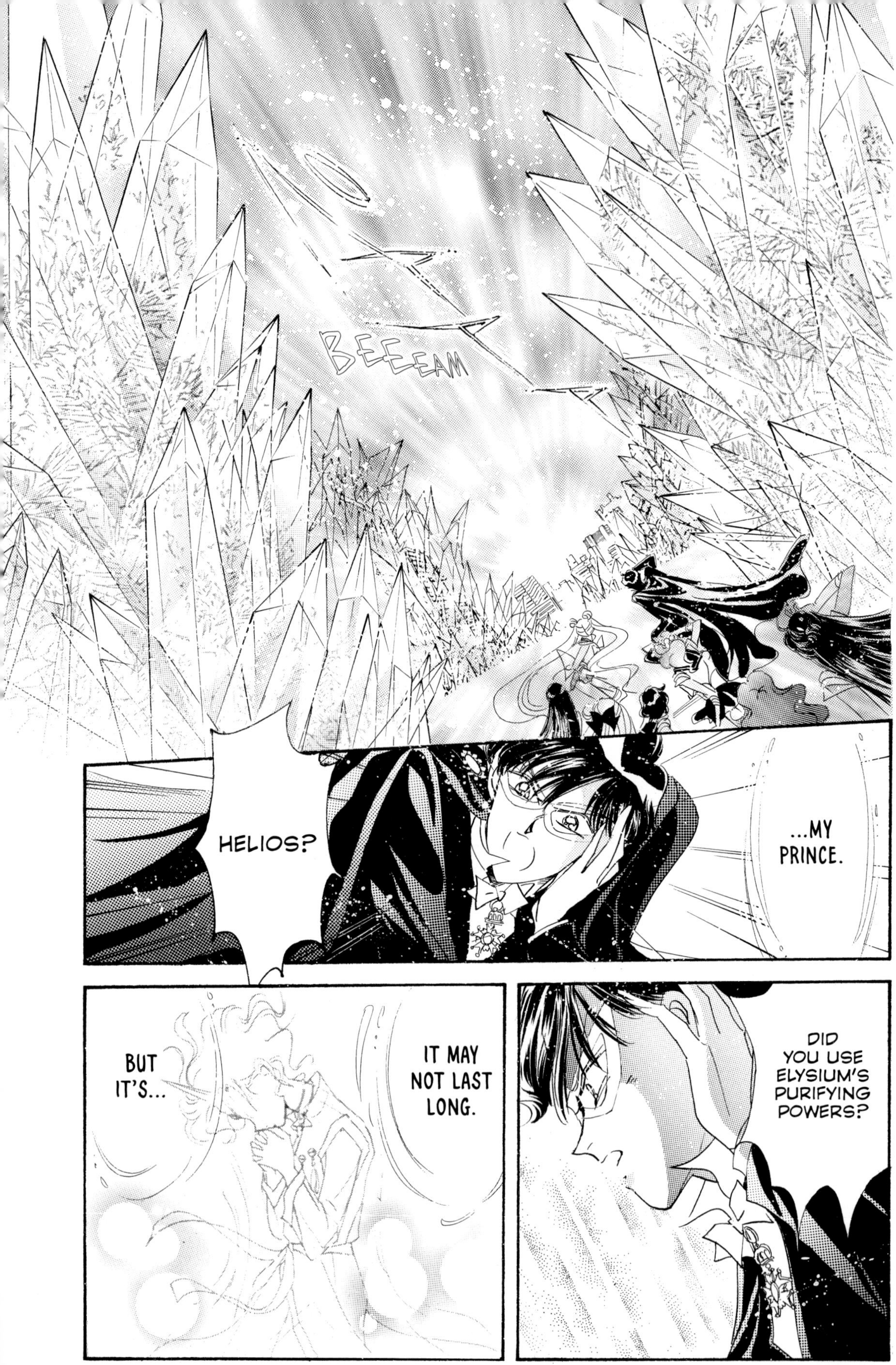
BEEEEAM
...MY PRINCE.
HELIOS?
DID YOU USE ELYSIUM'S PURIFYING POWERS?
IT MAY NOT LAST LONG.
BUT IT'S...

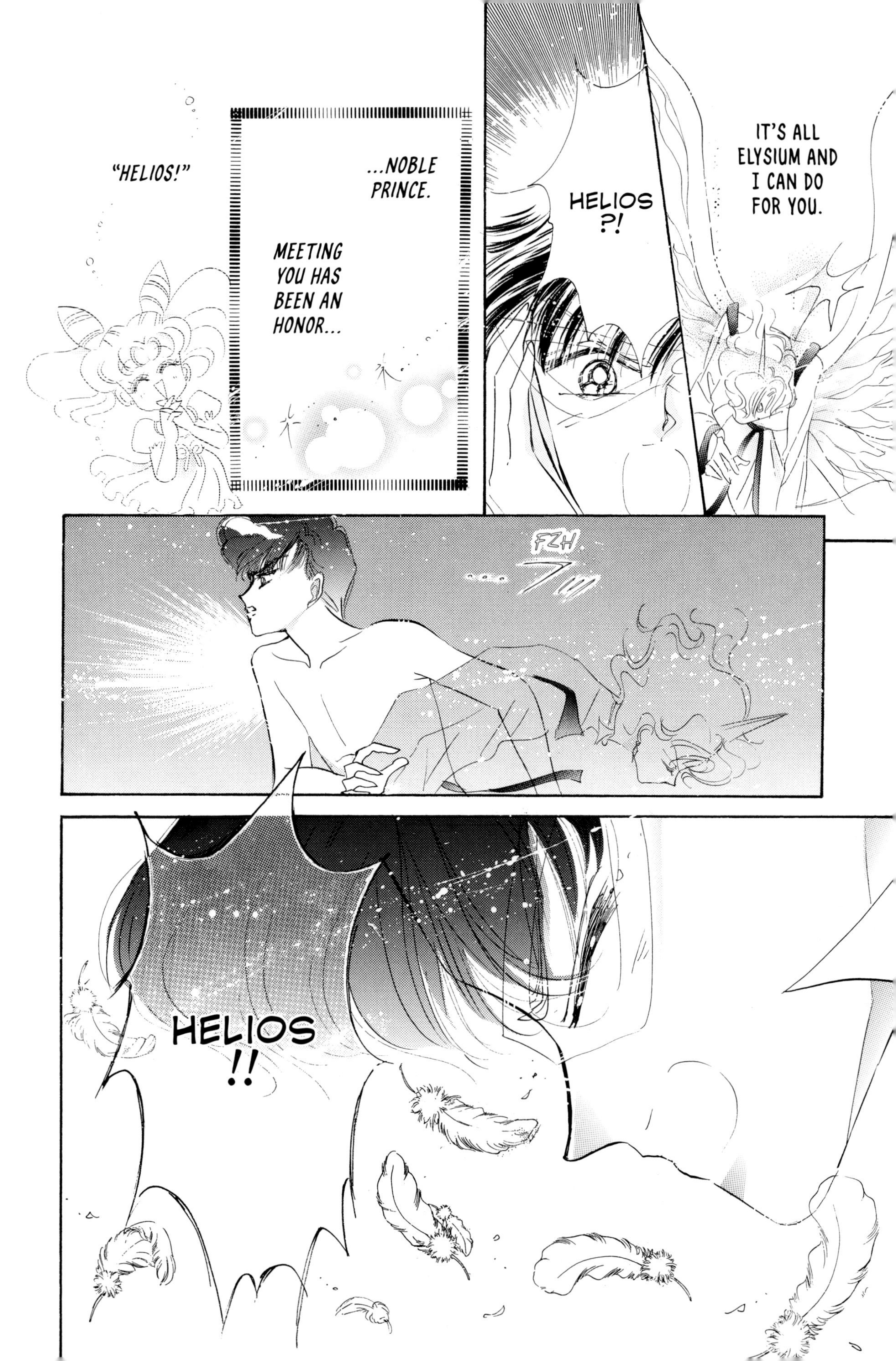
IT'S ALL ELYSIUM AND I CAN DO FOR YOU.
HELIOS ?!
...NOBLE PRINCE.
MEETING YOU HAS BEEN AN HONOR...
"HELIOS!"
FZH
HELIOS !!

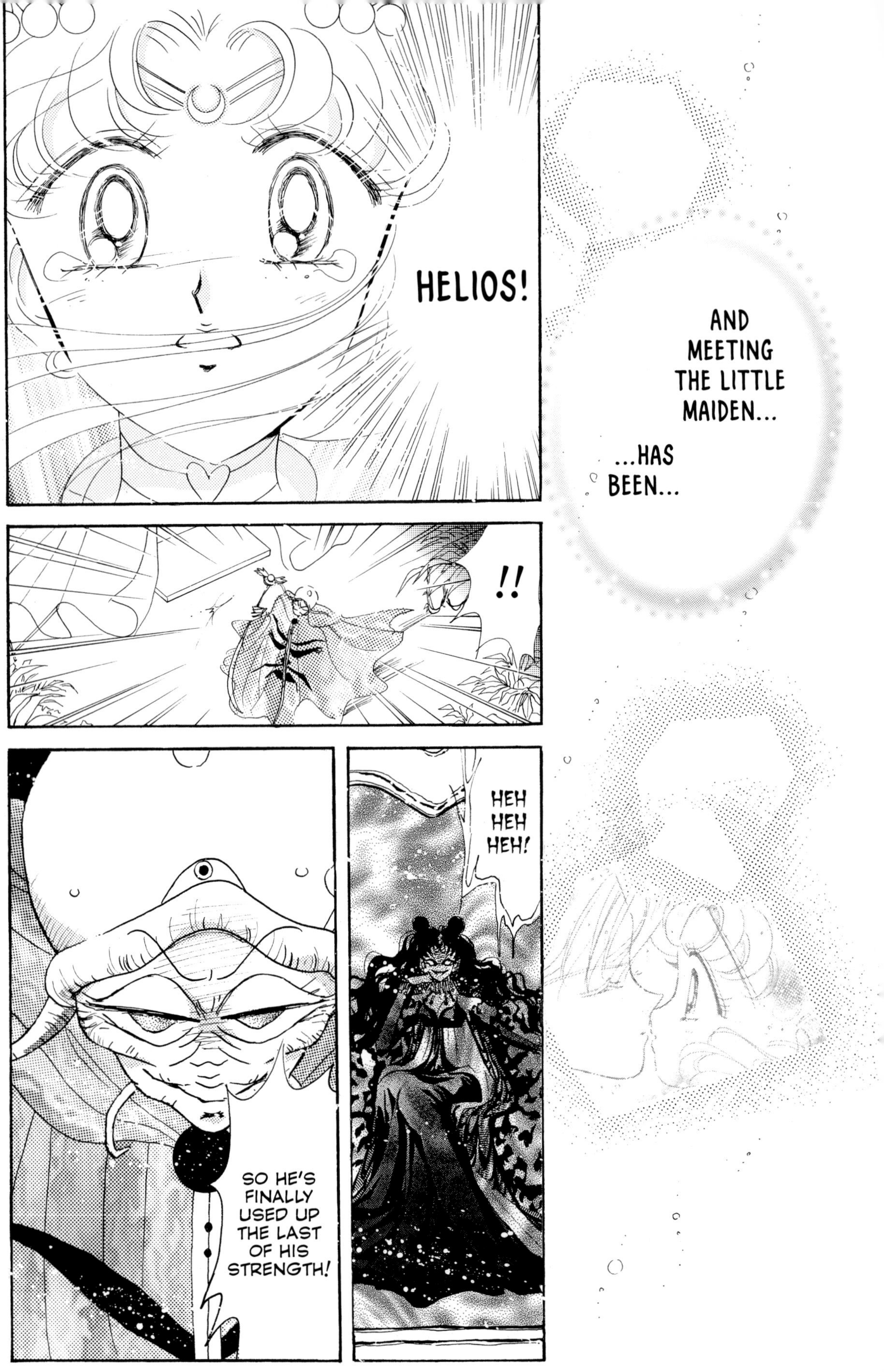
AND MEETING THE LITTLE MAIDEN...
...HAS BEEN...
HELIOS!
!!
HEH HEH HEH!
SO HE'S FINALLY USED UP THE LAST OF HIS STRENGTH!

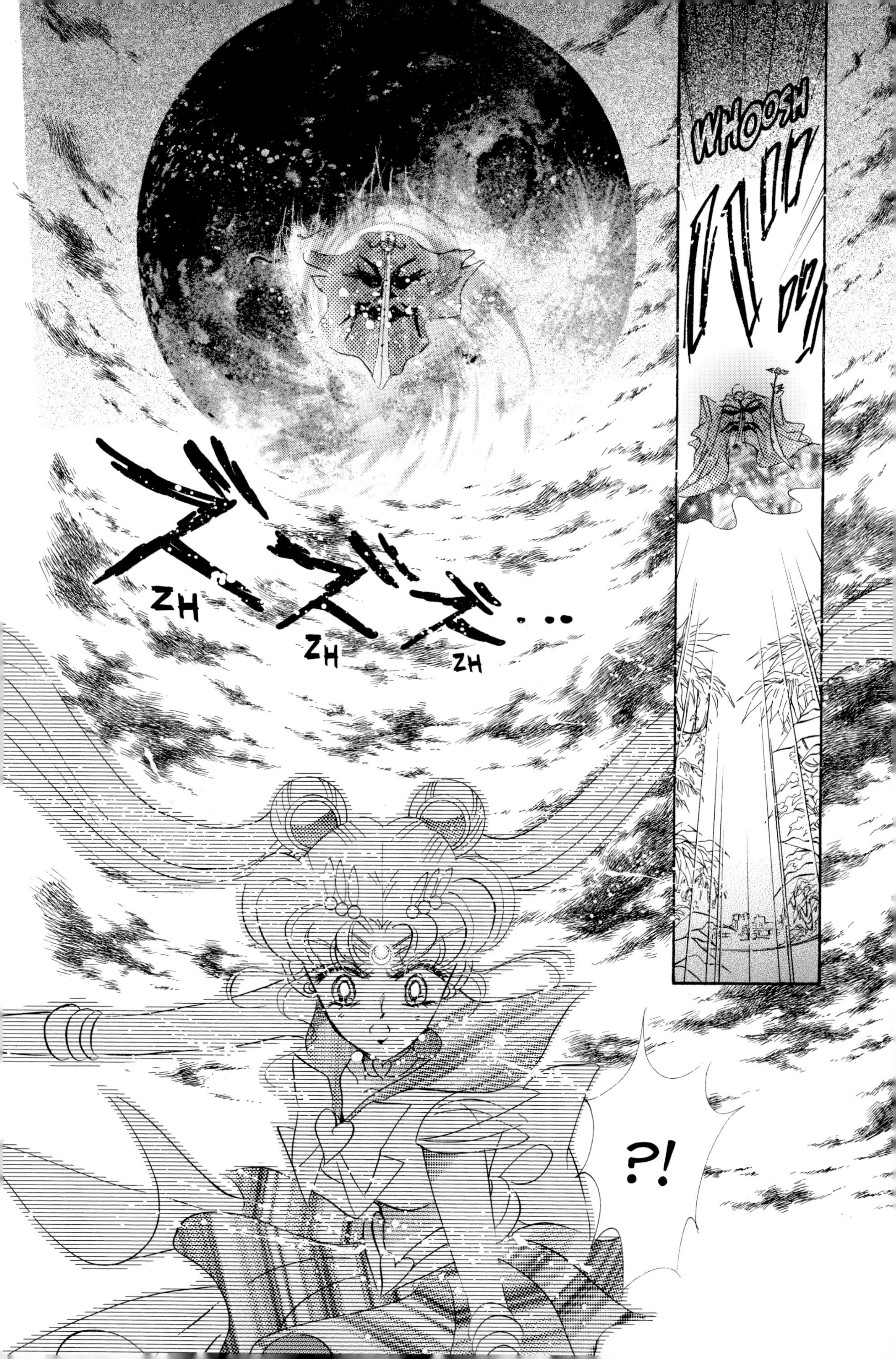
WHOOSH
ハッ
ズズズ…
ZH ZH ZH
?!

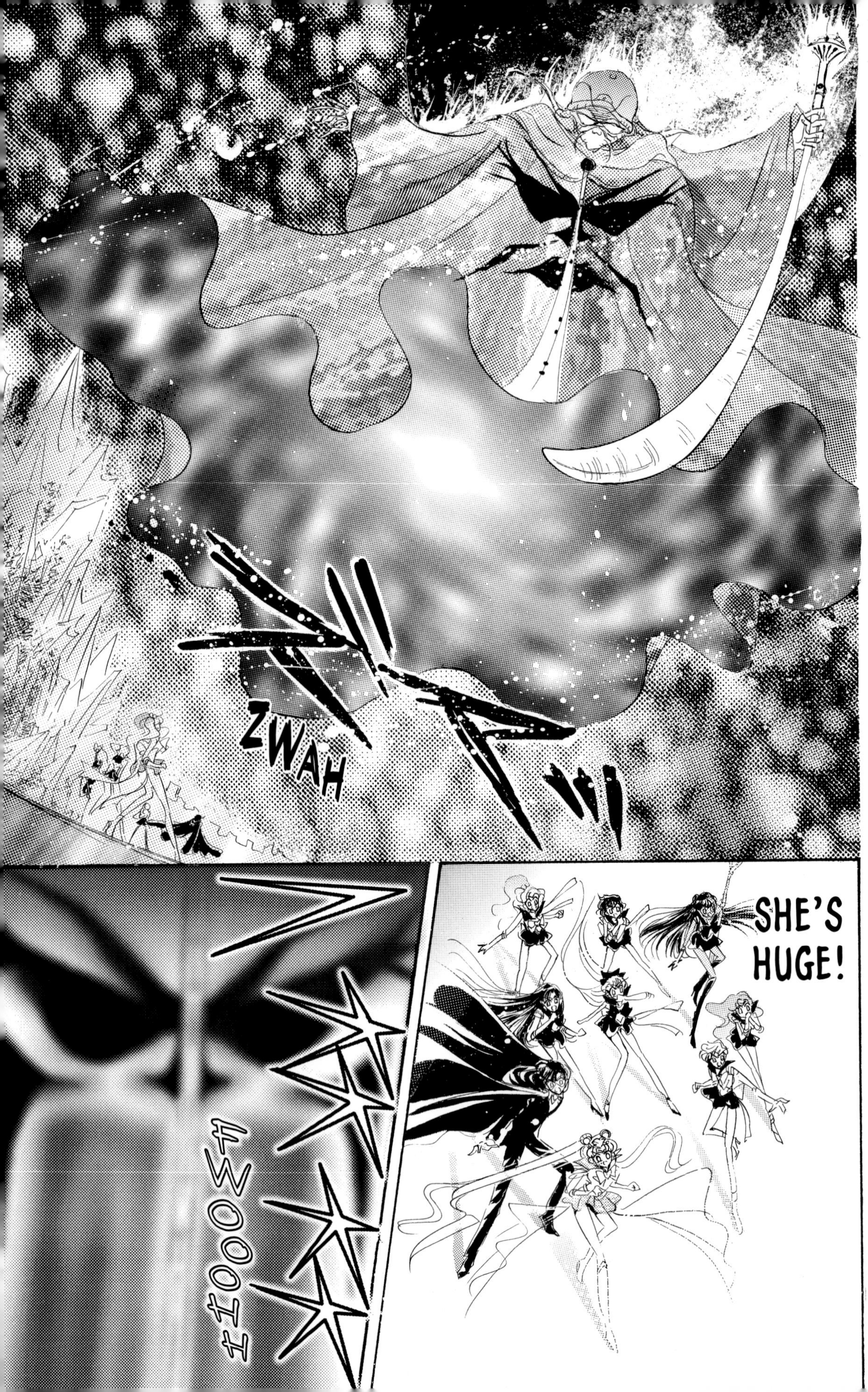
ZWAH
SHE'S HUGE!
FWOOOOH

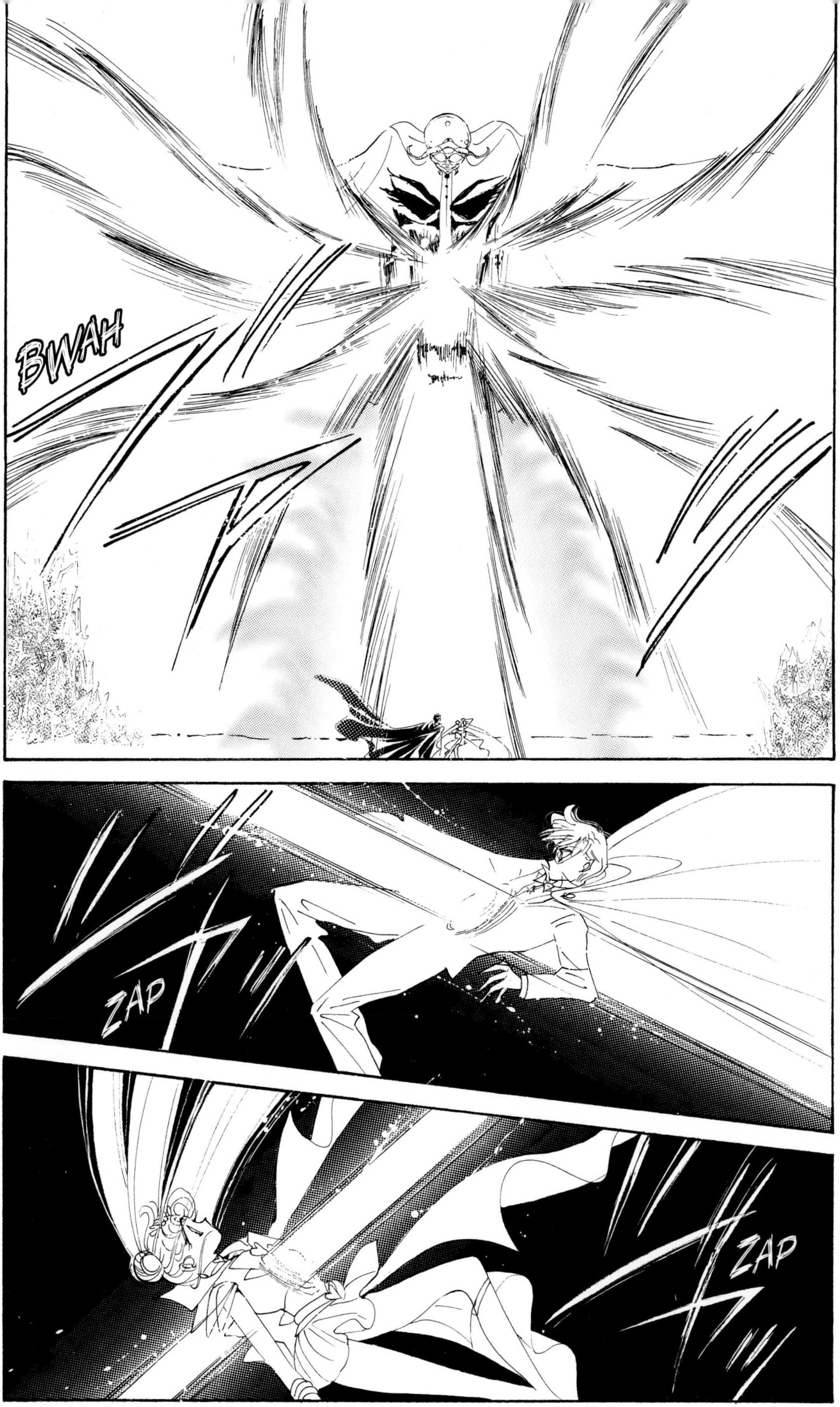
BWAH
ZAP
ZAP

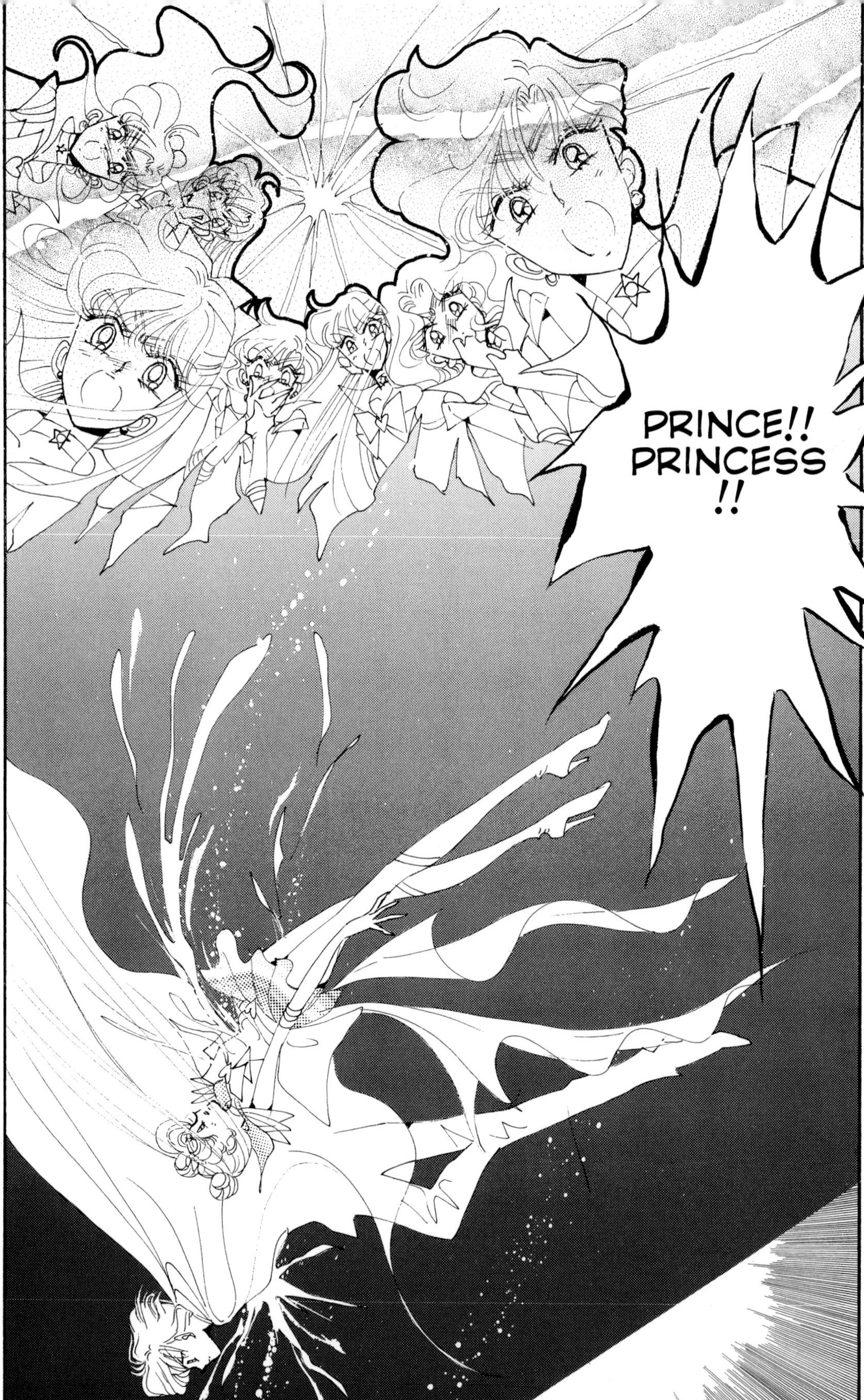
PRINCE!! PRINCESS !!

Pretty Guardian

Sailor Moon

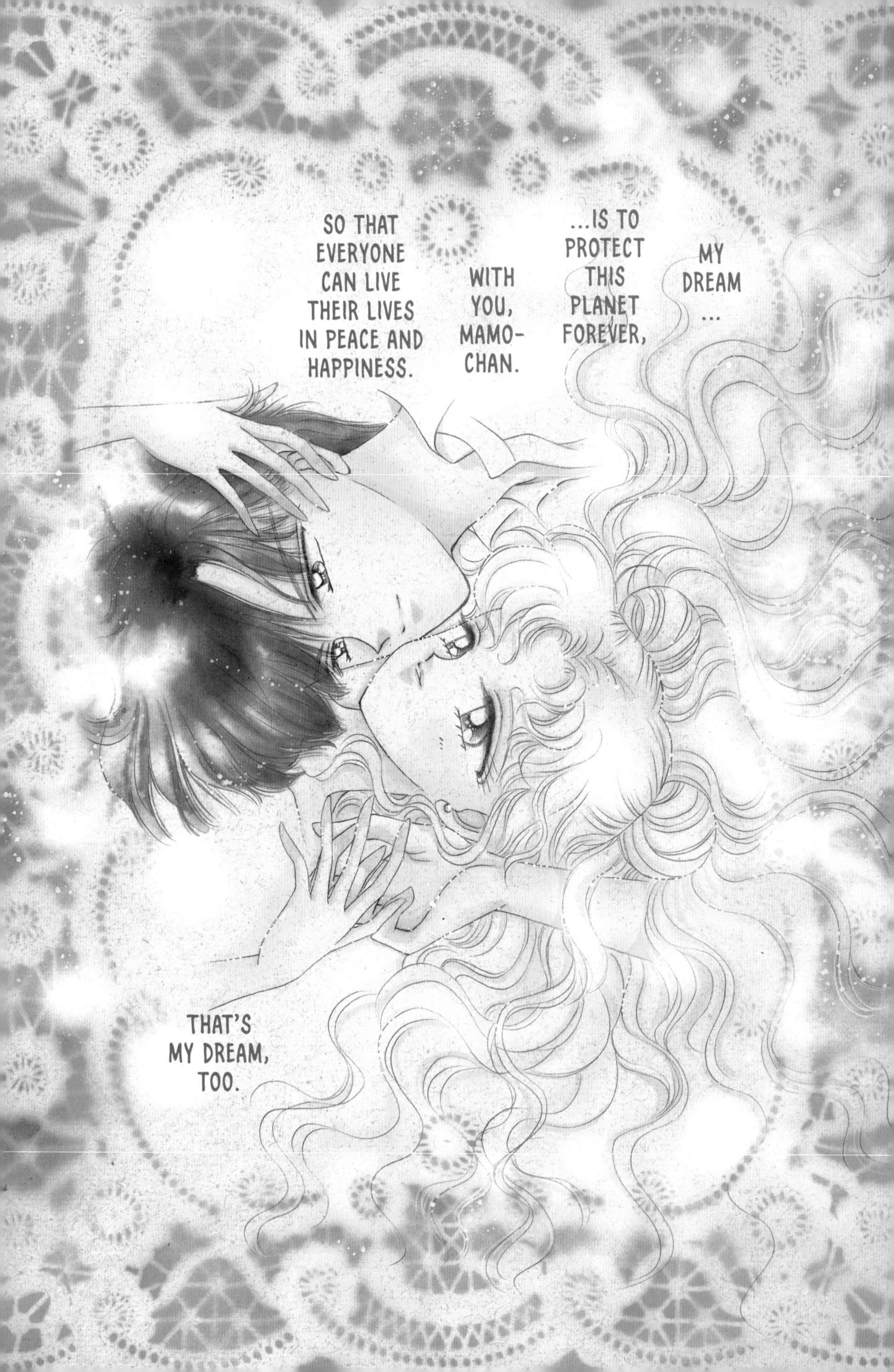
MY DREAM ...
...IS TO PROTECT THIS PLANET FOREVER,
WITH YOU, MAMO-CHAN.
SO THAT EVERYONE CAN LIVE THEIR LIVES IN PEACE AND HAPPINESS.
THAT'S MY DREAM, TOO.

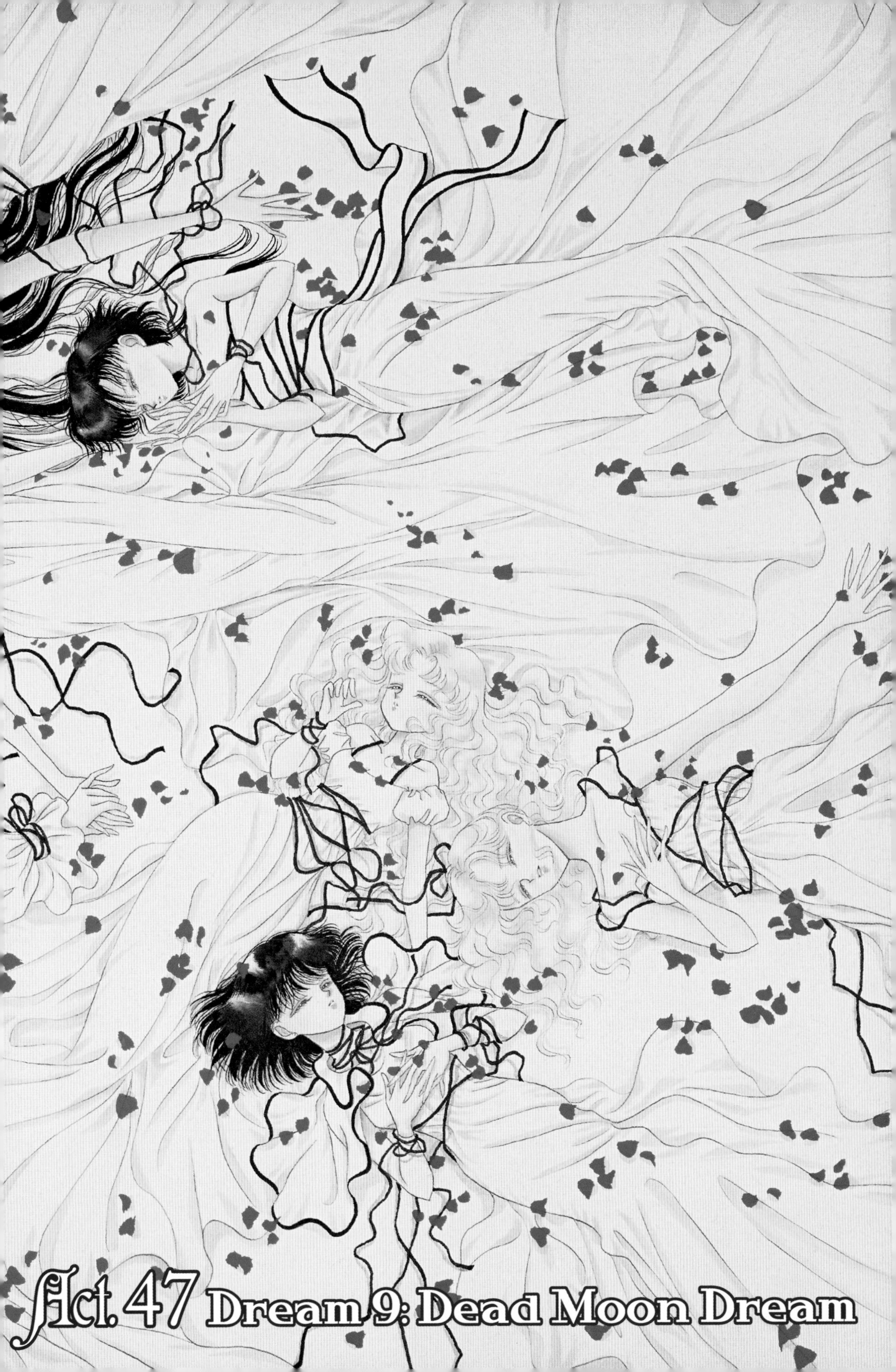

Act. 47 Dream 9: Dead Moon Dream

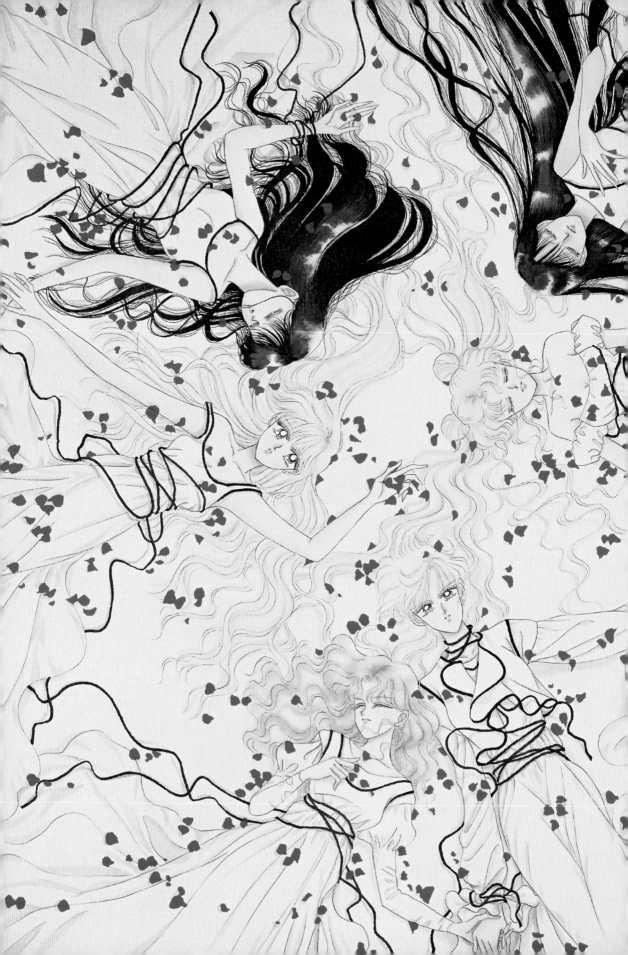

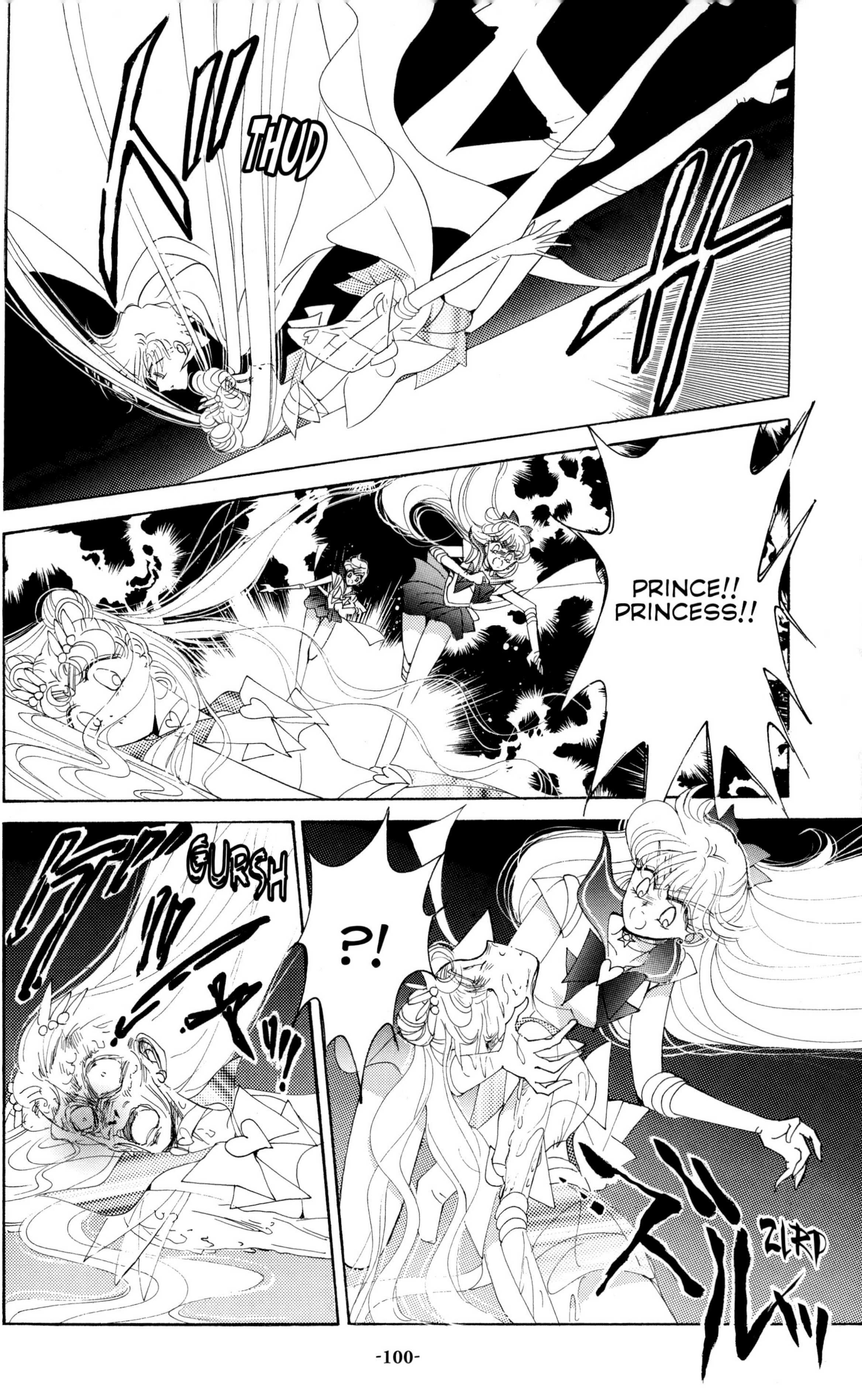
THUD
PRINCE!!
PRINCESS!!
?!
ZLRP
GURSH

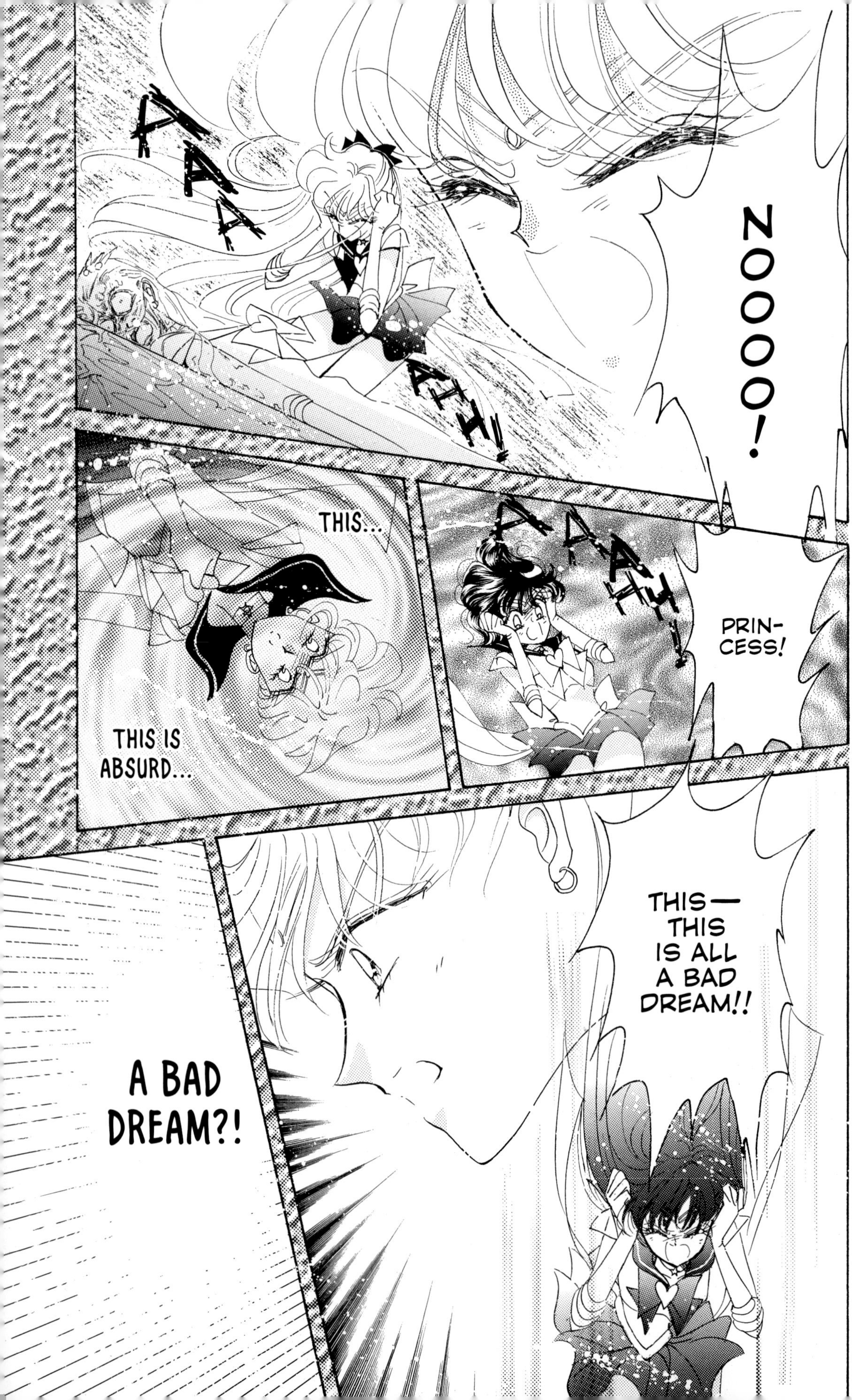
NOOOOO!
AAAAHH!!
AAAHH!
PRIN-CESS!
THIS...
THIS IS ABSURD...
THIS—THIS IS ALL A BAD DREAM!!
A BAD DREAM?!

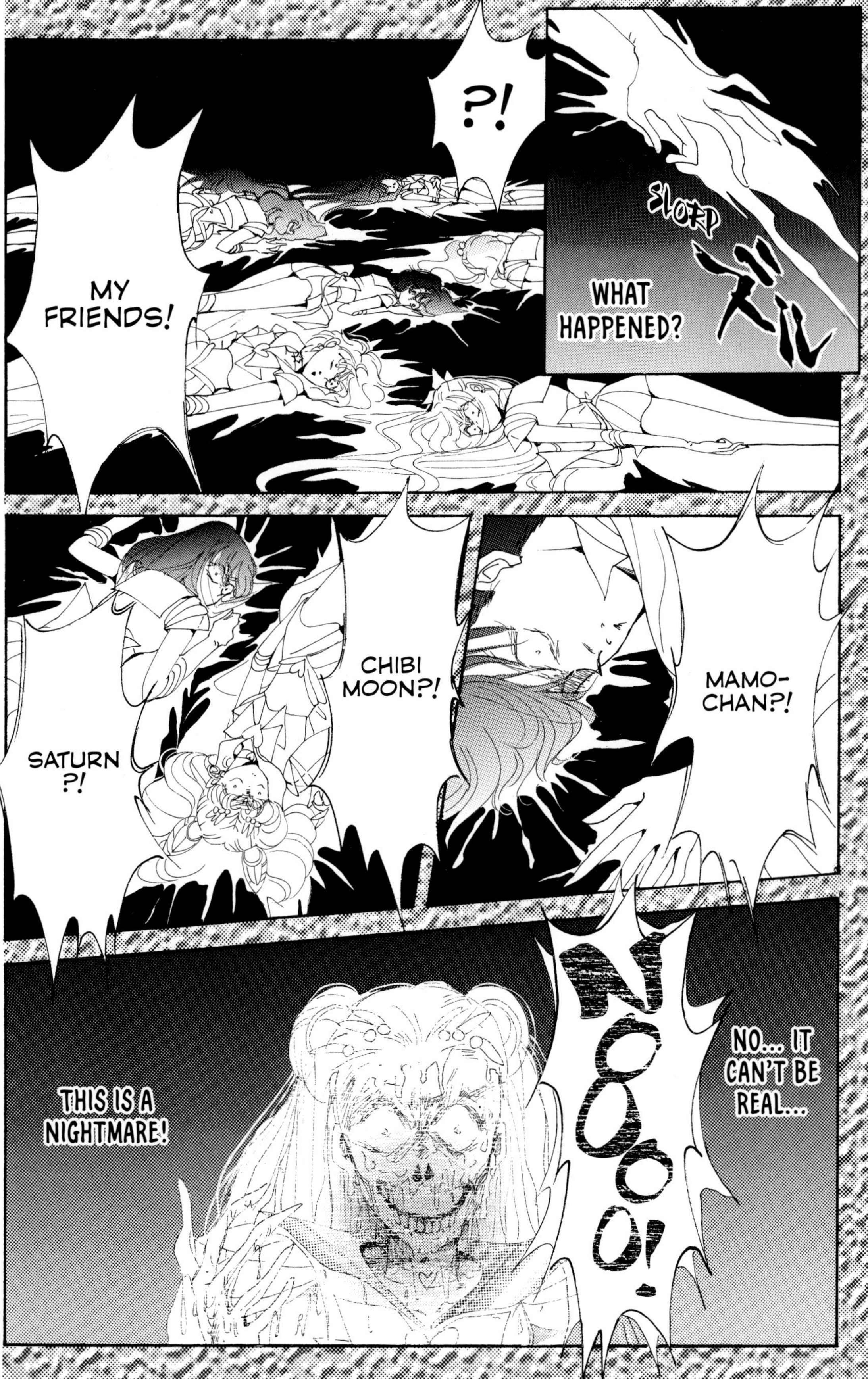
SLORP
ズル
WHAT HAPPENED?
?!
MY FRIENDS!
MAMO-CHAN?!
CHIBI MOON?!
SATURN ?!
NO... IT CAN'T BE REAL...
NOOOOO!
THIS IS A NIGHTMARE!

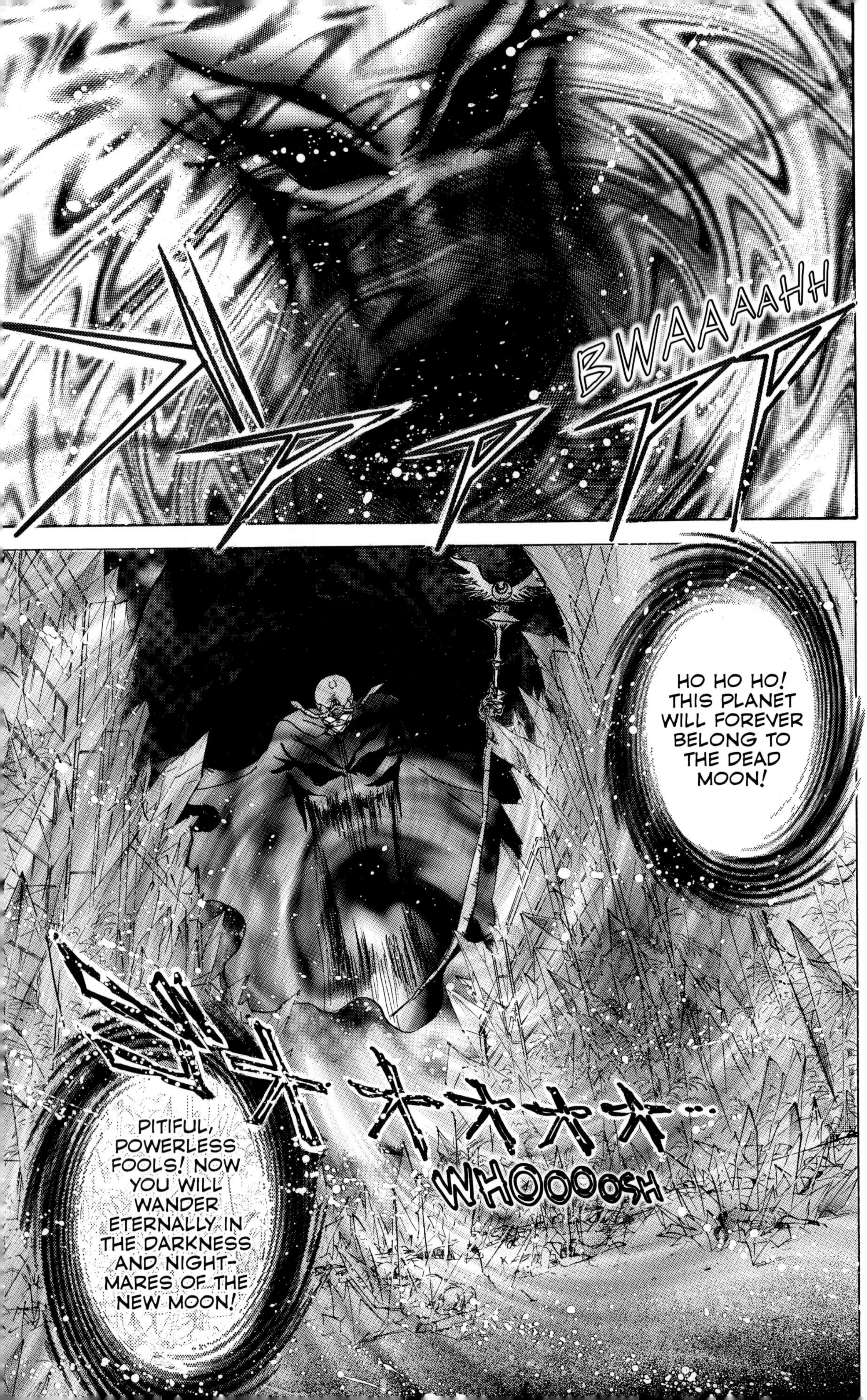
BWAAAAHH
HO HO HO! THIS PLANET WILL FOREVER BELONG TO THE DEAD MOON!
WHOOOOSH
PITIFUL, POWERLESS FOOLS! NOW YOU WILL WANDER ETERNALLY IN THE DARKNESS AND NIGHT-MARES OF THE NEW MOON!

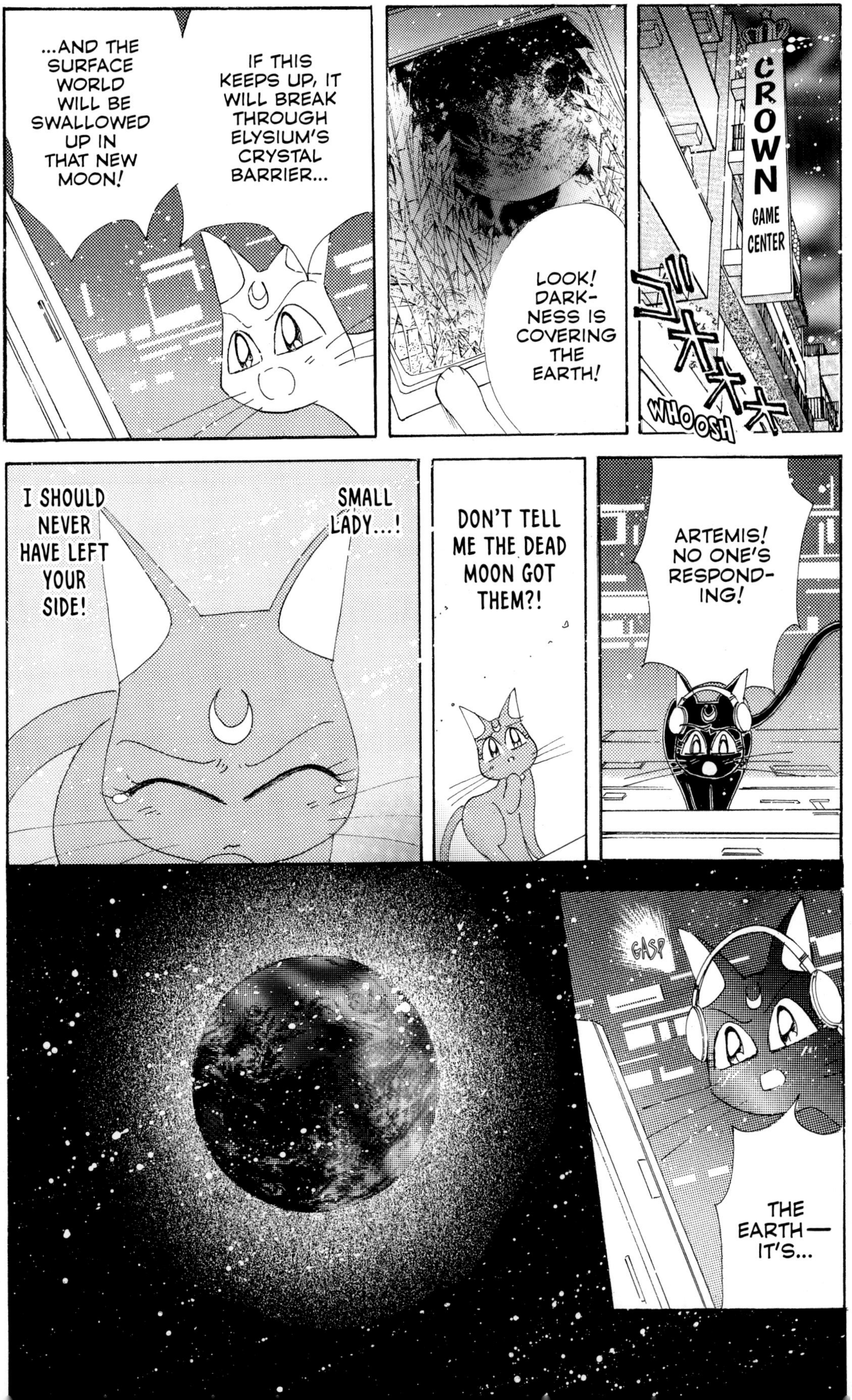
CROWN
GAME CENTER
WHOOSH
LOOK! DARKNESS IS COVERING THE EARTH!
IF THIS KEEPS UP, IT WILL BREAK THROUGH ELYSIUM'S CRYSTAL BARRIER...
...AND THE SURFACE WORLD WILL BE SWALLOWED UP IN THAT NEW MOON!
ARTEMIS! NO ONE'S RESPONDING!
DON'T TELL ME THE DEAD MOON GOT THEM?!
SMALL LADY...!
I SHOULD NEVER HAVE LEFT YOUR SIDE!
GASP
THE EARTH— IT'S...

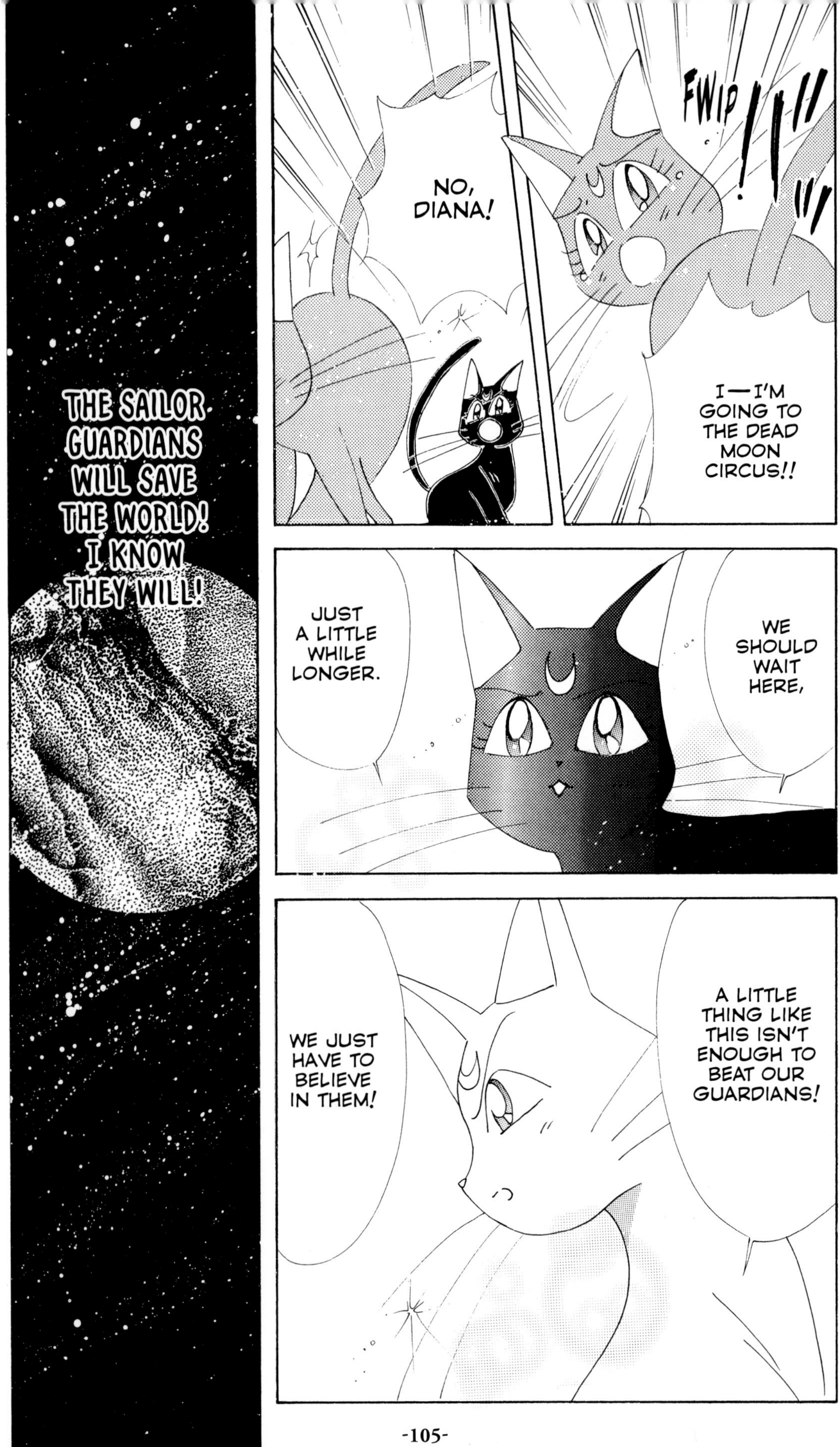
FWIP
I—I'M GOING TO THE DEAD MOON CIRCUS!!
NO, DIANA!
WE SHOULD WAIT HERE,
JUST A LITTLE WHILE LONGER.
A LITTLE THING LIKE THIS ISN'T ENOUGH TO BEAT OUR GUARDIANS!
WE JUST HAVE TO BELIEVE IN THEM!
THE SAILOR GUARDIANS WILL SAVE THE WORLD! I KNOW THEY WILL!

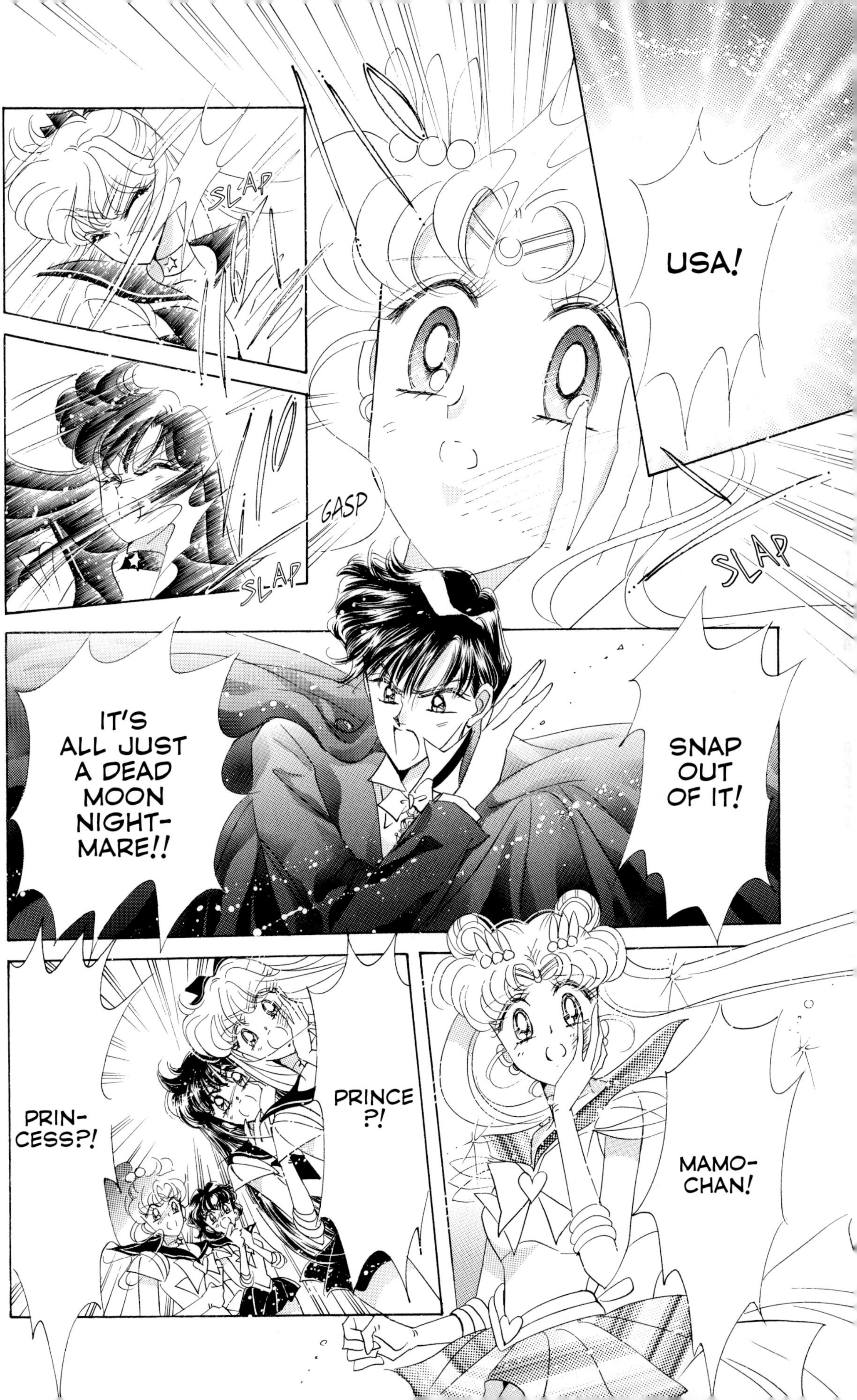
USA!
SLAP
SLAP
GASP
SLAP
SNAP OUT OF IT!
IT'S ALL JUST A DEAD MOON NIGHT-MARE!!
MAMO-CHAN!
PRINCE?!
PRIN-CESS?!

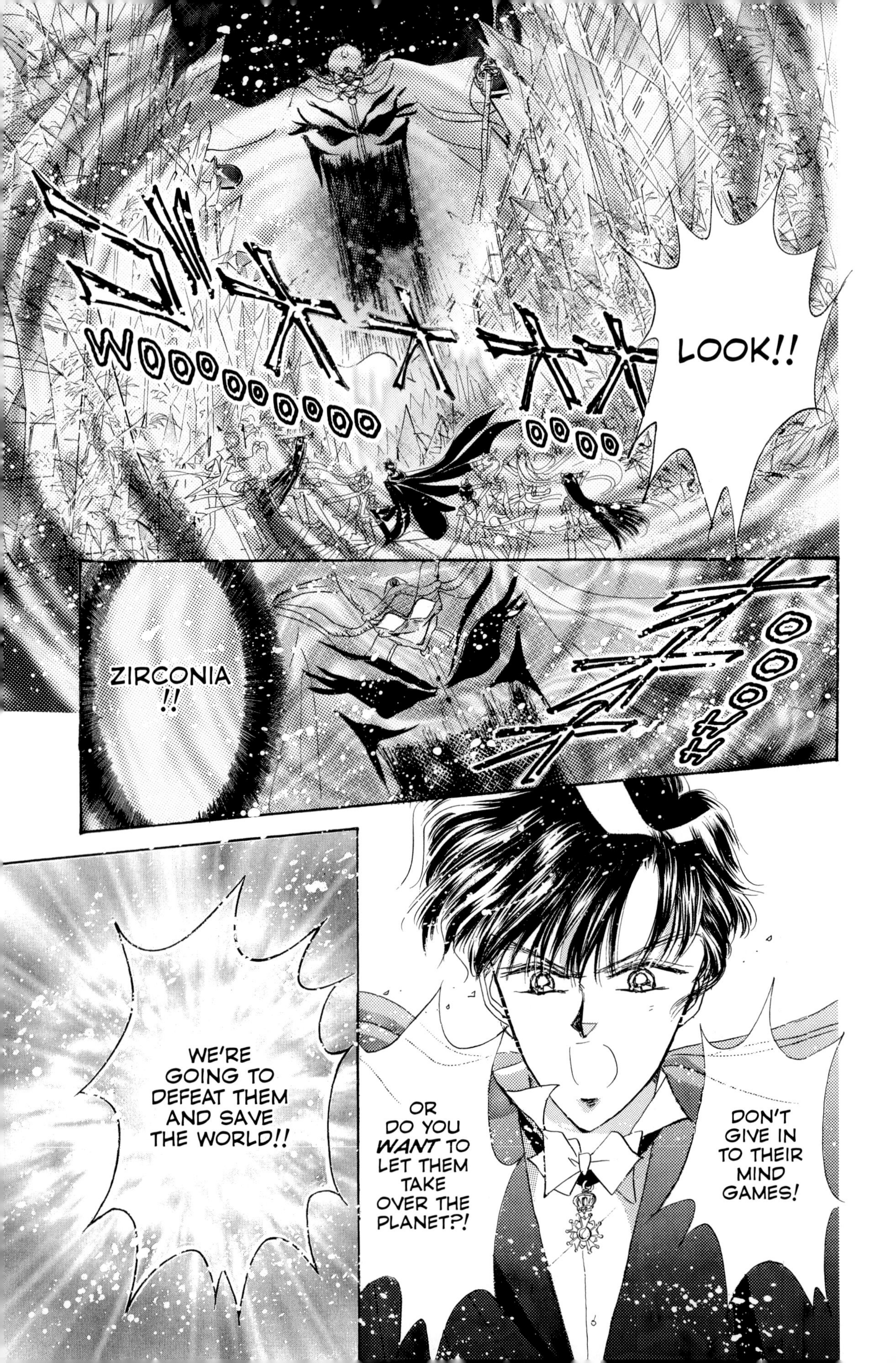
LOOK!!
WOOOOOOOOOOOOO
ZIRCONIA!!
OOOOOHH
DON'T GIVE IN TO THEIR MIND GAMES!
OR DO YOU *WANT* TO LET THEM TAKE OVER THE PLANET?!
WE'RE GOING TO DEFEAT THEM AND SAVE THE WORLD!!

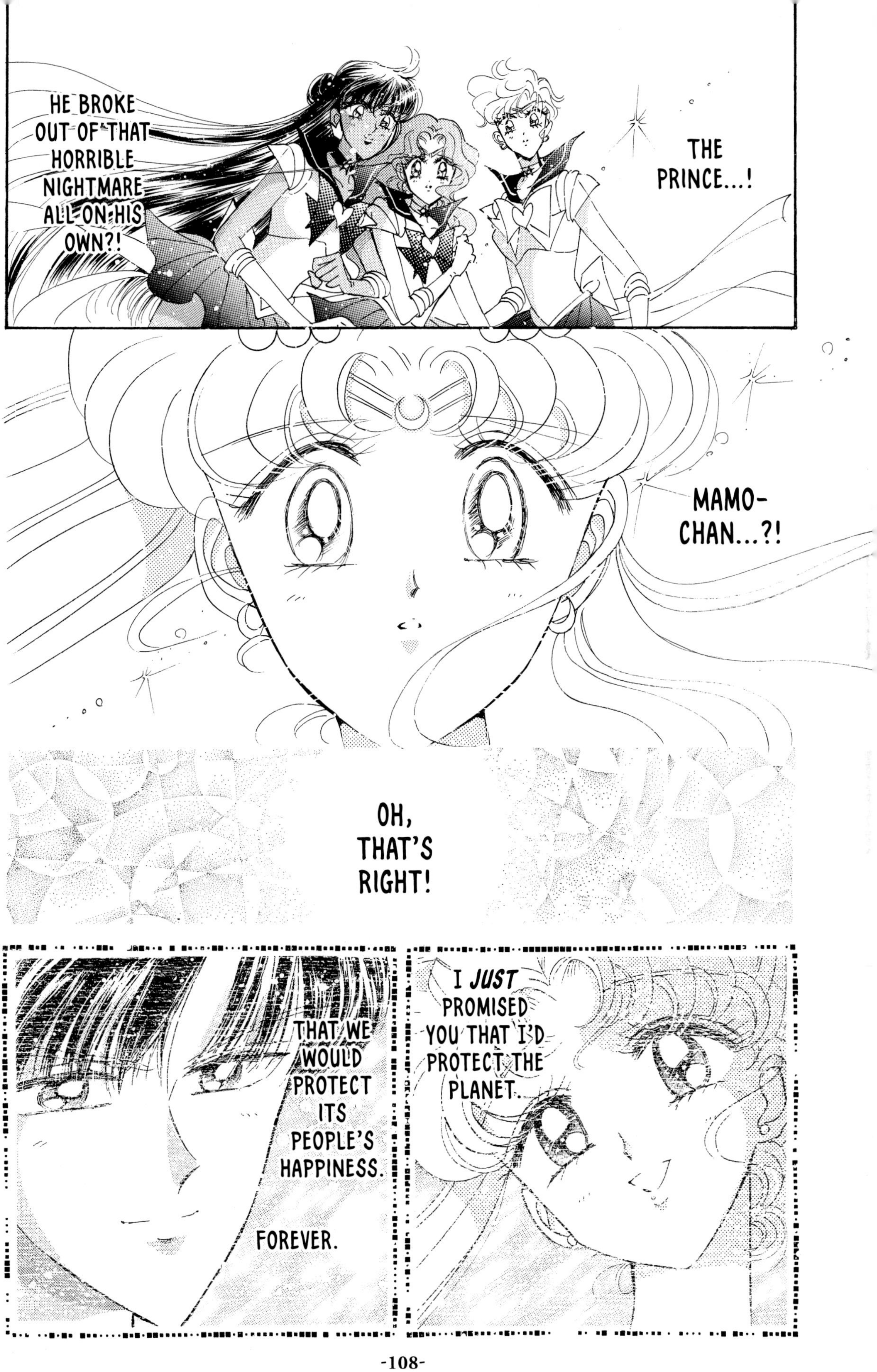
THE PRINCE...!
HE BROKE OUT OF THAT HORRIBLE NIGHTMARE ALL ON HIS OWN?!
MAMO-CHAN...?!
OH, THAT'S RIGHT!
I *JUST* PROMISED YOU THAT I'D PROTECT THE PLANET.
THAT WE WOULD PROTECT ITS PEOPLE'S HAPPINESS.
FOREVER.

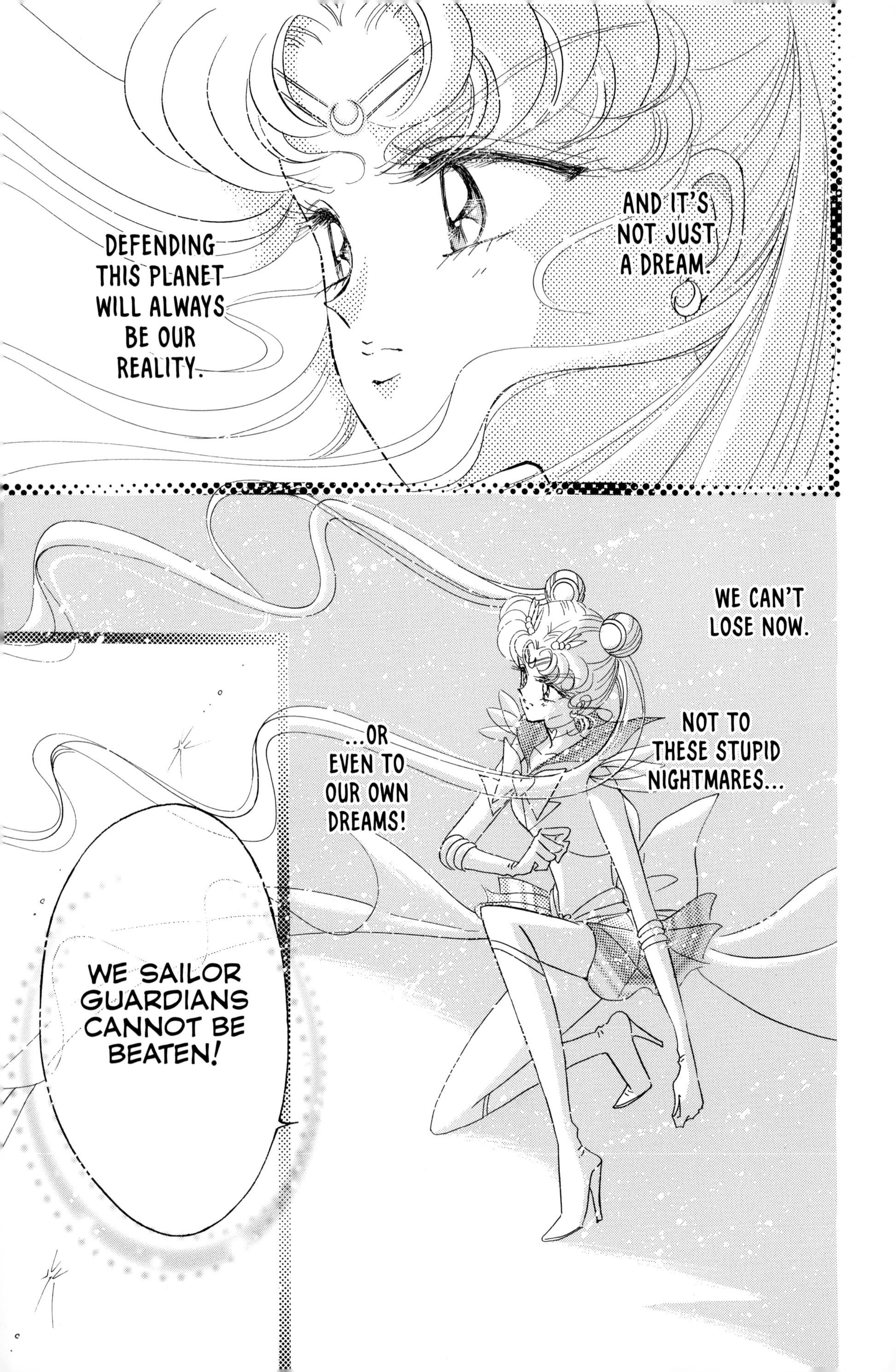
AND IT'S NOT JUST A DREAM.
DEFENDING THIS PLANET WILL ALWAYS BE OUR REALITY.
WE CAN'T LOSE NOW.
NOT TO THESE STUPID NIGHTMARES...
...OR EVEN TO OUR OWN DREAMS!
WE SAILOR GUARDIANS CANNOT BE BEATEN!

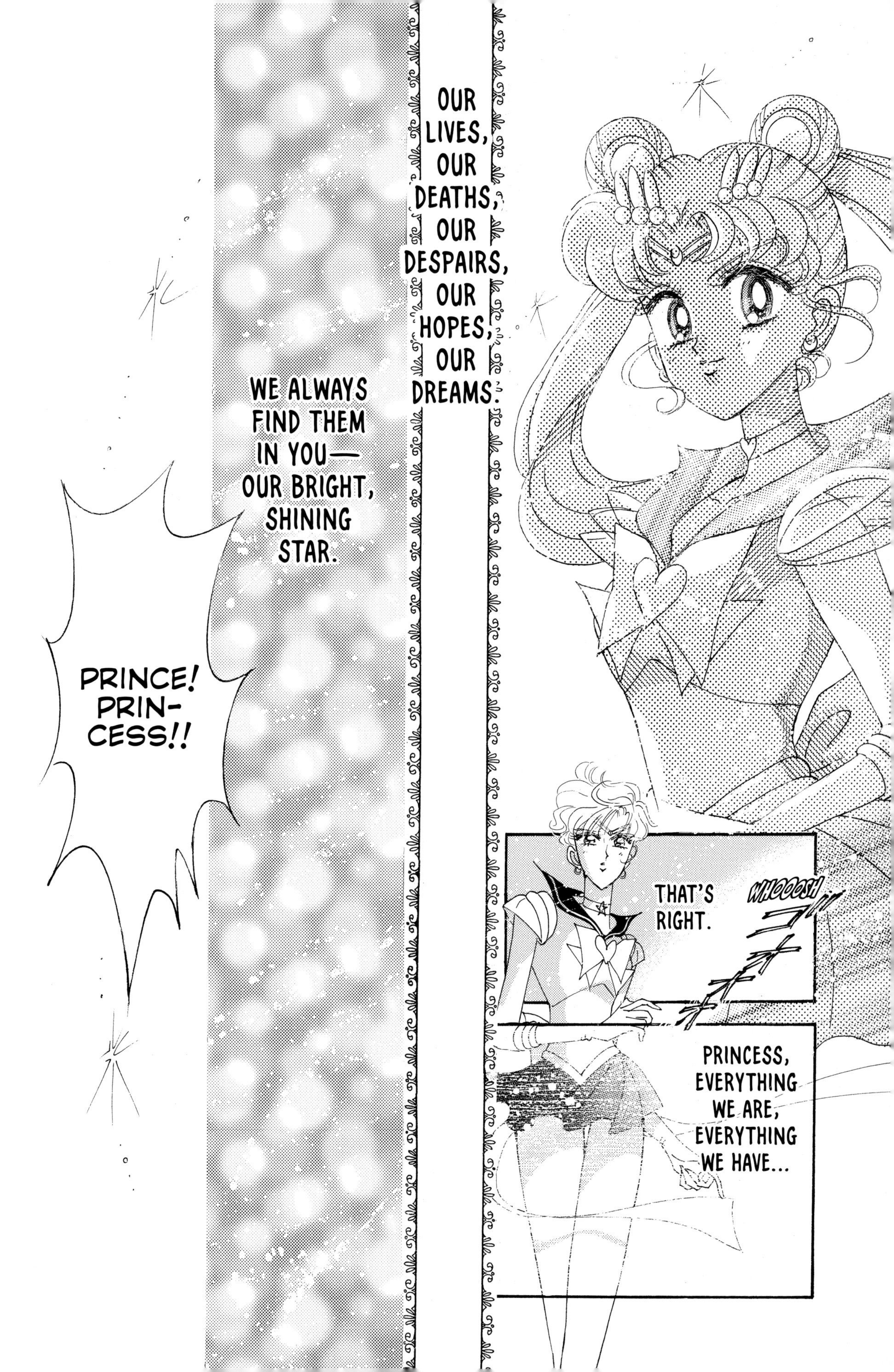
THAT'S RIGHT.
WHOOOSH
PRINCESS, EVERYTHING WE ARE, EVERYTHING WE HAVE...
OUR LIVES, OUR DEATHS, OUR DESPAIRS, OUR HOPES, OUR DREAMS.
WE ALWAYS FIND THEM IN YOU— OUR BRIGHT, SHINING STAR.
PRINCE! PRIN-CESS!!

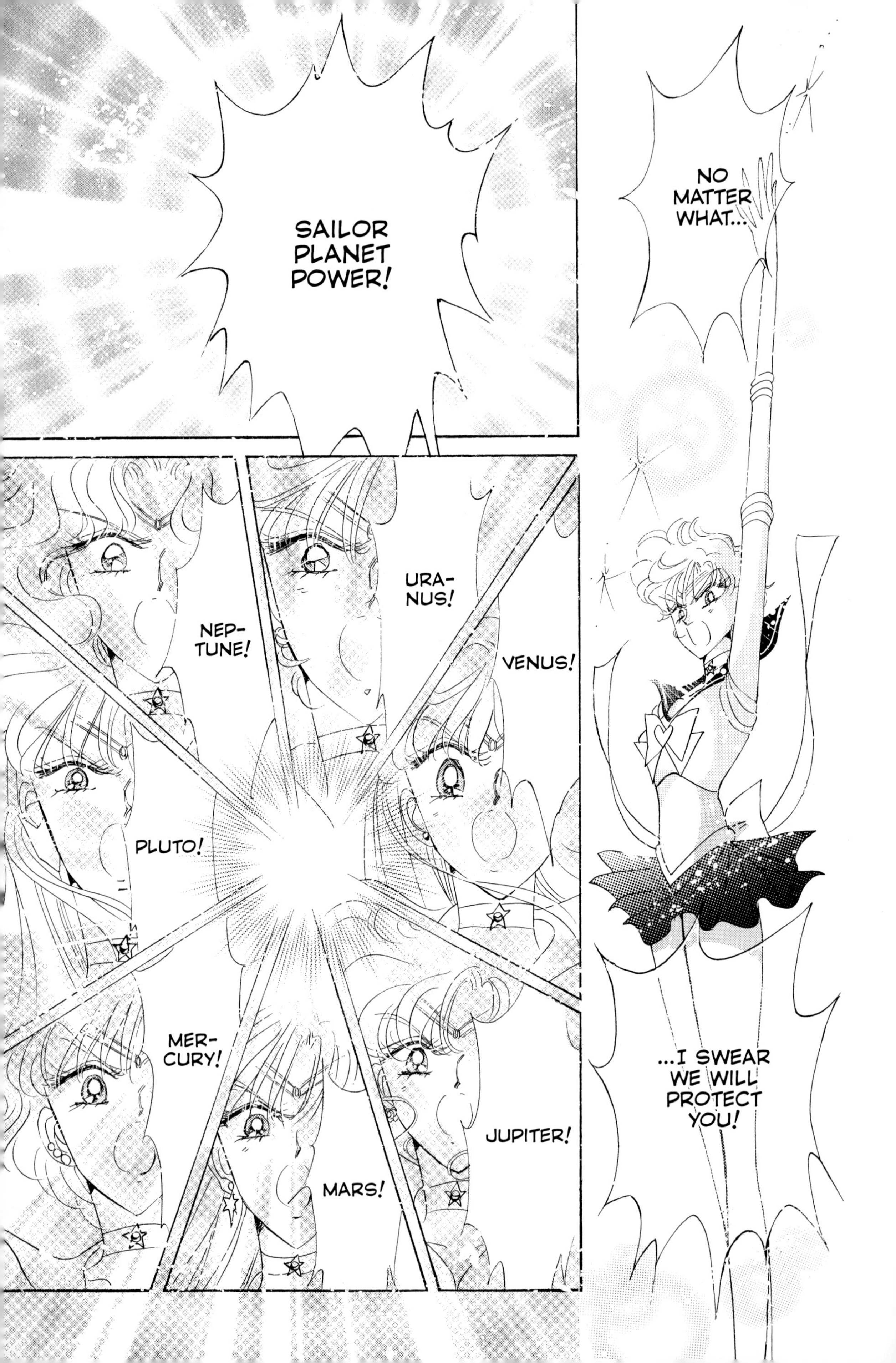
NO MATTER WHAT...
...I SWEAR WE WILL PROTECT YOU!
SAILOR PLANET POWER!
URA-NUS!
VENUS!
NEP-TUNE!
PLUTO!
JUPITER!
MER-CURY!
MARS!

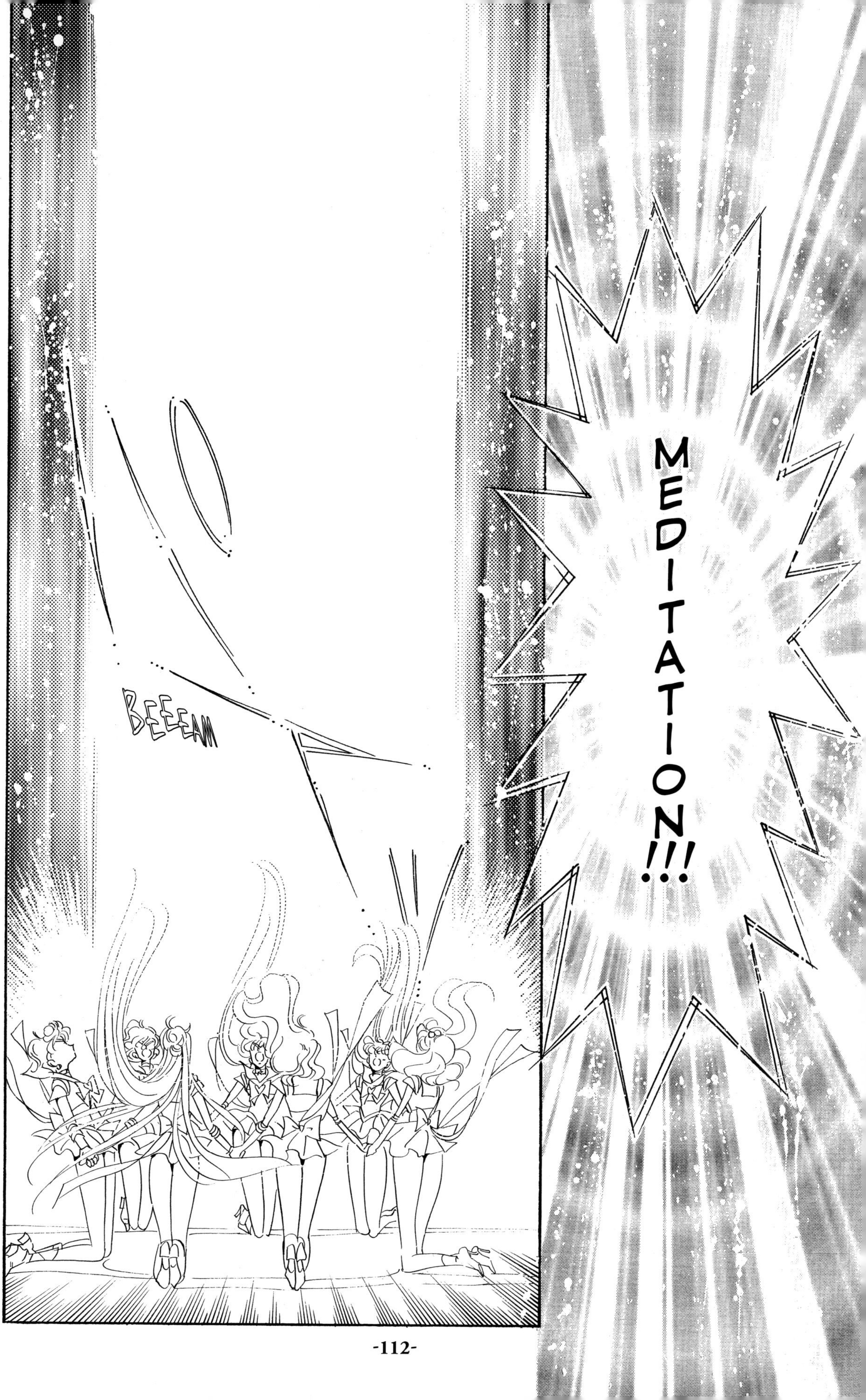
MEDITATION!!!
BEEEEAM

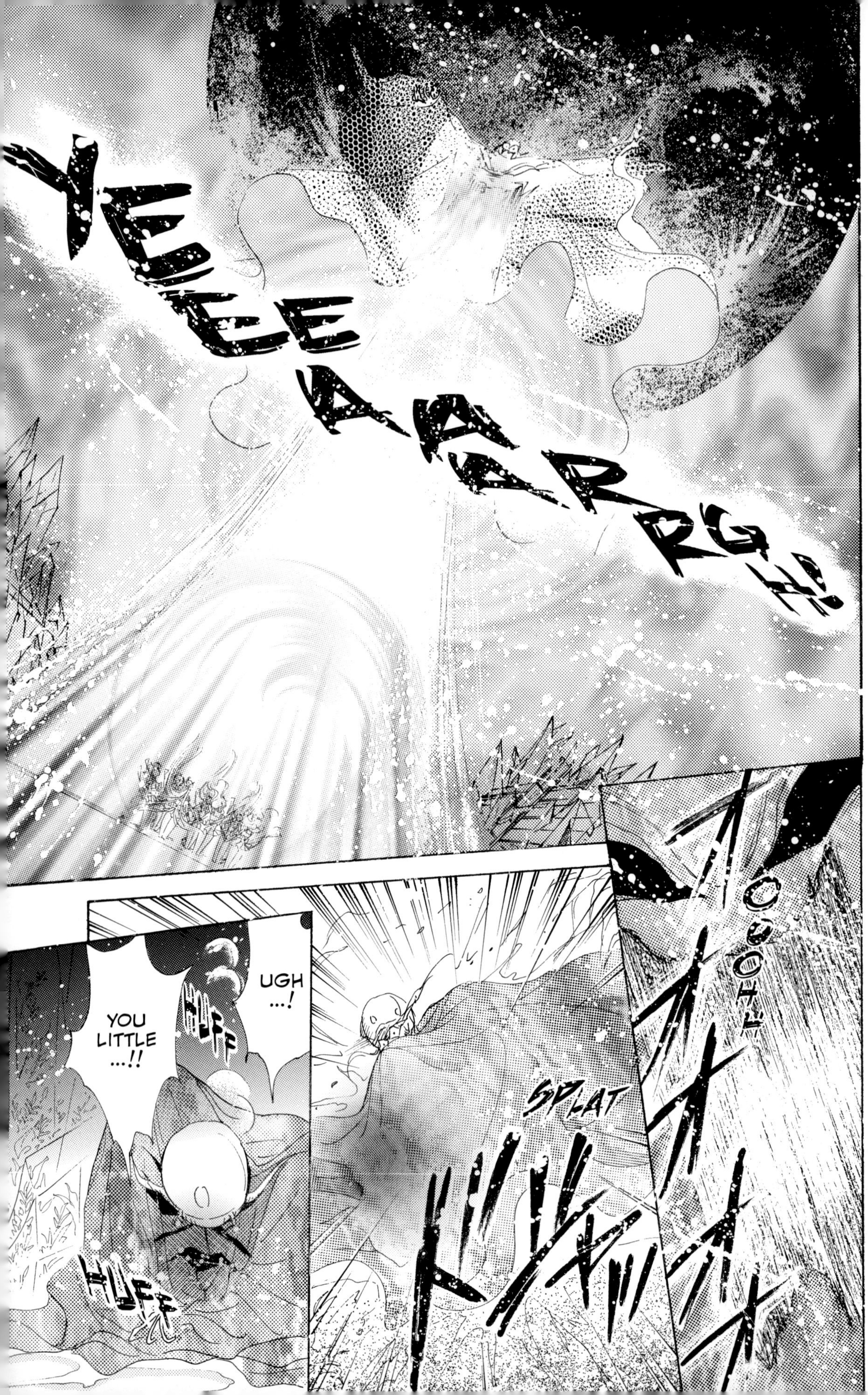
YEEEAAARRGH!!
OUCH!!
SPLAT
UGH ...!
YOU LITTLE ...!!
HUFF
HUFF

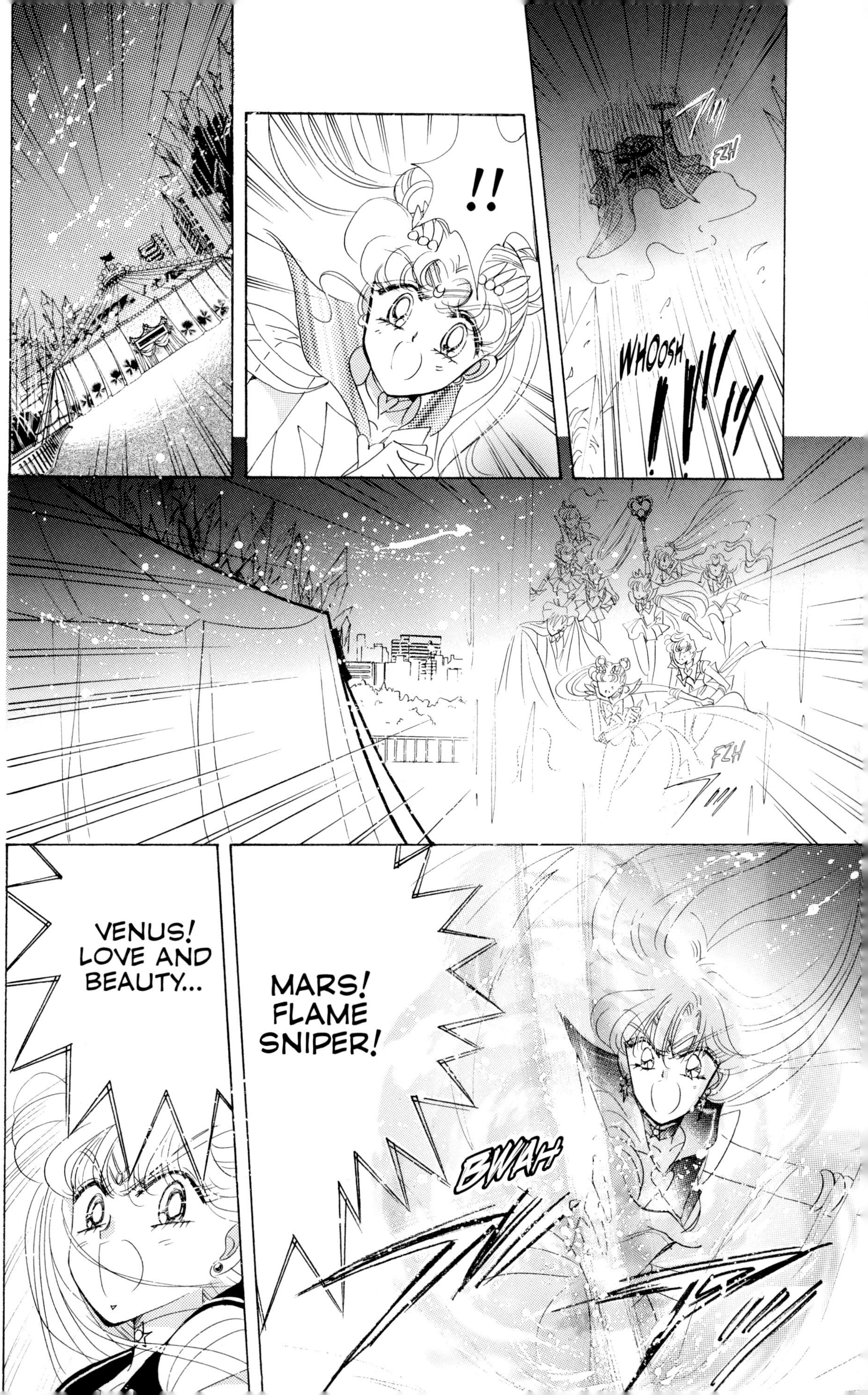
FZH
WHOOSH
!!
FZH
MARS! FLAME SNIPER!
BWAH
VENUS! LOVE AND BEAUTY...

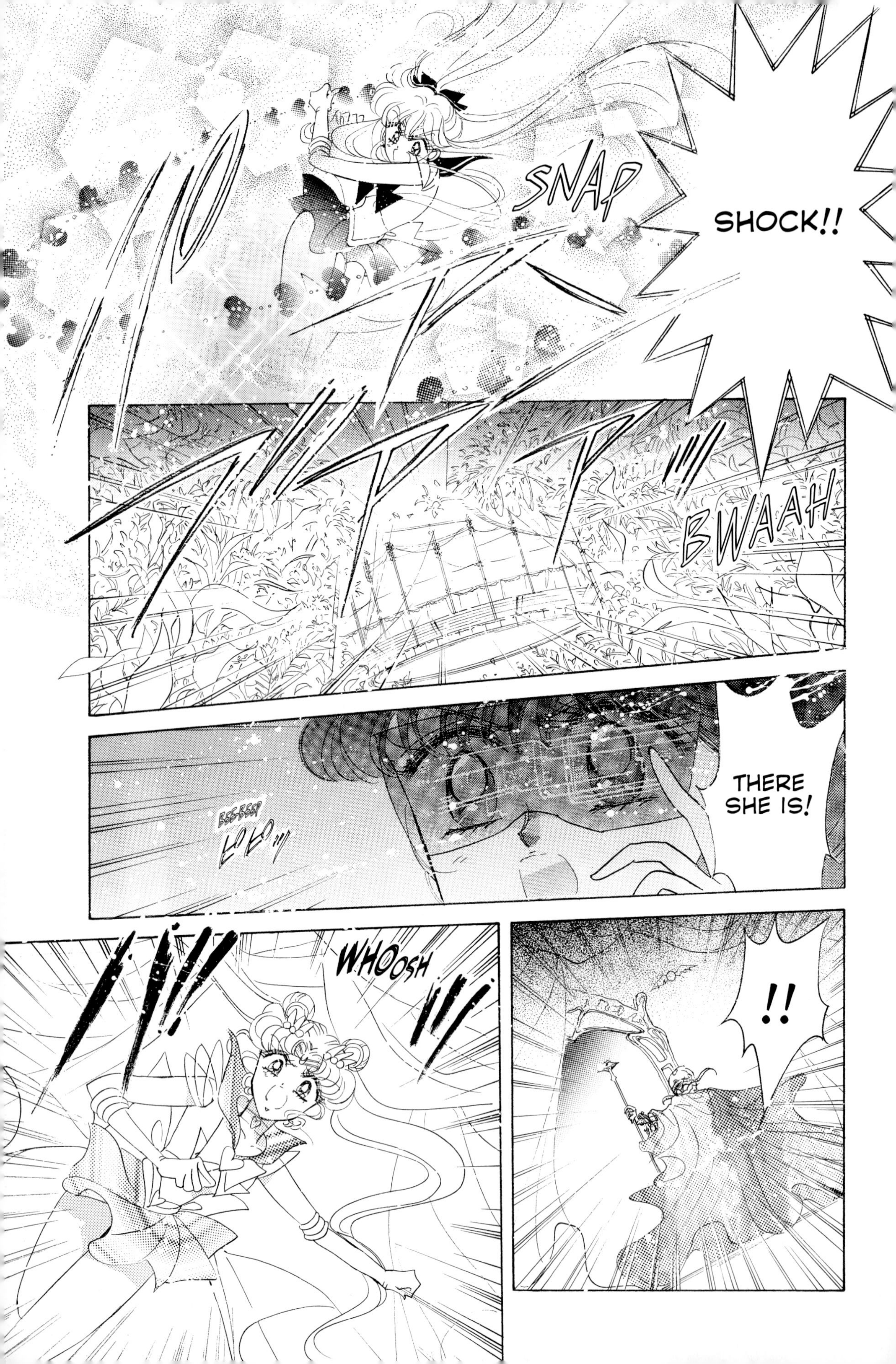
SHOCK!!
SNAP
BWAAH
THERE SHE IS!
BEEP BEEP
!!
WHOOSH

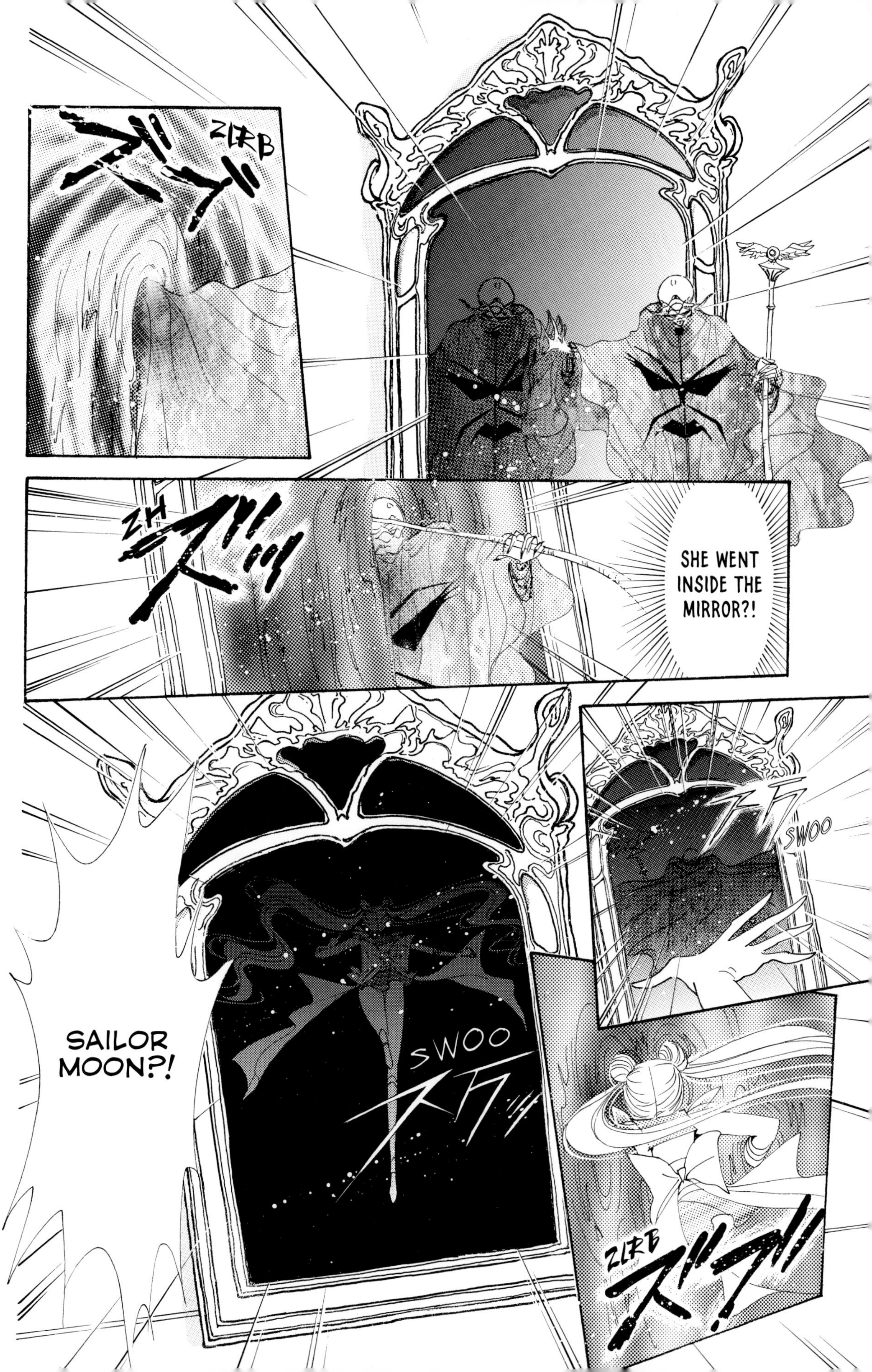

ZLRB
SHE WENT INSIDE THE MIRROR?!
ZH
SWOO
ZLRB
SWOO
SAILOR MOON?!

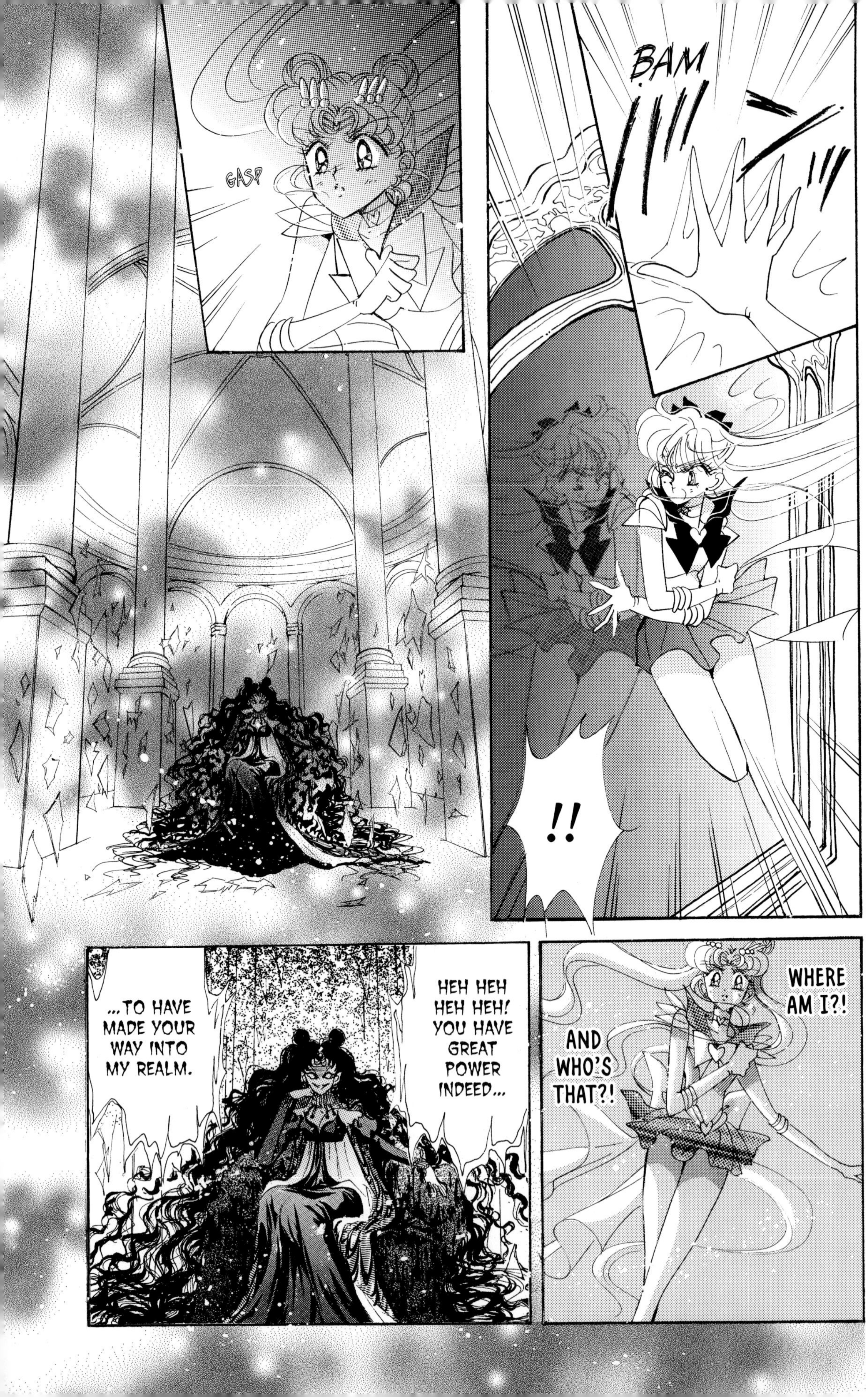
BAM
!!
GASP
WHERE AM I?!
AND WHO'S THAT?!
HEH HEH HEH HEH! YOU HAVE GREAT POWER INDEED...
...TO HAVE MADE YOUR WAY INTO MY REALM.

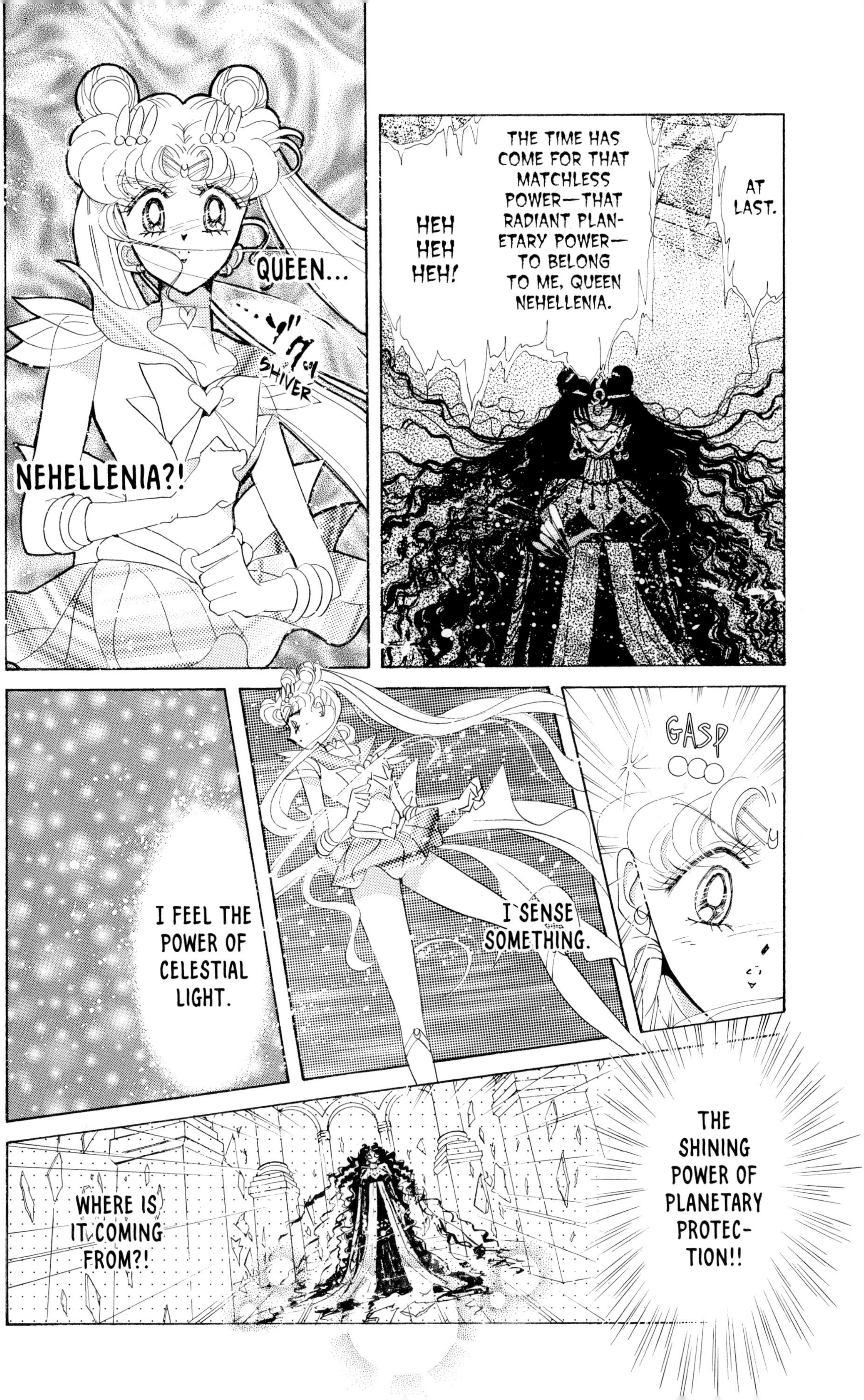
AT LAST.
THE TIME HAS COME FOR THAT MATCHLESS POWER—THAT RADIANT PLANETARY POWER—TO BELONG TO ME, QUEEN NEHELLENIA.
HEH HEH HEH!
QUEEN...
SHIVER
NEHELLENIA?!
GASP
I SENSE SOMETHING.
I FEEL THE POWER OF CELESTIAL LIGHT.
THE SHINING POWER OF PLANETARY PROTECTION!!
WHERE IS IT COMING FROM?!

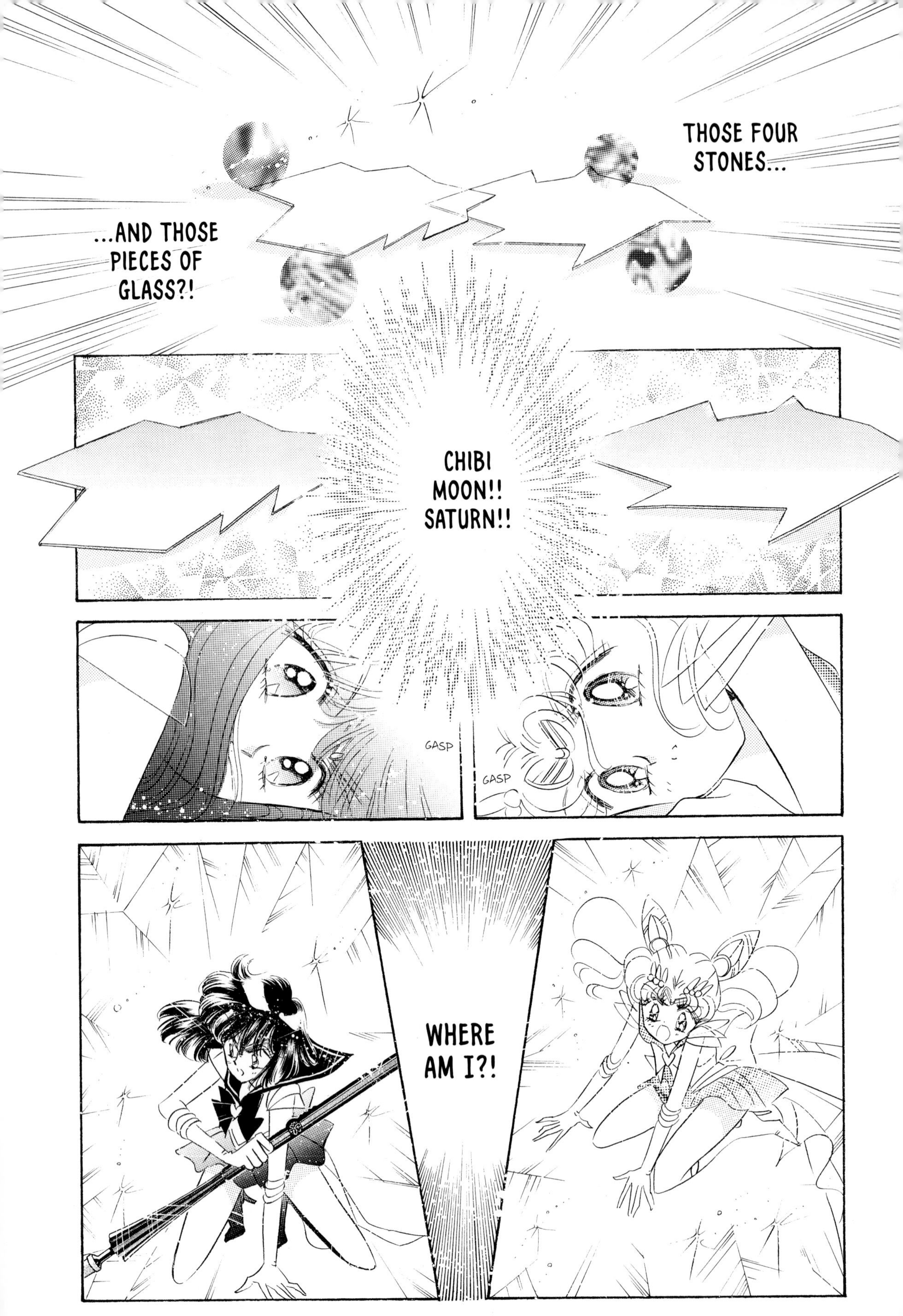
THOSE FOUR STONES...
...AND THOSE PIECES OF GLASS?!
CHIBI MOON!! SATURN!!
GASP
GASP
WHERE AM I?!

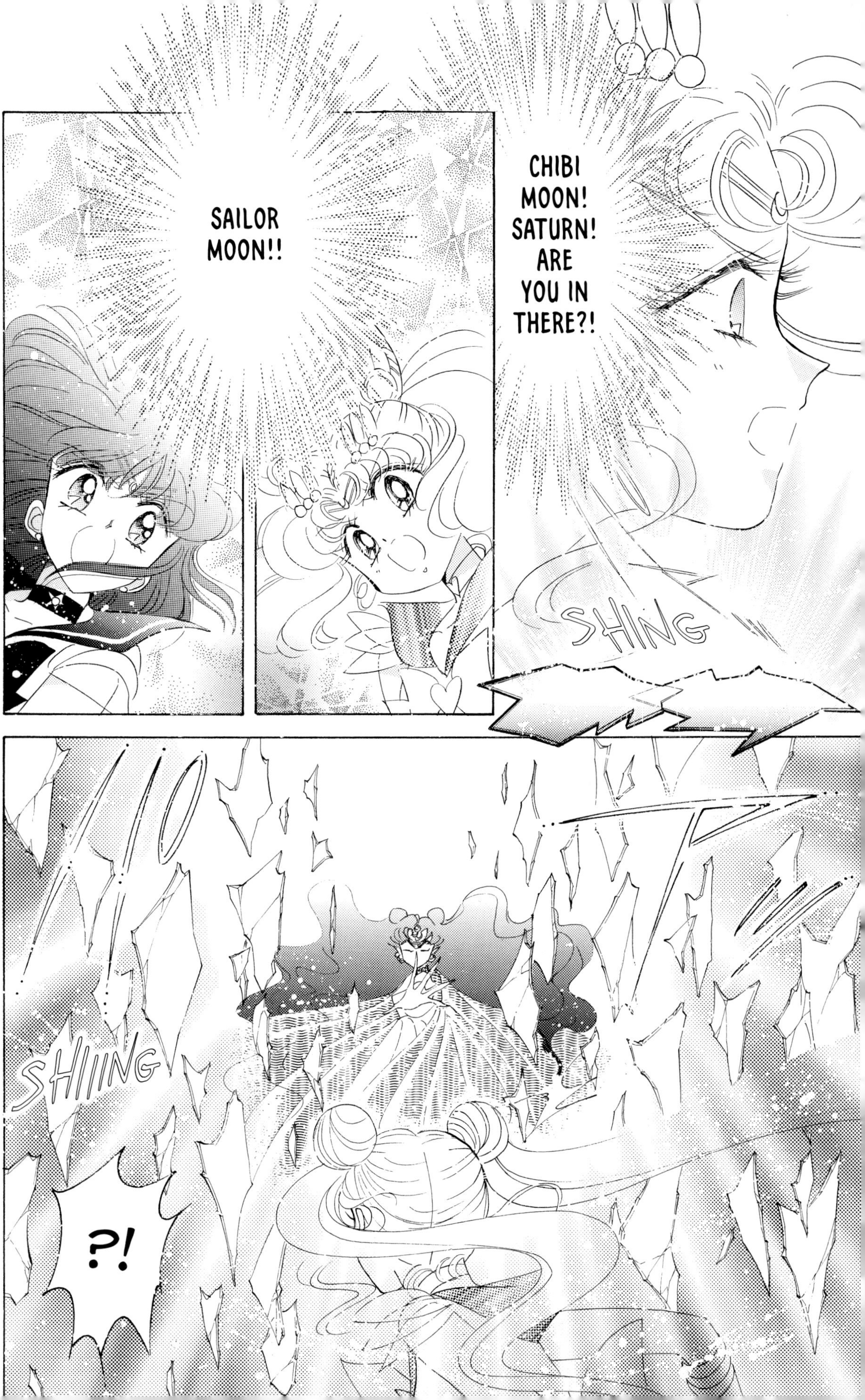
CHIBI MOON! SATURN! ARE YOU IN THERE?!
SHING
SAILOR MOON!!
SHIIING
?!

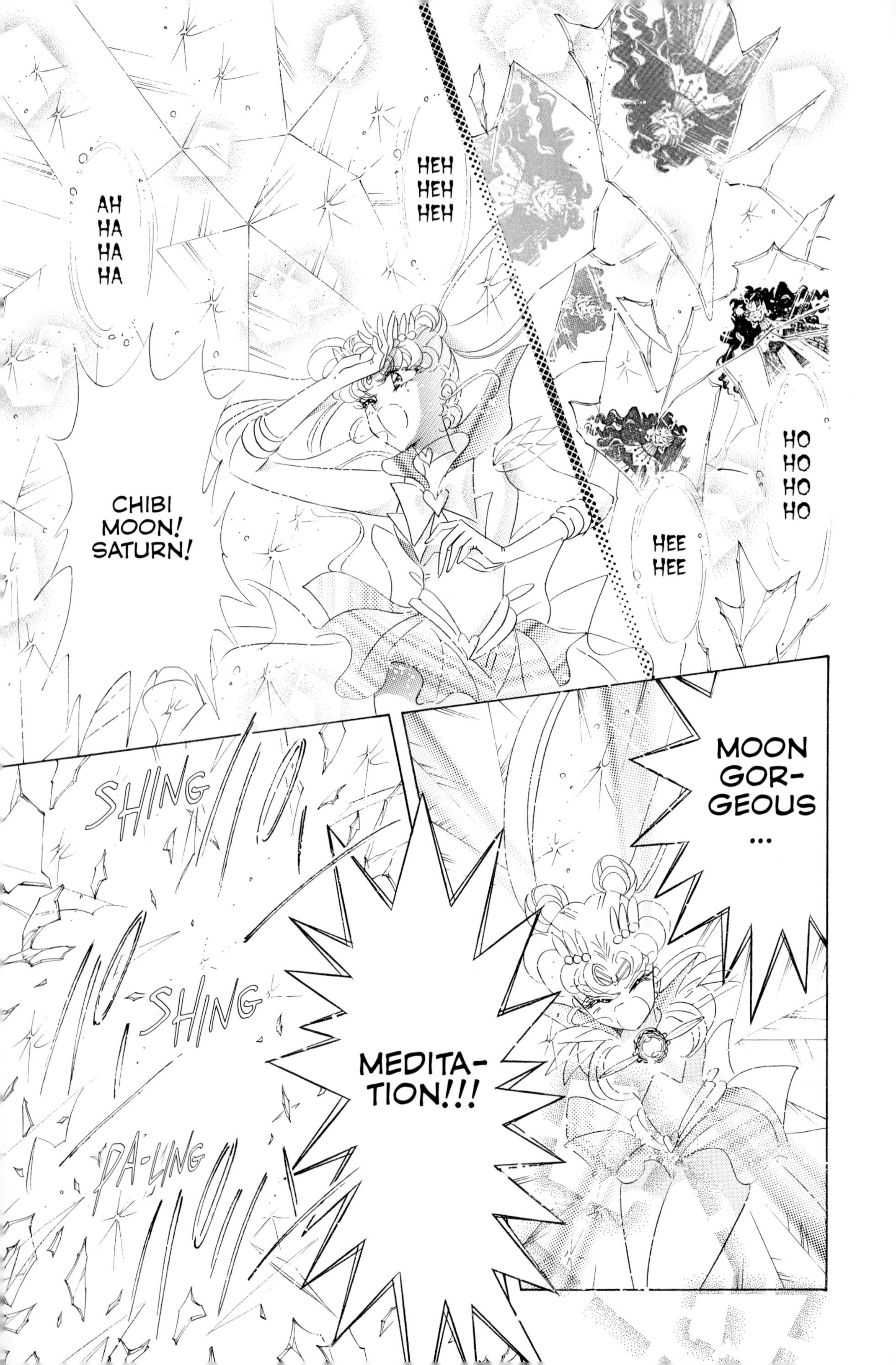
HO HO HO HO
HEH HEH HEH
HEE HEE
AH HA HA HA
CHIBI MOON! SATURN!
MOON GOR-GEOUS ...
MEDITA-TION!!!
SHING
SHING
PA-LING

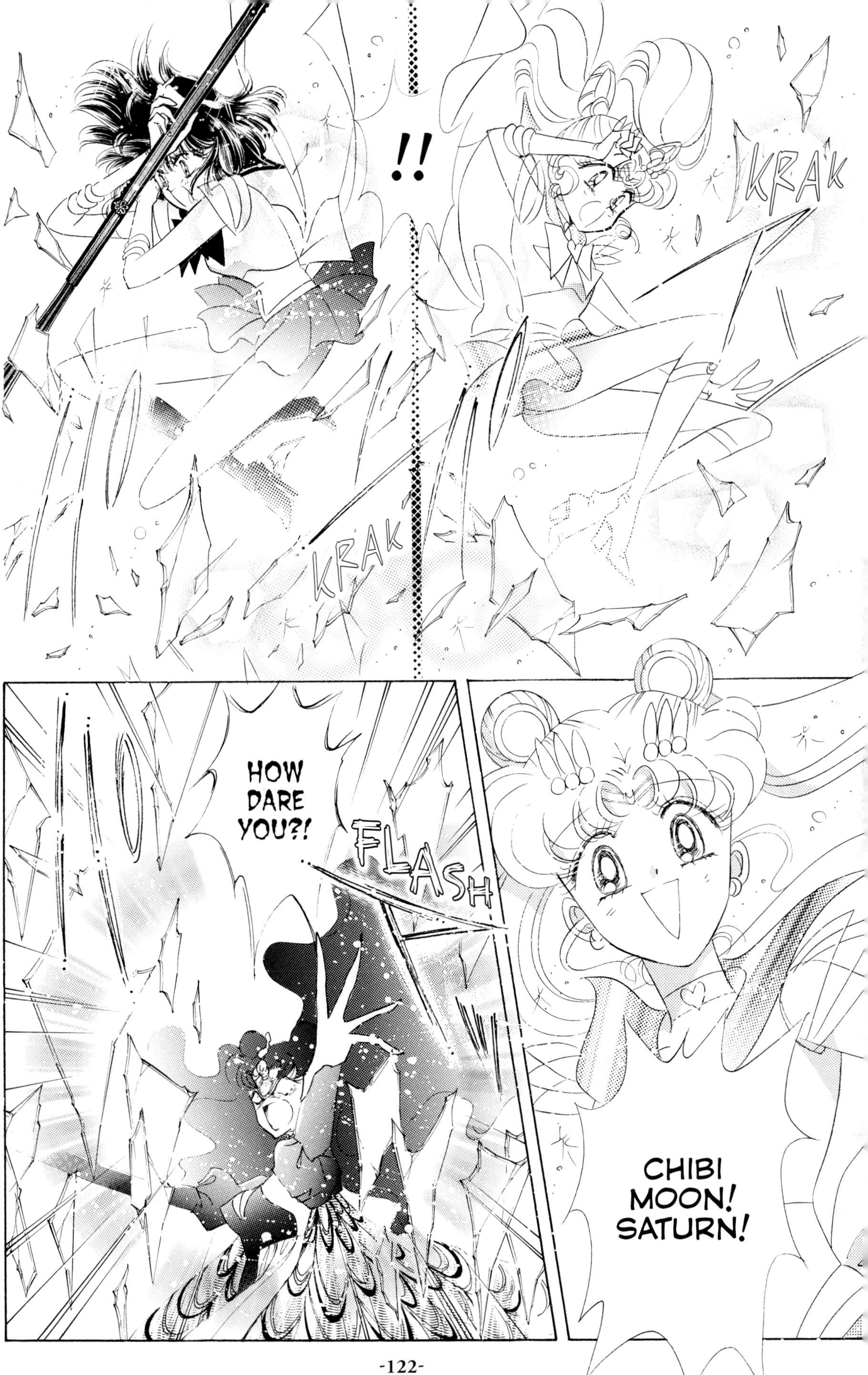
KRAK
!!
KRAK
CHIBI MOON! SATURN!
HOW DARE YOU?!
FLASH

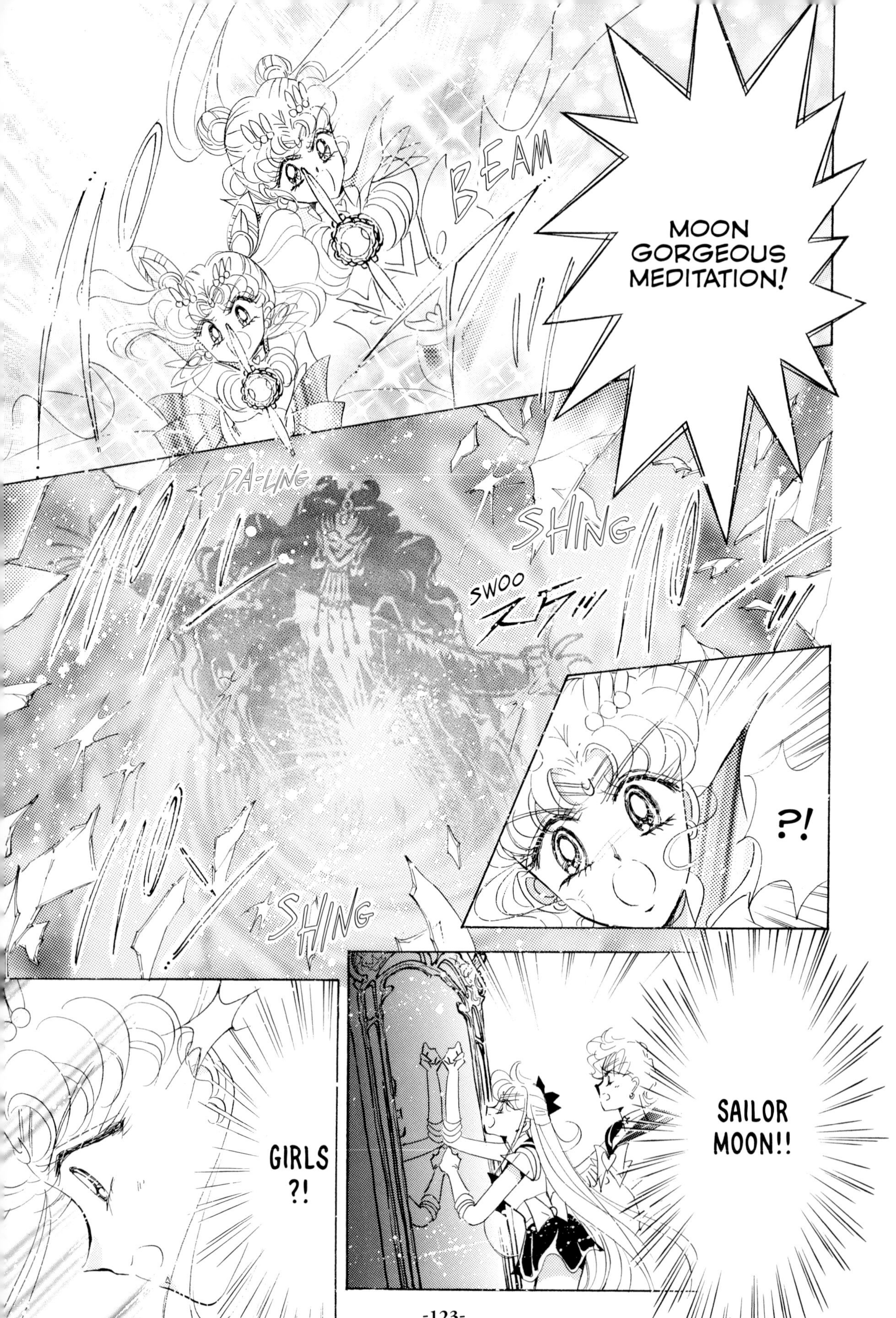
MOON GORGEOUS MEDITATION!
BEAM
PA-LING
SHING
SWOO
SHING
?!
SAILOR MOON!!
GIRLS ?!

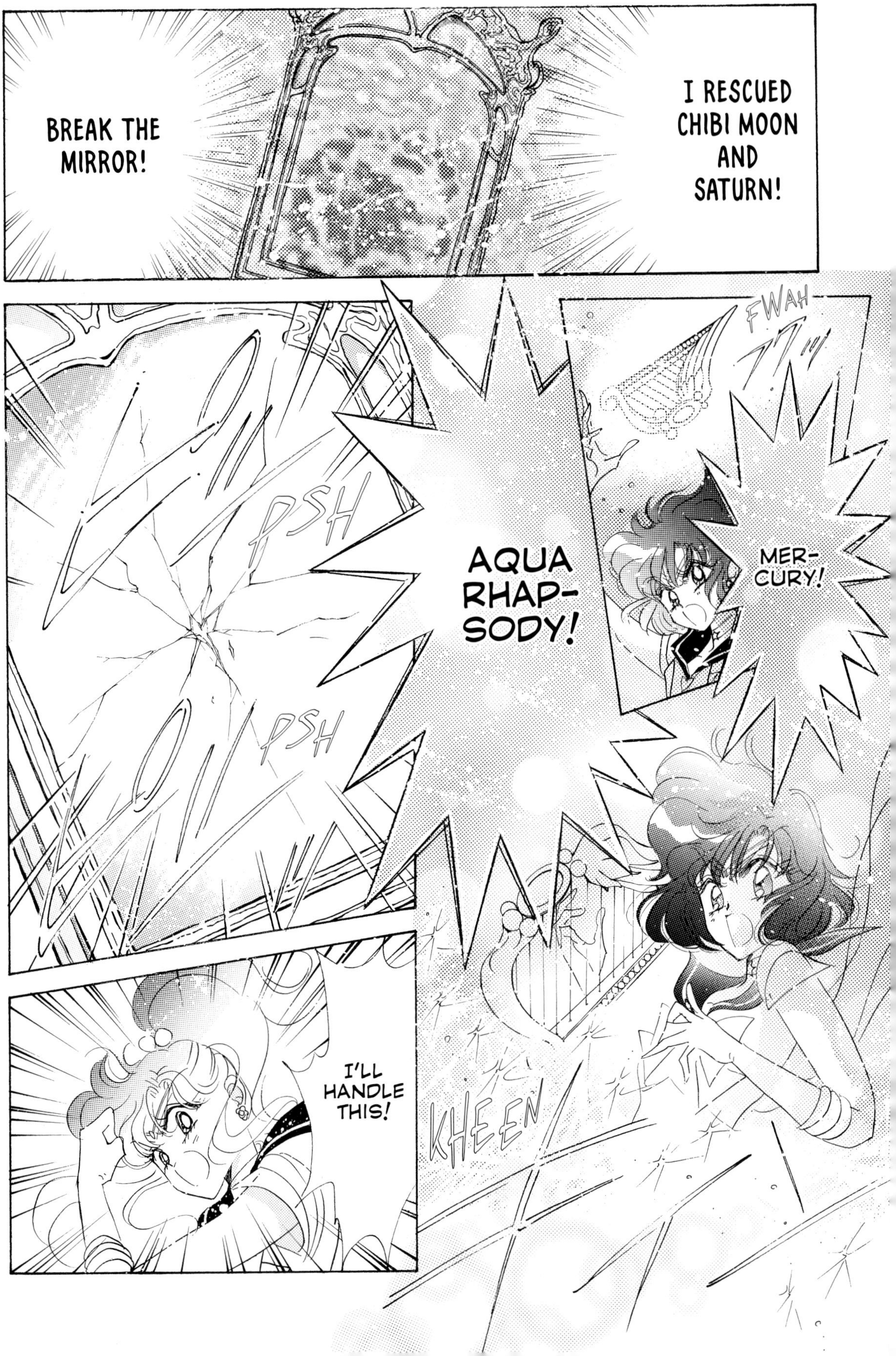
I RESCUED CHIBI MOON AND SATURN!
BREAK THE MIRROR!
FWAH
MER-CURY!
AQUA RHAP-SODY!
KHEEN
PSH
PSH
I'LL HANDLE THIS!

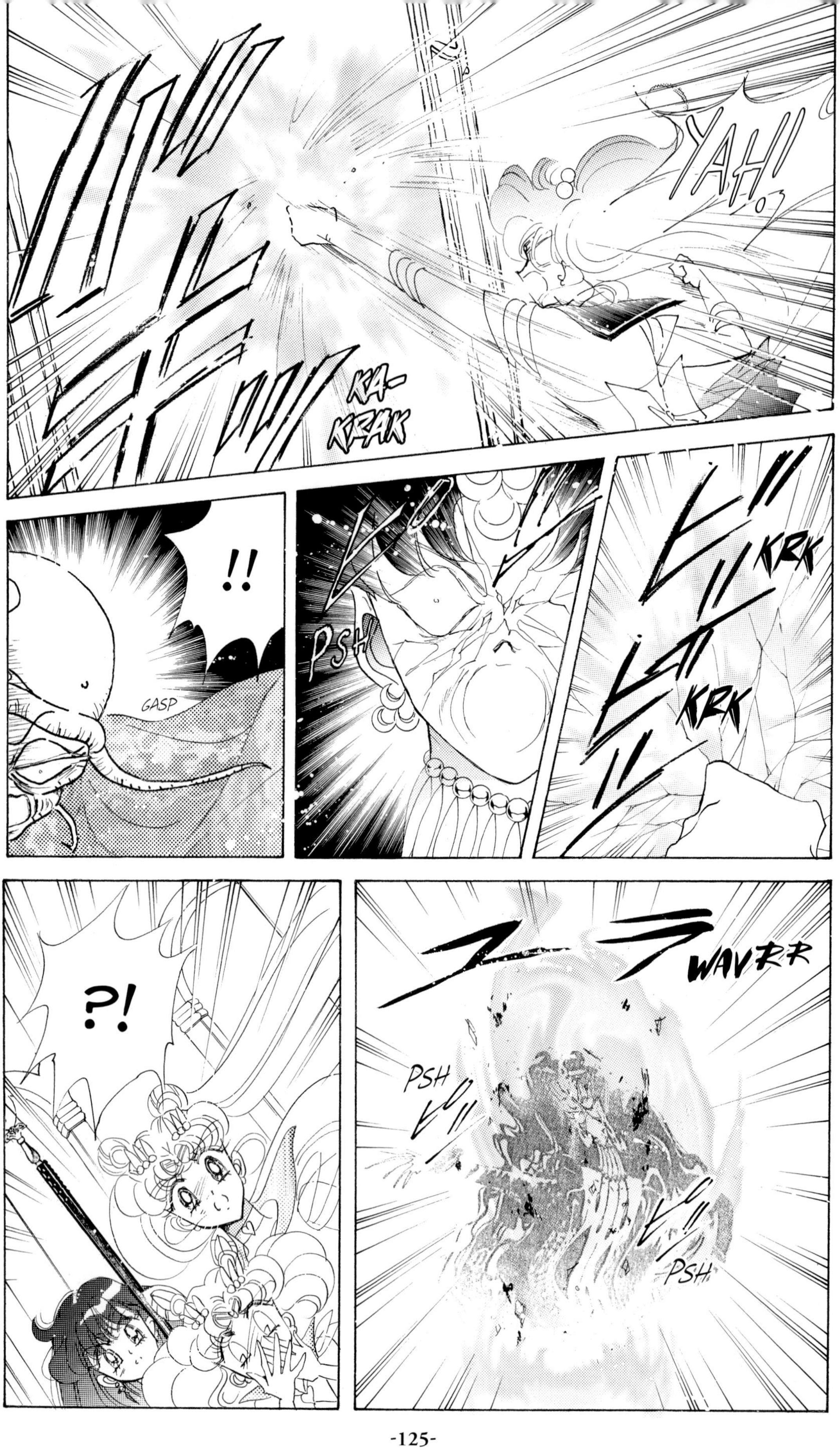
YAH!
KA-
KRAK
KRK
KRK
PSH
!!
GASP
WAVRR
PSH
PSH
?!

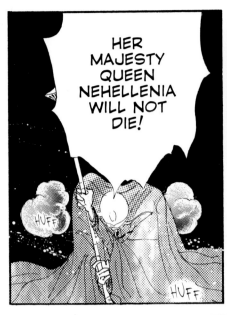

HER MAJESTY QUEEN NEHELLENIA WILL NOT DIE!

HUFF

HUFF

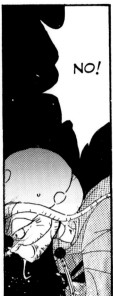

NO!

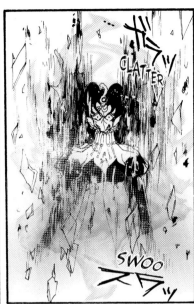

CLATTER

SWOO

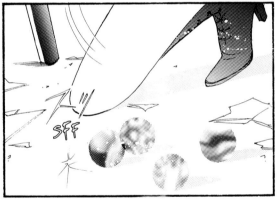

SFF

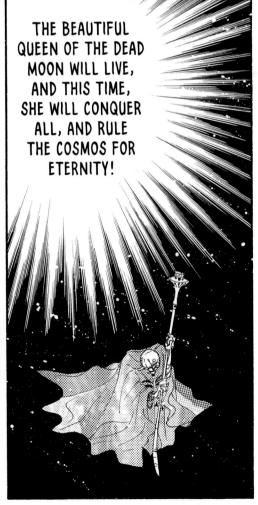

THE BEAUTIFUL QUEEN OF THE DEAD MOON WILL LIVE, AND THIS TIME, SHE WILL CONQUER ALL, AND RULE THE COSMOS FOR ETERNITY!

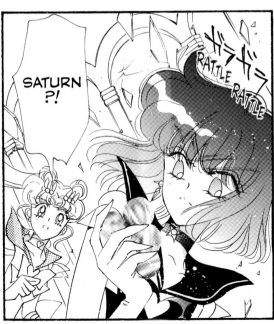

SATURN ?!

RATTLE RATTLE

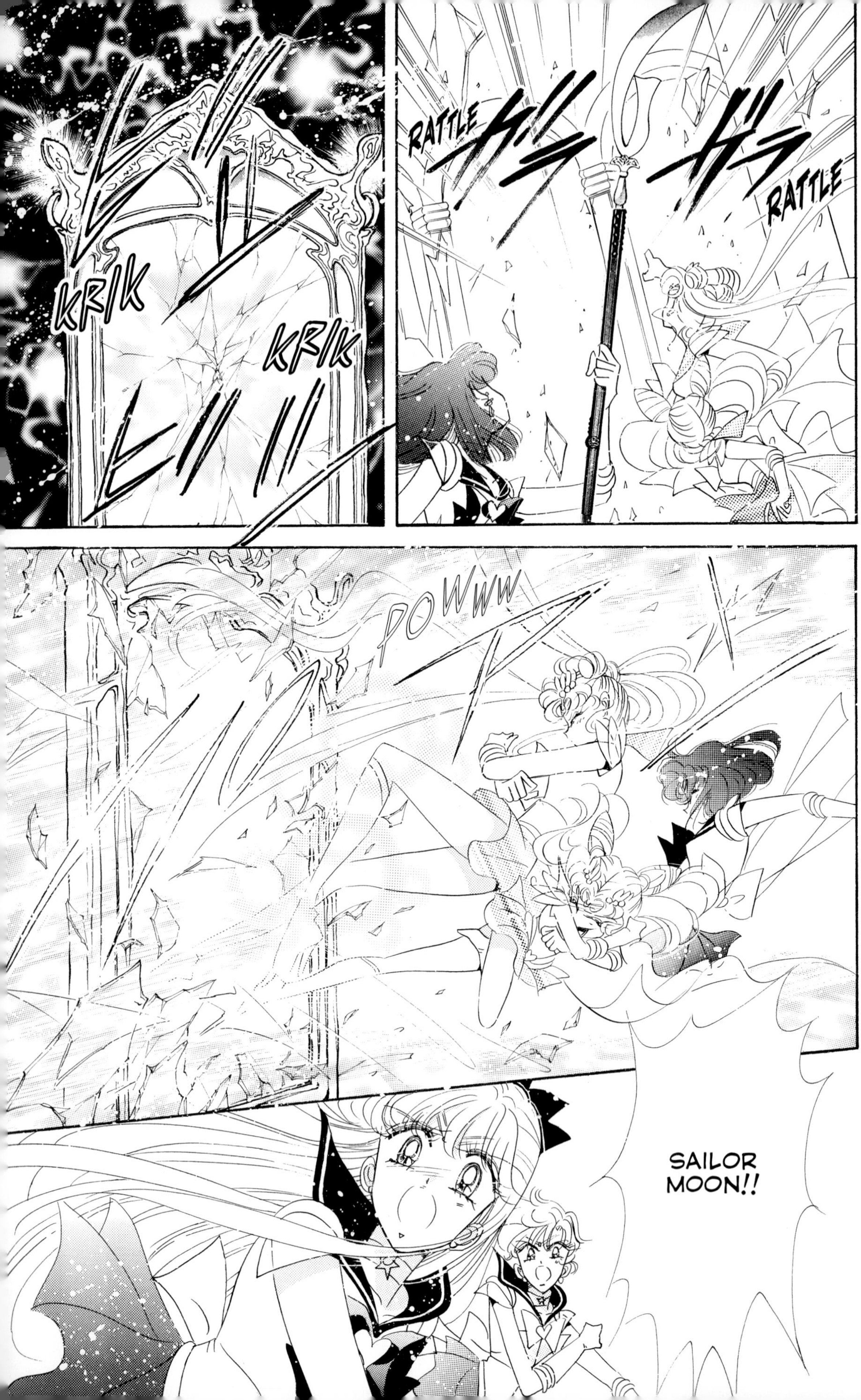
RATTLE
RATTLE
KRIK
KRIK
POWWW
SAILOR MOON!!

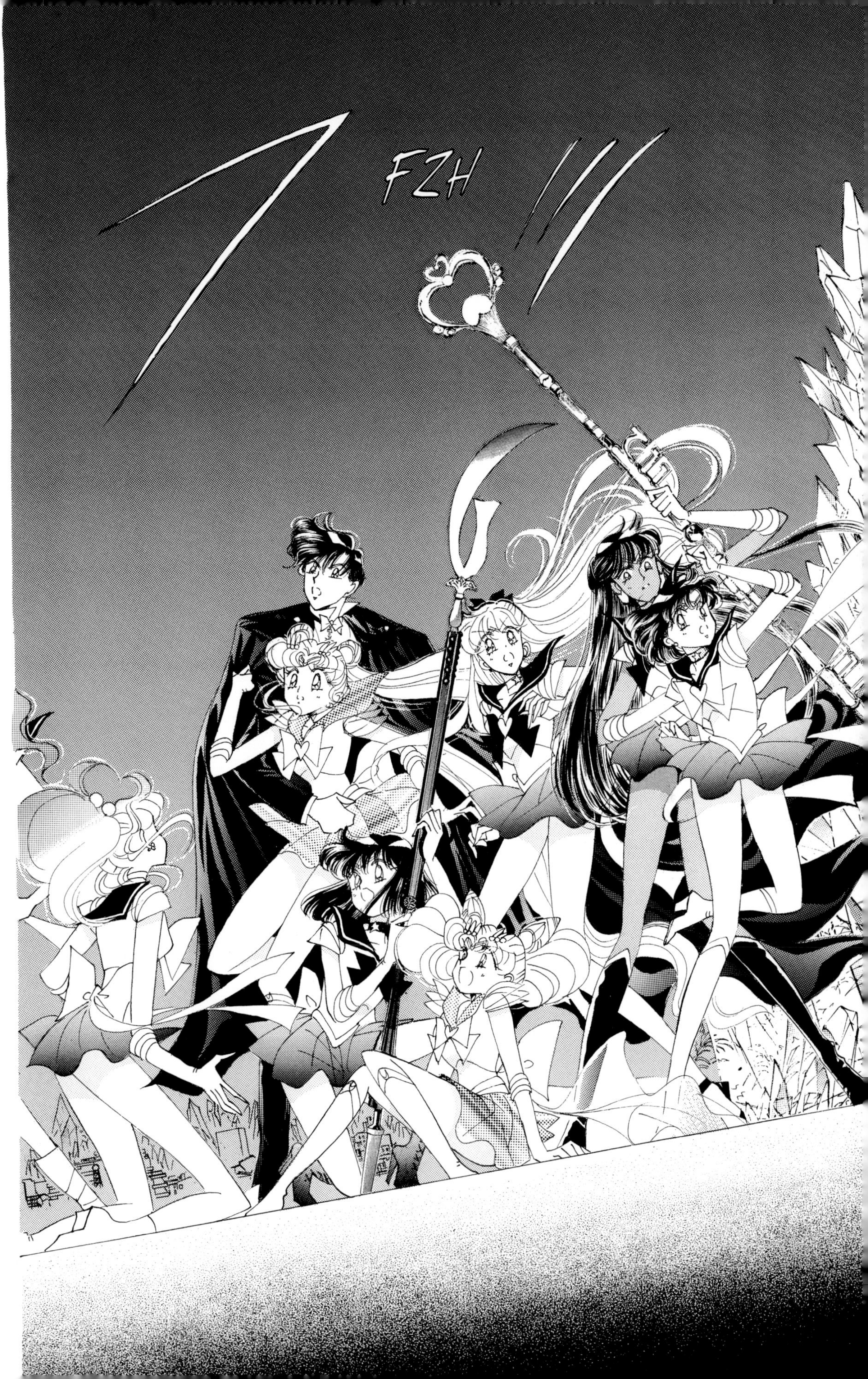
FZH

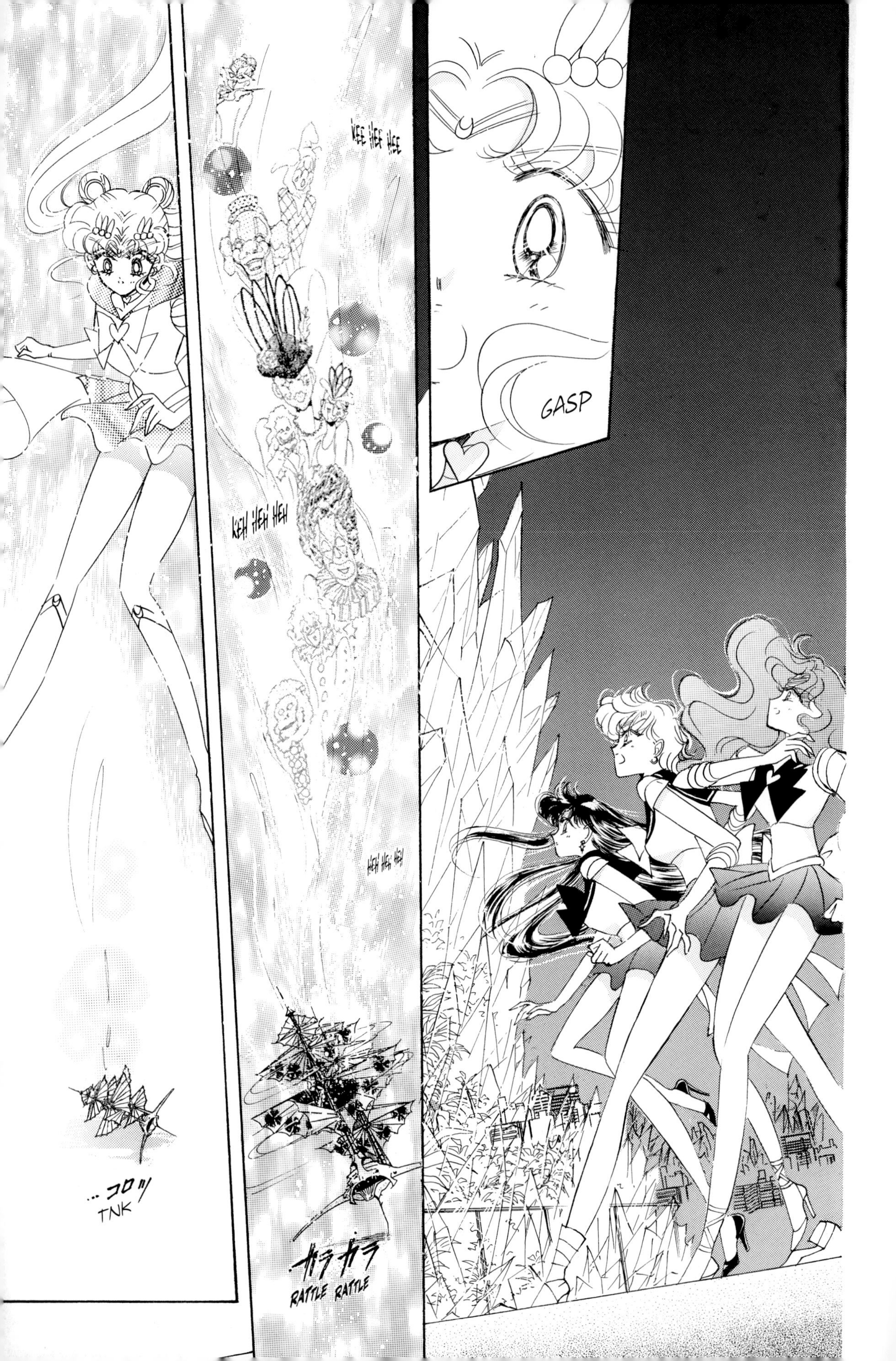
GASP
HEE HEE HEE
KEH HEH HEH
HEH HEH HEH
ガラガラ
RATTLE RATTLE
...コロッ
TNK

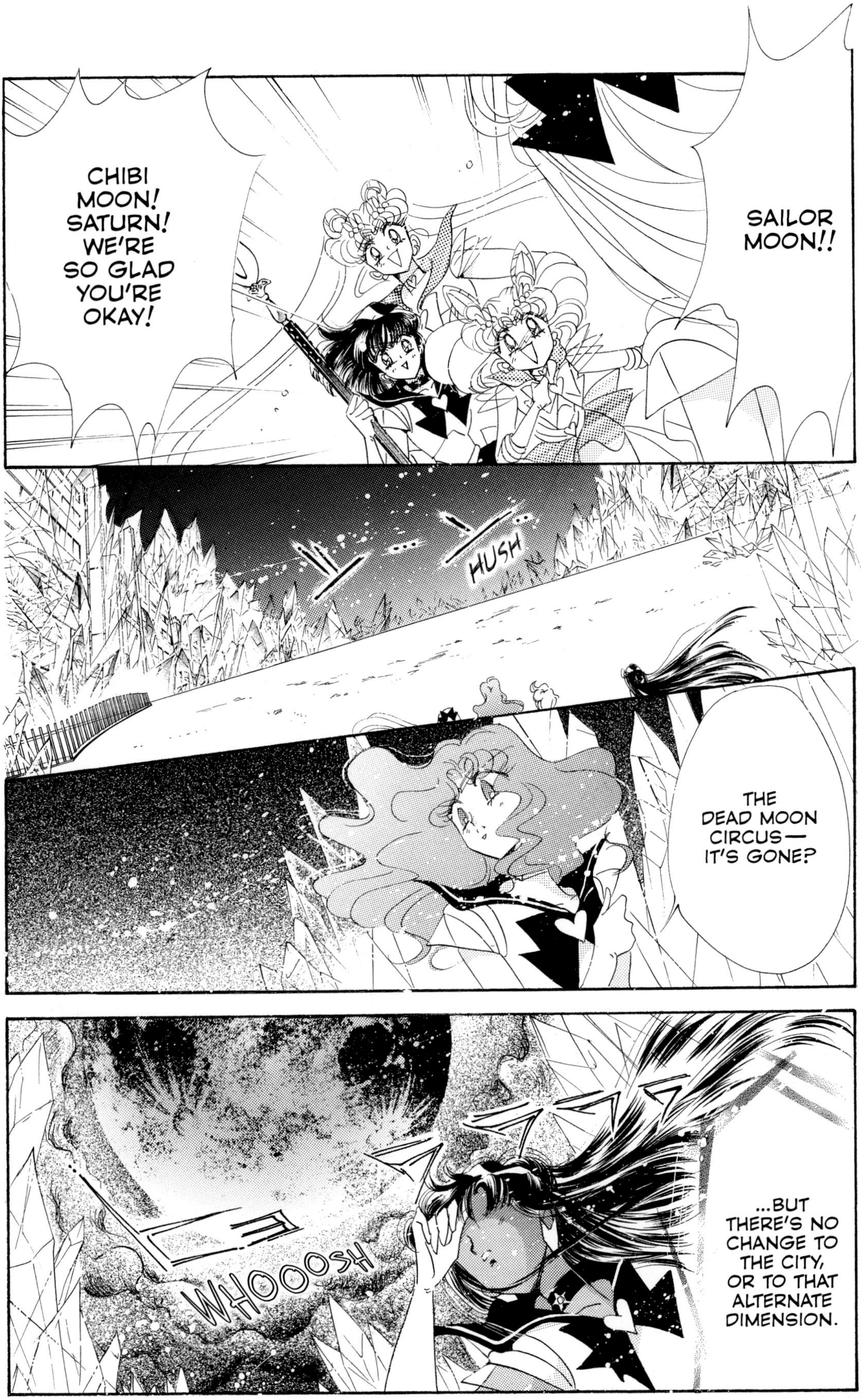
SAILOR MOON!!
CHIBI MOON! SATURN! WE'RE SO GLAD YOU'RE OKAY!
HUSH
THE DEAD MOON CIRCUS— IT'S GONE?
...BUT THERE'S NO CHANGE TO THE CITY, OR TO THAT ALTERNATE DIMENSION.
WHOOOSH

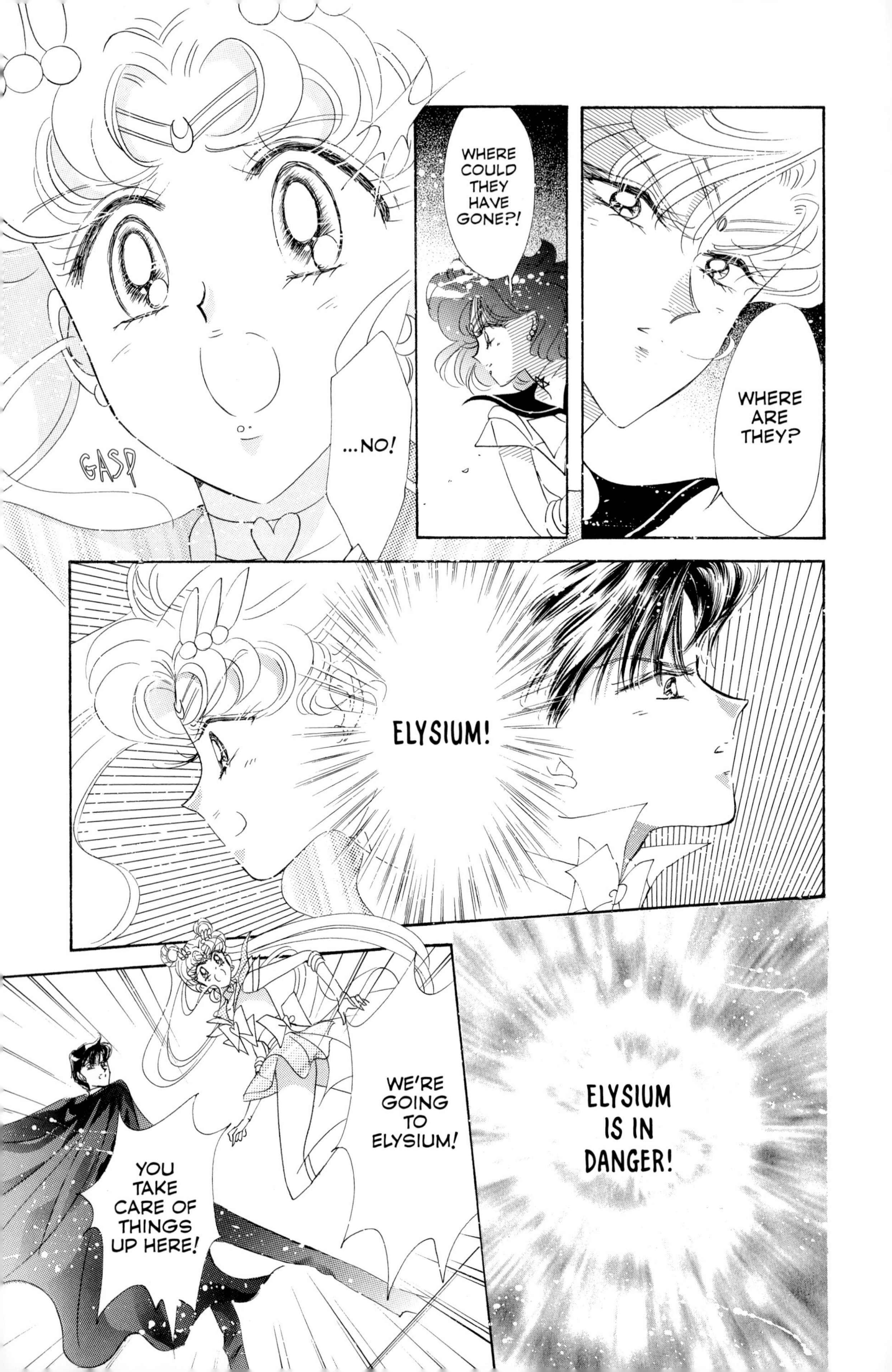
WHERE ARE THEY?
WHERE COULD THEY HAVE GONE?!
...NO!
GASP
ELYSIUM!
ELYSIUM IS IN DANGER!
WE'RE GOING TO ELYSIUM!
YOU TAKE CARE OF THINGS UP HERE!

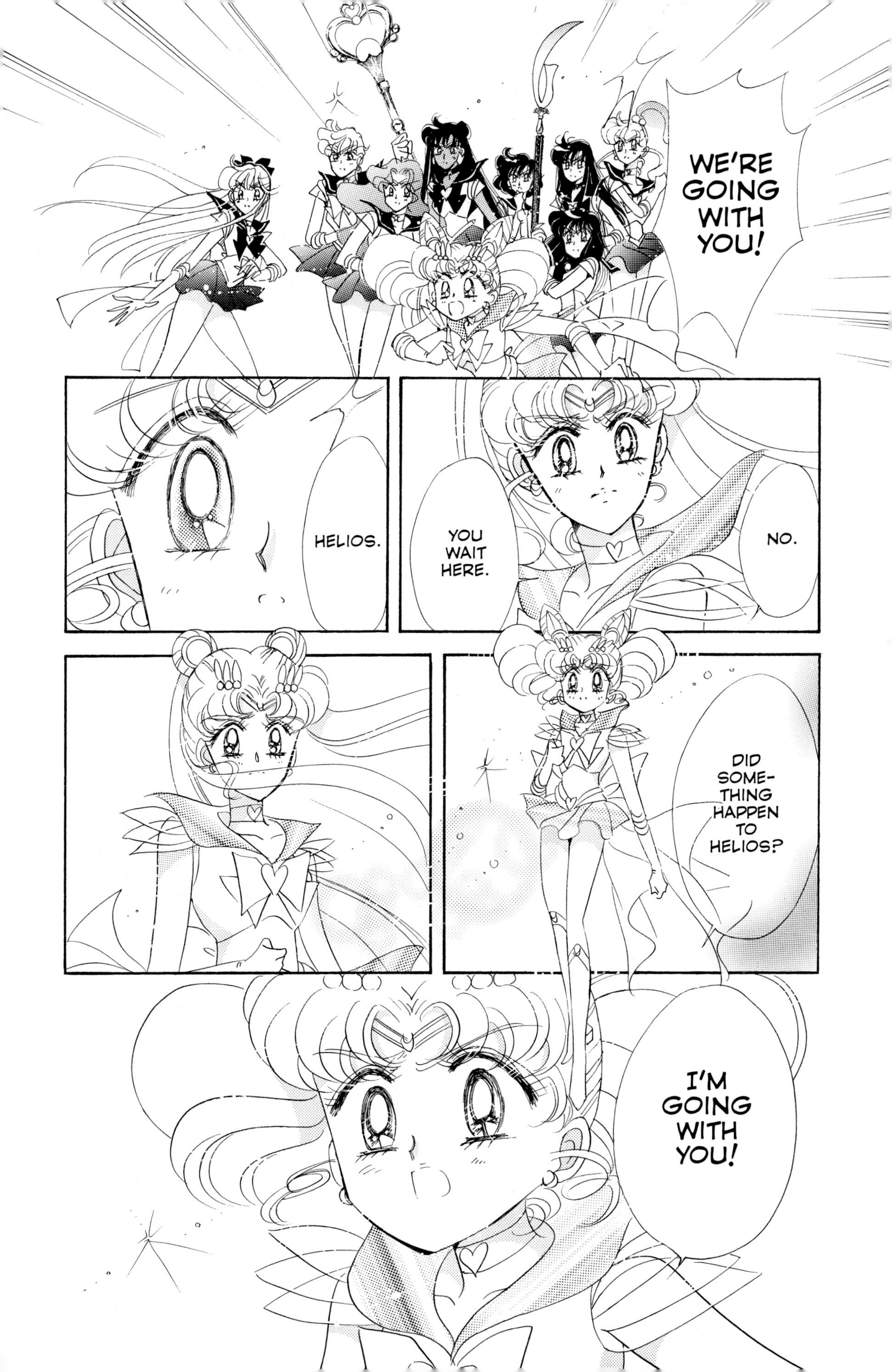
WE'RE GOING WITH YOU!
NO.
YOU WAIT HERE.
HELIOS.
DID SOME-THING HAPPEN TO HELIOS?
I'M GOING WITH YOU!

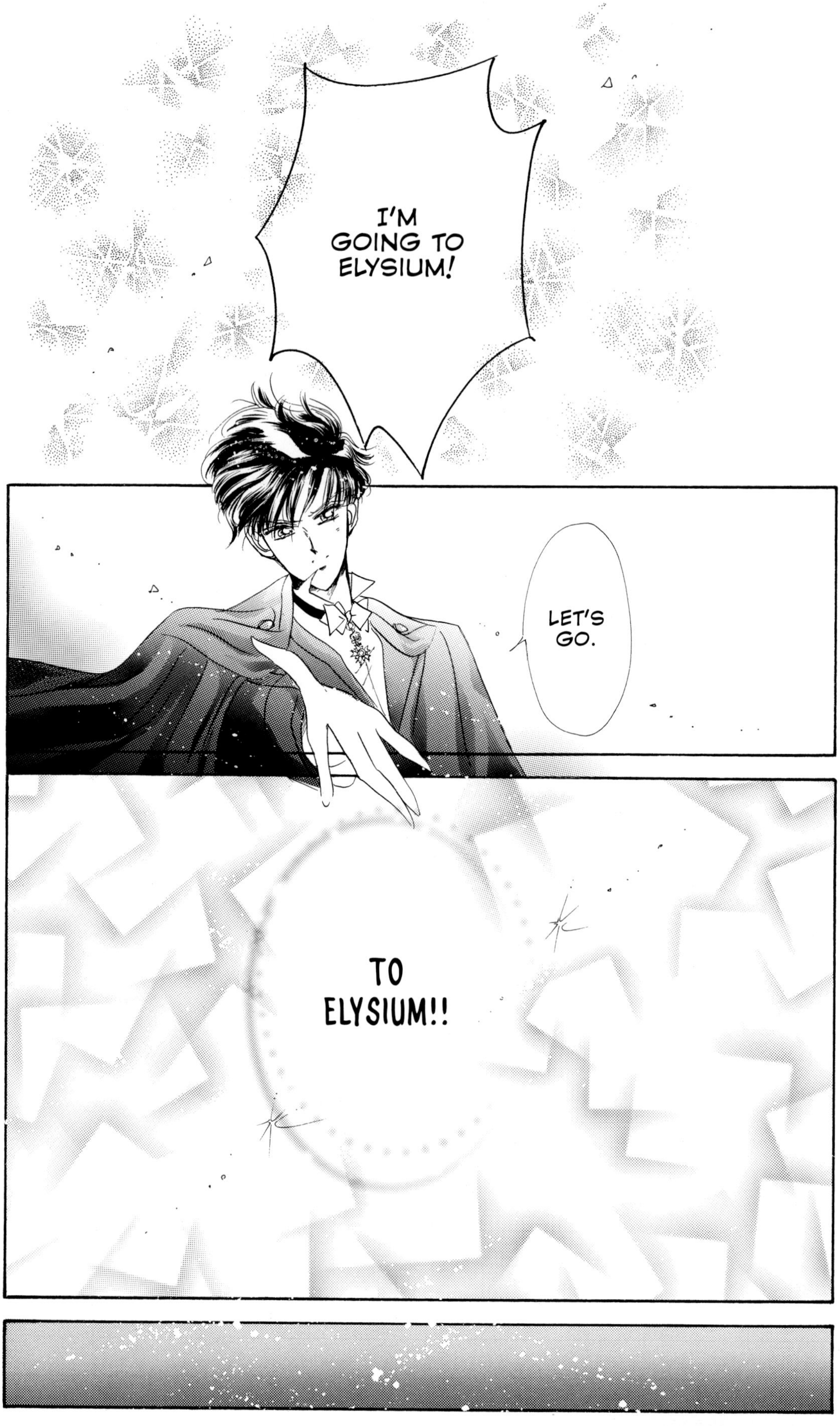
I'M GOING TO ELYSIUM!
LET'S GO.
TO ELYSIUM!!

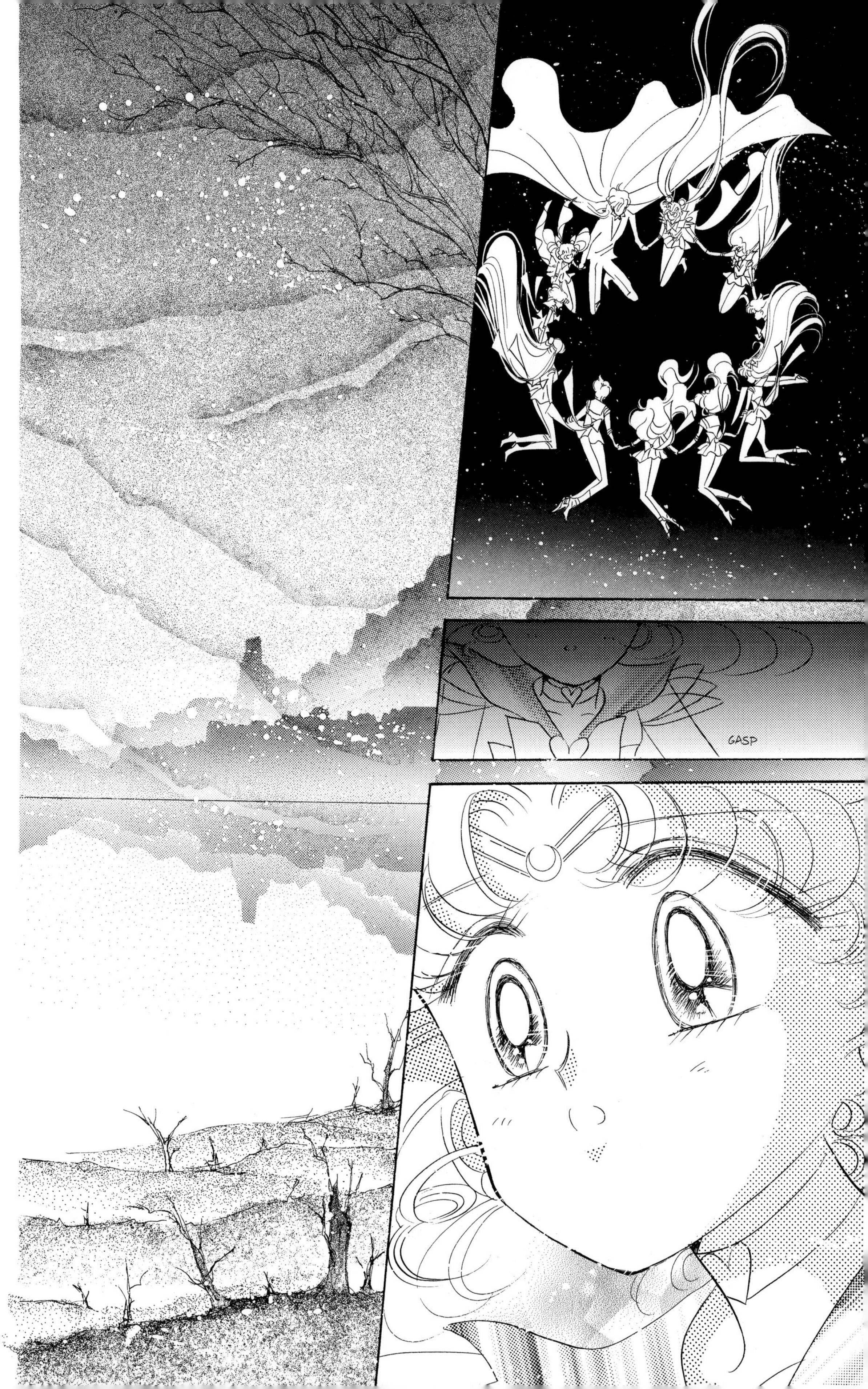
GASP

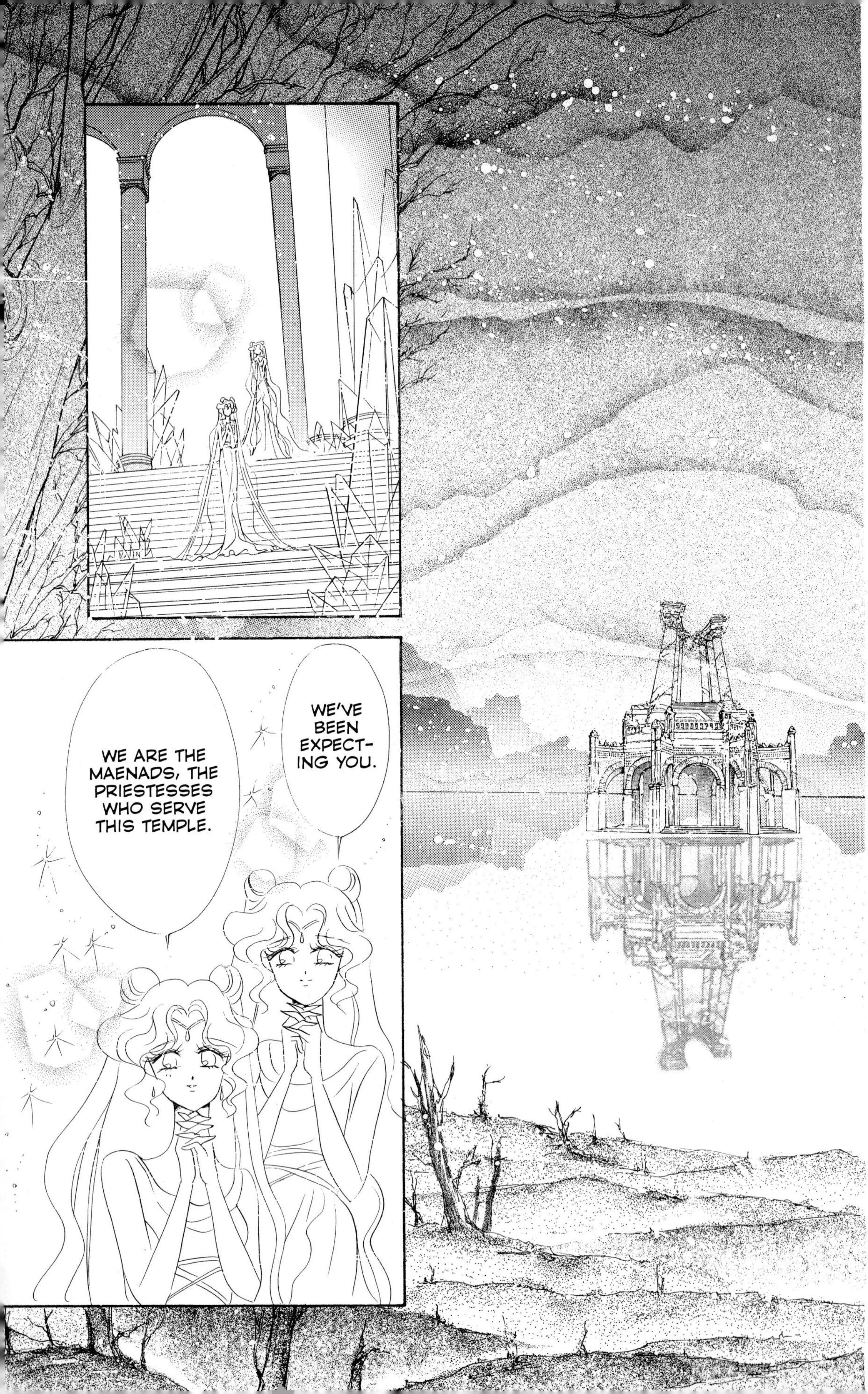
WE'VE BEEN EXPECTING YOU.
WE ARE THE MAENADS, THE PRIESTESSES WHO SERVE THIS TEMPLE.

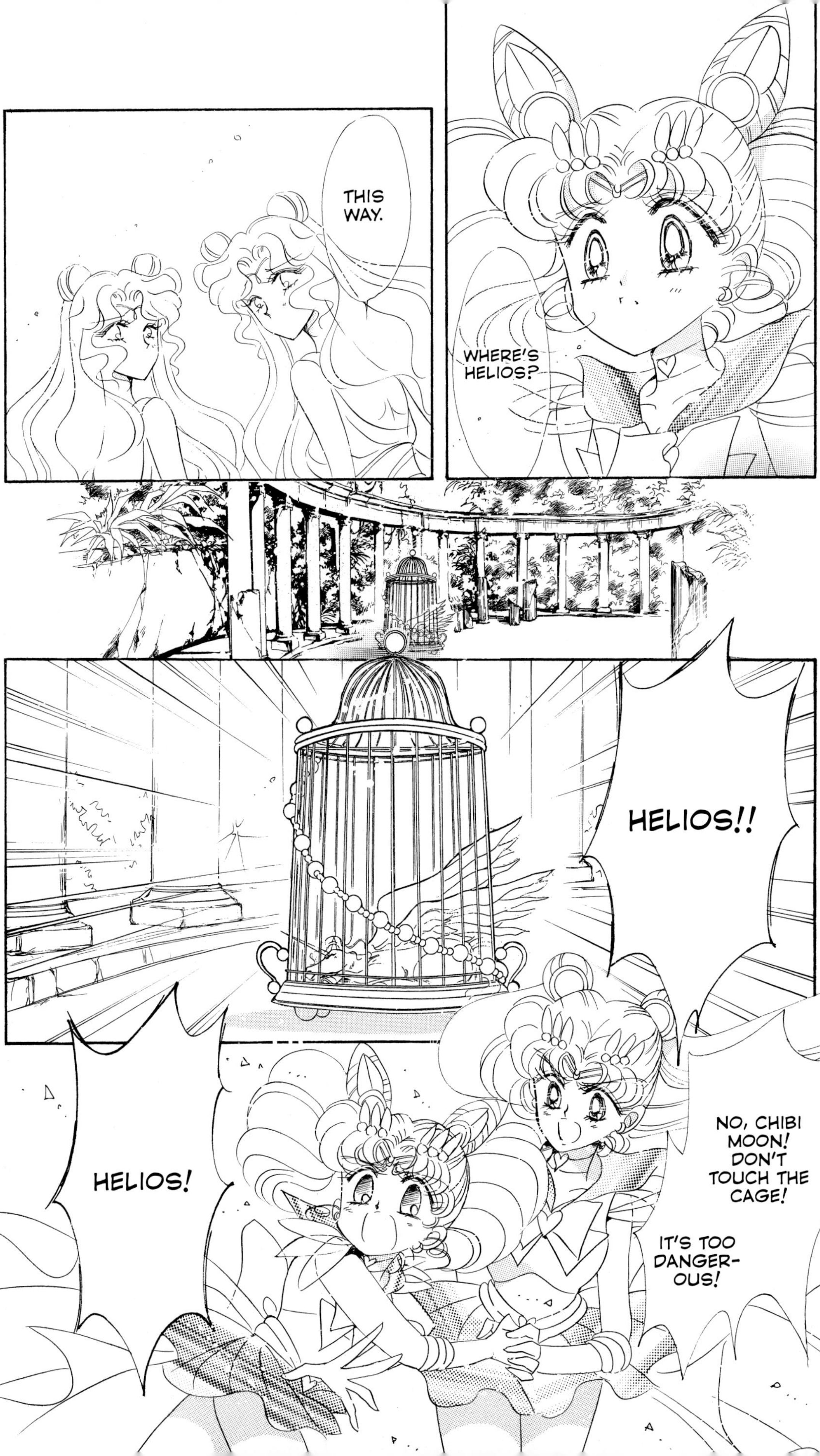
WHERE'S HELIOS?
THIS WAY.
HELIOS!!
NO, CHIBI MOON! DON'T TOUCH THE CAGE!
IT'S TOO DANGER-OUS!
HELIOS!

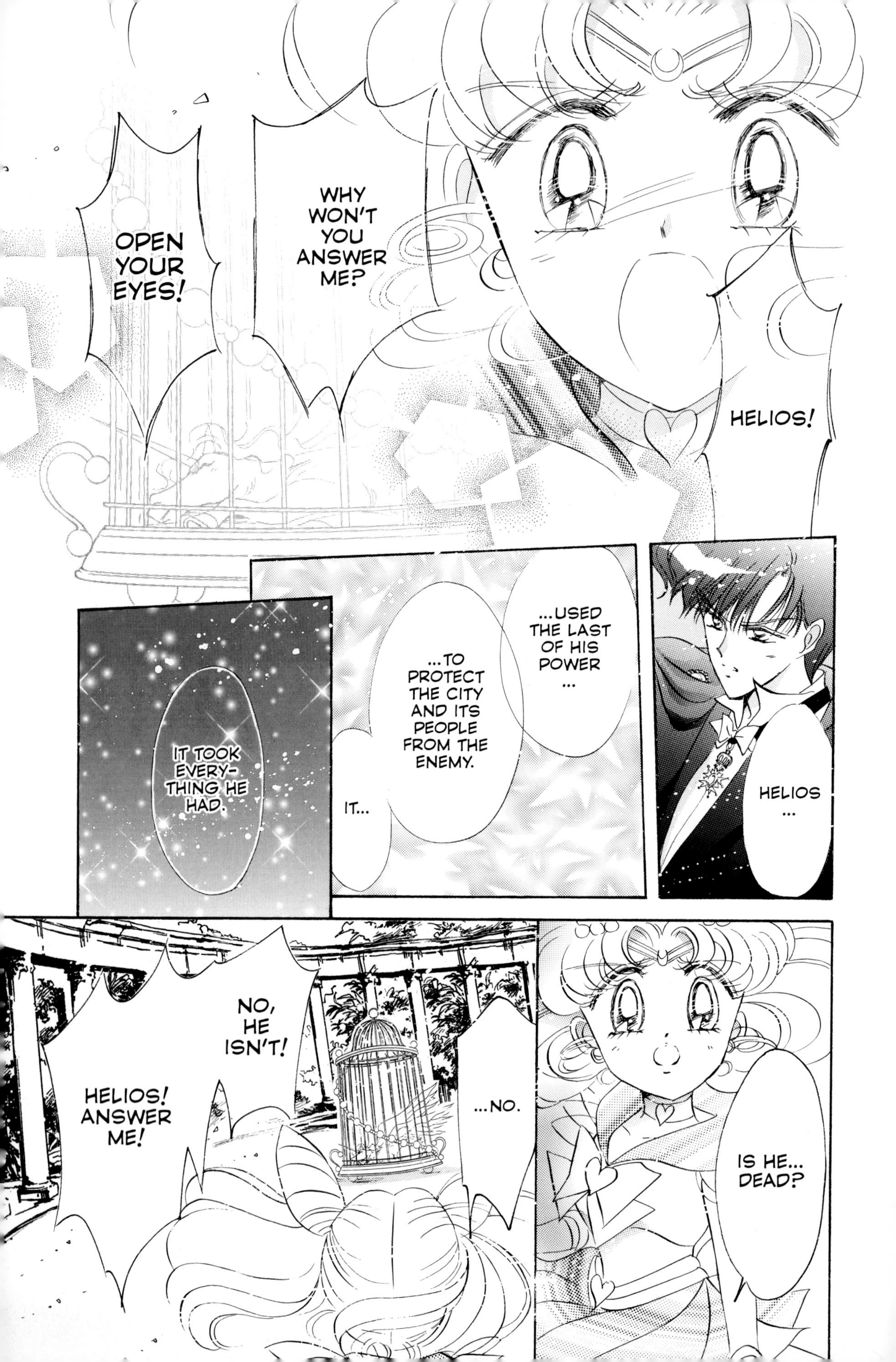
HELIOS!
WHY WON'T YOU ANSWER ME?
OPEN YOUR EYES!
HELIOS ...
...USED THE LAST OF HIS POWER ...
...TO PROTECT THE CITY AND ITS PEOPLE FROM THE ENEMY.
IT...
IT TOOK EVERY-THING HE HAD.
IS HE... DEAD?
...NO.
NO, HE ISN'T!
HELIOS! ANSWER ME!

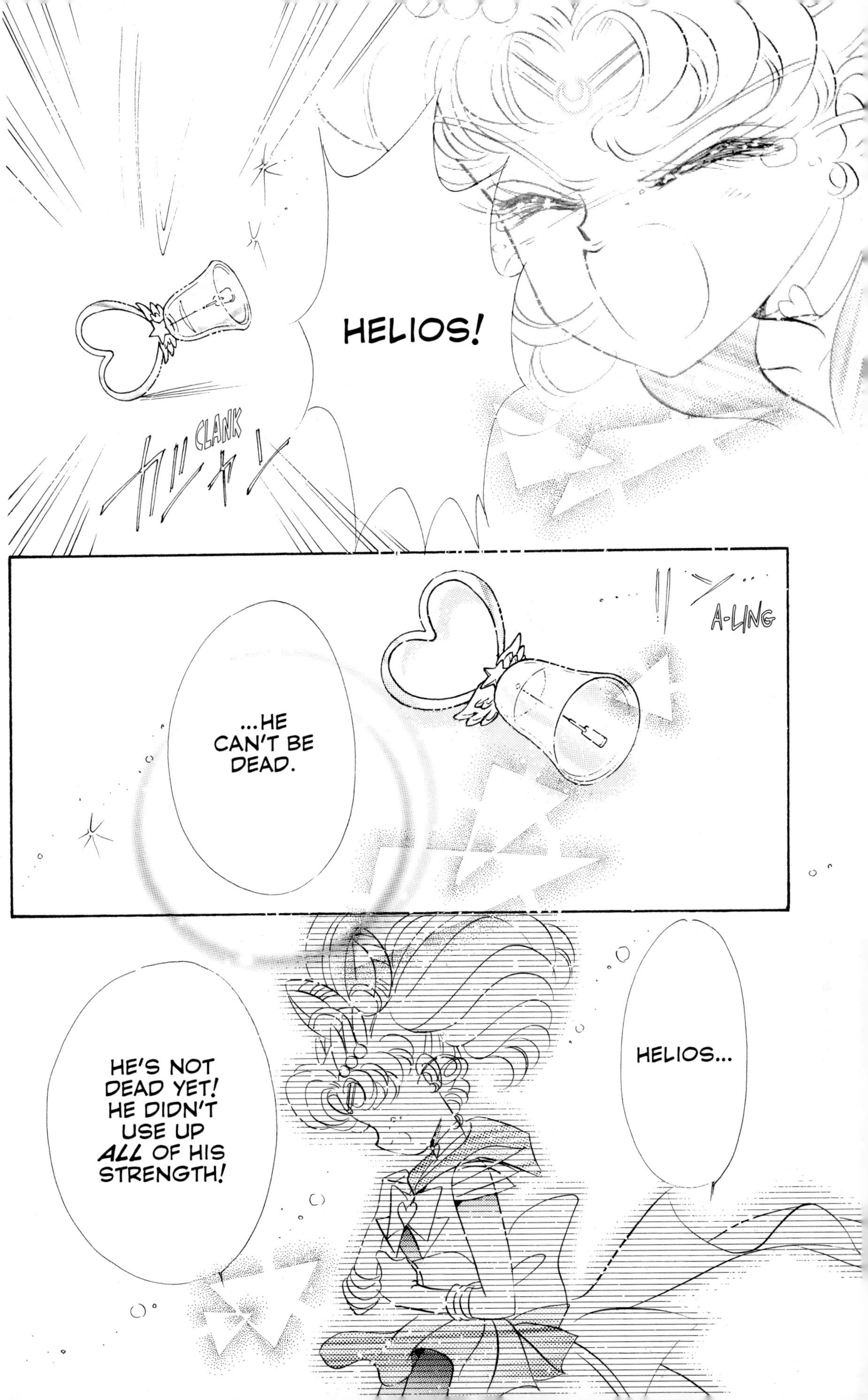
HELIOS!
CLANK
A-LING
...HE CAN'T BE DEAD.
HELIOS...
HE'S NOT DEAD YET! HE DIDN'T USE UP ALL OF HIS STRENGTH!

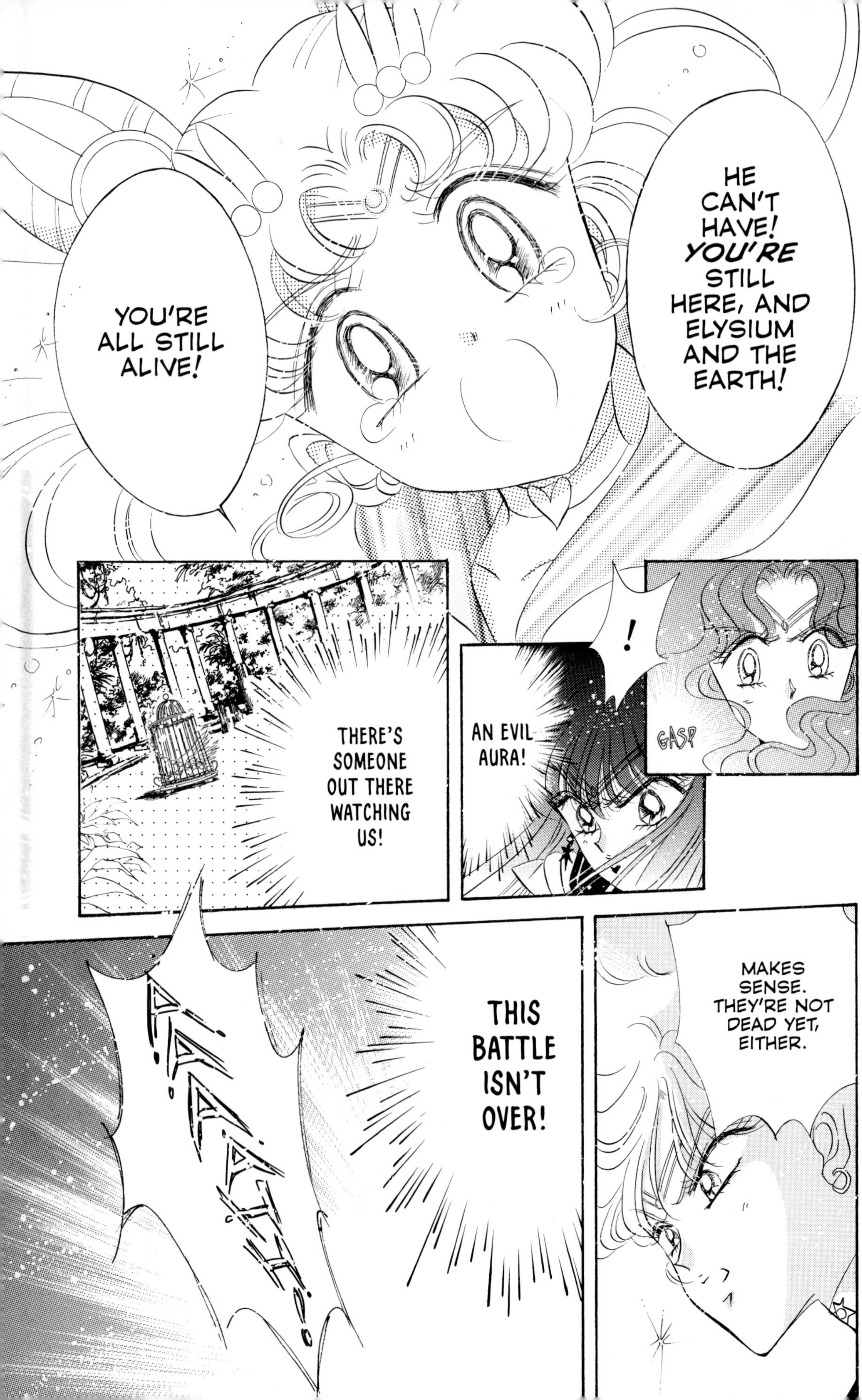
HE CAN'T HAVE! *YOU'RE* STILL HERE, AND ELYSIUM AND THE EARTH!
YOU'RE ALL STILL ALIVE!
GASP
!
AN EVIL AURA!
THERE'S SOMEONE OUT THERE WATCHING US!
MAKES SENSE. THEY'RE NOT DEAD YET, EITHER.
THIS BATTLE ISN'T OVER!

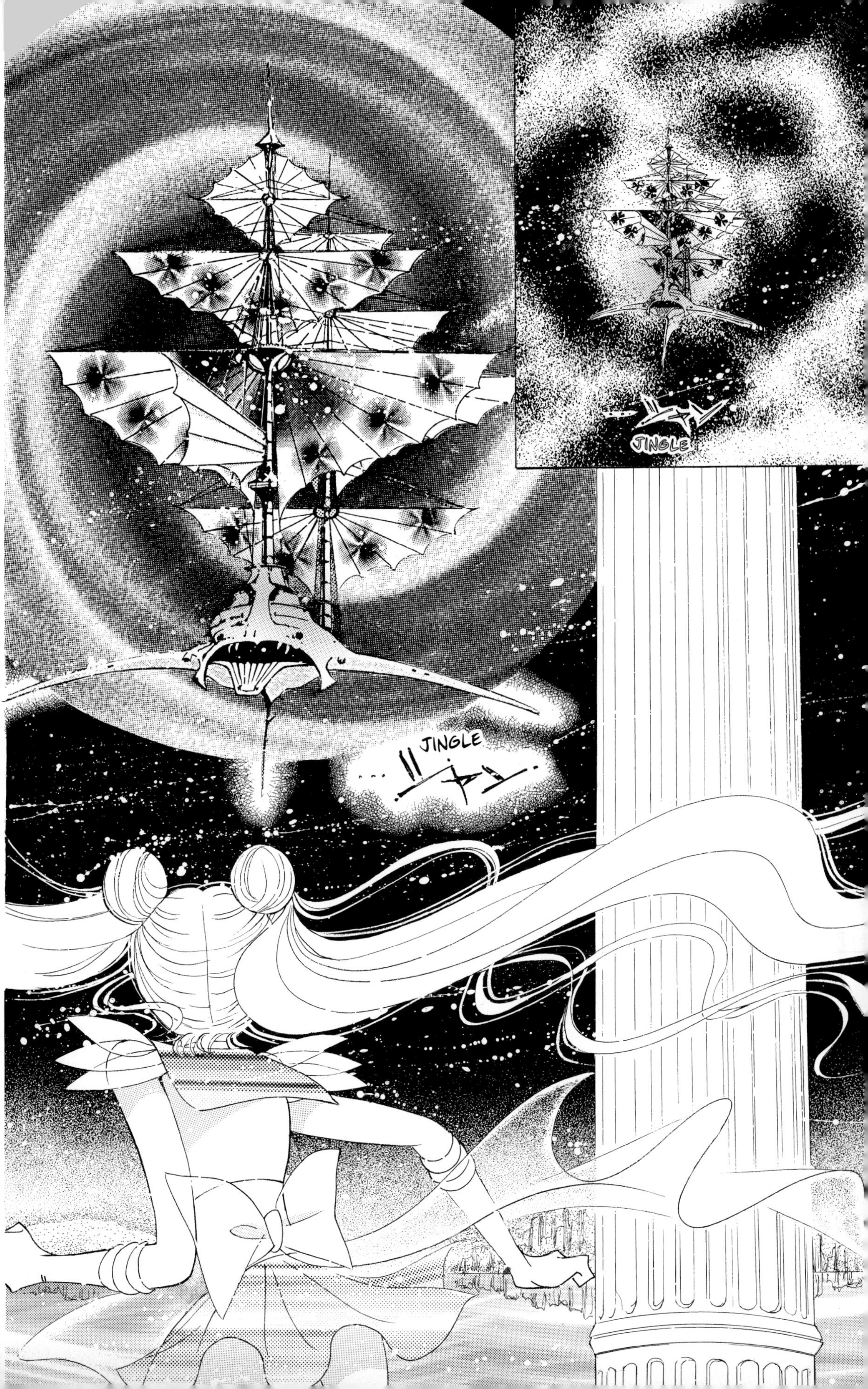
JINGLE
JINGLE

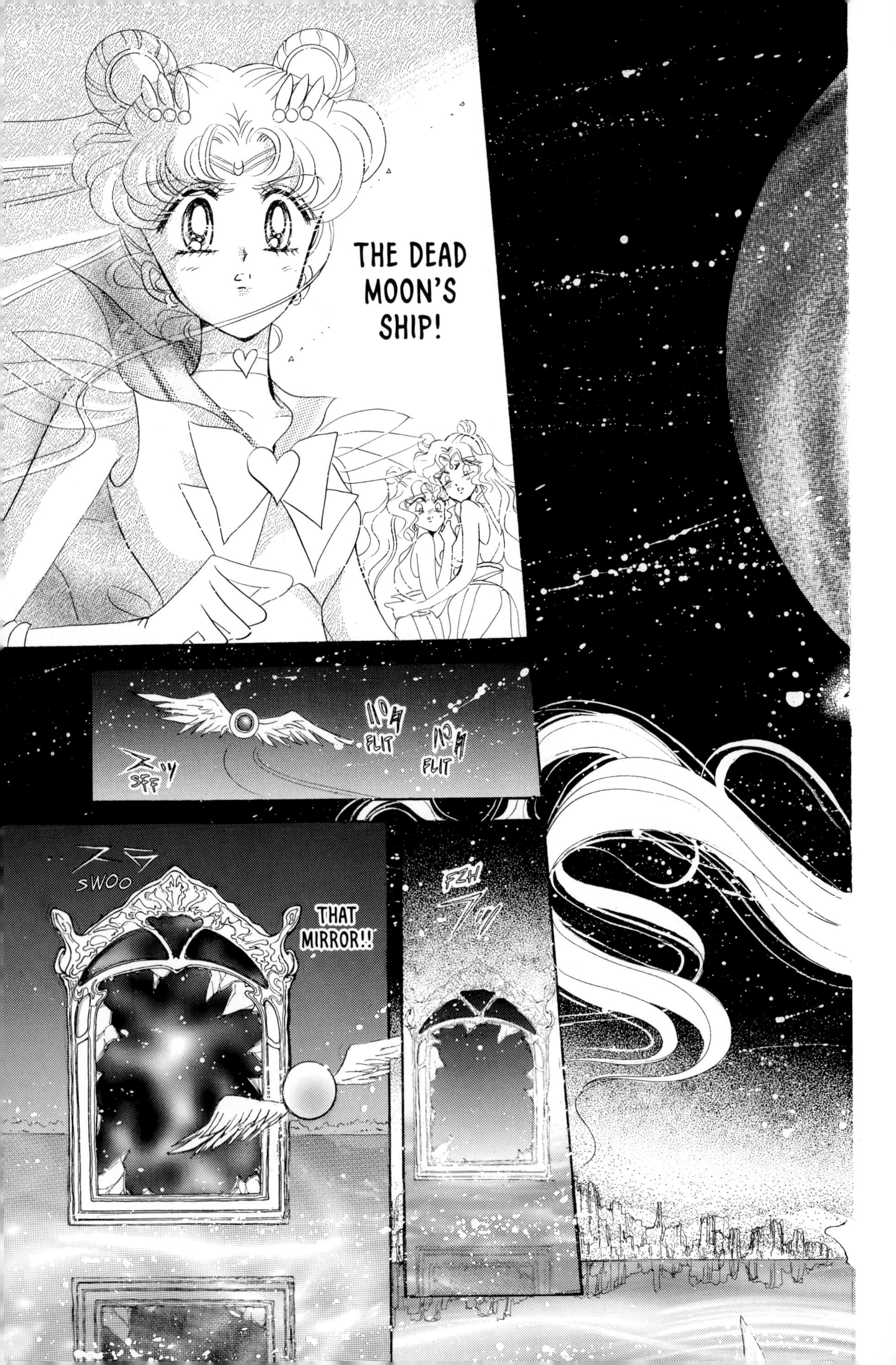
THE DEAD MOON'S SHIP!
FLIT
FLIT
SFF
FZH
SWOO
THAT MIRROR!!

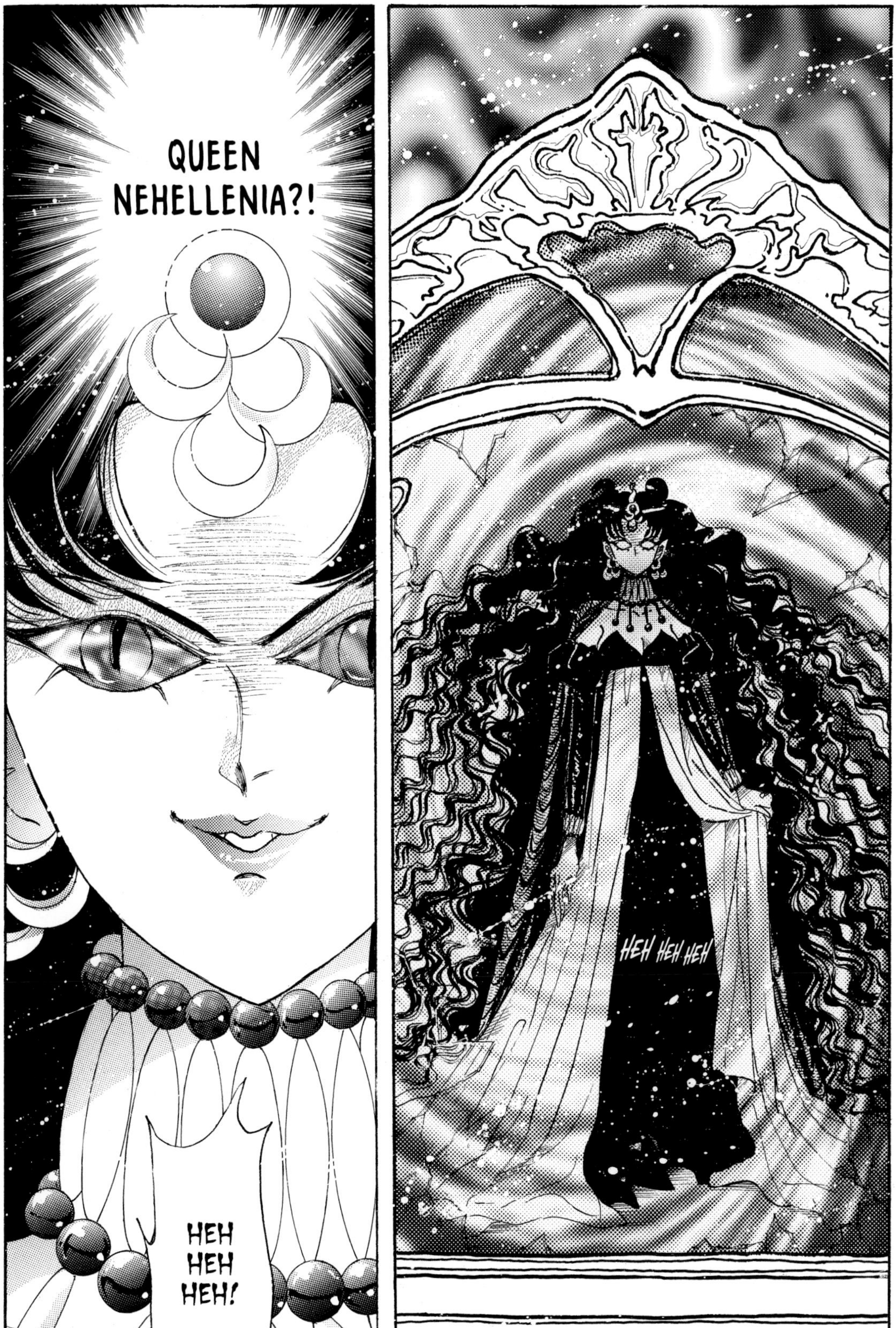
HEH HEH HEH
QUEEN NEHELLENIA?!
HEH HEH HEH!

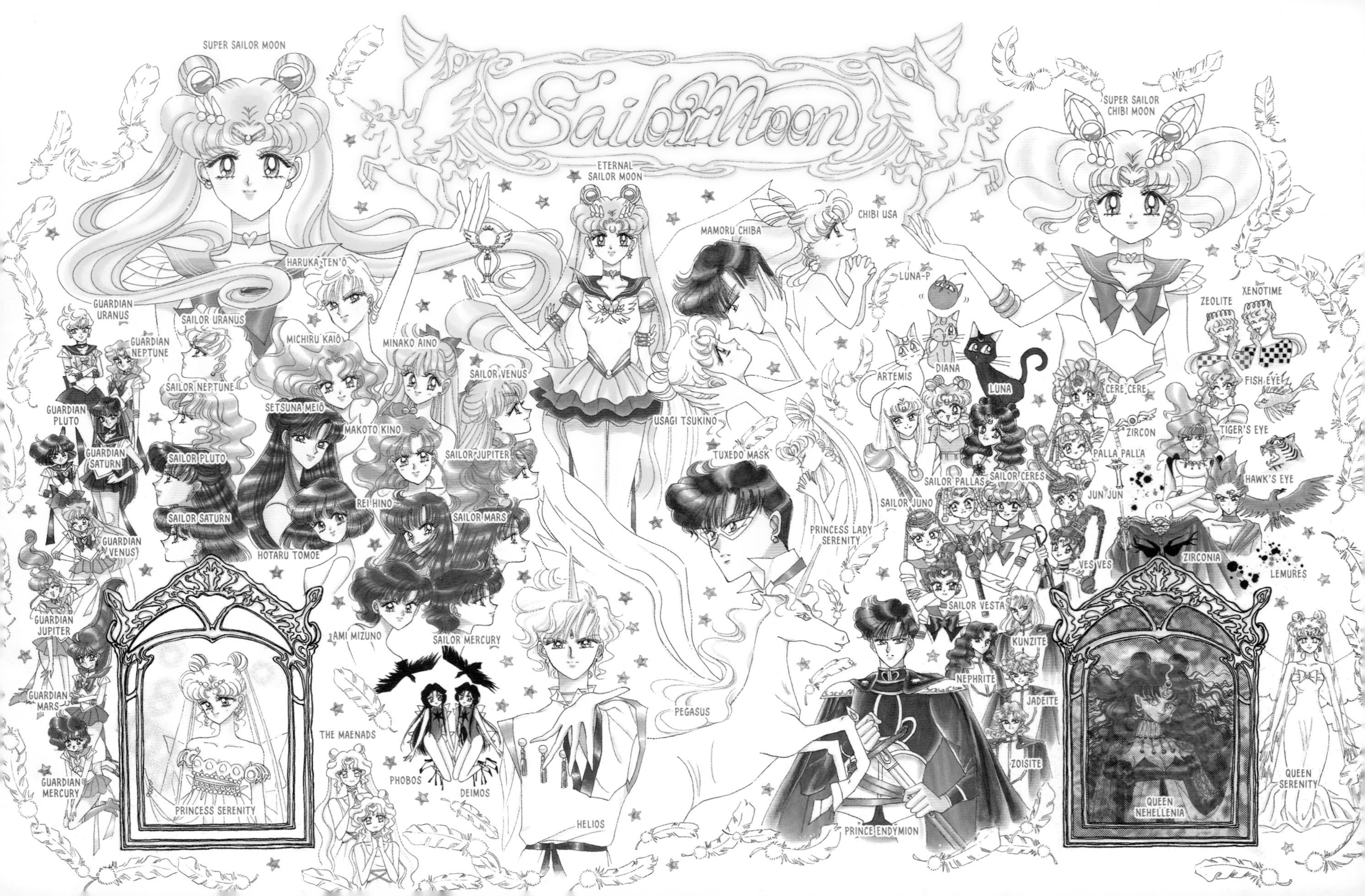
Sailor Moon
SUPER SAILOR MOON
ETERNAL SAILOR MOON
SUPER SAILOR CHIBI MOON
CHIBI USA
MAMORU CHIBA
HARUKA TEN'Ō
GUARDIAN URANUS
SAILOR URANUS
GUARDIAN NEPTUNE
MICHIRU KAIŌ
MINAKO AINO
SAILOR VENUS
SAILOR NEPTUNE
GUARDIAN PLUTO
SETSUNA MEIŌ
MAKOTO KINO
USAGI TSUKINO
LUNA-P
ARTEMIS
DIANA
LUNA
CERE CERE
ZEOLITE
XENOTIME
FISH EYE
ZIRCON
TIGER'S EYE
GUARDIAN SATURN
SAILOR PLUTO
SAILOR JUPITER
TUXEDO MASK
PALLA PALLA
SAILOR PALLAS
SAILOR CERES
JUN JUN
HAWK'S EYE
SAILOR JUNO
SAILOR SATURN
REI HINO
SAILOR MARS
PRINCESS LADY SERENITY
GUARDIAN VENUS
HOTARU TOMOE
VES VES
ZIRCONIA
LEMURES
SAILOR VESTA
GUARDIAN JUPITER
AMI MIZUNO
SAILOR MERCURY
KUNZITE
NEPHRITE
GUARDIAN MARS
JADEITE
PEGASUS
THE MAENADS
PHOBOS
DEIMOS
ZOISITE
QUEEN SERENITY
GUARDIAN MERCURY
PRINCESS SERENITY
QUEEN NEHELLENIA
HELIOS
PRINCE ENDYMION

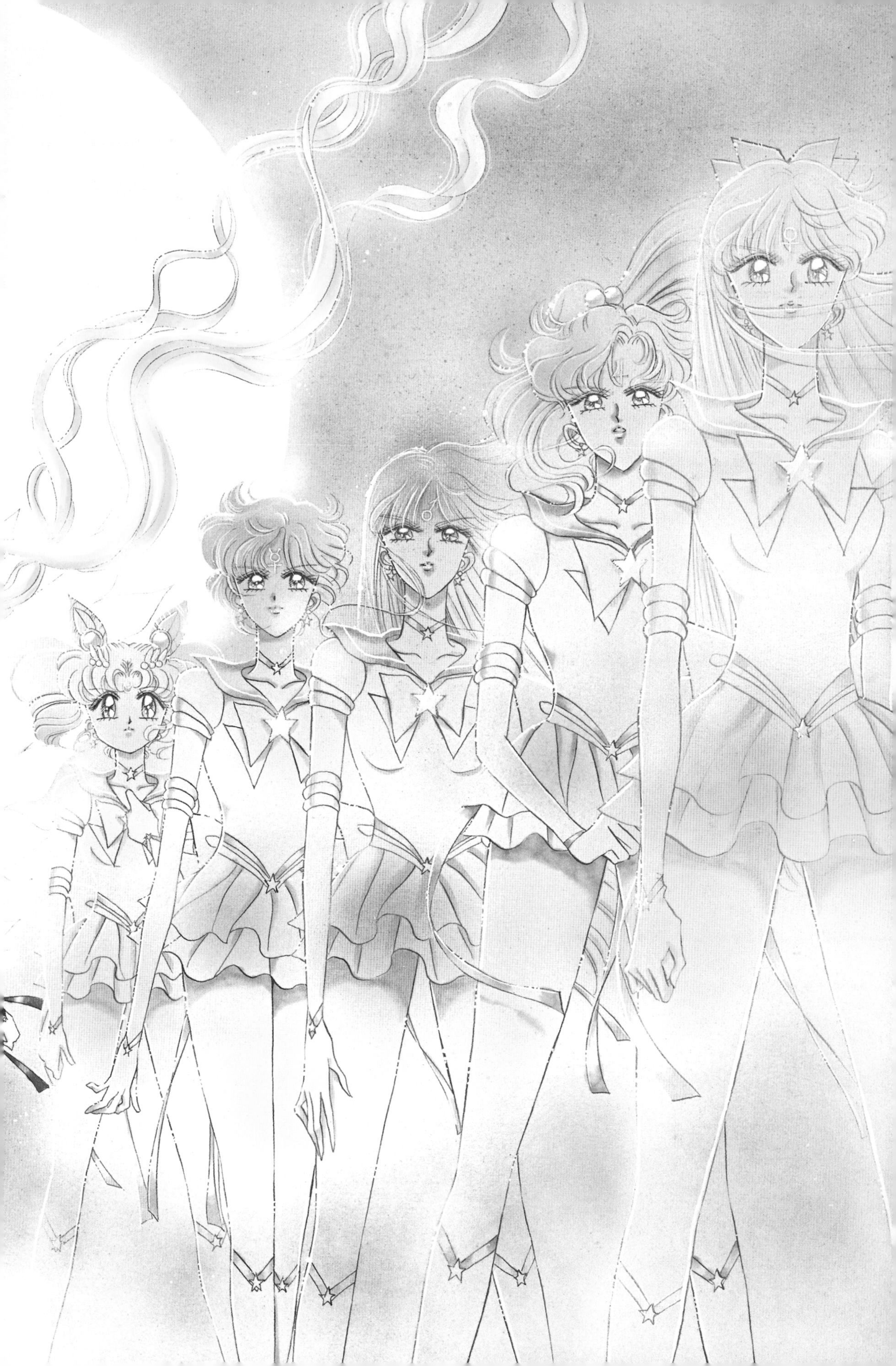

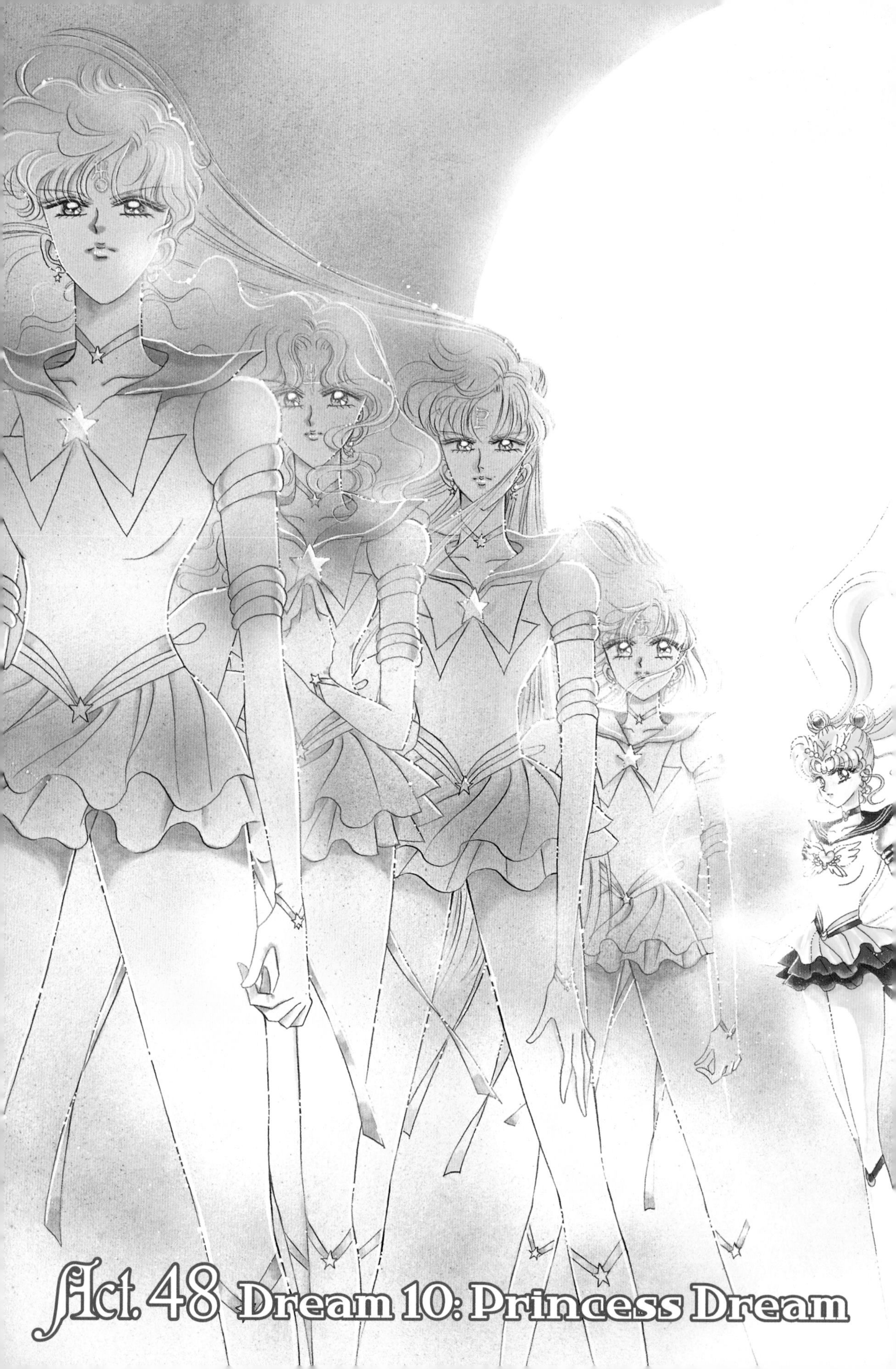

Act. 48 Dream 10: Princess Dream

Pretty Guardian

Sailor Moon

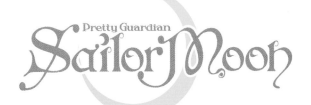

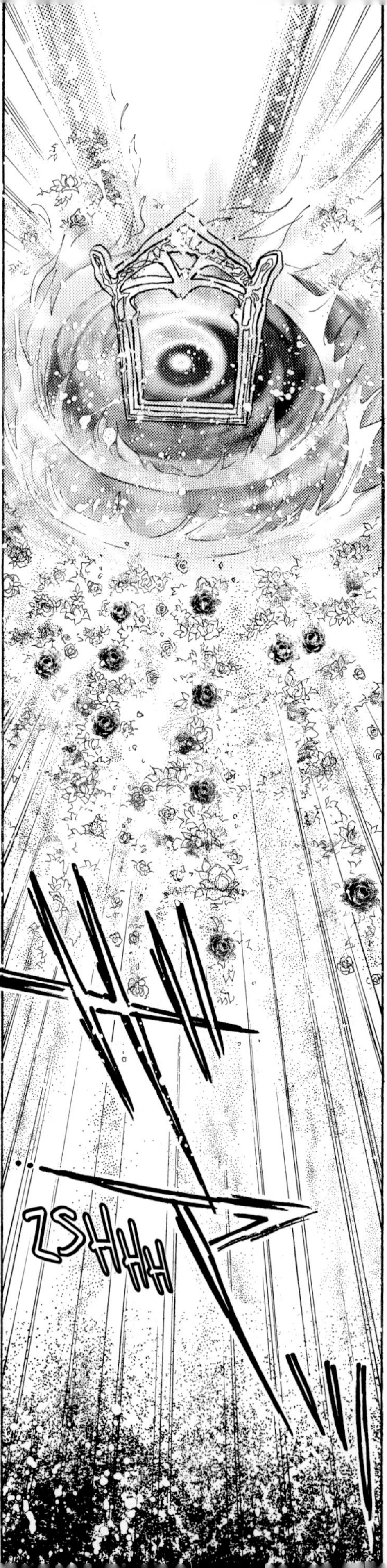
ZSHHH

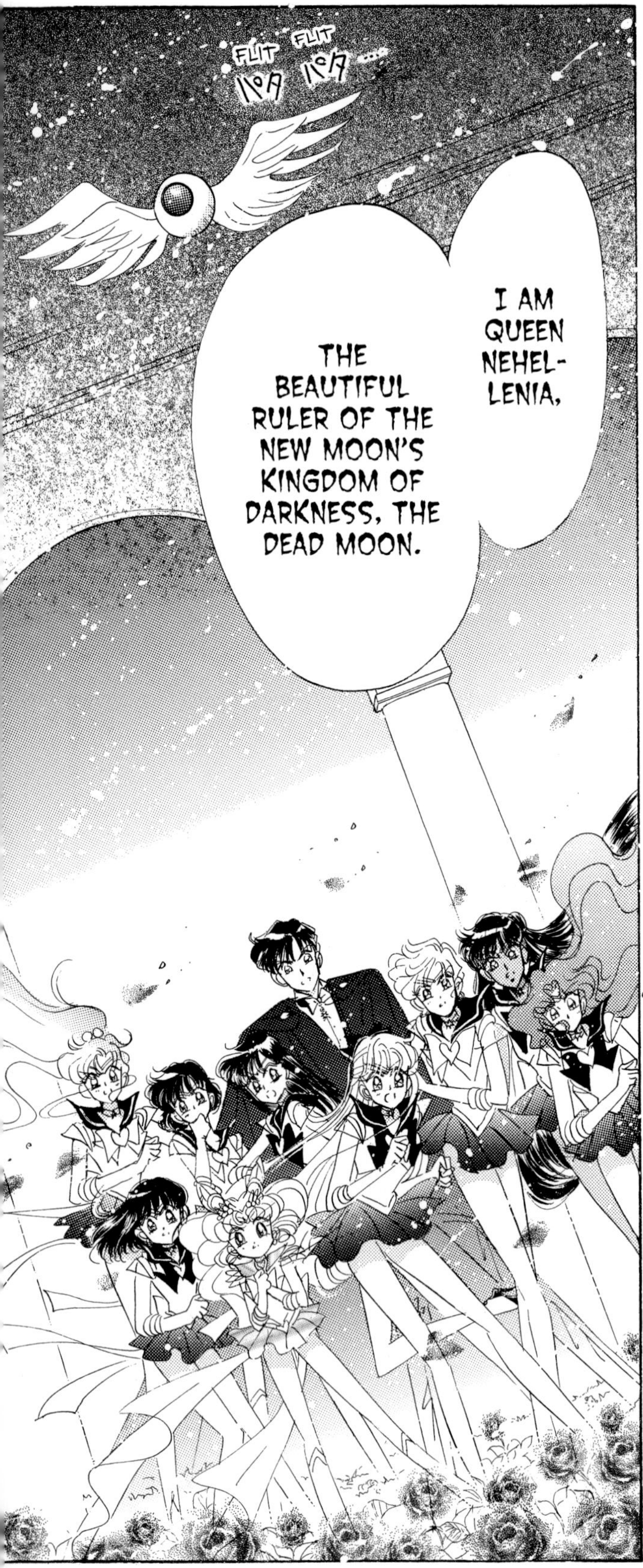
FLIT FLIT
パタ パタ……
I AM QUEEN NEHEL-LENIA,
THE BEAUTIFUL RULER OF THE NEW MOON'S KINGDOM OF DARKNESS, THE DEAD MOON.

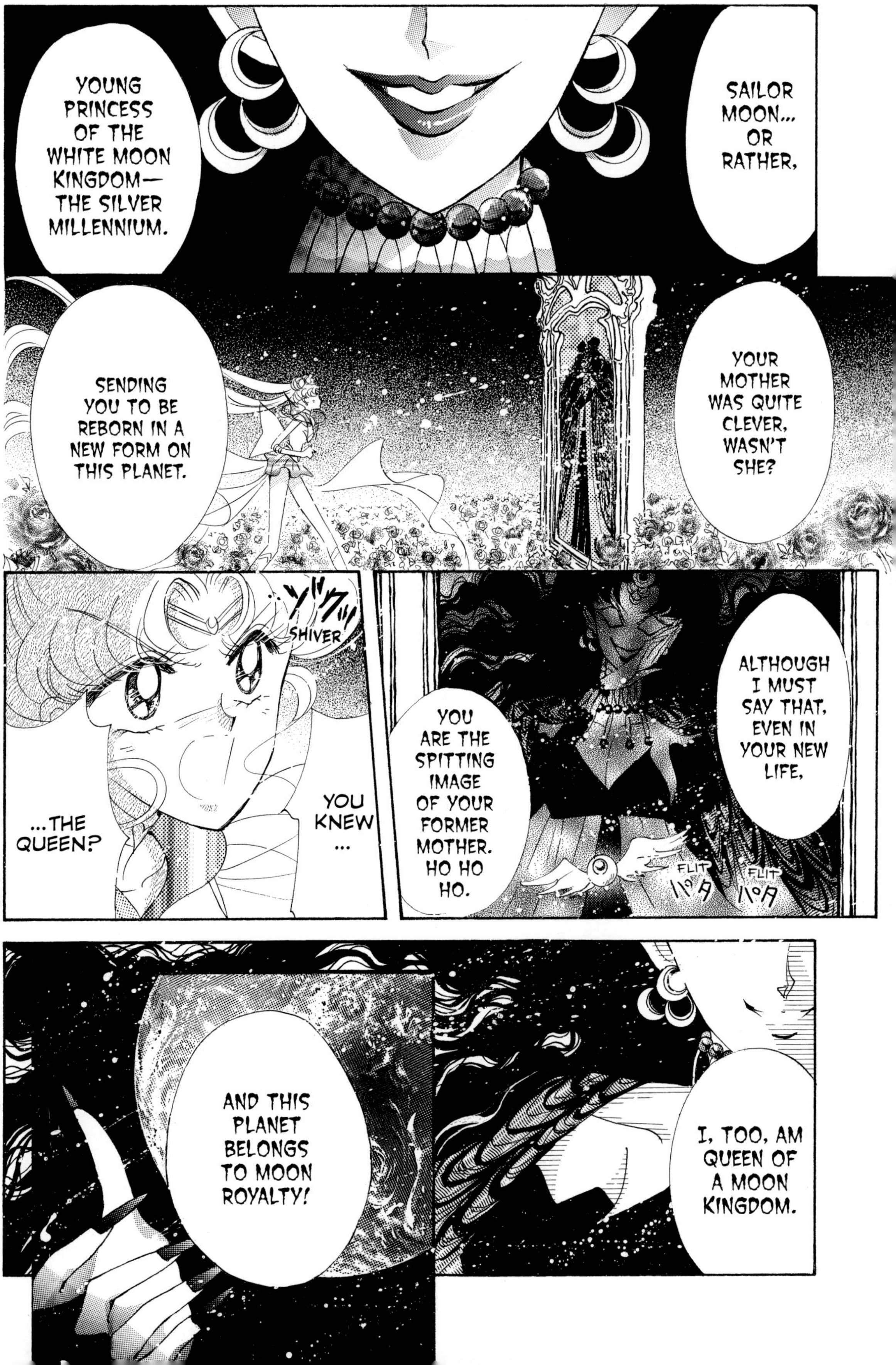

SAILOR MOON... OR RATHER,
YOUNG PRINCESS OF THE WHITE MOON KINGDOM—THE SILVER MILLENNIUM.
YOUR MOTHER WAS QUITE CLEVER, WASN'T SHE?
SENDING YOU TO BE REBORN IN A NEW FORM ON THIS PLANET.
ALTHOUGH I MUST SAY THAT, EVEN IN YOUR NEW LIFE,
YOU ARE THE SPITTING IMAGE OF YOUR FORMER MOTHER. HO HO HO.
FLIT パタ
FLIT パタ
SHIVER
YOU KNEW ...
...THE QUEEN?
I, TOO, AM QUEEN OF A MOON KINGDOM.
AND THIS PLANET BELONGS TO MOON ROYALTY!

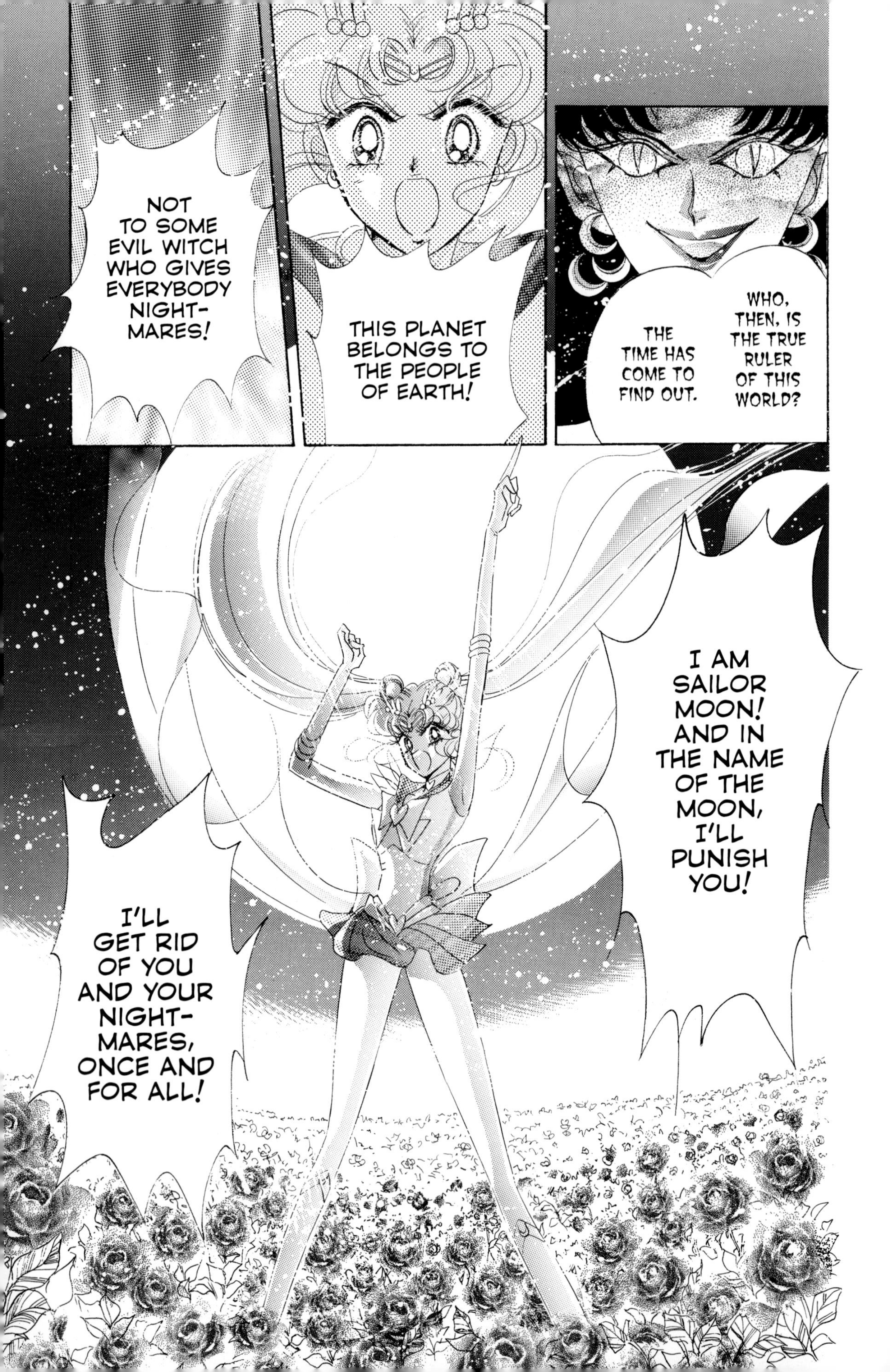
WHO, THEN, IS THE TRUE RULER OF THIS WORLD?
THE TIME HAS COME TO FIND OUT.
THIS PLANET BELONGS TO THE PEOPLE OF EARTH!
NOT TO SOME EVIL WITCH WHO GIVES EVERYBODY NIGHT-MARES!
I AM SAILOR MOON! AND IN THE NAME OF THE MOON, I'LL PUNISH YOU!
I'LL GET RID OF YOU AND YOUR NIGHT-MARES, ONCE AND FOR ALL!

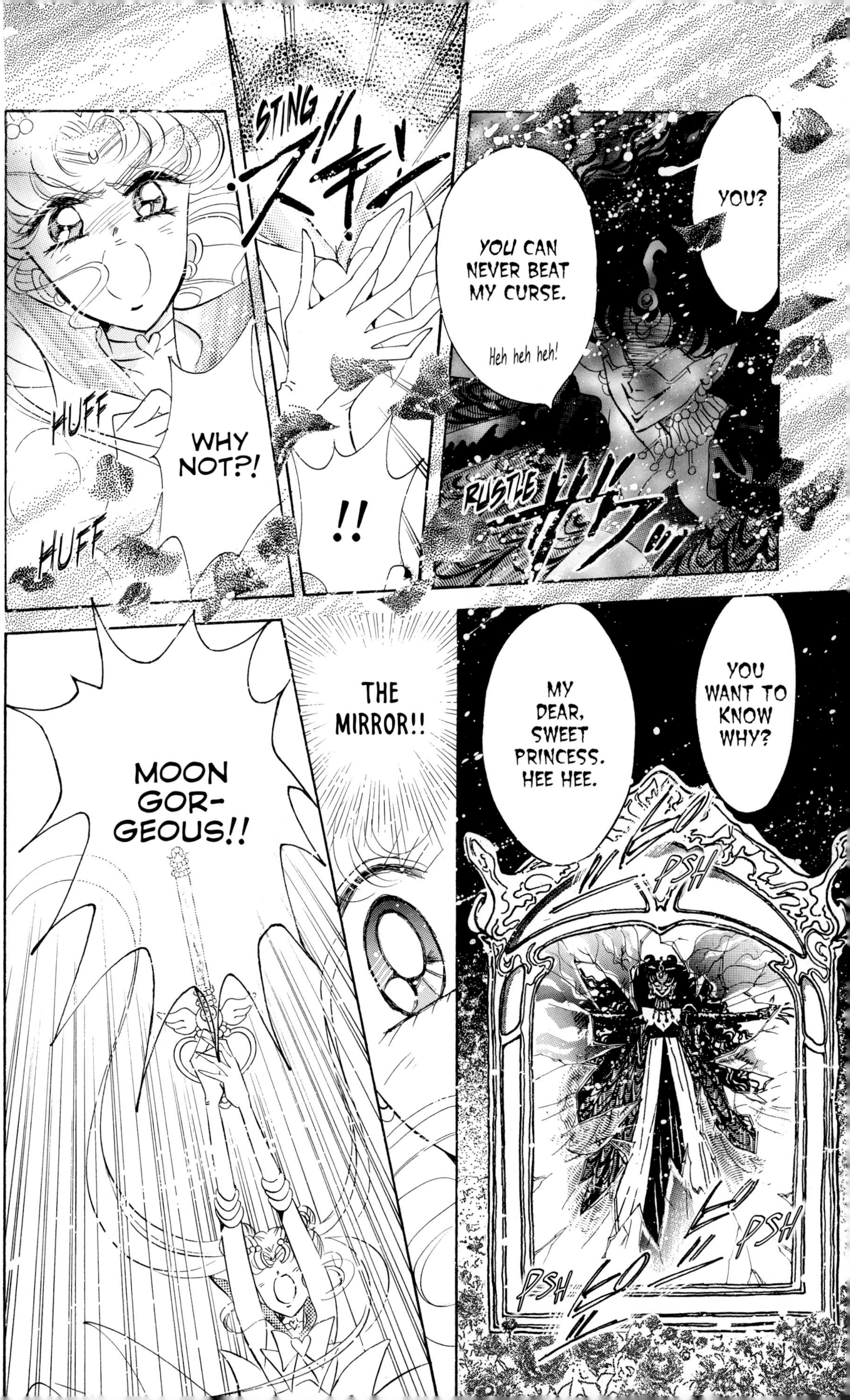

YOU?
YOU CAN NEVER BEAT MY CURSE.
Heh heh heh!
RUSTLE
STING
!!
WHY NOT?!
HUFF
HUFF
YOU WANT TO KNOW WHY?
MY DEAR, SWEET PRINCESS. HEE HEE.
PSH
PSH
PSH
THE MIRROR!!
MOON GOR-GEOUS!!

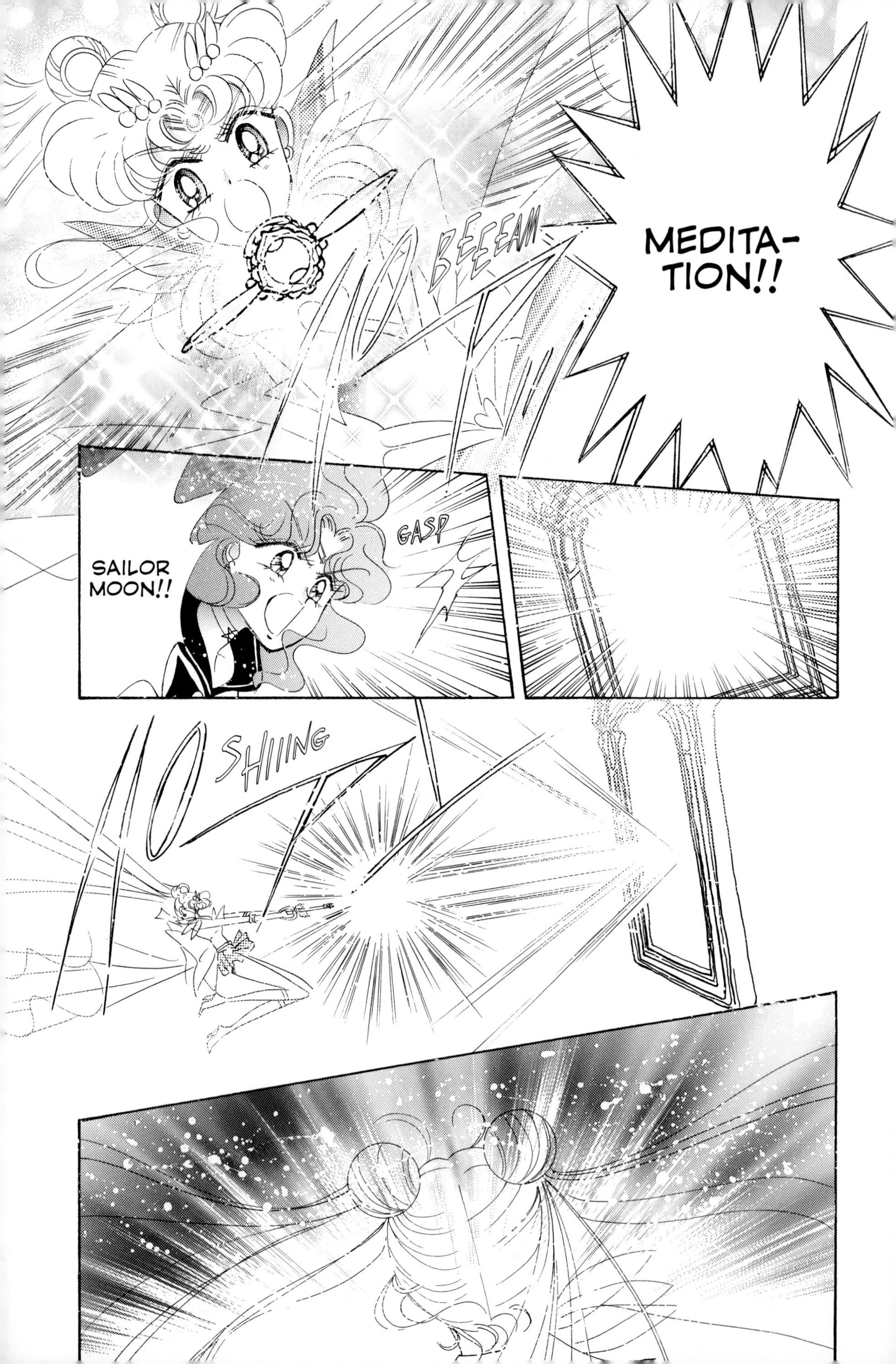
MEDITA-TION!!
BEEEAM
GASP
SAILOR MOON!!
SHIIING

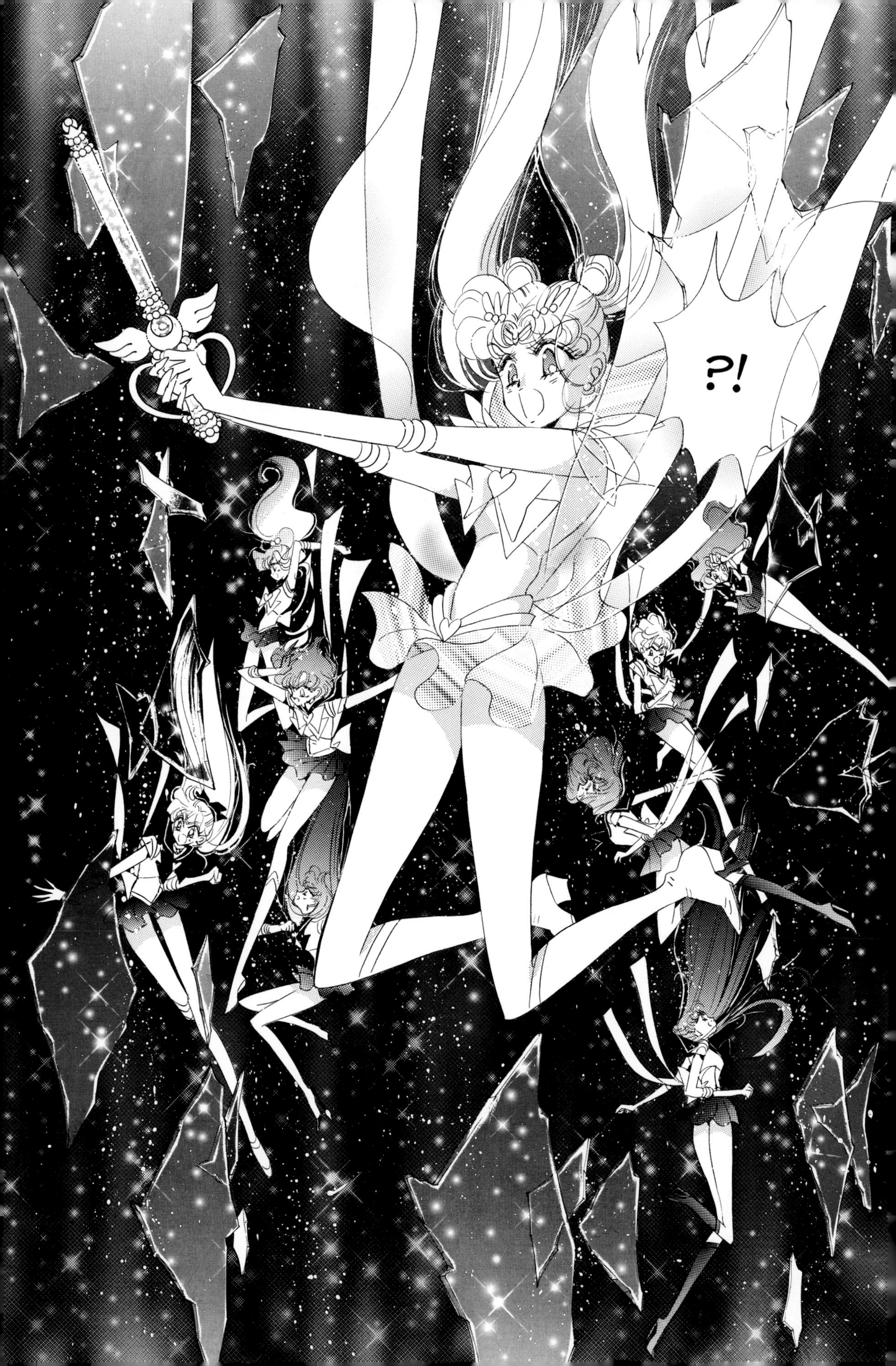
?!

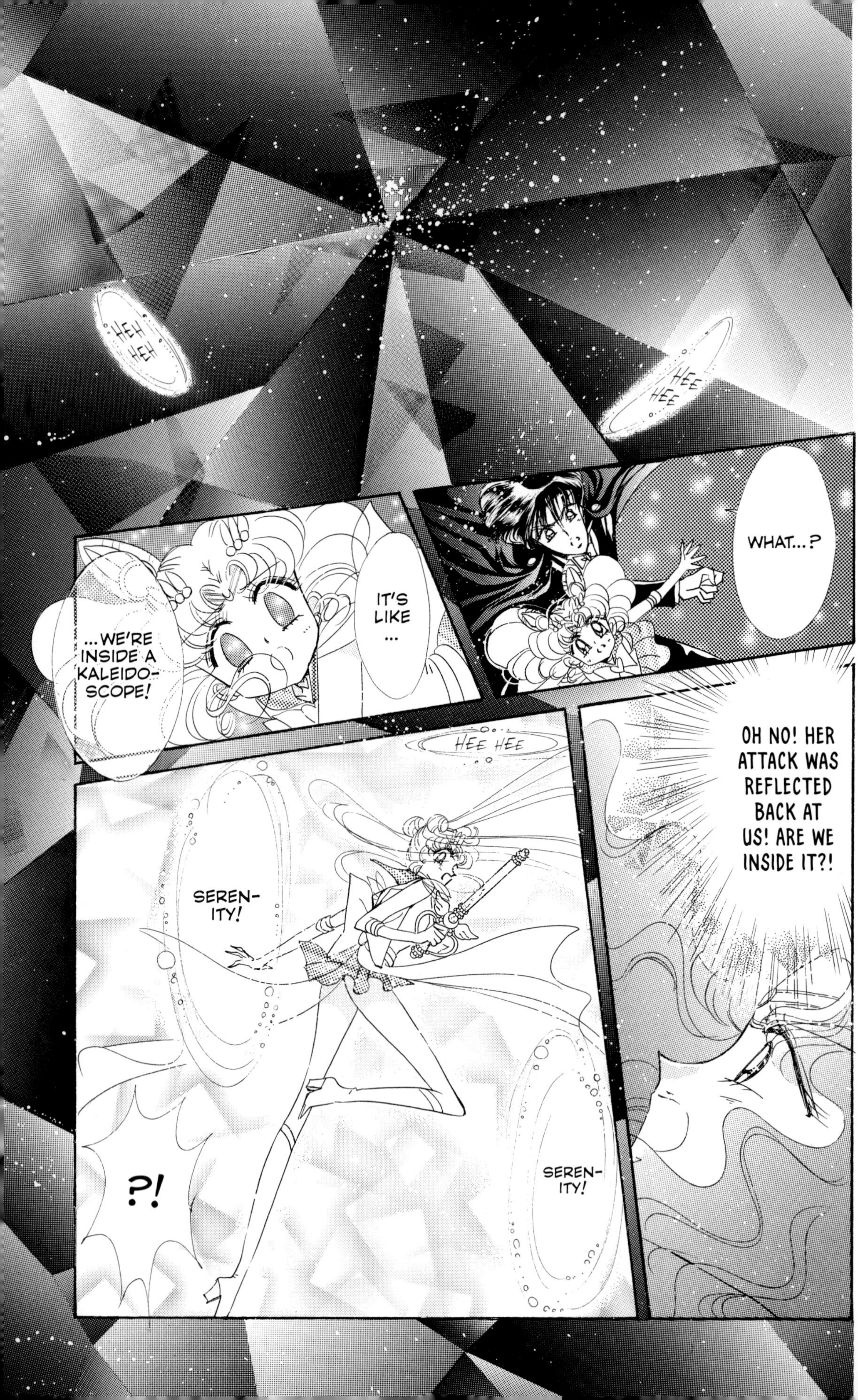
HEE HEE
HEH HEH
WHAT...?
IT'S LIKE ...
...WE'RE INSIDE A KALEIDO-SCOPE!
OH NO! HER ATTACK WAS REFLECTED BACK AT US! ARE WE INSIDE IT?!
HEE HEE
SEREN-ITY!
SEREN-ITY!
?!

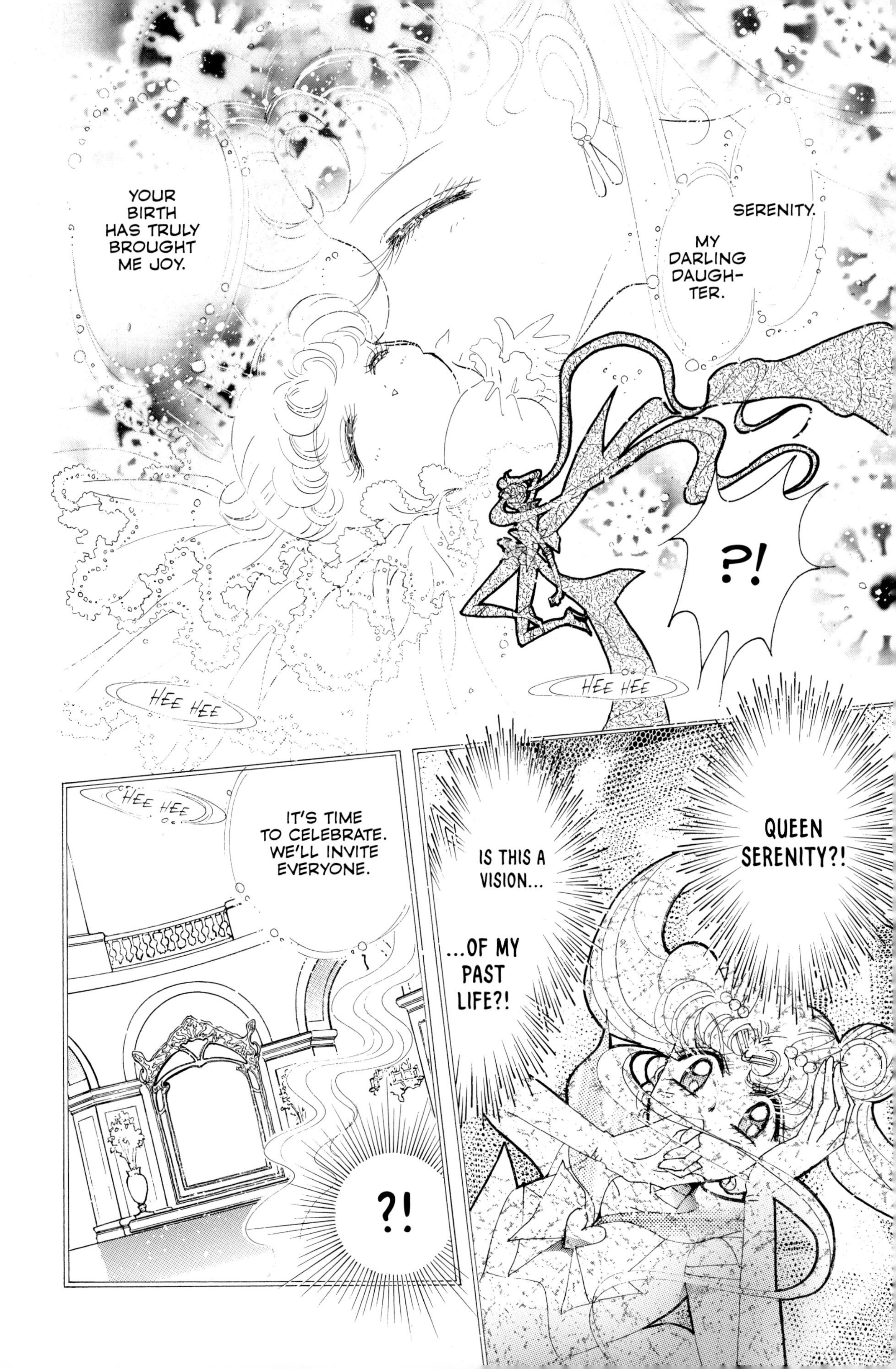
SERENITY.
MY DARLING DAUGHTER.
YOUR BIRTH HAS TRULY BROUGHT ME JOY.
?!
HEE HEE
HEE HEE
QUEEN SERENITY?!
IS THIS A VISION...
...OF MY PAST LIFE?!
HEE HEE
IT'S TIME TO CELEBRATE. WE'LL INVITE EVERYONE.
?!

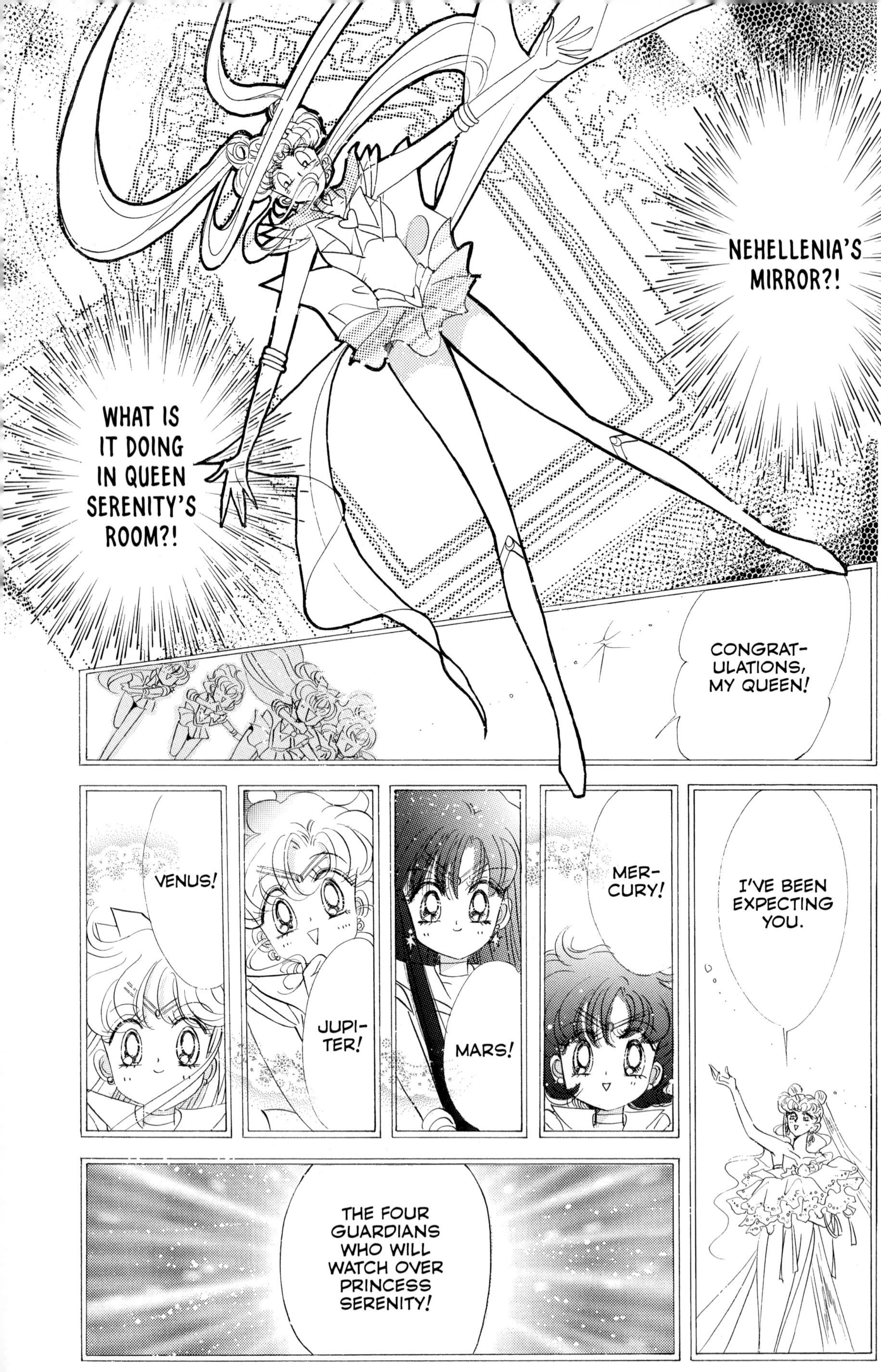
NEHELLENIA'S MIRROR?!
WHAT IS IT DOING IN QUEEN SERENITY'S ROOM?!
CONGRAT-ULATIONS, MY QUEEN!
I'VE BEEN EXPECTING YOU.
MER-CURY!
MARS!
JUPI-TER!
VENUS!
THE FOUR GUARDIANS WHO WILL WATCH OVER PRINCESS SERENITY!

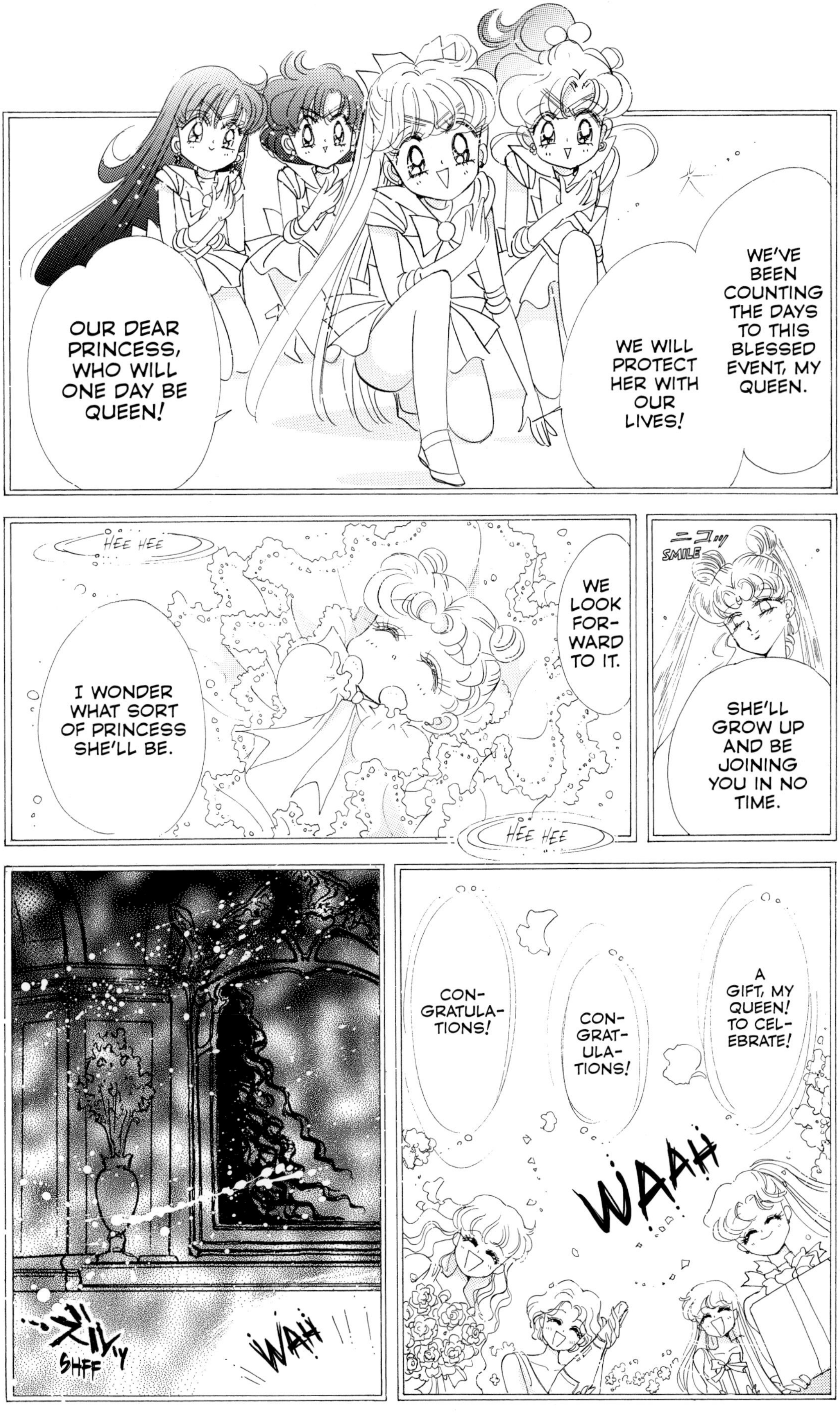
WE'VE BEEN COUNTING THE DAYS TO THIS BLESSED EVENT, MY QUEEN.
WE WILL PROTECT HER WITH OUR LIVES!
OUR DEAR PRINCESS, WHO WILL ONE DAY BE QUEEN!
ニコッ
SMILE
SHE'LL GROW UP AND BE JOINING YOU IN NO TIME.
WE LOOK FORWARD TO IT.
HEE HEE
I WONDER WHAT SORT OF PRINCESS SHE'LL BE.
HEE HEE
A GIFT, MY QUEEN! TO CELEBRATE!
CONGRATULATIONS!
CONGRATULATIONS!
WAAH
WAH
SHFF

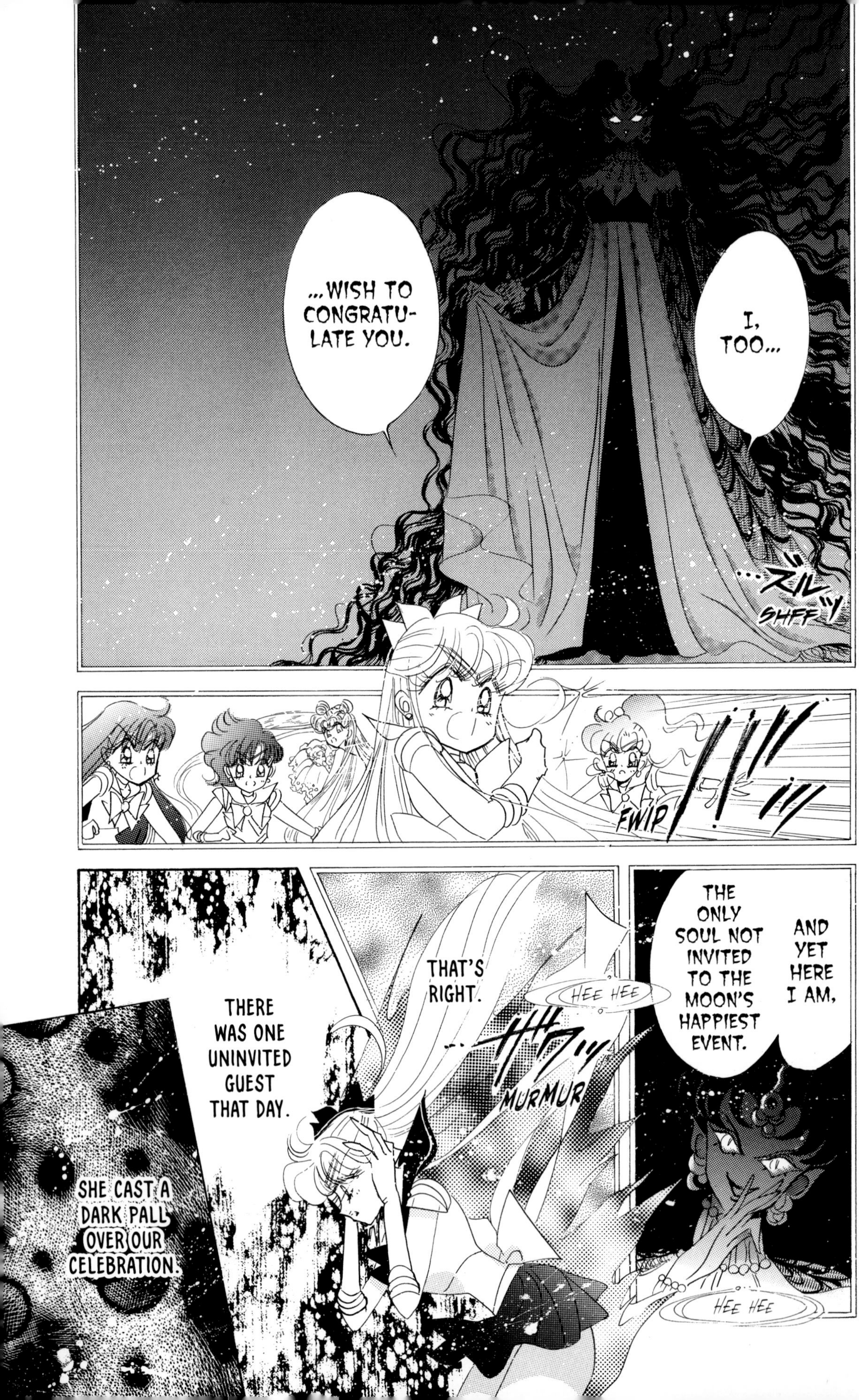
I, TOO...
...WISH TO CONGRATU-LATE YOU.
SHFF
FWIP
AND YET HERE I AM,
THE ONLY SOUL NOT INVITED TO THE MOON'S HAPPIEST EVENT.
HEE HEE
HEE HEE
THAT'S RIGHT.
MURMUR
THERE WAS ONE UNINVITED GUEST THAT DAY.
SHE CAST A DARK PALL OVER OUR CELEBRATION.

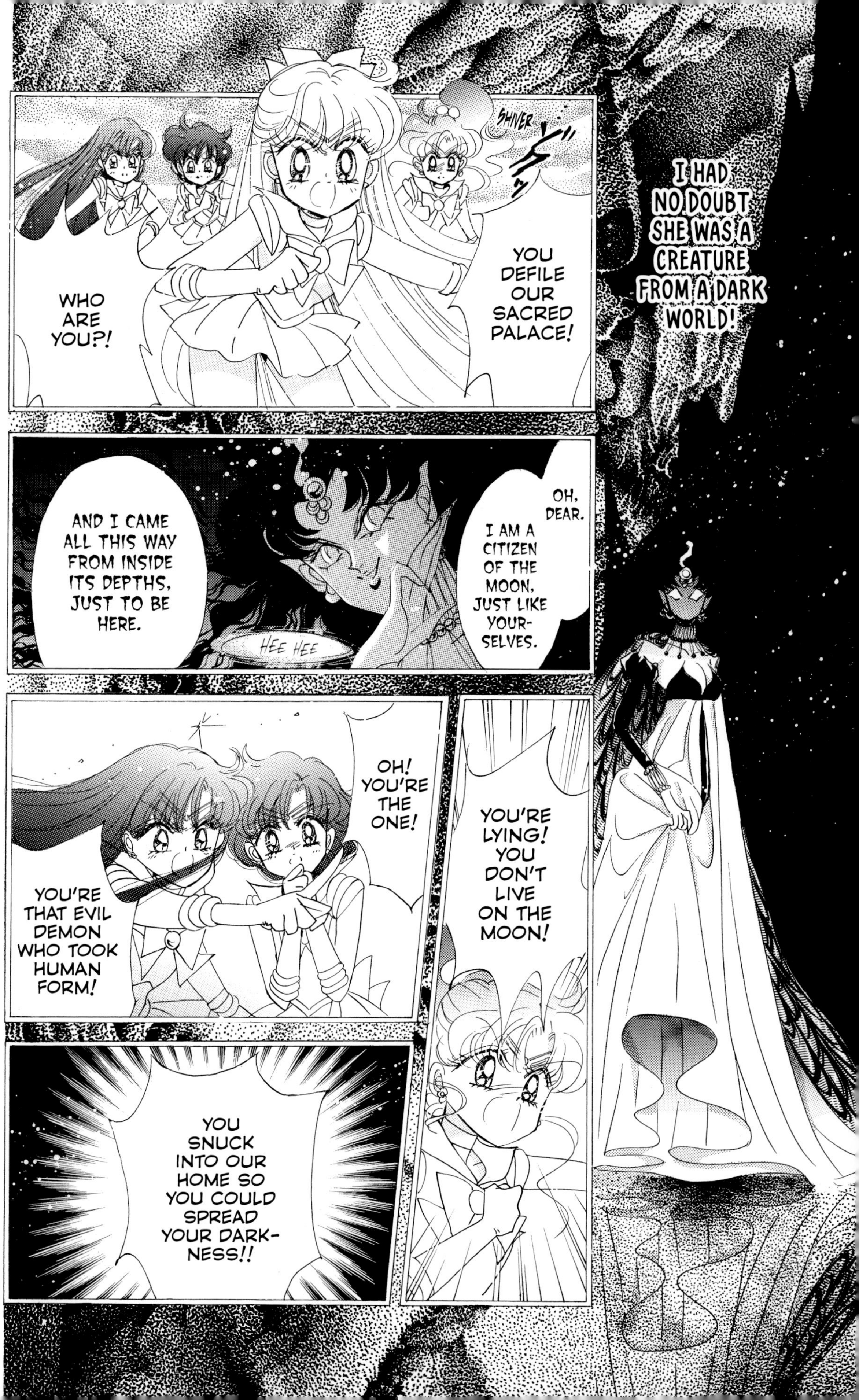
I HAD NO DOUBT SHE WAS A CREATURE FROM A DARK WORLD!
SHIVER
YOU DEFILE OUR SACRED PALACE!
WHO ARE YOU?!
OH, DEAR.
I AM A CITIZEN OF THE MOON, JUST LIKE YOUR-SELVES.
HEE HEE
AND I CAME ALL THIS WAY FROM INSIDE ITS DEPTHS, JUST TO BE HERE.
YOU'RE LYING! YOU DON'T LIVE ON THE MOON!
OH! YOU'RE THE ONE!
YOU'RE THAT EVIL DEMON WHO TOOK HUMAN FORM!
YOU SNUCK INTO OUR HOME SO YOU COULD SPREAD YOUR DARK-NESS!!

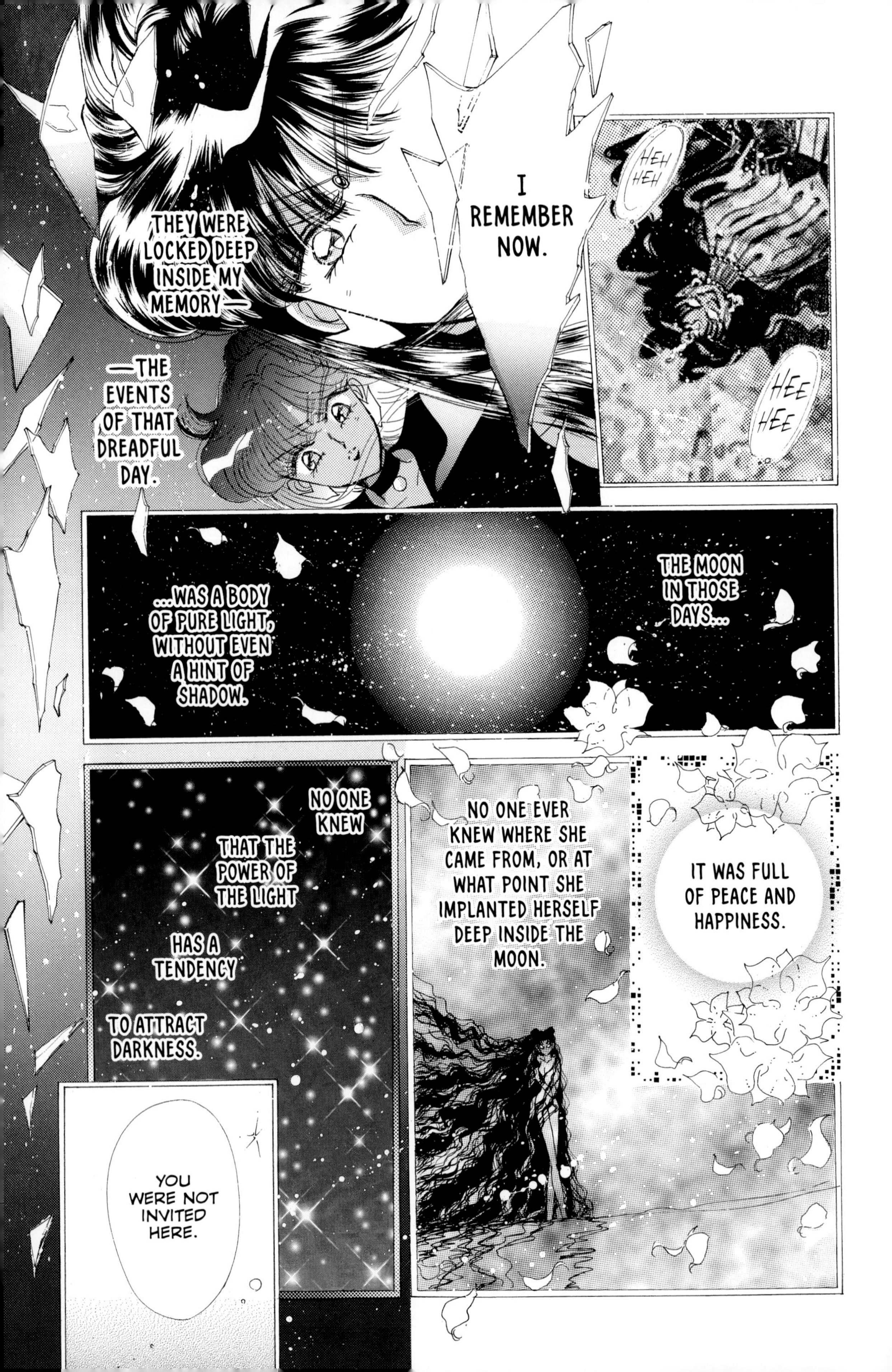
HEH HEH
HEE HEE
I REMEMBER NOW.
THEY WERE LOCKED DEEP INSIDE MY MEMORY—
—THE EVENTS OF THAT DREADFUL DAY.
THE MOON IN THOSE DAYS...
...WAS A BODY OF PURE LIGHT, WITHOUT EVEN A HINT OF SHADOW.
IT WAS FULL OF PEACE AND HAPPINESS.
NO ONE EVER KNEW WHERE SHE CAME FROM, OR AT WHAT POINT SHE IMPLANTED HERSELF DEEP INSIDE THE MOON.
NO ONE KNEW
THAT THE POWER OF THE LIGHT
HAS A TENDENCY
TO ATTRACT DARKNESS.
YOU WERE NOT INVITED HERE.

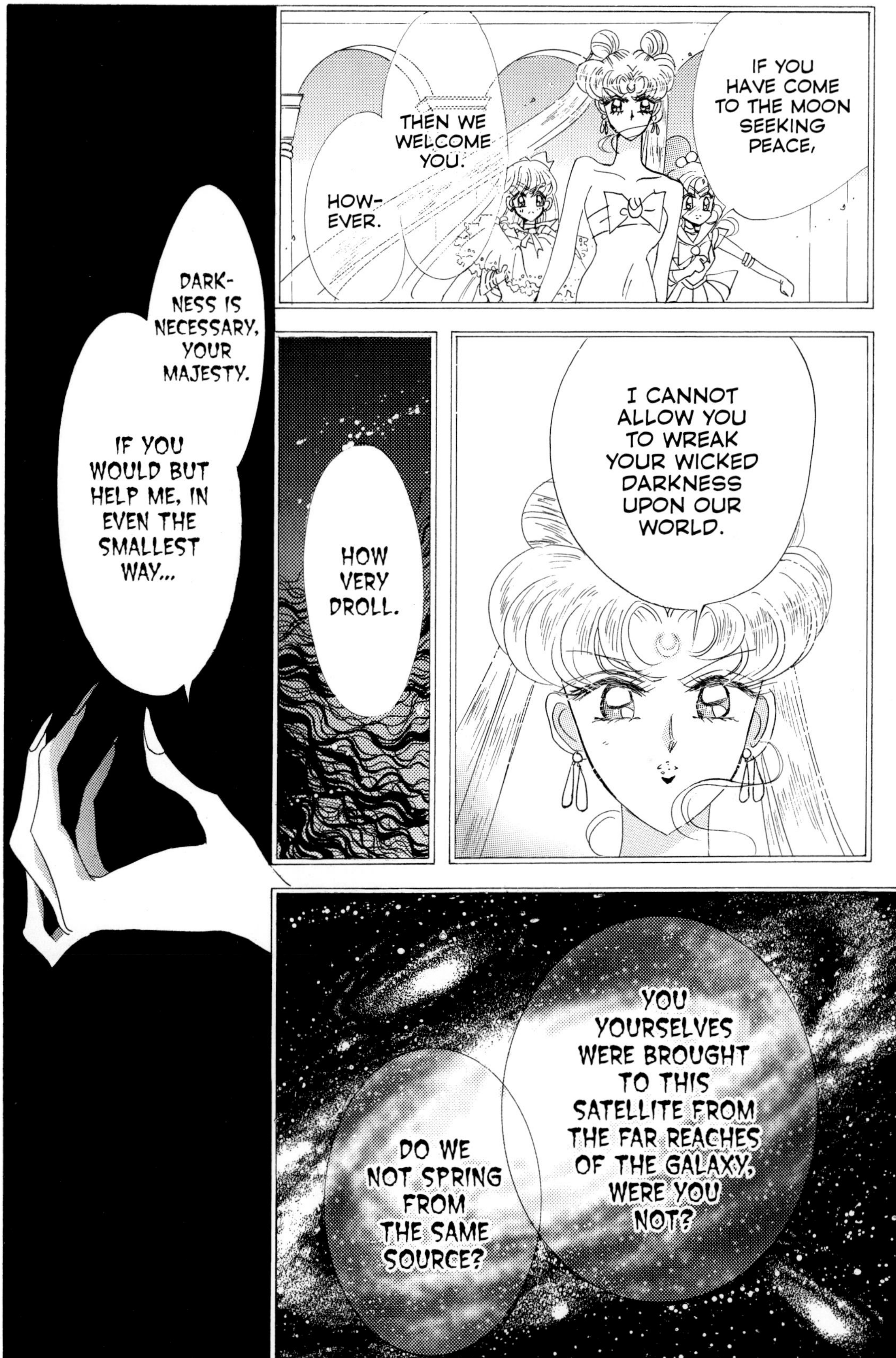
IF YOU HAVE COME TO THE MOON SEEKING PEACE,
THEN WE WELCOME YOU.
HOW-EVER.
I CANNOT ALLOW YOU TO WREAK YOUR WICKED DARKNESS UPON OUR WORLD.
HOW VERY DROLL.
YOU YOURSELVES WERE BROUGHT TO THIS SATELLITE FROM THE FAR REACHES OF THE GALAXY, WERE YOU NOT?
DO WE NOT SPRING FROM THE SAME SOURCE?
DARK-NESS IS NECESSARY, YOUR MAJESTY.
IF YOU WOULD BUT HELP ME, IN EVEN THE SMALLEST WAY...

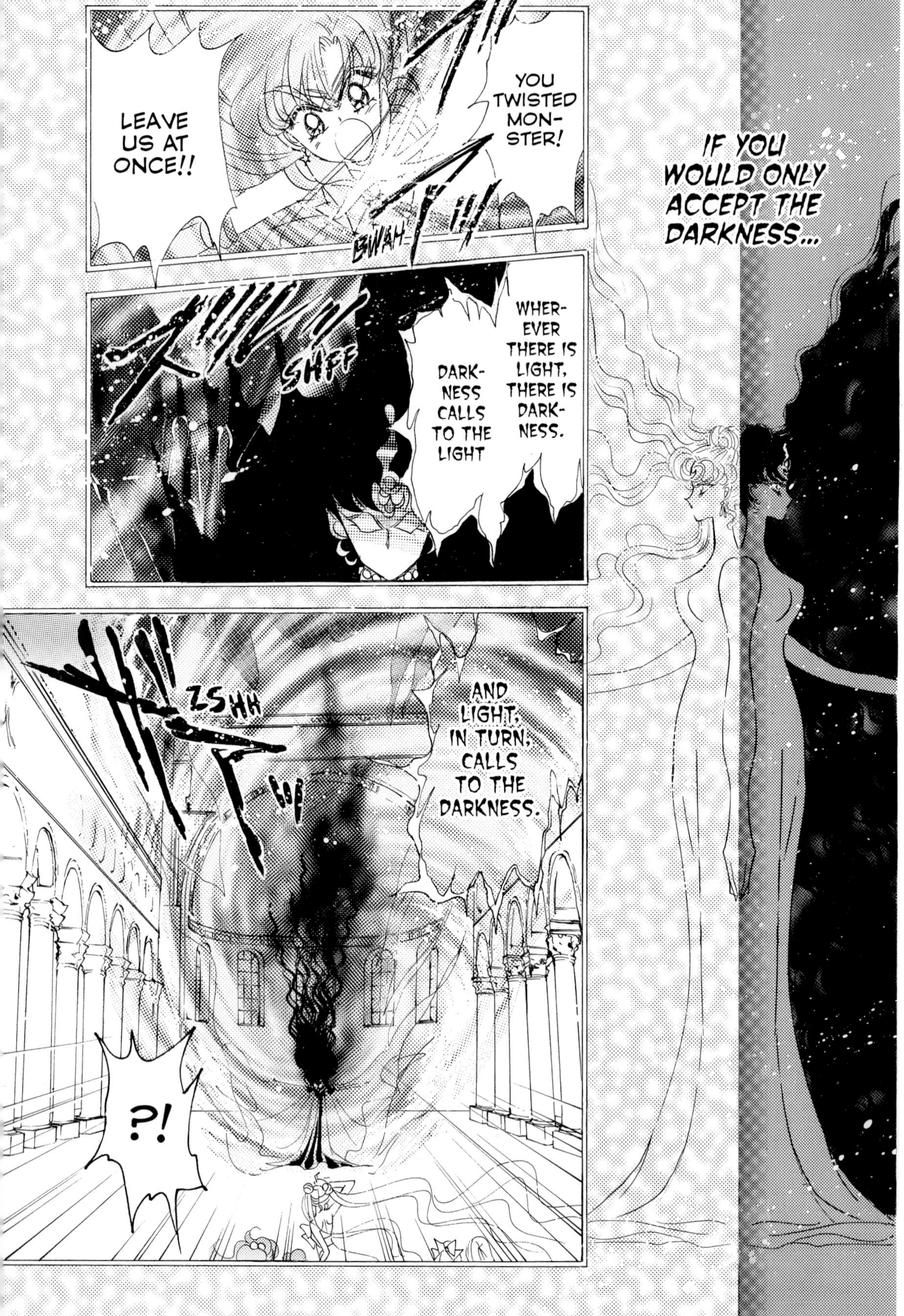
IF YOU WOULD ONLY ACCEPT THE DARKNESS...
YOU TWISTED MONSTER!
LEAVE US AT ONCE!!
BWAH
WHEREVER THERE IS LIGHT, THERE IS DARKNESS.
DARKNESS CALLS TO THE LIGHT
SHFF
AND LIGHT, IN TURN, CALLS TO THE DARKNESS.
ZSHH
?!

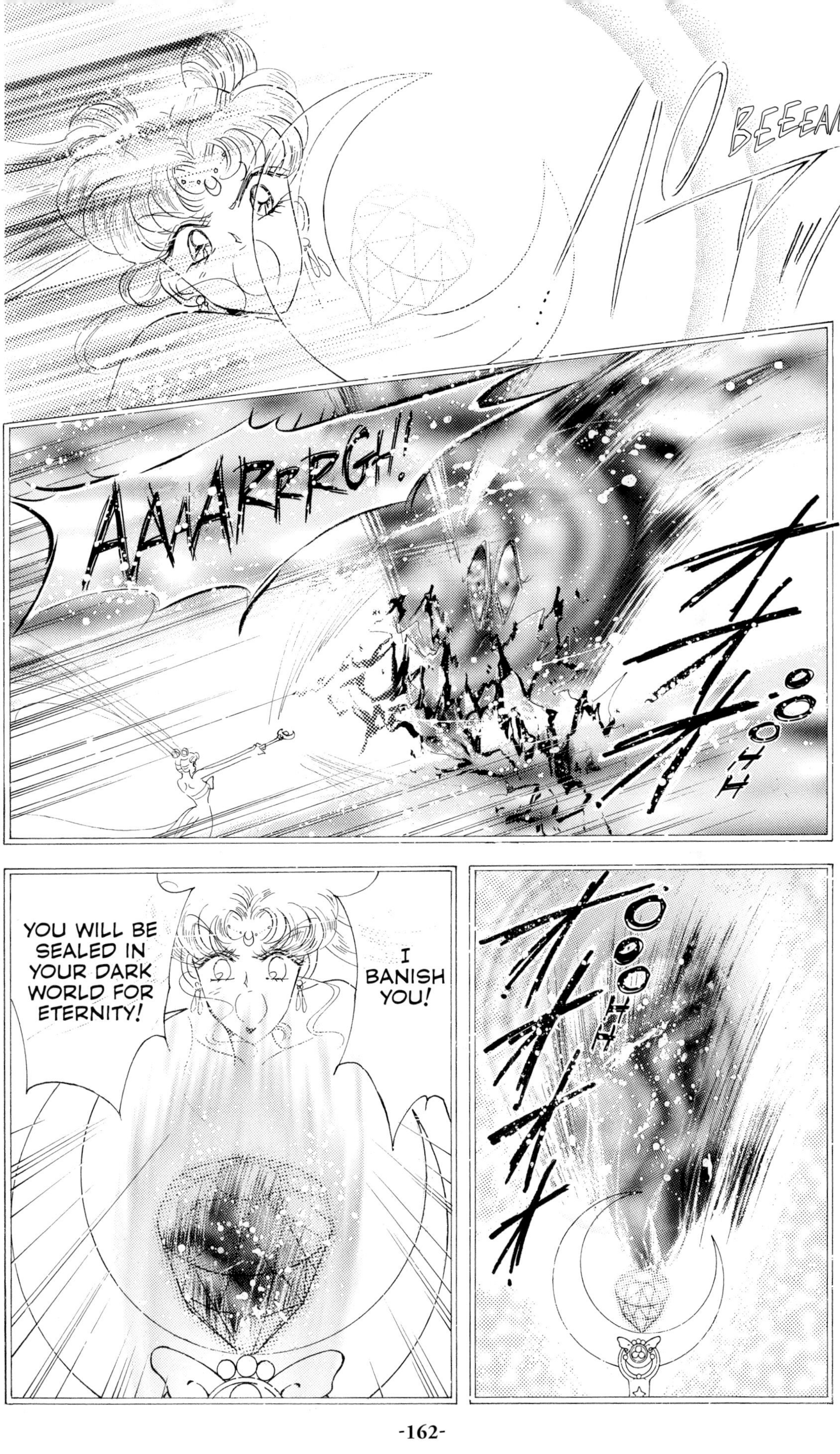
BEEEAM
OOOHH
AAAARRRGH!
OOOHH
I BANISH YOU!
YOU WILL BE SEALED IN YOUR DARK WORLD FOR ETERNITY!

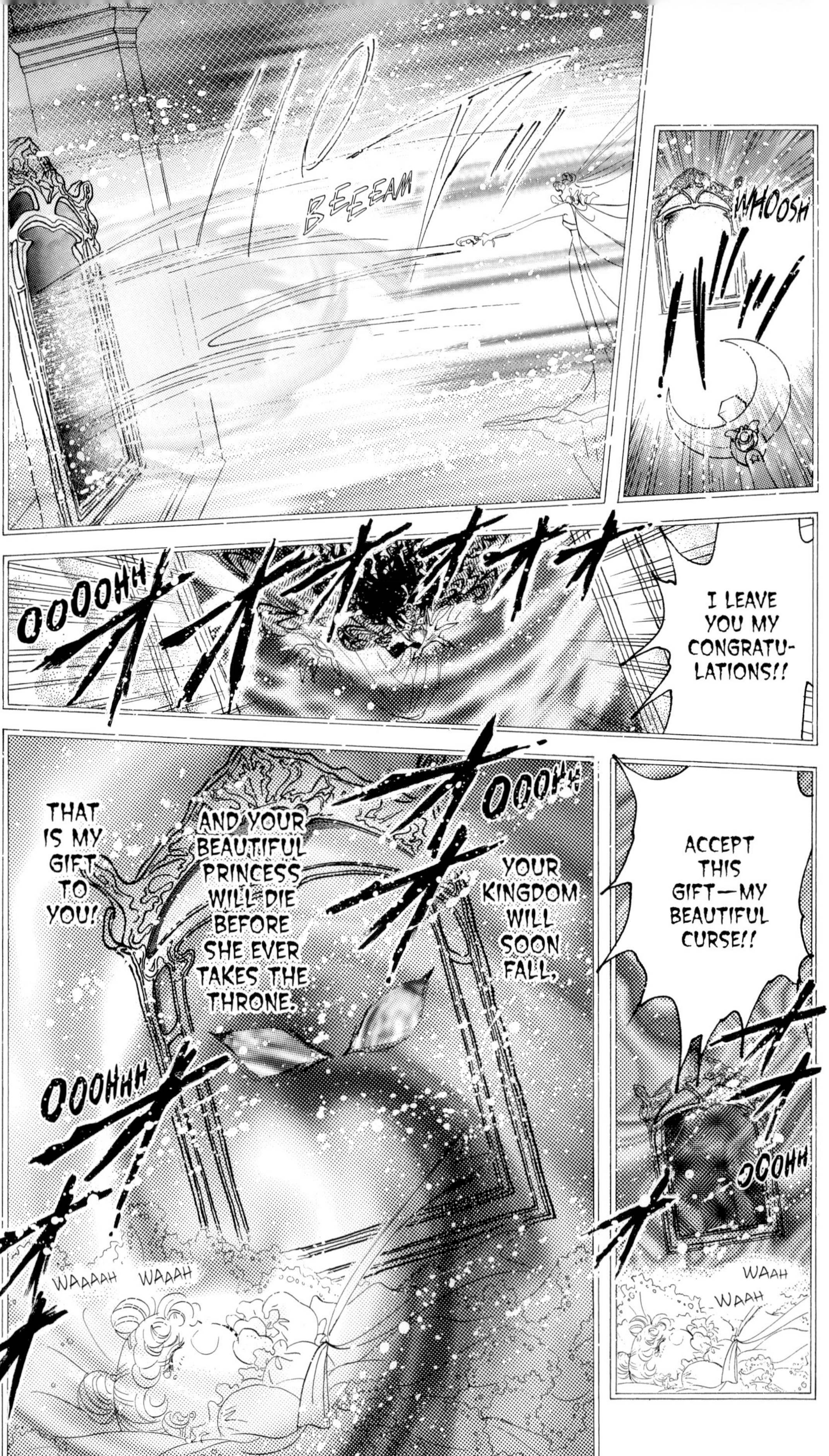

WHOOSH
BEEEAM
I LEAVE YOU MY CONGRATULATIONS!!
OOOOHH
ACCEPT THIS GIFT—MY BEAUTIFUL CURSE!!
OOOHH
WAAH
WAAH
YOUR KINGDOM WILL SOON FALL,
AND YOUR BEAUTIFUL PRINCESS WILL DIE BEFORE SHE EVER TAKES THE THRONE.
THAT IS MY GIFT TO YOU!
OOOHH
OOOHHH
WAAAAH
WAAH

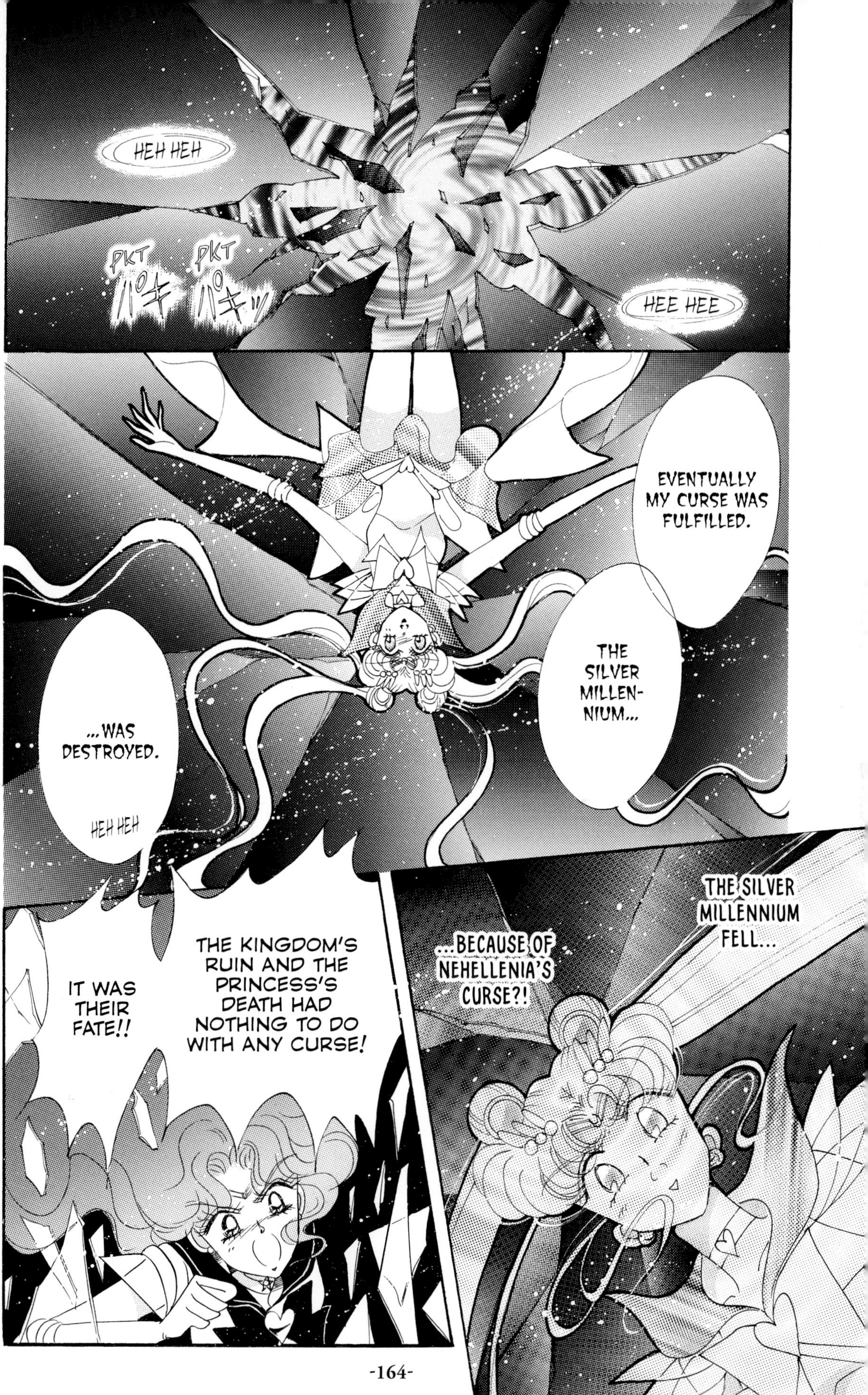
HEH HEH
PKT パキ
PKT パキッ
HEE HEE
EVENTUALLY MY CURSE WAS FULFILLED.
THE SILVER MILLEN-NIUM...
...WAS DESTROYED.
HEH HEH
THE SILVER MILLENNIUM FELL...
...BECAUSE OF NEHELLENIA'S CURSE?!
THE KINGDOM'S RUIN AND THE PRINCESS'S DEATH HAD NOTHING TO DO WITH ANY CURSE!
IT WAS THEIR FATE!!

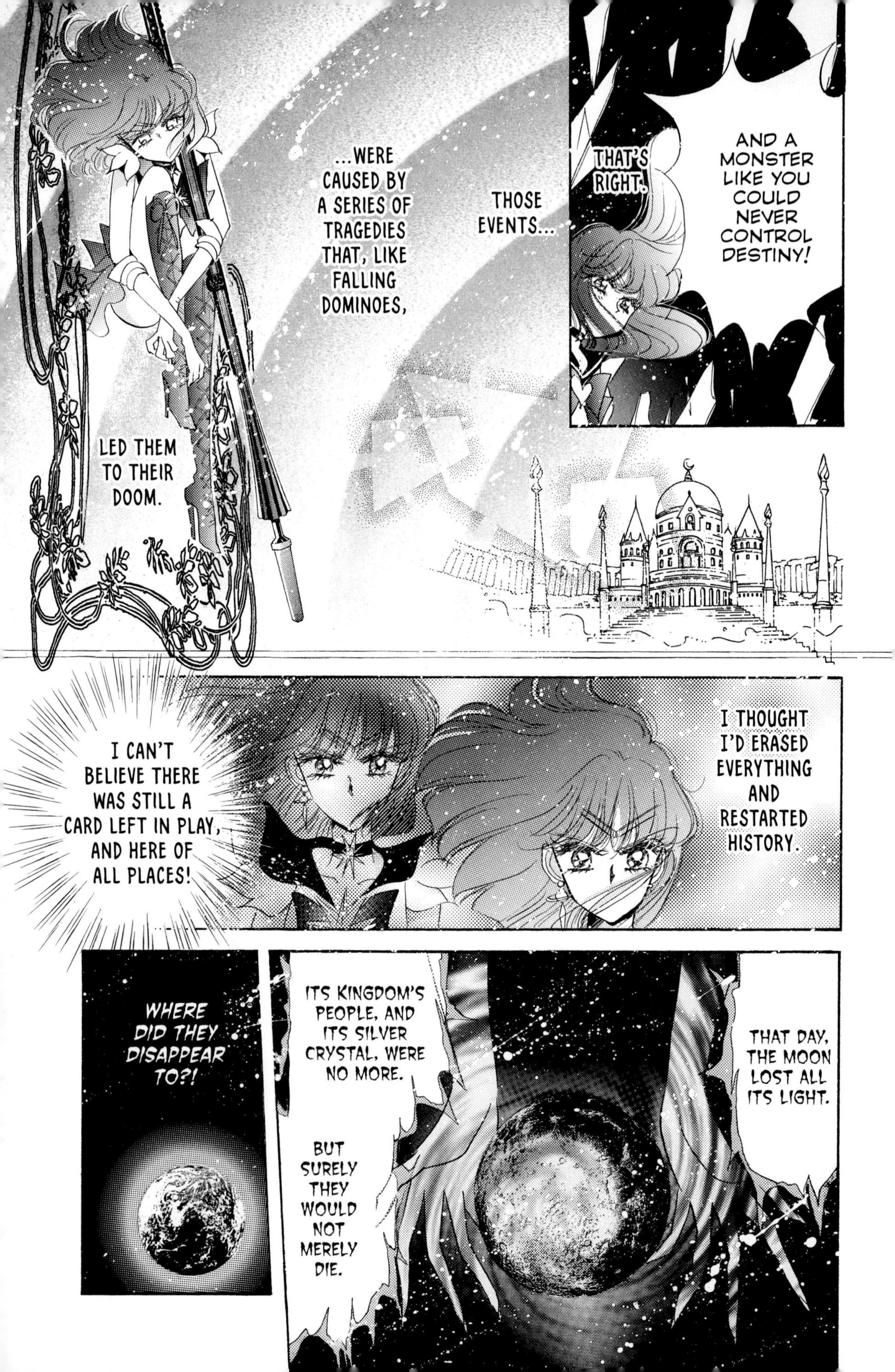
AND A MONSTER LIKE YOU COULD NEVER CONTROL DESTINY!
THAT'S RIGHT.
THOSE EVENTS...
...WERE CAUSED BY A SERIES OF TRAGEDIES THAT, LIKE FALLING DOMINOES,
LED THEM TO THEIR DOOM.
I THOUGHT I'D ERASED EVERYTHING AND RESTARTED HISTORY.
I CAN'T BELIEVE THERE WAS STILL A CARD LEFT IN PLAY, AND HERE OF ALL PLACES!
THAT DAY, THE MOON LOST ALL ITS LIGHT.
ITS KINGDOM'S PEOPLE, AND ITS SILVER CRYSTAL, WERE NO MORE.
BUT SURELY THEY WOULD NOT MERELY DIE.
WHERE DID THEY DISAPPEAR TO?!

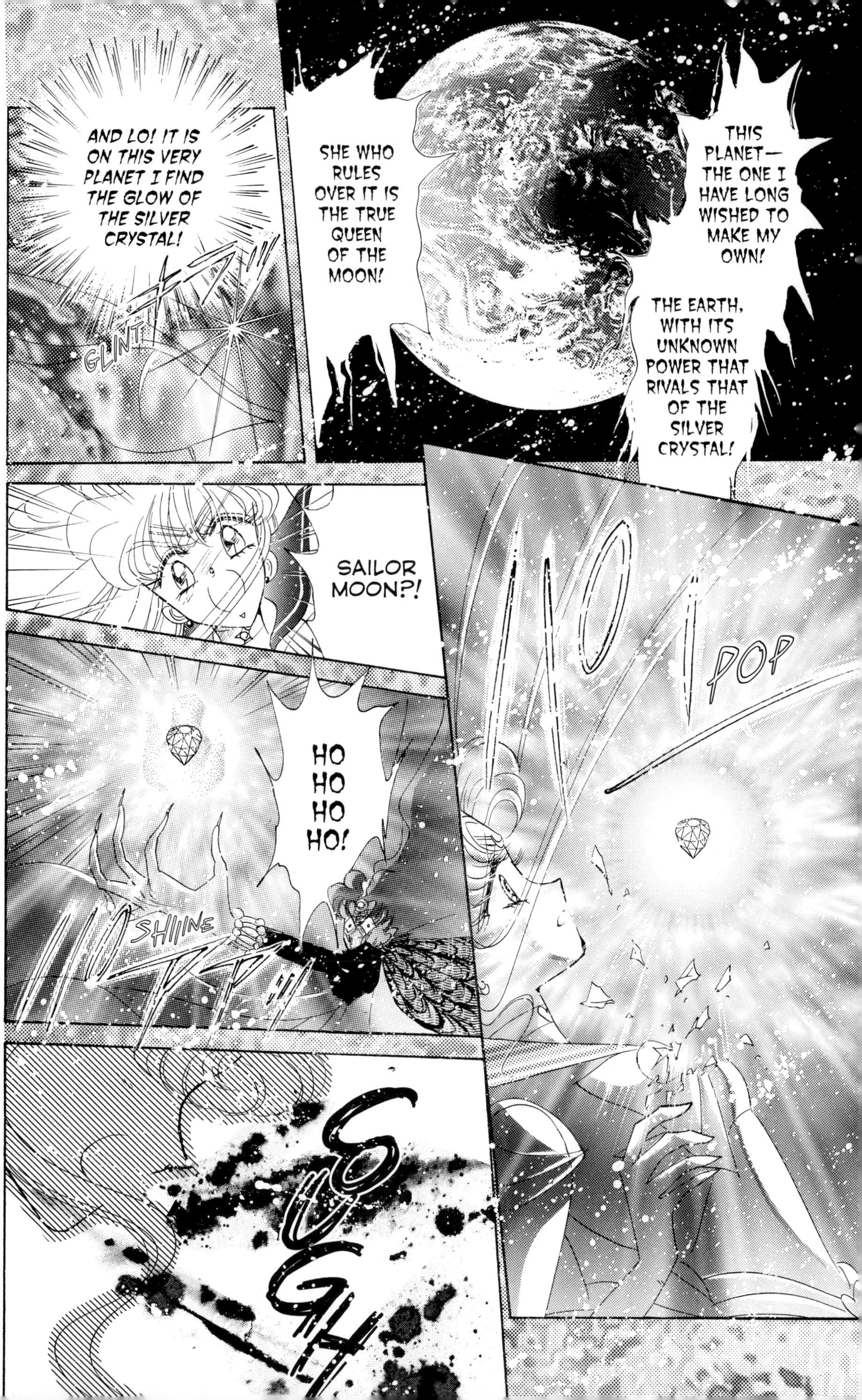
THIS PLANET—THE ONE I HAVE LONG WISHED TO MAKE MY OWN!
THE EARTH, WITH ITS UNKNOWN POWER THAT RIVALS THAT OF THE SILVER CRYSTAL!
SHE WHO RULES OVER IT IS THE TRUE QUEEN OF THE MOON!
AND LO! IT IS ON THIS VERY PLANET I FIND THE GLOW OF THE SILVER CRYSTAL!
GLINT
POP
SAILOR MOON?!
HO HO HO HO!
SHIIINE

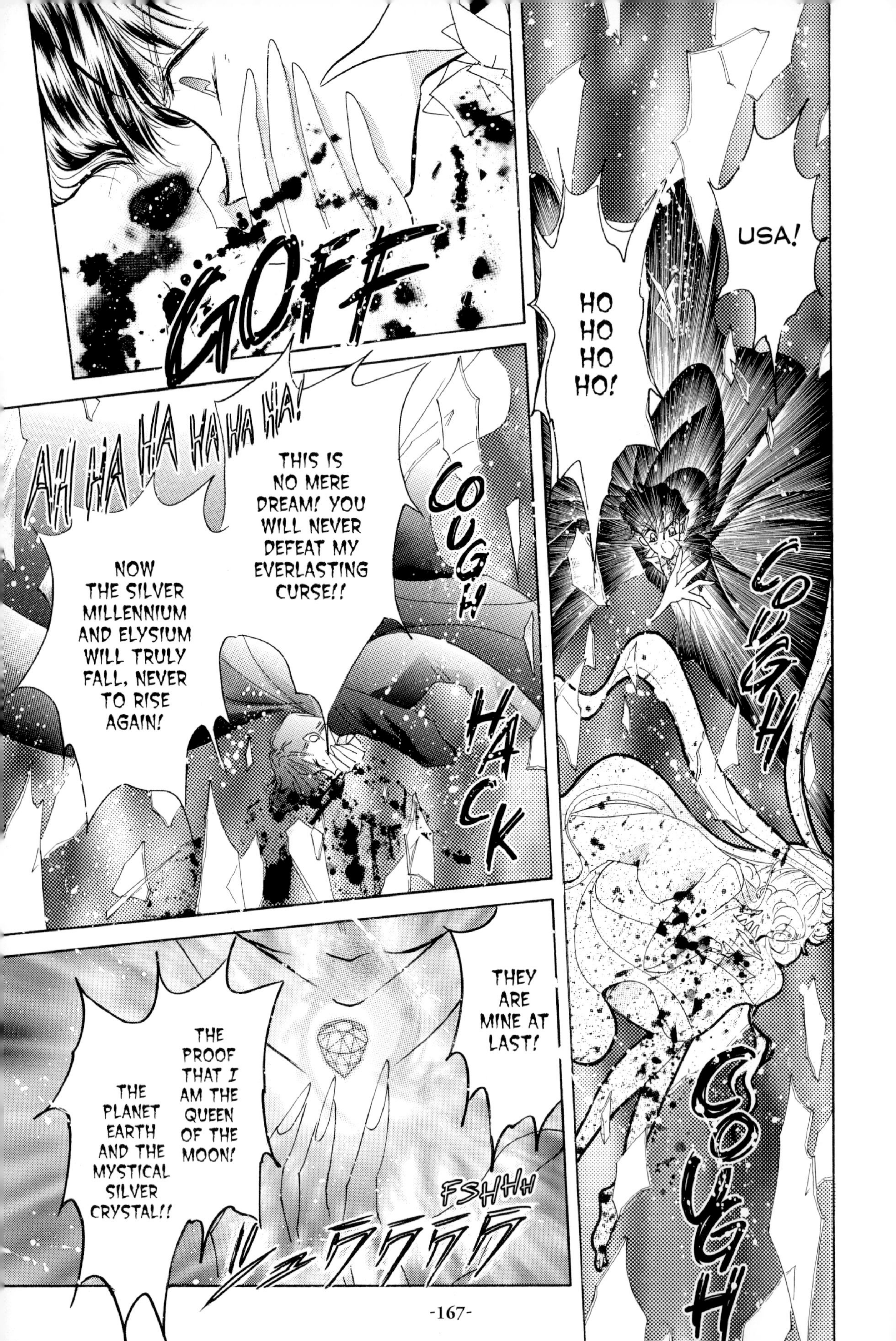
USA!
HO HO HO HO!
COUGH
COUGH
GOFF
COUGH
THIS IS NO MERE DREAM! YOU WILL NEVER DEFEAT MY EVERLASTING CURSE!!
AH HA HA HA HA HA!
NOW THE SILVER MILLENNIUM AND ELYSIUM WILL TRULY FALL, NEVER TO RISE AGAIN!
HACK
THEY ARE MINE AT LAST!
THE PROOF THAT I AM THE QUEEN OF THE MOON!
THE PLANET EARTH AND THE MYSTICAL SILVER CRYSTAL!!
FSHHH

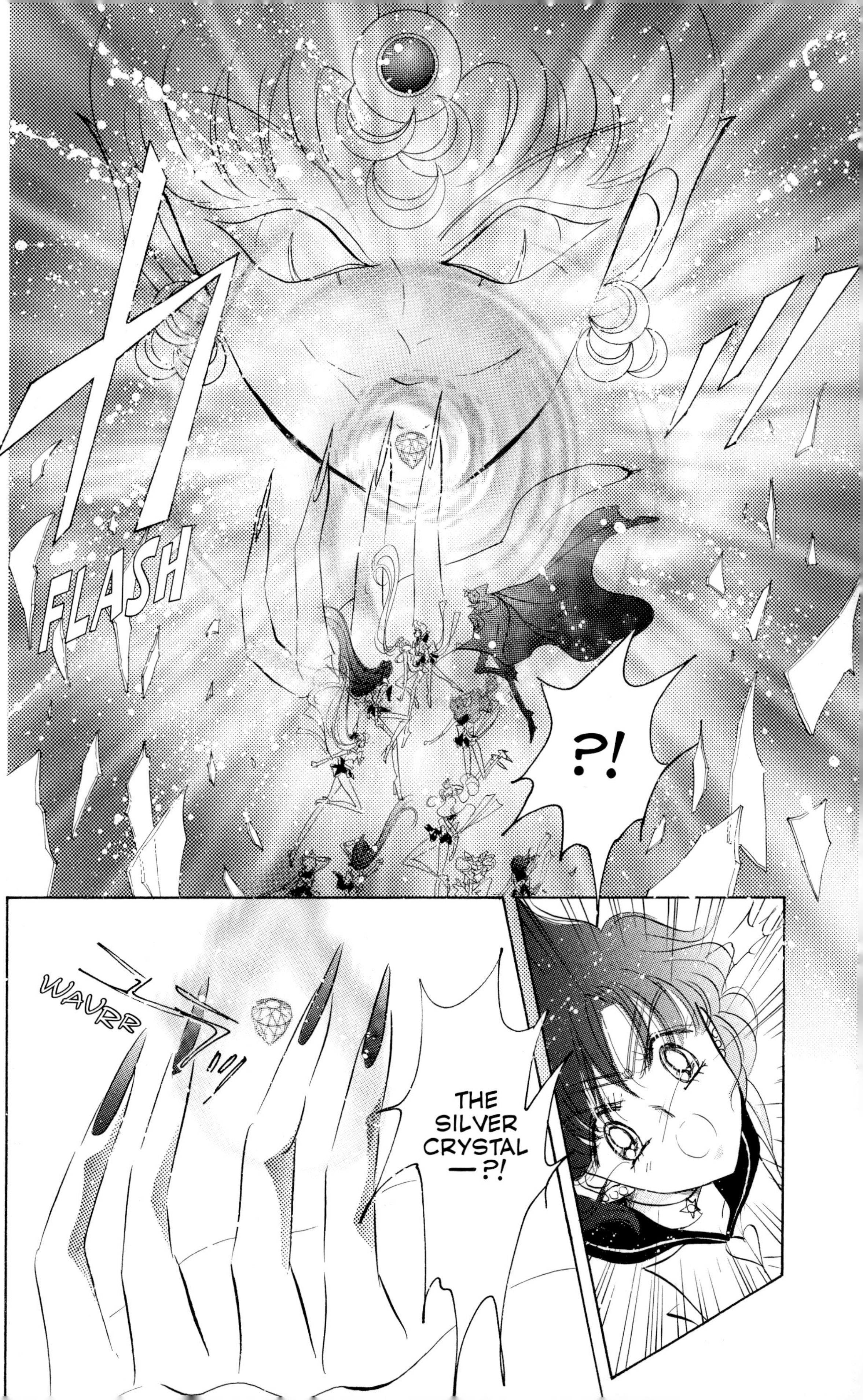
FLASH
?!
WAURR
THE SILVER CRYSTAL—?!

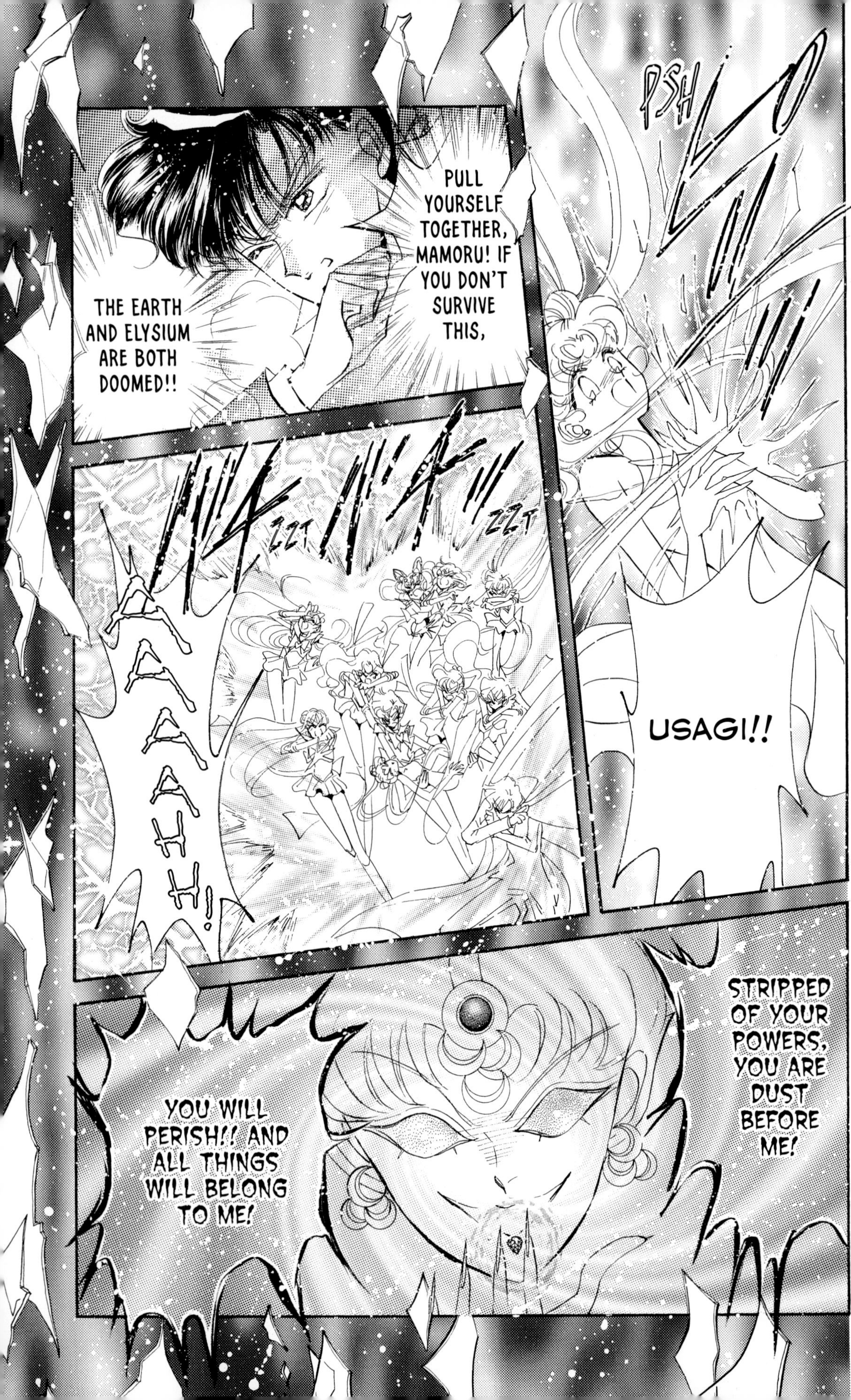
PSH
USAGI!!
PULL YOURSELF TOGETHER, MAMORU! IF YOU DON'T SURVIVE THIS,
THE EARTH AND ELYSIUM ARE BOTH DOOMED!!
ZZT
ZZT
AAAAHH!
STRIPPED OF YOUR POWERS, YOU ARE DUST BEFORE ME!
YOU WILL PERISH!! AND ALL THINGS WILL BELONG TO ME!

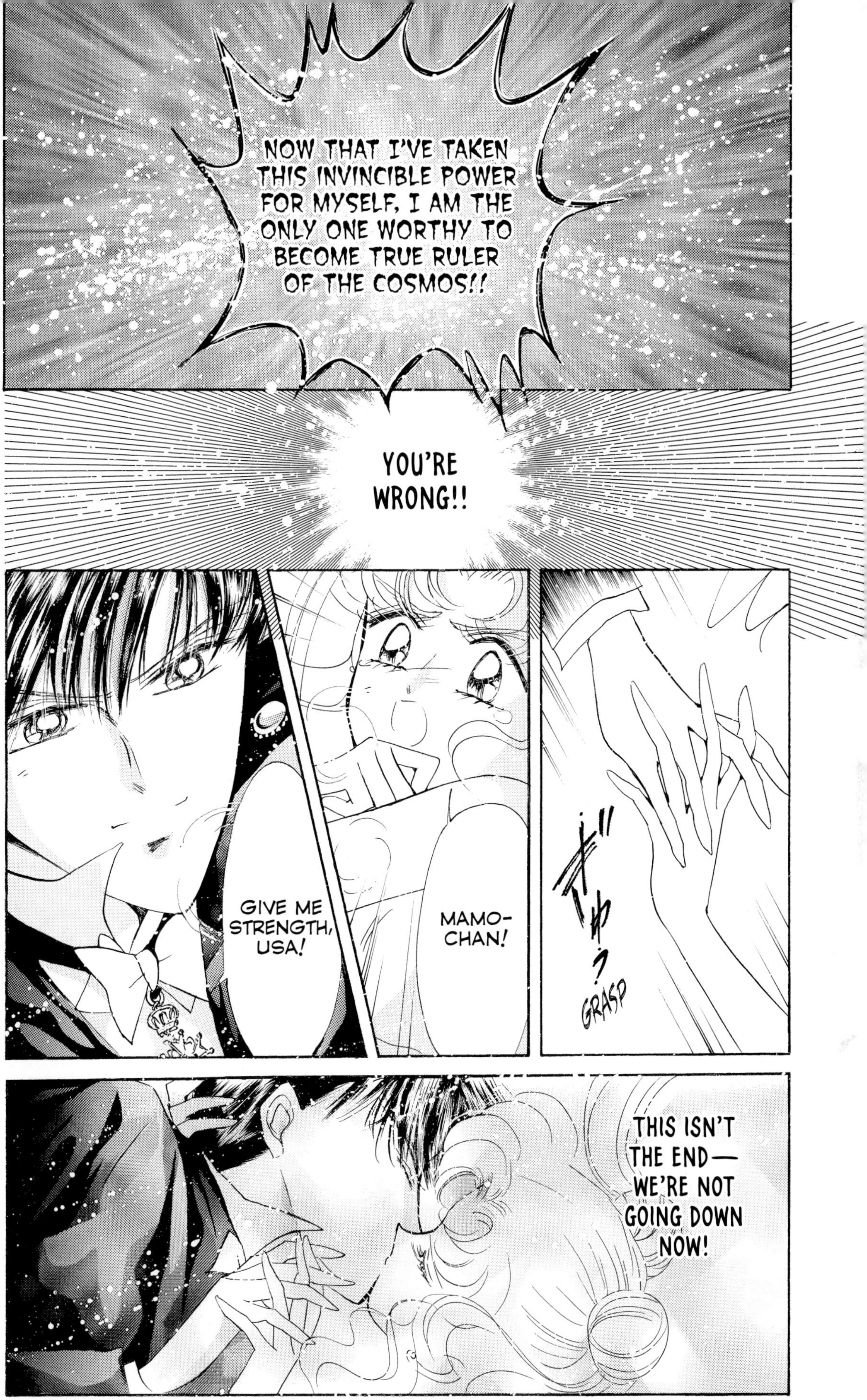
NOW THAT I'VE TAKEN THIS INVINCIBLE POWER FOR MYSELF, I AM THE ONLY ONE WORTHY TO BECOME TRUE RULER OF THE COSMOS!!
YOU'RE WRONG!!
GRASP
MAMO-CHAN!
GIVE ME STRENGTH, USA!
THIS ISN'T THE END— WE'RE NOT GOING DOWN NOW!

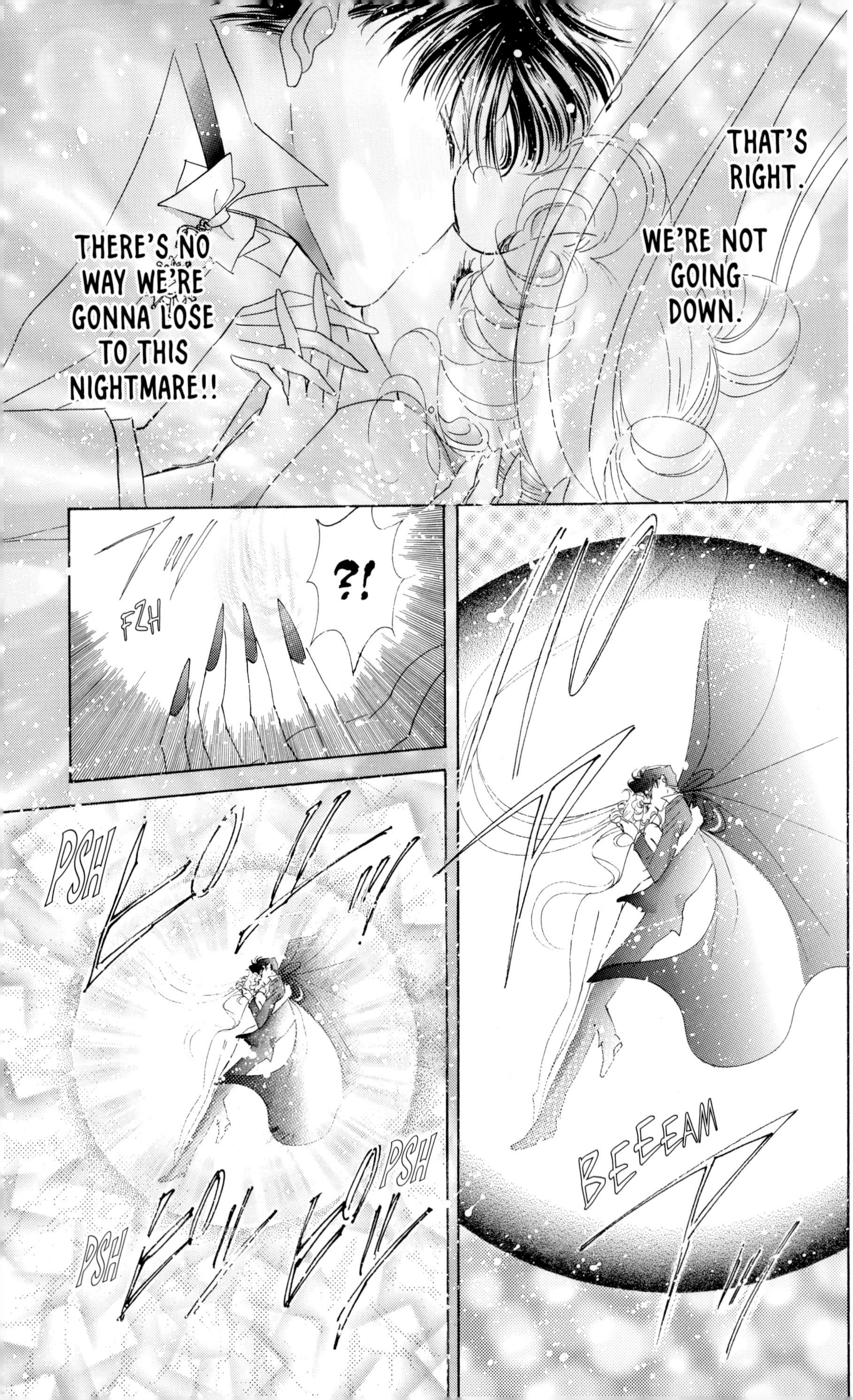
THAT'S RIGHT.
WE'RE NOT GOING DOWN.
THERE'S NO WAY WE'RE GONNA LOSE TO THIS NIGHTMARE!!
BEEEAM
FZH
?!
PSH
PSH
PSH

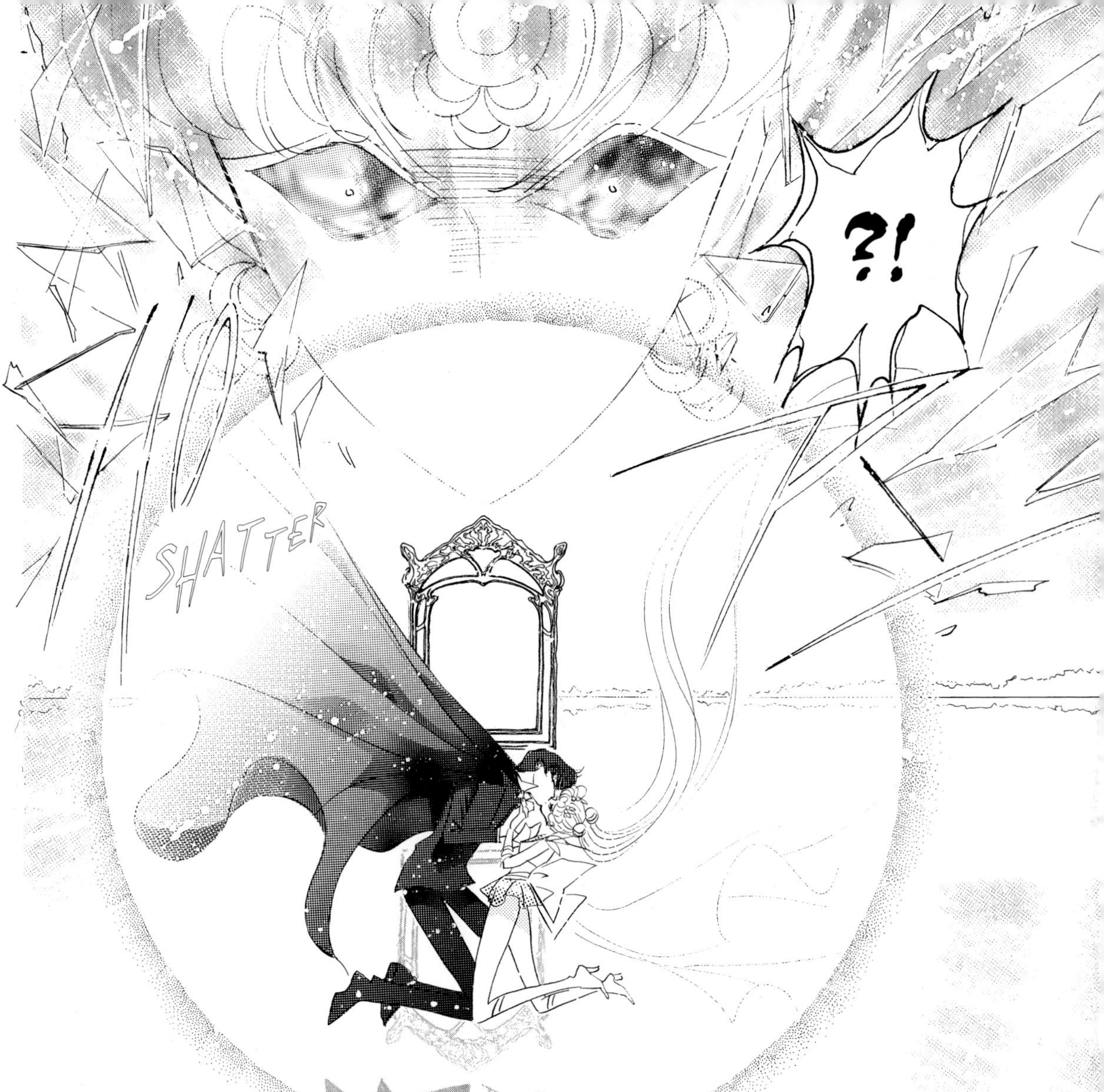
?!
SHATTER
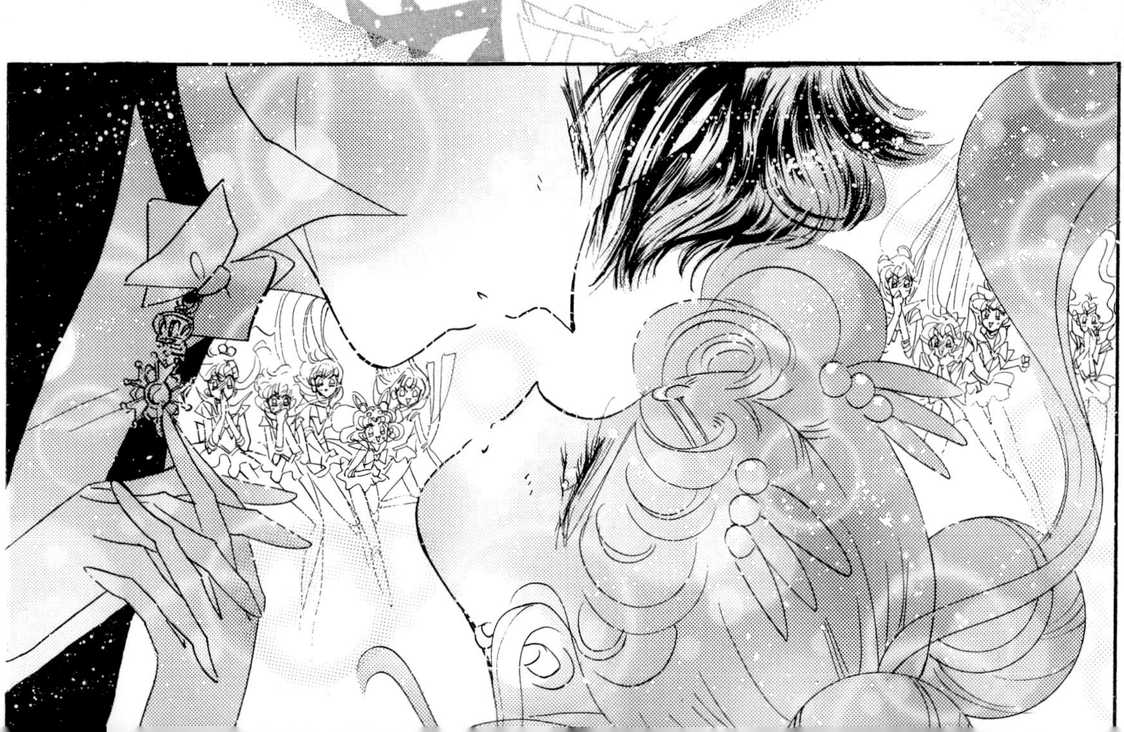

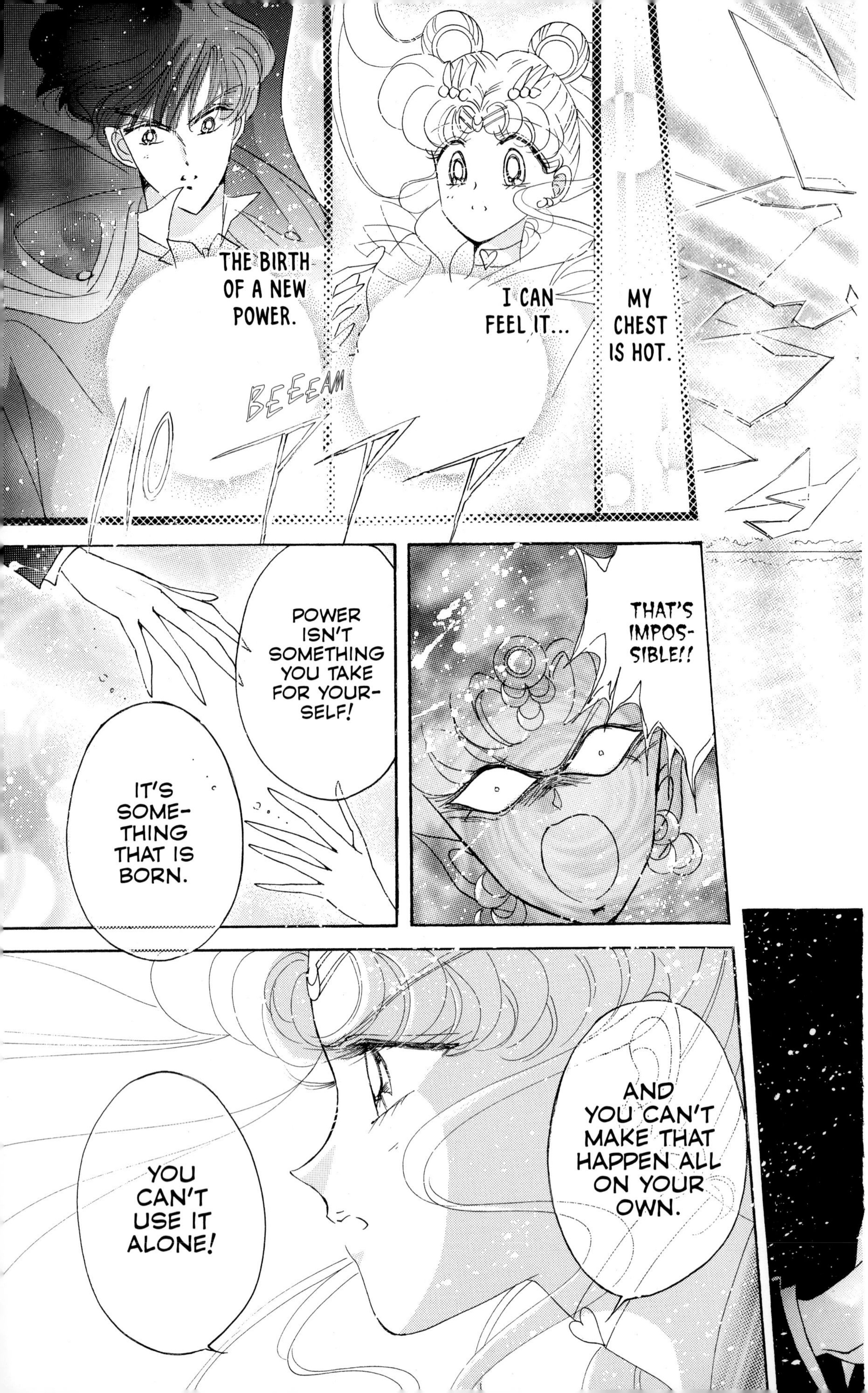
MY CHEST IS HOT.
I CAN FEEL IT...
BEEEAM
THE BIRTH OF A NEW POWER.
THAT'S IMPOSSIBLE!!
POWER ISN'T SOMETHING YOU TAKE FOR YOURSELF!
IT'S SOMETHING THAT IS BORN.
AND YOU CAN'T MAKE THAT HAPPEN ALL ON YOUR OWN.
YOU CAN'T USE IT ALONE!

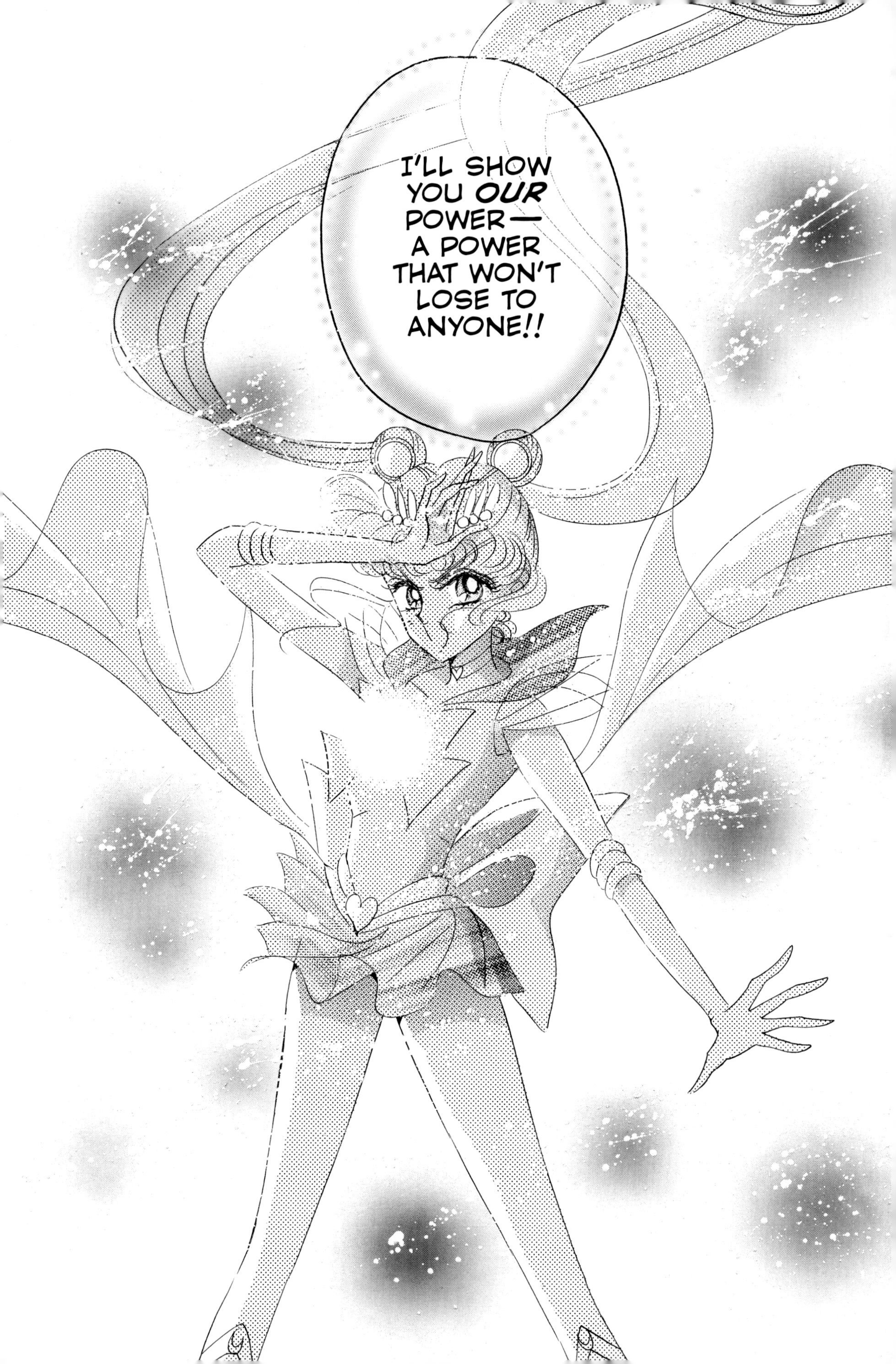
I'LL SHOW YOU OUR POWER— A POWER THAT WON'T LOSE TO ANYONE!!

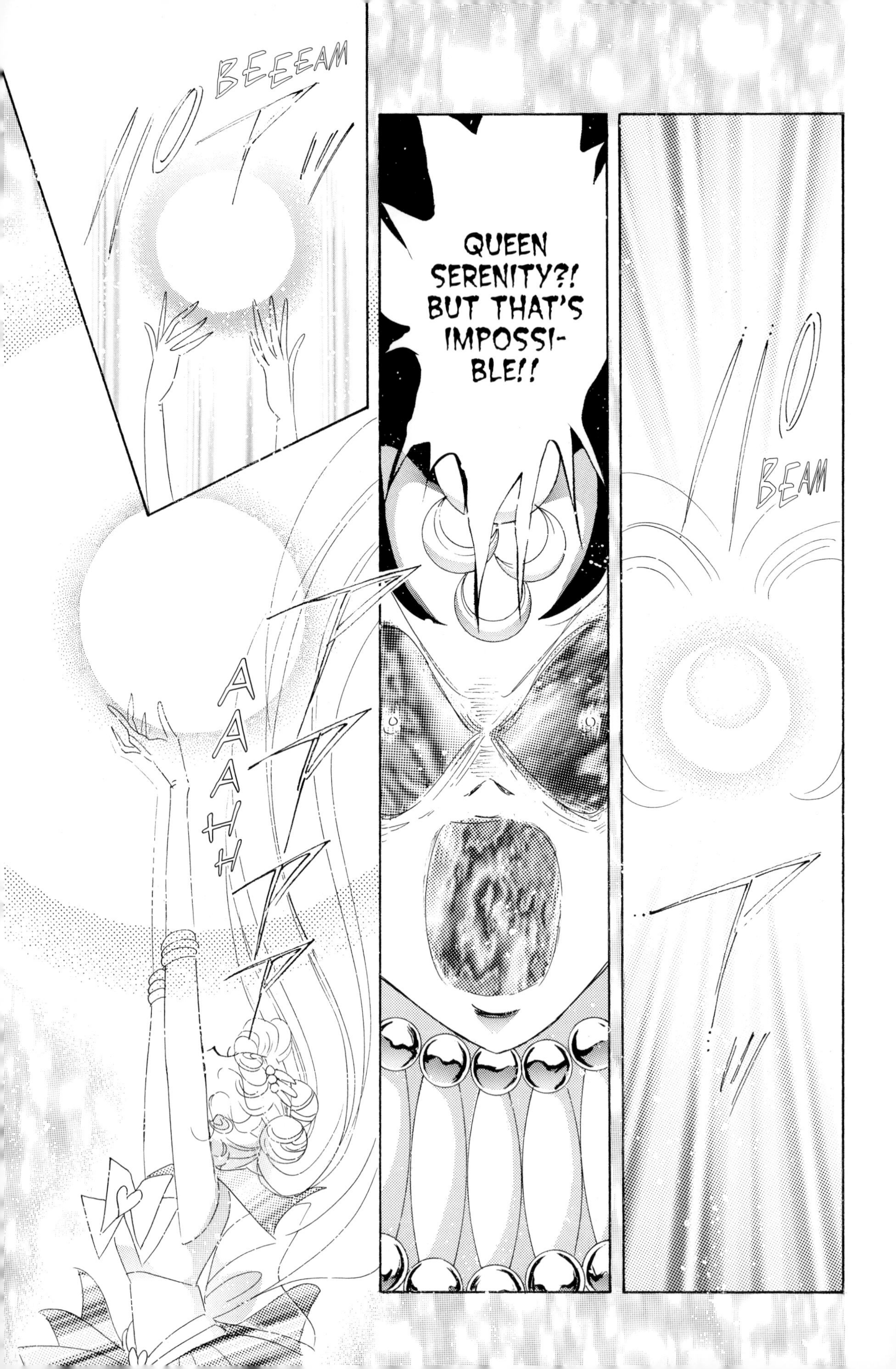
BEAM
QUEEN SERENITY?! BUT THAT'S IMPOSSI-BLE!!
BEEEEAM
AAAAHH

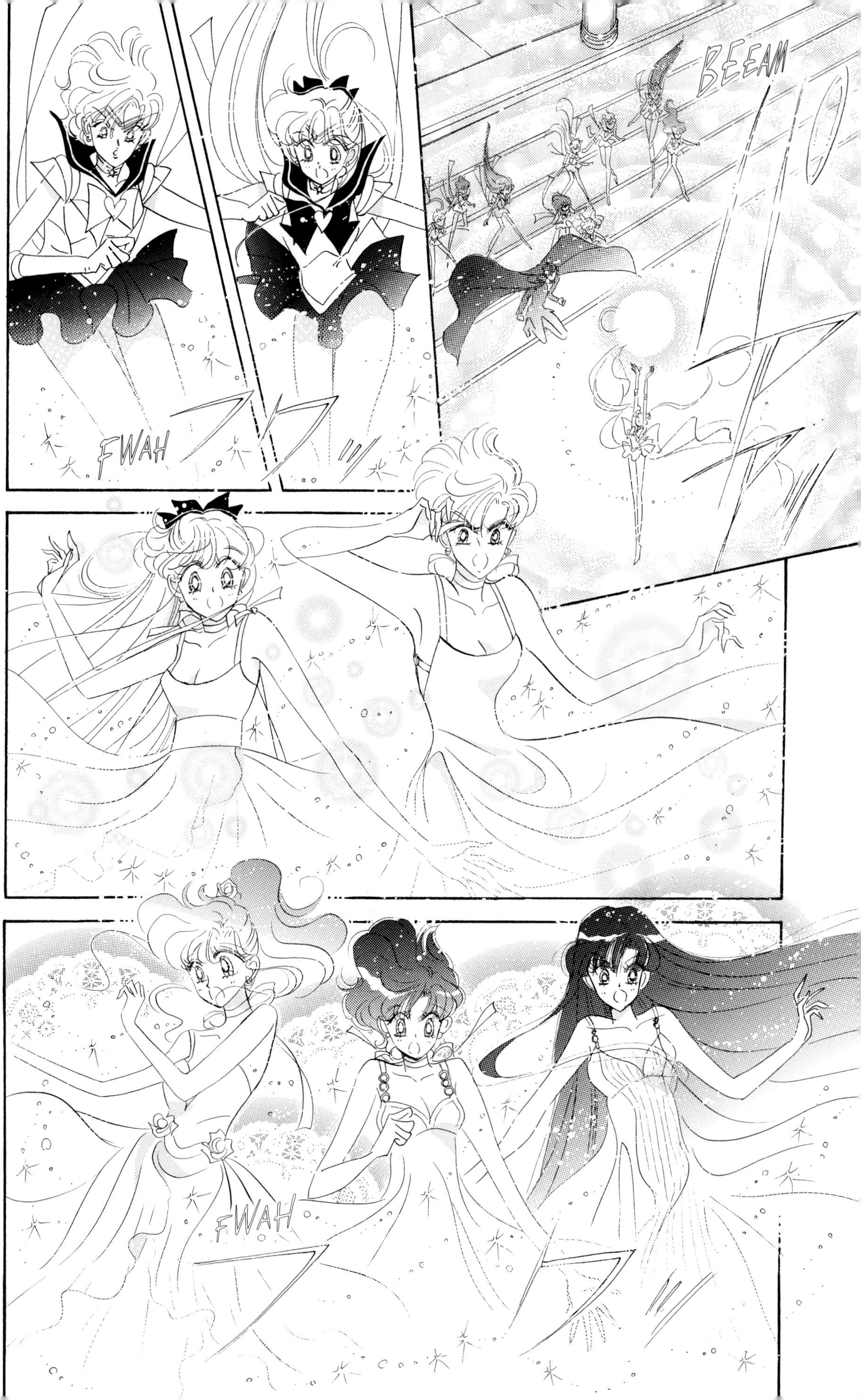
BEEAM
FWAH
FWAH

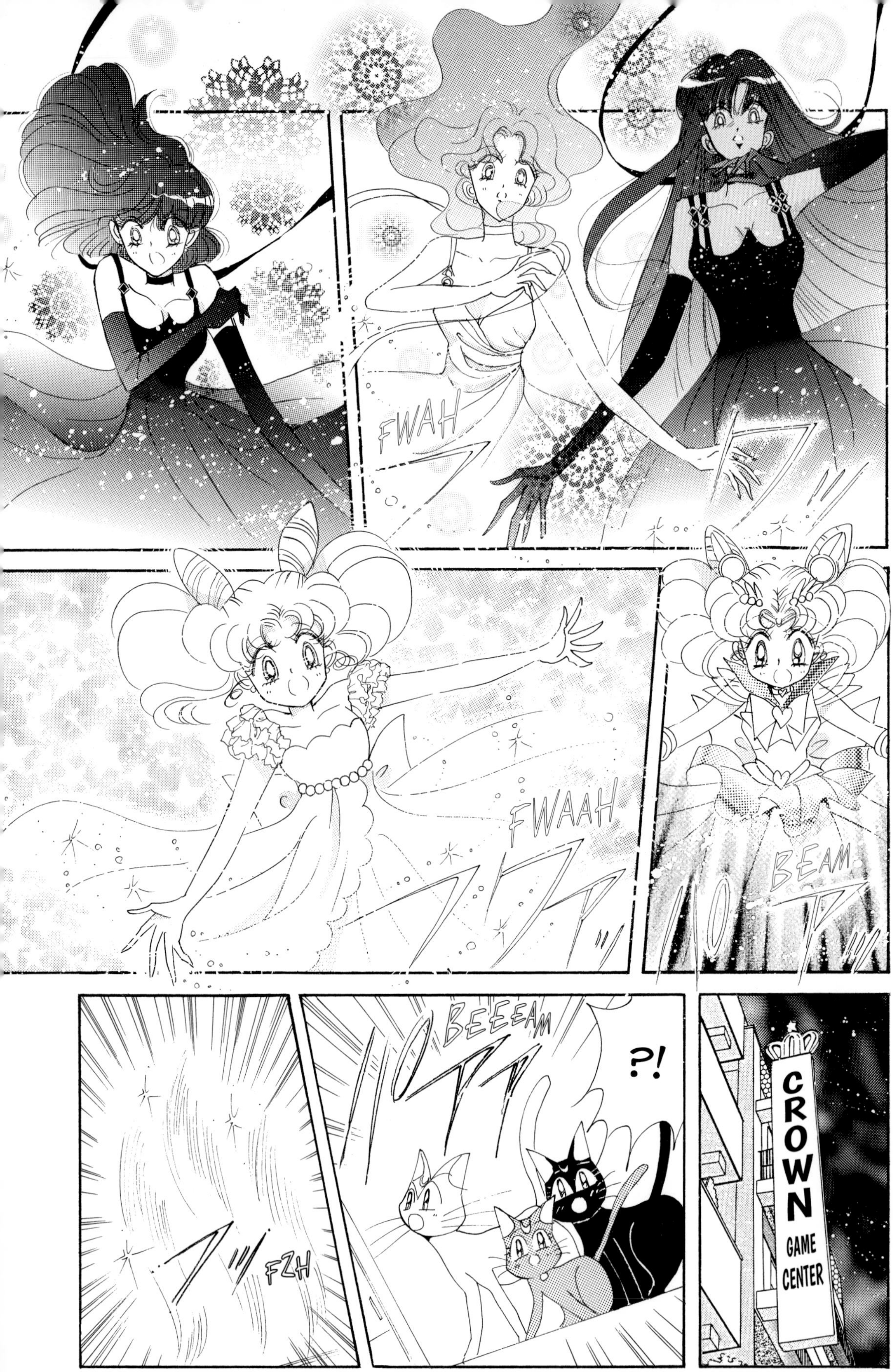
FWAH
BEAM
FWAAH
CROWN
GAME CENTER
?!
BEEEAM
FZH

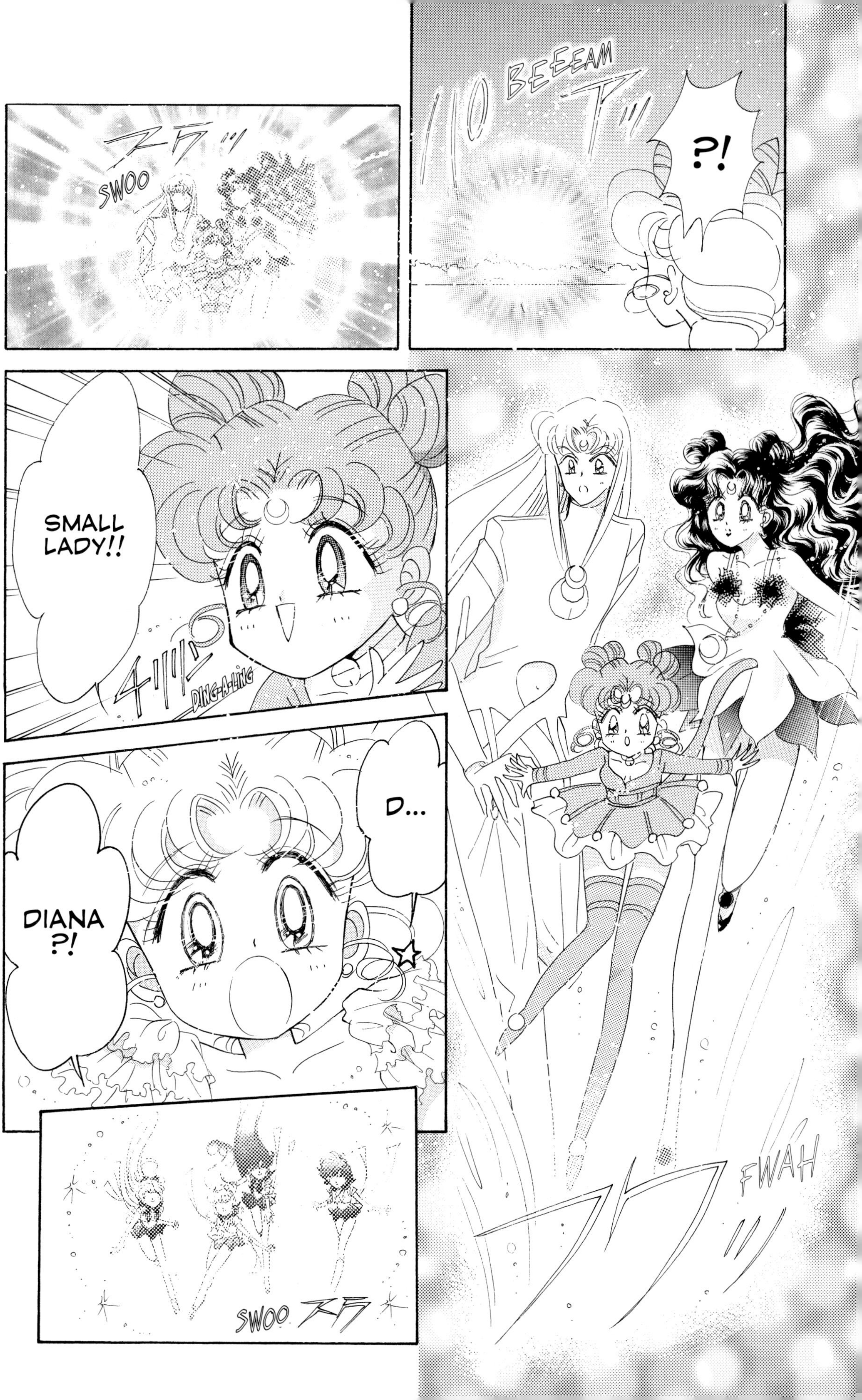
BEEEAM
?!
SWOO
FWAH
SMALL LADY!!
DING-A-LING
D...
DIANA ?!
SWOO

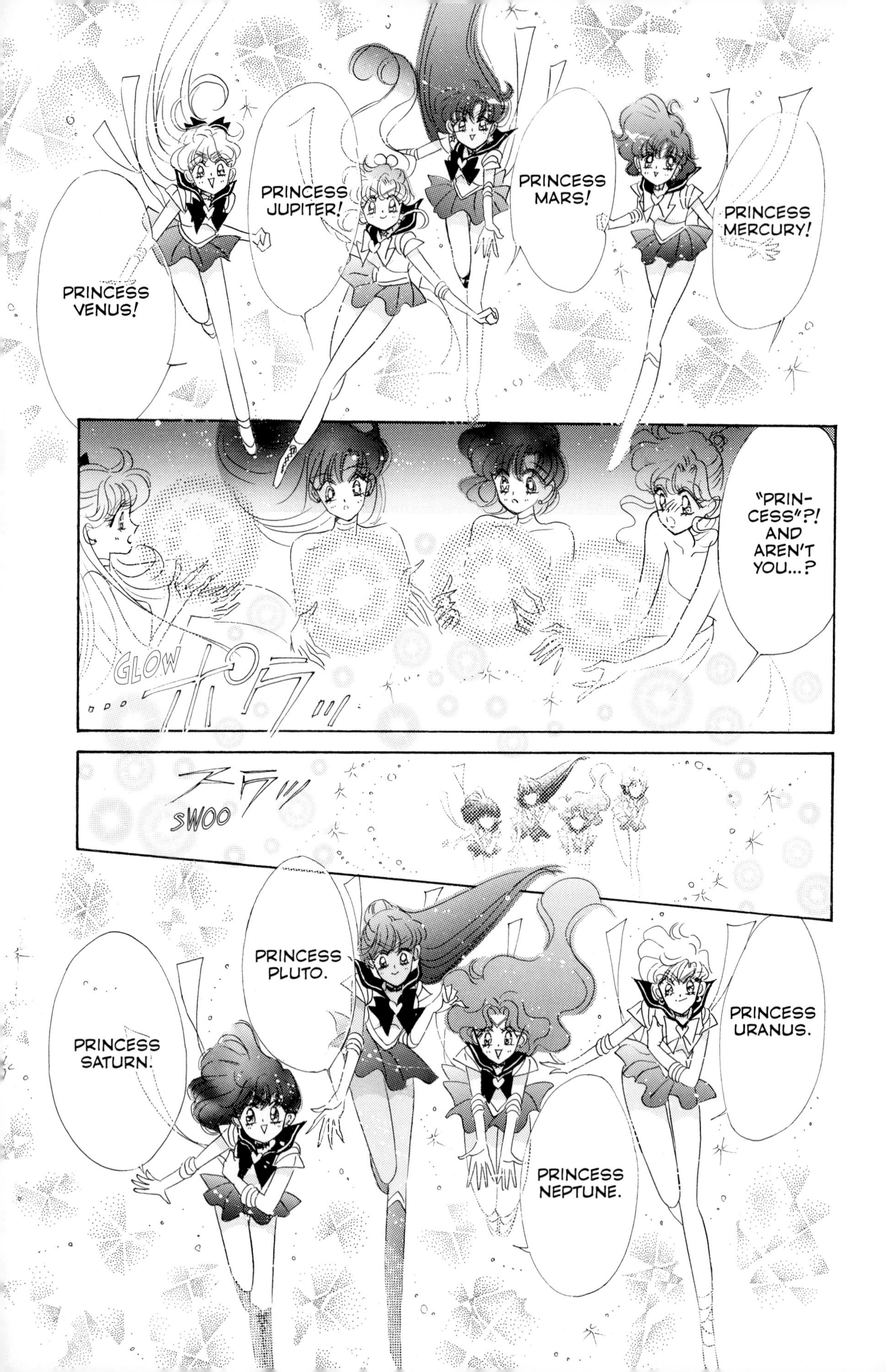

PRINCESS MERCURY!
PRINCESS MARS!
PRINCESS JUPITER!
PRINCESS VENUS!
"PRIN-CESS"?! AND AREN'T YOU...?
GLOW
SWOO
PRINCESS URANUS.
PRINCESS NEPTUNE.
PRINCESS PLUTO.
PRINCESS SATURN.

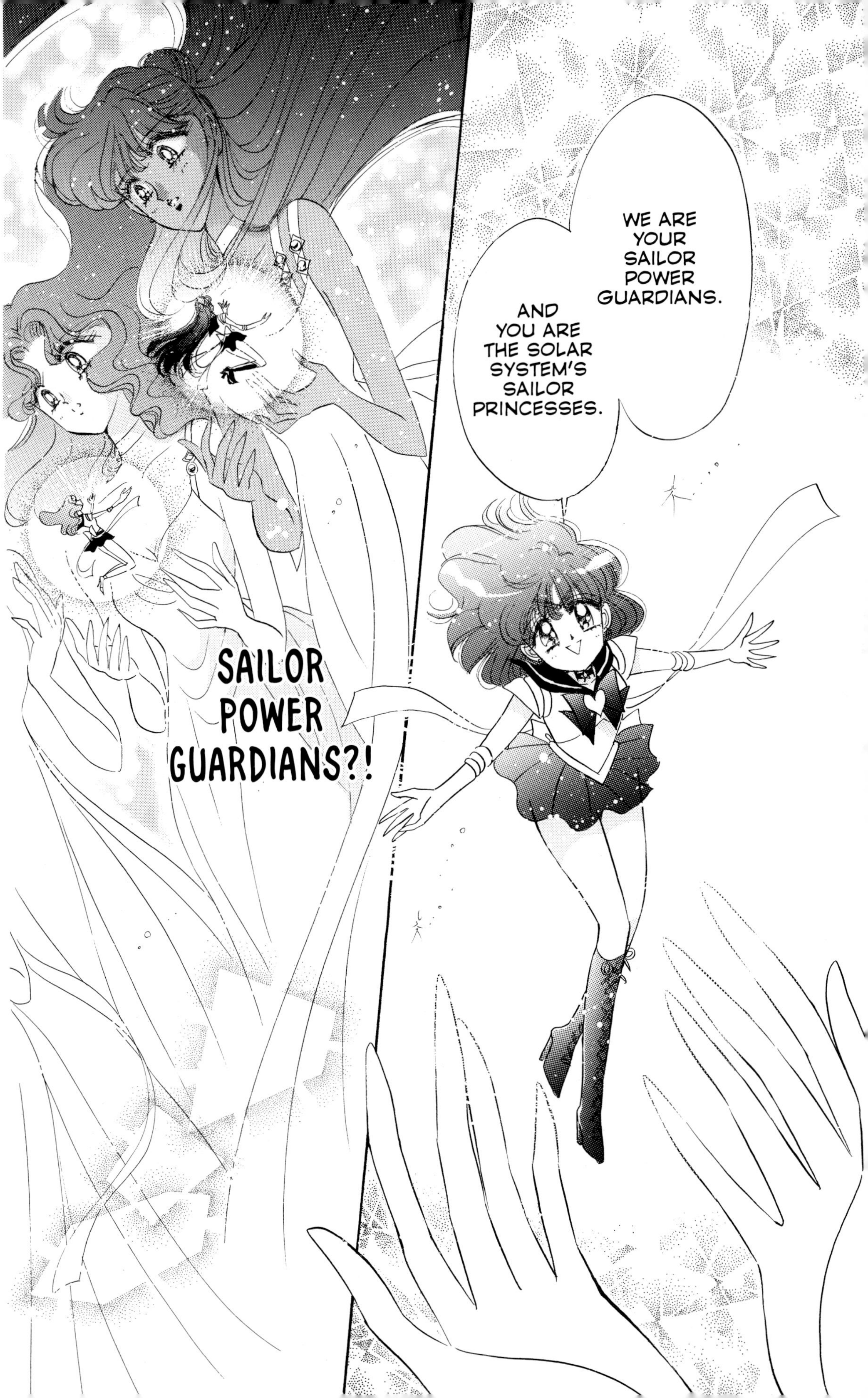
WE ARE YOUR SAILOR POWER GUARDIANS.
AND YOU ARE THE SOLAR SYSTEM'S SAILOR PRINCESSES.
SAILOR POWER GUARDIANS?!

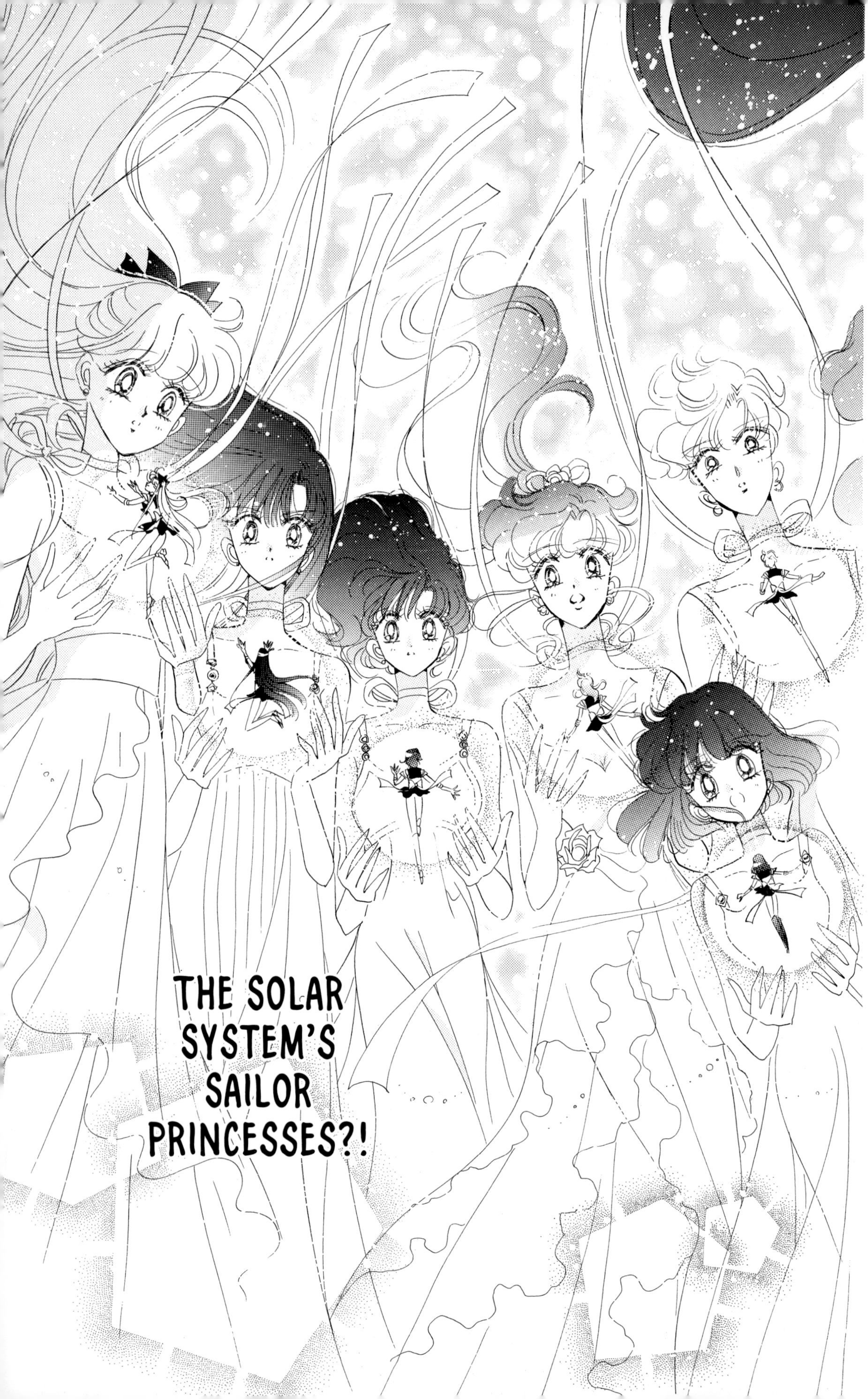
THE SOLAR SYSTEM'S SAILOR PRINCESSES?!

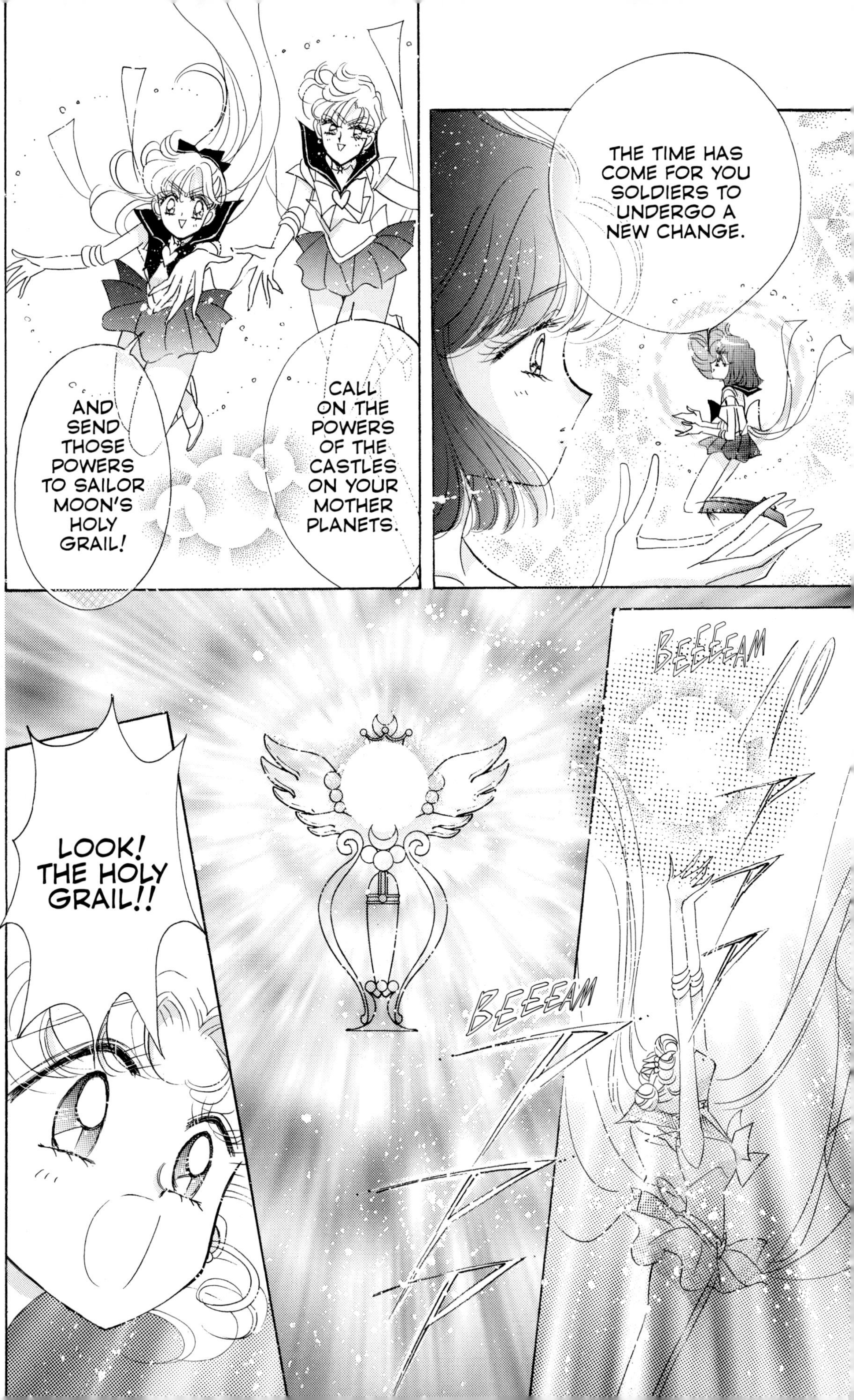
THE TIME HAS COME FOR YOU SOLDIERS TO UNDERGO A NEW CHANGE.
CALL ON THE POWERS OF THE CASTLES ON YOUR MOTHER PLANETS.
AND SEND THOSE POWERS TO SAILOR MOON'S HOLY GRAIL!
BEEEEAM
BEEEEAM
LOOK! THE HOLY GRAIL!!

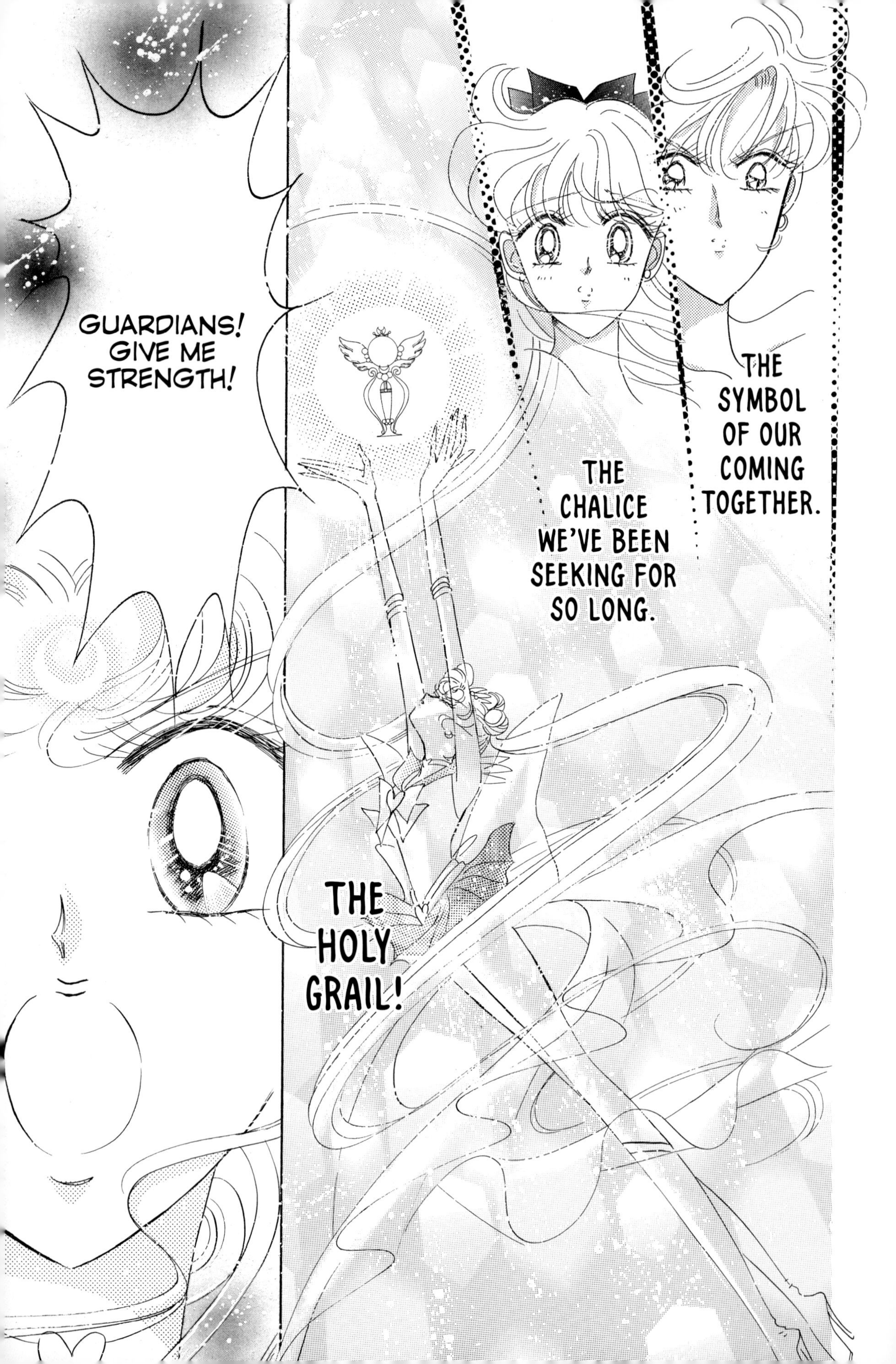
THE SYMBOL OF OUR COMING TOGETHER.
THE CHALICE WE'VE BEEN SEEKING FOR SO LONG.
THE HOLY GRAIL!
GUARDIANS! GIVE ME STRENGTH!

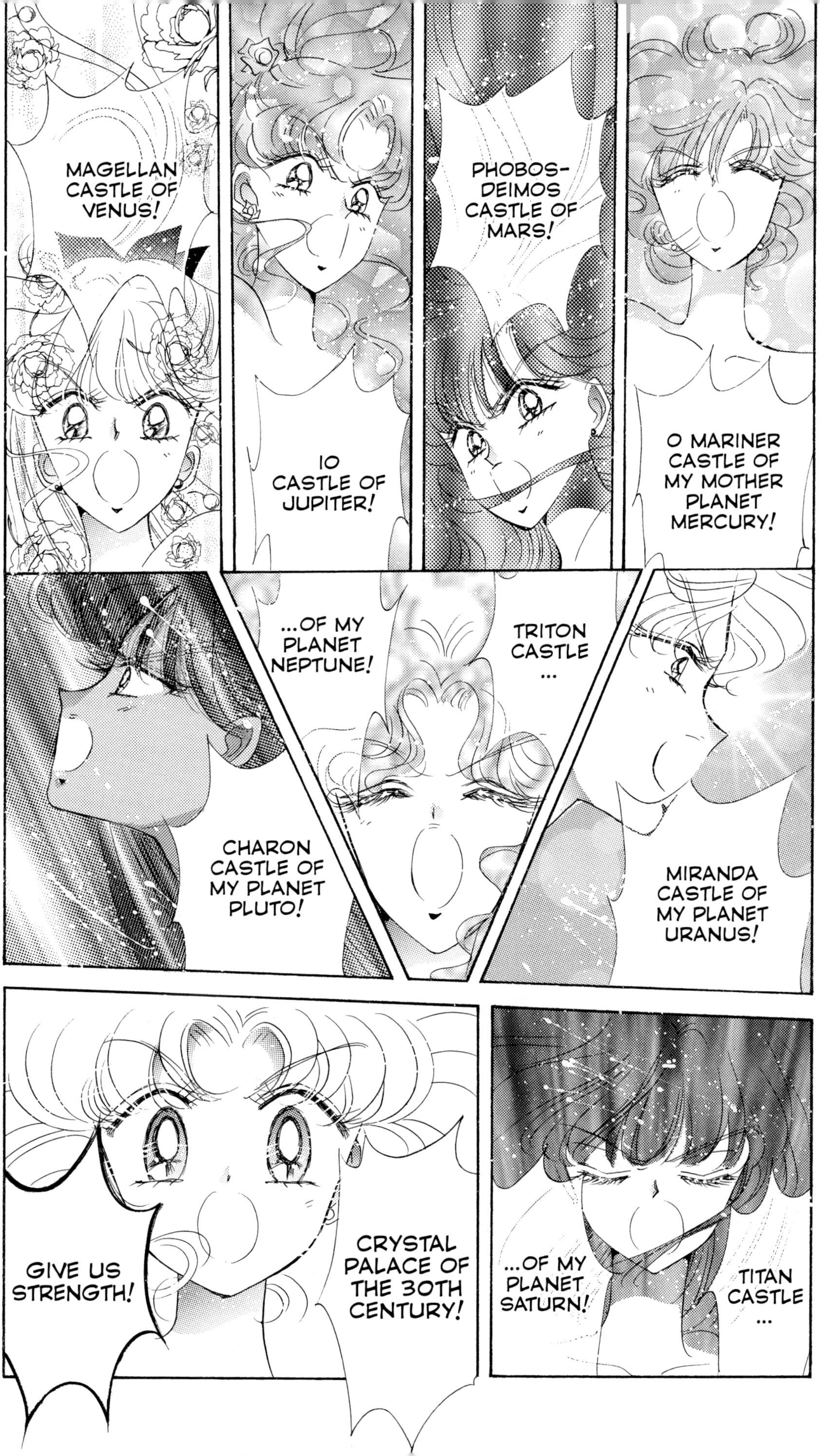
O MARINER CASTLE OF MY MOTHER PLANET MERCURY!
PHOBOS-DEIMOS CASTLE OF MARS!
IO CASTLE OF JUPITER!
MAGELLAN CASTLE OF VENUS!
MIRANDA CASTLE OF MY PLANET URANUS!
TRITON CASTLE ...
...OF MY PLANET NEPTUNE!
CHARON CASTLE OF MY PLANET PLUTO!
TITAN CASTLE ...
...OF MY PLANET SATURN!
CRYSTAL PALACE OF THE 30TH CENTURY!
GIVE US STRENGTH!

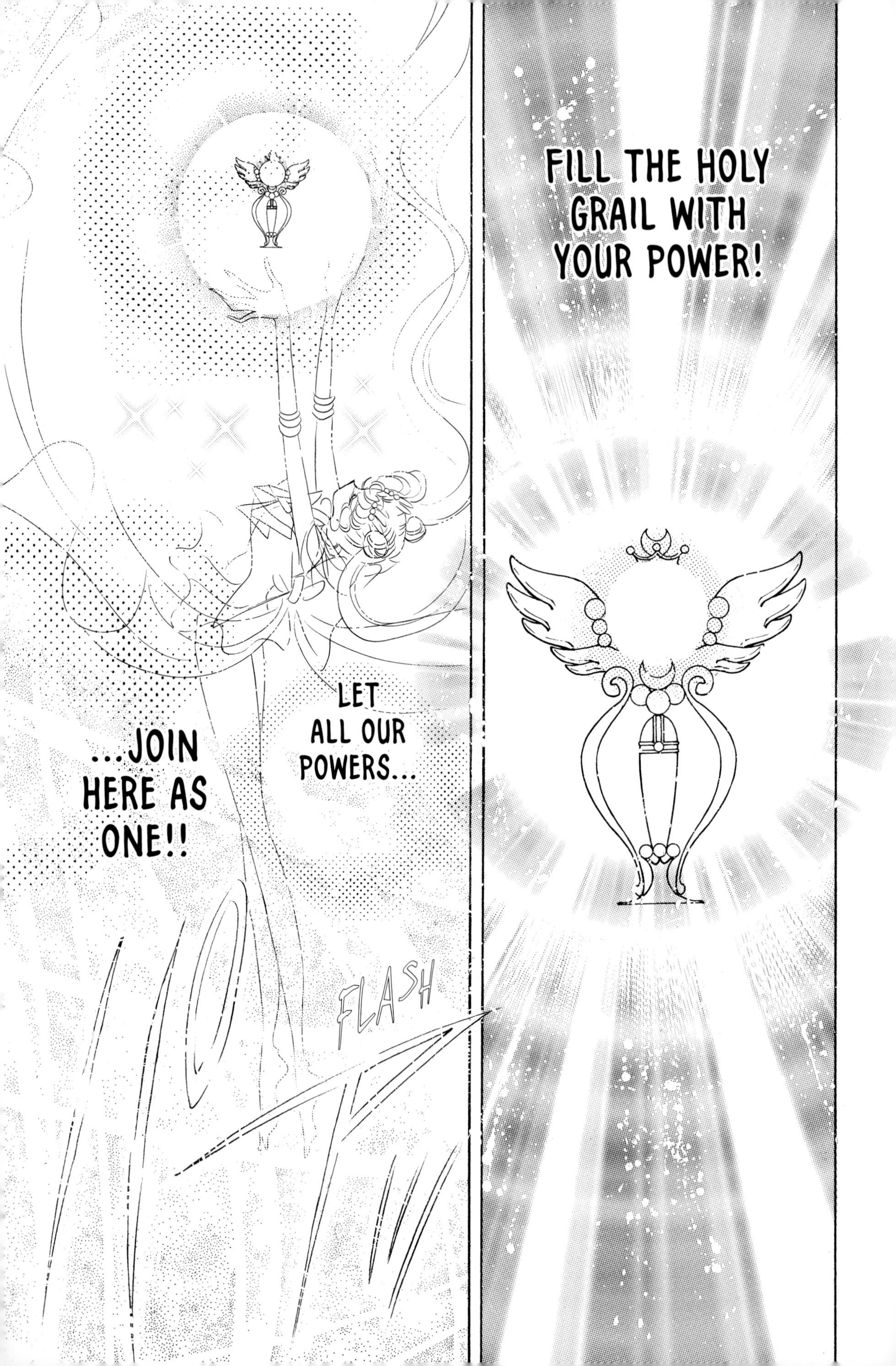
FILL THE HOLY GRAIL WITH YOUR POWER!
LET ALL OUR POWERS...
...JOIN HERE AS ONE!!
FLASH

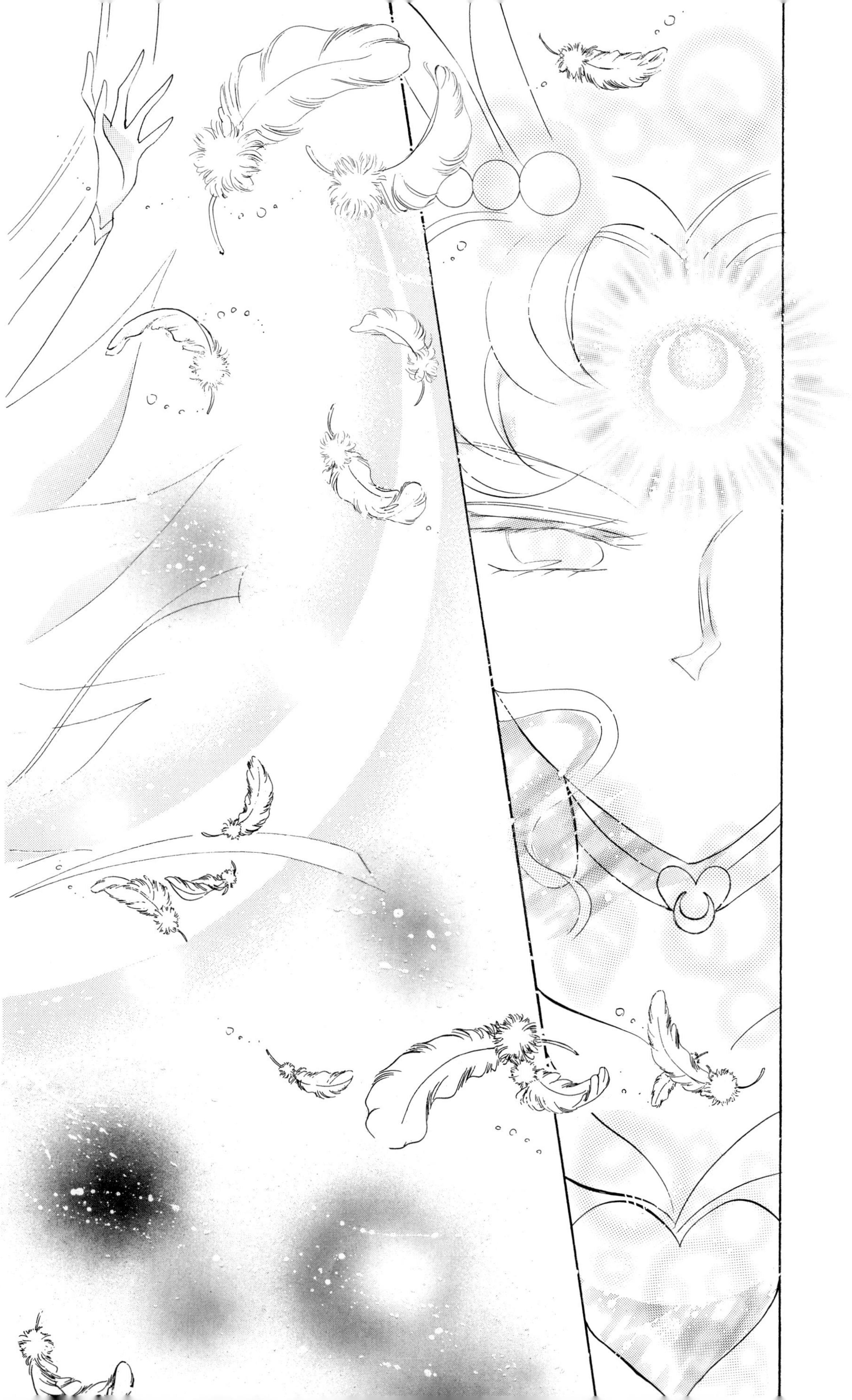

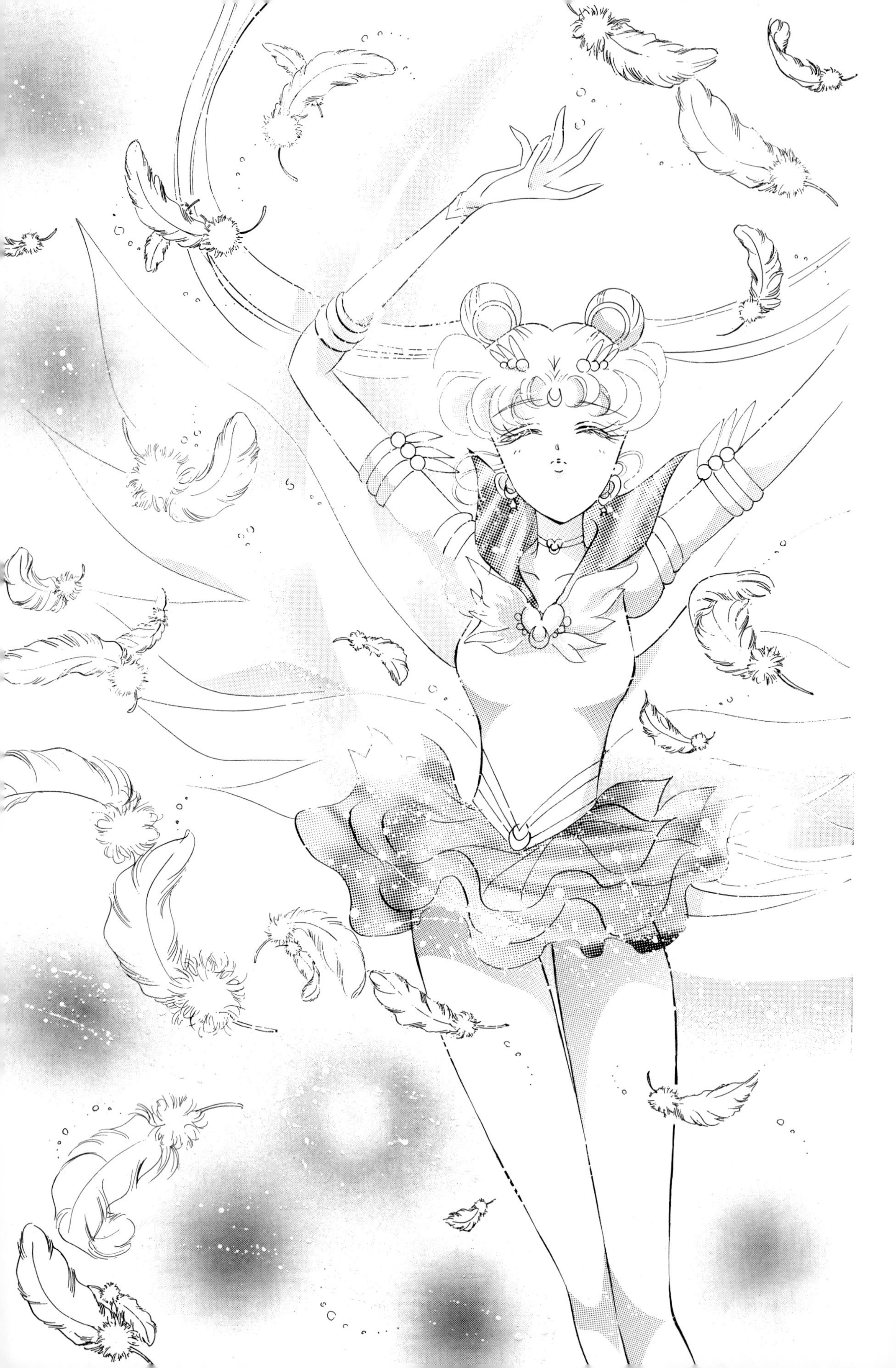

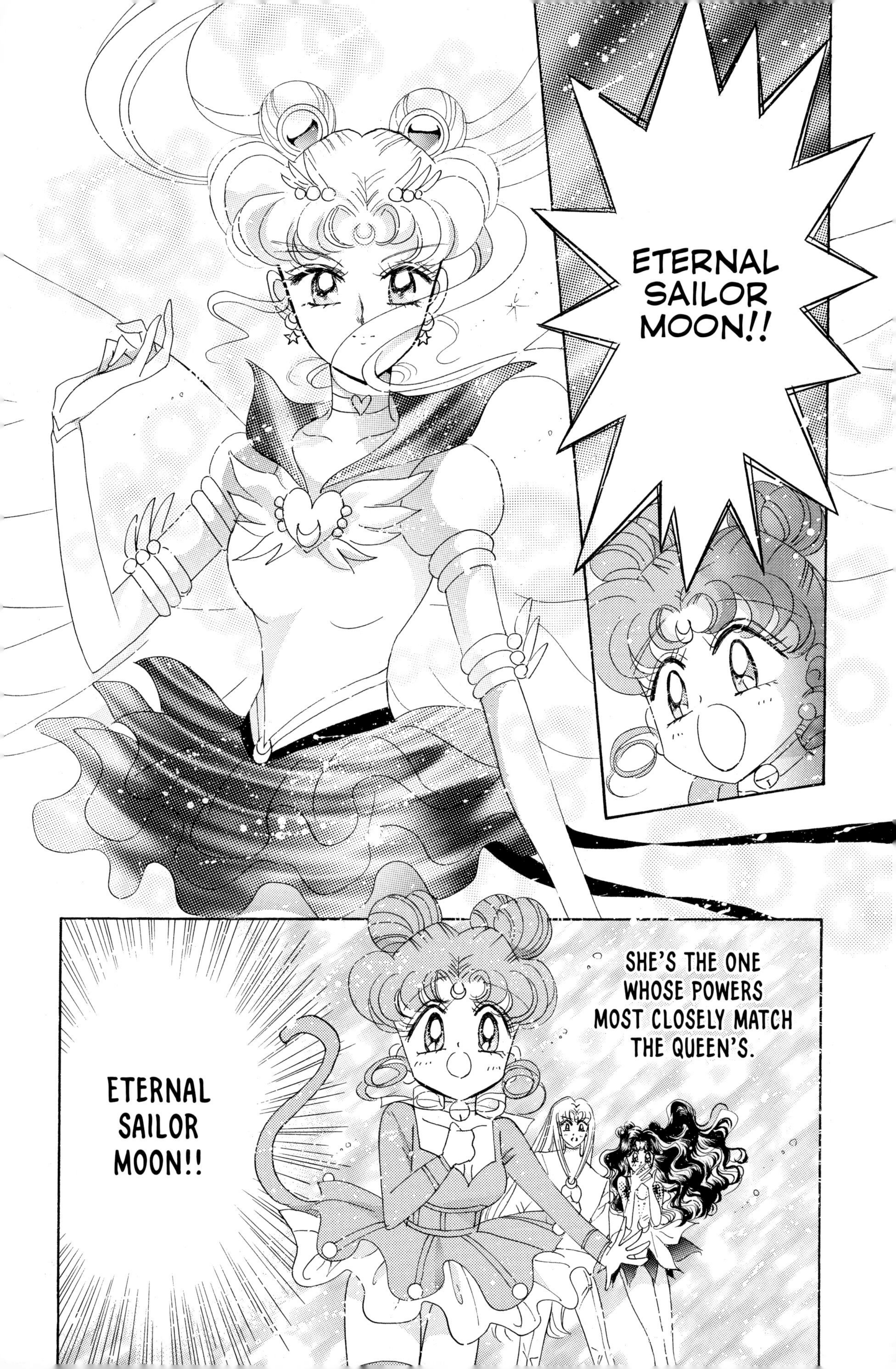
ETERNAL SAILOR MOON!!
SHE'S THE ONE WHOSE POWERS MOST CLOSELY MATCH THE QUEEN'S.
ETERNAL SAILOR MOON!!

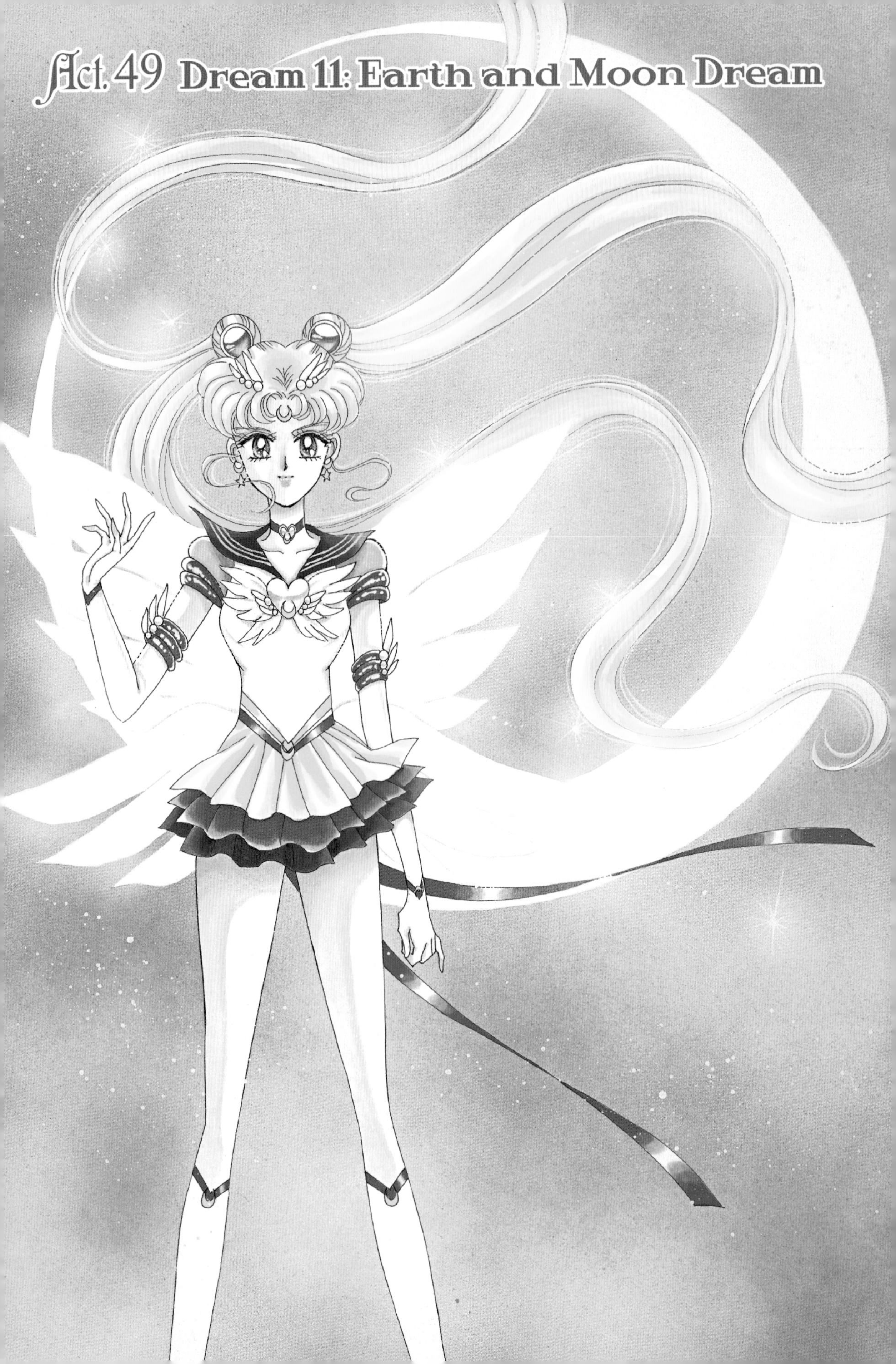
Act.49 Dream 11: Earth and Moon Dream

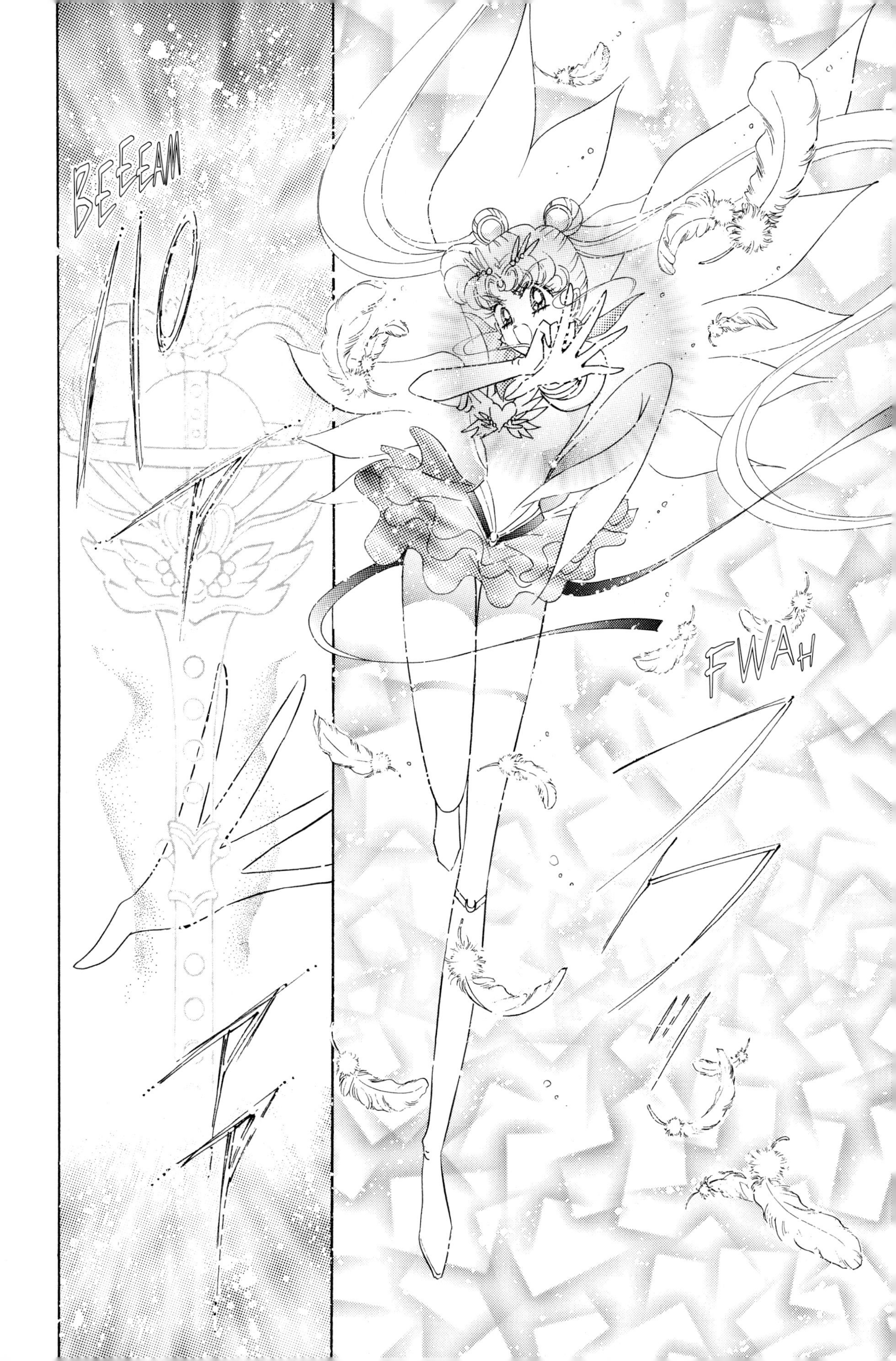
FWAH
BEEEAM

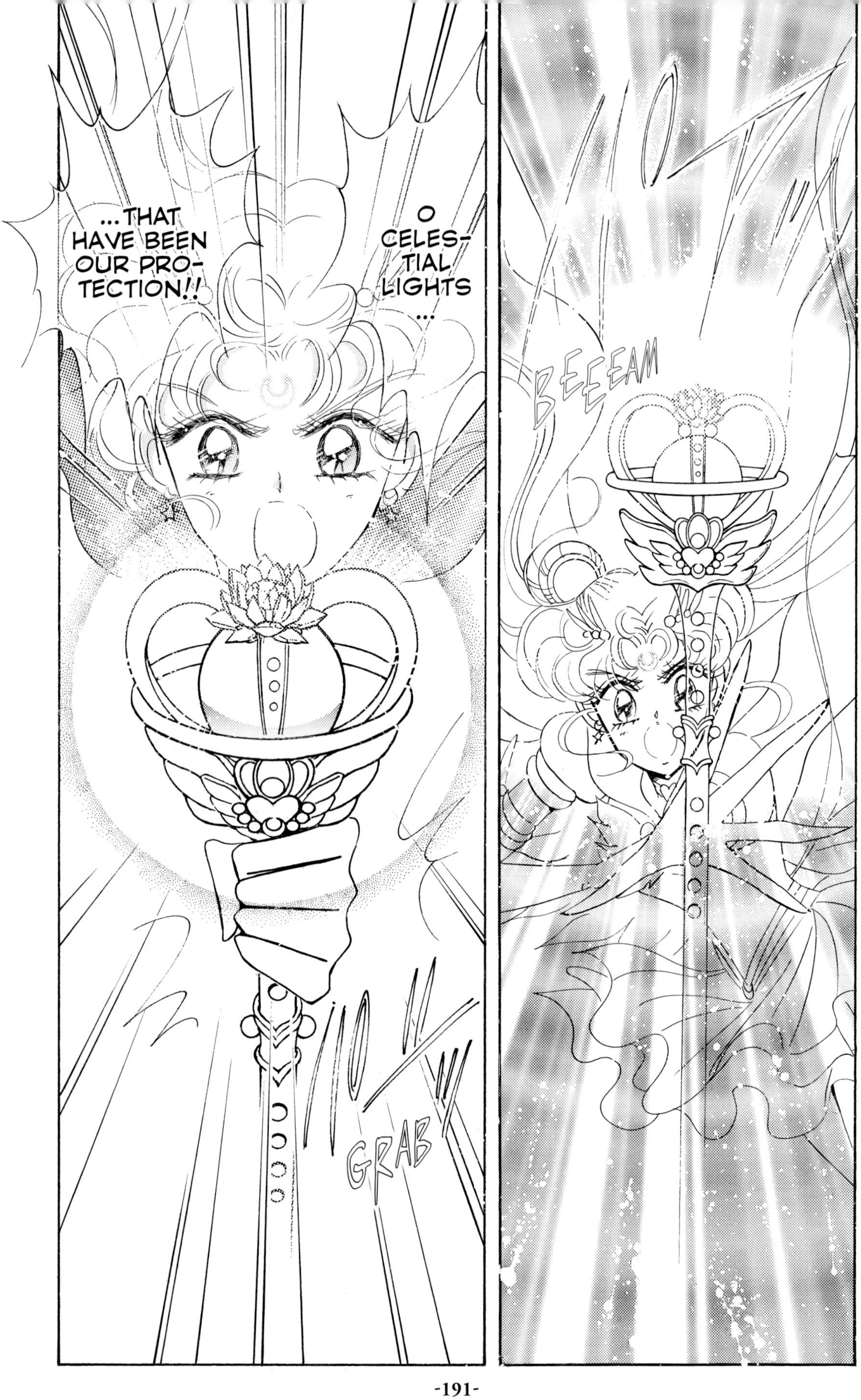
BEEEEAM
O CELESTIAL LIGHTS...
...THAT HAVE BEEN OUR PROTECTION!!
GRAB

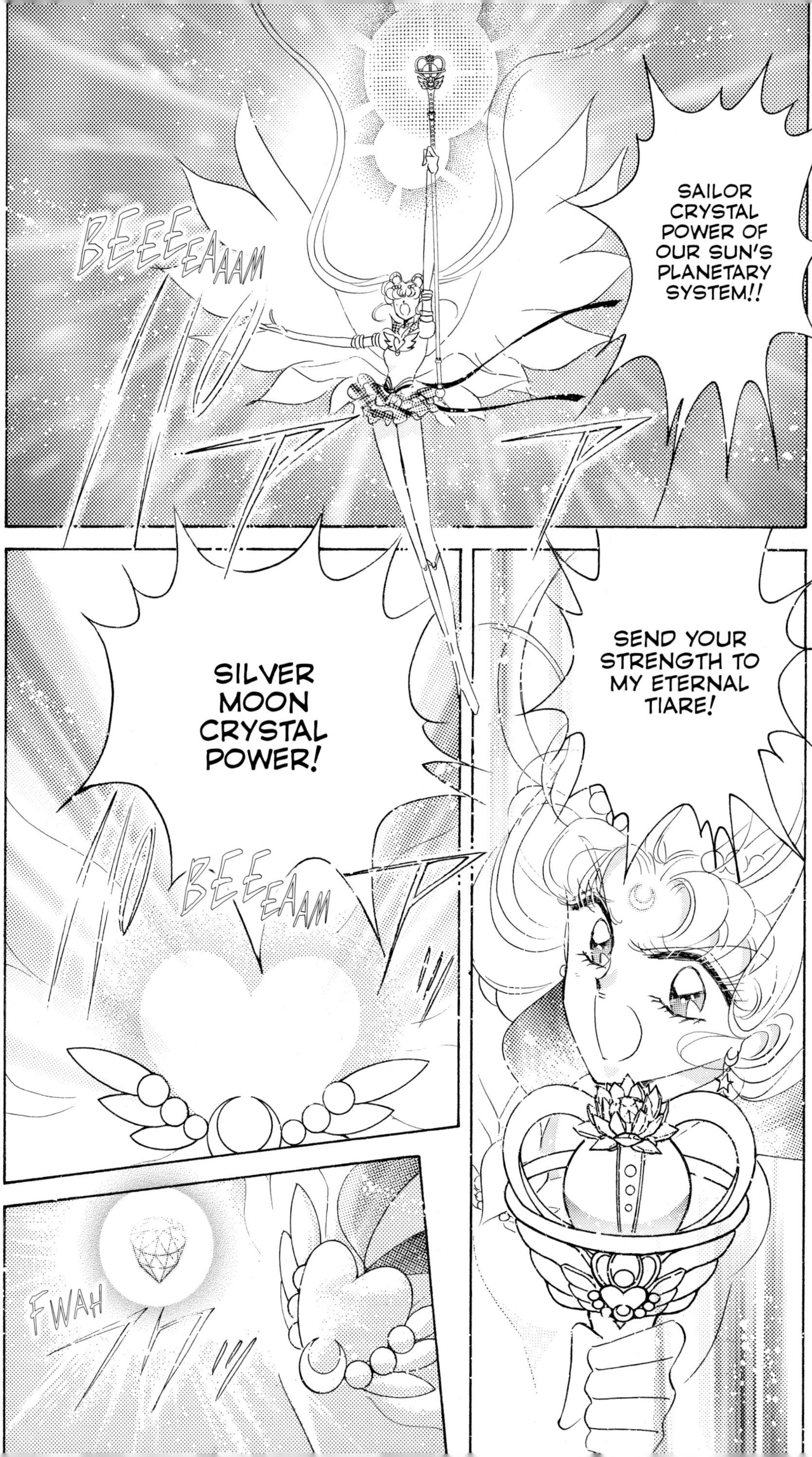
SAILOR CRYSTAL POWER OF OUR SUN'S PLANETARY SYSTEM!!
BEEEEAAAM
SEND YOUR STRENGTH TO MY ETERNAL TIARE!
SILVER MOON CRYSTAL POWER!
BEEEAAM
FWAH

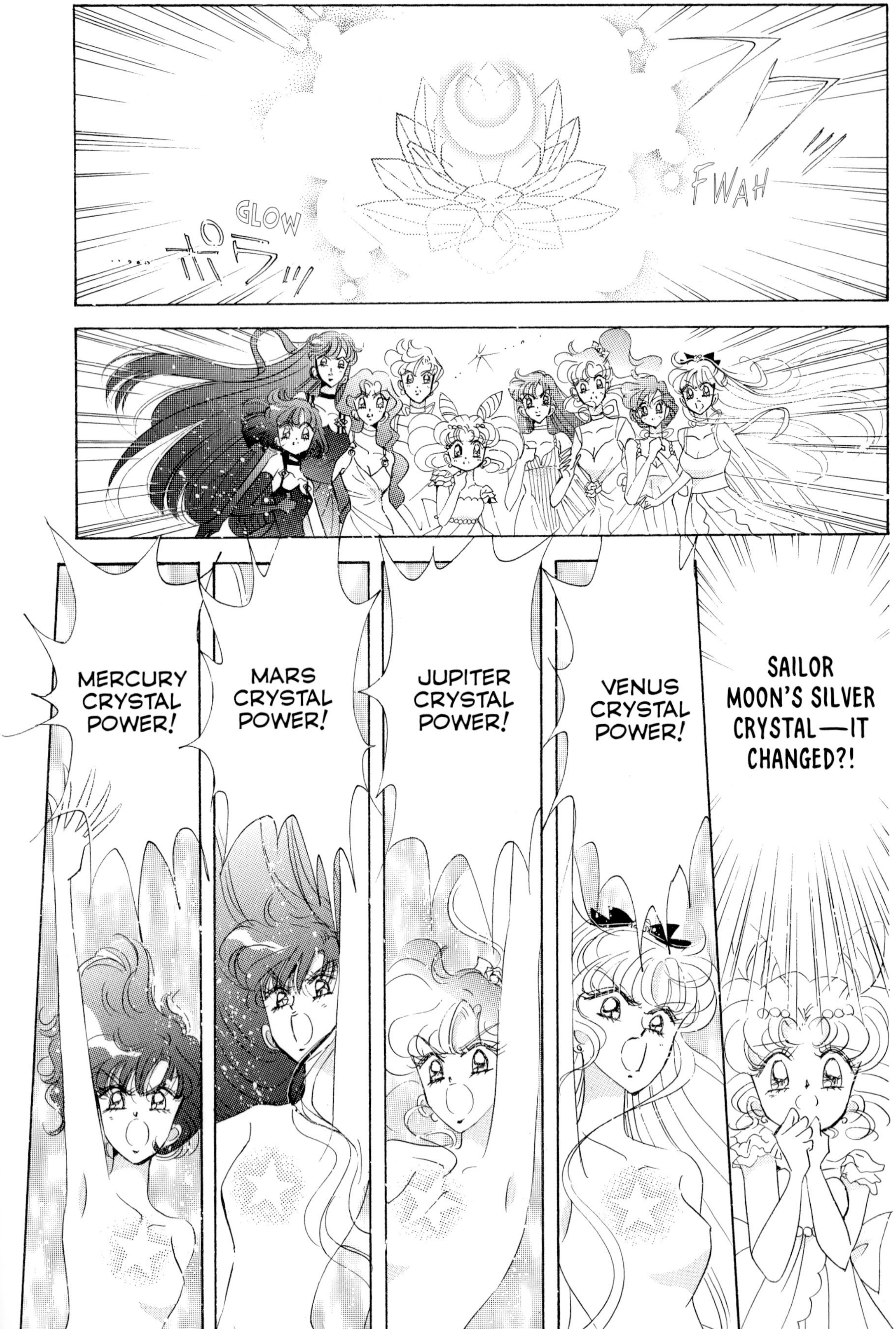
FWAH
GLOW
SAILOR MOON'S SILVER CRYSTAL—IT CHANGED?!
VENUS CRYSTAL POWER!
JUPITER CRYSTAL POWER!
MARS CRYSTAL POWER!
MERCURY CRYSTAL POWER!

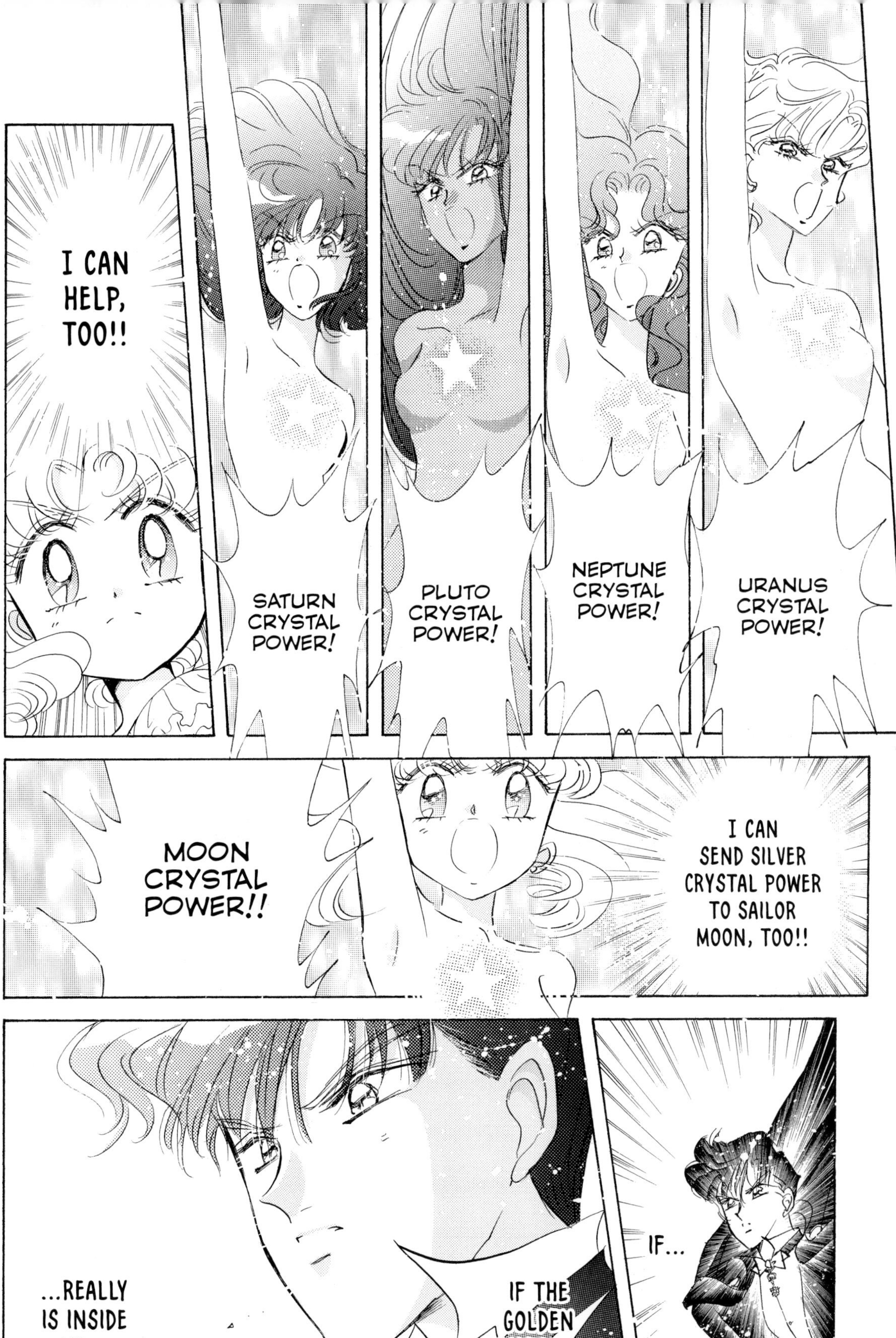
URANUS CRYSTAL POWER!
NEPTUNE CRYSTAL POWER!
PLUTO CRYSTAL POWER!
SATURN CRYSTAL POWER!
I CAN HELP, TOO!!
I CAN SEND SILVER CRYSTAL POWER TO SAILOR MOON, TOO!!
MOON CRYSTAL POWER!!
IF...
IF THE GOLDEN CRYSTAL...
...REALLY IS INSIDE ME...

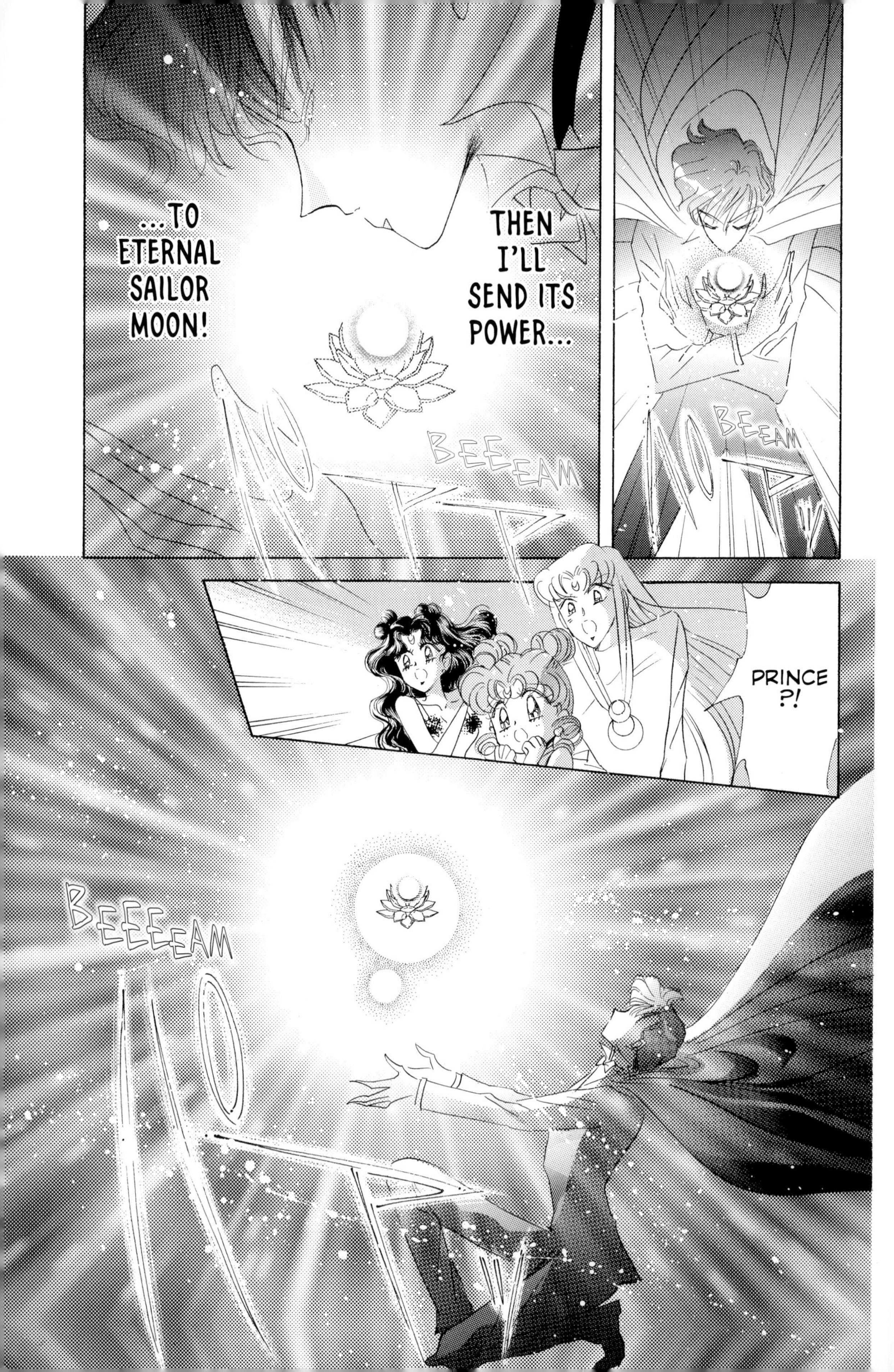
BEEEAM
THEN I'LL SEND ITS POWER...
...TO ETERNAL SAILOR MOON!
BEEEAM
PRINCE ?!
BEEEEEAM

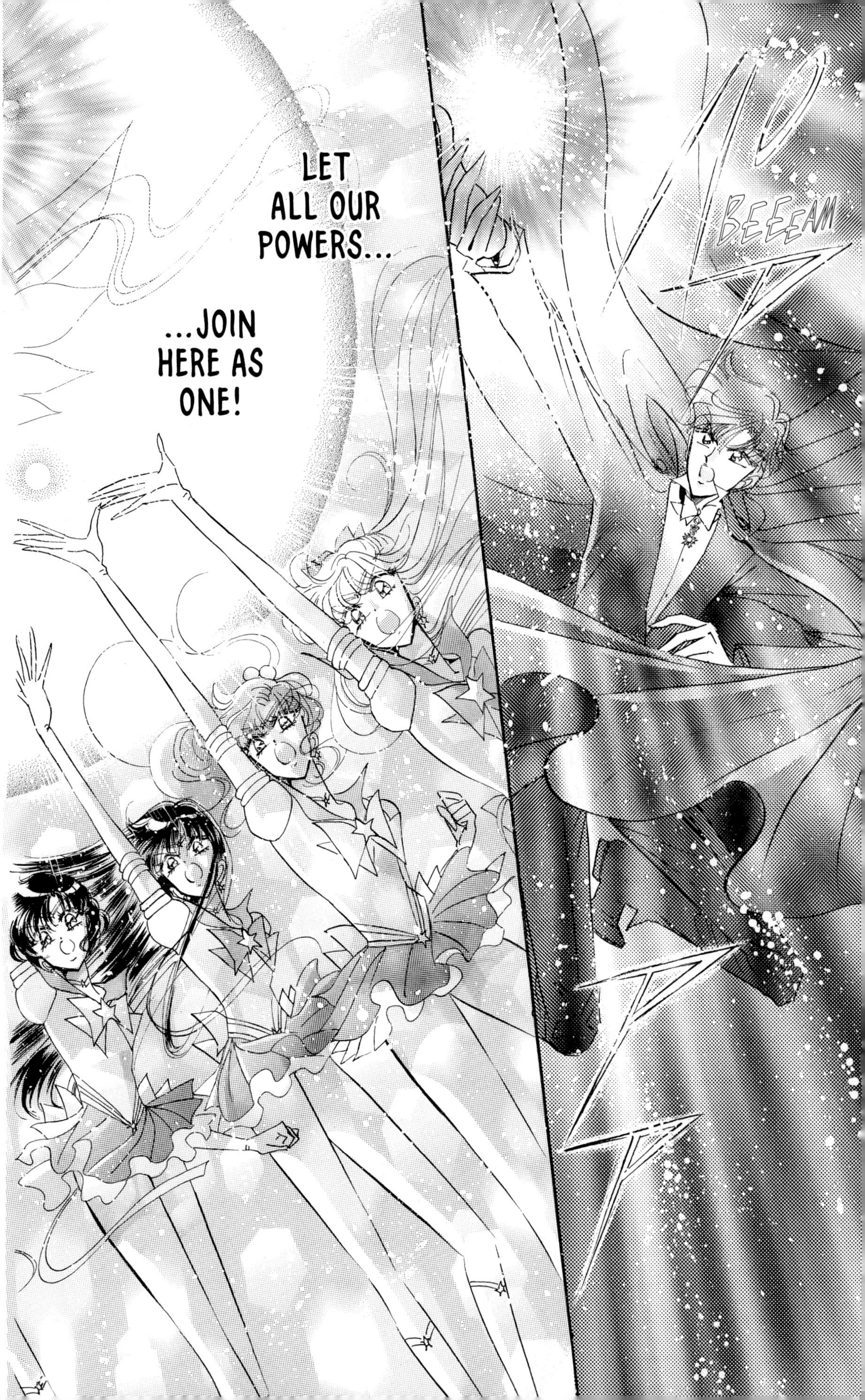
BEEEAM
LET ALL OUR POWERS...
...JOIN HERE AS ONE!

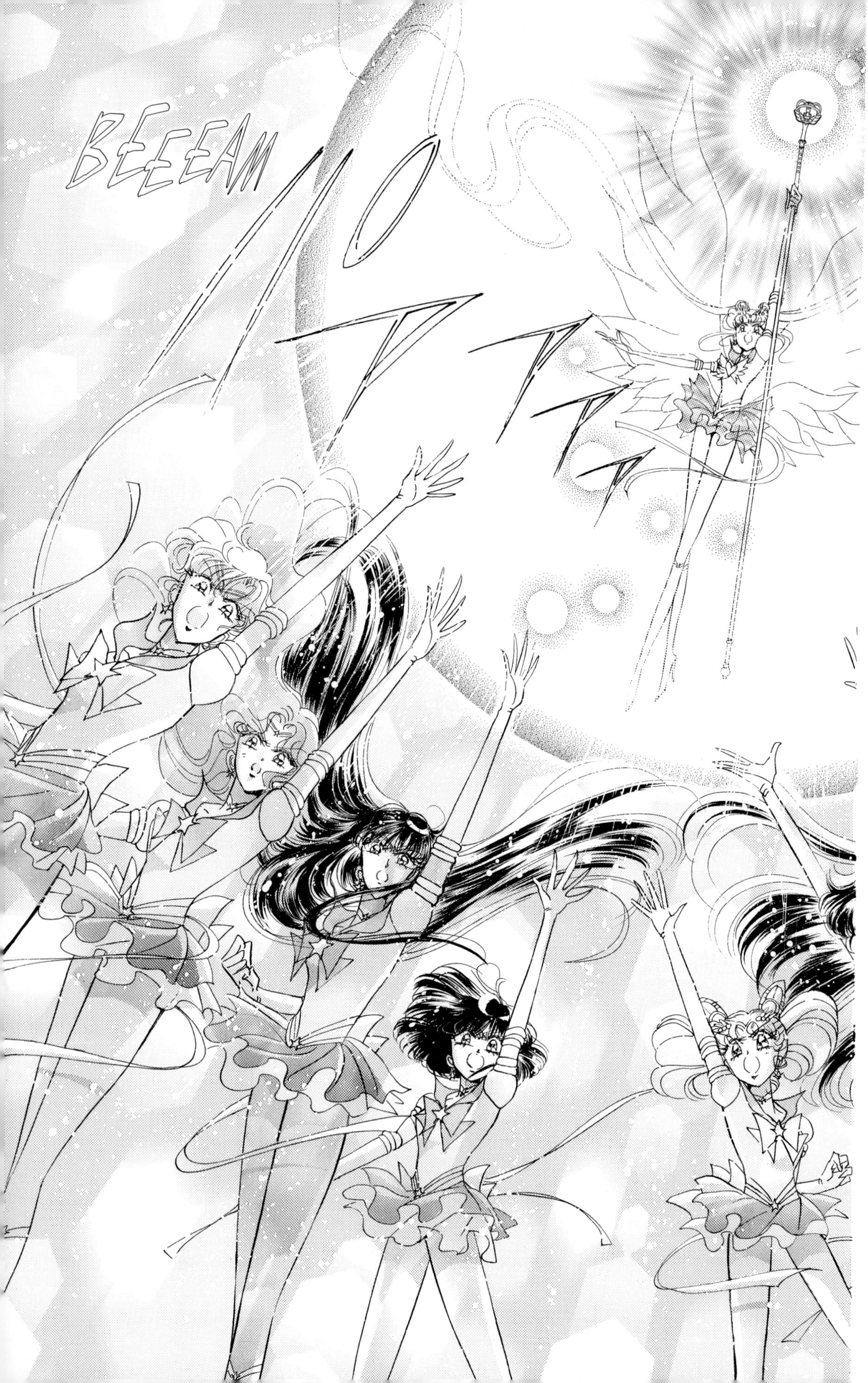
BEEEAM

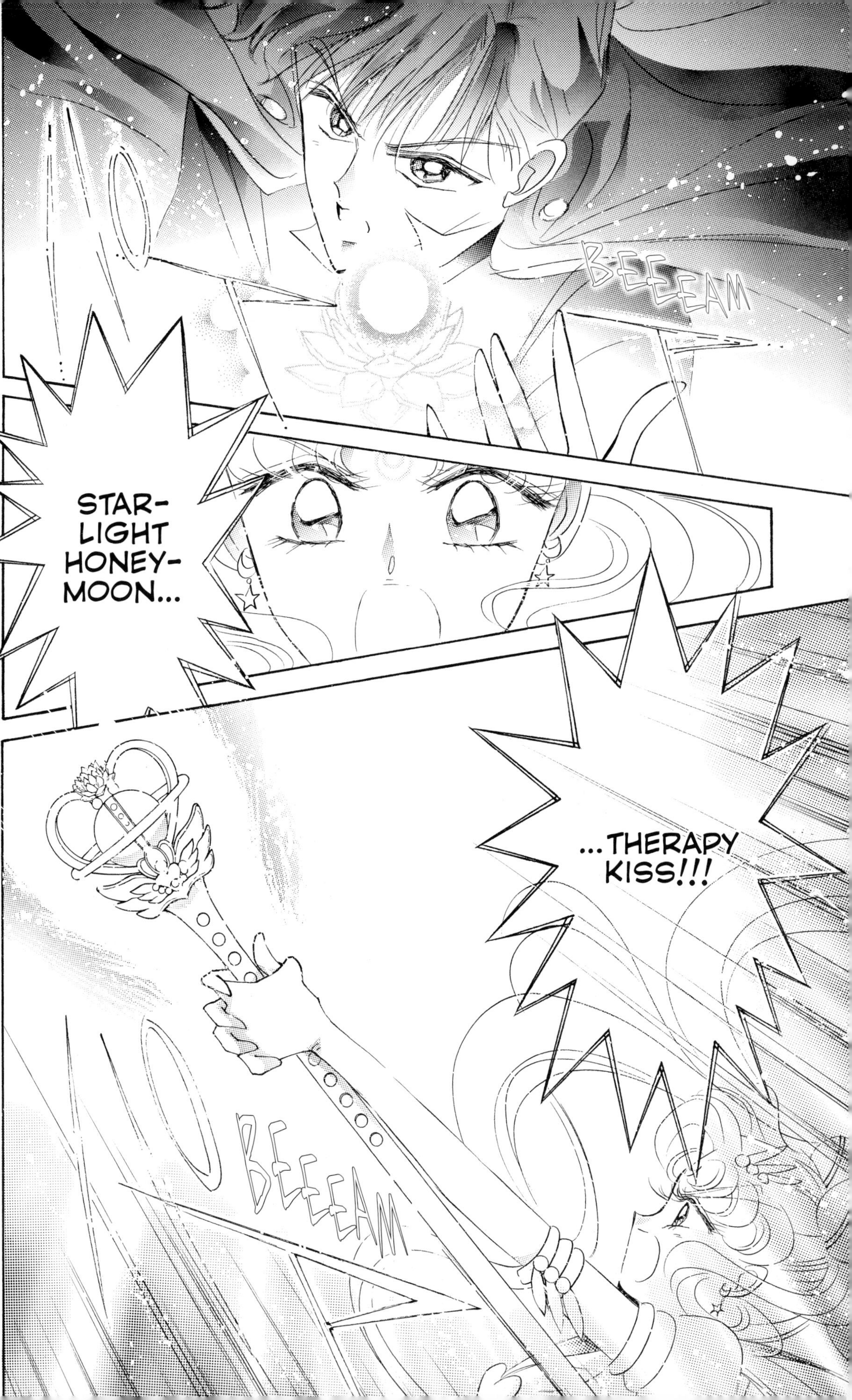
BEEEAM
STAR-LIGHT HONEY-MOON...
...THERAPY KISS!!!
BEEEAM

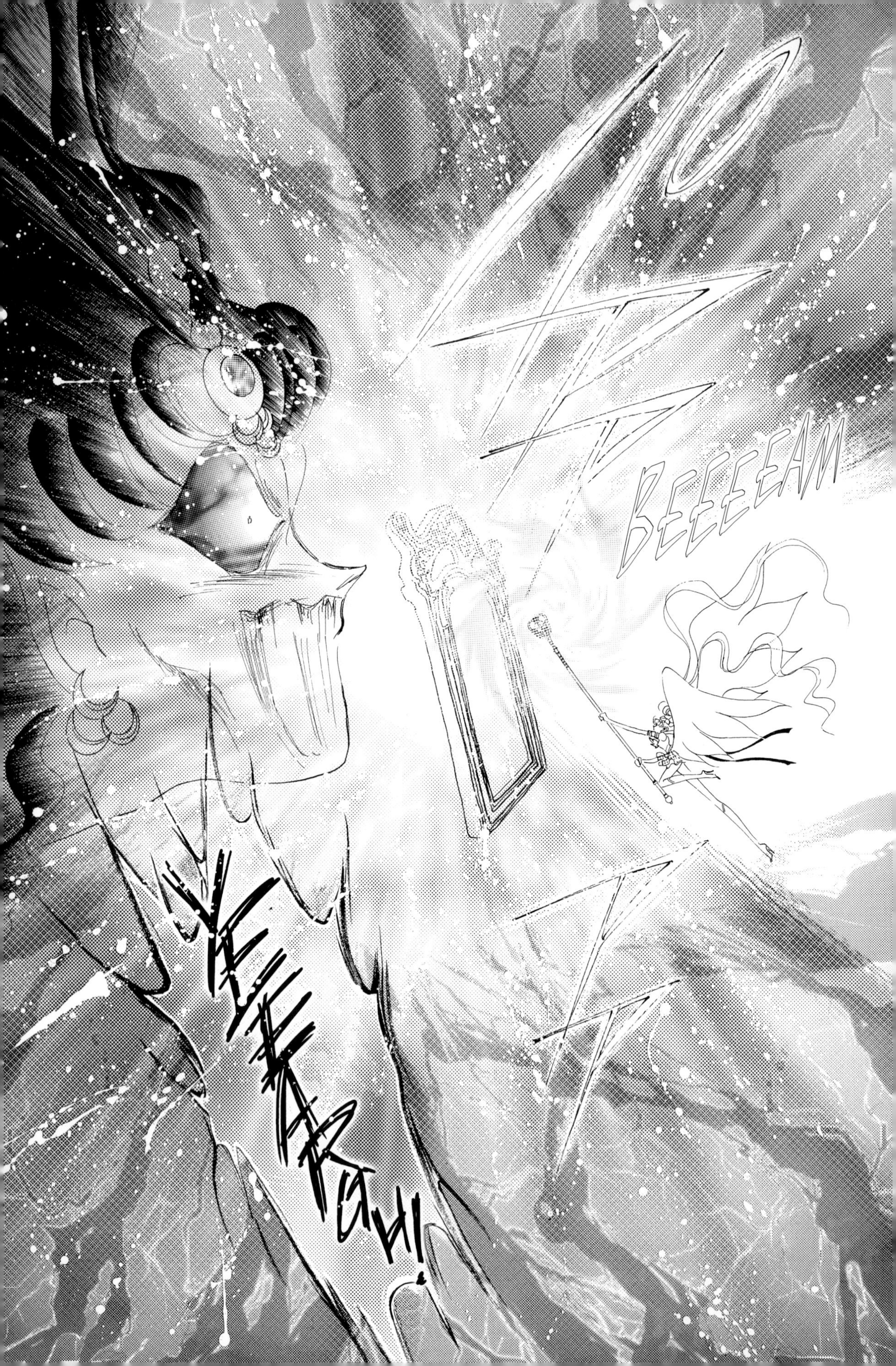
BEEEEAM
YEEEARGH!

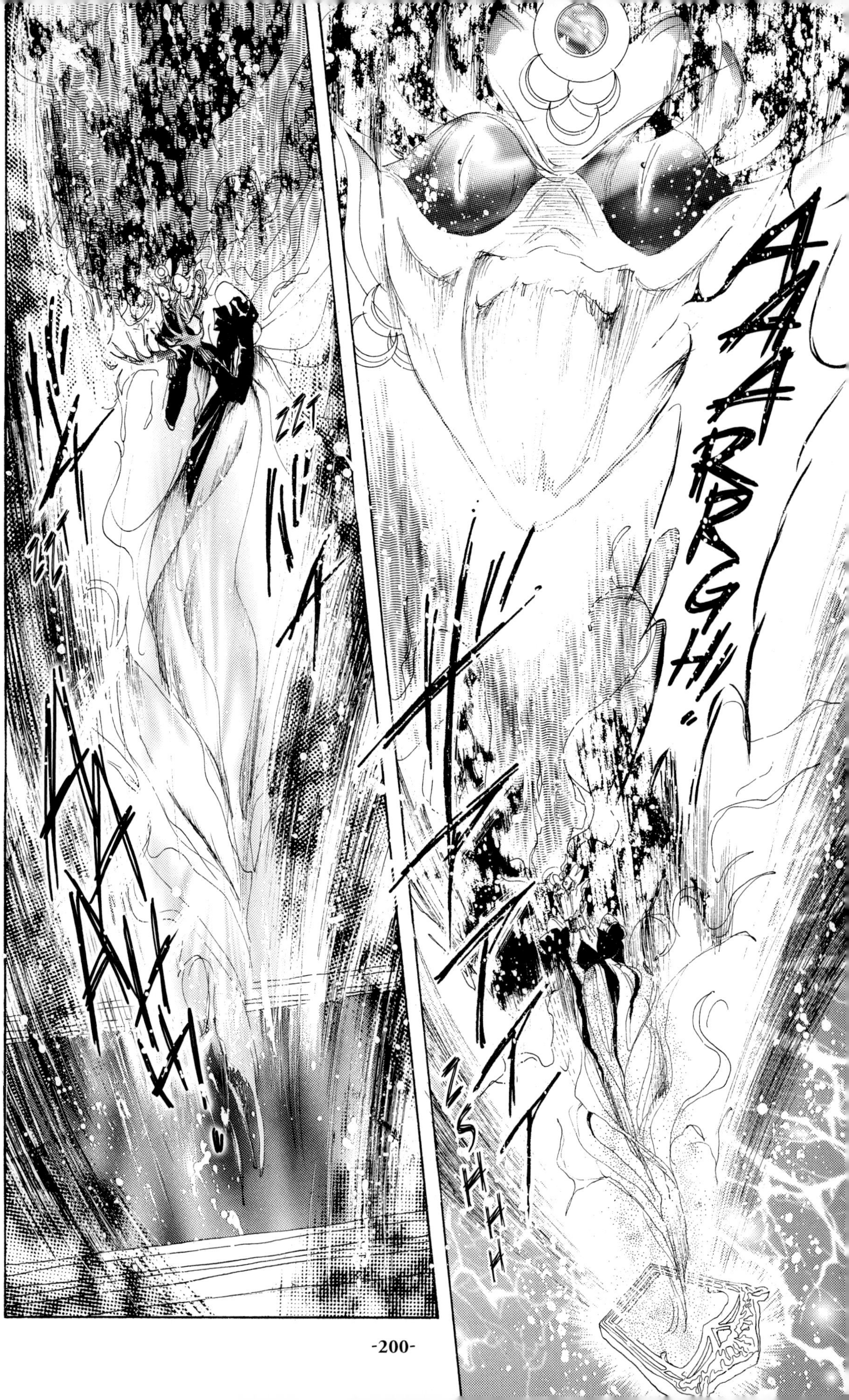
AAARRGH!!
ZSHHHH
ZZT
ZZT
AAAAHH!!

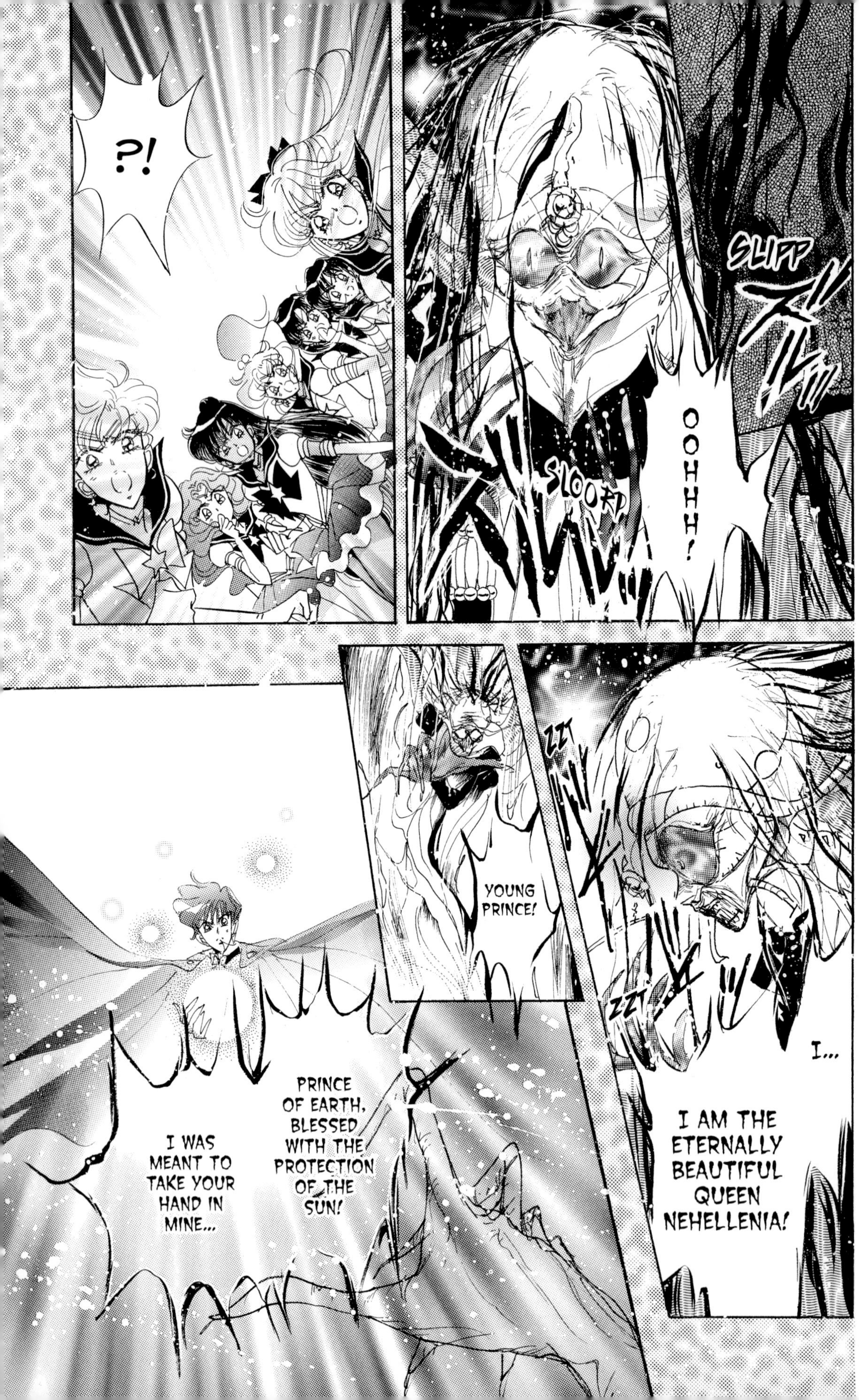
SLIPP
OOHHH!
SLOORP
?!
ZZT
ZZT
I...
I AM THE ETERNALLY BEAUTIFUL QUEEN NEHELLENIA!
YOUNG PRINCE!
PRINCE OF EARTH, BLESSED WITH THE PROTECTION OF THE SUN!
I WAS MEANT TO TAKE YOUR HAND IN MINE...

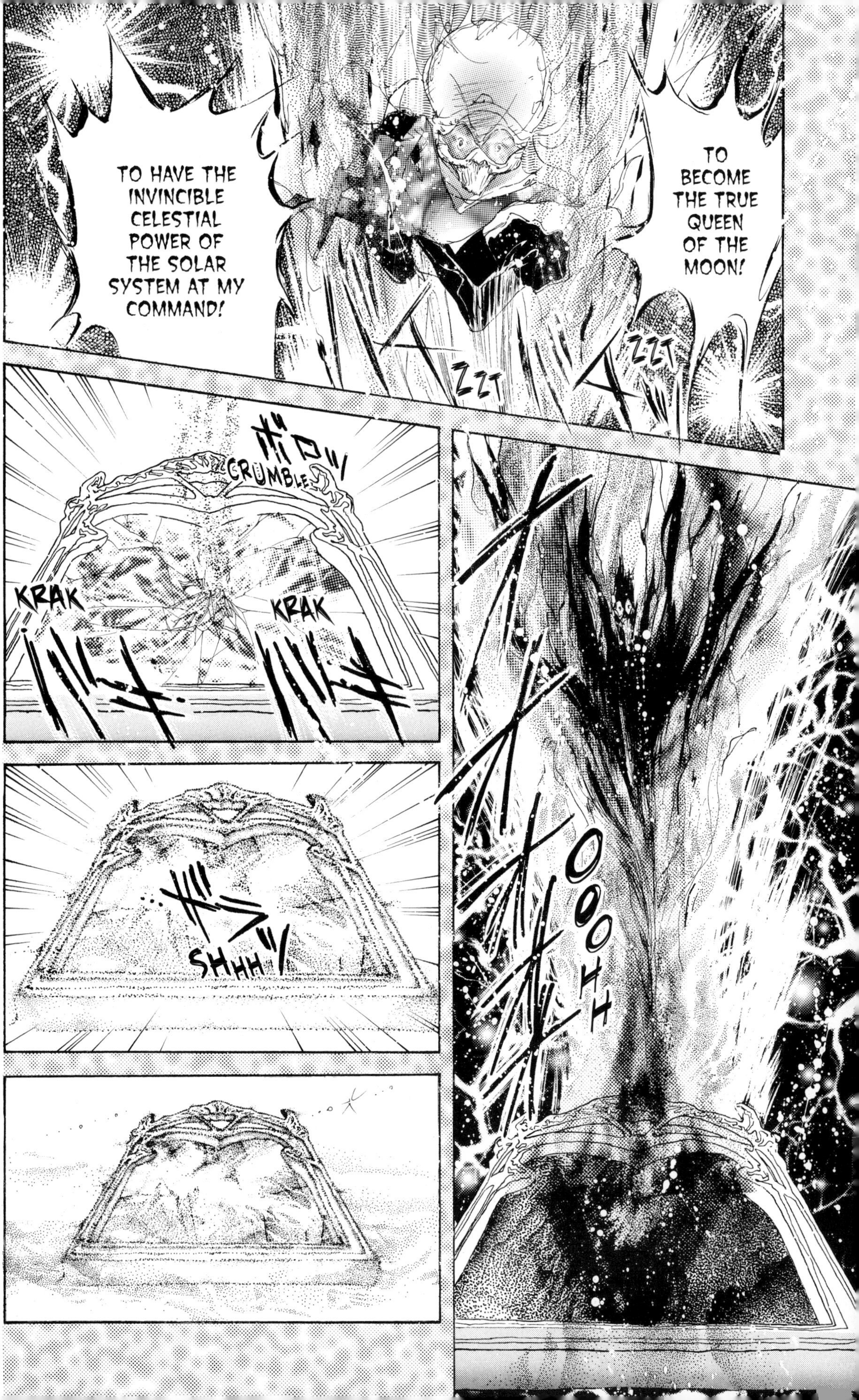
TO BECOME THE TRUE QUEEN OF THE MOON!
TO HAVE THE INVINCIBLE CELESTIAL POWER OF THE SOLAR SYSTEM AT MY COMMAND!
ZZZT
ZZZT
OOOOHH
CRUMBLE
KRAK
KRAK
SHHH

BEEEAM
FZH
GLINT
FZH
BEEEAM

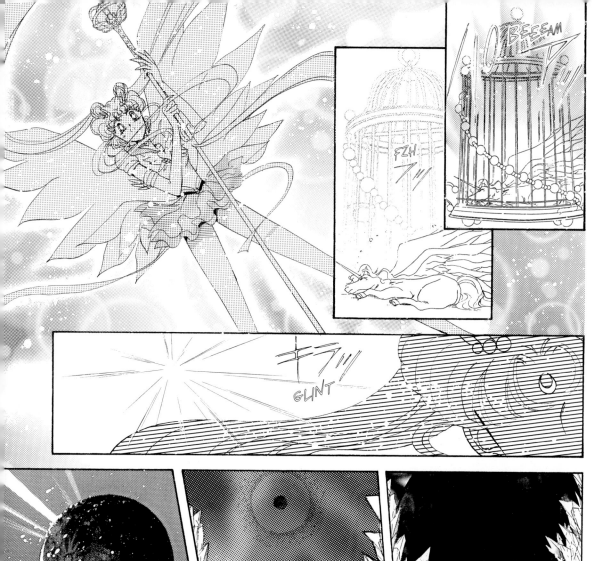

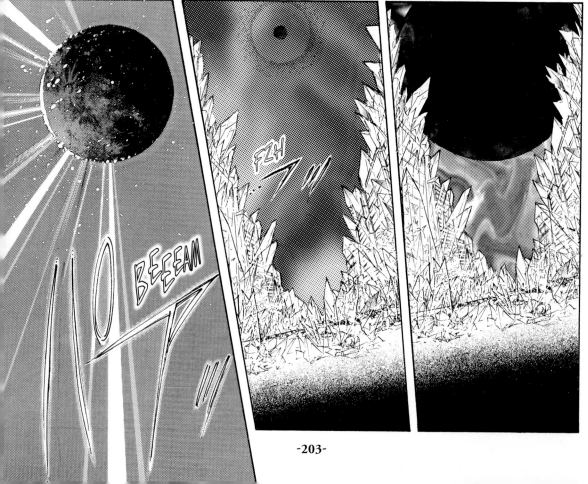

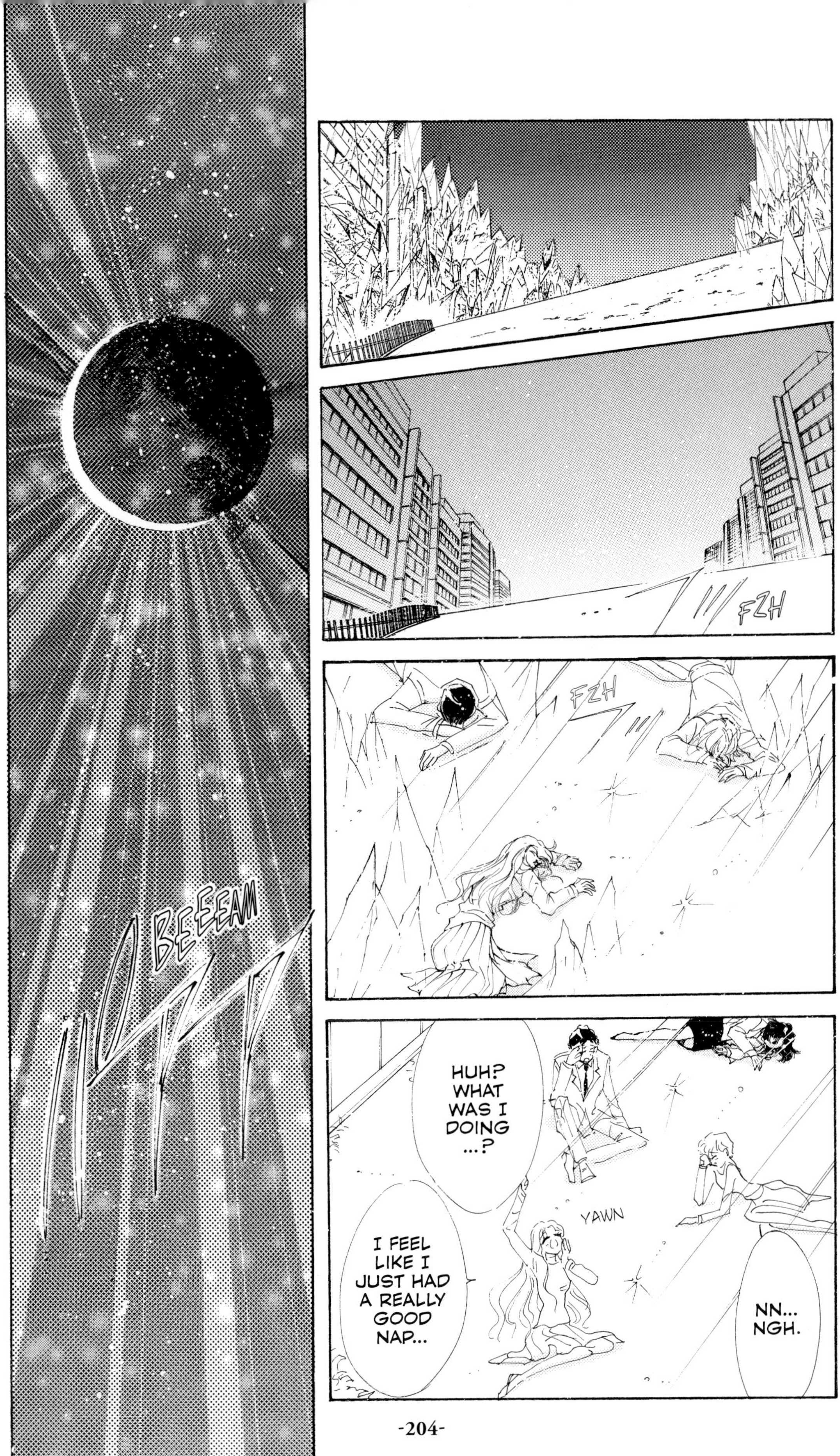
FZH
FZH
HUH? WHAT WAS I DOING ...?
NN... NGH.
YAWN
I FEEL LIKE I JUST HAD A REALLY GOOD NAP...
BEEEAM

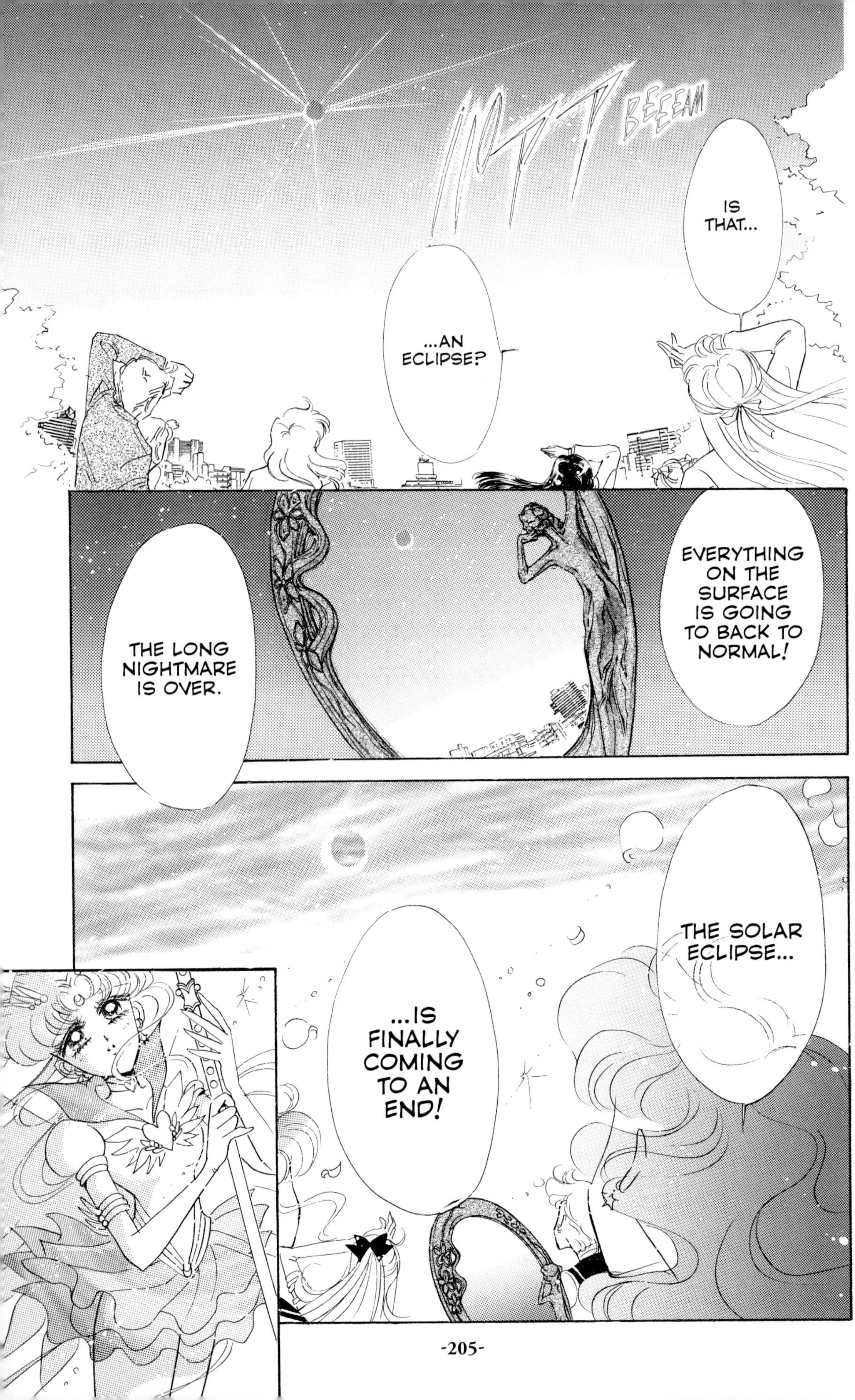
BEEEAM
IS THAT...
...AN ECLIPSE?
EVERYTHING ON THE SURFACE IS GOING TO BACK TO NORMAL!
THE LONG NIGHTMARE IS OVER.
THE SOLAR ECLIPSE...
...IS FINALLY COMING TO AN END!

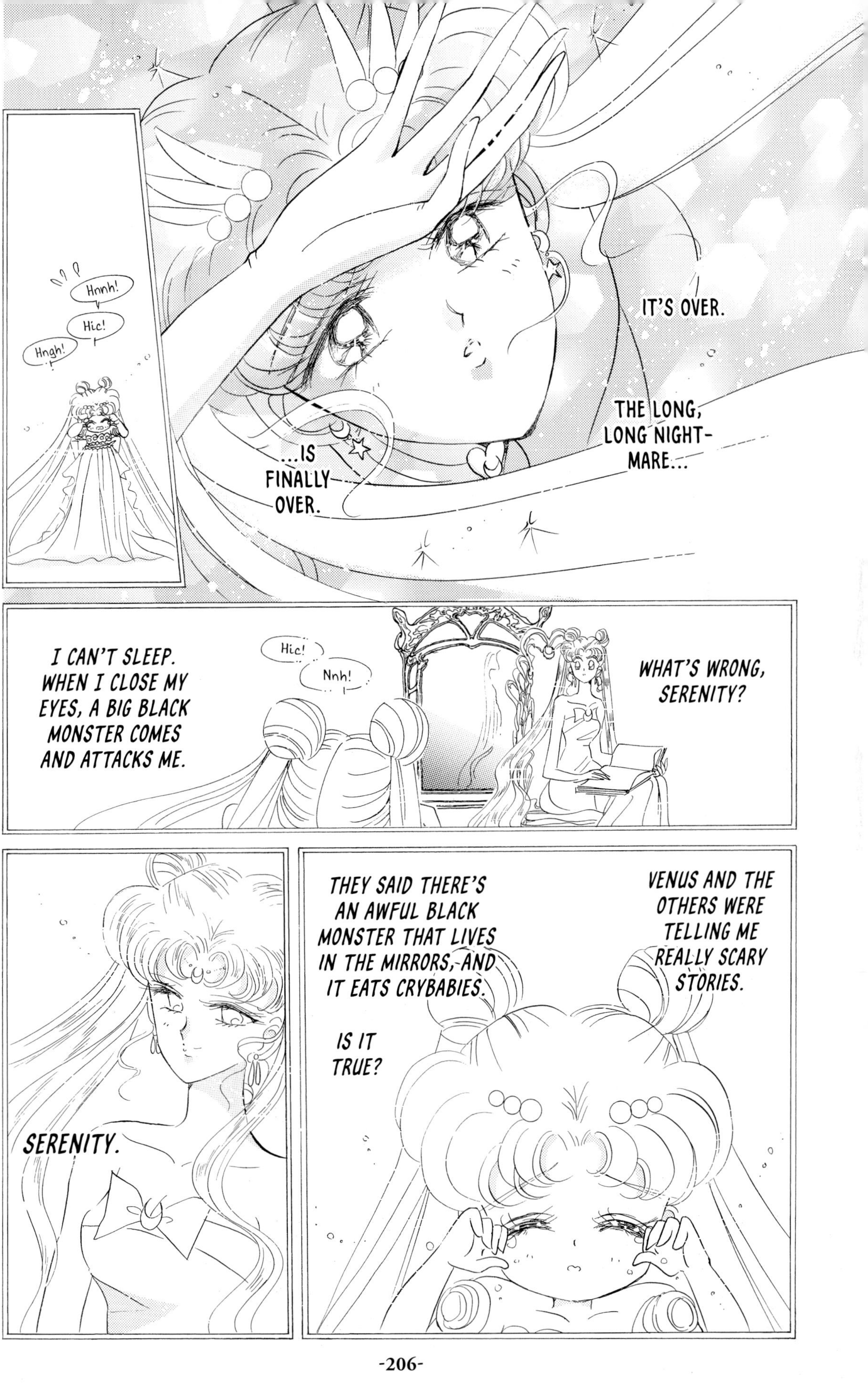
IT'S OVER.
THE LONG, LONG NIGHTMARE...
...IS FINALLY OVER.
Hnnh!
Hic!
Hngh!
WHAT'S WRONG, SERENITY?
Hic!
Nnh!
I CAN'T SLEEP. WHEN I CLOSE MY EYES, A BIG BLACK MONSTER COMES AND ATTACKS ME.
VENUS AND THE OTHERS WERE TELLING ME REALLY SCARY STORIES.
THEY SAID THERE'S AN AWFUL BLACK MONSTER THAT LIVES IN THE MIRRORS, AND IT EATS CRYBABIES.
IS IT TRUE?
SERENITY.

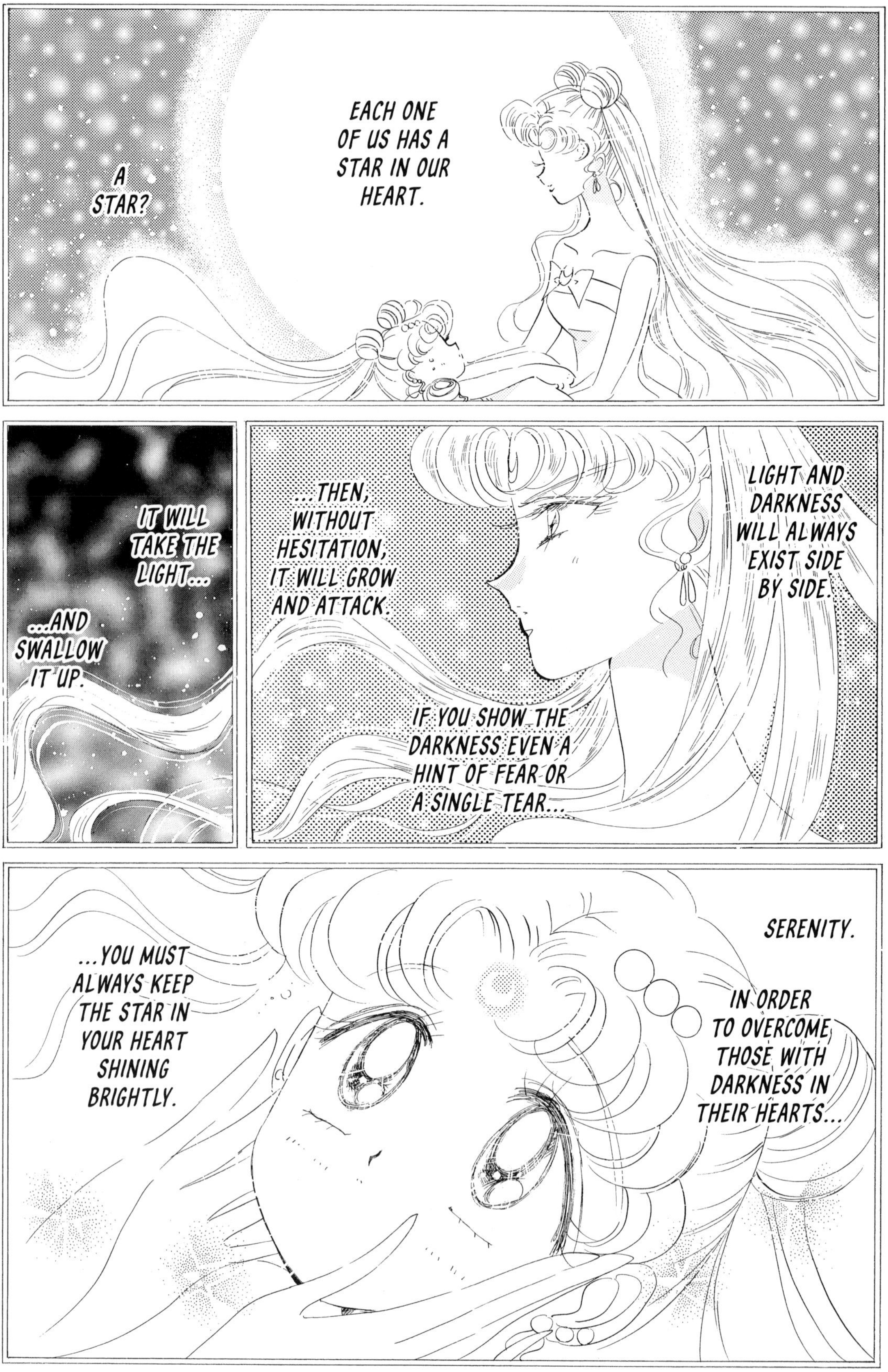
EACH ONE OF US HAS A STAR IN OUR HEART.
A STAR?
LIGHT AND DARKNESS WILL ALWAYS EXIST SIDE BY SIDE.
...THEN, WITHOUT HESITATION, IT WILL GROW AND ATTACK.
IF YOU SHOW THE DARKNESS EVEN A HINT OF FEAR OR A SINGLE TEAR...
IT WILL TAKE THE LIGHT...
...AND SWALLOW IT UP.
SERENITY.
IN ORDER TO OVERCOME THOSE WITH DARKNESS IN THEIR HEARTS...
...YOU MUST ALWAYS KEEP THE STAR IN YOUR HEART SHINING BRIGHTLY.

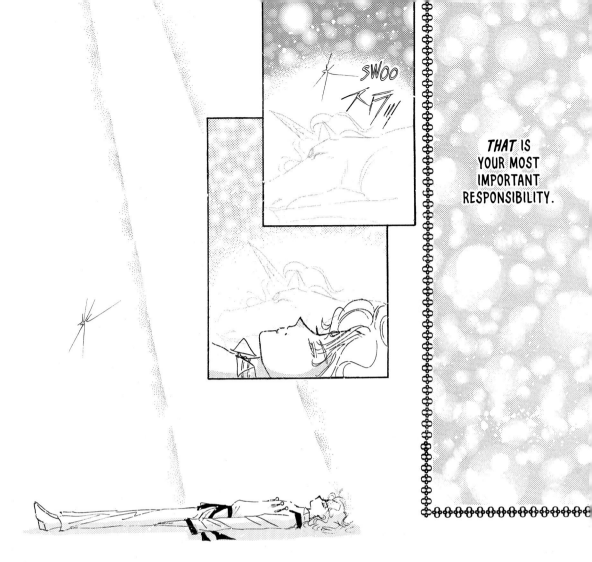

SWOO
RG!!!

THAT IS
YOUR MOST
IMPORTANT
RESPONSIBILITY.

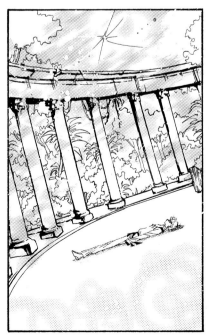

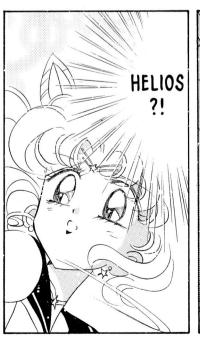

HELIOS
?!

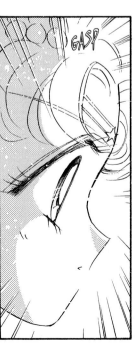

GASP

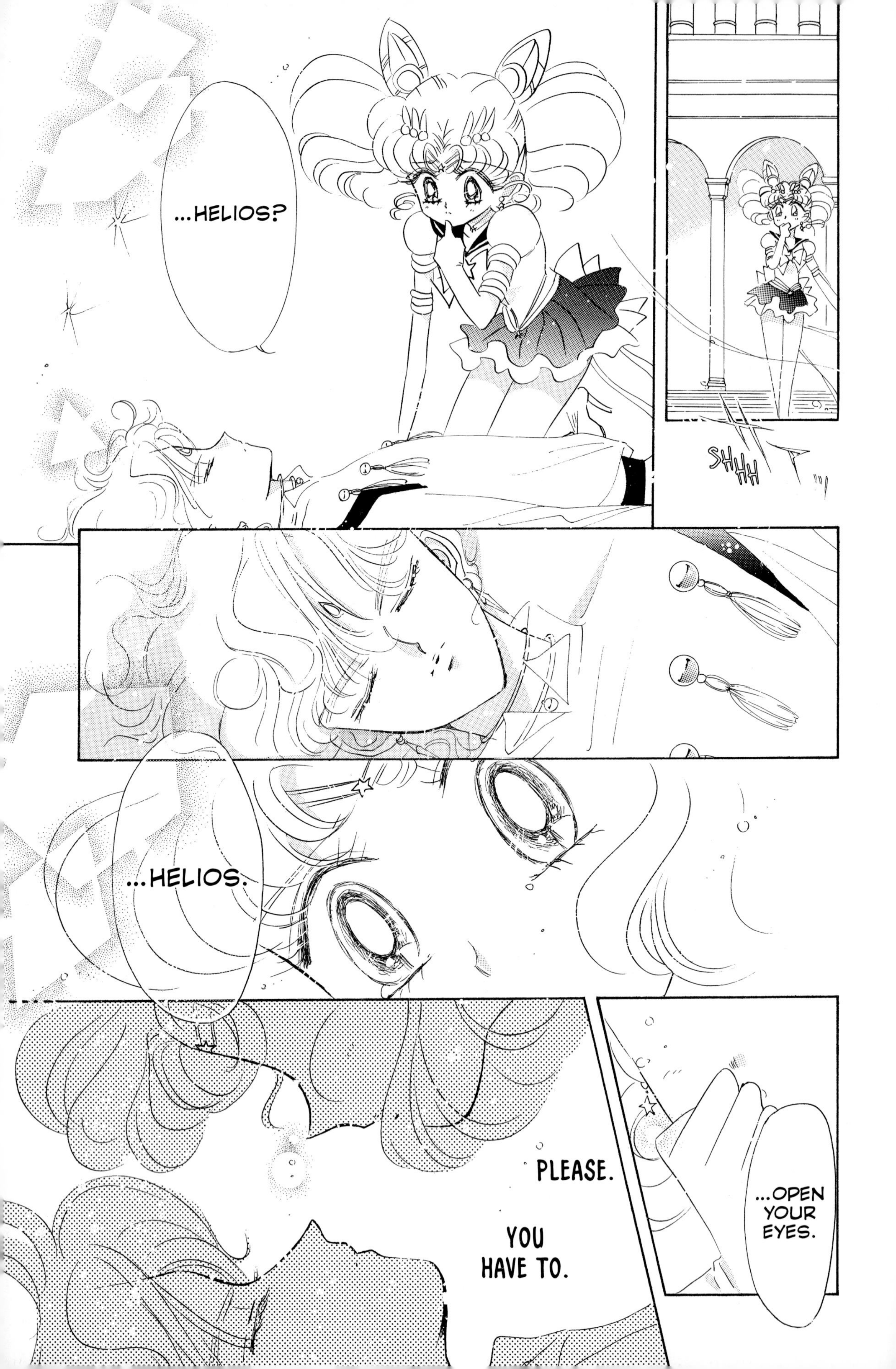
SHHHH
...HELIOS?
...HELIOS.
...OPEN YOUR EYES.
PLEASE.
YOU HAVE TO.

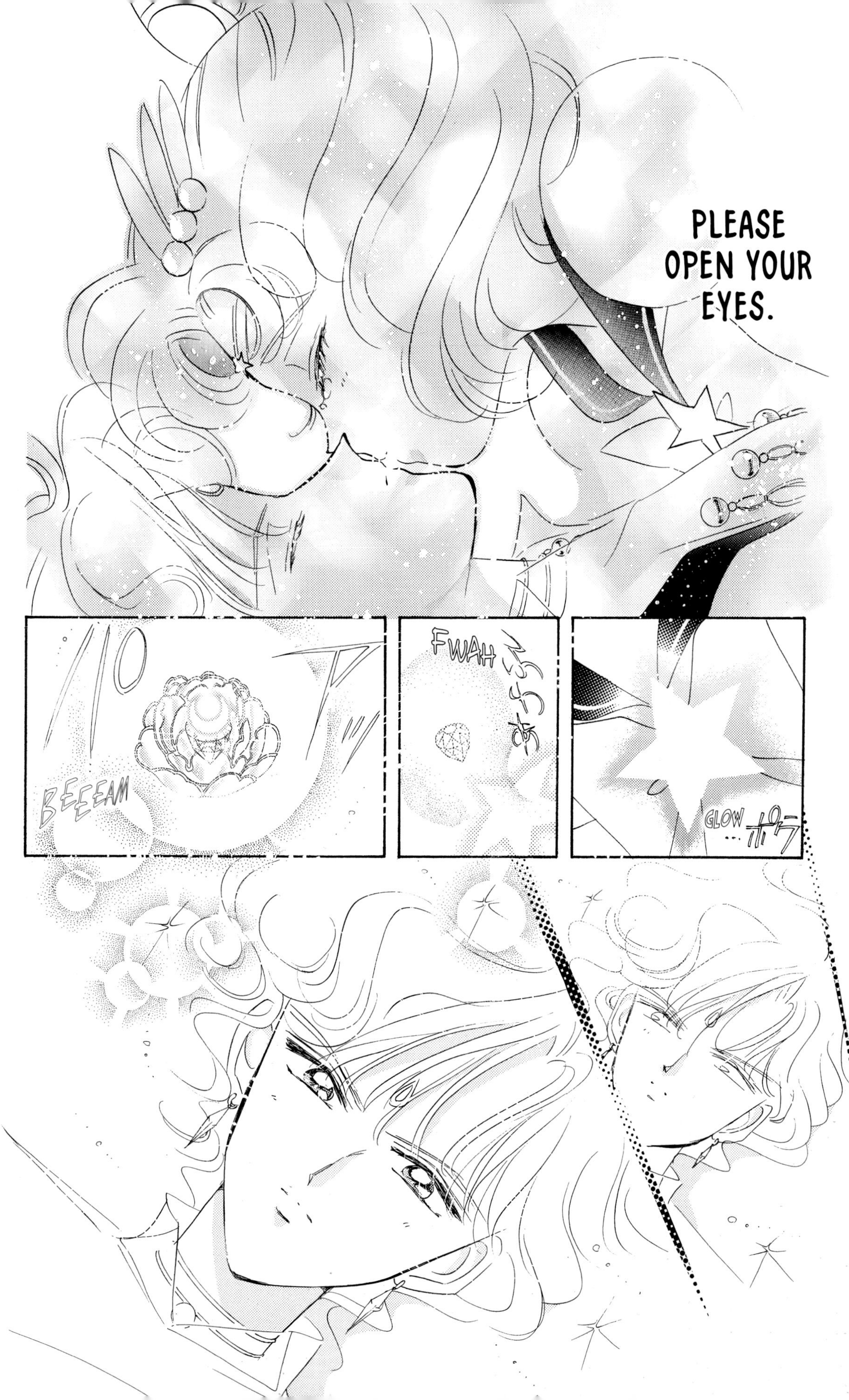
PLEASE OPEN YOUR EYES.
GLOW...
FWAH
BEEEAM

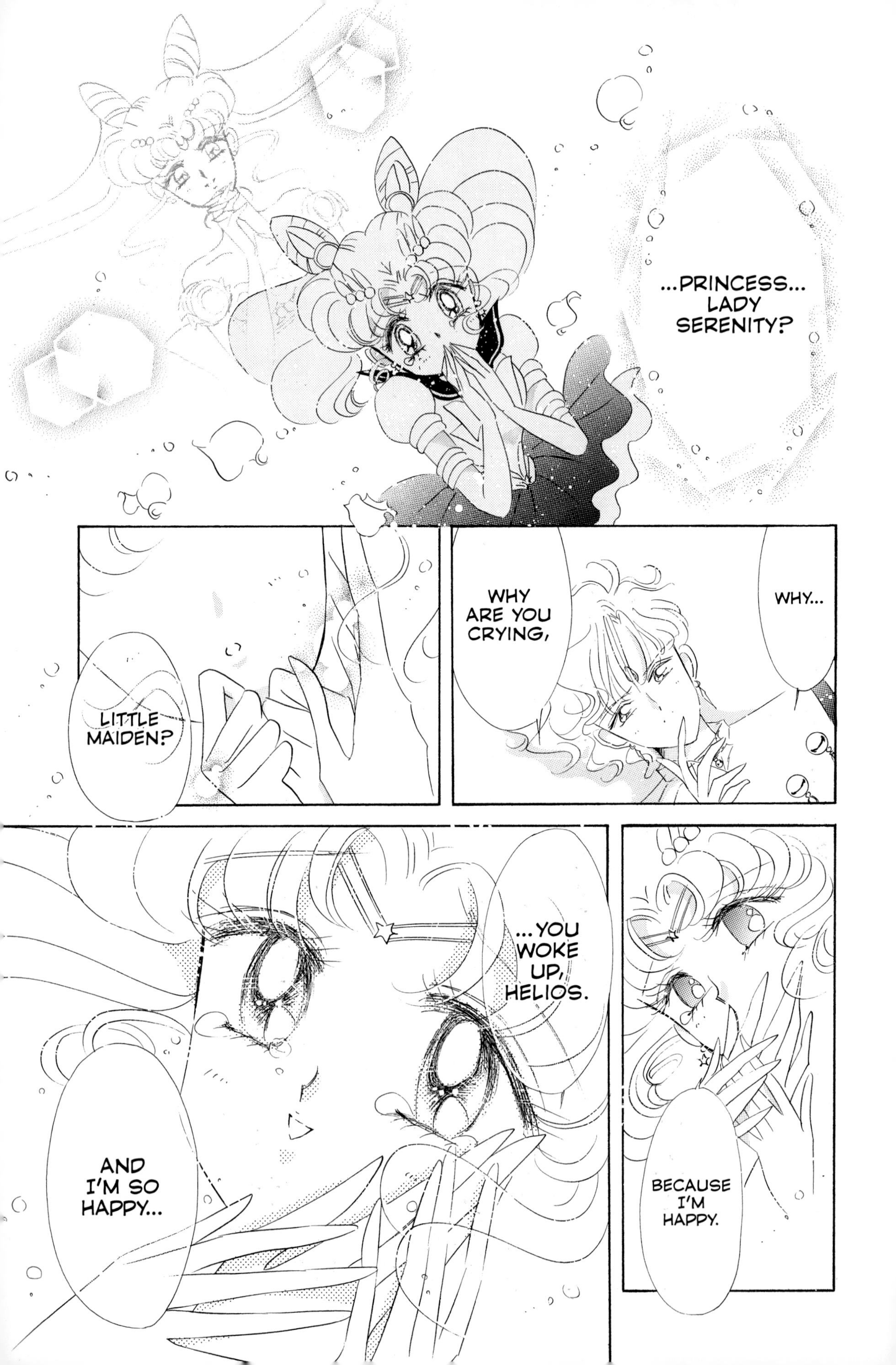
...PRINCESS... LADY SERENITY?
WHY...
WHY ARE YOU CRYING,
LITTLE MAIDEN?
BECAUSE I'M HAPPY.
...YOU WOKE UP, HELIOS.
AND I'M SO HAPPY...

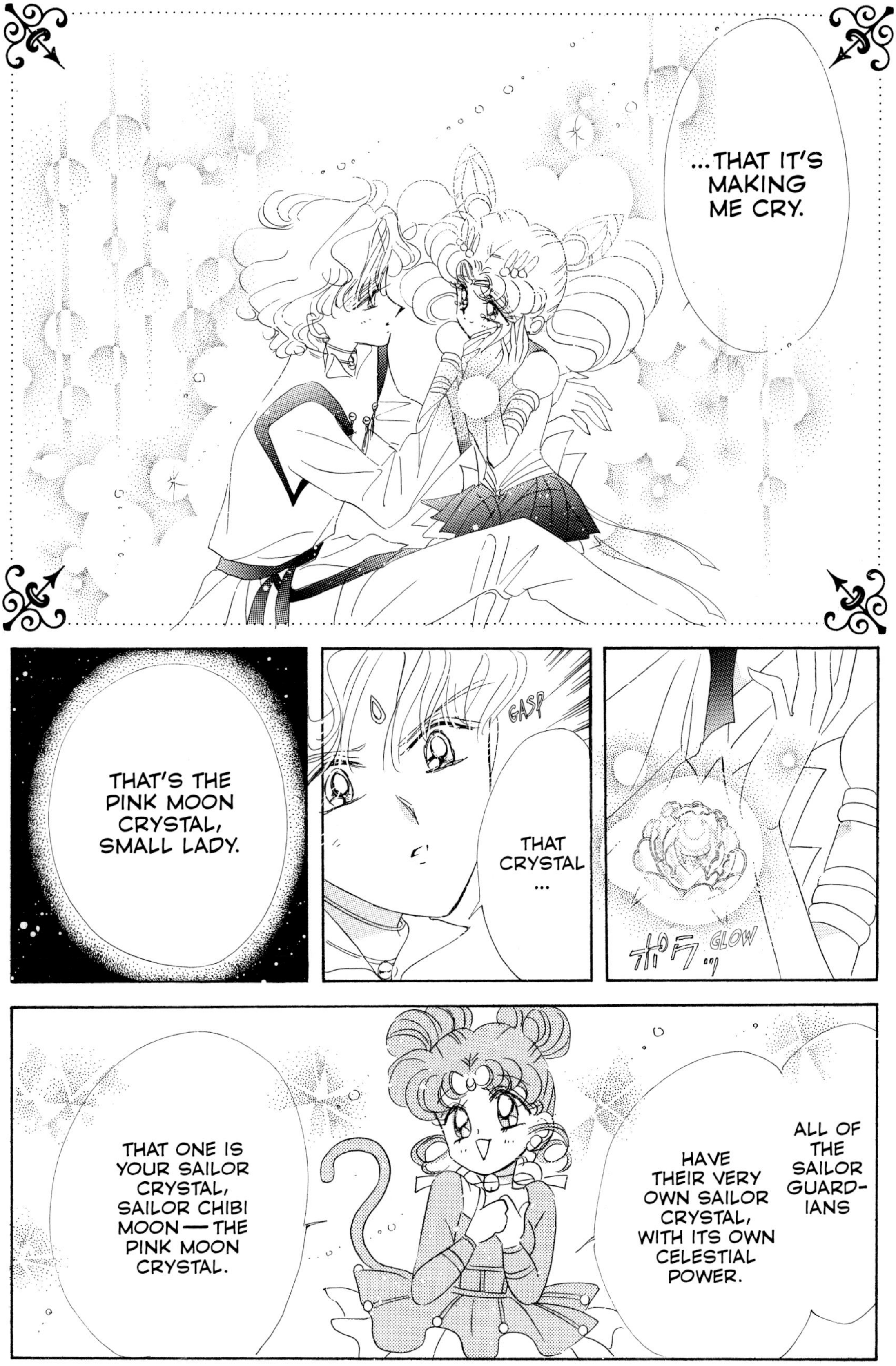
...THAT IT'S MAKING ME CRY.
GLOW
GASP
THAT CRYSTAL ...
THAT'S THE PINK MOON CRYSTAL, SMALL LADY.
ALL OF THE SAILOR GUARDIANS
HAVE THEIR VERY OWN SAILOR CRYSTAL, WITH ITS OWN CELESTIAL POWER.
THAT ONE IS YOUR SAILOR CRYSTAL, SAILOR CHIBI MOON — THE PINK MOON CRYSTAL.

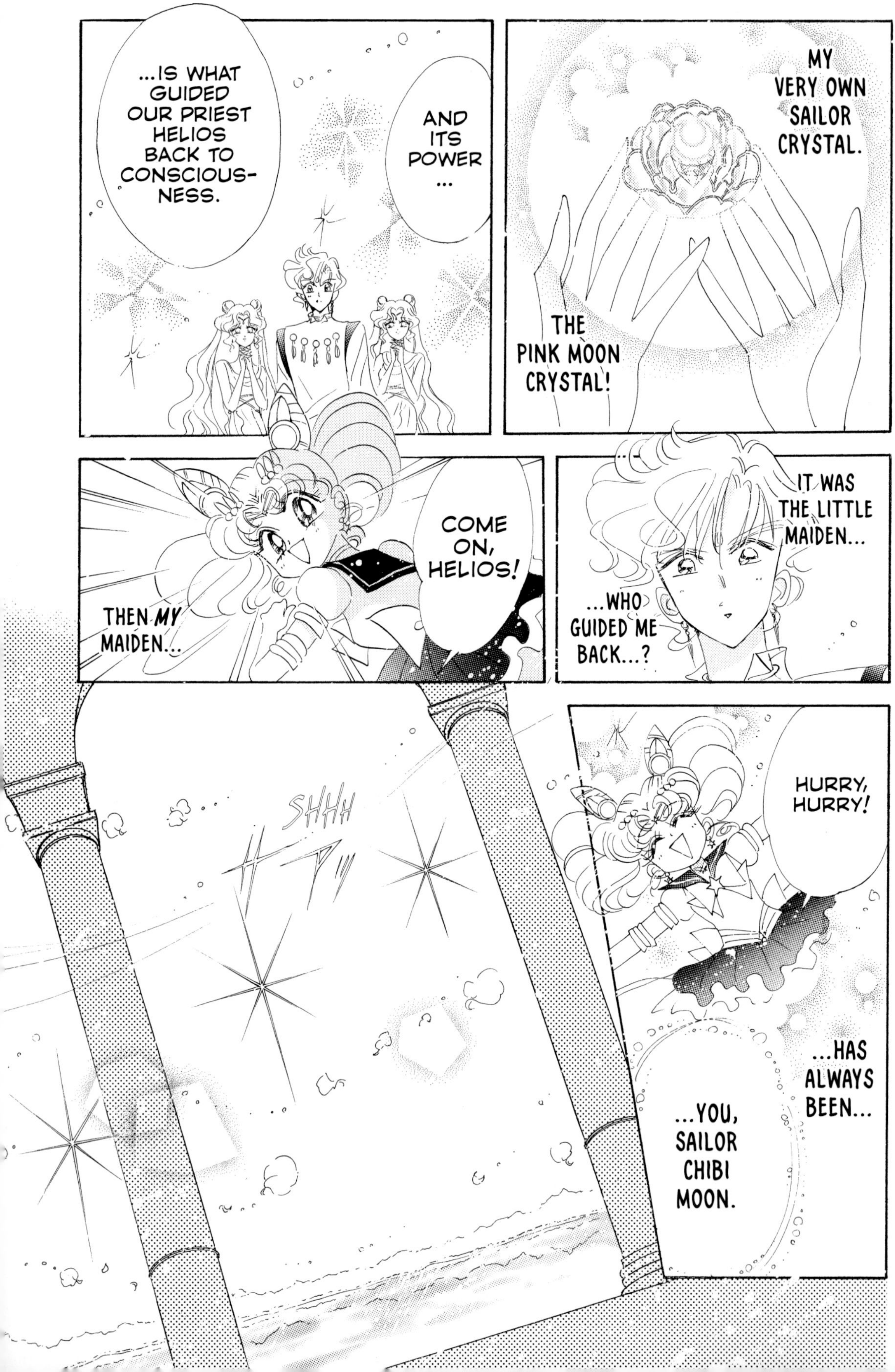
MY VERY OWN SAILOR CRYSTAL.
THE PINK MOON CRYSTAL!
AND ITS POWER ...
...IS WHAT GUIDED OUR PRIEST HELIOS BACK TO CONSCIOUS-NESS.
IT WAS THE LITTLE MAIDEN...
...WHO GUIDED ME BACK...?
COME ON, HELIOS!
THEN MY MAIDEN...
HURRY, HURRY!
...HAS ALWAYS BEEN...
...YOU, SAILOR CHIBI MOON.
SHHH

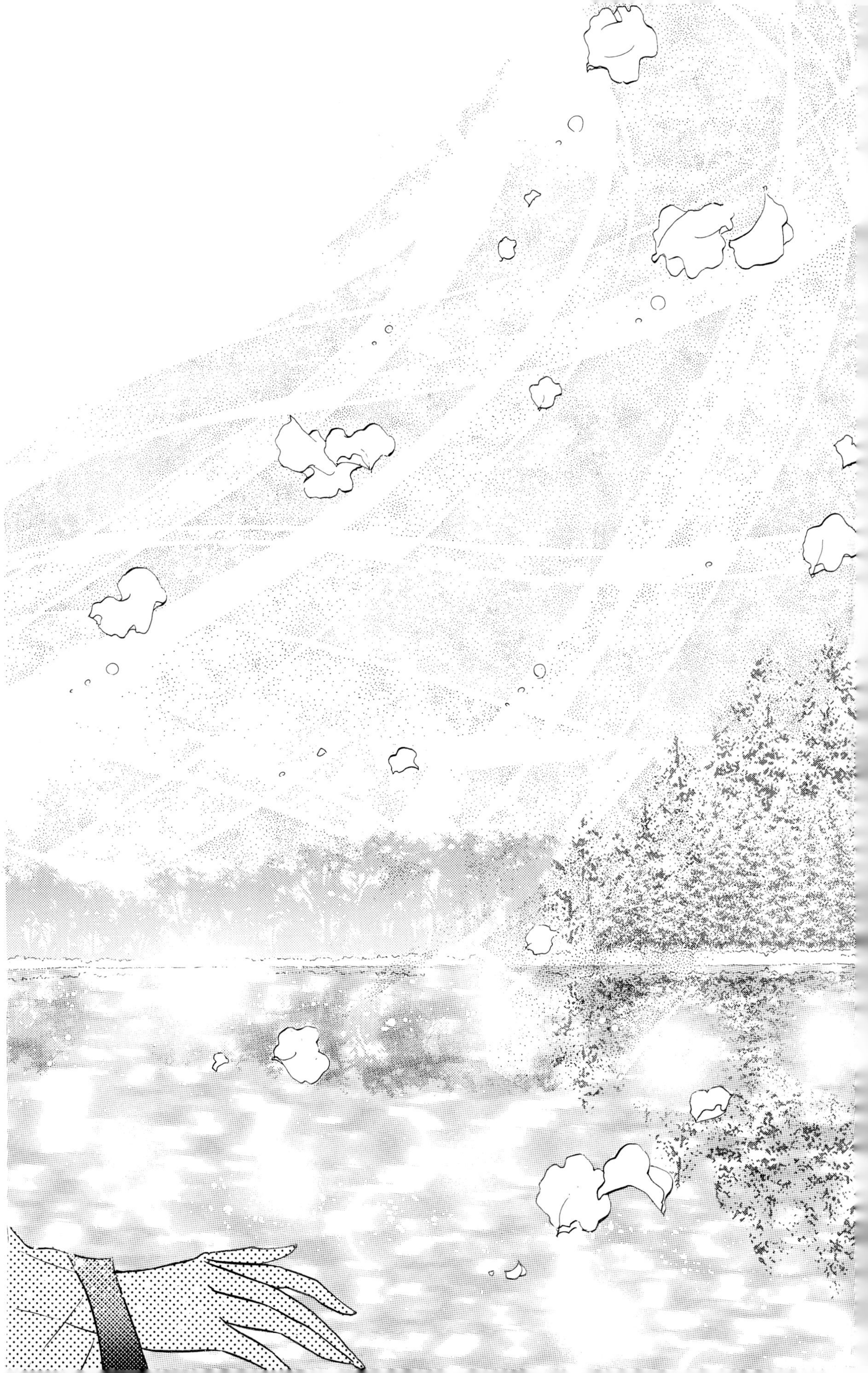

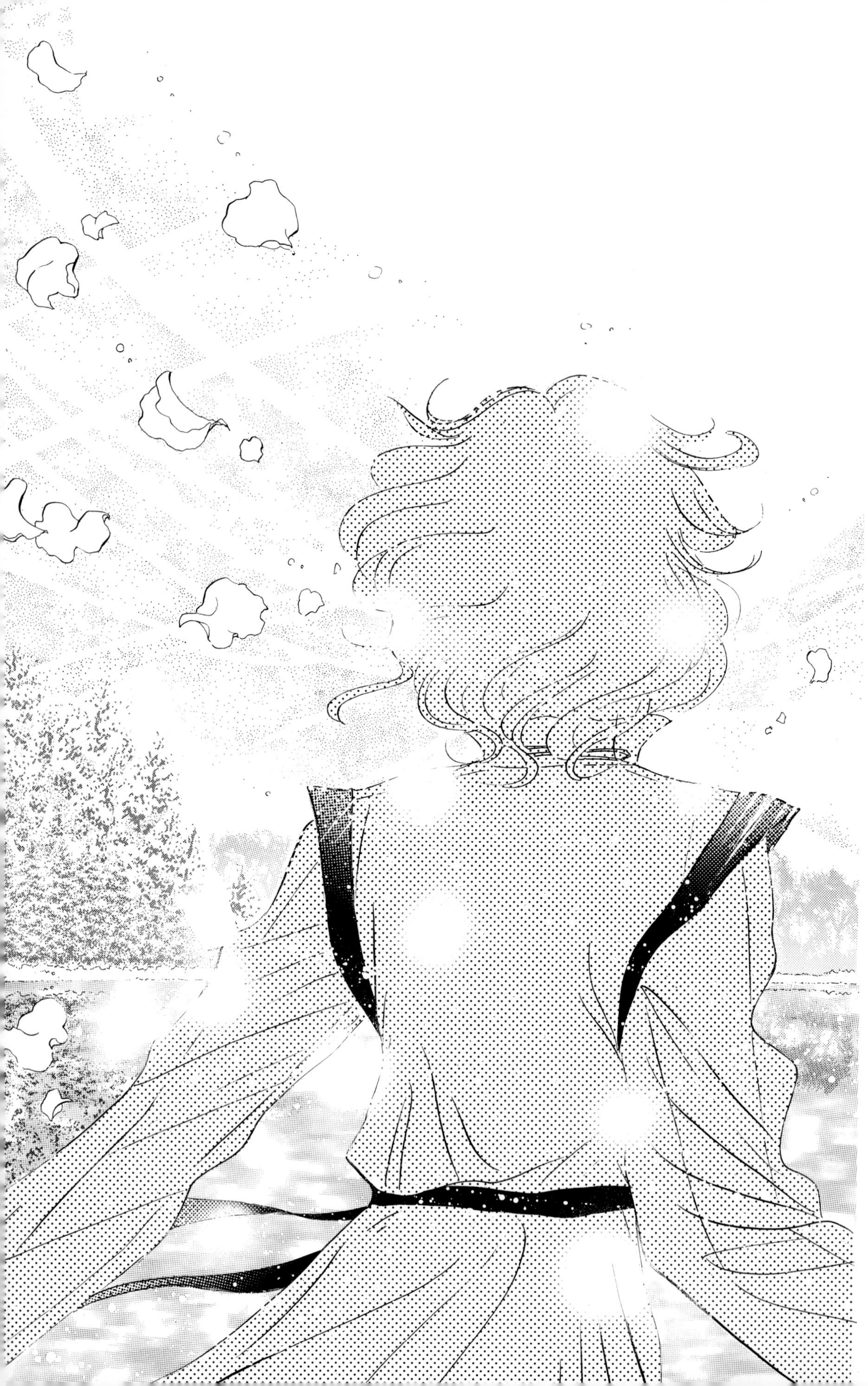

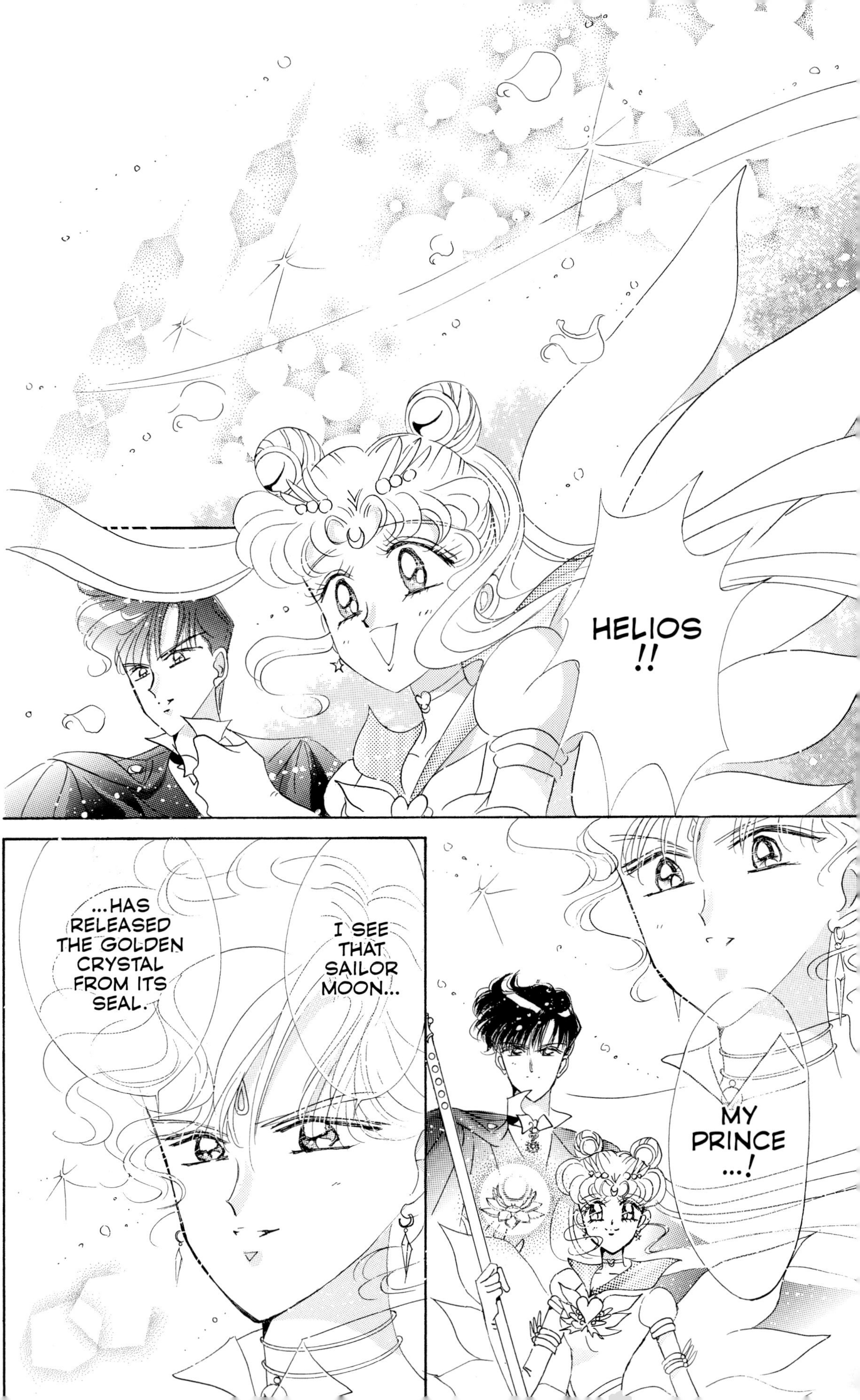
HELIOS !!
MY PRINCE ...!
I SEE THAT SAILOR MOON...
...HAS RELEASED THE GOLDEN CRYSTAL FROM ITS SEAL.

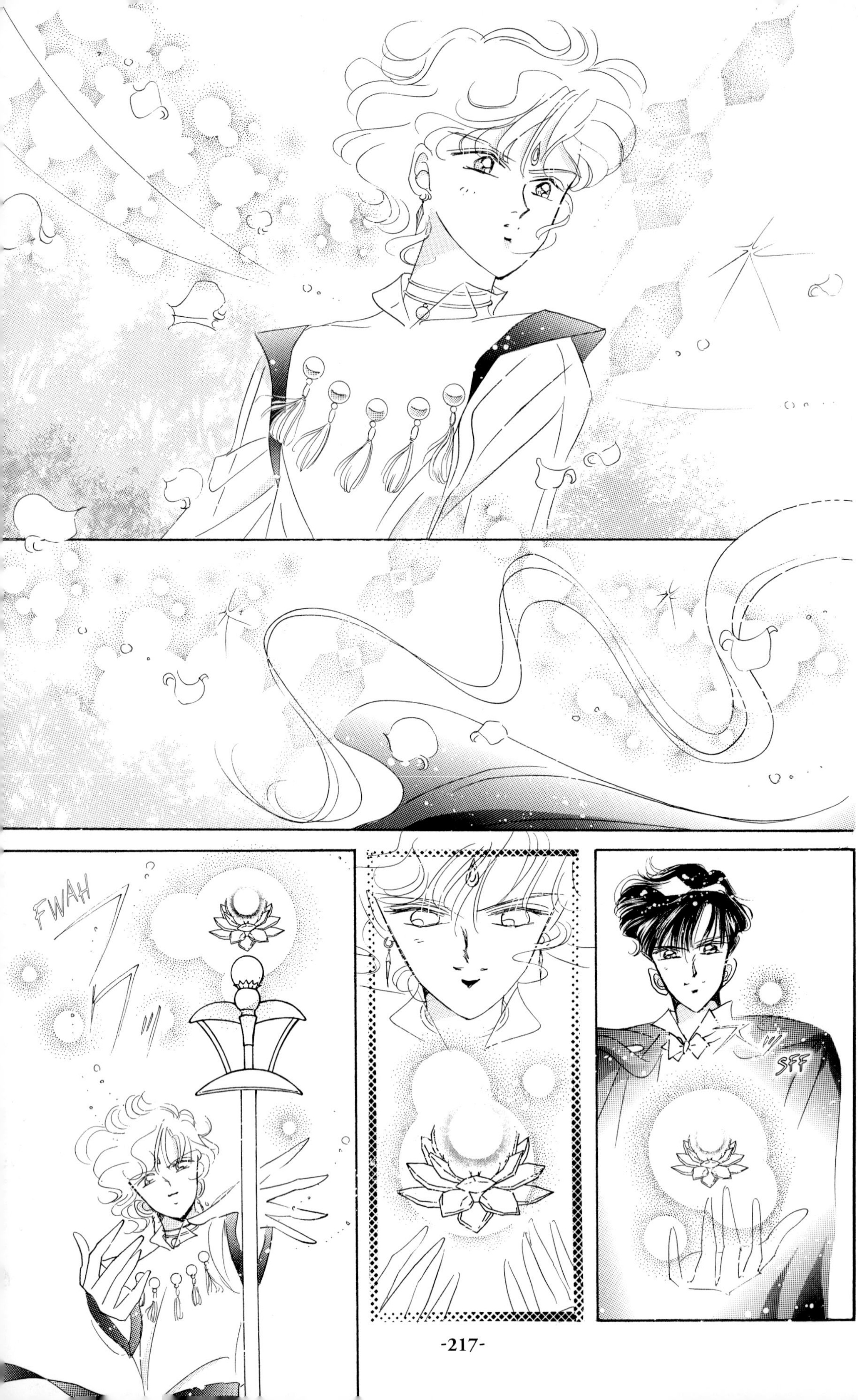
SFF
FWAH

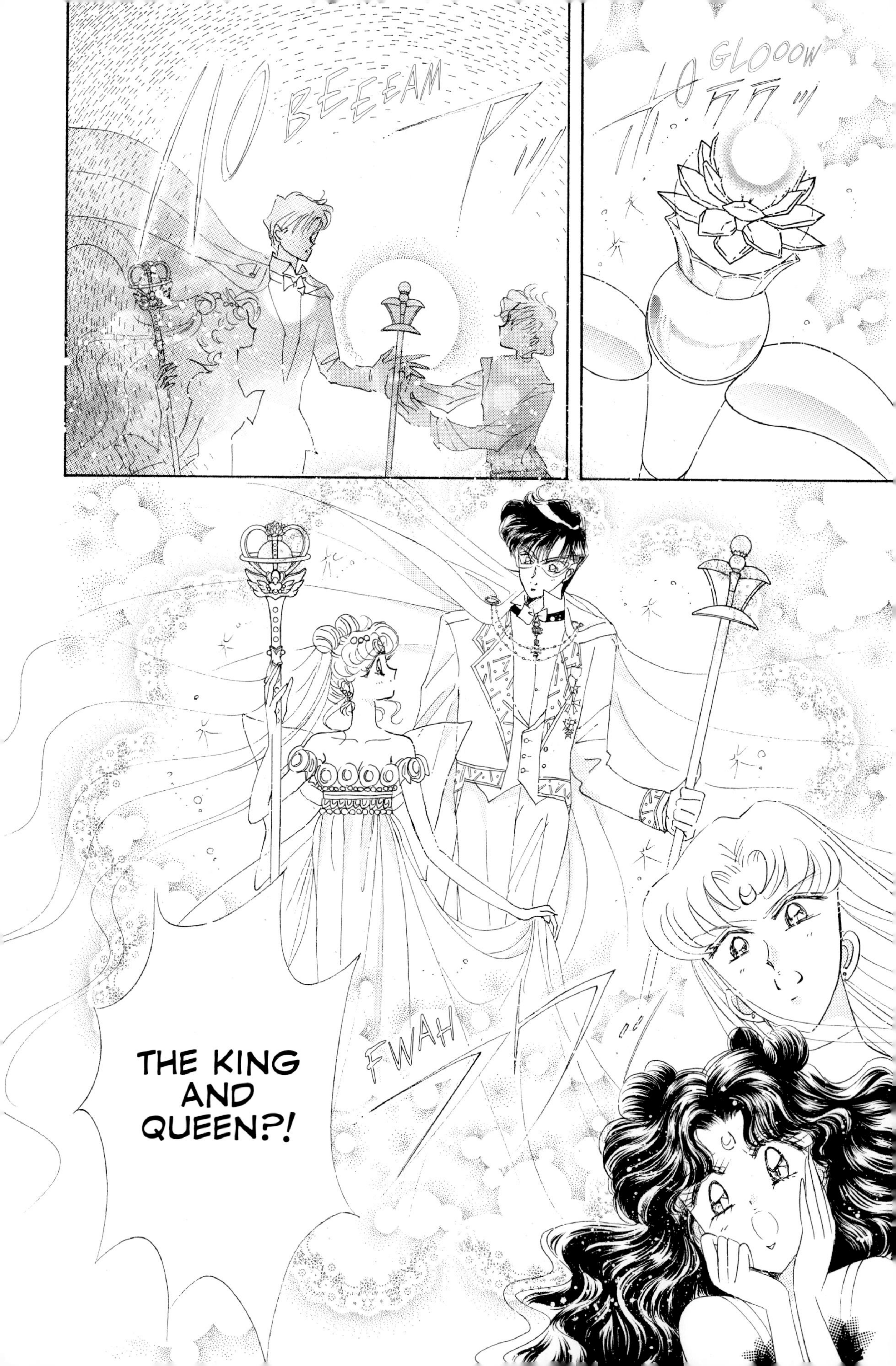
GLOOOW
BEEEAM
FWAH
THE KING AND QUEEN?!

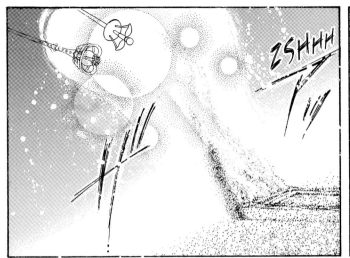
ZSHHH

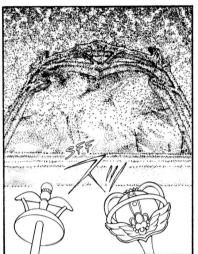
SFF

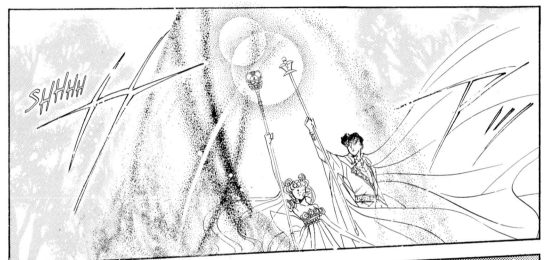
SHHHH

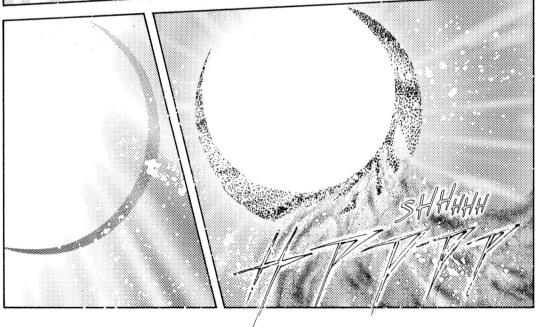
SHHHHH

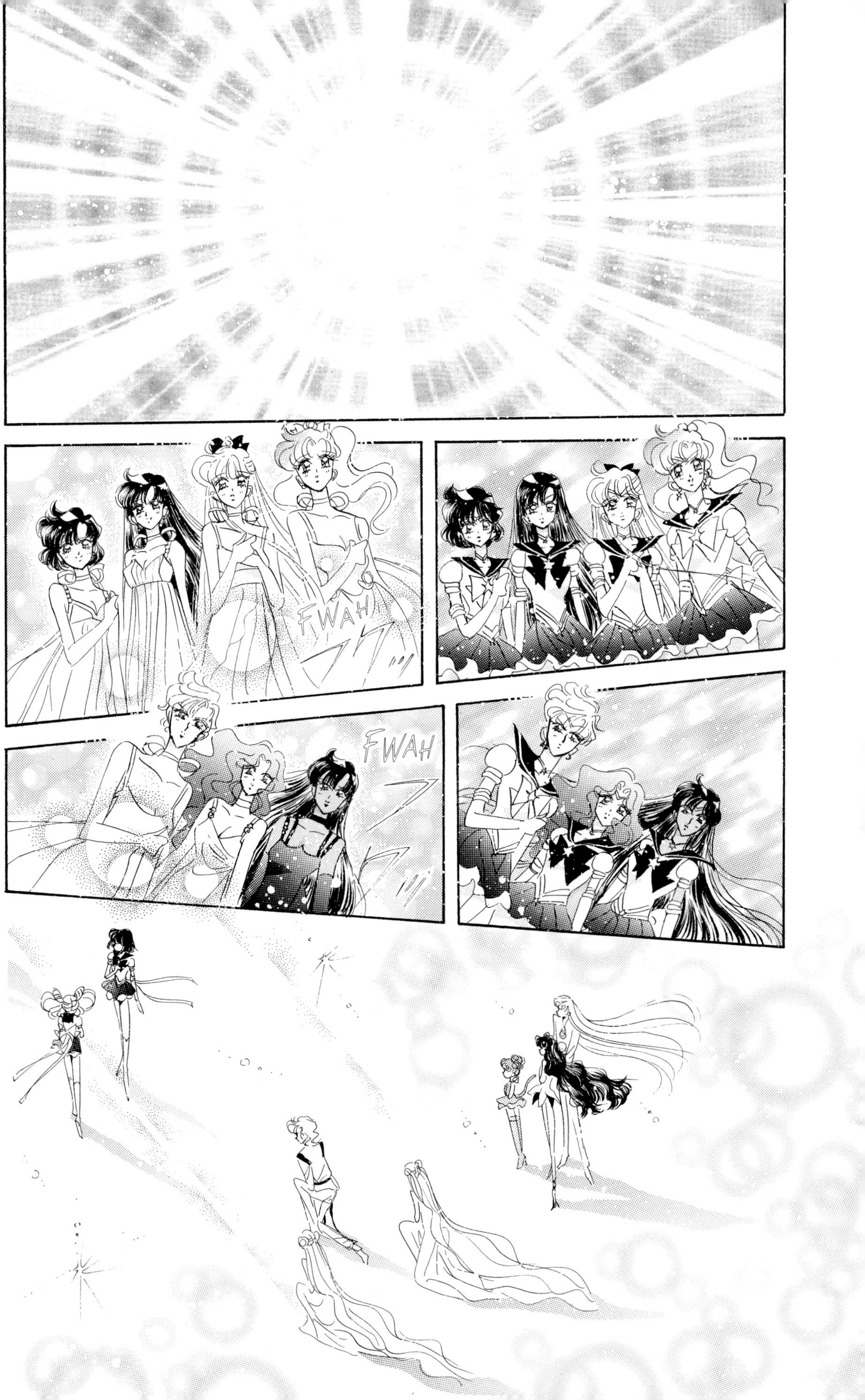
FWAH
FWAH

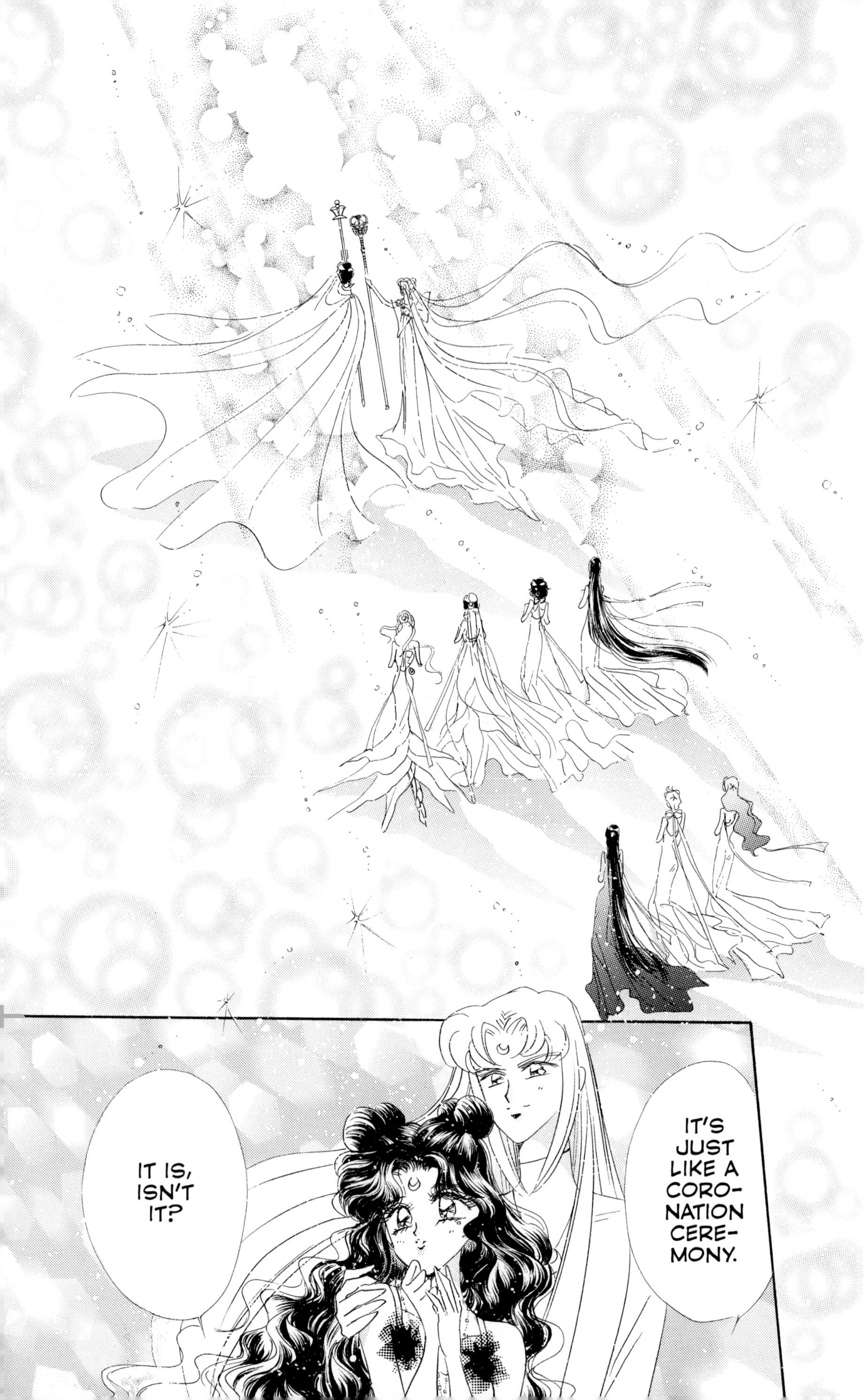
IT'S JUST LIKE A CORONATION CEREMONY.
IT IS, ISN'T IT?

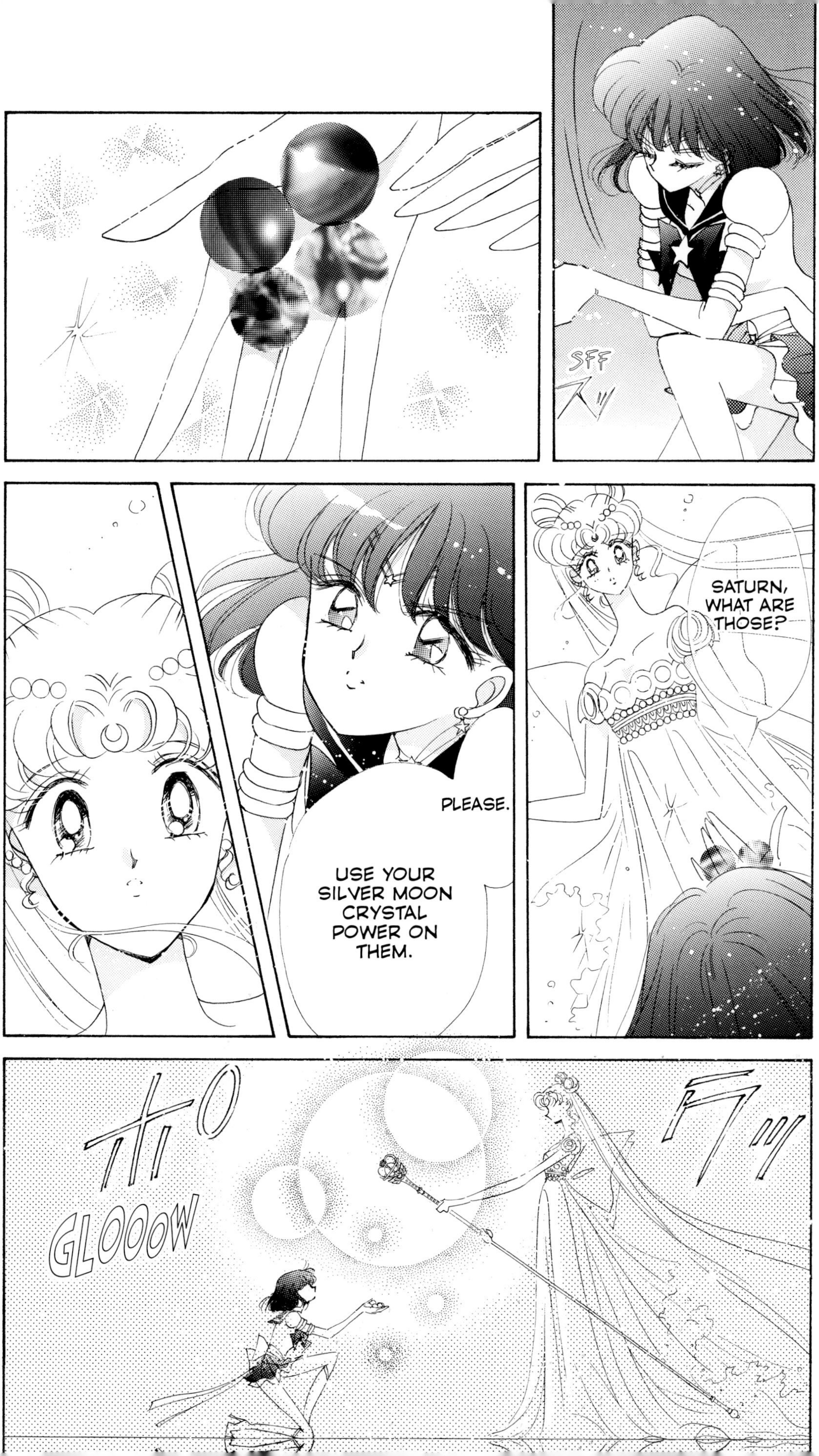
SFF
SATURN, WHAT ARE THOSE?
PLEASE.
USE YOUR SILVER MOON CRYSTAL POWER ON THEM.
GLOOOW

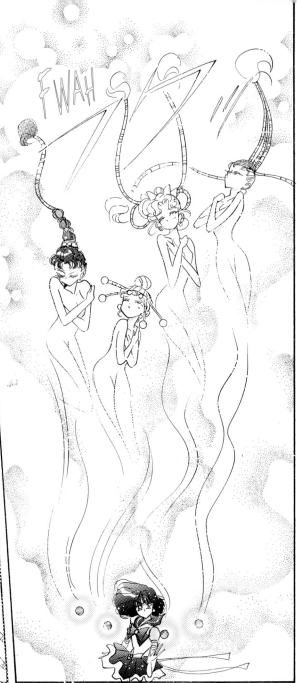

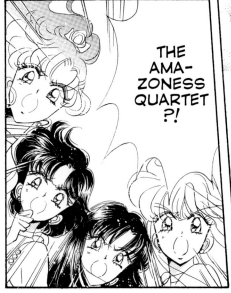

THE AMA-ZONESS QUARTET ?!

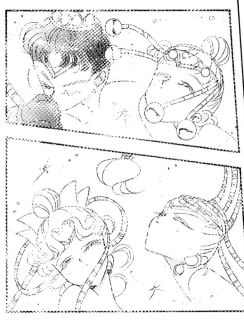

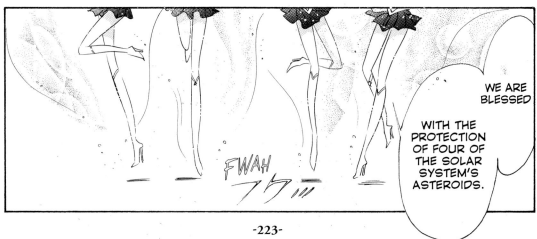

WE ARE BLESSED

WITH THE PROTECTION OF FOUR OF THE SOLAR SYSTEM'S ASTEROIDS.

FWAH

FWAH

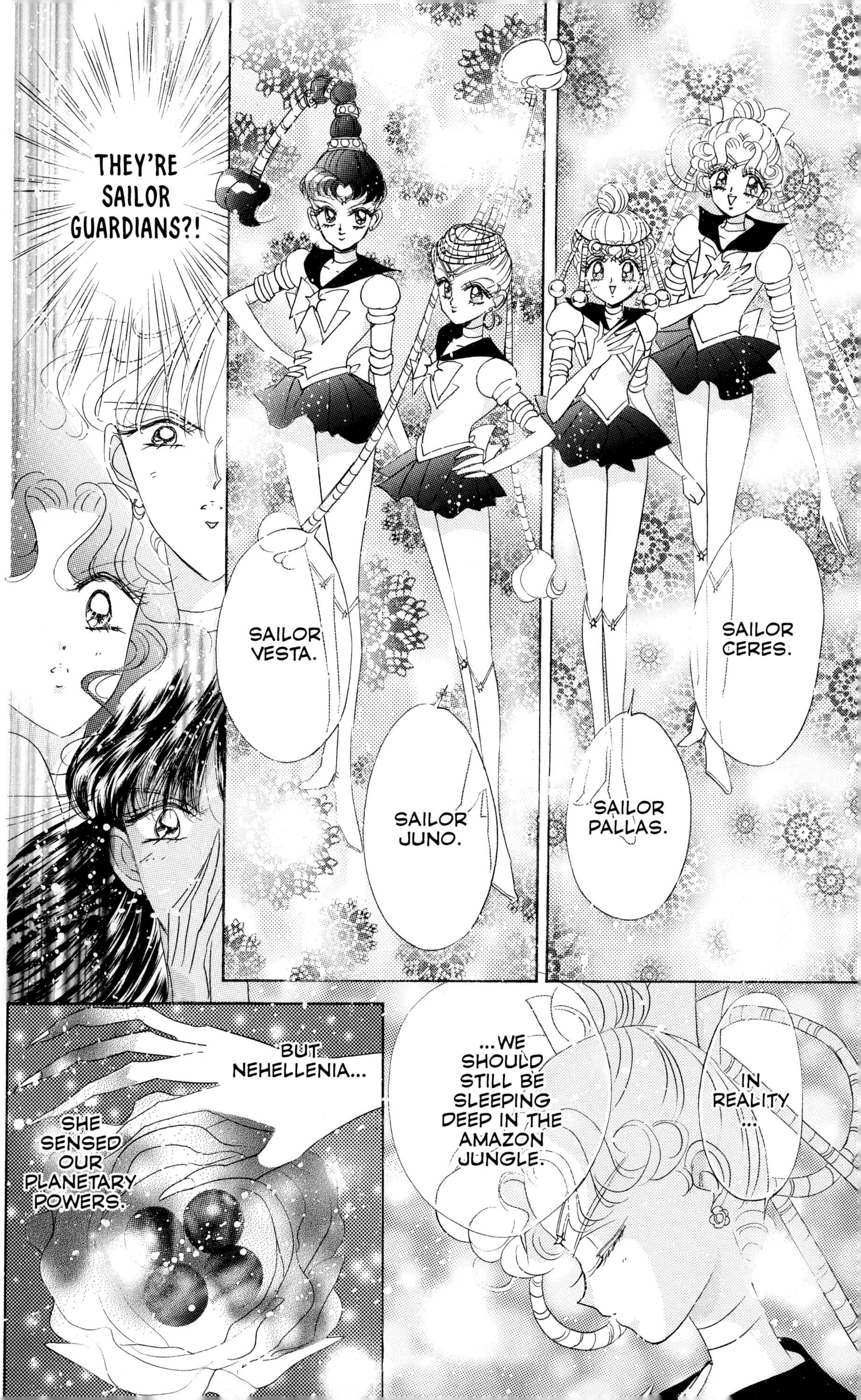
SAILOR CERES.
SAILOR PALLAS.
SAILOR VESTA.
SAILOR JUNO.
THEY'RE SAILOR GUARDIANS?!
IN REALITY...
...WE SHOULD STILL BE SLEEPING DEEP IN THE AMAZON JUNGLE.
BUT NEHELLENIA...
SHE SENSED OUR PLANETARY POWERS.

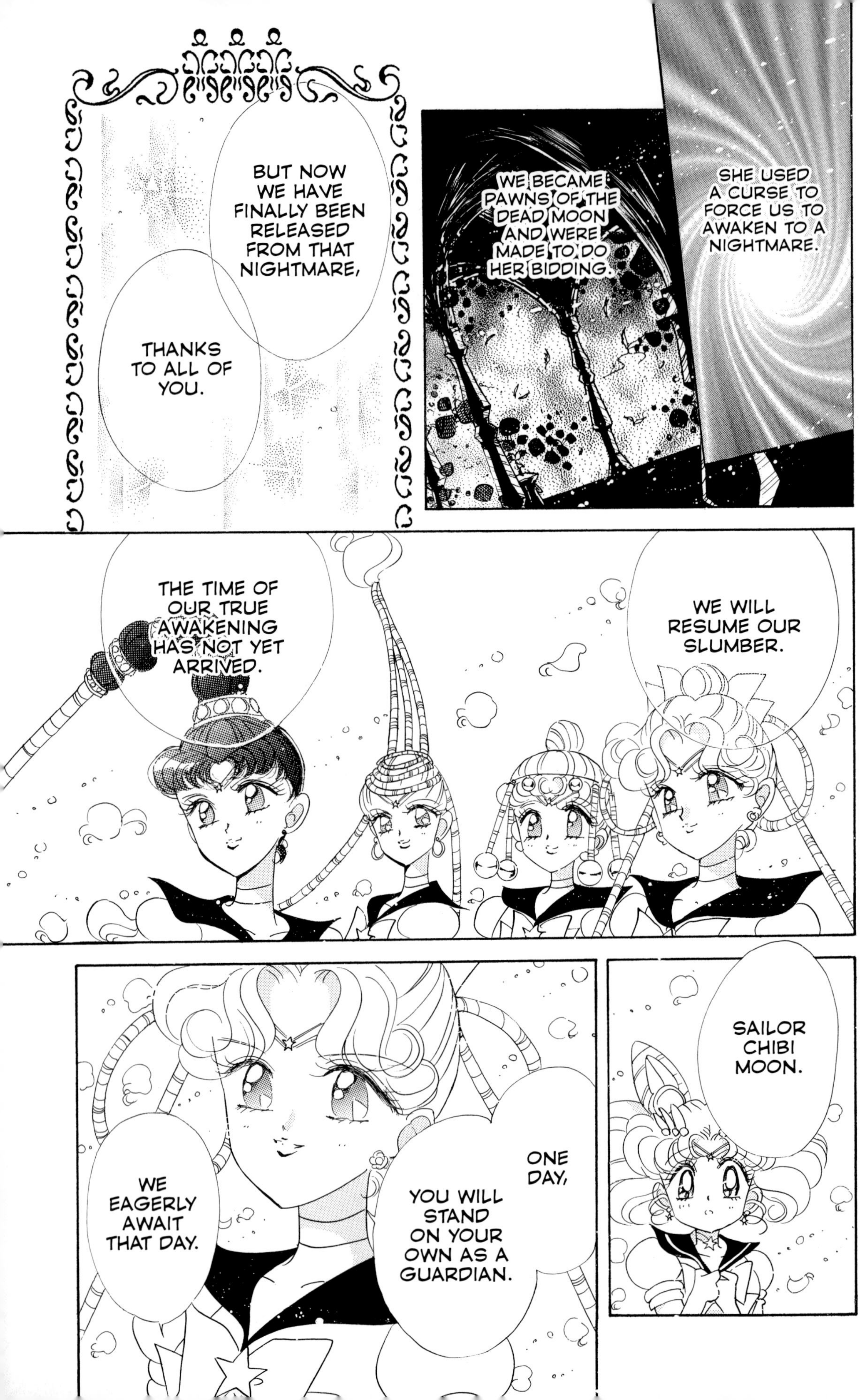
SHE USED A CURSE TO FORCE US TO AWAKEN TO A NIGHTMARE.
WE BECAME PAWNS OF THE DEAD MOON AND WERE MADE TO DO HER BIDDING.
BUT NOW WE HAVE FINALLY BEEN RELEASED FROM THAT NIGHTMARE,
THANKS TO ALL OF YOU.
WE WILL RESUME OUR SLUMBER.
THE TIME OF OUR TRUE AWAKENING HAS NOT YET ARRIVED.
SAILOR CHIBI MOON.
ONE DAY,
YOU WILL STAND ON YOUR OWN AS A GUARDIAN.
WE EAGERLY AWAIT THAT DAY.

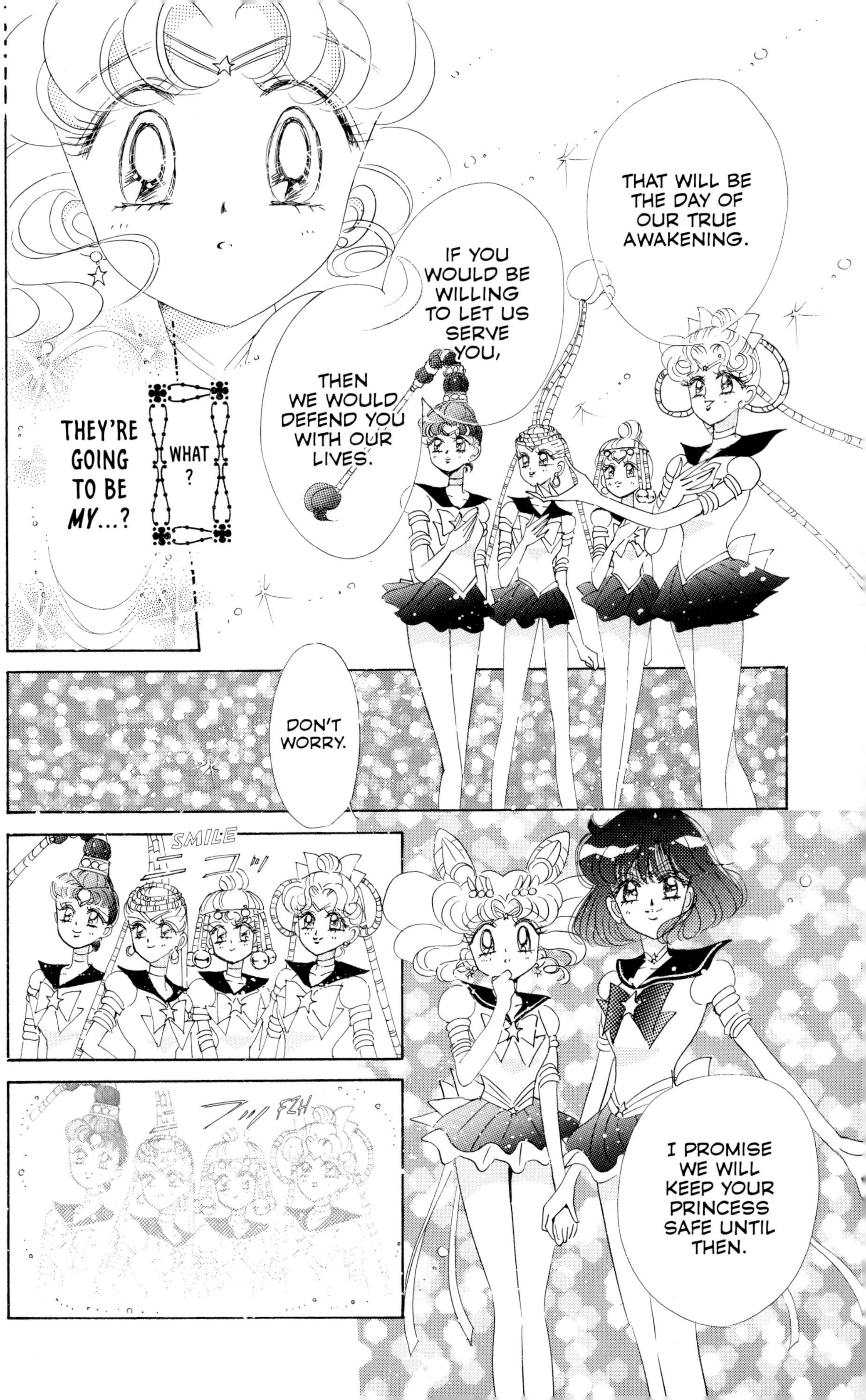
THAT WILL BE THE DAY OF OUR TRUE AWAKENING.
IF YOU WOULD BE WILLING TO LET US SERVE YOU,
THEN WE WOULD DEFEND YOU WITH OUR LIVES.
WHAT?
THEY'RE GOING TO BE *MY*...?
DON'T WORRY.
I PROMISE WE WILL KEEP YOUR PRINCESS SAFE UNTIL THEN.
SMILE
FZH

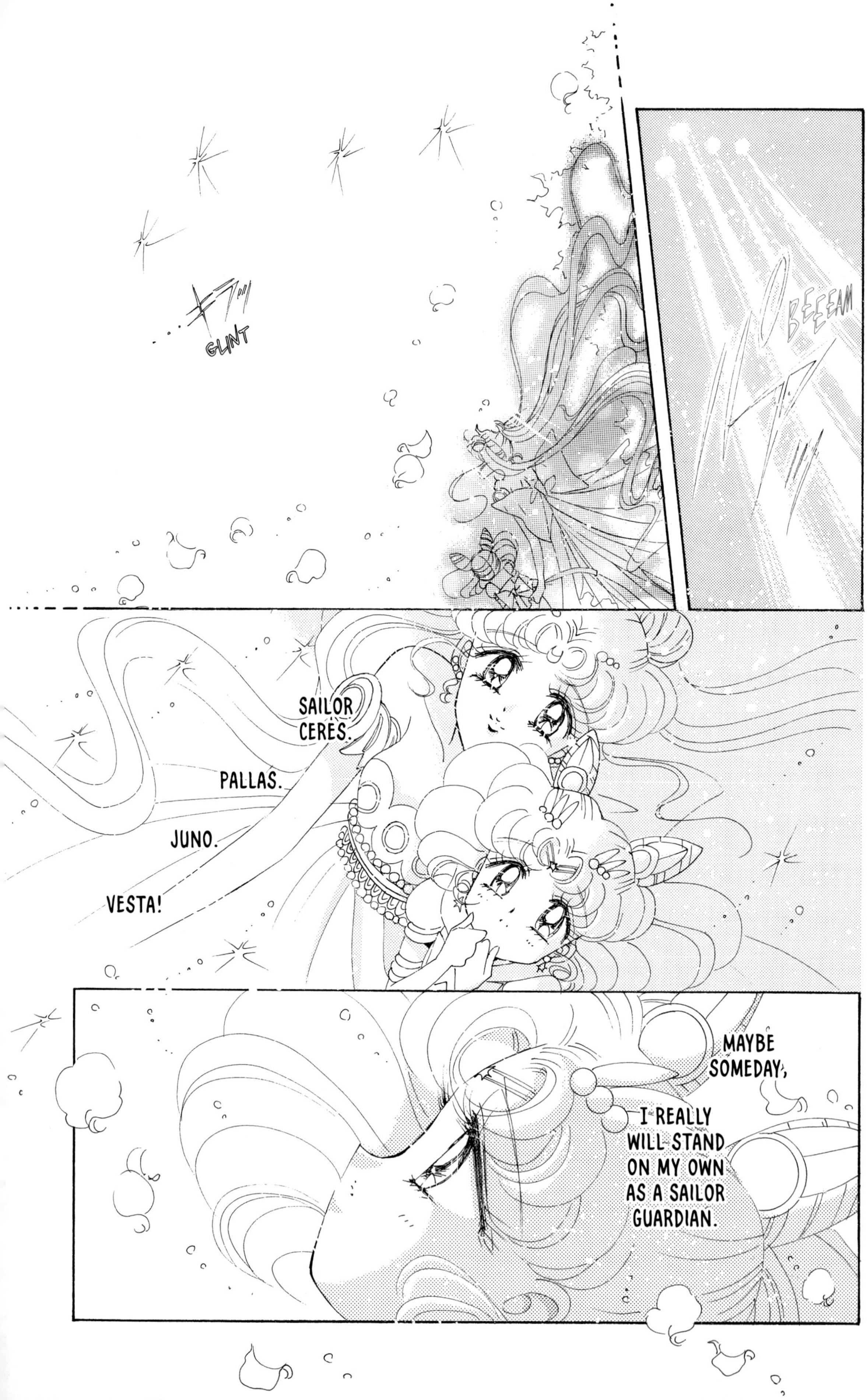
BEEEAM
GLINT
SAILOR CERES.
PALLAS.
JUNO.
VESTA!
MAYBE SOMEDAY,
I REALLY WILL STAND ON MY OWN AS A SAILOR GUARDIAN.

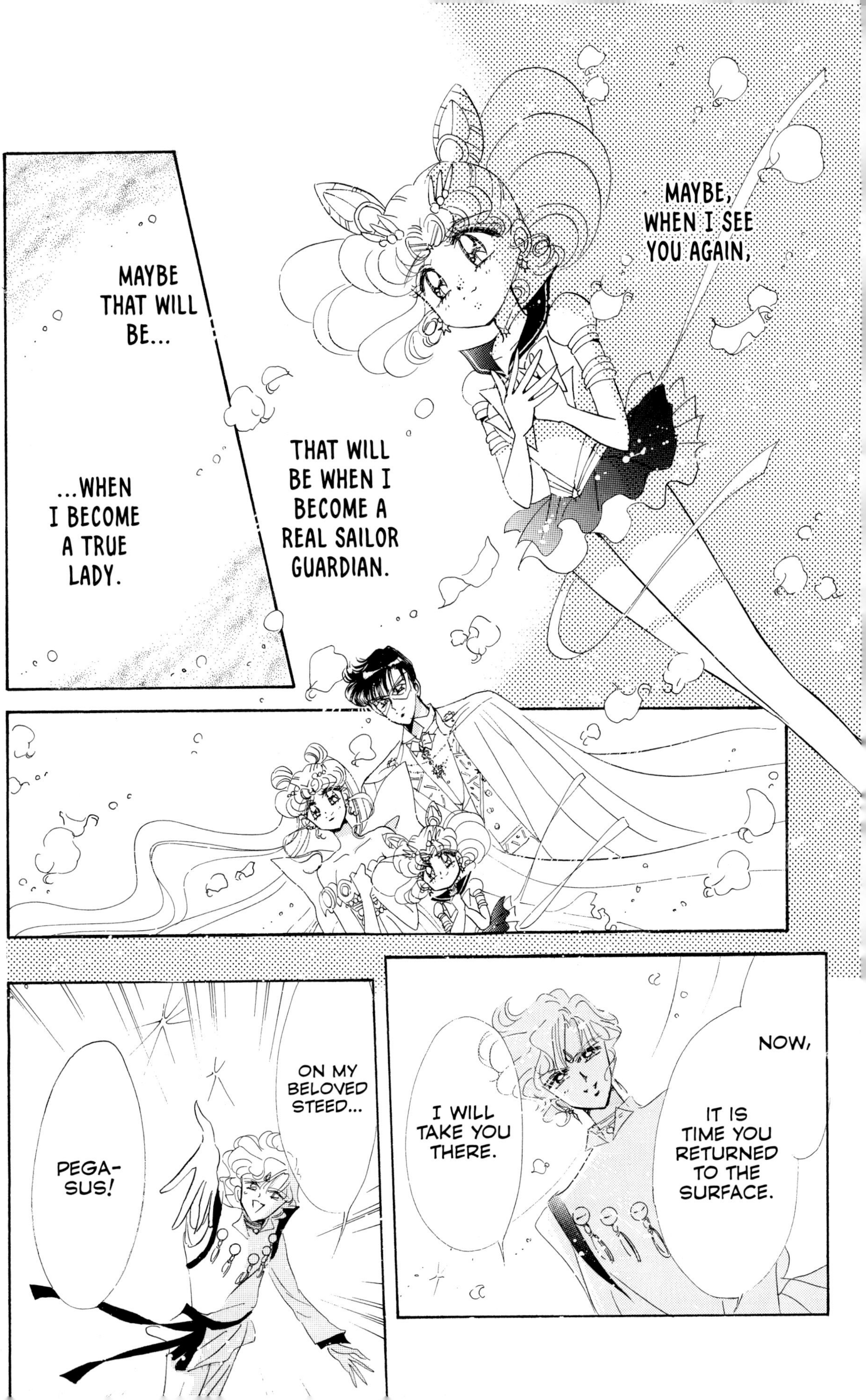
MAYBE, WHEN I SEE YOU AGAIN,
THAT WILL BE WHEN I BECOME A REAL SAILOR GUARDIAN.
MAYBE THAT WILL BE...
...WHEN I BECOME A TRUE LADY.
NOW,
IT IS TIME YOU RETURNED TO THE SURFACE.
I WILL TAKE YOU THERE.
ON MY BELOVED STEED...
PEGA-SUS!

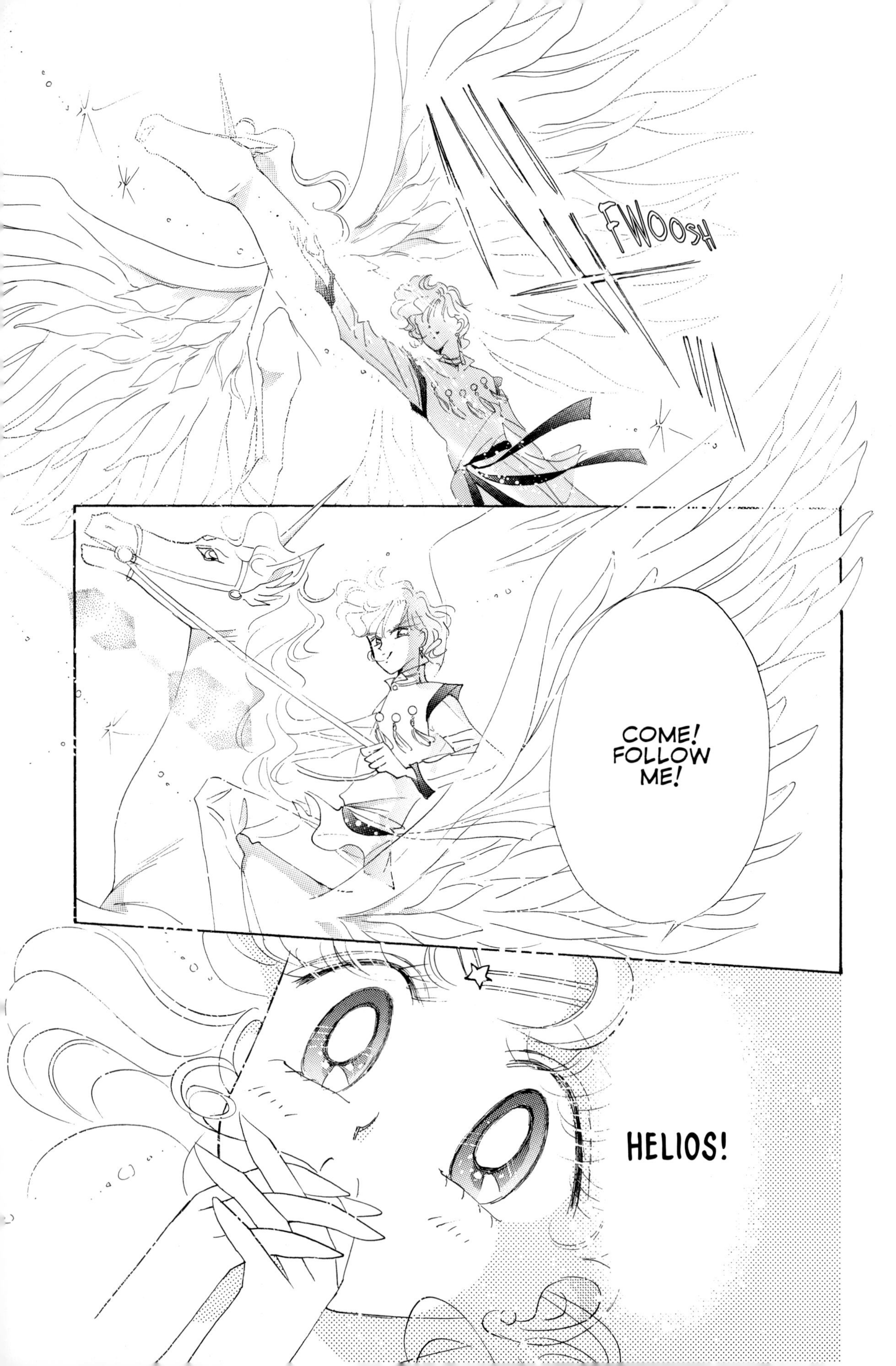
FWOOSH
COME! FOLLOW ME!
HELIOS!

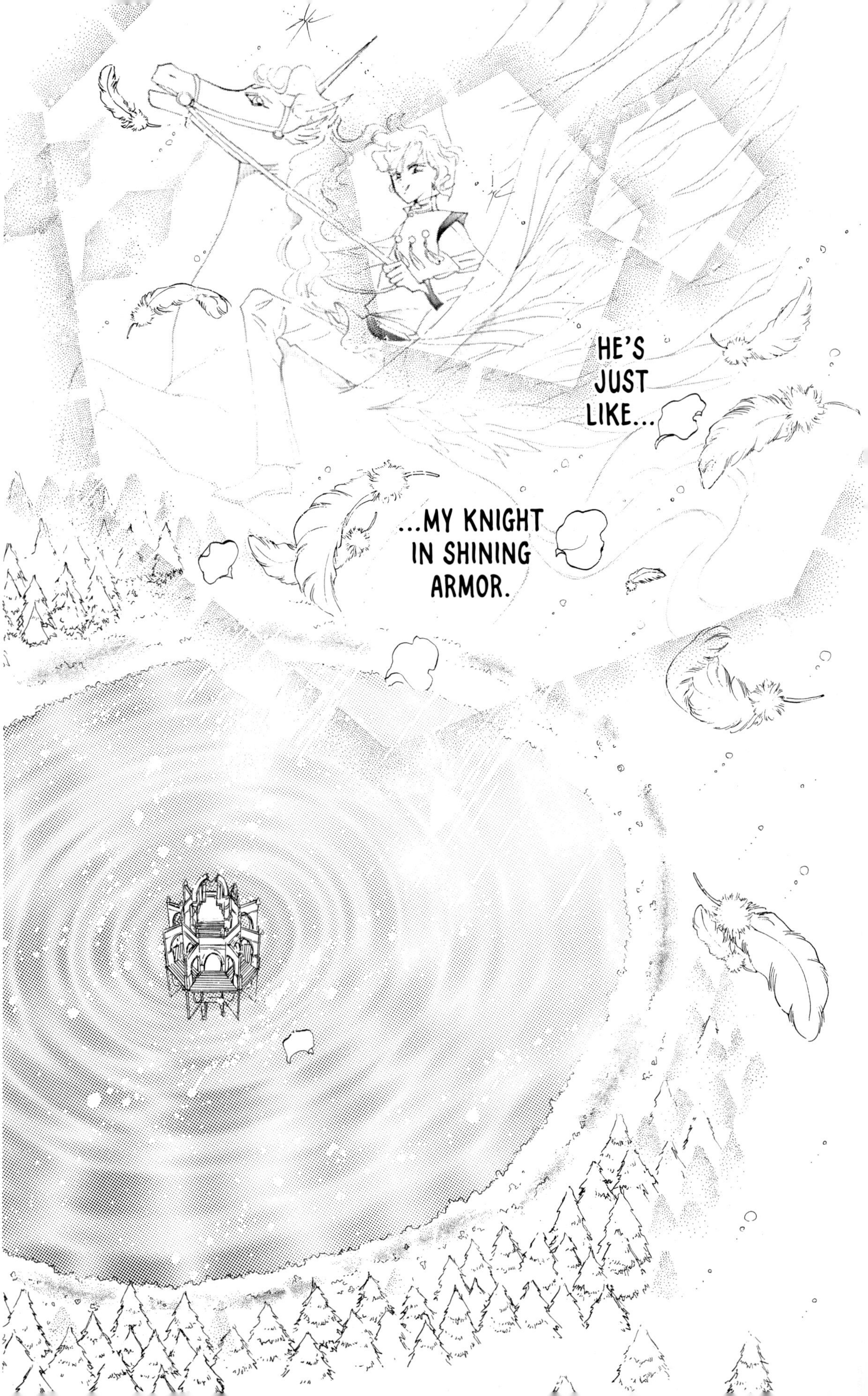
HE'S JUST LIKE...
...MY KNIGHT IN SHINING ARMOR.

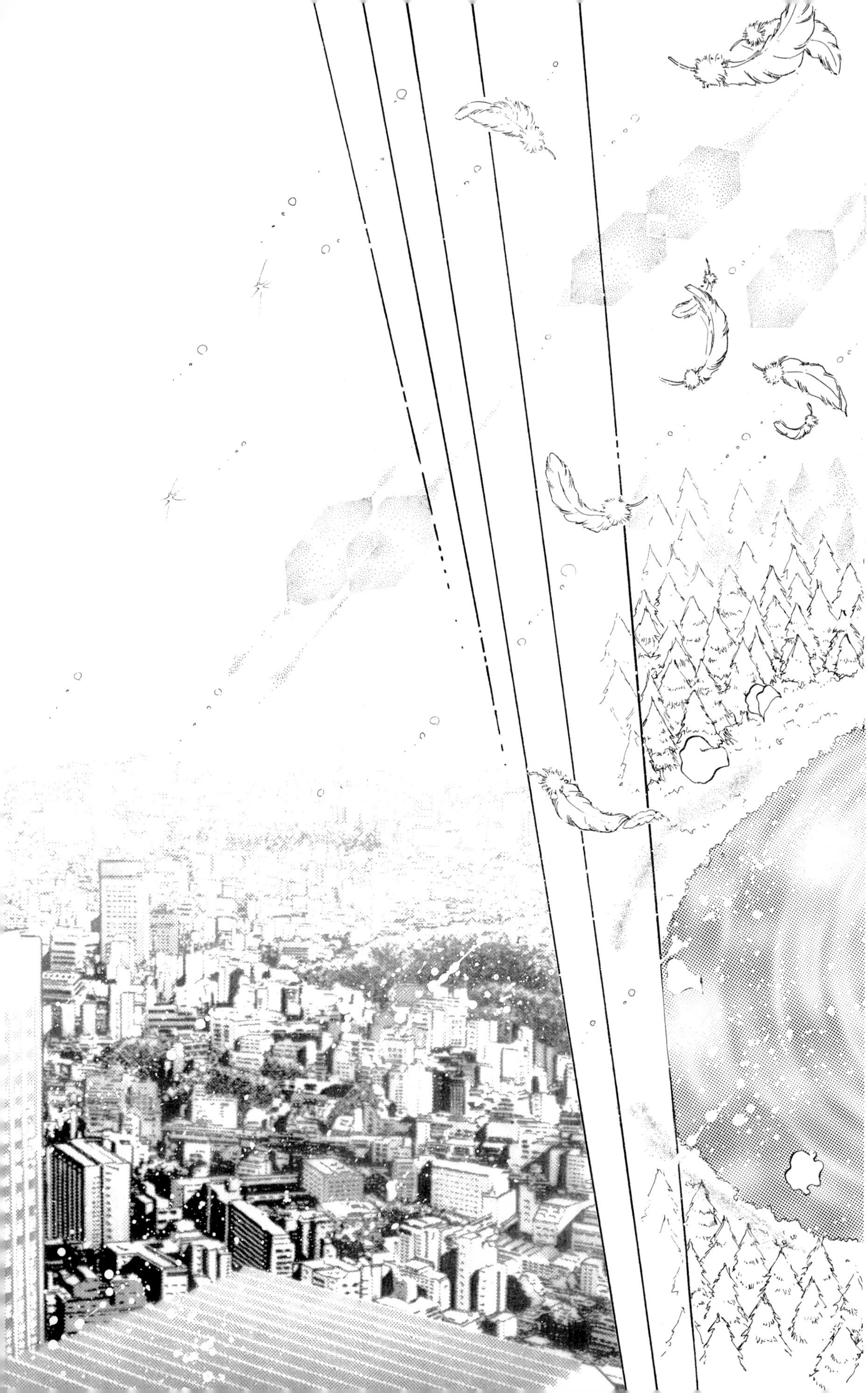

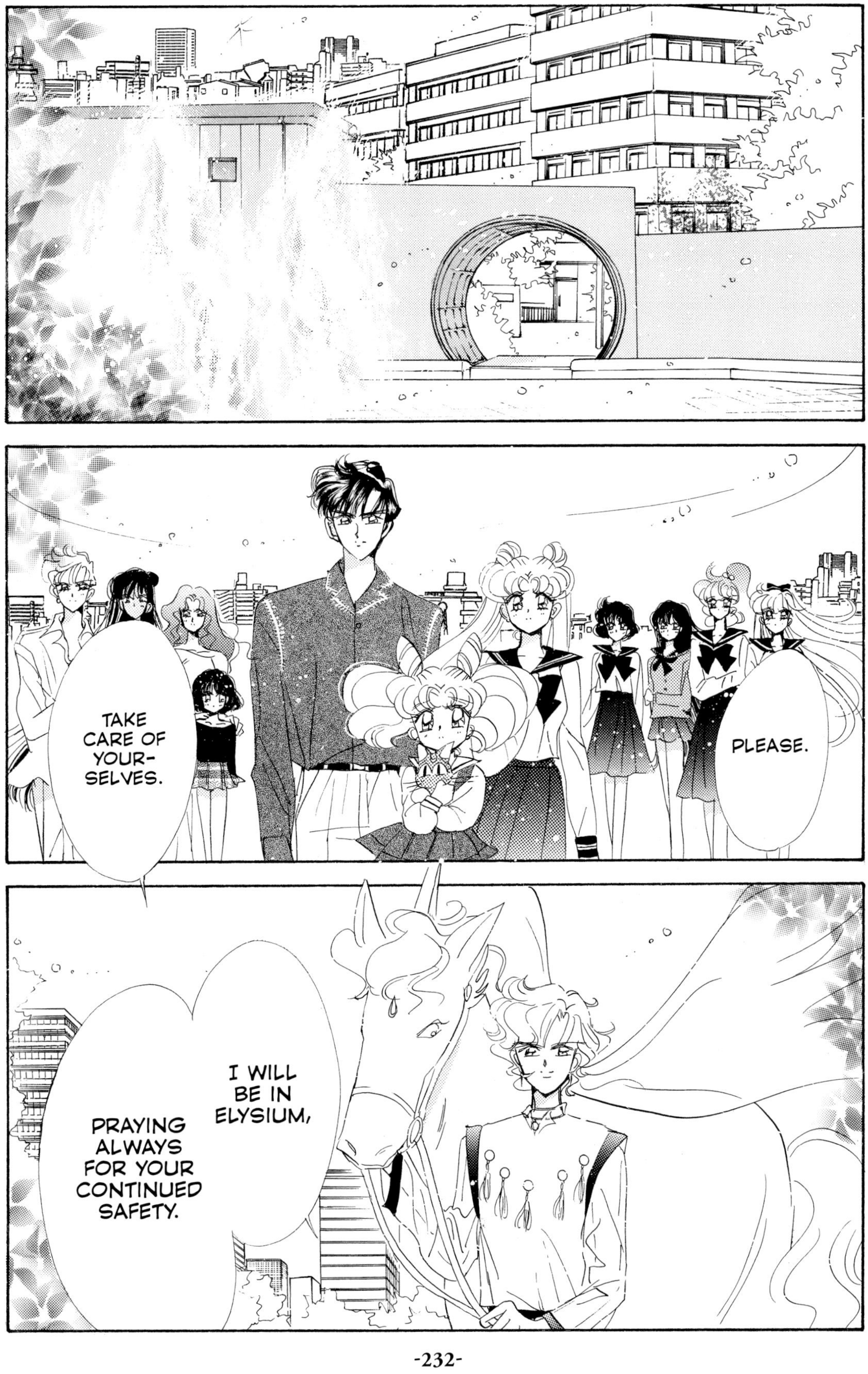
PLEASE.
TAKE CARE OF YOUR-SELVES.
I WILL BE IN ELYSIUM,
PRAYING ALWAYS FOR YOUR CONTINUED SAFETY.

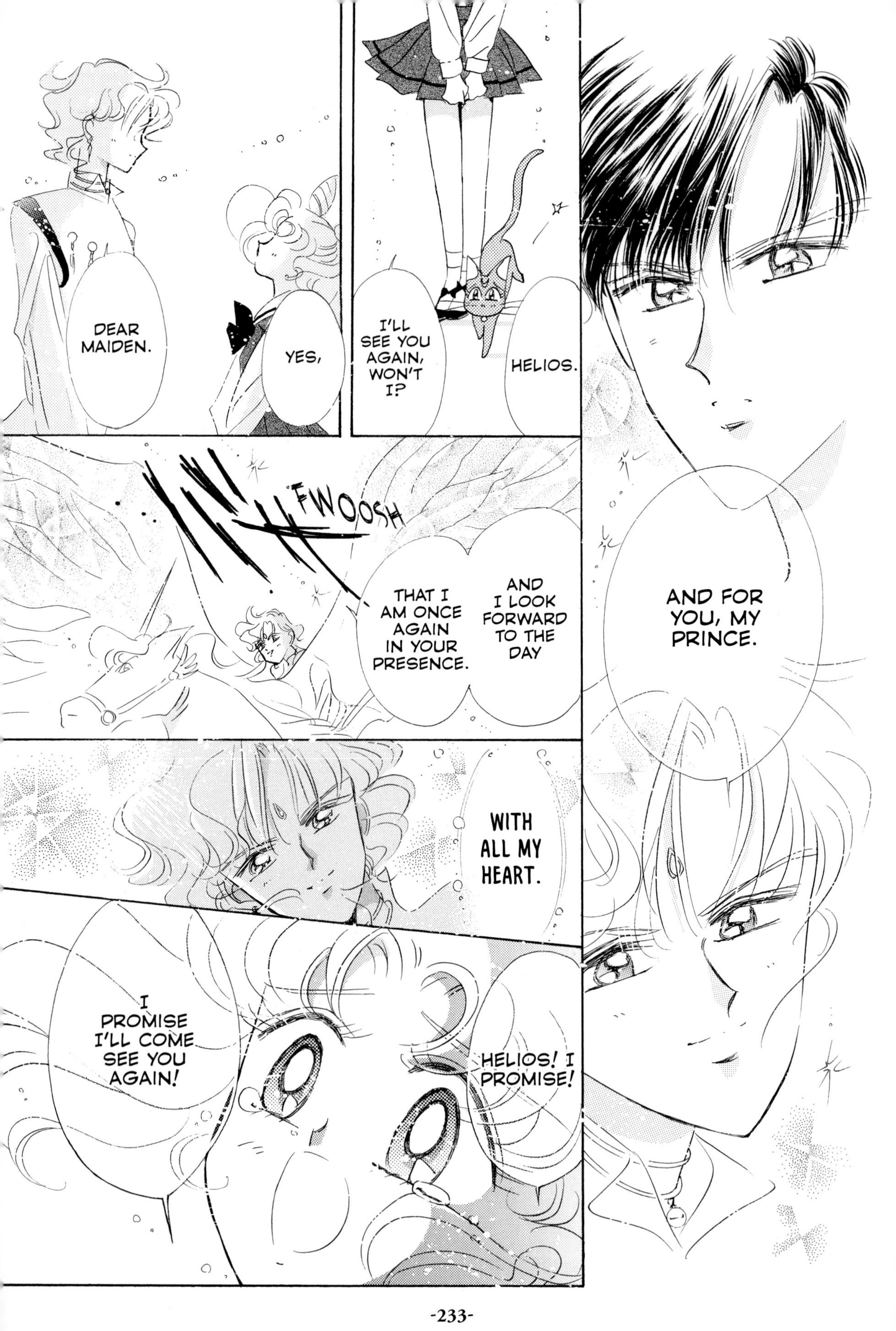
AND FOR YOU, MY PRINCE.
HELIOS.
I'LL SEE YOU AGAIN, WON'T I?
YES,
DEAR MAIDEN.
FWOOSH
AND I LOOK FORWARD TO THE DAY
THAT I AM ONCE AGAIN IN YOUR PRESENCE.
WITH ALL MY HEART.
HELIOS! I PROMISE!
I PROMISE I'LL COME SEE YOU AGAIN!

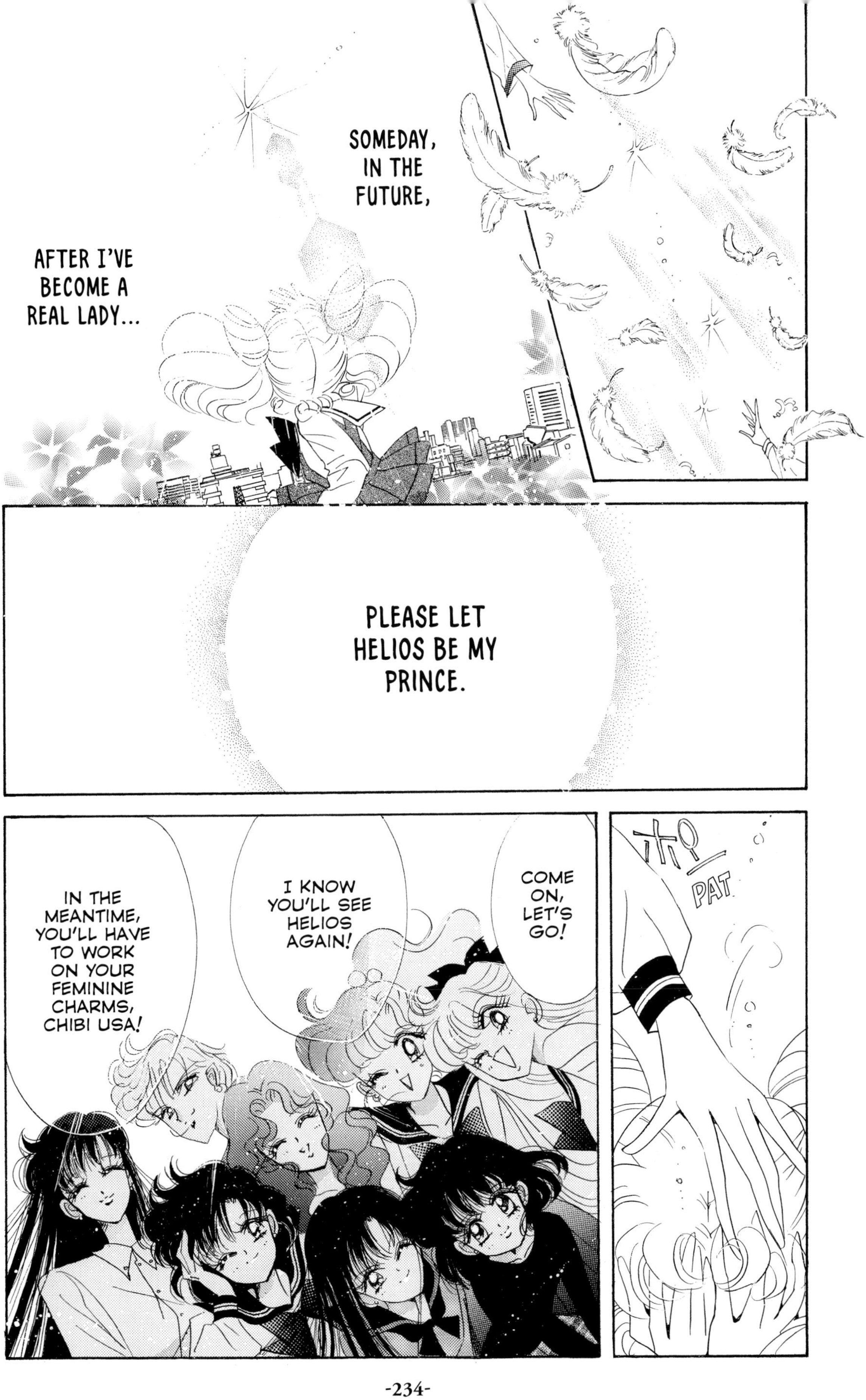
SOMEDAY, IN THE FUTURE,
AFTER I'VE BECOME A REAL LADY...
PLEASE LET HELIOS BE MY PRINCE.
PAT
COME ON, LET'S GO!
I KNOW YOU'LL SEE HELIOS AGAIN!
IN THE MEANTIME, YOU'LL HAVE TO WORK ON YOUR FEMININE CHARMS, CHIBI USA!

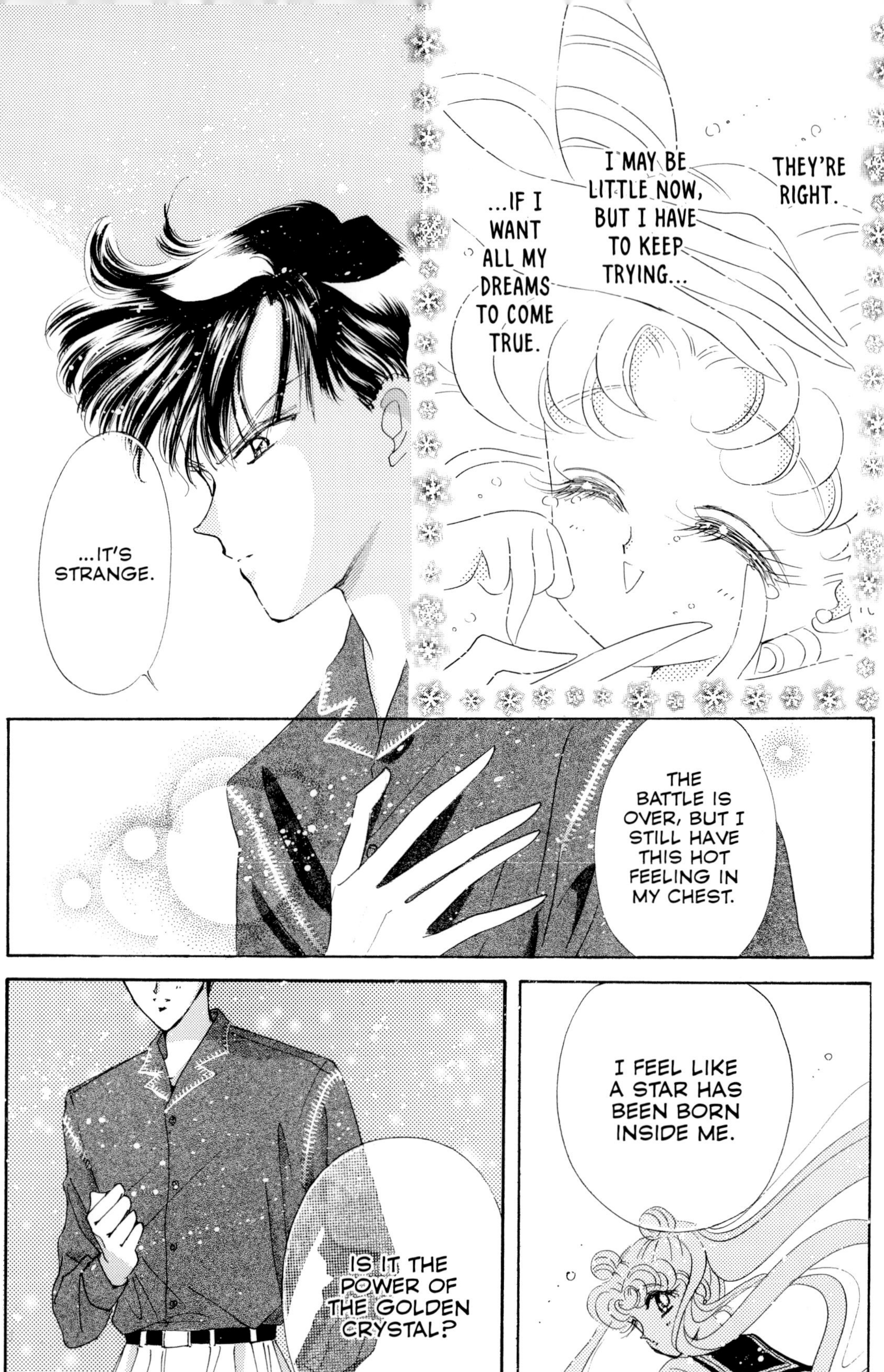
THEY'RE RIGHT.
I MAY BE LITTLE NOW, BUT I HAVE TO KEEP TRYING...
...IF I WANT ALL MY DREAMS TO COME TRUE.
...IT'S STRANGE.
THE BATTLE IS OVER, BUT I STILL HAVE THIS HOT FEELING IN MY CHEST.
I FEEL LIKE A STAR HAS BEEN BORN INSIDE ME.
IS IT THE POWER OF THE GOLDEN CRYSTAL?

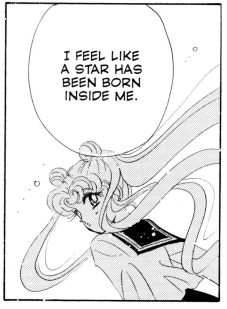

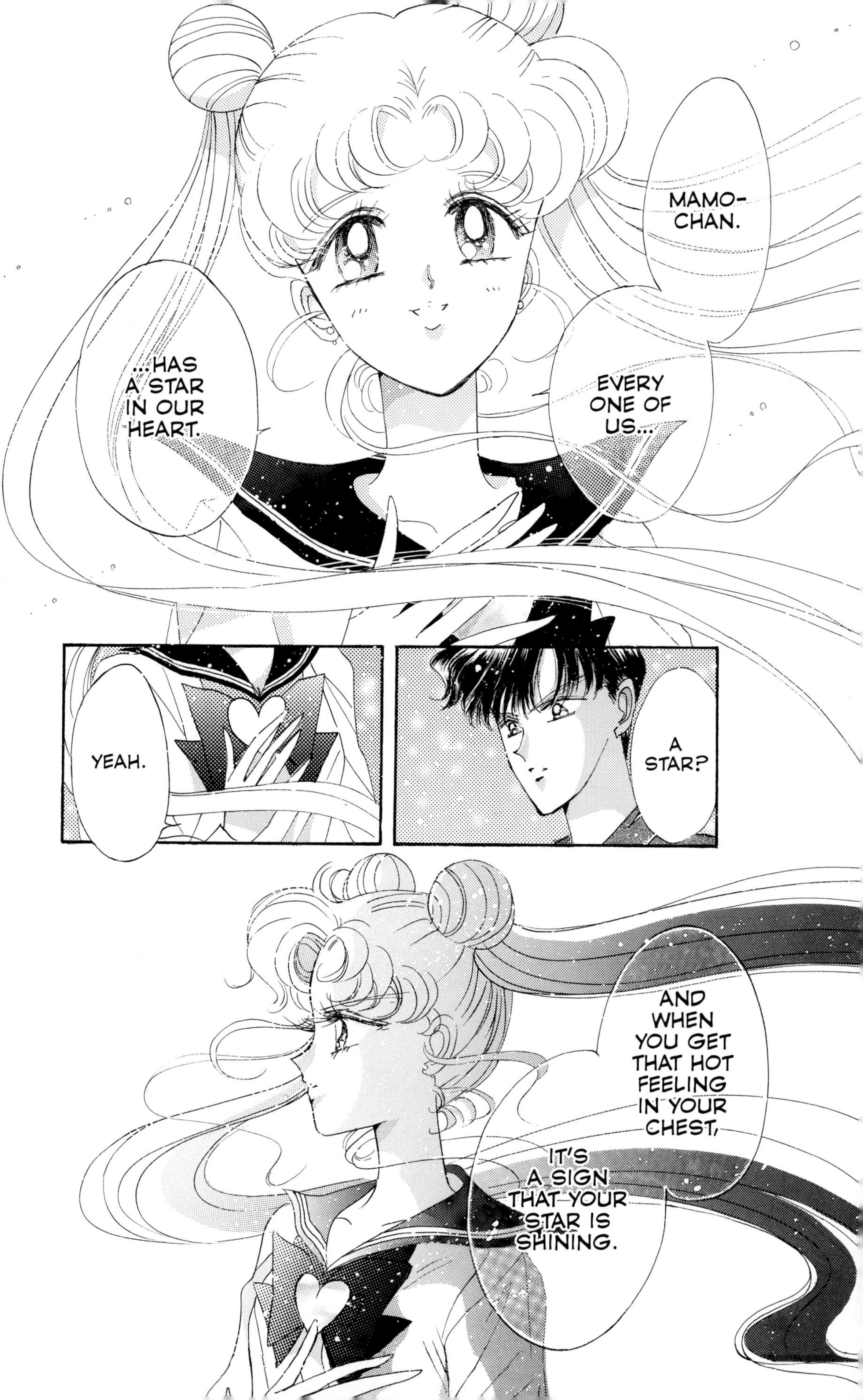
MAMO-CHAN.
EVERY ONE OF US...
...HAS A STAR IN OUR HEART.
A STAR?
YEAH.
AND WHEN YOU GET THAT HOT FEELING IN YOUR CHEST,
IT'S A SIGN THAT YOUR STAR IS SHINING.

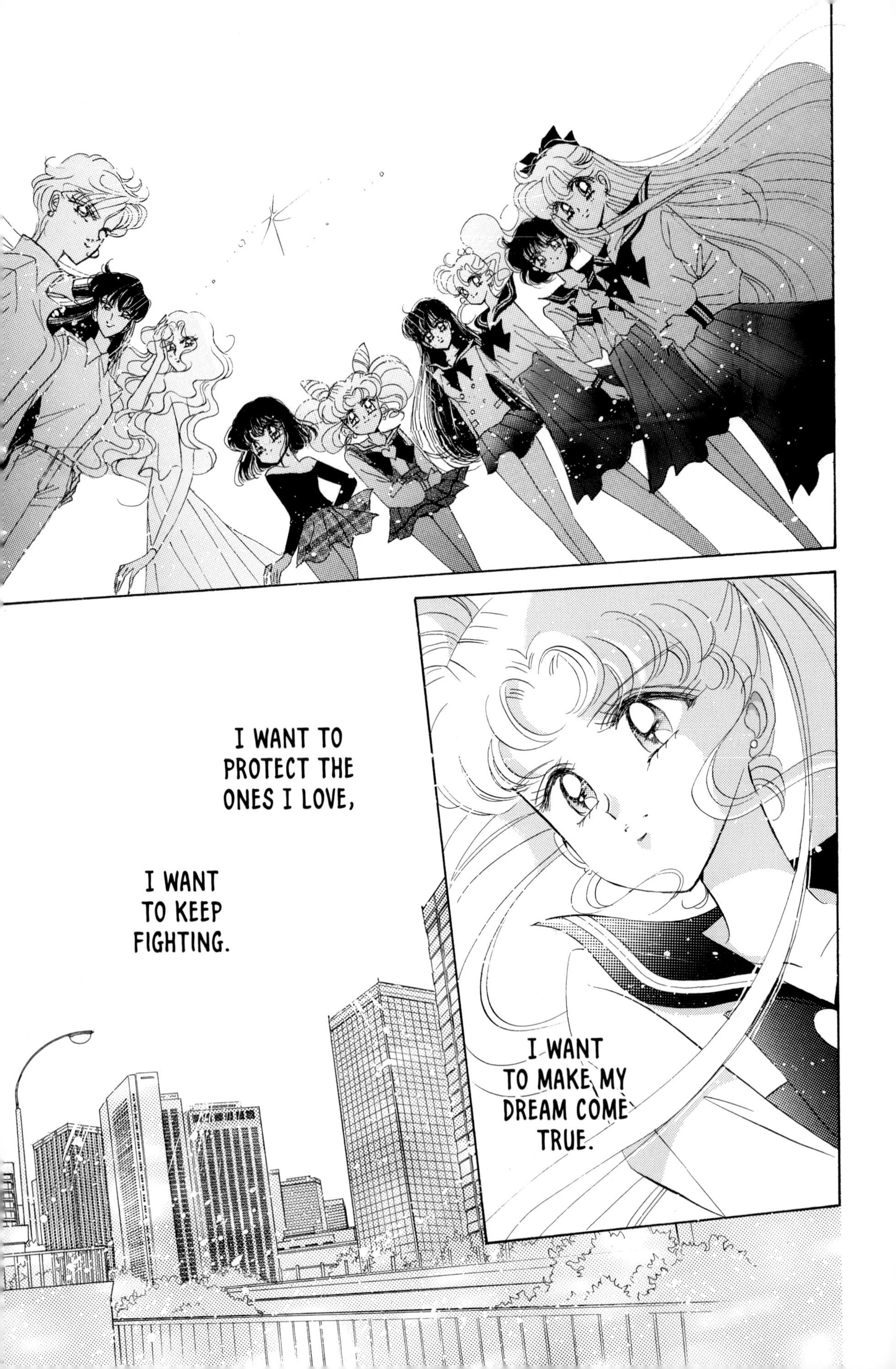
I WANT TO PROTECT THE ONES I LOVE,
I WANT TO KEEP FIGHTING.
I WANT TO MAKE MY DREAM COME TRUE.

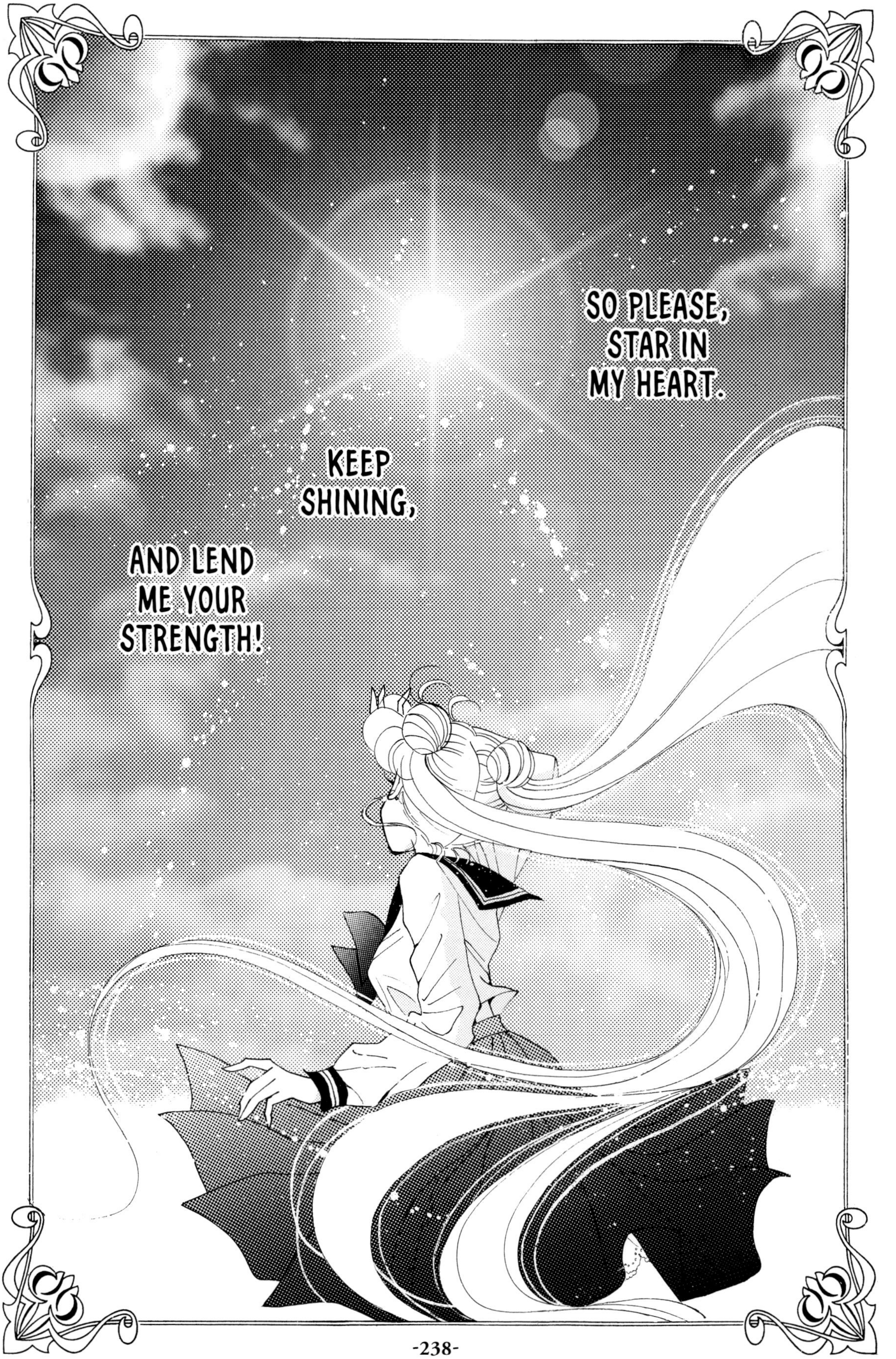
SO PLEASE, STAR IN MY HEART.
KEEP SHINING,
AND LEND ME YOUR STRENGTH!

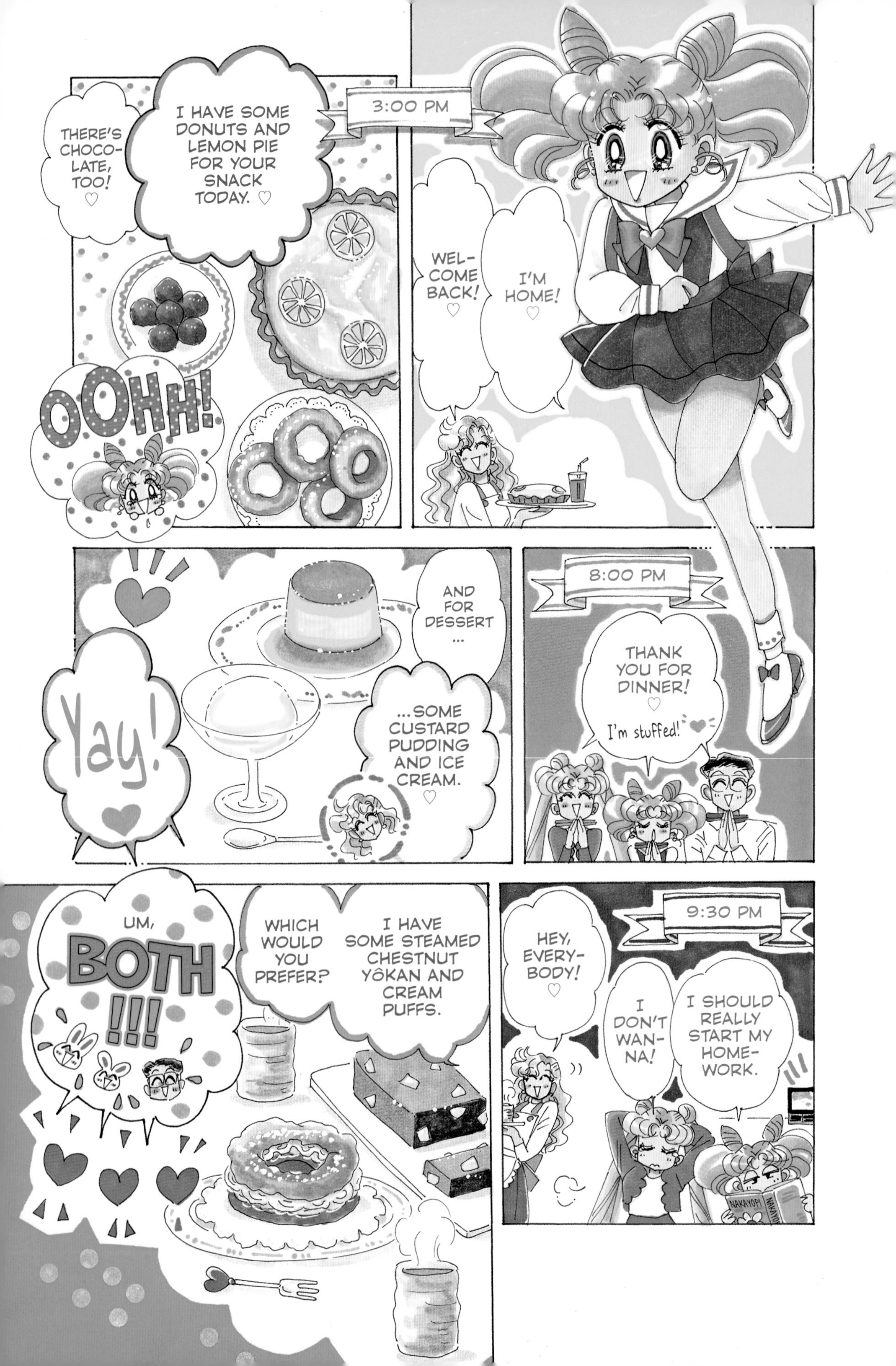
3:00 PM
I'M HOME! ♡
WEL-COME BACK! ♡
I HAVE SOME DONUTS AND LEMON PIE FOR YOUR SNACK TODAY. ♡
THERE'S CHOCO-LATE, TOO! ♡
OOHH!
8:00 PM
THANK YOU FOR DINNER! ♡
I'm stuffed!
AND FOR DESSERT ...
...SOME CUSTARD PUDDING AND ICE CREAM. ♡
Yay!
9:30 PM
I SHOULD REALLY START MY HOME-WORK.
I DON'T WAN-NA!
HEY, EVERY-BODY! ♡
I HAVE SOME STEAMED CHESTNUT YÔKAN AND CREAM PUFFS.
WHICH WOULD YOU PREFER?
UM, BOTH!!!

Beware of Cavities!

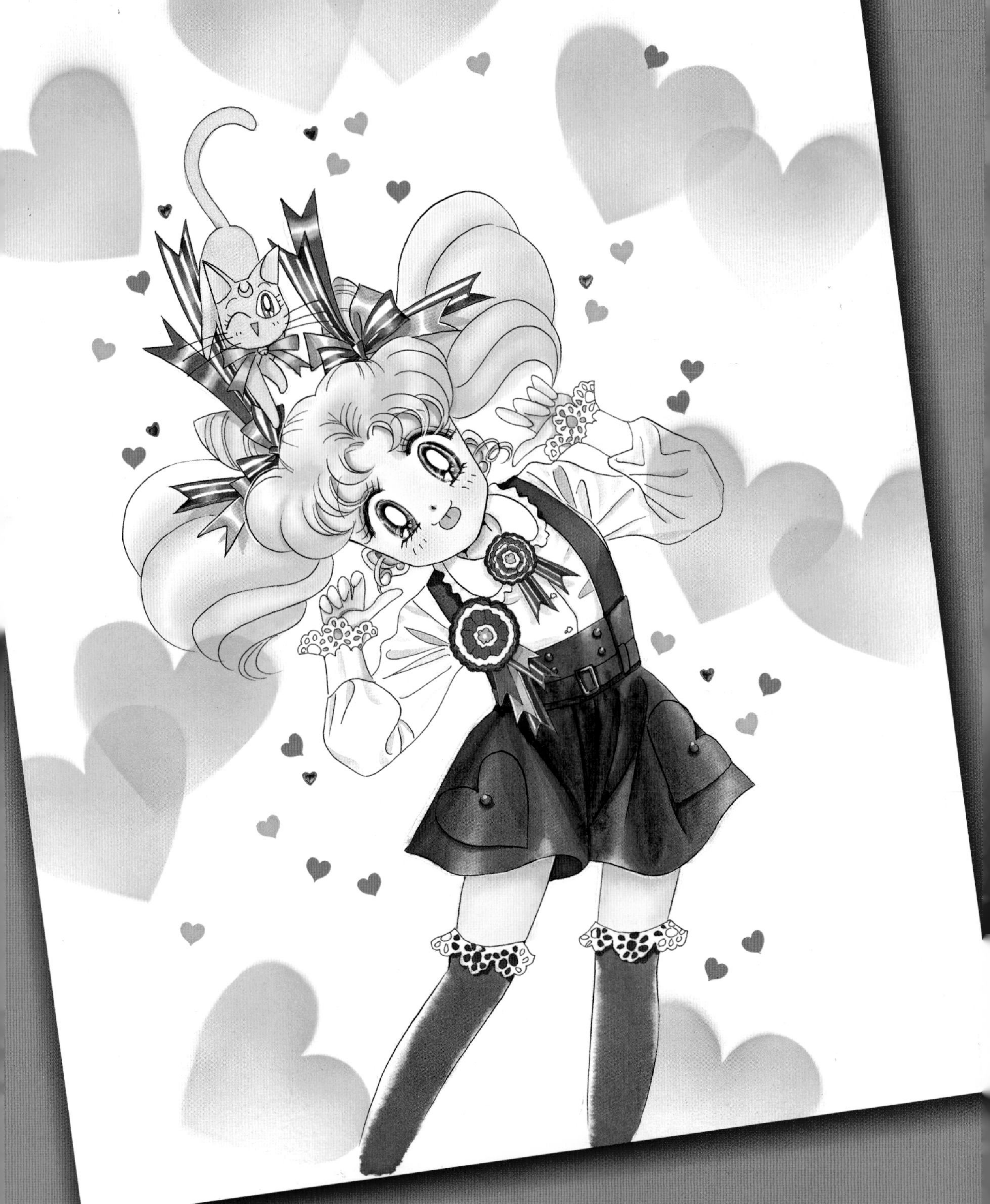

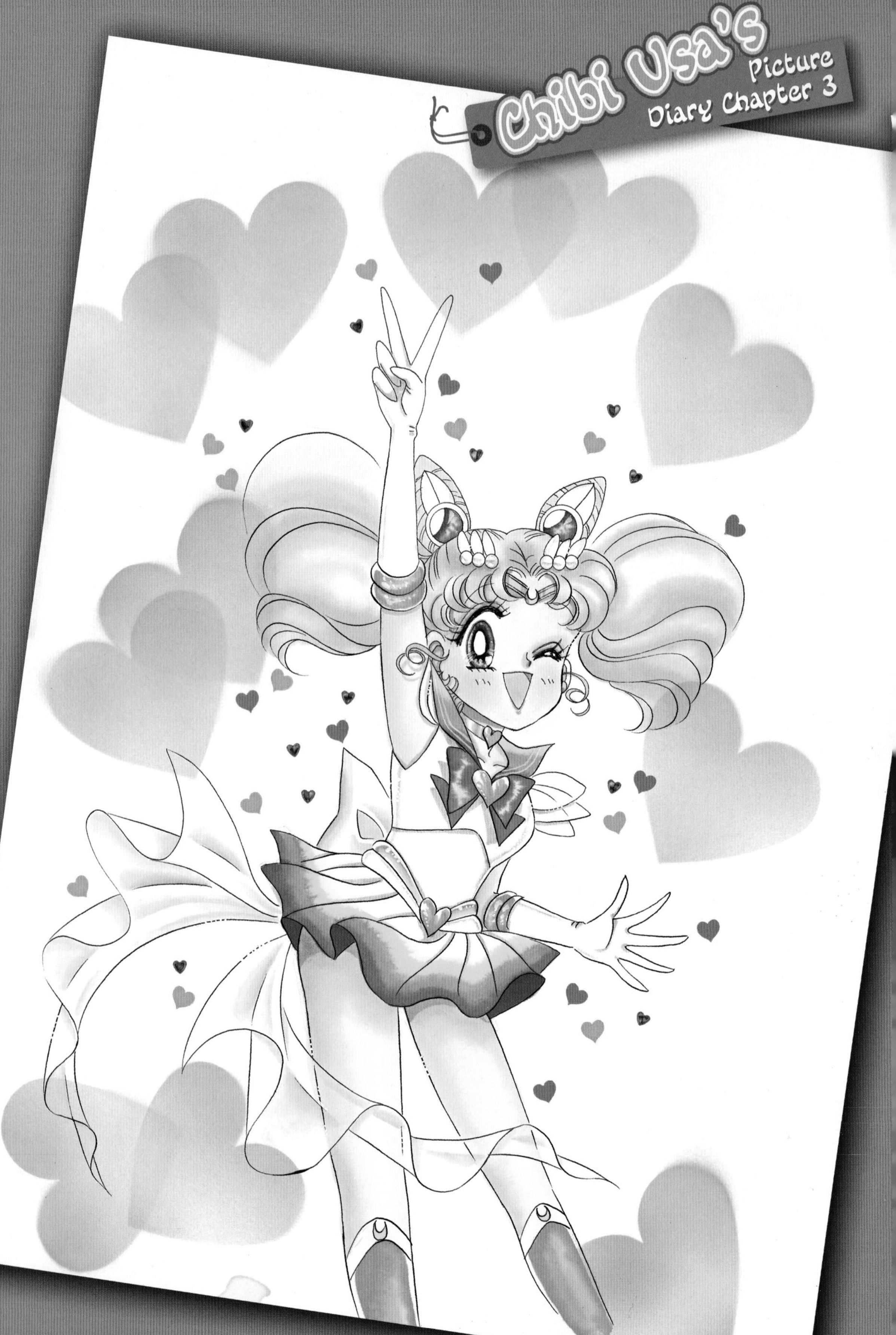
Chibi Usa's
Picture
Diary Chapter 3

Pretty Guardian
Sailor Moon

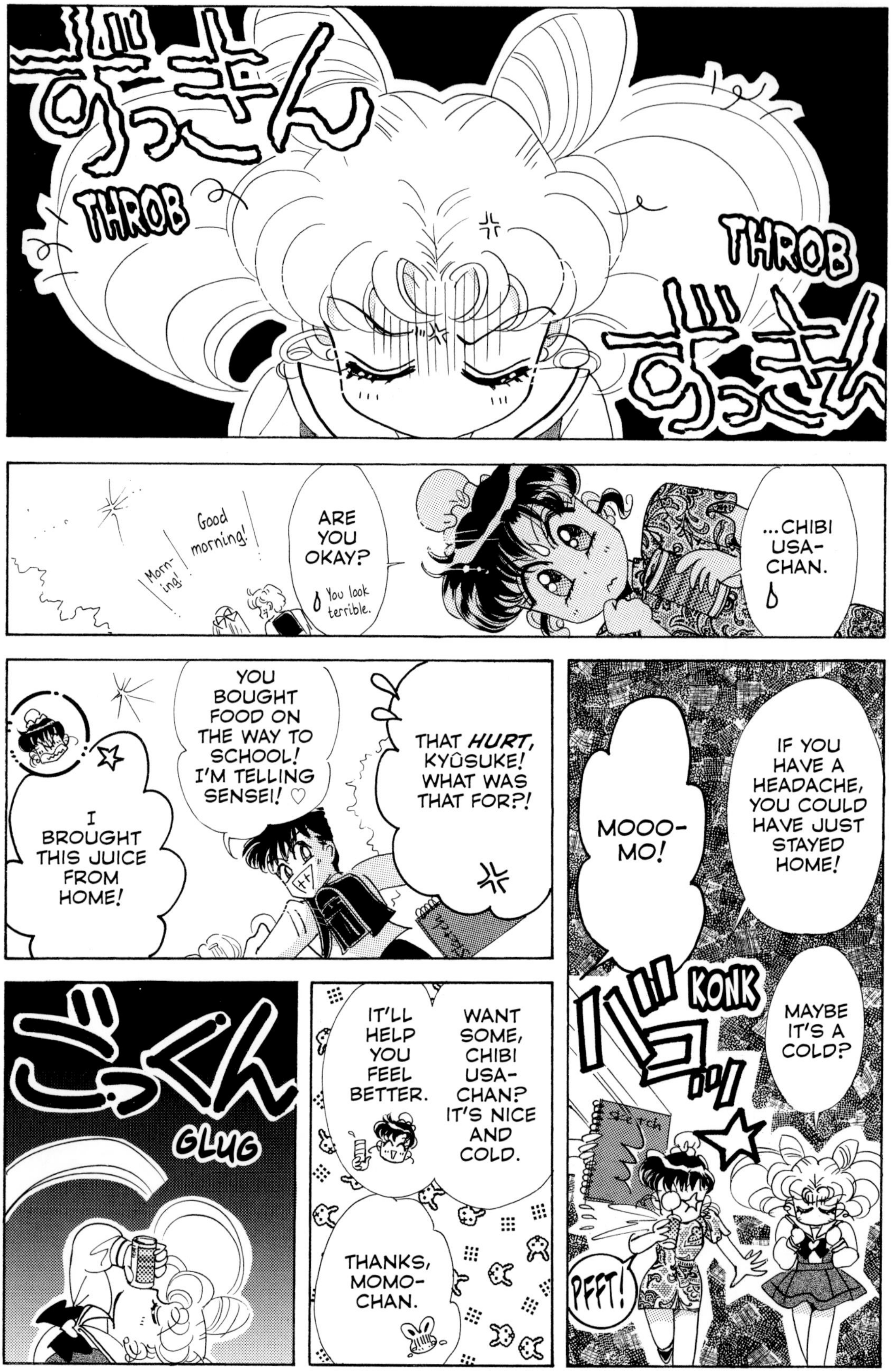
ずっきん
THROB
ずっきん
THROB
...CHIBI USA-CHAN.
ARE YOU OKAY?
You look terrible.
Good morning!
Morning!
IF YOU HAVE A HEADACHE, YOU COULD HAVE JUST STAYED HOME!
MOOO-MO!
KONK
バコッ
MAYBE IT'S A COLD?
PFFT!
THAT *HURT*, KYÛSUKE! WHAT WAS THAT FOR?!
YOU BOUGHT FOOD ON THE WAY TO SCHOOL! I'M TELLING SENSEI! ♡
I BROUGHT THIS JUICE FROM HOME!
WANT SOME, CHIBI USA-CHAN? IT'S NICE AND COLD.
IT'LL HELP YOU FEEL BETTER.
THANKS, MOMO-CHAN.
ごっくん
GLUG

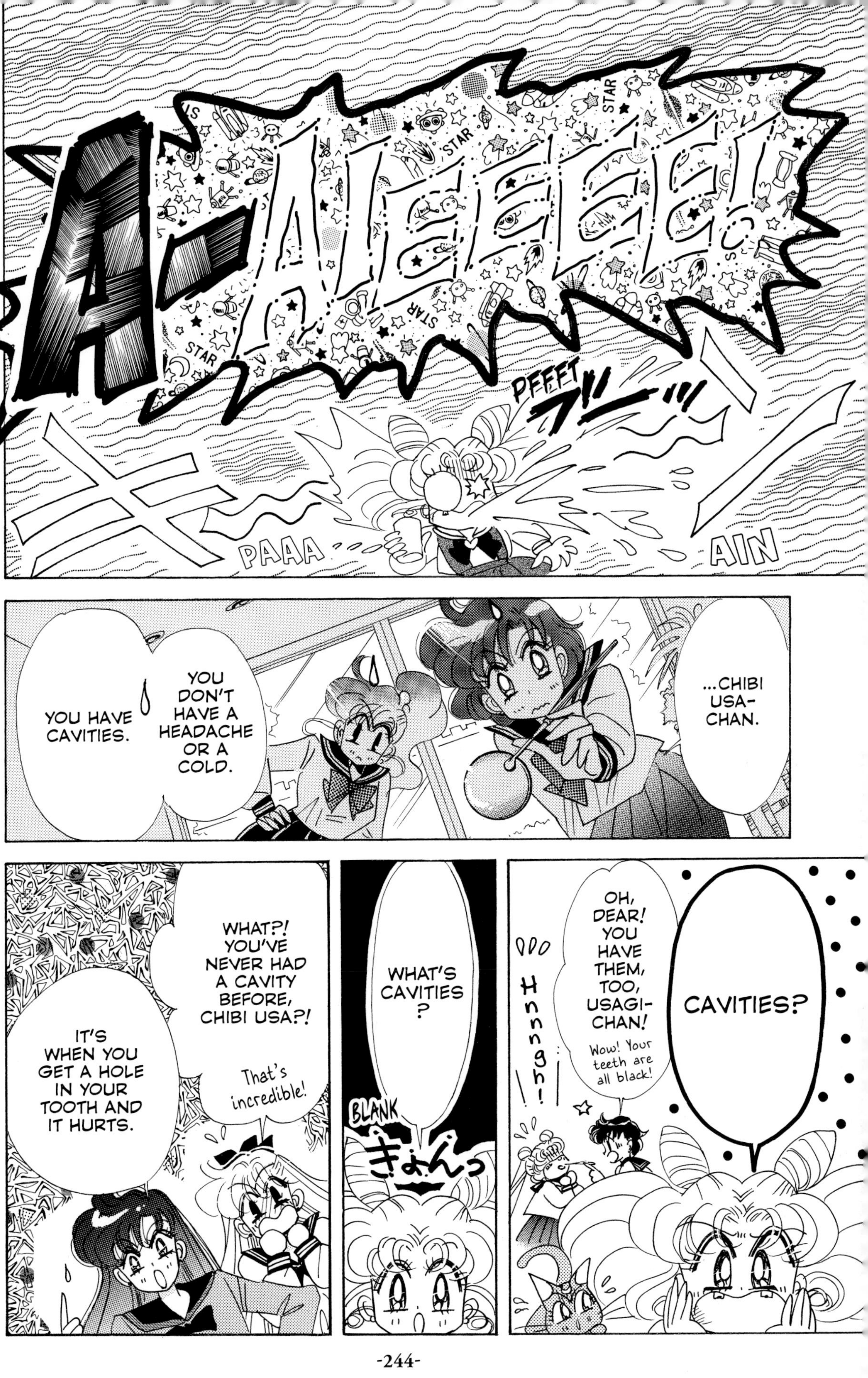
PFFFT
A-AIEEEE!
PAAA
AIN
...CHIBI USA-CHAN.
YOU DON'T HAVE A HEADACHE OR A COLD.
YOU HAVE CAVITIES.
CAVITIES?
OH, DEAR! YOU HAVE THEM, TOO, USAGI-CHAN!
Wow! Your teeth are all black!
Hnnngh!
WHAT'S CAVITIES?
BLANK
きょんっ
WHAT?! YOU'VE NEVER HAD A CAVITY BEFORE, CHIBI USA?!
That's incredible!
IT'S WHEN YOU GET A HOLE IN YOUR TOOTH AND IT HURTS.

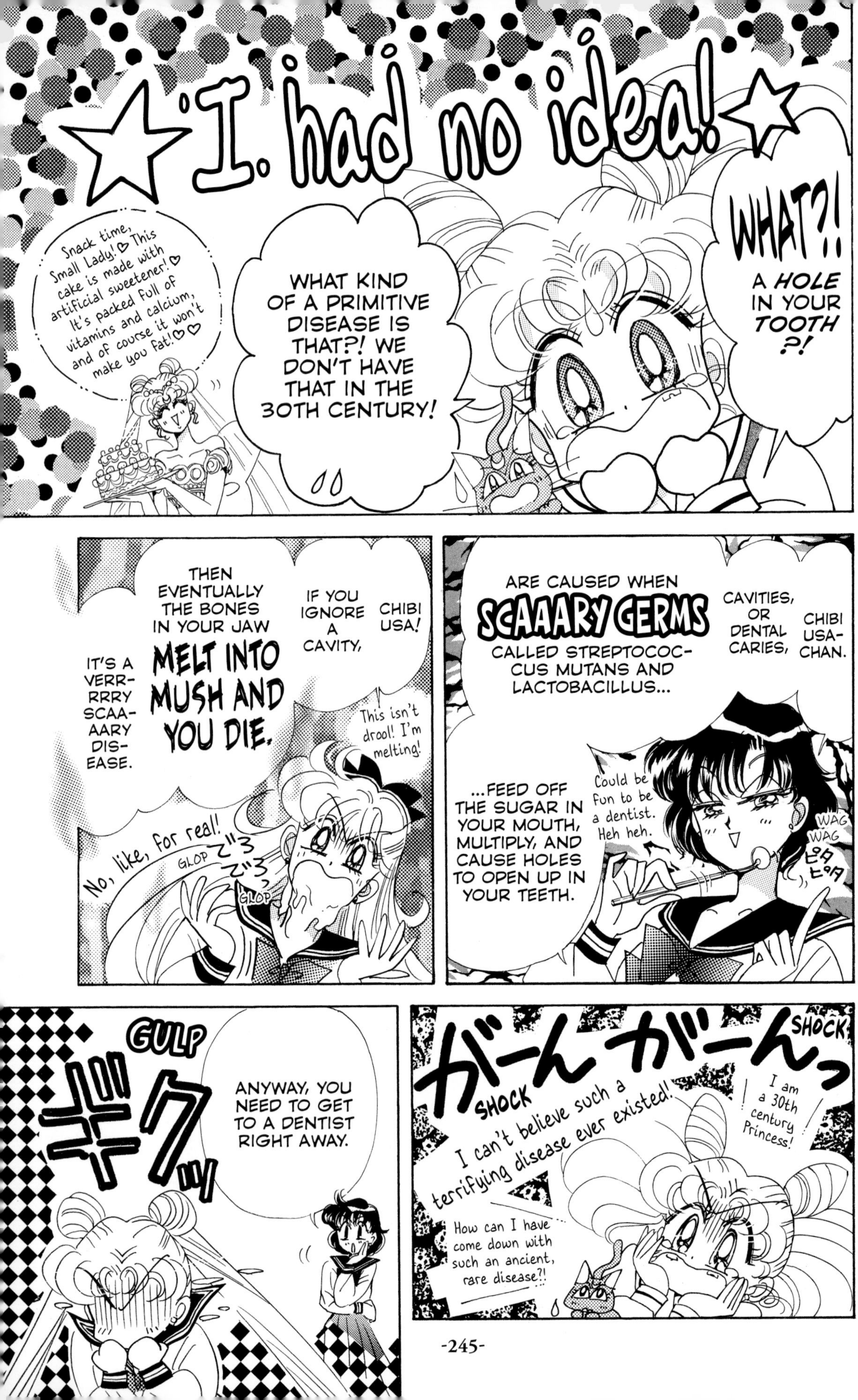
☆I had no idea!☆
WHAT?!
A HOLE IN YOUR TOOTH?!
WHAT KIND OF A PRIMITIVE DISEASE IS THAT?! WE DON'T HAVE THAT IN THE 30TH CENTURY!
Snack time, Small Lady! ♡ This cake is made with artificial sweetener! ♡ It's packed full of vitamins and calcium, and of course it won't make you fat! ♡♡
CHIBI USA-CHAN.
CAVITIES, OR DENTAL CARIES,
ARE CAUSED WHEN SCAAARY GERMS CALLED STREPTOCOCCUS MUTANS AND LACTOBACILLUS...
...FEED OFF THE SUGAR IN YOUR MOUTH, MULTIPLY, AND CAUSE HOLES TO OPEN UP IN YOUR TEETH.
Could be fun to be a dentist. Heh heh.
WAG WAG
ピタ ピタ
CHIBI USA!
IF YOU IGNORE A CAVITY,
THEN EVENTUALLY THE BONES IN YOUR JAW MELT INTO MUSH AND YOU DIE.
IT'S A VERRRRRY SCAAAARY DISEASE.
This isn't drool! I'm melting!
No, like, for real!
どろ GLOP
どろ GLOP
がーん SHOCK がーんっ SHOCK
I am a 30th century Princess!
I can't believe such a terrifying disease ever existed!
How can I have come down with such an ancient, rare disease?!
ANYWAY, YOU NEED TO GET TO A DENTIST RIGHT AWAY.
GULP
ギクッ

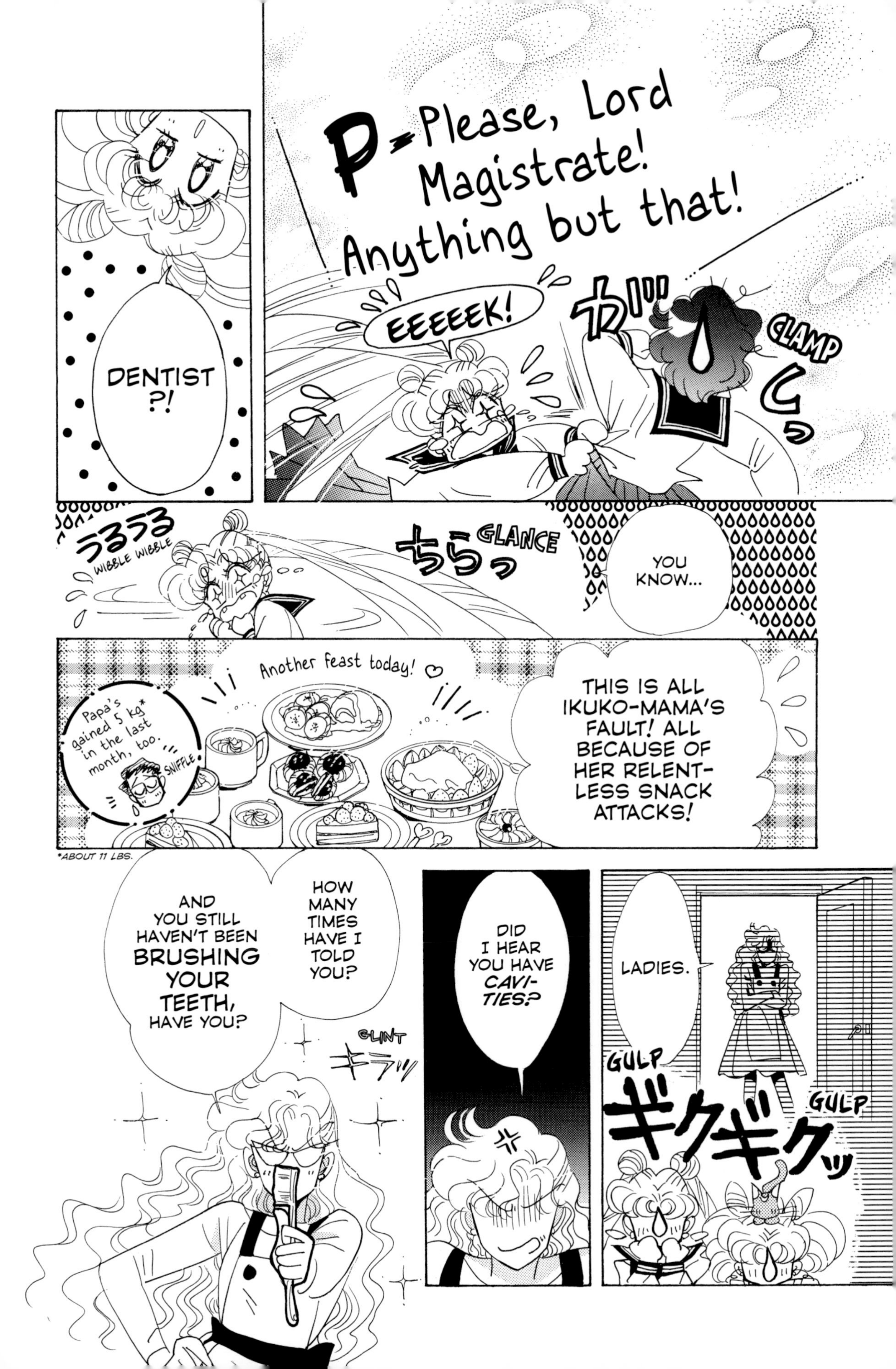
P-Please, Lord Magistrate! Anything but that!
EEEEEK!
CLAMP
DENTIST?!
YOU KNOW...
GLANCE
WIBBLE WIBBLE
THIS IS ALL IKUKO-MAMA'S FAULT! ALL BECAUSE OF HER RELENTLESS SNACK ATTACKS!
Another feast today!
Papa's gained 5 kg* in the last month, too.
SNIFFLE
LADIES.
GULP
GULP
DID I HEAR YOU HAVE CAVITIES?
HOW MANY TIMES HAVE I TOLD YOU?
AND YOU STILL HAVEN'T BEEN BRUSHING YOUR TEETH, HAVE YOU?
GLINT

*ABOUT 11 LBS.

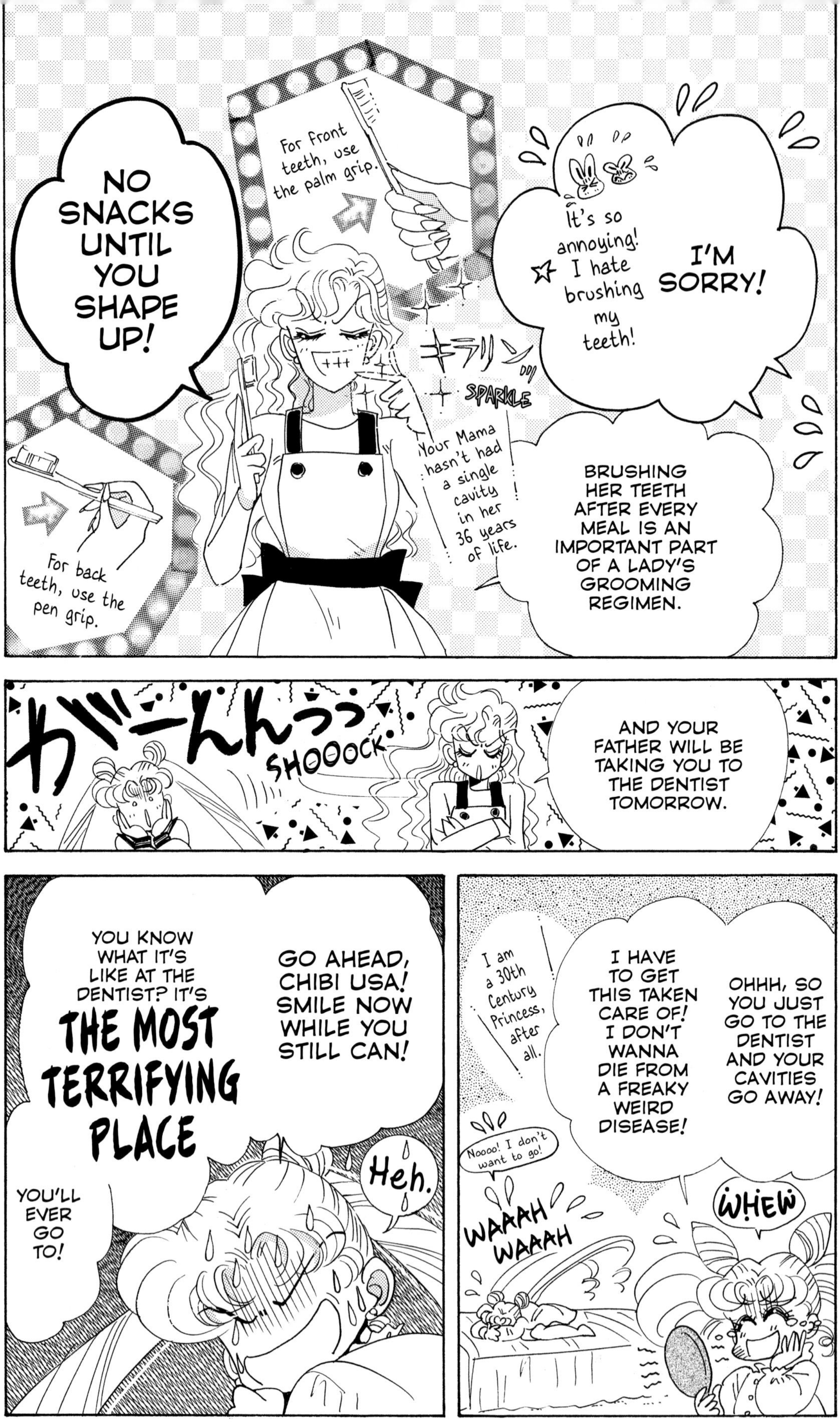
I'M SORRY!
It's so annoying! I hate brushing my teeth!
BRUSHING HER TEETH AFTER EVERY MEAL IS AN IMPORTANT PART OF A LADY'S GROOMING REGIMEN.
Your Mama hasn't had a single cavity in her 36 years of life.
キラリン
SPARKLE
For front teeth, use the palm grip.
NO SNACKS UNTIL YOU SHAPE UP!
For back teeth, use the pen grip.
AND YOUR FATHER WILL BE TAKING YOU TO THE DENTIST TOMORROW.
がーんんっっ
SHOOOCK
OHHH, SO YOU JUST GO TO THE DENTIST AND YOUR CAVITIES GO AWAY!
I HAVE TO GET THIS TAKEN CARE OF! I DON'T WANNA DIE FROM A FREAKY WEIRD DISEASE!
I am a 30th Century Princess, after all.
WHEW
Noooo! I don't want to go!
WAAAH WAAAH
GO AHEAD, CHIBI USA! SMILE NOW WHILE YOU STILL CAN!
YOU KNOW WHAT IT'S LIKE AT THE DENTIST? IT'S THE MOST TERRIFYING PLACE
YOU'LL EVER GO TO!
Heh.

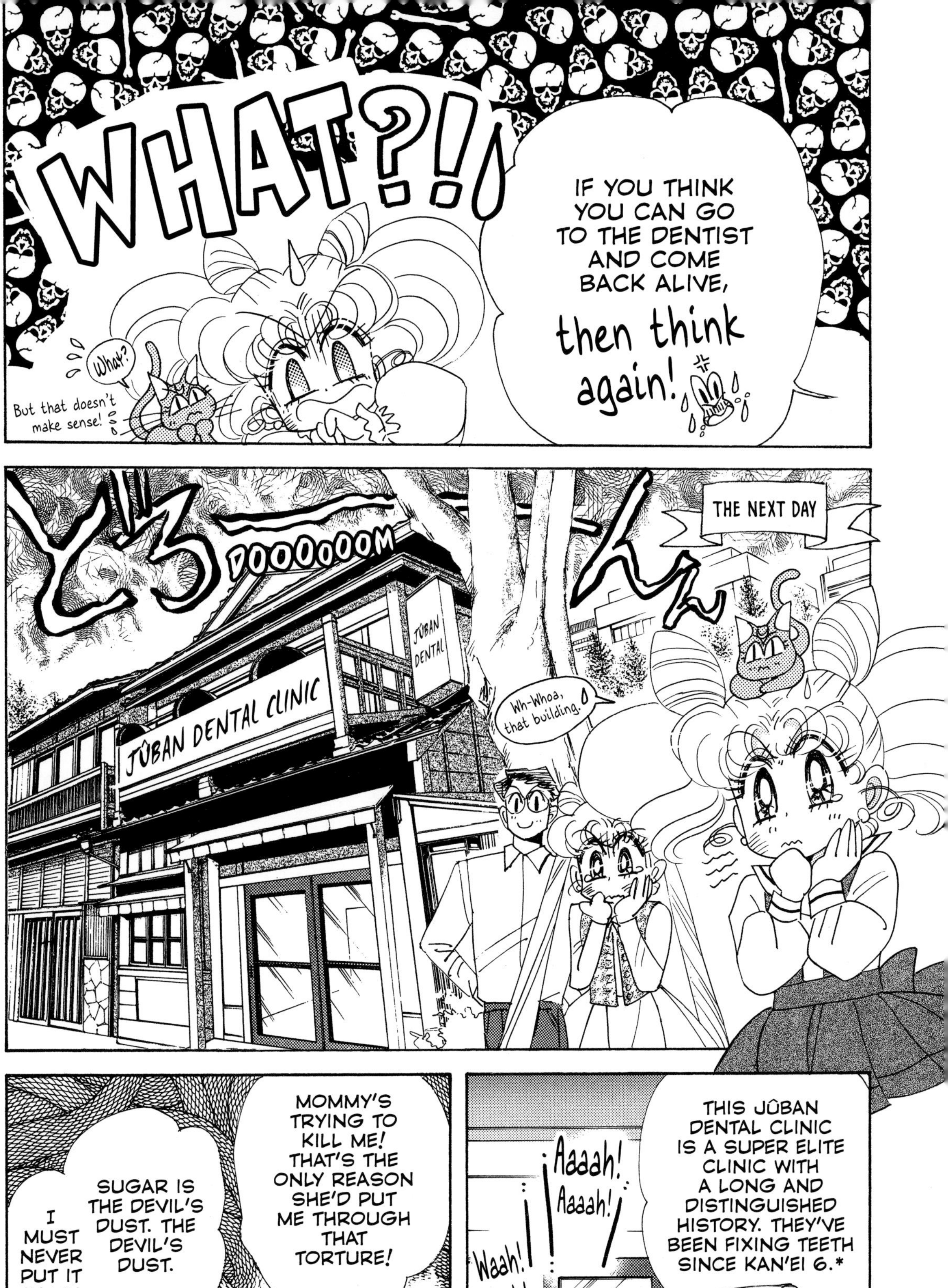
IF YOU THINK YOU CAN GO TO THE DENTIST AND COME BACK ALIVE, then think again!
WHAT?!!
What?
But that doesn't make sense!
THE NEXT DAY
どろーん DOOOOOOM
JÛBAN DENTAL
Wh-Whoa, that building.
JÛBAN DENTAL CLINIC
THIS JÛBAN DENTAL CLINIC IS A SUPER ELITE CLINIC WITH A LONG AND DISTINGUISHED HISTORY. THEY'VE BEEN FIXING TEETH SINCE KAN'EI 6.*
Aaaah! Aaaah!
Waah! Waah!
MOMMY'S TRYING TO KILL ME! THAT'S THE ONLY REASON SHE'D PUT ME THROUGH THAT TORTURE!
Waaah! Waaah!
SUGAR IS THE DEVIL'S DUST. THE DEVIL'S DUST.
I MUST NEVER PUT IT IN MY MOUTH AGAIN.
STAGGER フラフラ STAGGER
MUTTER MUTTER ブツブツ

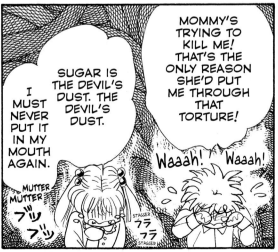

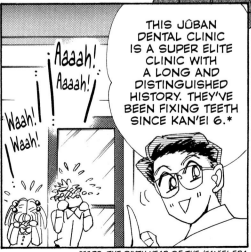

*1629, THE SIXTH YEAR OF THE KAN'EI ERA.

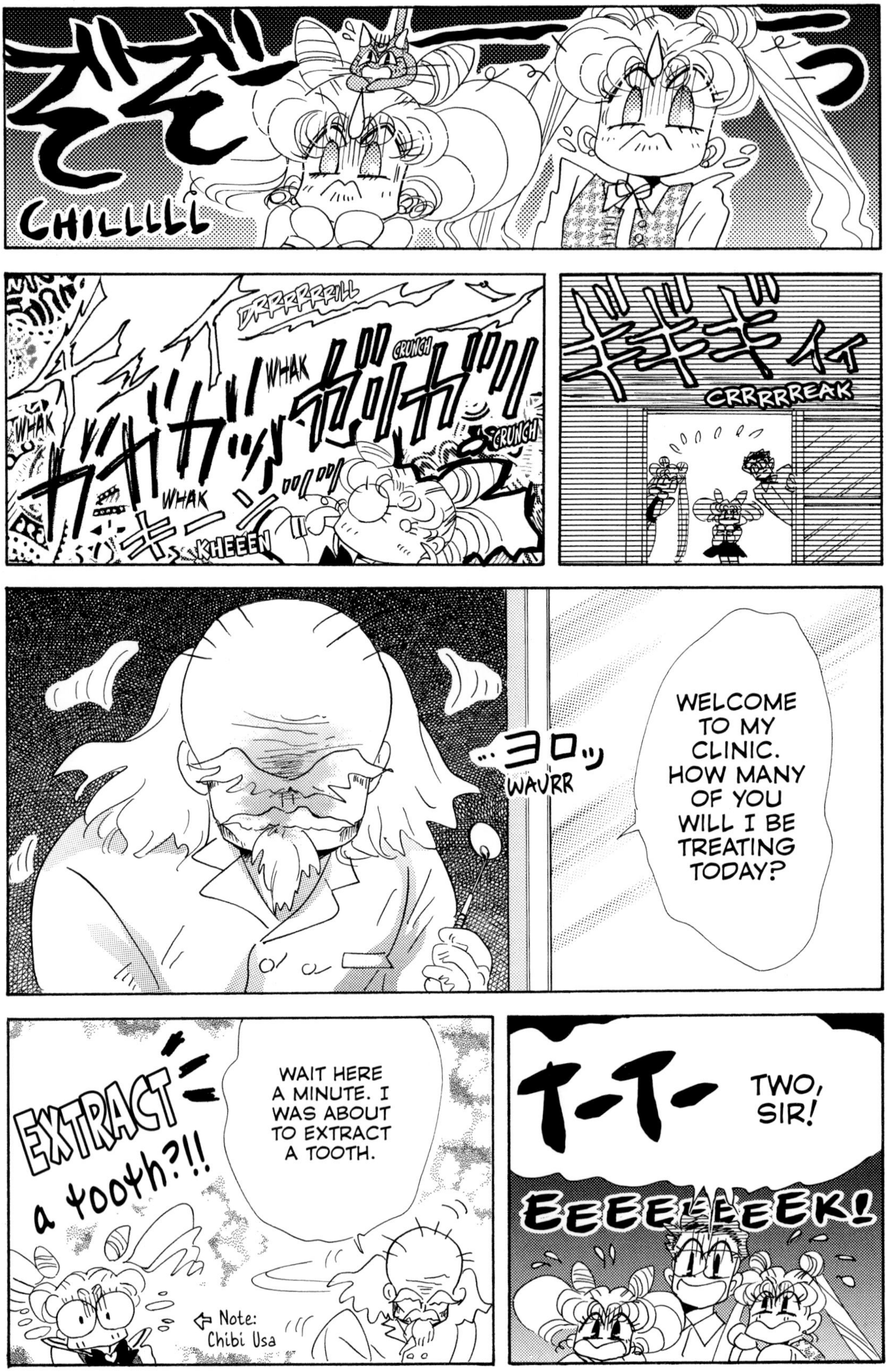
CHILLLLL
CRRRRREAK
DRRRRRRILL
WHAK
CRUNCH
WHAK
CRUNCH
WHAK
KHEEEN
WELCOME TO MY CLINIC. HOW MANY OF YOU WILL I BE TREATING TODAY?
ヨロッ
WAURR
TWO, SIR!
EEEEEEEEK!
WAIT HERE A MINUTE. I WAS ABOUT TO EXTRACT A TOOTH.
EXTRACT a tooth?!!
Note: Chibi Usa

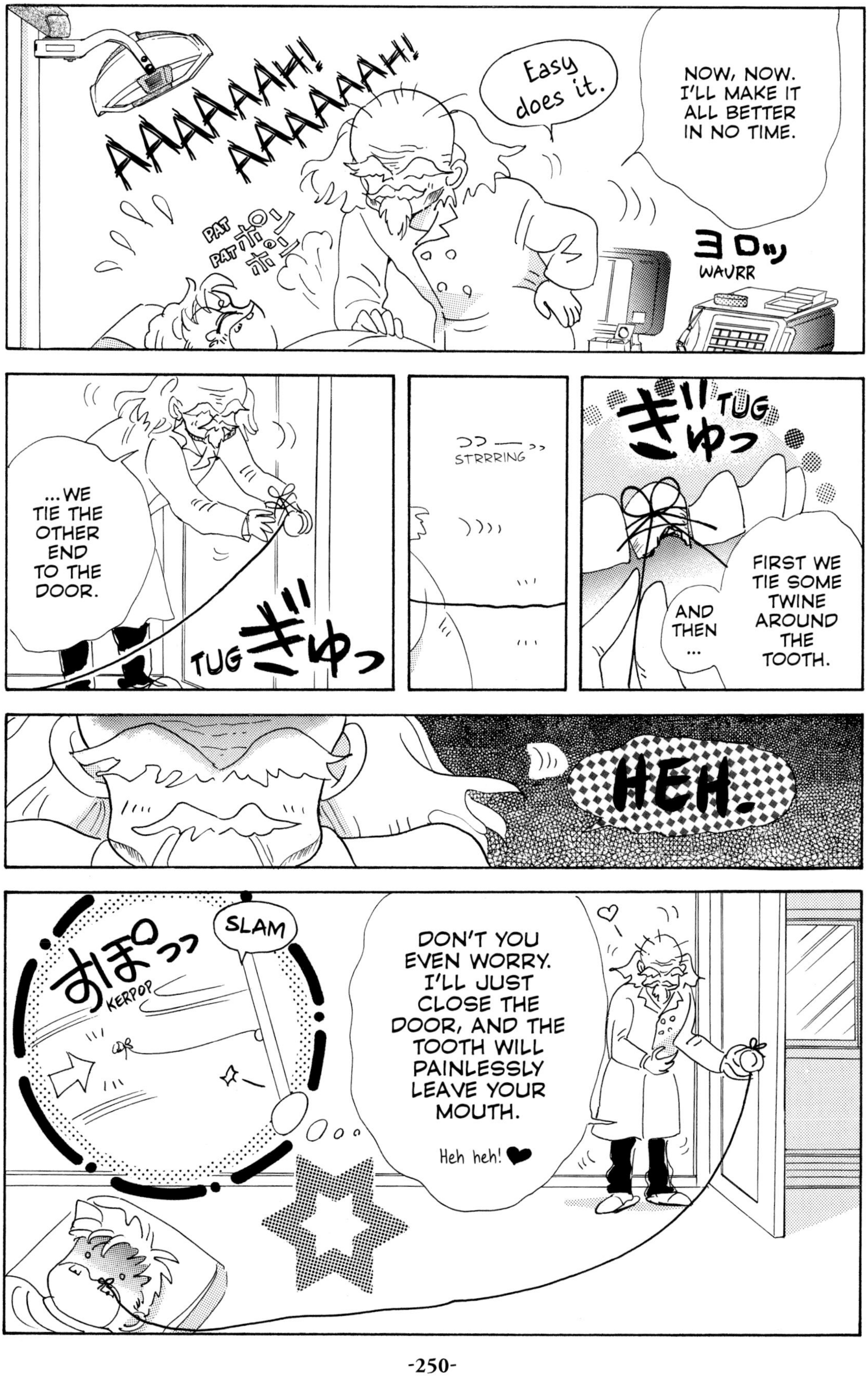
ヨロッ
WAURR
NOW, NOW. I'LL MAKE IT ALL BETTER IN NO TIME.
Easy does it.
AAAAAAH! AAAAAAH!
PAT PAT ポンポン
TUG ぎゅっ
FIRST WE TIE SOME TWINE AROUND THE TOOTH.
AND THEN...
つつ—
STRRRING
...WE TIE THE OTHER END TO THE DOOR.
TUG ぎゅっ
HEH.
DON'T YOU EVEN WORRY. I'LL JUST CLOSE THE DOOR, AND THE TOOTH WILL PAINLESSLY LEAVE YOUR MOUTH.
Heh heh!
SLAM
すぽっっっ
KERPOP

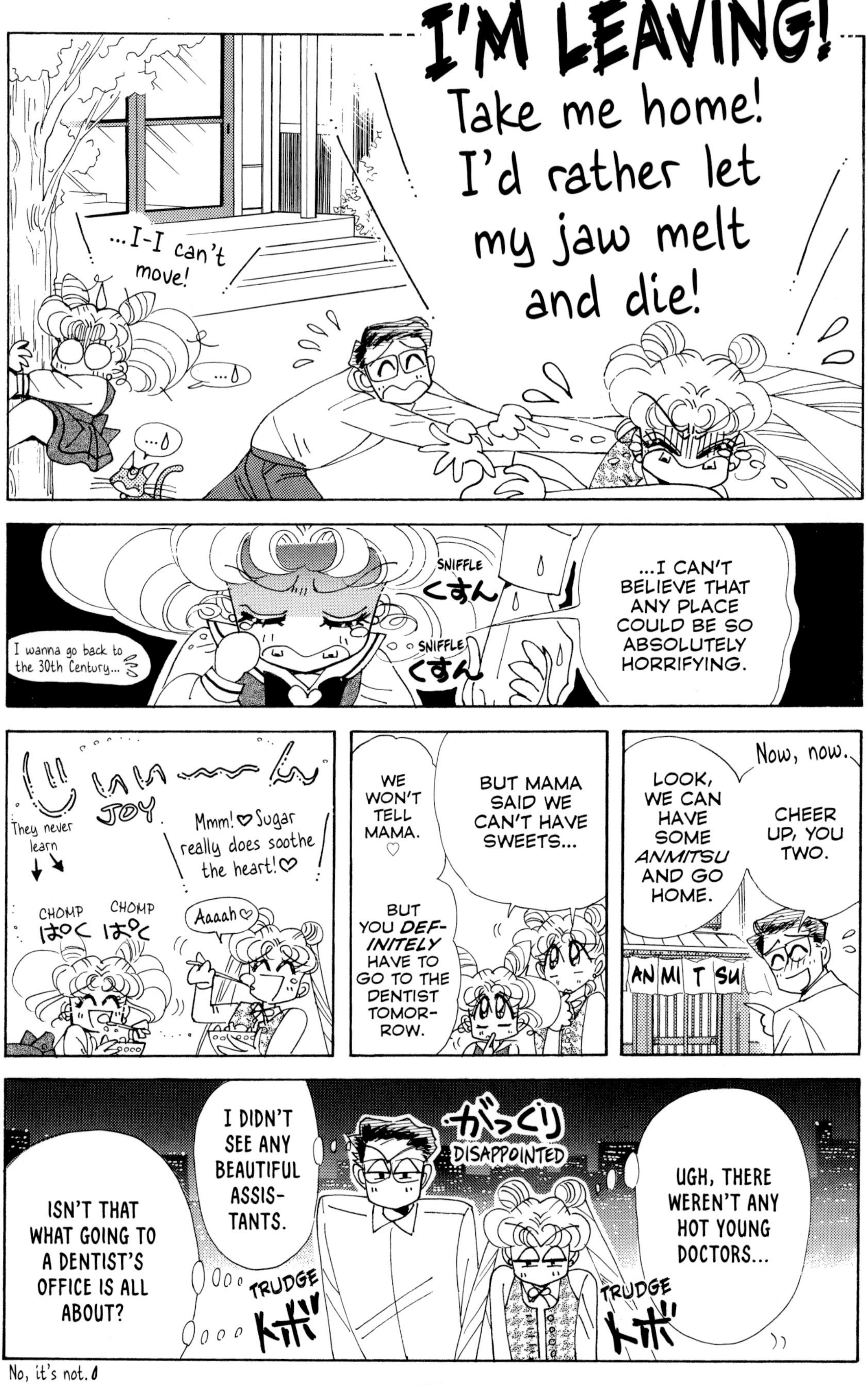
I'M LEAVING!
Take me home! I'd rather let my jaw melt and die!
...I-I can't move!
...
...
...I CAN'T BELIEVE THAT ANY PLACE COULD BE SO ABSOLUTELY HORRIFYING.
SNIFFLE くすん
SNIFFLE くすん
I wanna go back to the 30th Century...
Now, now.
CHEER UP, YOU TWO.
LOOK, WE CAN HAVE SOME *ANMITSU* AND GO HOME.
AN MI T SU
BUT MAMA SAID WE CAN'T HAVE SWEETS...
WE WON'T TELL MAMA. ♡
BUT YOU *DEFINITELY* HAVE TO GO TO THE DENTIST TOMORROW.
JOY
Mmm! ♡ Sugar really does soothe the heart! ♡
Aaaah ♡
They never learn
CHOMP ぱく
CHOMP ぱく
UGH, THERE WEREN'T ANY HOT YOUNG DOCTORS...
がっくり DISAPPOINTED
I DIDN'T SEE ANY BEAUTIFUL ASSIS-TANTS.
ISN'T THAT WHAT GOING TO A DENTIST'S OFFICE IS ALL ABOUT?
TRUDGE トボ
TRUDGE トボ

No, it's not.

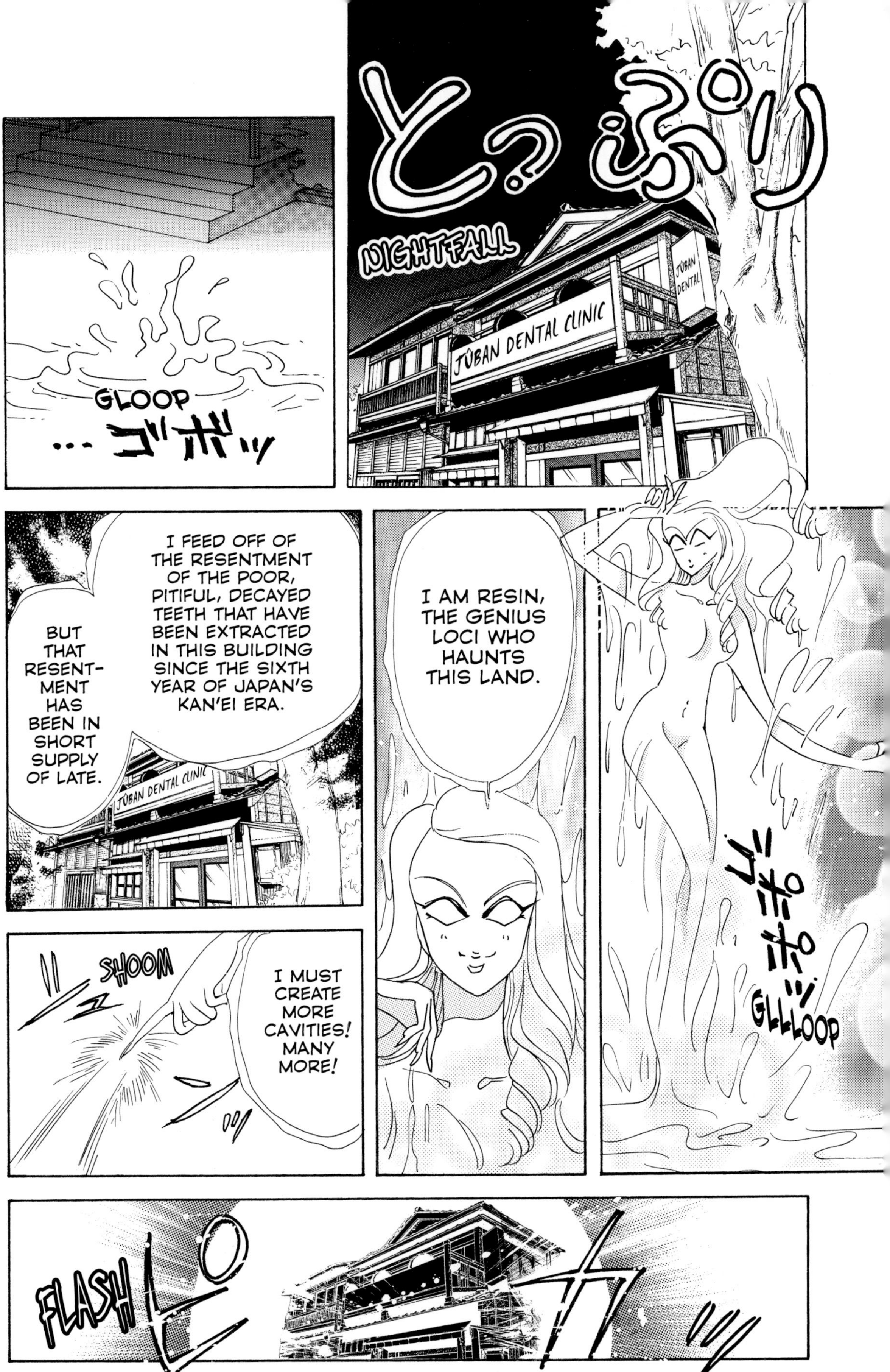
とっぷり
NIGHTFALL
JÛBAN DENTAL CLINIC
JÛBAN DENTAL
GLOOP
…ゴボッ
ゴポポッ
GLLLOOP
I AM RESIN, THE GENIUS LOCI WHO HAUNTS THIS LAND.
I FEED OFF OF THE RESENTMENT OF THE POOR, PITIFUL, DECAYED TEETH THAT HAVE BEEN EXTRACTED IN THIS BUILDING SINCE THE SIXTH YEAR OF JAPAN'S KAN'EI ERA.
BUT THAT RESENT-MENT HAS BEEN IN SHORT SUPPLY OF LATE.
JÛBAN DENTAL CLINIC
SHOOM
I MUST CREATE MORE CAVITIES! MANY MORE!
FLASH
ピカッ

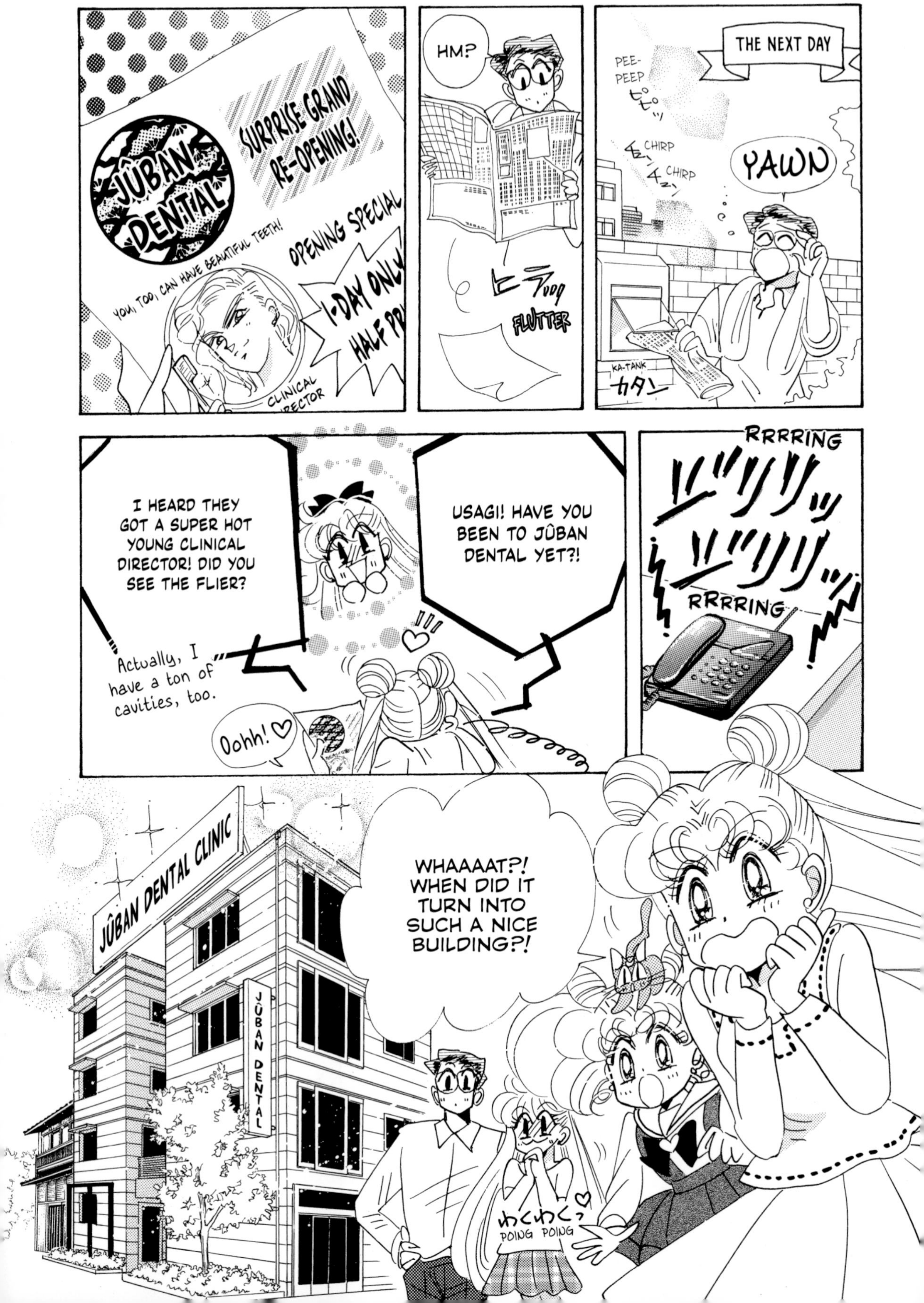

THE NEXT DAY
PEE-PEEP
ピピッ
CHIRP
CHIRP
YAWN
KA-TANK
カタン
HM?
ヒラッ
FLUTTER
JÛBAN DENTAL
SURPRISE GRAND RE-OPENING!
YOU, TOO, CAN HAVE BEAUTIFUL TEETH!
OPENING SPECIAL
1-DAY ONLY
CLINICAL
RRRRING
ジリリリッ
RRRRING
USAGI! HAVE YOU BEEN TO JÛBAN DENTAL YET?!
I HEARD THEY GOT A SUPER HOT YOUNG CLINICAL DIRECTOR! DID YOU SEE THE FLIER?
Actually, I have a ton of cavities, too.
Oohh! ♡
WHAAAAT?! WHEN DID IT TURN INTO SUCH A NICE BUILDING?!
JÛBAN DENTAL CLINIC
JÛBAN DENTAL
わくわくっ
POING POING

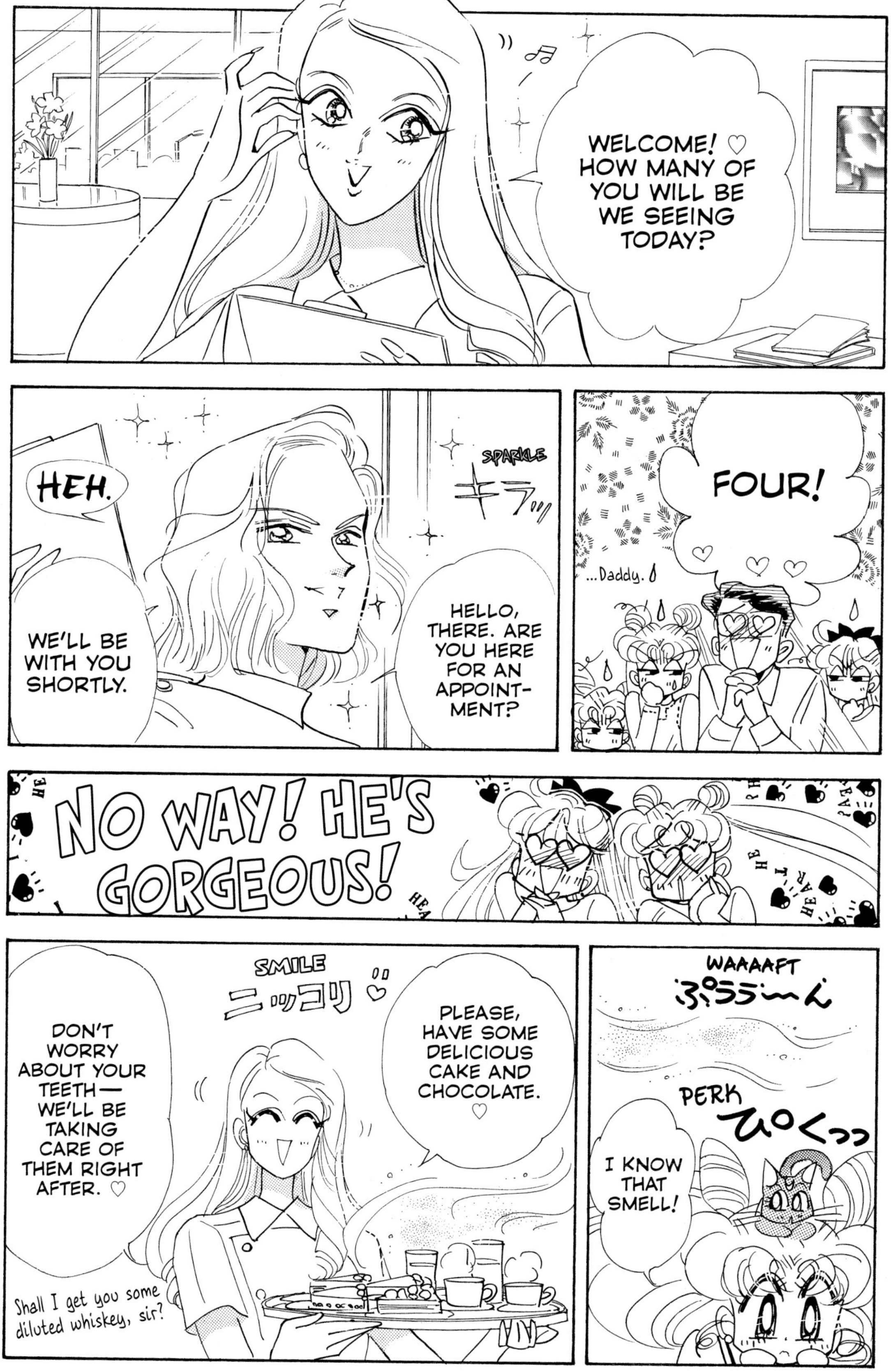

WELCOME! ♡ HOW MANY OF YOU WILL BE WE SEEING TODAY?
FOUR!
...Daddy.
SPARKLE
キラッ
HELLO, THERE. ARE YOU HERE FOR AN APPOINT-MENT?
HEH.
WE'LL BE WITH YOU SHORTLY.
NO WAY! HE'S GORGEOUS!
WAAAAFT
PERK
ぴくっ
I KNOW THAT SMELL!
SMILE
ニッコリ
PLEASE, HAVE SOME DELICIOUS CAKE AND CHOCOLATE. ♡
DON'T WORRY ABOUT YOUR TEETH— WE'LL BE TAKING CARE OF THEM RIGHT AFTER. ♡
Shall I get you some diluted whiskey, sir?

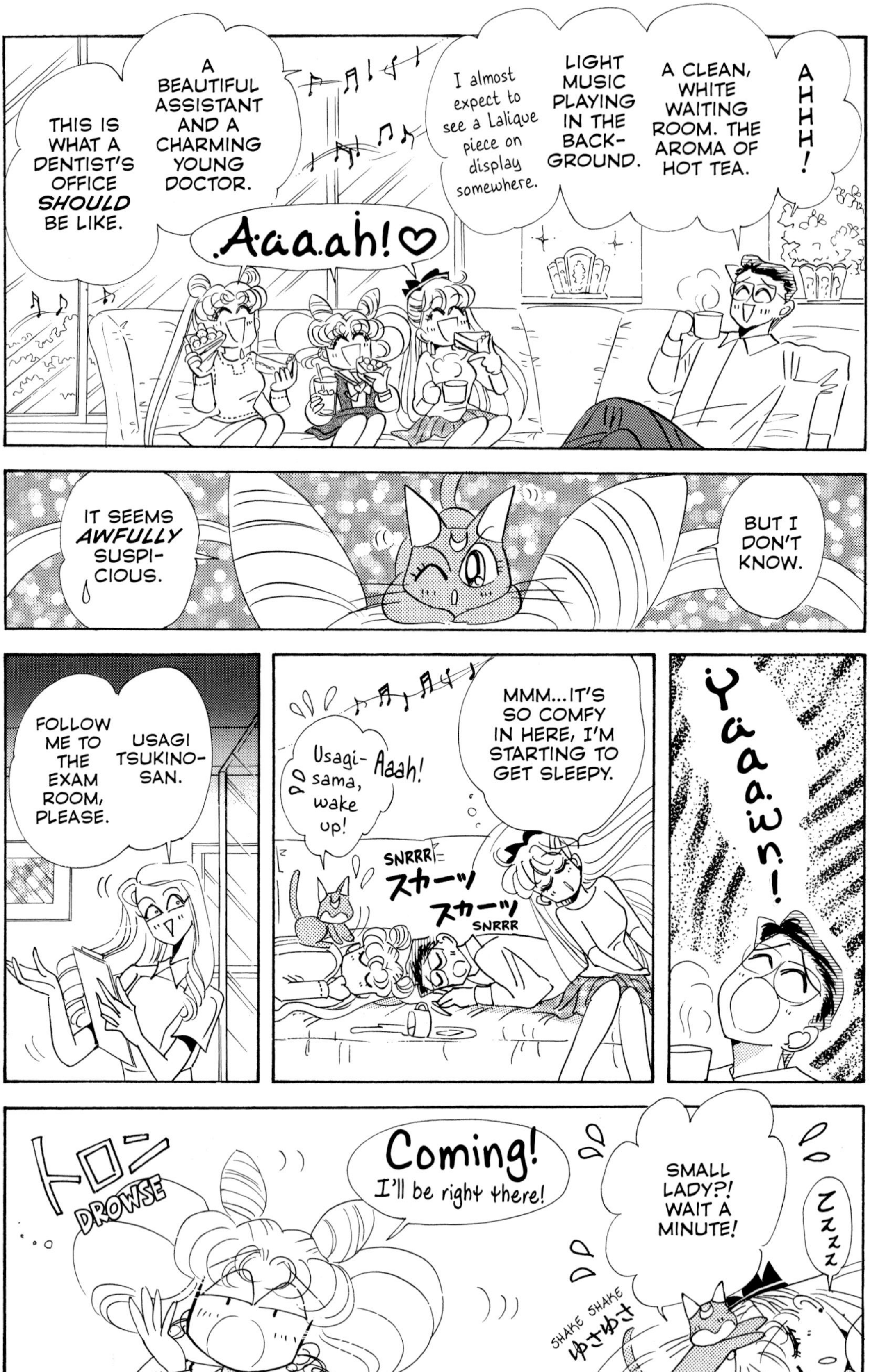
AHHH!
A CLEAN, WHITE WAITING ROOM. THE AROMA OF HOT TEA.
LIGHT MUSIC PLAYING IN THE BACKGROUND.
I almost expect to see a Lalique piece on display somewhere.
A BEAUTIFUL ASSISTANT AND A CHARMING YOUNG DOCTOR.
THIS IS WHAT A DENTIST'S OFFICE *SHOULD* BE LIKE.
Aaaah!♡
BUT I DON'T KNOW.
IT SEEMS *AWFULLY* SUSPICIOUS.
Yaaawn!
MMM...IT'S SO COMFY IN HERE, I'M STARTING TO GET SLEEPY.
Aaah!
Usagi-sama, wake up!
スカーッ SNRRR
スカーッ SNRRR
USAGI TSUKINO-SAN.
FOLLOW ME TO THE EXAM ROOM, PLEASE.
zzz
SMALL LADY?! WAIT A MINUTE!
ゆさゆさ SHAKE SHAKE
Coming! I'll be right there!
トロン DROWSE

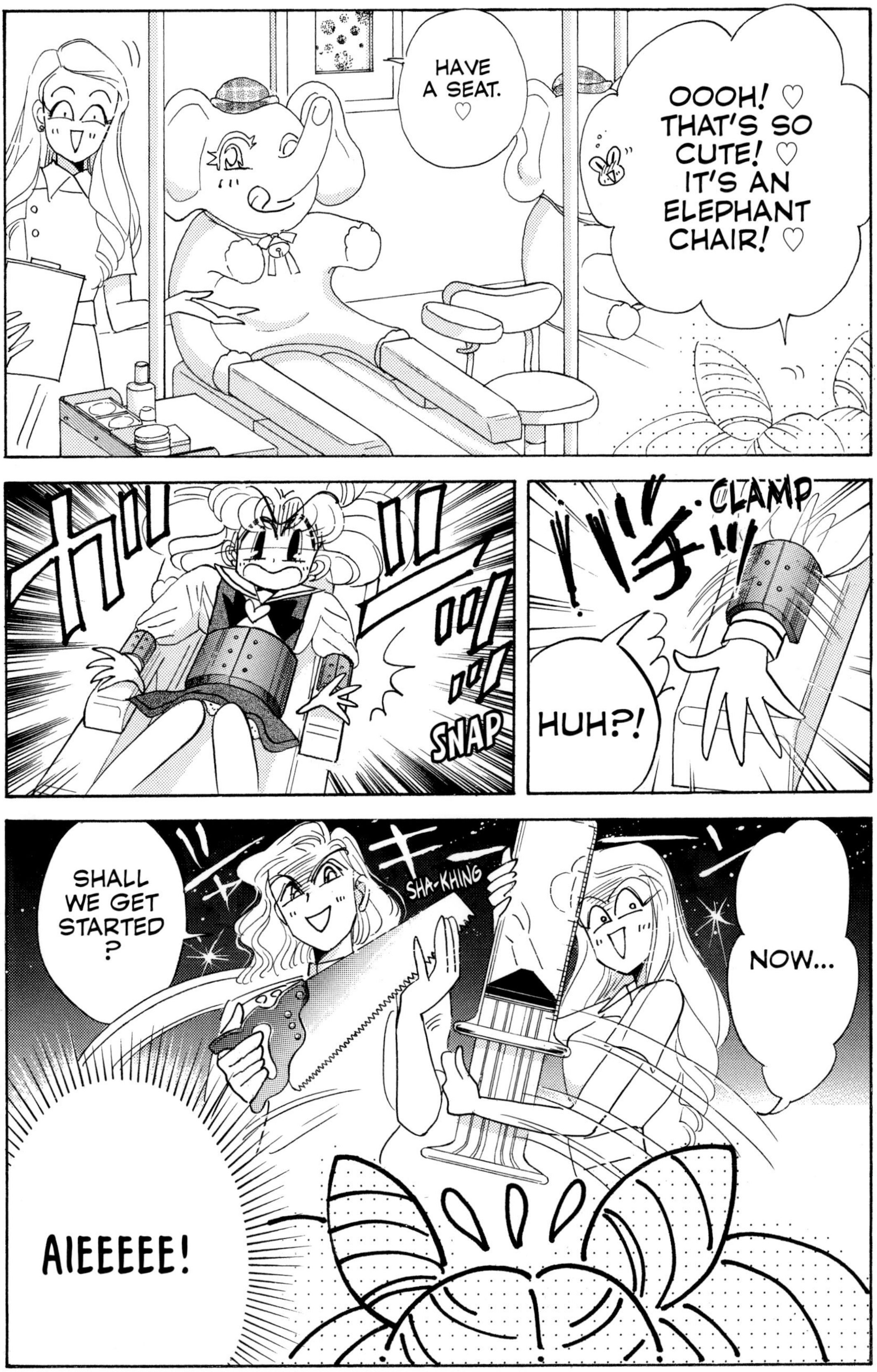
OOOH! ♡ THAT'S SO CUTE! ♡ IT'S AN ELEPHANT CHAIR! ♡
HAVE A SEAT. ♡
CLAMP
HUH?!
SNAP
NOW...
SHA-KHING
SHALL WE GET STARTED?
AIEEEEE!

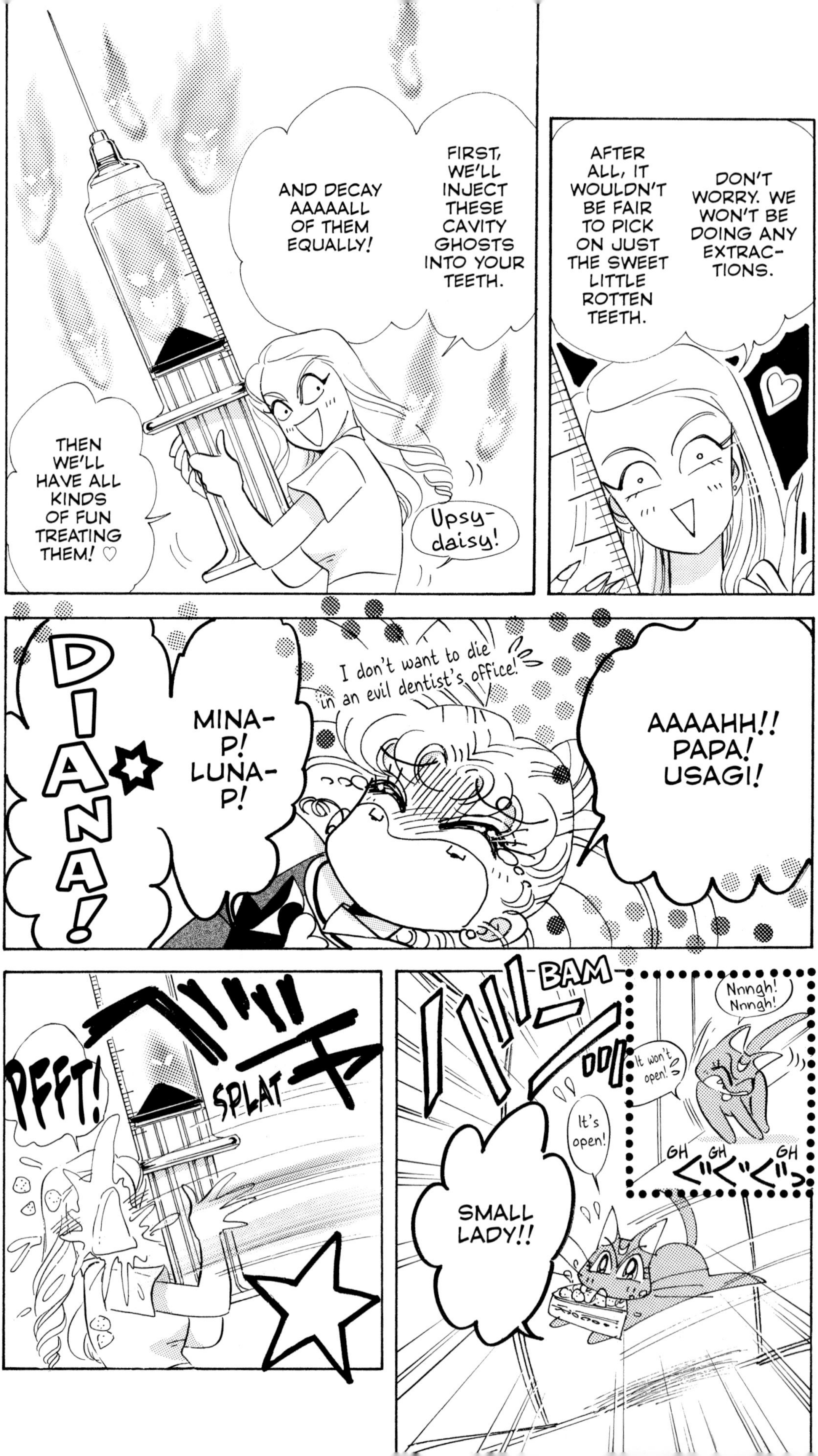

DON'T WORRY. WE WON'T BE DOING ANY EXTRAC-TIONS.
AFTER ALL, IT WOULDN'T BE FAIR TO PICK ON JUST THE SWEET LITTLE ROTTEN TEETH.
FIRST, WE'LL INJECT THESE CAVITY GHOSTS INTO YOUR TEETH.
AND DECAY AAAAALL OF THEM EQUALLY!
Upsy-daisy!
THEN WE'LL HAVE ALL KINDS OF FUN TREATING THEM! ♡
AAAAHH!! PAPA! USAGI!
I don't want to die in an evil dentist's office!
MINA-P! LUNA-P!
DIANA!
BAM
Nnngh! Nnngh!
It won't open!
GH GH GH
It's open!
SMALL LADY!!
SPLAT
PFFT!

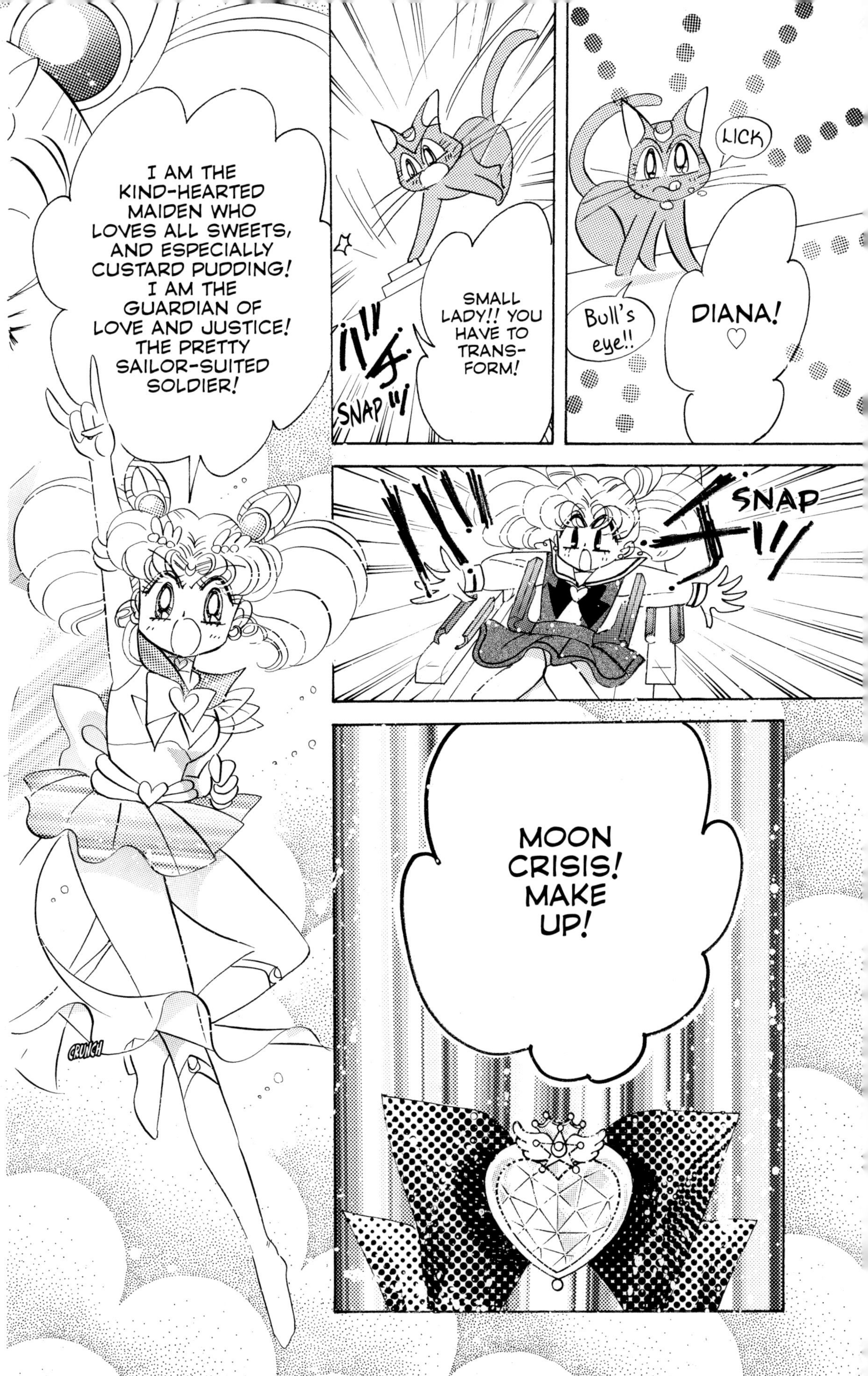
LICK
DIANA! ♡
Bull's eye!!
SMALL LADY!! YOU HAVE TO TRANS-FORM!
SNAP
SNAP
MOON CRISIS! MAKE UP!
I AM THE KIND-HEARTED MAIDEN WHO LOVES ALL SWEETS, AND ESPECIALLY CUSTARD PUDDING! I AM THE GUARDIAN OF LOVE AND JUSTICE! THE PRETTY SAILOR-SUITED SOLDIER!
CRUNCH

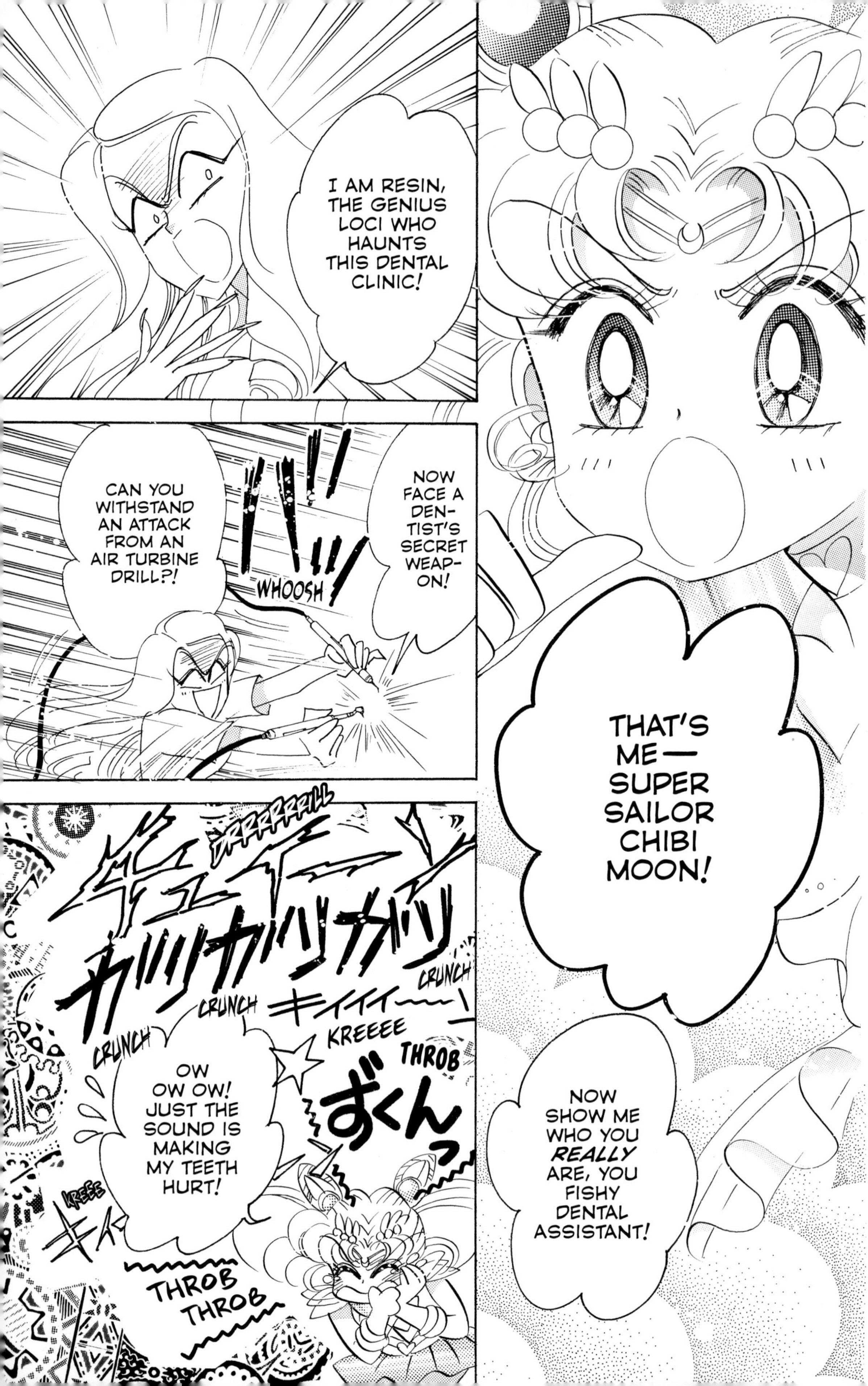
THAT'S ME—SUPER SAILOR CHIBI MOON!
NOW SHOW ME WHO YOU *REALLY* ARE, YOU FISHY DENTAL ASSISTANT!
I AM RESIN, THE GENIUS LOCI WHO HAUNTS THIS DENTAL CLINIC!
NOW FACE A DENTIST'S SECRET WEAPON!
WHOOSH
CAN YOU WITHSTAND AN ATTACK FROM AN AIR TURBINE DRILL?!
DRRRRRRILL
CRUNCH
CRUNCH
CRUNCH
KREEEE
THROB
OW OW OW! JUST THE SOUND IS MAKING MY TEETH HURT!
KREEE
THROB THROB

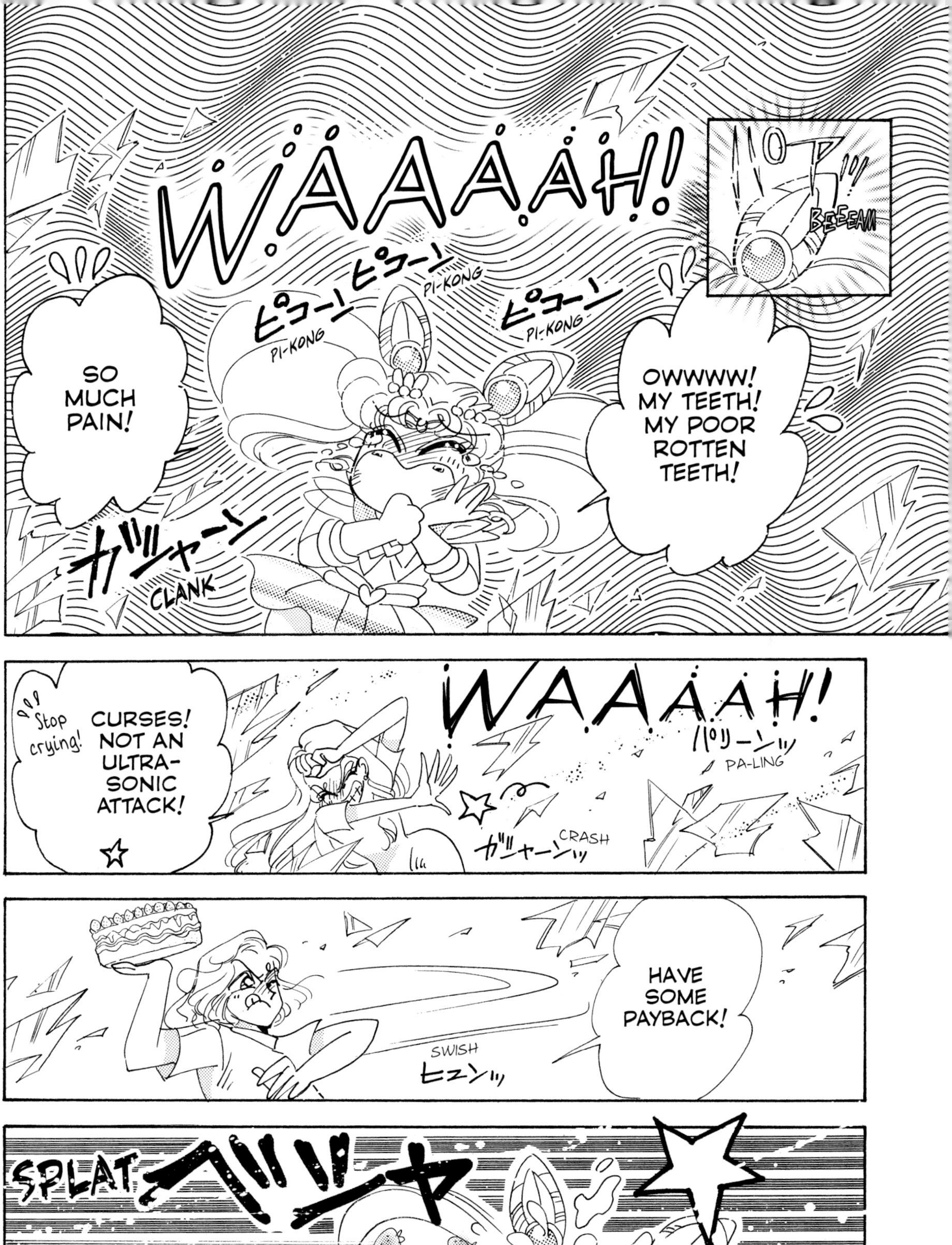
BEEEAM
WAAAAH!
ピコーン PI-KONG
ピコーン PI-KONG
ピコーン PI-KONG
OWWWW! MY TEETH! MY POOR ROTTEN TEETH!
SO MUCH PAIN!
ガシャーン CLANK
WAAAAH!
パリーンッ PA-LING
ガシャーンッ CRASH
CURSES! NOT AN ULTRA-SONIC ATTACK!
Stop crying!
HAVE SOME PAYBACK!
ヒュンッ SWISH
ベシャ SPLAT
BFFT!

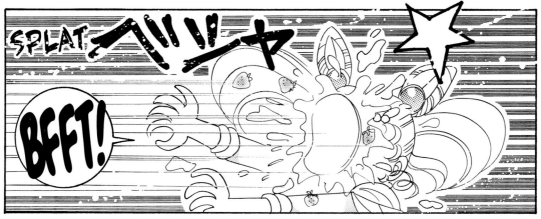

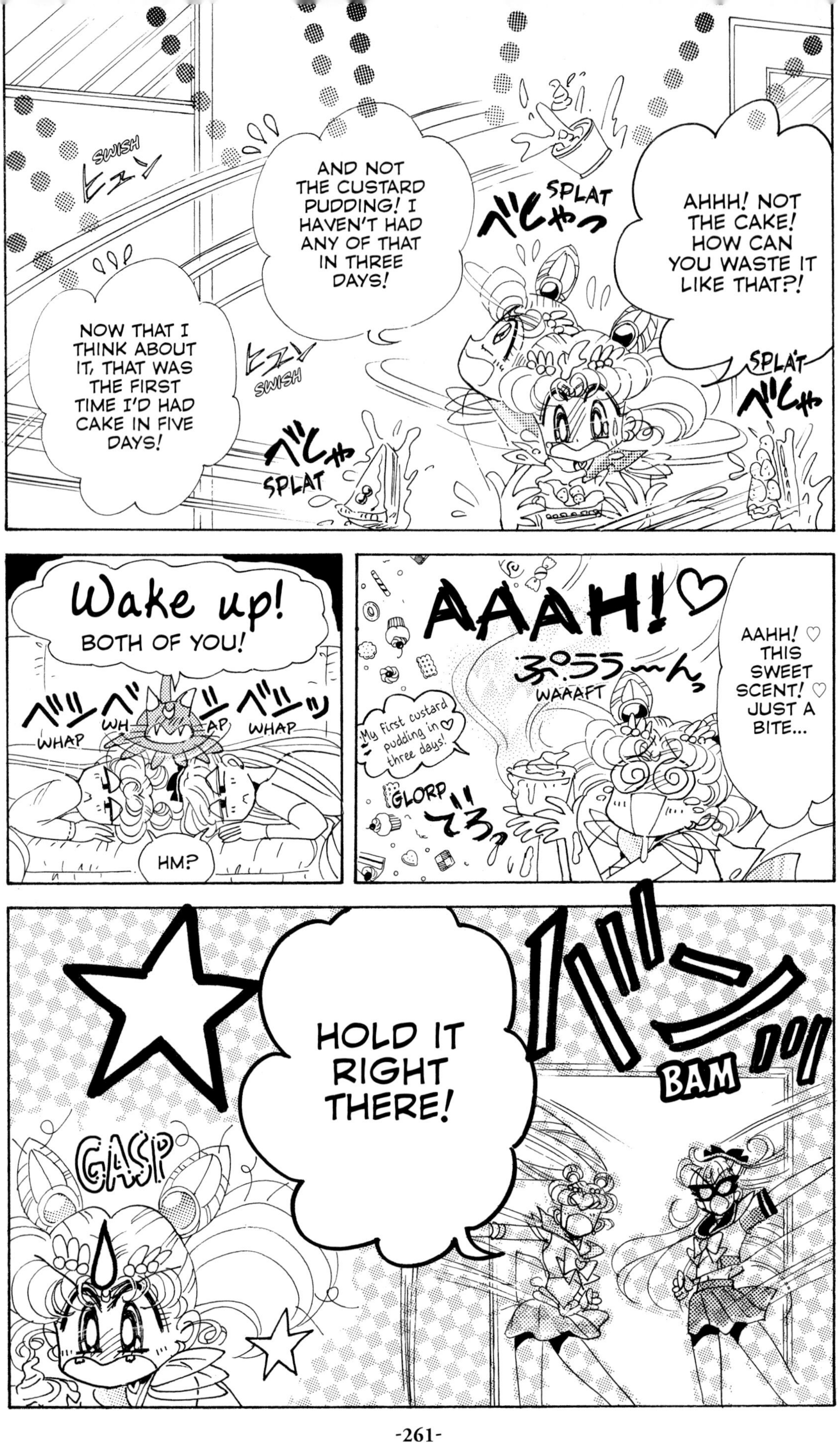

SPLAT
AHHH! NOT THE CAKE! HOW CAN YOU WASTE IT LIKE THAT?!
SPLAT
AND NOT THE CUSTARD PUDDING! I HAVEN'T HAD ANY OF THAT IN THREE DAYS!
SWISH
SWISH
NOW THAT I THINK ABOUT IT, THAT WAS THE FIRST TIME I'D HAD CAKE IN FIVE DAYS!
SPLAT
AAAH!♡
AAHH! ♡ THIS SWEET SCENT! ♡ JUST A BITE...
WAAAFT
My first custard pudding in♡ three days!
GLORP
Wake up! BOTH OF YOU!
WHAP
WH
AP
WHAP
HM?
BAM
HOLD IT RIGHT THERE!
GASP

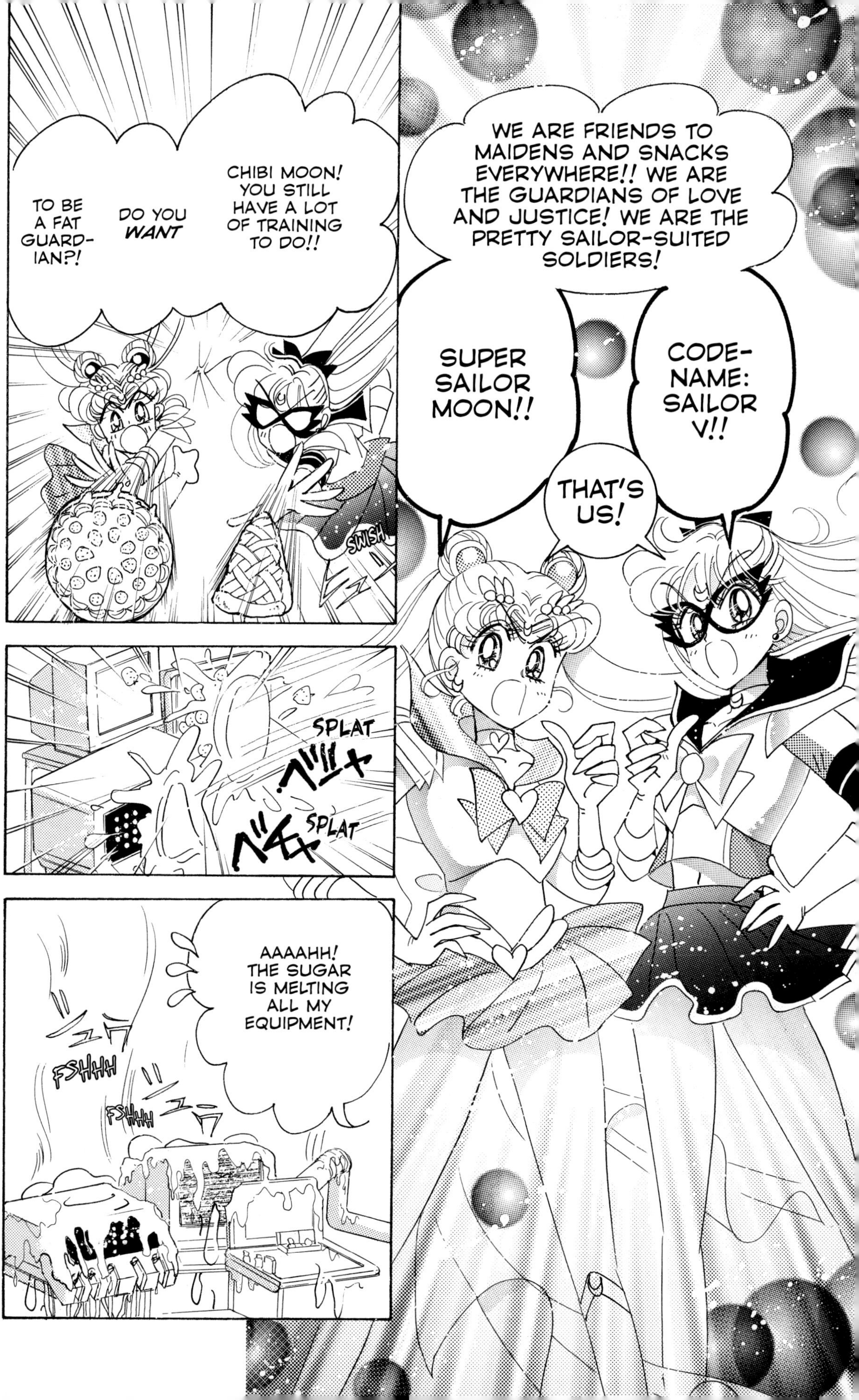
WE ARE FRIENDS TO MAIDENS AND SNACKS EVERYWHERE!! WE ARE THE GUARDIANS OF LOVE AND JUSTICE! WE ARE THE PRETTY SAILOR-SUITED SOLDIERS!
CODE-NAME: SAILOR V!!
SUPER SAILOR MOON!!
THAT'S US!
CHIBI MOON! YOU STILL HAVE A LOT OF TRAINING TO DO!!
DO YOU *WANT*
TO BE A FAT GUARDIAN?!
SWISH
SPLAT
SPLAT
AAAAHH! THE SUGAR IS MELTING ALL MY EQUIPMENT!
FSHHH
FSHHH

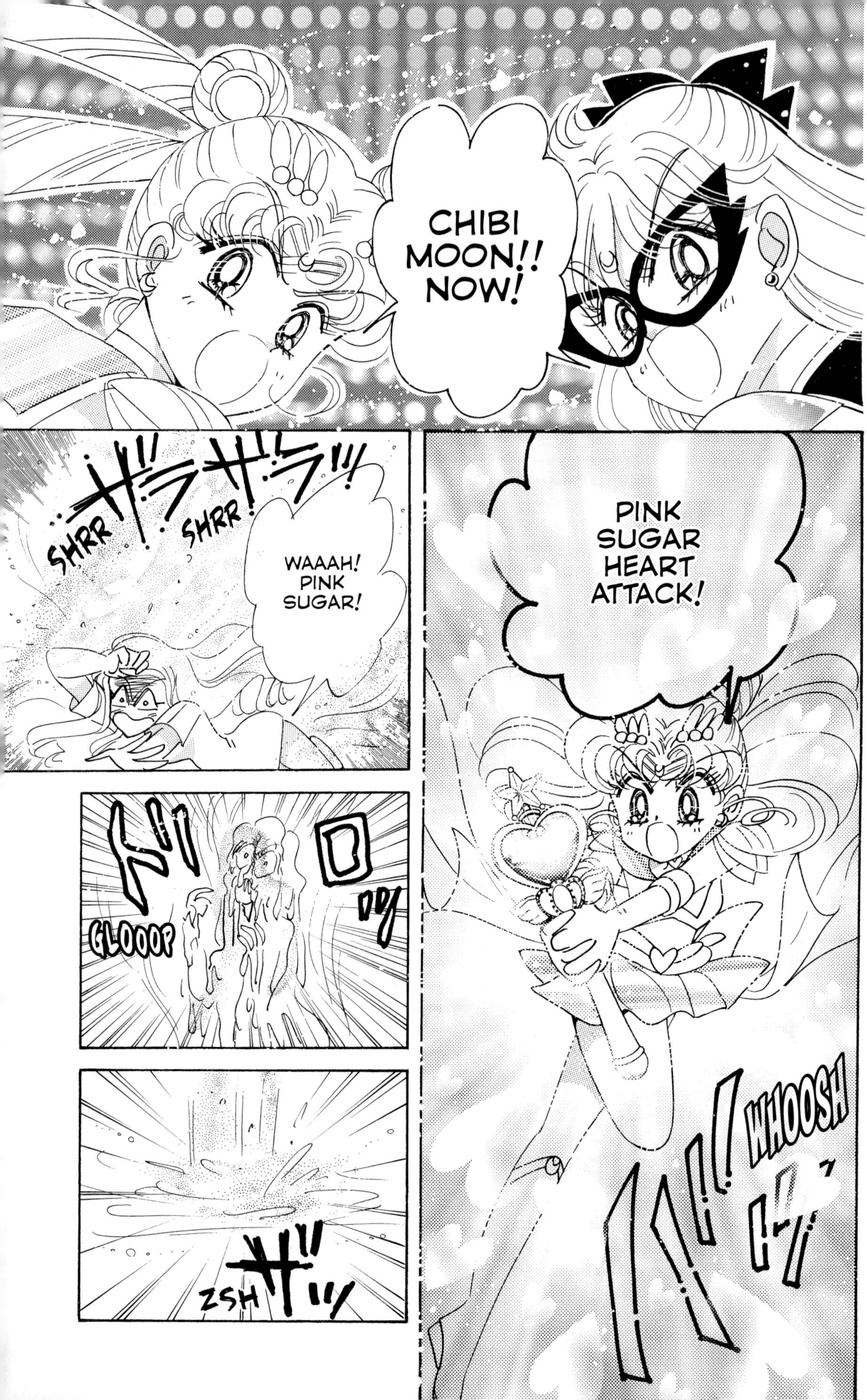
CHIBI MOON!! NOW!
PINK SUGAR HEART ATTACK!
WHOOSH
SHRR
SHRR
WAAAH! PINK SUGAR!
GLOOOP
ZSH

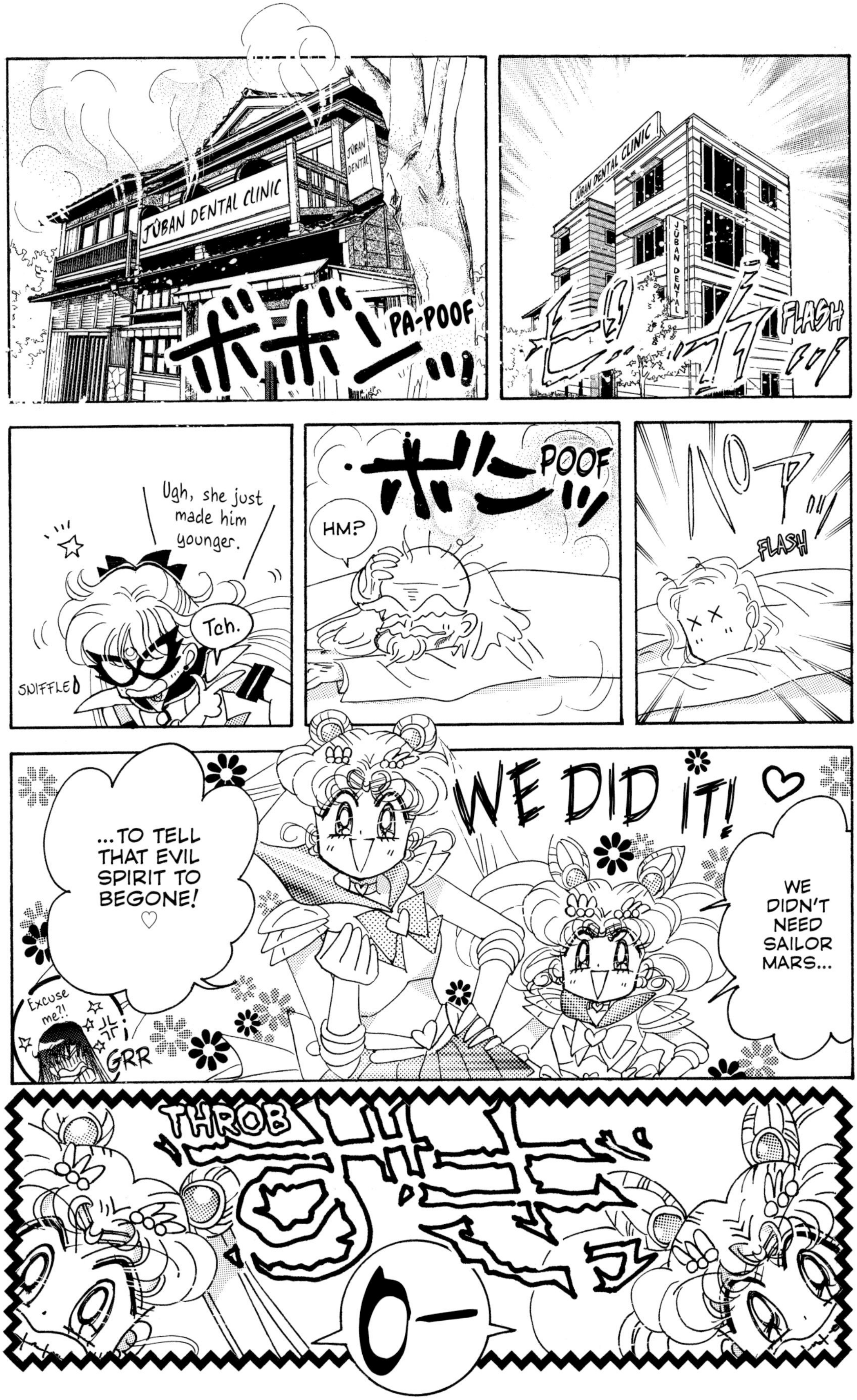
JÛBAN DENTAL CLINIC
JÛBAN DENTAL
FLASH
JÛBAN DENTAL CLINIC
JÛBAN DENTAL
PA-POOF
FLASH
POOF
HM?
Ugh, she just made him younger.
Tch.
SNIFFLED
WE DID IT!
WE DIDN'T NEED SAILOR MARS...
...TO TELL THAT EVIL SPIRIT TO BEGONE! ♡
Excuse me?!
GRR
THROB

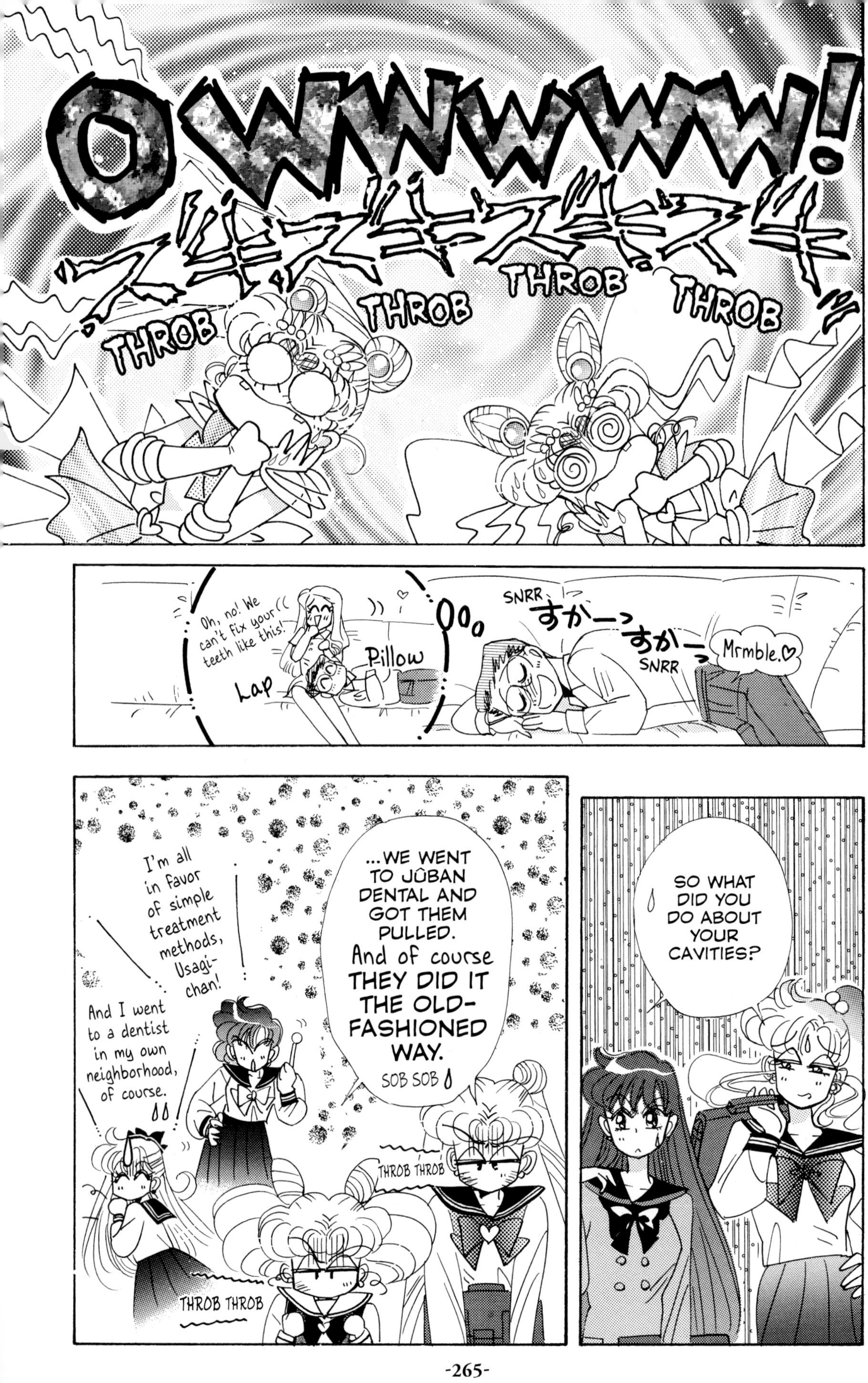
OWWWWW!
ズキズキズキズキ
THROB
THROB
THROB
THROB
SNRR
すかー
すかー
SNRR
Mrmble.♡
Oh, no! We can't fix your teeth like this!
Pillow
Lap
SO WHAT DID YOU DO ABOUT YOUR CAVITIES?
...WE WENT TO JÛBAN DENTAL AND GOT THEM PULLED. And of course THEY DID IT THE OLD-FASHIONED WAY.
SOB SOB
I'm all in favor of simple treatment methods, Usagi-chan!
And I went to a dentist in my own neighborhood, of course.
THROB THROB
THROB THROB

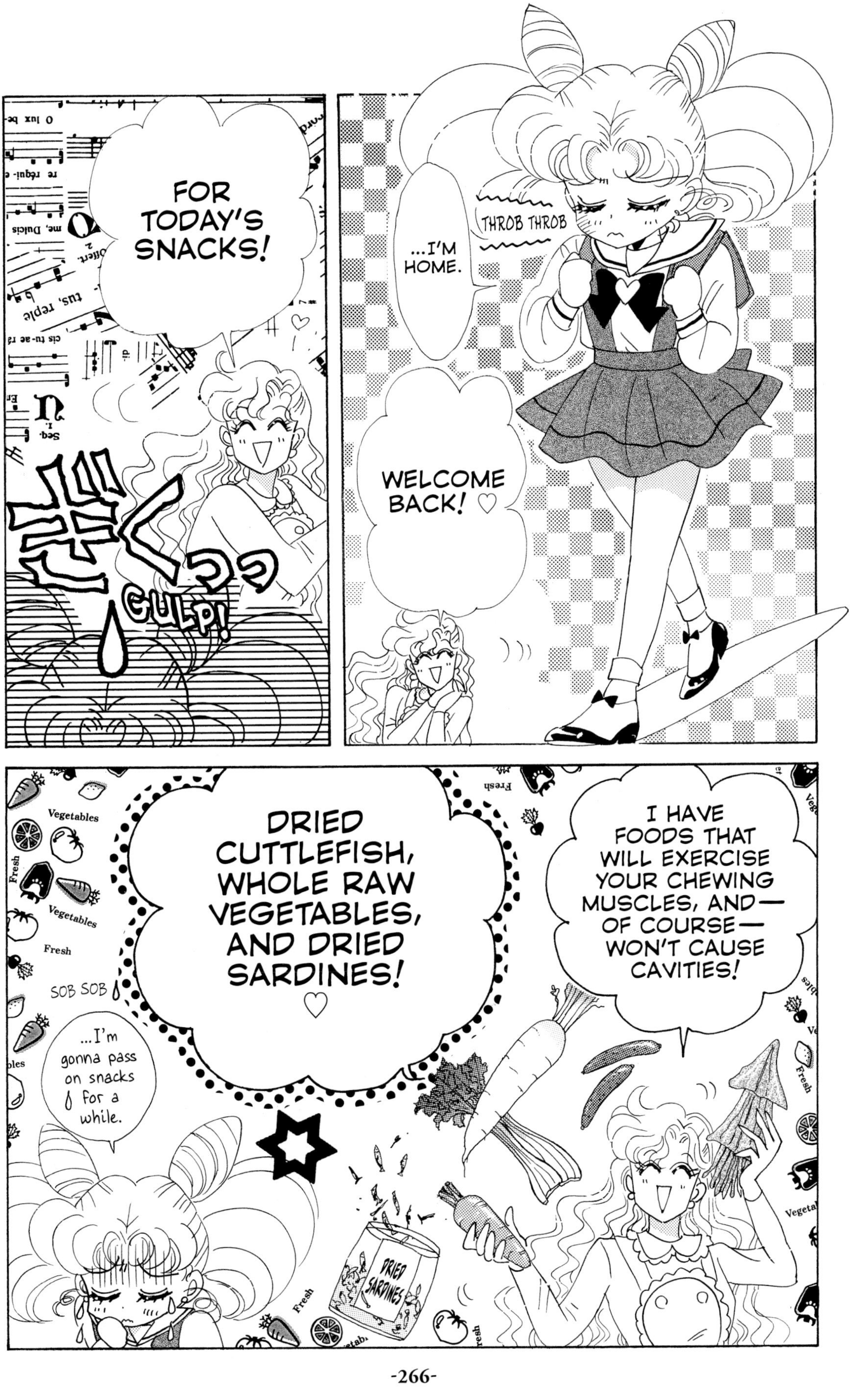
...I'M HOME.
THROB THROB
WELCOME BACK! ♡
FOR TODAY'S SNACKS!
GULP!
I HAVE FOODS THAT WILL EXERCISE YOUR CHEWING MUSCLES, AND—OF COURSE—WON'T CAUSE CAVITIES!
DRIED CUTTLEFISH, WHOLE RAW VEGETABLES, AND DRIED SARDINES! ♡
DRIED SARDINES
...I'm gonna pass on snacks for a while.
SOB SOB

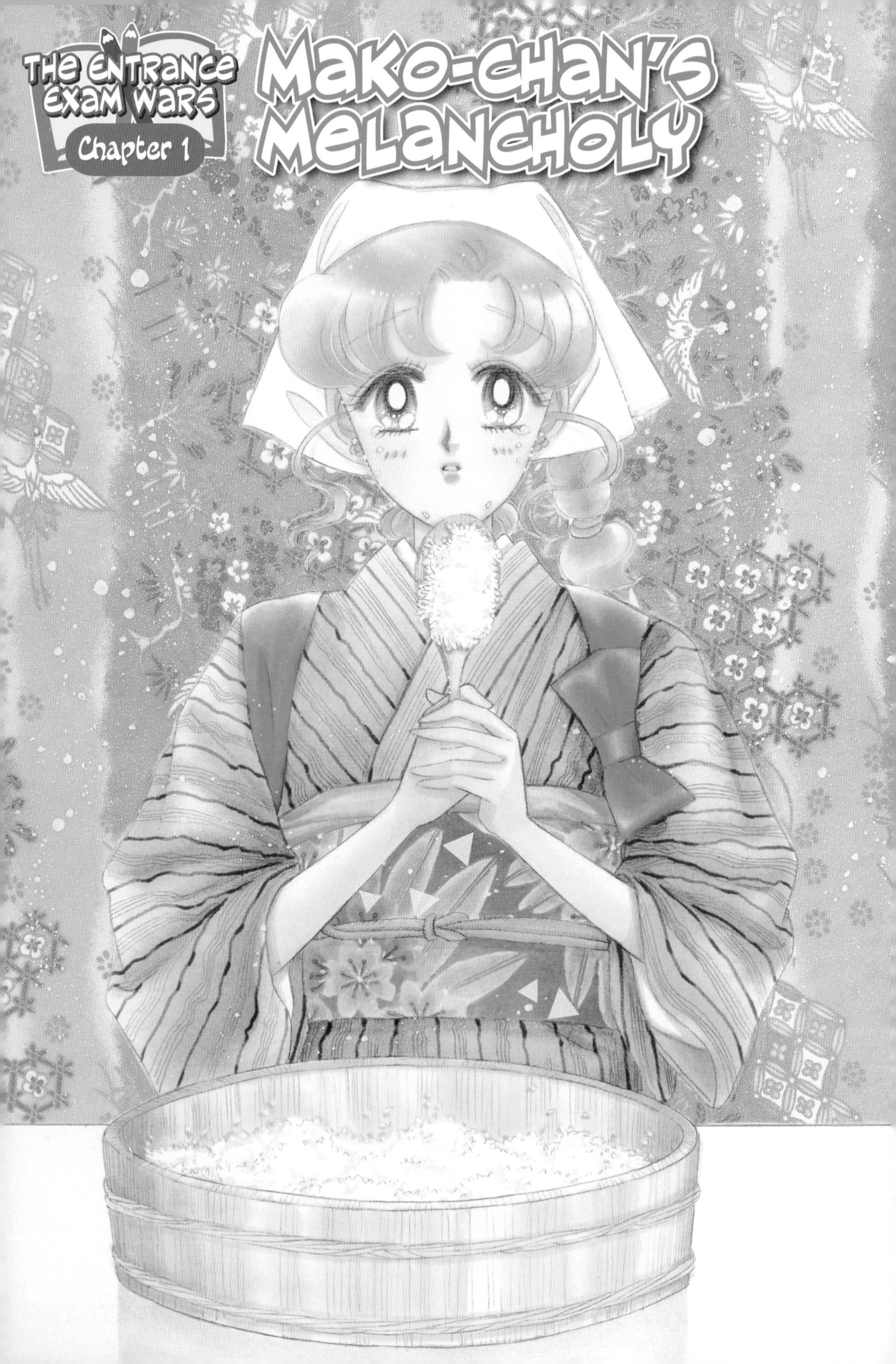
The Entrance Exam Wars
Chapter 1
Mako-chan's Melancholy

Pretty Guardian
Sailor Moon

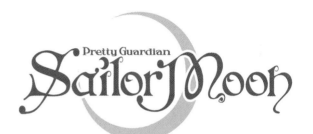

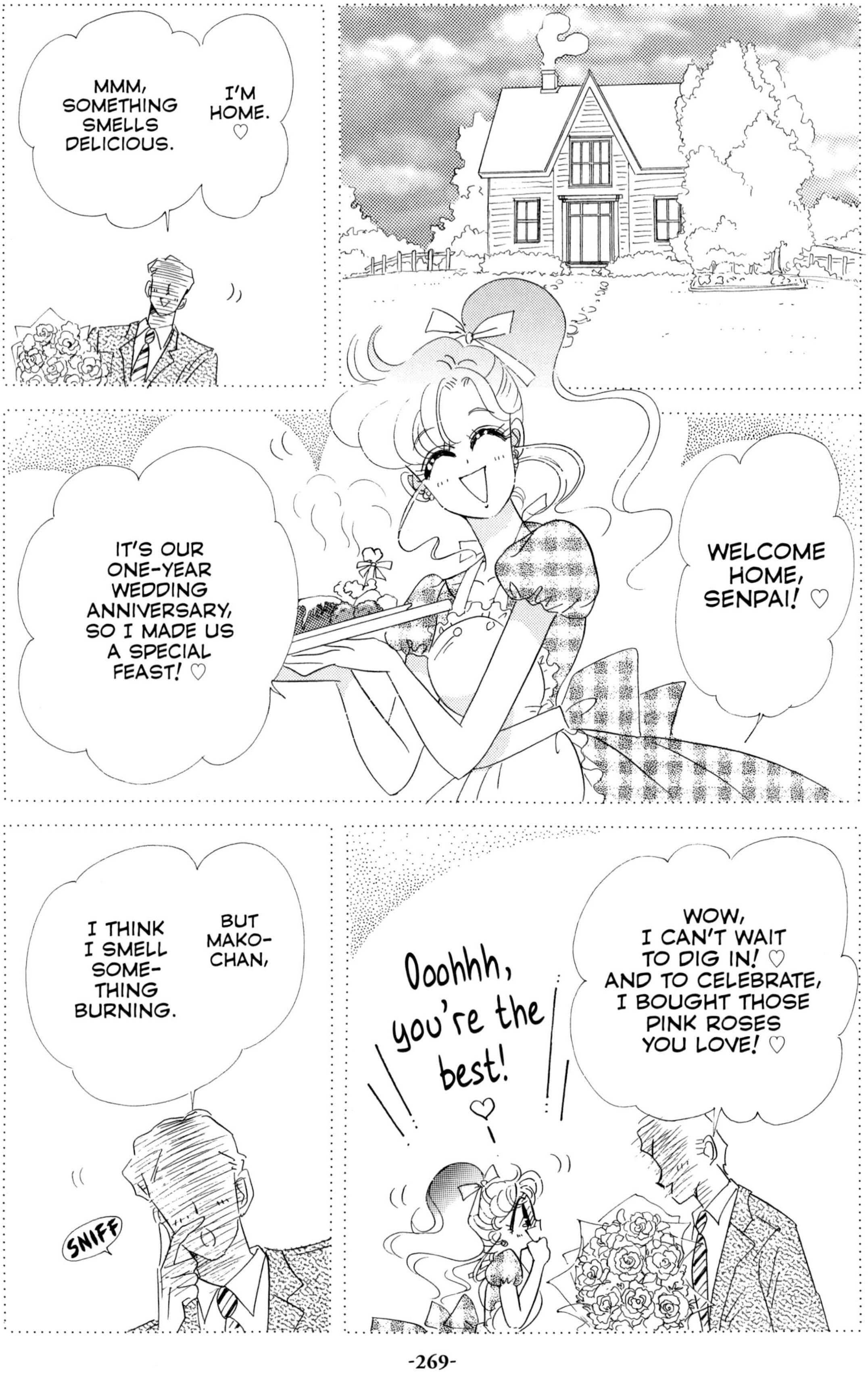
I'M HOME. ♡
MMM, SOMETHING SMELLS DELICIOUS.
WELCOME HOME, SENPAI! ♡
IT'S OUR ONE-YEAR WEDDING ANNIVERSARY, SO I MADE US A SPECIAL FEAST! ♡
WOW, I CAN'T WAIT TO DIG IN! ♡ AND TO CELEBRATE, I BOUGHT THOSE PINK ROSES YOU LOVE! ♡
Ooohhh, you're the best! ♡
BUT MAKO-CHAN,
I THINK I SMELL SOME-THING BURNING.
SNIFF

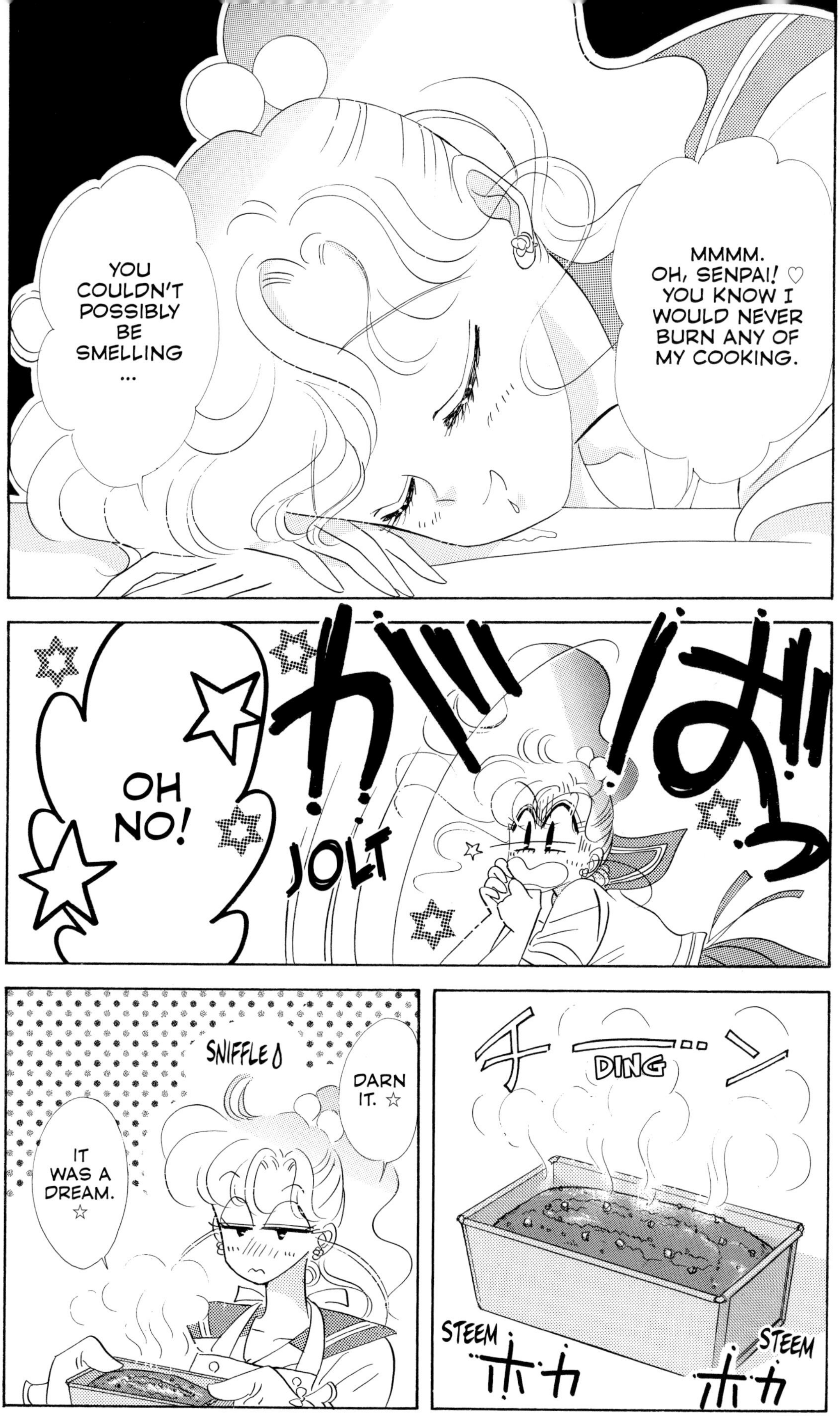
MMMM. OH, SENPAI! ♡ YOU KNOW I WOULD NEVER BURN ANY OF MY COOKING.
YOU COULDN'T POSSIBLY BE SMELLING ...
がばっ
JOLT
OH NO!
チーン
DING
STEEM
ホカ
STEEM
ホカ
DARN IT. ☆
SNIFFLE
IT WAS A DREAM. ☆

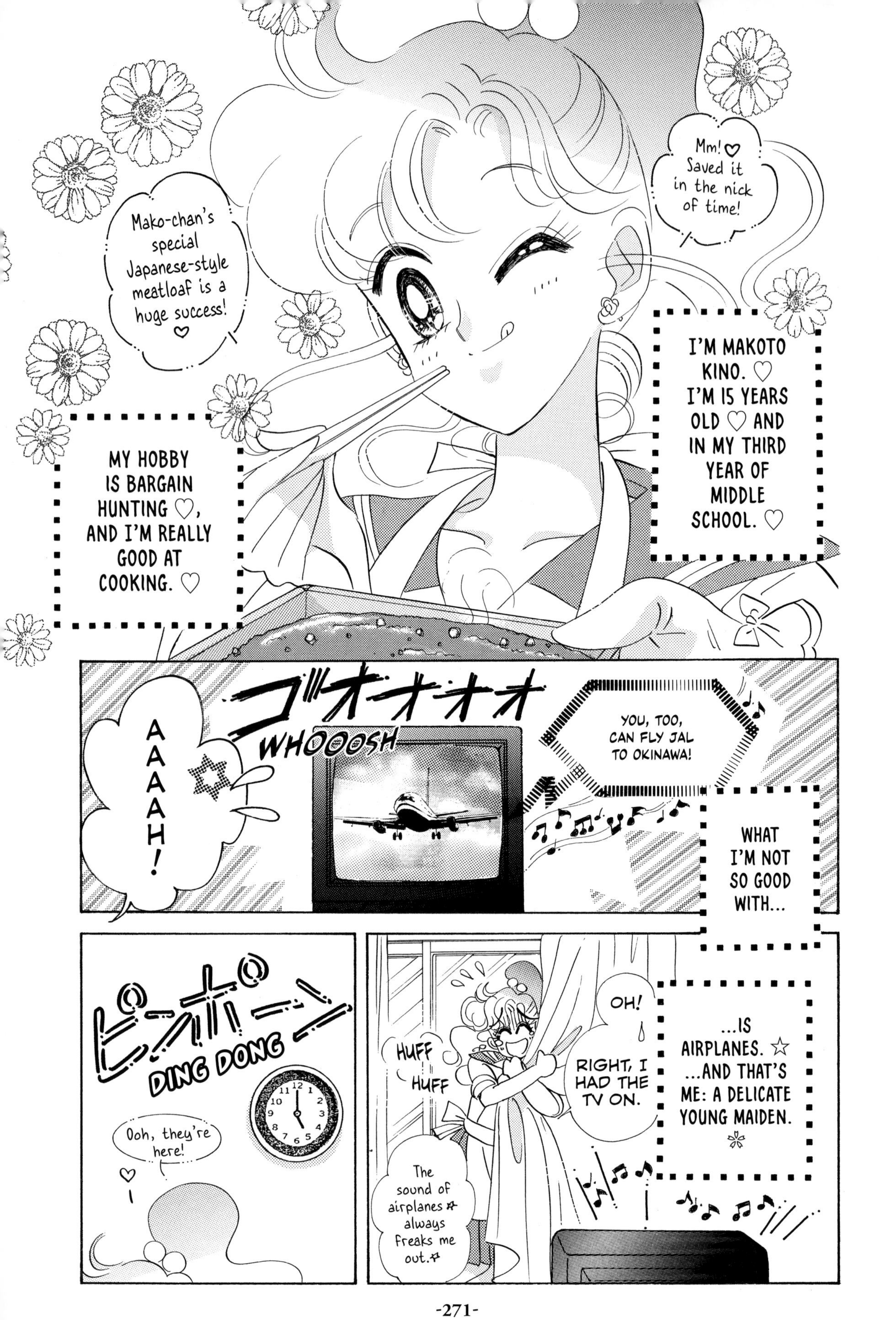
Mm! ♡ Saved it in the nick of time!
I'M MAKOTO KINO. ♡ I'M 15 YEARS OLD ♡ AND IN MY THIRD YEAR OF MIDDLE SCHOOL. ♡
Mako-chan's special Japanese-style meatloaf is a huge success! ♡
MY HOBBY IS BARGAIN HUNTING ♡, AND I'M REALLY GOOD AT COOKING. ♡
YOU, TOO, CAN FLY JAL TO OKINAWA!
ゴオオオオ
WHOOOSH
AAAAH!
WHAT I'M NOT SO GOOD WITH...
...IS AIRPLANES. ☆ ...AND THAT'S ME: A DELICATE YOUNG MAIDEN.
OH!
RIGHT, I HAD THE TV ON.
HUFF HUFF
The sound of airplanes always freaks me out.
ピンポーン
DING DONG
Ooh, they're here!

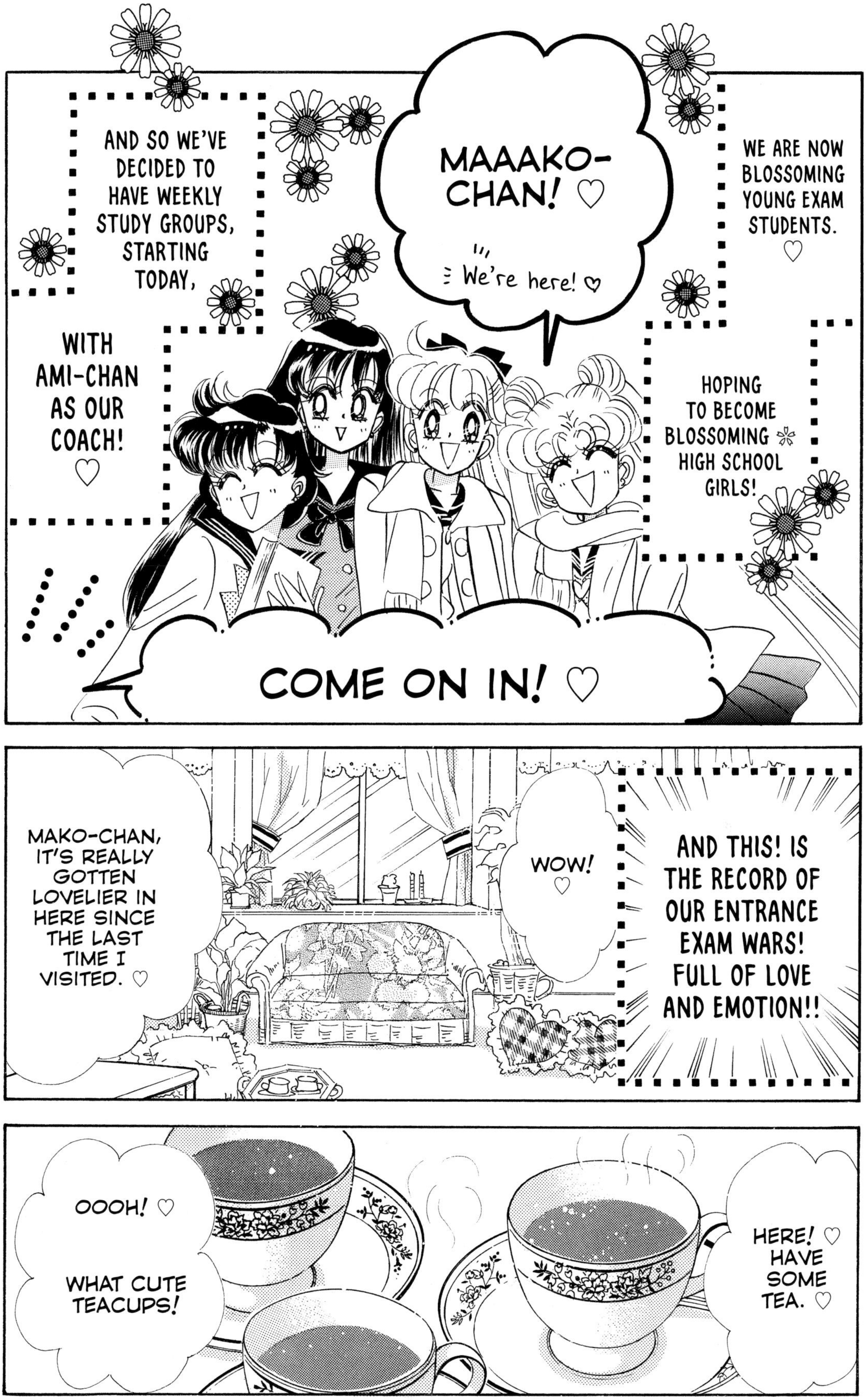

WE ARE NOW BLOSSOMING YOUNG EXAM STUDENTS. ♡
MAAAKO-CHAN! ♡
We're here! ♡
AND SO WE'VE DECIDED TO HAVE WEEKLY STUDY GROUPS, STARTING TODAY,
WITH AMI-CHAN AS OUR COACH! ♡
HOPING TO BECOME BLOSSOMING ✲ HIGH SCHOOL GIRLS!
COME ON IN! ♡
AND THIS! IS THE RECORD OF OUR ENTRANCE EXAM WARS! FULL OF LOVE AND EMOTION!!
WOW! ♡
MAKO-CHAN, IT'S REALLY GOTTEN LOVELIER IN HERE SINCE THE LAST TIME I VISITED. ♡
HERE! ♡ HAVE SOME TEA. ♡
OOOH! ♡
WHAT CUTE TEACUPS!

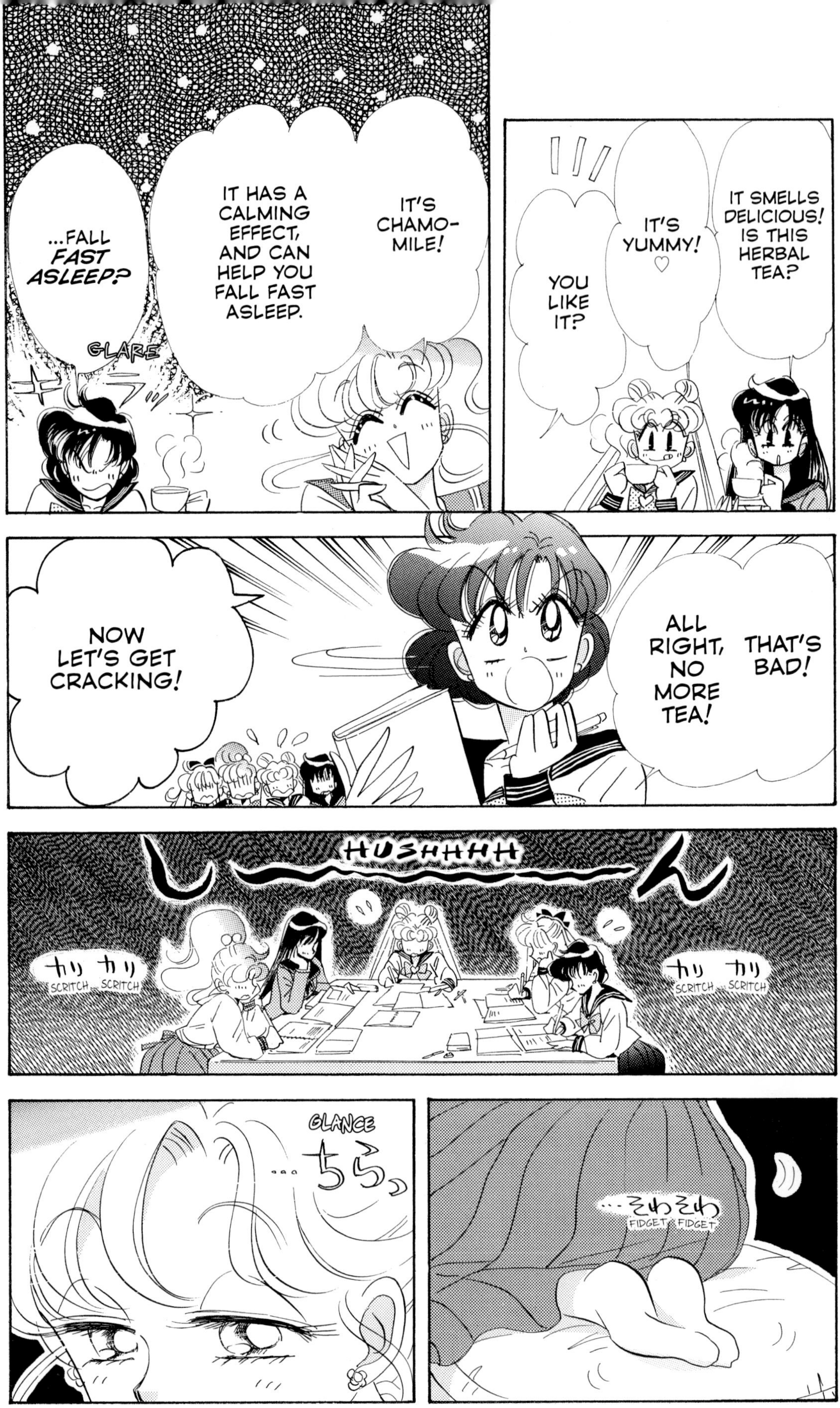
IT SMELLS DELICIOUS! IS THIS HERBAL TEA?
IT'S YUMMY! ♡
YOU LIKE IT?
IT'S CHAMO-MILE!
IT HAS A CALMING EFFECT, AND CAN HELP YOU FALL FAST ASLEEP.
GLARE
...FALL *FAST ASLEEP?*
THAT'S BAD!
ALL RIGHT, NO MORE TEA!
NOW LET'S GET CRACKING!
HUSHHHH
しーーん
カリ カリ
SCRITCH SCRITCH
カリ カリ
SCRITCH SCRITCH
...そわそわ
FIDGET FIDGET
GLANCE
...ちらっ

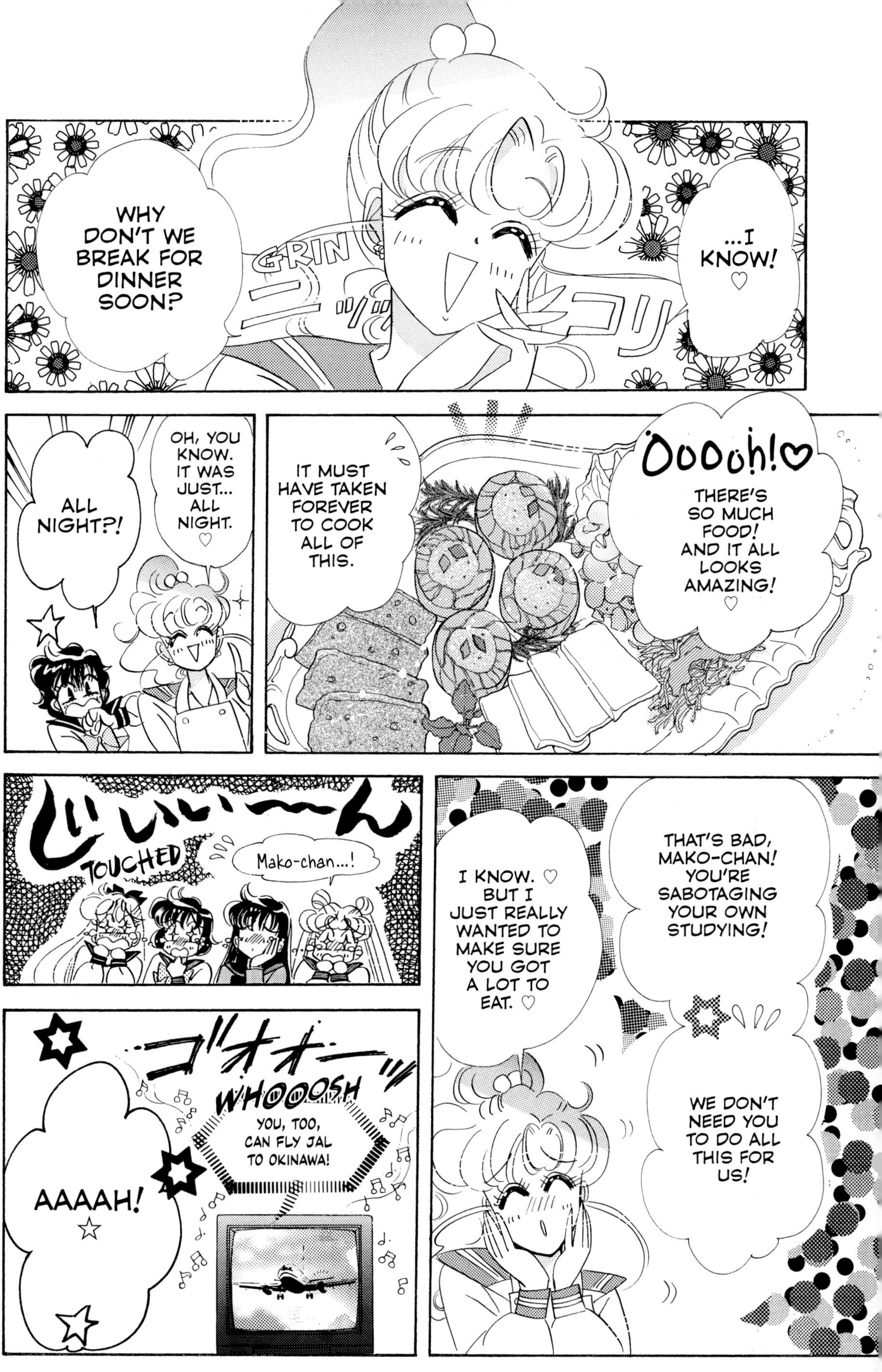
...I KNOW! ♡
WHY DON'T WE BREAK FOR DINNER SOON?
ニッコリ
GRIN
Ooooh!♡
THERE'S SO MUCH FOOD! AND IT ALL LOOKS AMAZING! ♡
IT MUST HAVE TAKEN FOREVER TO COOK ALL OF THIS.
OH, YOU KNOW. IT WAS JUST... ALL NIGHT. ♡
ALL NIGHT?!
THAT'S BAD, MAKO-CHAN! YOU'RE SABOTAGING YOUR OWN STUDYING!
I KNOW. ♡ BUT I JUST REALLY WANTED TO MAKE SURE YOU GOT A LOT TO EAT. ♡
WE DON'T NEED YOU TO DO ALL THIS FOR US!
じいいーーん
TOUCHED
Mako-chan...!
ゴオオー
WHOOOSH
YOU, TOO, CAN FLY JAL TO OKINAWA!
AAAAH! ☆

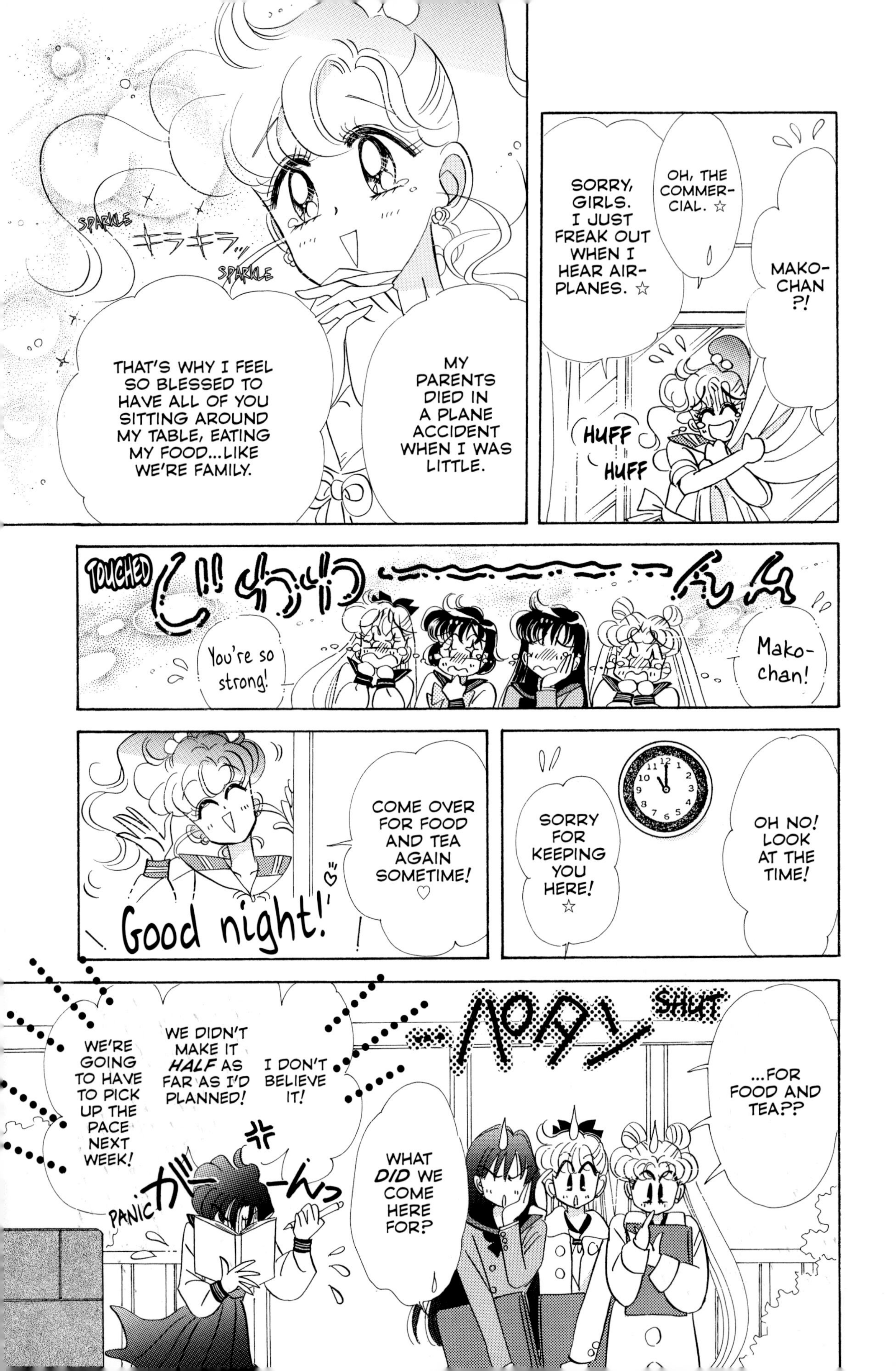
MAKO-CHAN?!
OH, THE COMMERCIAL. ☆
SORRY, GIRLS. I JUST FREAK OUT WHEN I HEAR AIRPLANES. ☆
HUFF HUFF
SPARKLE
SPARKLE
MY PARENTS DIED IN A PLANE ACCIDENT WHEN I WAS LITTLE.
THAT'S WHY I FEEL SO BLESSED TO HAVE ALL OF YOU SITTING AROUND MY TABLE, EATING MY FOOD...LIKE WE'RE FAMILY.
Mako-chan!
You're so strong!
TOUCHED
OH NO! LOOK AT THE TIME!
SORRY FOR KEEPING YOU HERE! ☆
COME OVER FOR FOOD AND TEA AGAIN SOMETIME! ♡
Good night!
...FOR FOOD AND TEA??
SHUT
WHAT DID WE COME HERE FOR?
I DON'T BELIEVE IT!
WE DIDN'T MAKE IT HALF AS FAR AS I'D PLANNED!
WE'RE GOING TO HAVE TO PICK UP THE PACE NEXT WEEK!
PANIC

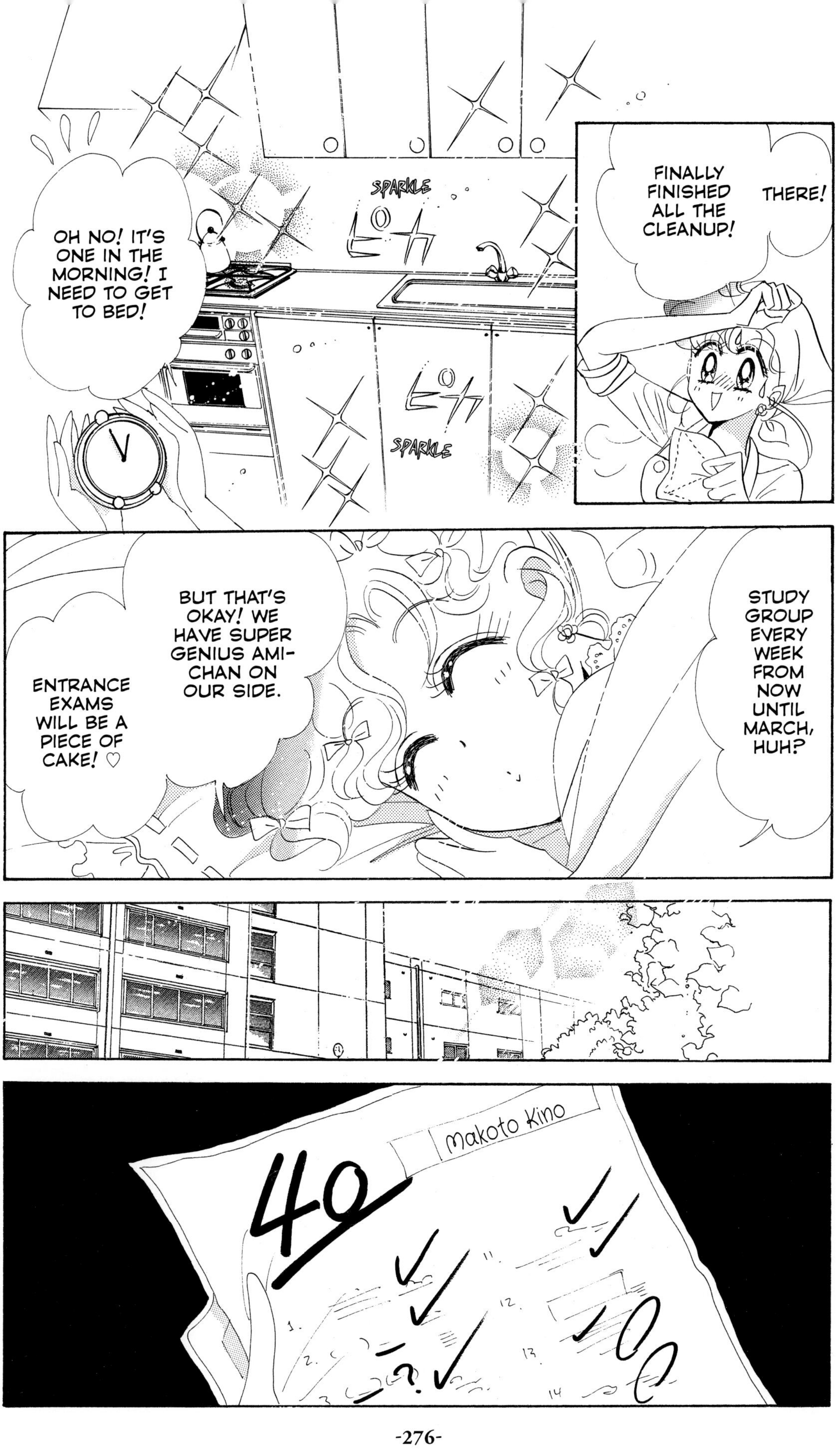
THERE!
FINALLY FINISHED ALL THE CLEANUP!
SPARKLE
ピカ
OH NO! IT'S ONE IN THE MORNING! I NEED TO GET TO BED!
ピカ
SPARKLE
STUDY GROUP EVERY WEEK FROM NOW UNTIL MARCH, HUH?
BUT THAT'S OKAY! WE HAVE SUPER GENIUS AMI-CHAN ON OUR SIDE.
ENTRANCE EXAMS WILL BE A PIECE OF CAKE! ♡
40
Makoto Kino

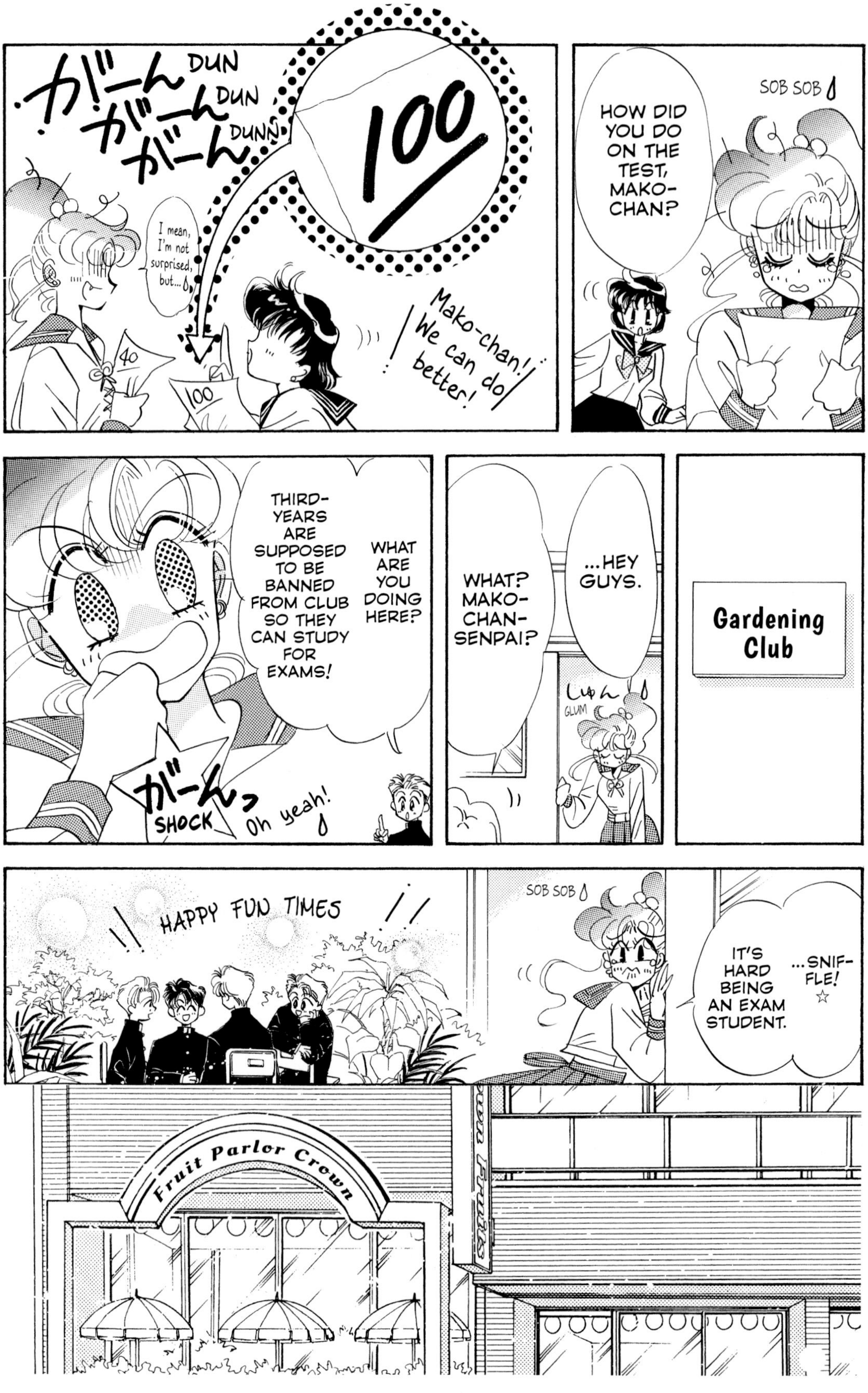
SOB SOB
HOW DID YOU DO ON THE TEST, MAKO-CHAN?
がーん DUN がーん DUN がーん DUNN
100
Mako-chan! We can do better!
I mean, I'm not surprised, but...
40
100
Gardening Club
...HEY GUYS.
WHAT? MAKO-CHAN-SENPAI?
しゅん GLUM
WHAT ARE YOU DOING HERE?
THIRD-YEARS ARE SUPPOSED TO BE BANNED FROM CLUB SO THEY CAN STUDY FOR EXAMS!
がーん SHOCK
Oh yeah!
...SNIF-FLE! ☆
IT'S HARD BEING AN EXAM STUDENT.
SOB SOB
HAPPY FUN TIMES
Fruit Parlor Crown

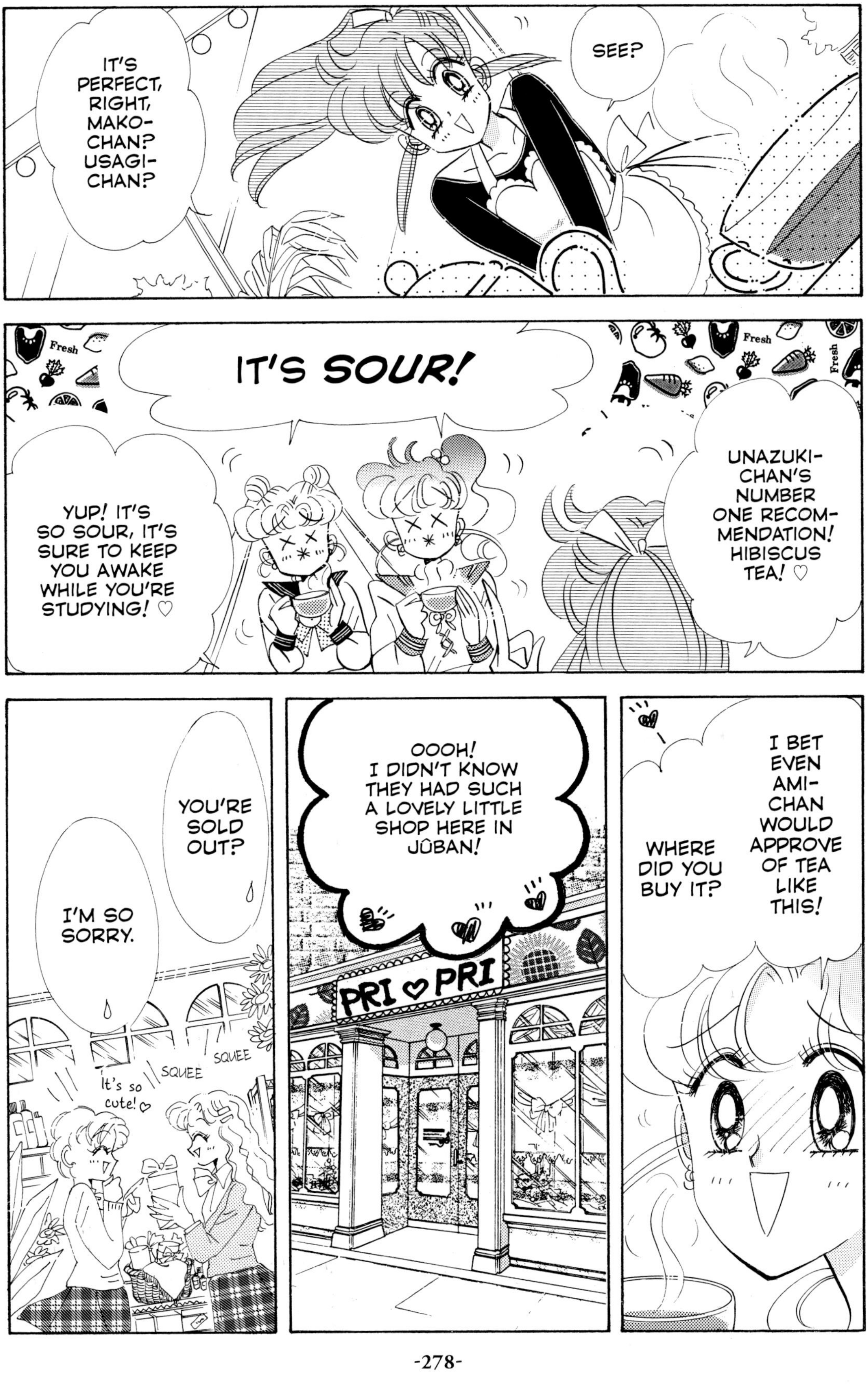
SEE?
IT'S PERFECT, RIGHT, MAKO-CHAN? USAGI-CHAN?
Fresh
UNAZUKI-CHAN'S NUMBER ONE RECOMMENDATION! HIBISCUS TEA! ♡
IT'S SOUR!
YUP! IT'S SO SOUR, IT'S SURE TO KEEP YOU AWAKE WHILE YOU'RE STUDYING! ♡
I BET EVEN AMI-CHAN WOULD APPROVE OF TEA LIKE THIS!
WHERE DID YOU BUY IT?
OOOH! I DIDN'T KNOW THEY HAD SUCH A LOVELY LITTLE SHOP HERE IN JÛBAN!
PRI ♡ PRI
YOU'RE SOLD OUT?
I'M SO SORRY.
SQUEE
SQUEE
It's so cute! ♡

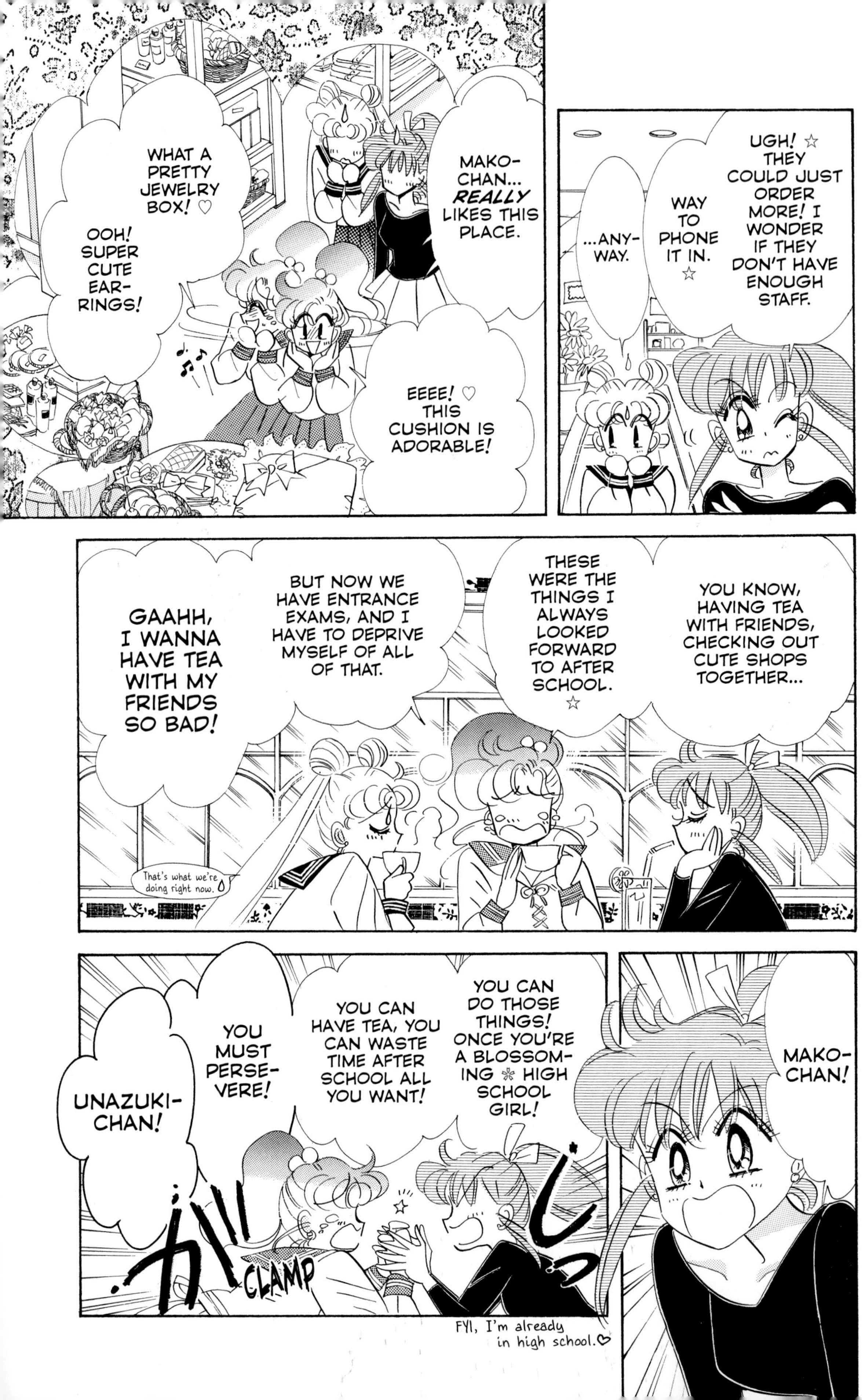
UGH! ☆ THEY COULD JUST ORDER MORE! I WONDER IF THEY DON'T HAVE ENOUGH STAFF.
WAY TO PHONE IT IN. ☆
...ANY-WAY.
MAKO-CHAN... *REALLY* LIKES THIS PLACE.
WHAT A PRETTY JEWELRY BOX! ♡
OOH! SUPER CUTE EAR-RINGS!
EEEE! ♡ THIS CUSHION IS ADORABLE!
YOU KNOW, HAVING TEA WITH FRIENDS, CHECKING OUT CUTE SHOPS TOGETHER...
THESE WERE THE THINGS I ALWAYS LOOKED FORWARD TO AFTER SCHOOL. ☆
BUT NOW WE HAVE ENTRANCE EXAMS, AND I HAVE TO DEPRIVE MYSELF OF ALL OF THAT.
GAAHH, I WANNA HAVE TEA WITH MY FRIENDS SO BAD!
That's what we're doing right now.
MAKO-CHAN!
YOU CAN DO THOSE THINGS! ONCE YOU'RE A BLOSSOM-ING ✼ HIGH SCHOOL GIRL!
YOU CAN HAVE TEA, YOU CAN WASTE TIME AFTER SCHOOL ALL YOU WANT!
YOU MUST PERSE-VERE!
UNAZUKI-CHAN!
CLAMP
FYI, I'm already in high school.♡

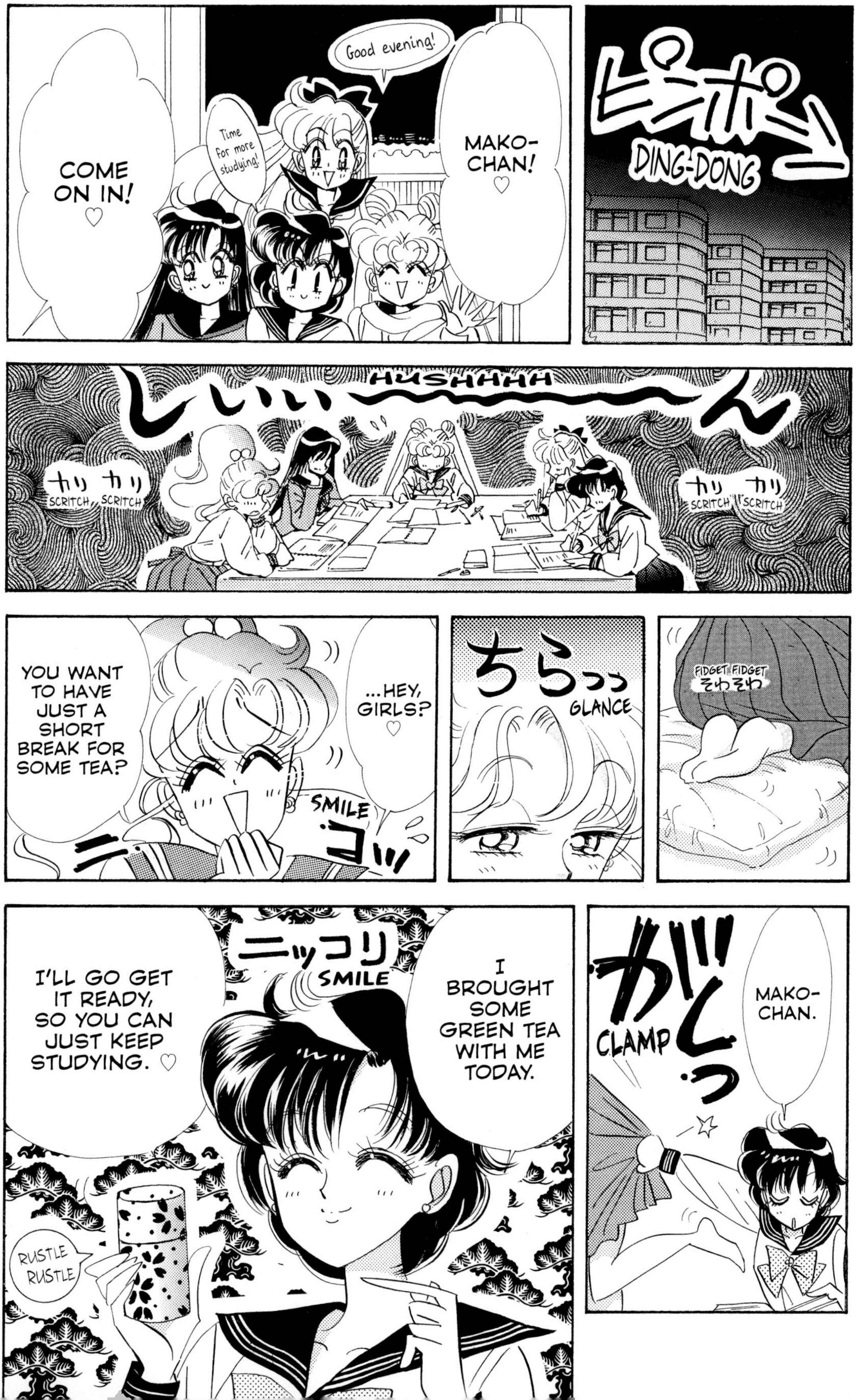

ピンポン
DING-DONG
MAKO-CHAN! ♡
Good evening!
Time for more studying!
COME ON IN! ♡
しいい〜〜〜ん
HUSHHHH
カリ カリ
SCRITCH SCRITCH
カリ カリ
SCRITCH SCRITCH
FIDGET FIDGET
そわそわ
ちらっっ
GLANCE
...HEY, GIRLS? ♡
SMILE
ニコッ
YOU WANT TO HAVE JUST A SHORT BREAK FOR SOME TEA?
MAKO-CHAN.
がしっ
CLAMP
I BROUGHT SOME GREEN TEA WITH ME TODAY.
ニッコリ
SMILE
I'LL GO GET IT READY, SO YOU CAN JUST KEEP STUDYING. ♡
RUSTLE RUSTLE

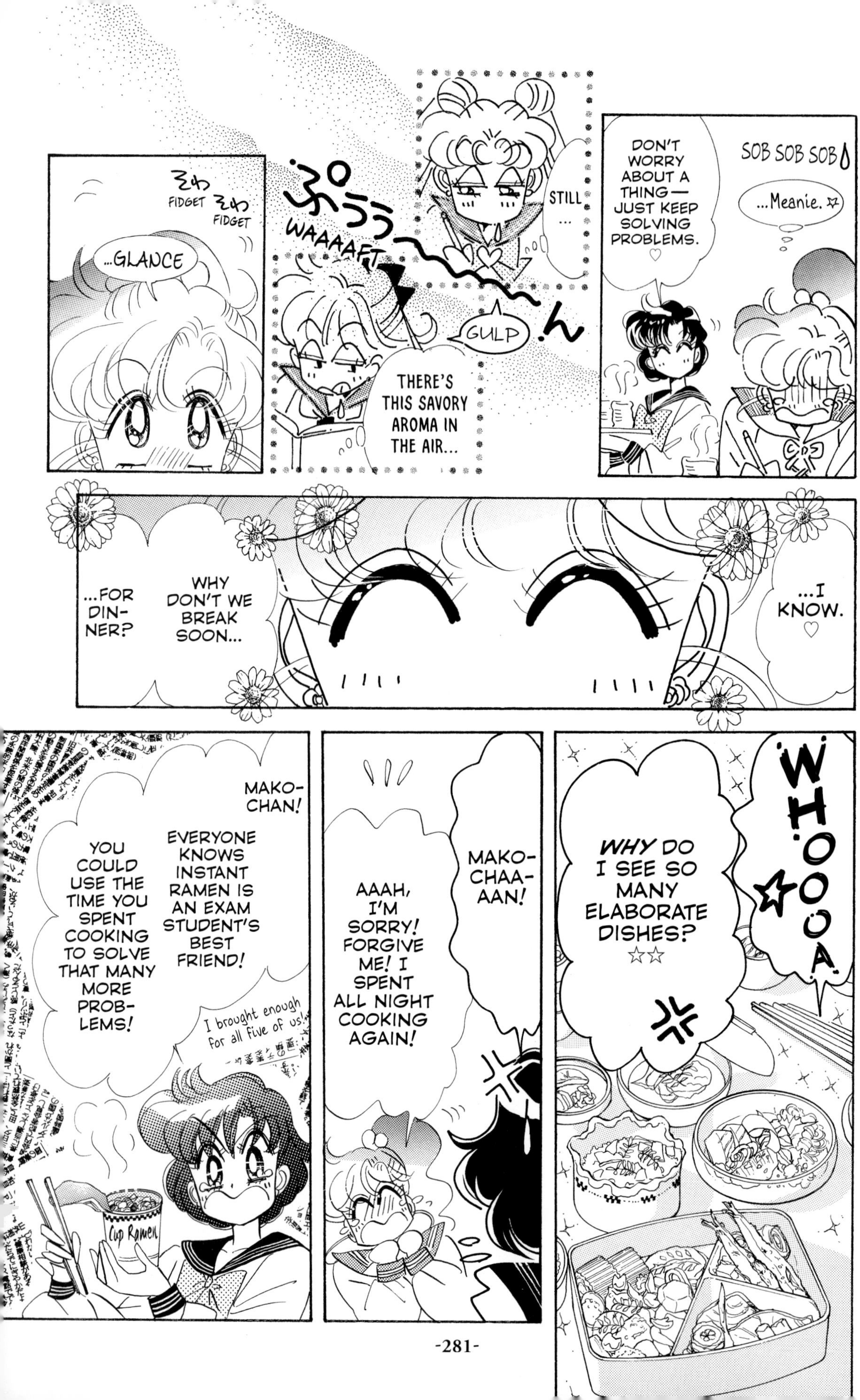
SOB SOB SOB
DON'T WORRY ABOUT A THING—JUST KEEP SOLVING PROBLEMS. ♡
...Meanie. ☆
STILL ...
ぷううう
WAAAAFT
ん
GULP
THERE'S THIS SAVORY AROMA IN THE AIR...
そわ FIDGET
そわ FIDGET
...GLANCE
...I KNOW. ♡
WHY DON'T WE BREAK SOON...
...FOR DINNER?
WHOOOA ☆
WHY DO I SEE SO MANY ELABORATE DISHES? ☆☆
MAKO-CHAAAAN!
AAAH, I'M SORRY! FORGIVE ME! I SPENT ALL NIGHT COOKING AGAIN!
MAKO-CHAN!
EVERYONE KNOWS INSTANT RAMEN IS AN EXAM STUDENT'S BEST FRIEND!
YOU COULD USE THE TIME YOU SPENT COOKING TO SOLVE THAT MANY MORE PROBLEMS!
I brought enough for all five of us!
Cup Ramen

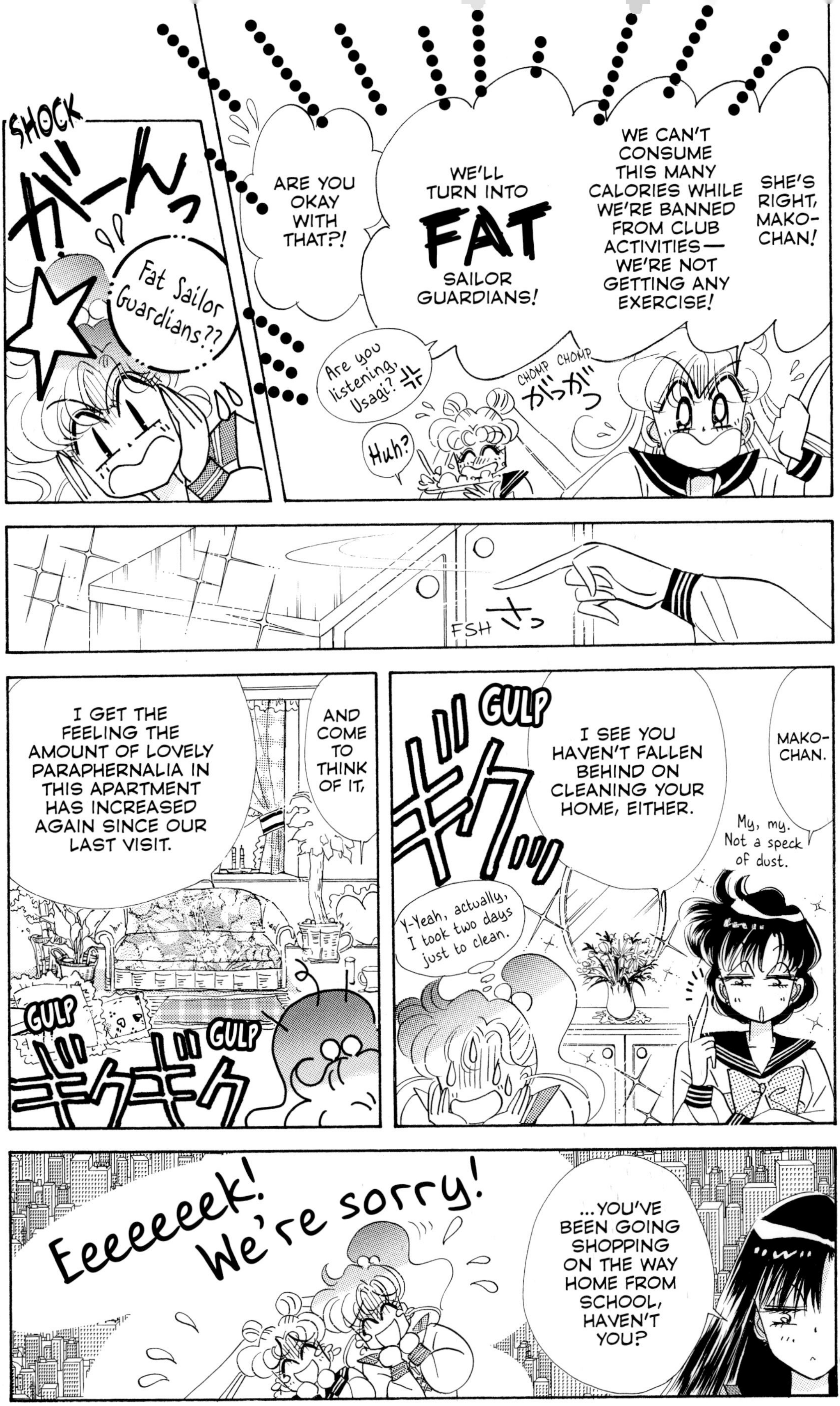

SHE'S RIGHT, MAKO-CHAN!
WE CAN'T CONSUME THIS MANY CALORIES WHILE WE'RE BANNED FROM CLUB ACTIVITIES—WE'RE NOT GETTING ANY EXERCISE!
WE'LL TURN INTO FAT SAILOR GUARDIANS!
ARE YOU OKAY WITH THAT?!
CHOMP CHOMP
がつがつ
Are you listening, Usagi?
Huh?
SHOCK
がーんっ
Fat Sailor Guardians??
FSH
さっ
MAKO-CHAN.
I SEE YOU HAVEN'T FALLEN BEHIND ON CLEANING YOUR HOME, EITHER.
My, my. Not a speck of dust.
GULP
ギクッ
Y-Yeah, actually, I took two days just to clean.
AND COME TO THINK OF IT,
I GET THE FEELING THE AMOUNT OF LOVELY PARAPHERNALIA IN THIS APARTMENT HAS INCREASED AGAIN SINCE OUR LAST VISIT.
GULP
GULP
ギクギク
...YOU'VE BEEN GOING SHOPPING ON THE WAY HOME FROM SCHOOL, HAVEN'T YOU?
Eeeeeeek! We're sorry!

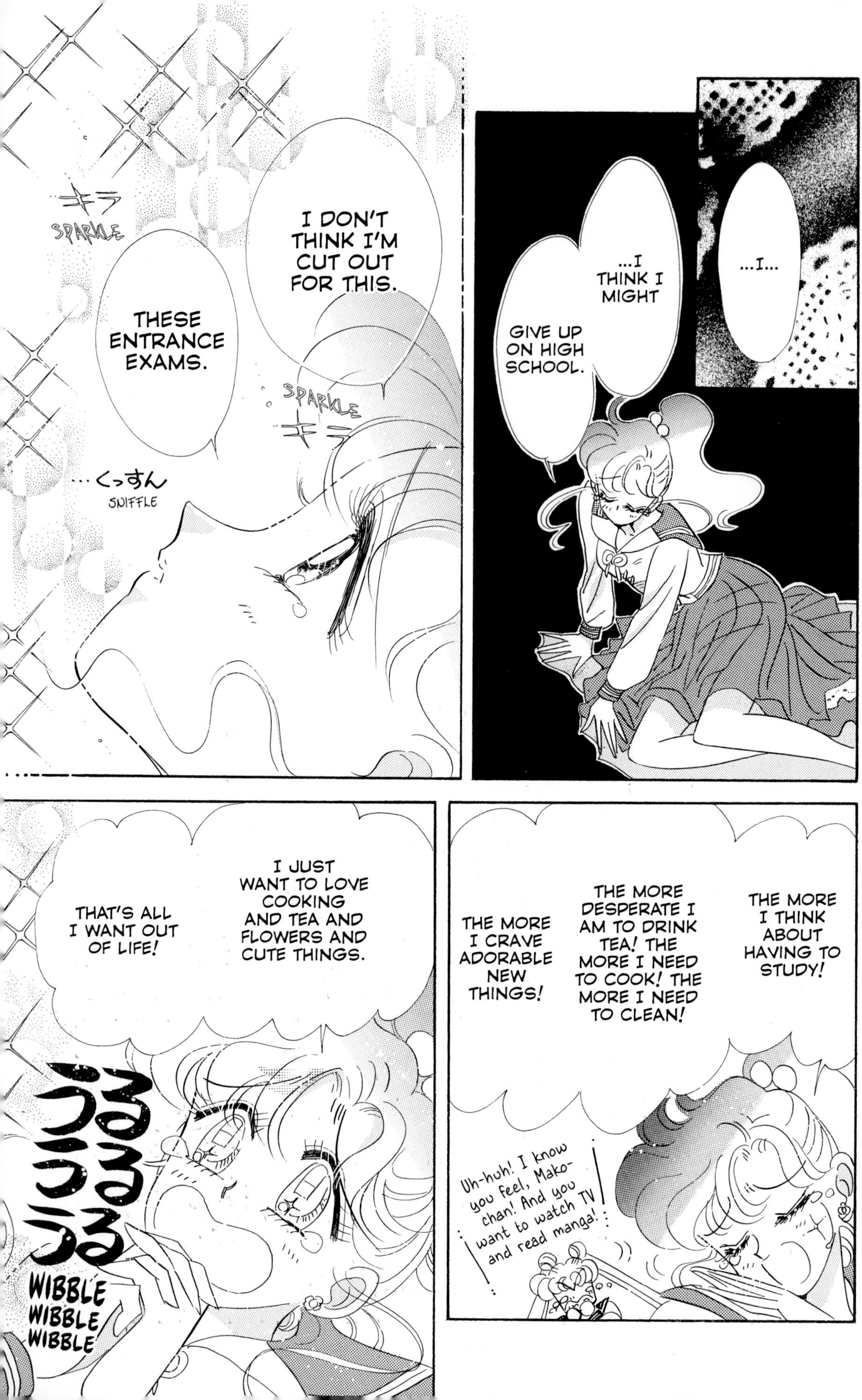
...I...
...I THINK I MIGHT
GIVE UP ON HIGH SCHOOL.
キラ
SPARKLE
I DON'T THINK I'M CUT OUT FOR THIS.
キラ
SPARKLE
THESE ENTRANCE EXAMS.
...くっすん
SNIFFLE
THE MORE I THINK ABOUT HAVING TO STUDY!
THE MORE DESPERATE I AM TO DRINK TEA! THE MORE I NEED TO COOK! THE MORE I NEED TO CLEAN!
THE MORE I CRAVE ADORABLE NEW THINGS!
Uh-huh! I know how you feel, Mako-chan! And you want to watch TV and read manga!
I JUST WANT TO LOVE COOKING AND TEA AND FLOWERS AND CUTE THINGS.
THAT'S ALL I WANT OUT OF LIFE!
うるうるうる
WIBBLE WIBBLE WIBBLE

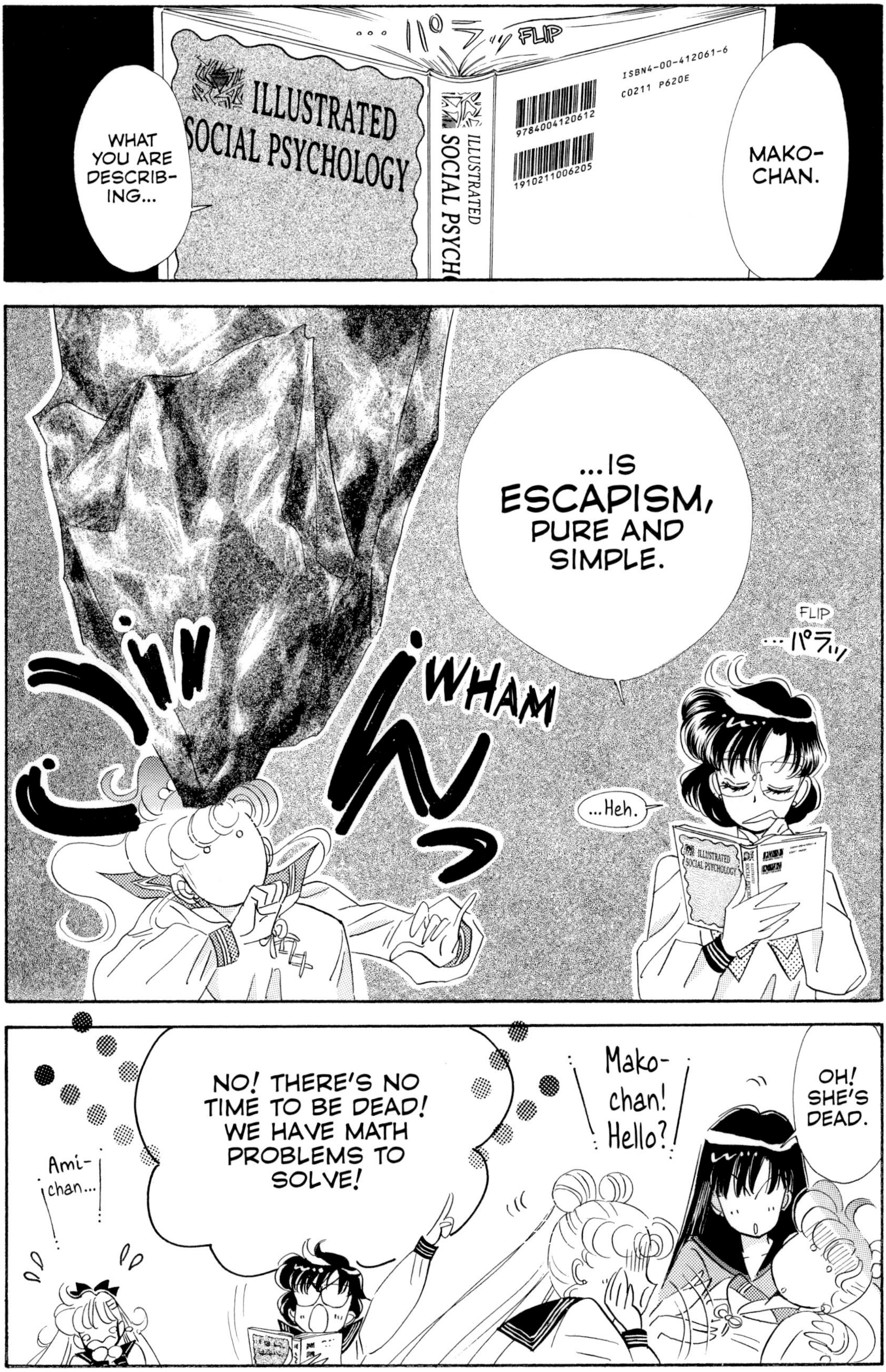
MAKO-CHAN.
...パラッ FLIP
ISBN4-00-412061-6
C0211 P620E
ILLUSTRATED SOCIAL PSYCHOLOGY
WHAT YOU ARE DESCRIB-ING...
...IS ESCAPISM, PURE AND SIMPLE.
FLIP ...パラッ
...Heh.
WHAM
OH! SHE'S DEAD.
Mako-chan! Hello?
NO! THERE'S NO TIME TO BE DEAD! WE HAVE MATH PROBLEMS TO SOLVE!
Ami-chan...

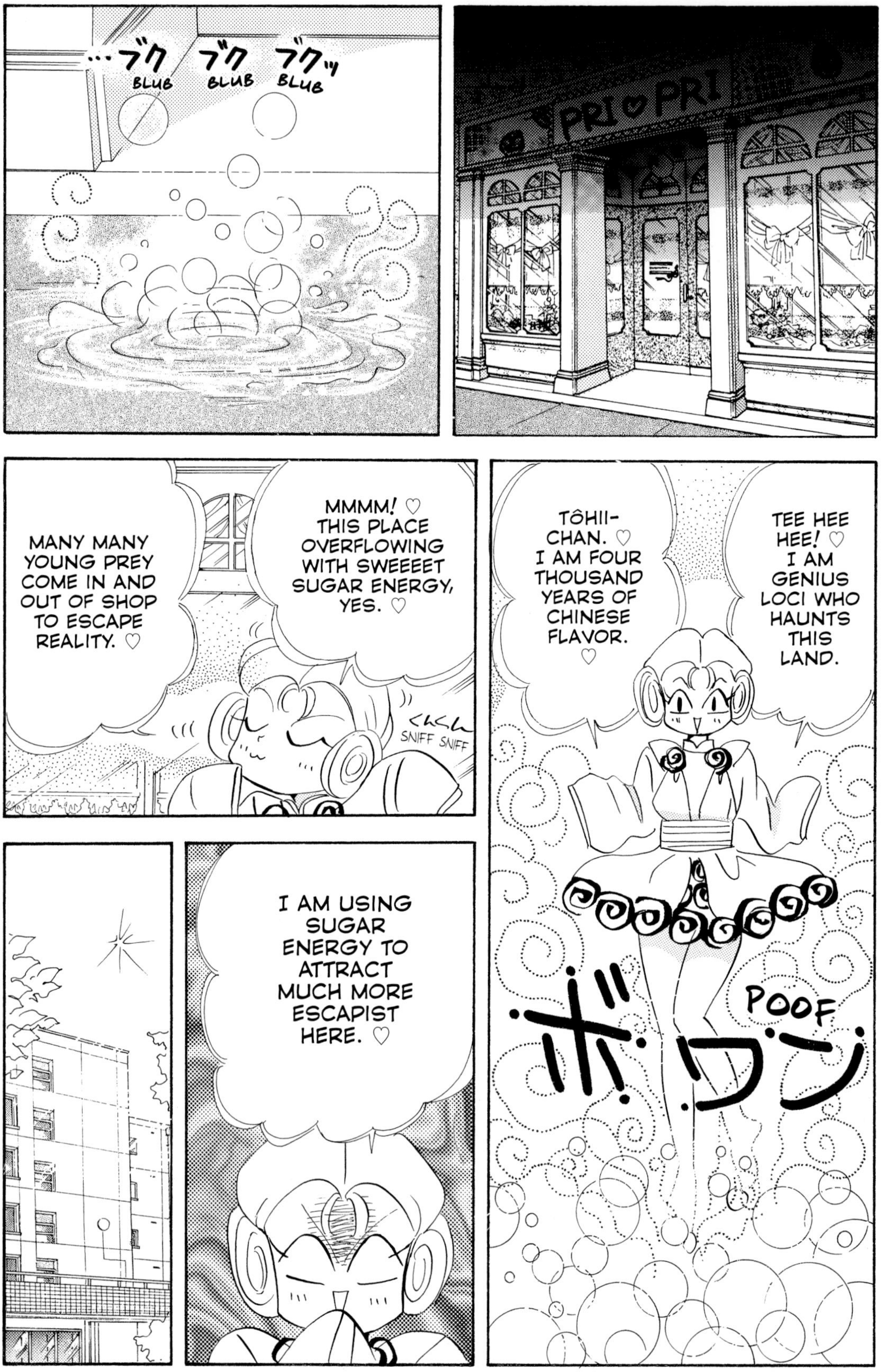
PRI♡PRI
…ブク ブク ブクッ
BLUB BLUB BLUB
TEE HEE HEE! ♡ I AM GENIUS LOCI WHO HAUNTS THIS LAND.
TÔHII-CHAN. ♡ I AM FOUR THOUSAND YEARS OF CHINESE FLAVOR. ♡
ボワン
POOF
MMMM! ♡ THIS PLACE OVERFLOWING WITH SWEEEET SUGAR ENERGY, YES. ♡
MANY MANY YOUNG PREY COME IN AND OUT OF SHOP TO ESCAPE REALITY. ♡
くんくん
SNIFF SNIFF
I AM USING SUGAR ENERGY TO ATTRACT MUCH MORE ESCAPIST HERE. ♡

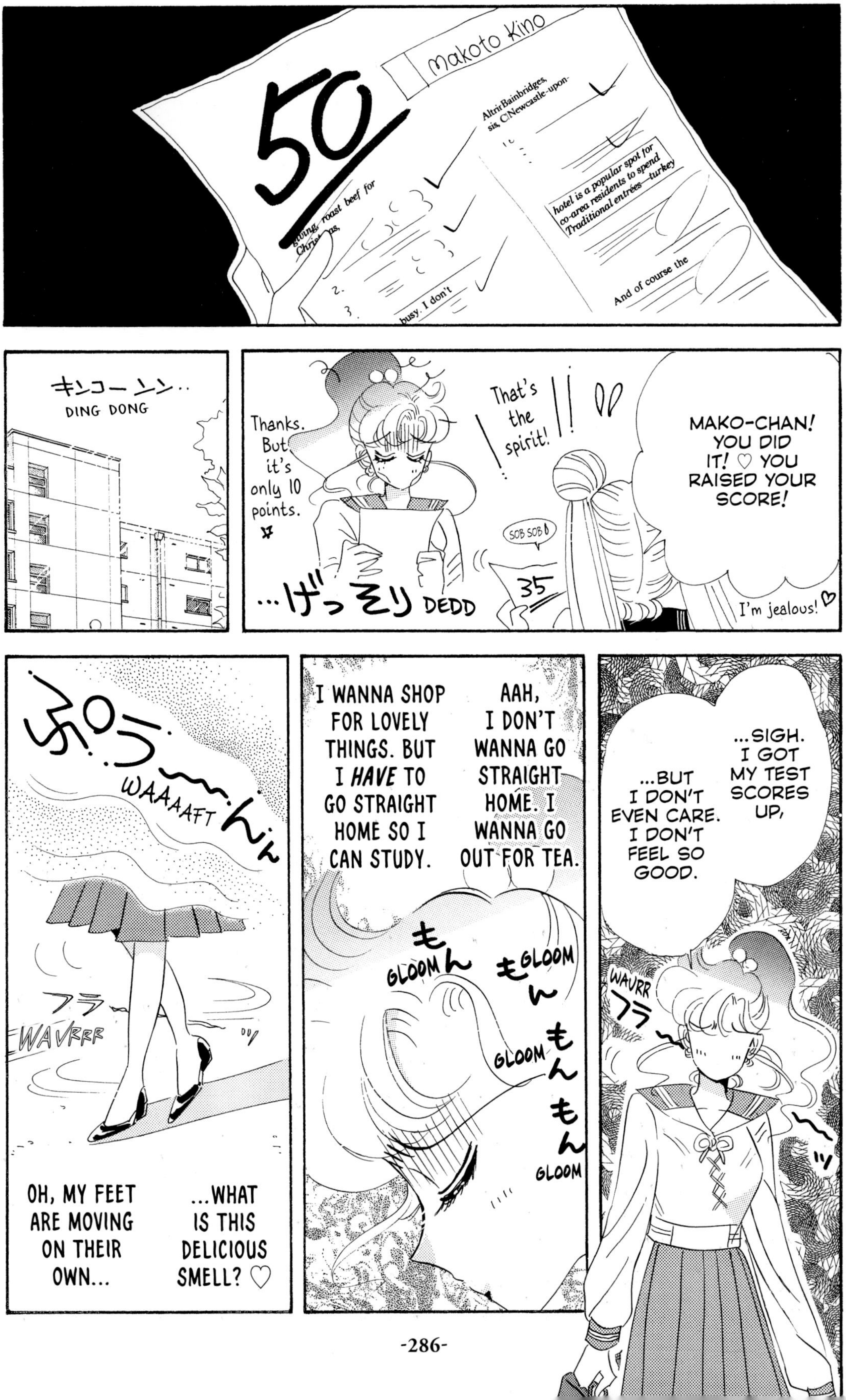

Makoto Kino
50
giving, roast beef for Christmas,
busy. I don't
AltrirBainbridges, sis, C'Newcastle-upon-
hotel is a popular spot for co-area residents to spend Traditional entrées—turkey
And of course the
MAKO-CHAN! YOU DID IT! ♡ YOU RAISED YOUR SCORE!
I'm jealous! ♡
That's the spirit!
SOB SOB
35
Thanks. But it's only 10 points.
…げっそり DEDD
キンコーンン‥
DING DONG
...SIGH. I GOT MY TEST SCORES UP,
...BUT I DON'T EVEN CARE. I DON'T FEEL SO GOOD.
WAURR フラ〜ッ
AAH, I DON'T WANNA GO STRAIGHT HOME. I WANNA GO OUT FOR TEA.
I WANNA SHOP FOR LOVELY THINGS. BUT I *HAVE* TO GO STRAIGHT HOME SO I CAN STUDY.
もん GLOOM
もん GLOOM
もん GLOOM
もん GLOOM
ふら〜〜ん WAAAAAFT
フラ〜 WAVRRR
...WHAT IS THIS DELICIOUS SMELL? ♡
OH, MY FEET ARE MOVING ON THEIR OWN...

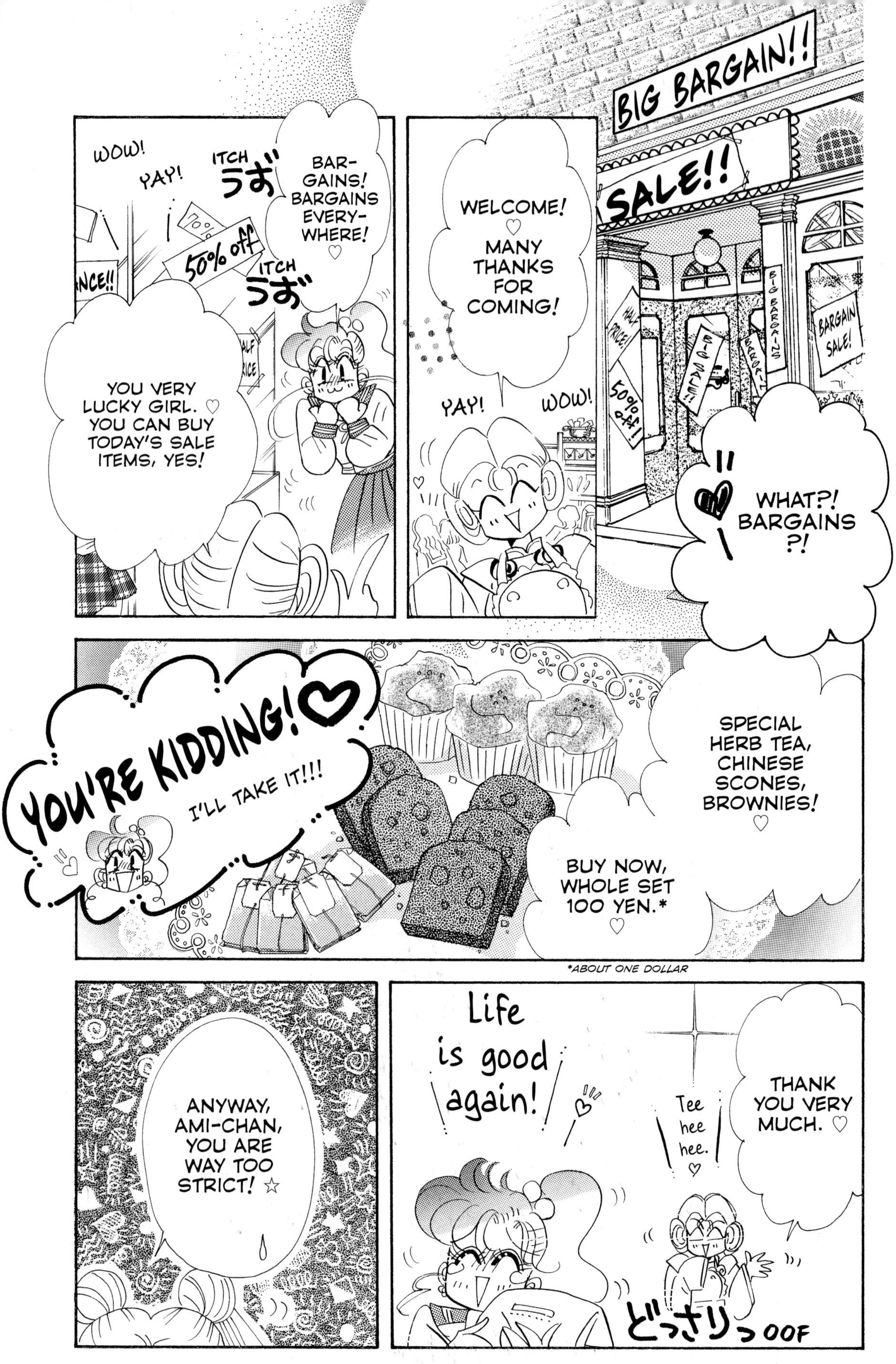
BIG BARGAIN!!
SALE!!
HALF PRICE!
BIG BARGAINS
BIG SALE!!
BARGAIN!
BARGAIN SALE!
50% off!!
WHAT?! BARGAINS ?!
WELCOME! ♡ MANY THANKS FOR COMING!
WOW!
YAY!
BAR-GAINS! BARGAINS EVERY-WHERE! ♡
ITCH うず
ITCH うず
WOW!
YAY!
50% off
70%
HALF PRICE
YOU VERY LUCKY GIRL. ♡ YOU CAN BUY TODAY'S SALE ITEMS, YES!
SPECIAL HERB TEA, CHINESE SCONES, BROWNIES! ♡
BUY NOW, WHOLE SET 100 YEN.* ♡
YOU'RE KIDDING!♡
I'LL TAKE IT!!!
THANK YOU VERY MUCH. ♡
Tee hee hee. ♡
Life is good again!
どっさりっ OOF
ANYWAY, AMI-CHAN, YOU ARE WAY TOO STRICT! ☆

*ABOUT ONE DOLLAR

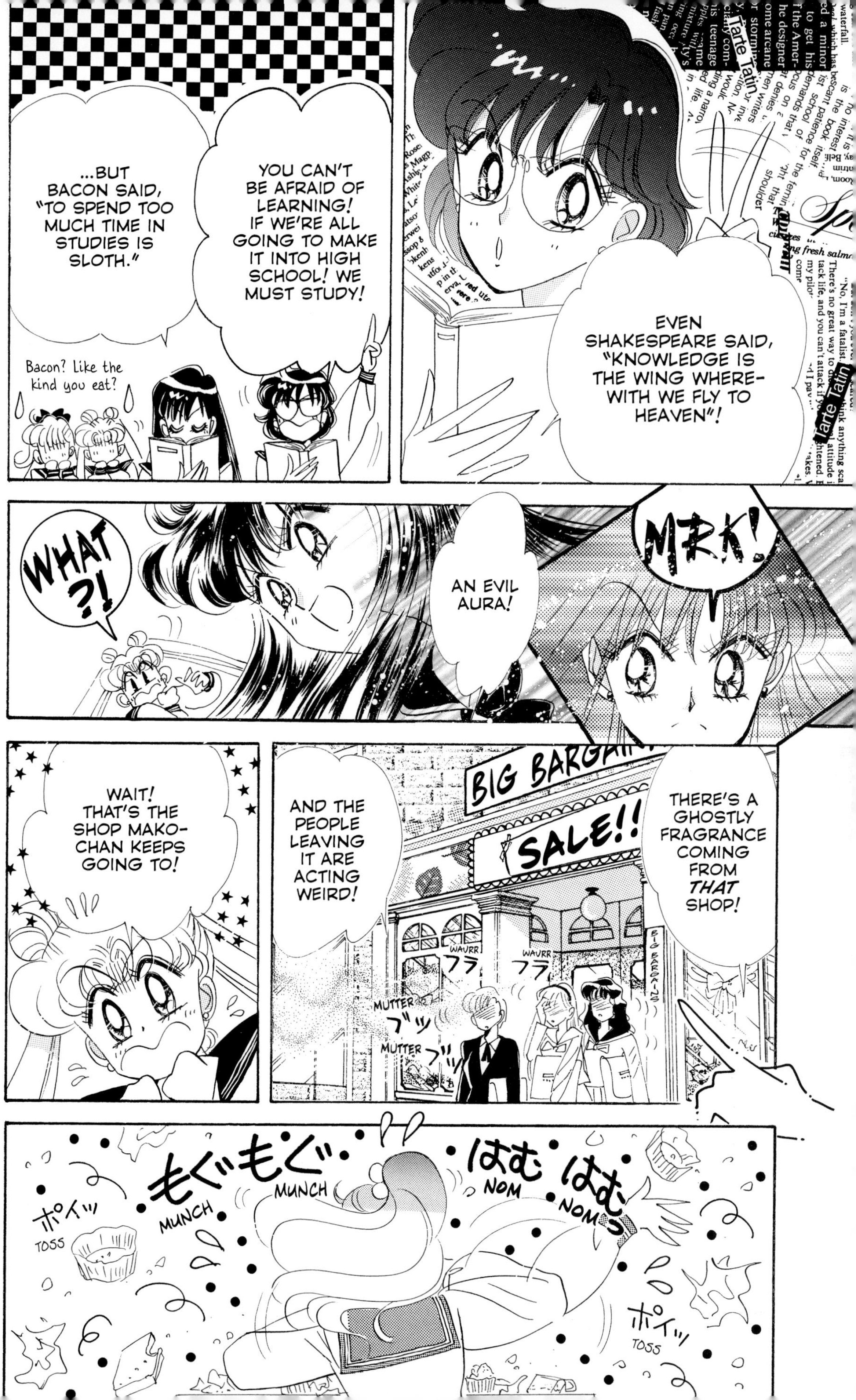
Tarte Tatin
EVEN SHAKESPEARE SAID, "KNOWLEDGE IS THE WING WHEREWITH WE FLY TO HEAVEN"!
YOU CAN'T BE AFRAID OF LEARNING! IF WE'RE ALL GOING TO MAKE IT INTO HIGH SCHOOL! WE MUST STUDY!
...BUT BACON SAID, "TO SPEND TOO MUCH TIME IN STUDIES IS SLOTH."
Bacon? Like the kind you eat?
MRK!
AN EVIL AURA!
WHAT?!
THERE'S A GHOSTLY FRAGRANCE COMING FROM *THAT* SHOP!
SALE!!
AND THE PEOPLE LEAVING IT ARE ACTING WEIRD!
WAURR フラ
WAURR フラ
MUTTER ブツ
MUTTER ブツ
WAIT! THAT'S THE SHOP MAKO-CHAN KEEPS GOING TO!
はむ はむ
NOM NOM
もぐもぐ
MUNCH MUNCH
ポイッ
TOSS
ポイッ
TOSS

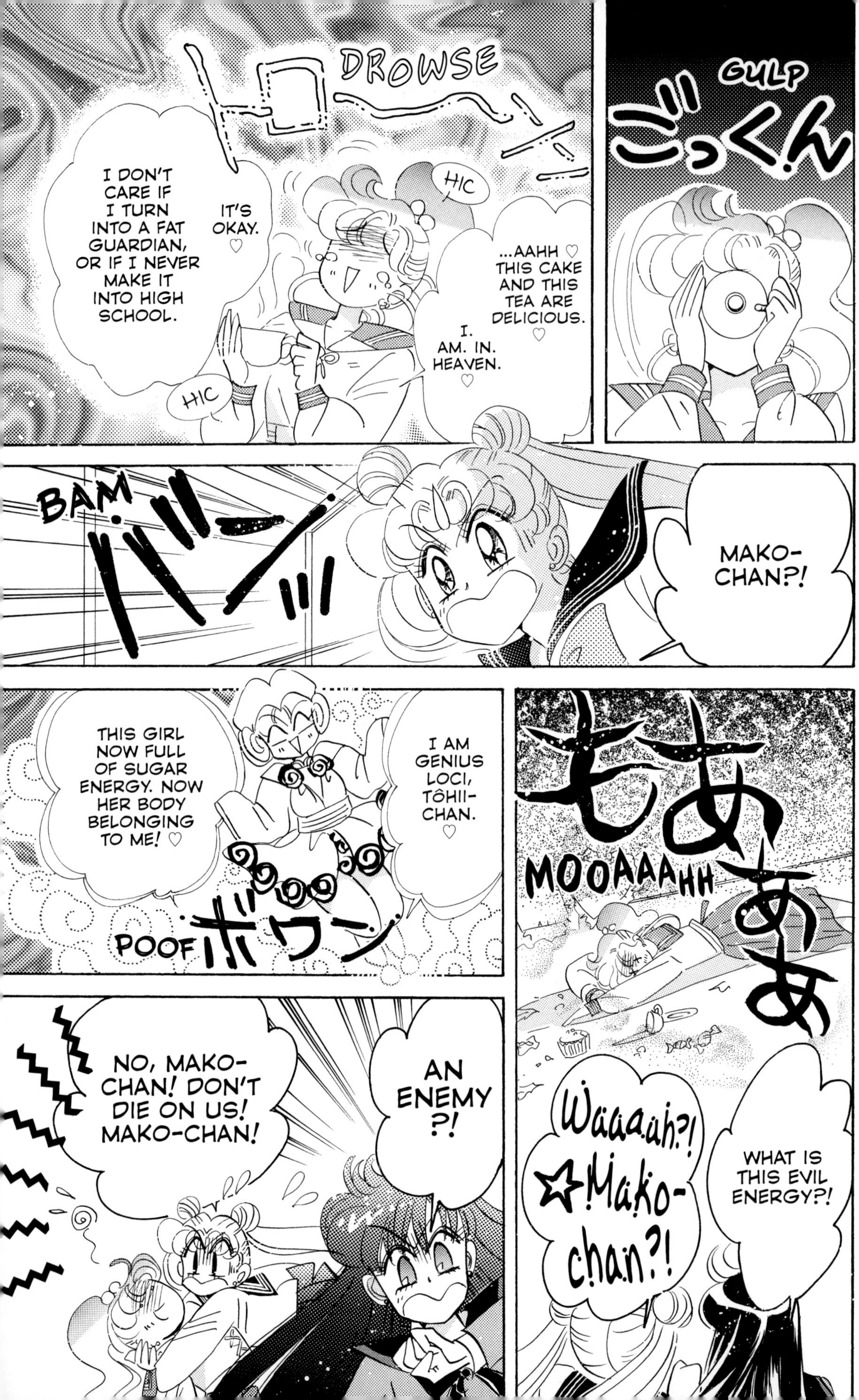
GULP
ごっくん
HIC
...AAHH ♡ THIS CAKE AND THIS TEA ARE DELICIOUS. ♡
I. AM. IN. HEAVEN. ♡
DROWSE
トロ～ン
IT'S OKAY. ♡
I DON'T CARE IF I TURN INTO A FAT GUARDIAN, OR IF I NEVER MAKE IT INTO HIGH SCHOOL.
HIC
MAKO-CHAN?!
BAM
バン
もあああ
MOOAAAHH
WHAT IS THIS EVIL ENERGY?!
Waaaah?! ☆ Mako-chan?!
I AM GENIUS LOCI, TÔHII-CHAN. ♡
THIS GIRL NOW FULL OF SUGAR ENERGY. NOW HER BODY BELONGING TO ME! ♡
POOF
ボワーン
AN ENEMY?!
NO, MAKO-CHAN! DON'T DIE ON US! MAKO-CHAN!

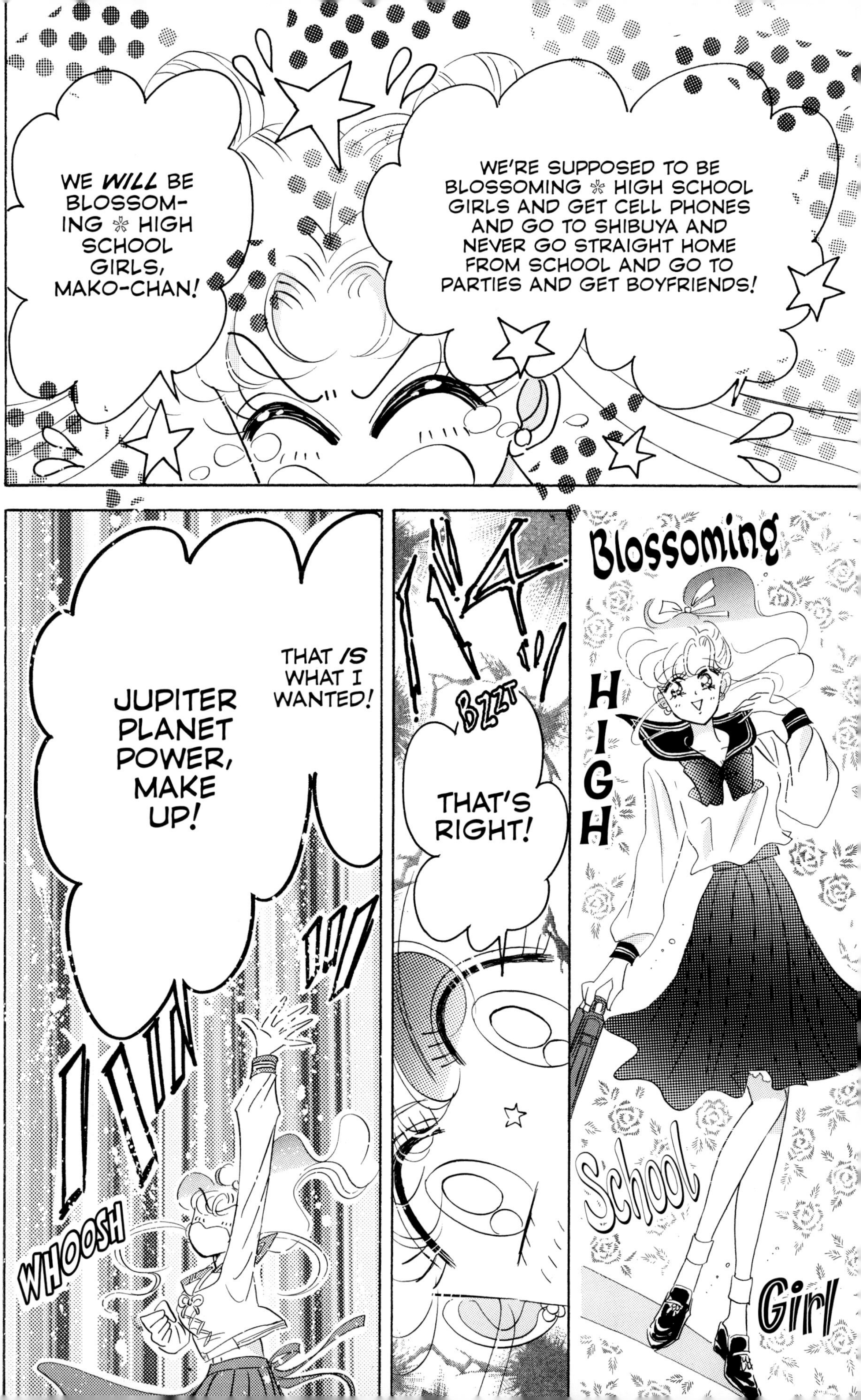
WE'RE SUPPOSED TO BE BLOSSOMING ❀ HIGH SCHOOL GIRLS AND GET CELL PHONES AND GO TO SHIBUYA AND NEVER GO STRAIGHT HOME FROM SCHOOL AND GO TO PARTIES AND GET BOYFRIENDS!
WE *WILL* BE BLOSSOMING ❀ HIGH SCHOOL GIRLS, MAKO-CHAN!
Blossoming
HIGH
School
Girl
BZZT
THAT'S RIGHT!
THAT *IS* WHAT I WANTED!
JUPITER PLANET POWER, MAKE UP!
WHOOSH

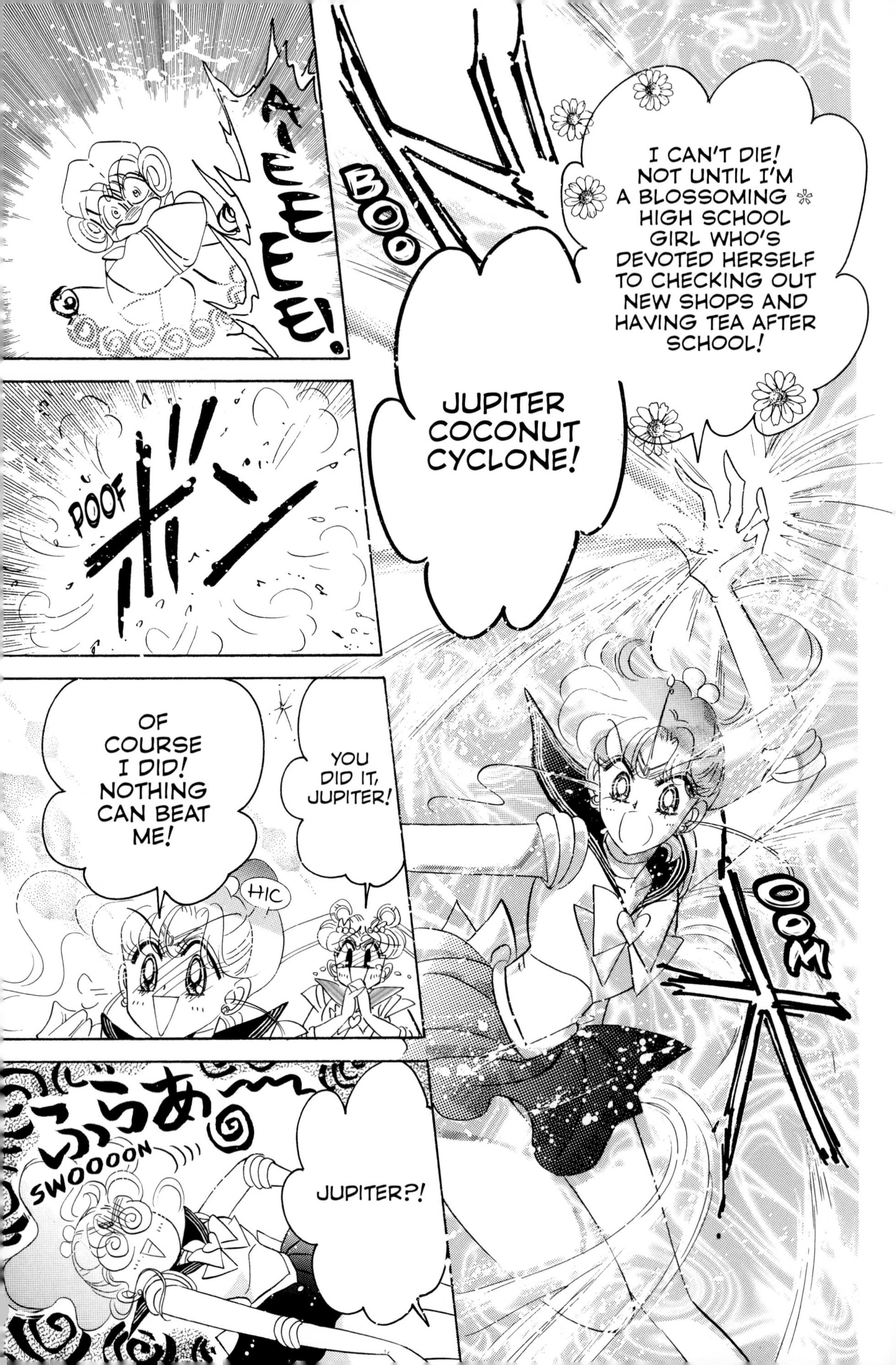
I CAN'T DIE! NOT UNTIL I'M A BLOSSOMING HIGH SCHOOL GIRL WHO'S DEVOTED HERSELF TO CHECKING OUT NEW SHOPS AND HAVING TEA AFTER SCHOOL!
JUPITER COCONUT CYCLONE!
BOOO
OOOM
A-EEEEE!
POOF
YOU DID IT, JUPITER!
OF COURSE I DID! NOTHING CAN BEAT ME!
HIC
SWOOOON
JUPITER?!

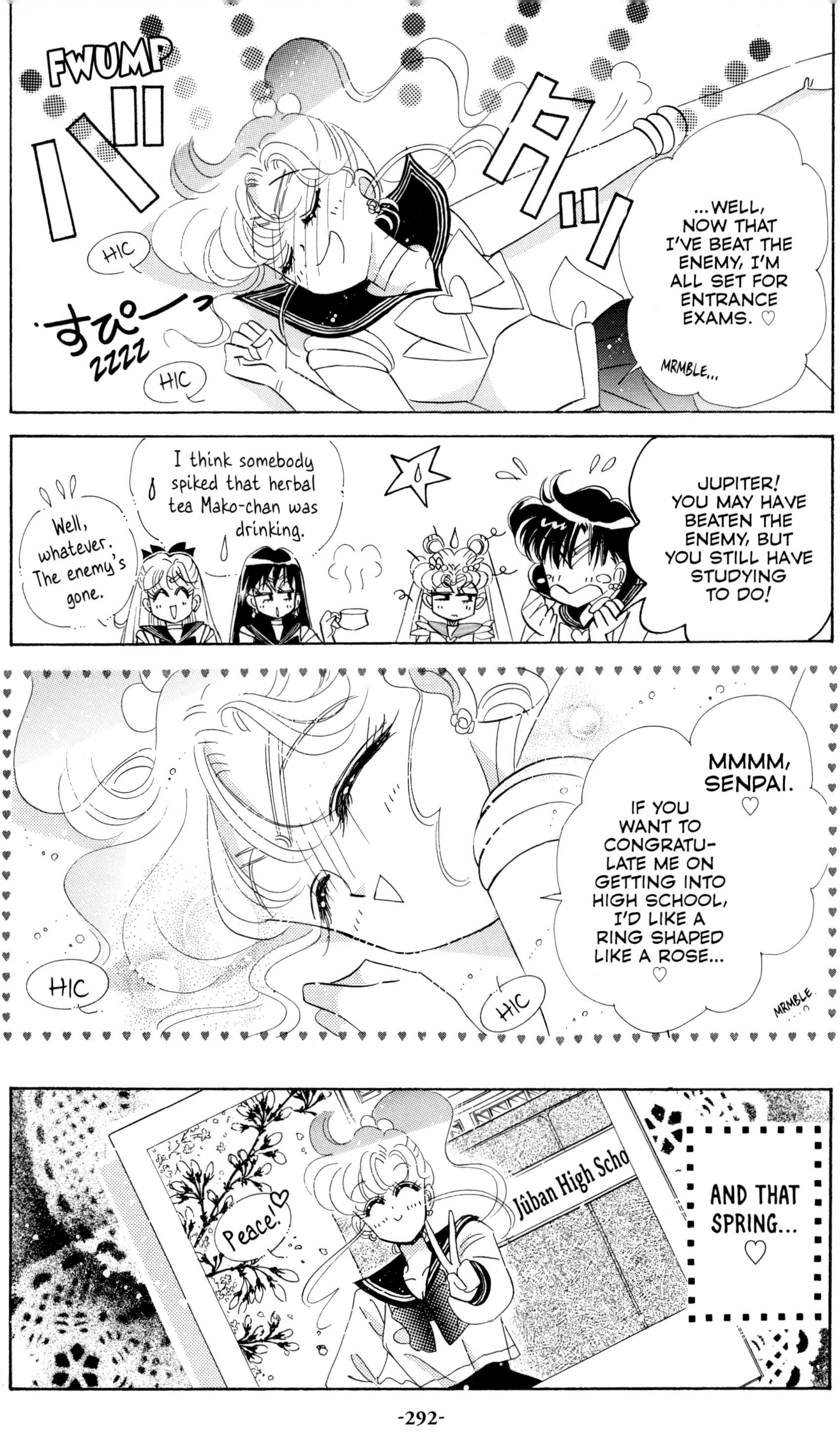
...WELL, NOW THAT I'VE BEAT THE ENEMY, I'M ALL SET FOR ENTRANCE EXAMS. ♡
MRMBLE...
FWUMP
HIC
すぴーっ
ZZZZ
HIC
JUPITER! YOU MAY HAVE BEATEN THE ENEMY, BUT YOU STILL HAVE STUDYING TO DO!
I think somebody spiked that herbal tea Mako-chan was drinking.
Well, whatever. The enemy's gone.
MMMM, SENPAI. ♡
IF YOU WANT TO CONGRATU-LATE ME ON GETTING INTO HIGH SCHOOL, I'D LIKE A RING SHAPED LIKE A ROSE... ♡
MRMBLE...
HIC
HIC
AND THAT SPRING... ♡
Jûban High Scho
Peace! ♡

The Entrance Exam Wars

Chapter 2

Ami-chan's First Love

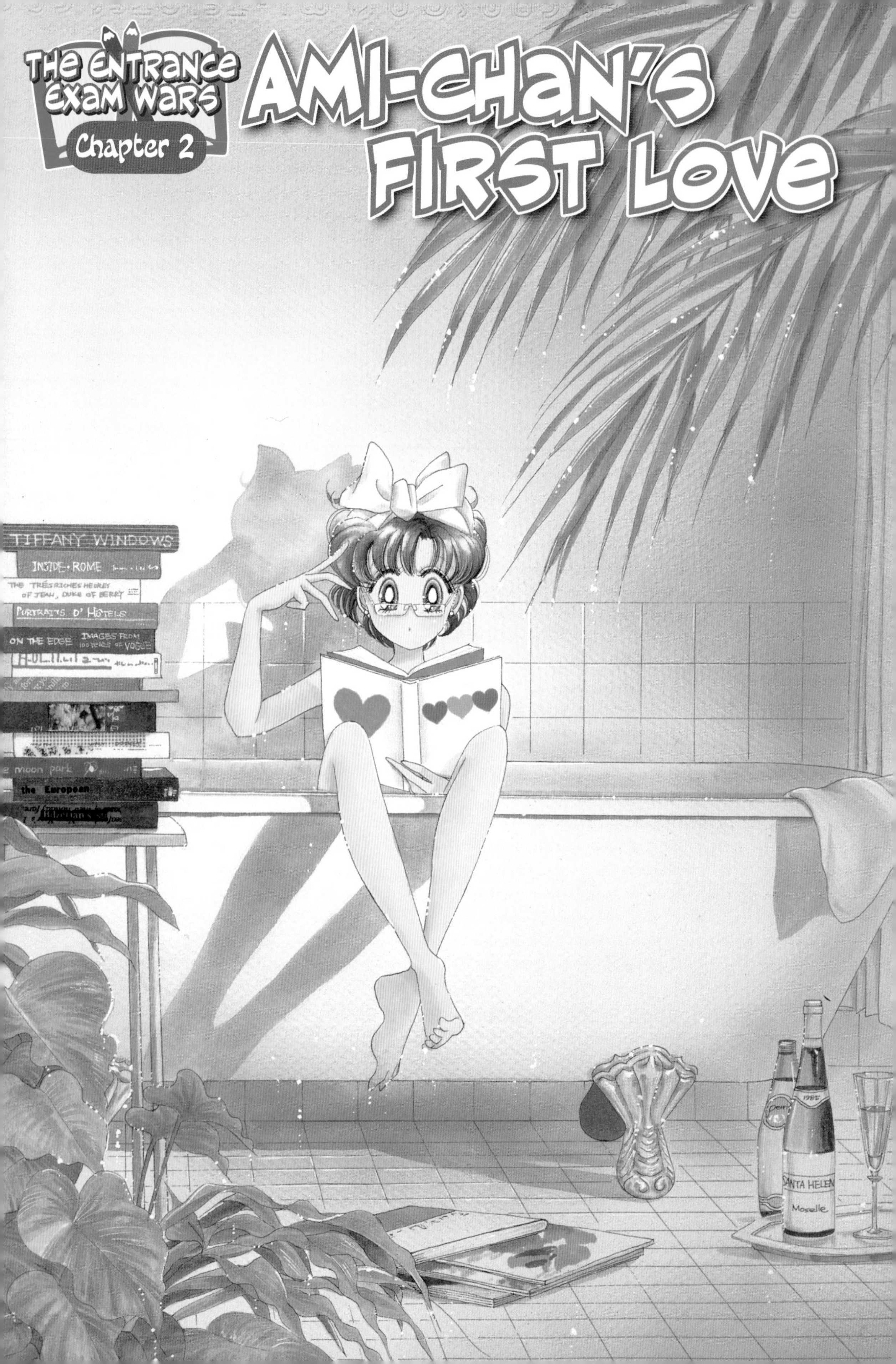
TIFFANY WINDOWS
INSIDE·ROME
THE TRÈS RICHES HEURES OF JEAN, DUKE OF BERRY
PORTRAITS O' HOTELS
ON THE EDGE
IMAGES FROM 100 YEARS OF VOGUE
moon park
the European
1985
SANTA HELEN
Moselle

Pretty Guardian

Sailor Moon

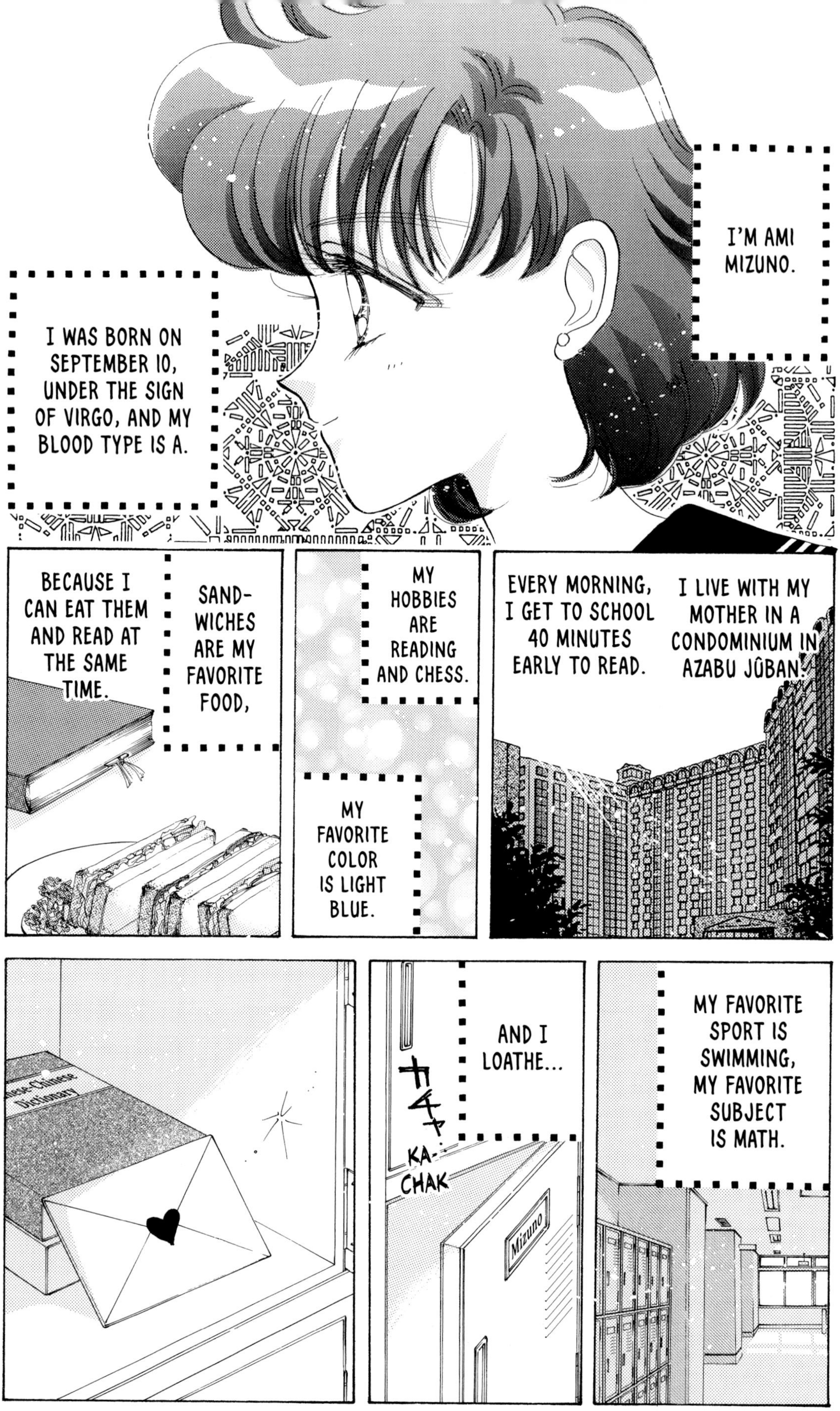
I'M AMI MIZUNO.
I WAS BORN ON SEPTEMBER 10, UNDER THE SIGN OF VIRGO, AND MY BLOOD TYPE IS A.
I LIVE WITH MY MOTHER IN A CONDOMINIUM IN AZABU JÛBAN.
EVERY MORNING, I GET TO SCHOOL 40 MINUTES EARLY TO READ.
MY HOBBIES ARE READING AND CHESS.
MY FAVORITE COLOR IS LIGHT BLUE.
SAND-WICHES ARE MY FAVORITE FOOD,
BECAUSE I CAN EAT THEM AND READ AT THE SAME TIME.
MY FAVORITE SPORT IS SWIMMING, MY FAVORITE SUBJECT IS MATH.
AND I LOATHE...
KA-CHAK
Mizuno
Dictionary

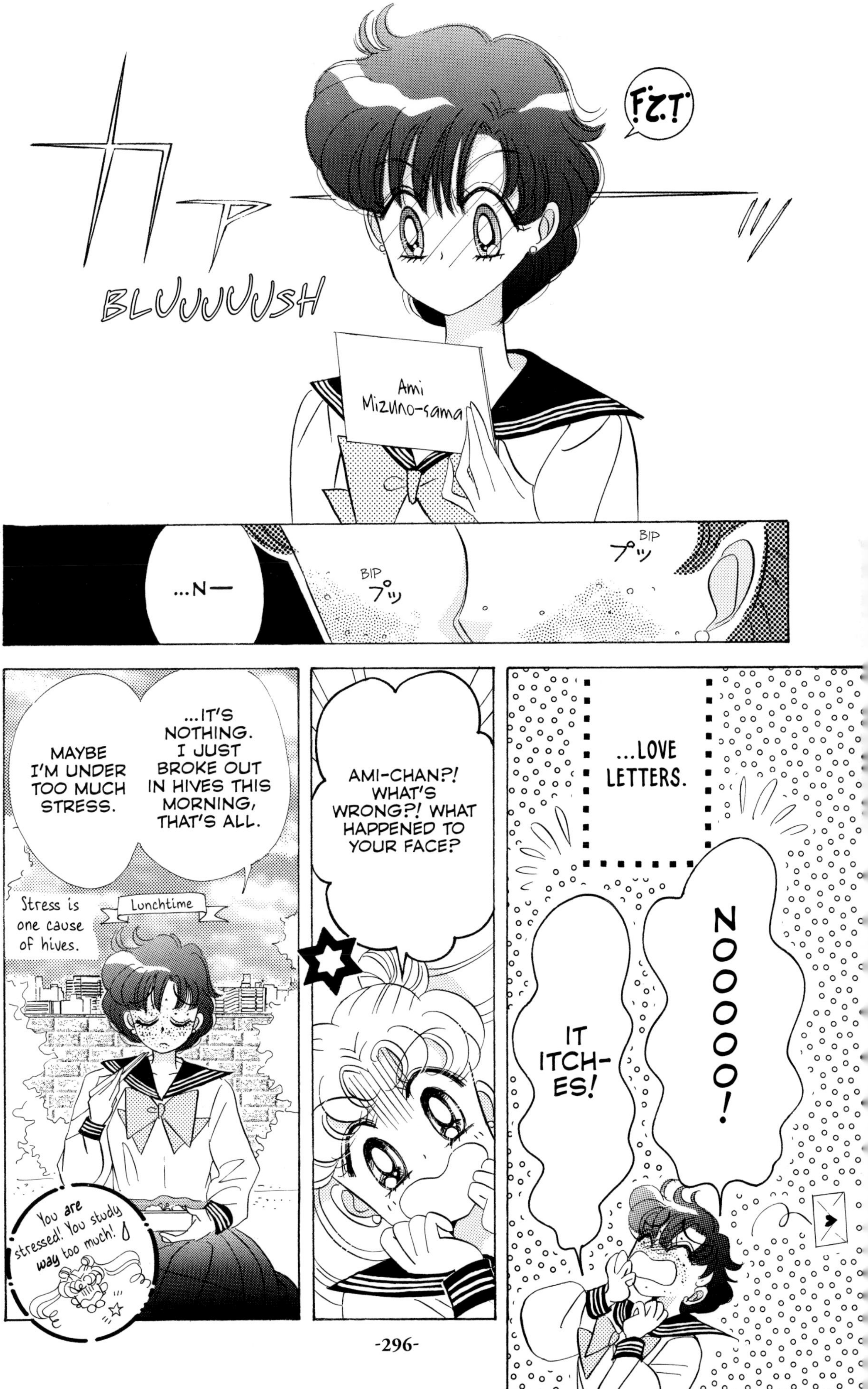
FZT
カァ
BLUUUUUSH
Ami Mizuno-sama
BIP
プッ
BIP
プッ
...N—
...LOVE LETTERS.
NOOOOOO!
IT ITCH-ES!
AMI-CHAN?! WHAT'S WRONG?! WHAT HAPPENED TO YOUR FACE?
...IT'S NOTHING. I JUST BROKE OUT IN HIVES THIS MORNING, THAT'S ALL.
MAYBE I'M UNDER TOO MUCH STRESS.
Lunchtime
Stress is one cause of hives.
You are stressed! You study way too much!

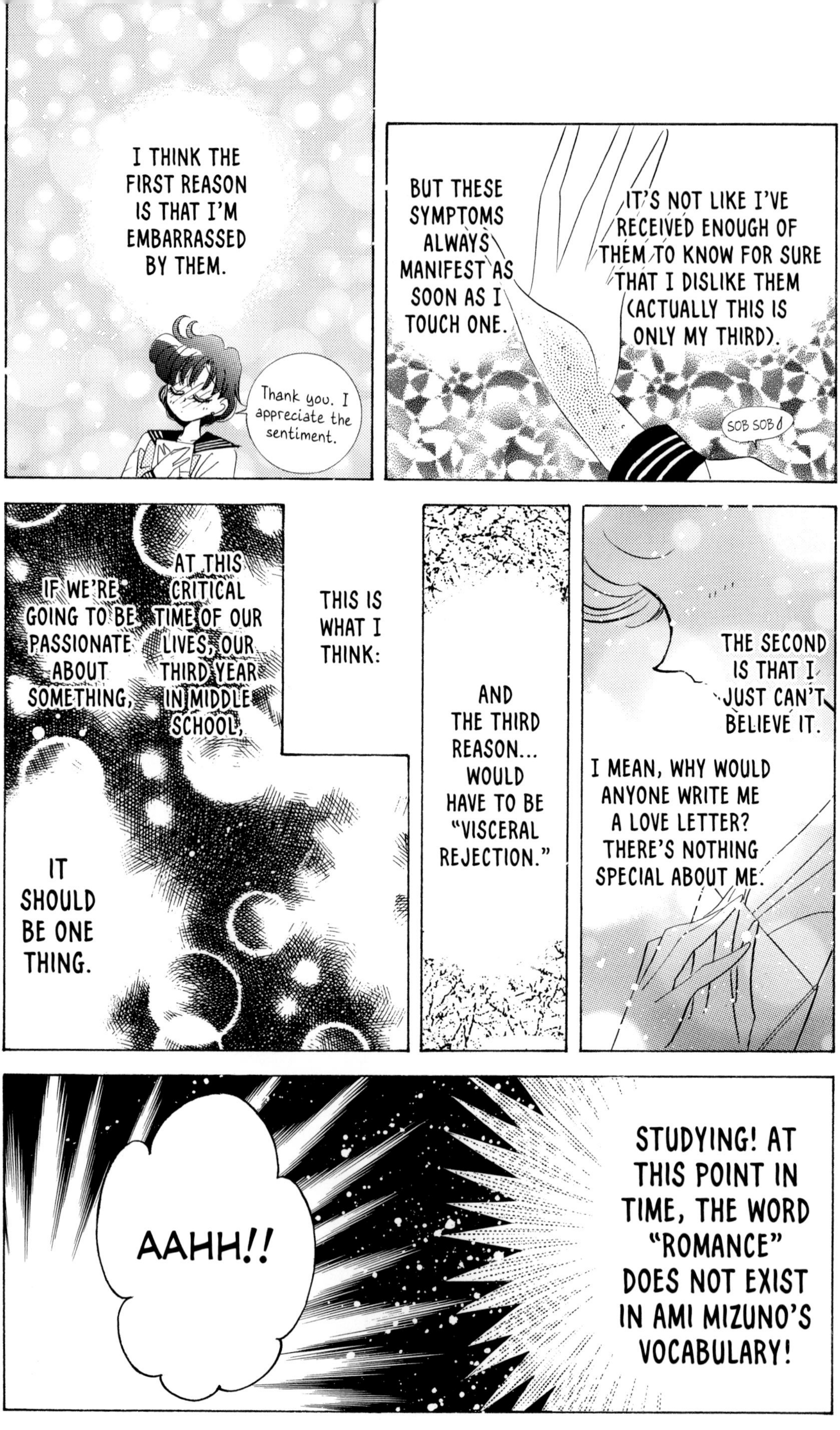
IT'S NOT LIKE I'VE RECEIVED ENOUGH OF THEM TO KNOW FOR SURE THAT I DISLIKE THEM (ACTUALLY THIS IS ONLY MY THIRD).
BUT THESE SYMPTOMS ALWAYS MANIFEST AS SOON AS I TOUCH ONE.
SOB SOB
I THINK THE FIRST REASON IS THAT I'M EMBARRASSED BY THEM.
Thank you. I appreciate the sentiment.
THE SECOND IS THAT I JUST CAN'T BELIEVE IT.
I MEAN, WHY WOULD ANYONE WRITE ME A LOVE LETTER? THERE'S NOTHING SPECIAL ABOUT ME.
AND THE THIRD REASON... WOULD HAVE TO BE "VISCERAL REJECTION."
THIS IS WHAT I THINK:
AT THIS CRITICAL TIME OF OUR LIVES, OUR THIRD YEAR IN MIDDLE SCHOOL,
IF WE'RE GOING TO BE PASSIONATE ABOUT SOMETHING,
IT SHOULD BE ONE THING.
STUDYING! AT THIS POINT IN TIME, THE WORD "ROMANCE" DOES NOT EXIST IN AMI MIZUNO'S VOCABULARY!
AAHH!!

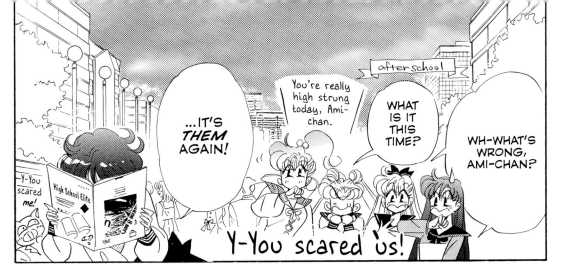

WH-WHAT'S WRONG, AMI-CHAN?

WHAT IS IT THIS TIME?

You're really high strung today, Ami-chan.

...IT'S **THEM** AGAIN!

Y-You scared me!

Y-You scared us!

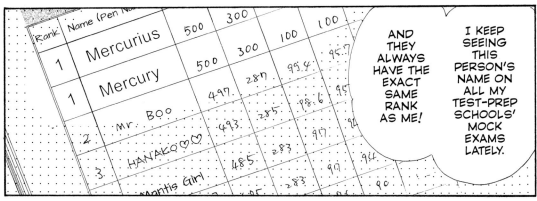

Rank	Name (Pen Na...					
1	Mercurius	500	300	100	100	95.7
1	Mercury	500	300	287	99.4	95
2	Mr. BOO	497.	285.	98.6	94	
	HANAKO♡♡	493	283	91.7		
3.		485.	283	91	94	
	Mantis Girl			90		

AND THEY ALWAYS HAVE THE EXACT SAME RANK AS ME!

I KEEP SEEING THIS PERSON'S NAME ON ALL MY TEST-PREP SCHOOLS' MOCK EXAMS LATELY.

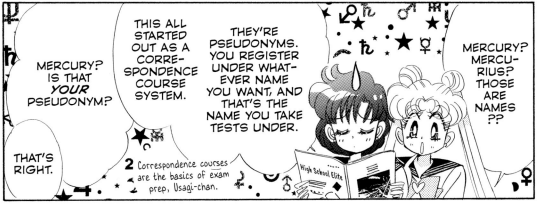

MERCURY? IS THAT **YOUR** PSEUDONYM?

THAT'S RIGHT.

THIS ALL STARTED OUT AS A CORRESPONDENCE COURSE SYSTEM.

THEY'RE PSEUDONYMS. YOU REGISTER UNDER WHATEVER NAME YOU WANT, AND THAT'S THE NAME YOU TAKE TESTS UNDER.

2 Correspondence courses are the basics of exam prep, Usagi-chan.

MERCURY? MERCURIUS? THOSE ARE NAMES ??

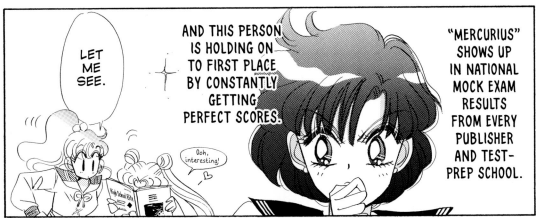

LET ME SEE.

AND THIS PERSON IS HOLDING ON TO FIRST PLACE BY CONSTANTLY GETTING PERFECT SCORES.

Ooh, interesting!

"MERCURIUS" SHOWS UP IN NATIONAL MOCK EXAM RESULTS FROM EVERY PUBLISHER AND TEST-PREP SCHOOL.

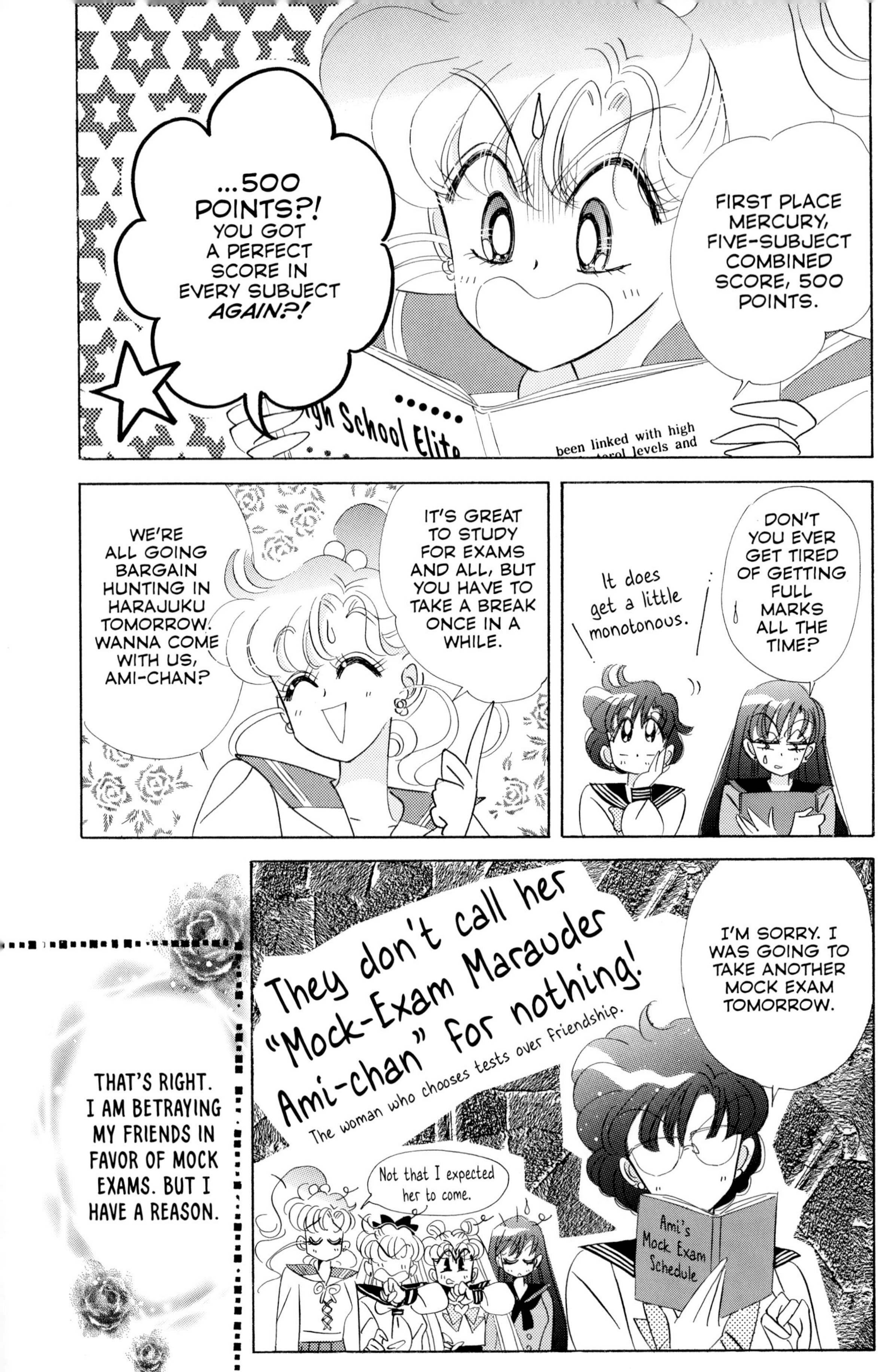
FIRST PLACE MERCURY, FIVE-SUBJECT COMBINED SCORE, 500 POINTS.
...500 POINTS?! YOU GOT A PERFECT SCORE IN EVERY SUBJECT *AGAIN?!*
been linked with high
DON'T YOU EVER GET TIRED OF GETTING FULL MARKS ALL THE TIME?
It does get a little monotonous.
IT'S GREAT TO STUDY FOR EXAMS AND ALL, BUT YOU HAVE TO TAKE A BREAK ONCE IN A WHILE.
WE'RE ALL GOING BARGAIN HUNTING IN HARAJUKU TOMORROW. WANNA COME WITH US, AMI-CHAN?
I'M SORRY. I WAS GOING TO TAKE ANOTHER MOCK EXAM TOMORROW.
They don't call her "Mock-Exam Marauder Ami-chan" for nothing!
The woman who chooses tests over friendship.
Not that I expected her to come.
Ami's Mock Exam Schedule
THAT'S RIGHT. I AM BETRAYING MY FRIENDS IN FAVOR OF MOCK EXAMS. BUT I HAVE A REASON.

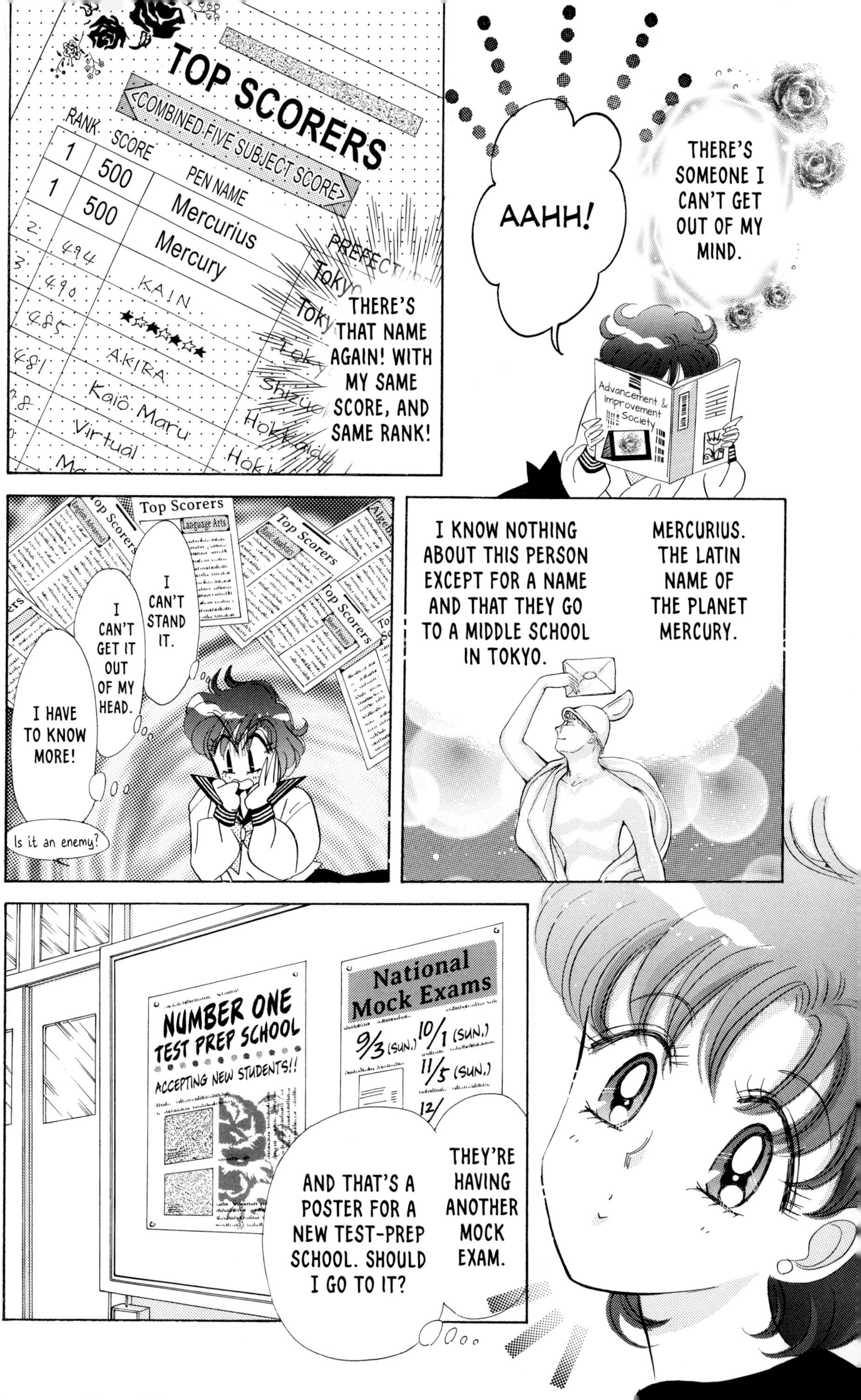
THERE'S SOMEONE I CAN'T GET OUT OF MY MIND.
AAHH!
Advancement & Improvement Society
TOP SCORERS
<COMBINED FIVE SUBJECT SCORE>
RANK SCORE PEN NAME PREFECTURE
1 500 Mercurius Tokyo
1 500 Mercury Tokyo
2. 494 KAIN
3. 490 ★☆★☆★☆
485 AKIRA
481 Kaiô Maru
Virtual
THERE'S THAT NAME AGAIN! WITH MY SAME SCORE, AND SAME RANK!
MERCURIUS. THE LATIN NAME OF THE PLANET MERCURY.
I KNOW NOTHING ABOUT THIS PERSON EXCEPT FOR A NAME AND THAT THEY GO TO A MIDDLE SCHOOL IN TOKYO.
Top Scorers
I CAN'T STAND IT.
I CAN'T GET IT OUT OF MY HEAD.
I HAVE TO KNOW MORE!
Is it an enemy?
National Mock Exams
9/3 (SUN.) 10/1 (SUN.) 11/5 (SUN.) 12/
NUMBER ONE TEST PREP SCHOOL
ACCEPTING NEW STUDENTS!!
THEY'RE HAVING ANOTHER MOCK EXAM.
AND THAT'S A POSTER FOR A NEW TEST-PREP SCHOOL. SHOULD I GO TO IT?

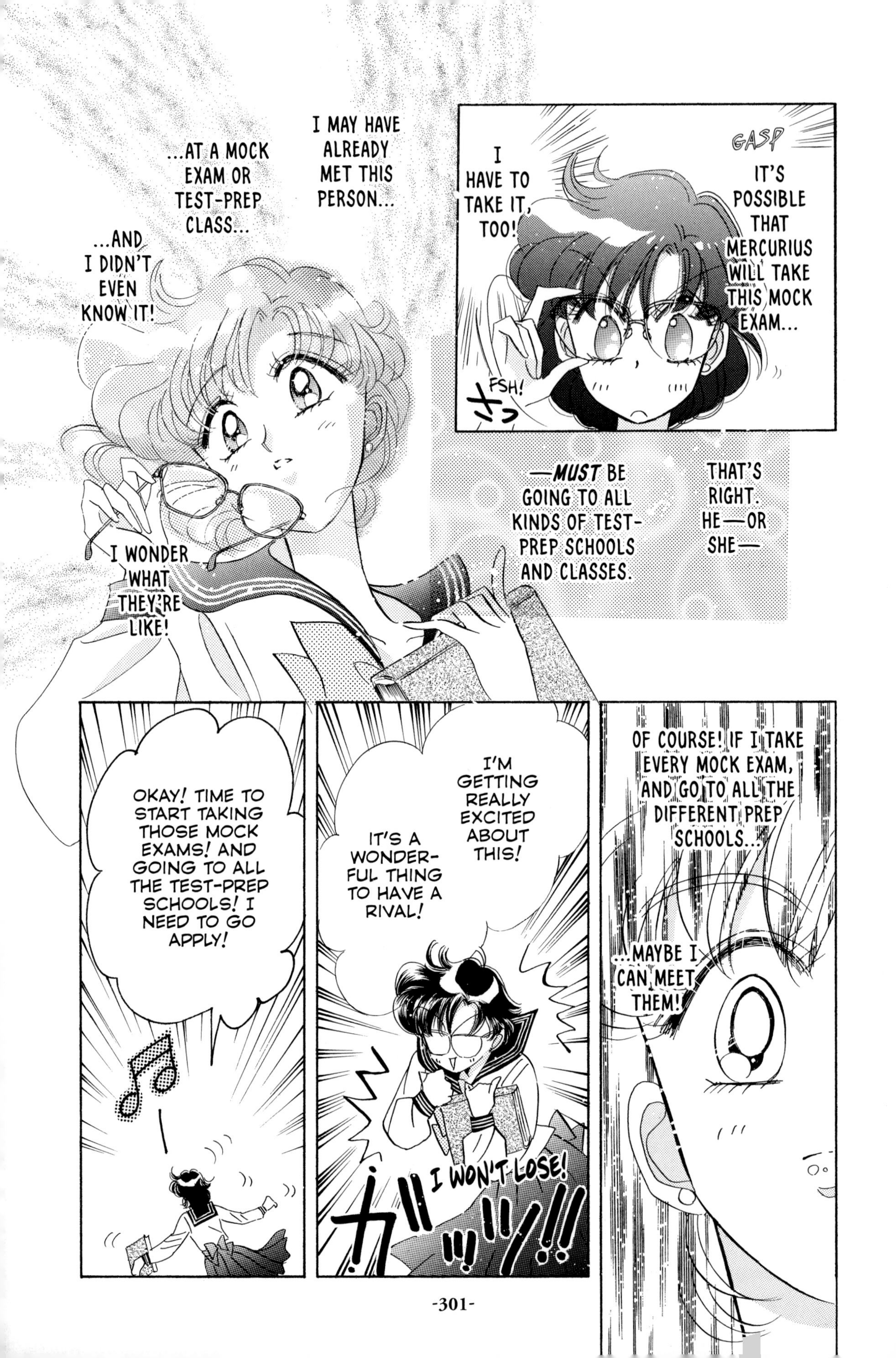
GASP
IT'S POSSIBLE THAT MERCURIUS WILL TAKE THIS MOCK EXAM...
I HAVE TO TAKE IT, TOO!
FSH!
THAT'S RIGHT. HE—OR SHE—
—*MUST* BE GOING TO ALL KINDS OF TEST-PREP SCHOOLS AND CLASSES.
I MAY HAVE ALREADY MET THIS PERSON...
...AT A MOCK EXAM OR TEST-PREP CLASS...
...AND I DIDN'T EVEN KNOW IT!
I WONDER WHAT THEY'RE LIKE!
OF COURSE! IF I TAKE EVERY MOCK EXAM, AND GO TO ALL THE DIFFERENT PREP SCHOOLS...
...MAYBE I CAN MEET THEM!
I'M GETTING REALLY EXCITED ABOUT THIS!
IT'S A WONDERFUL THING TO HAVE A RIVAL!
I WON'T LOSE!
OKAY! TIME TO START TAKING THOSE MOCK EXAMS! AND GOING TO ALL THE TEST-PREP SCHOOLS! I NEED TO GO APPLY!

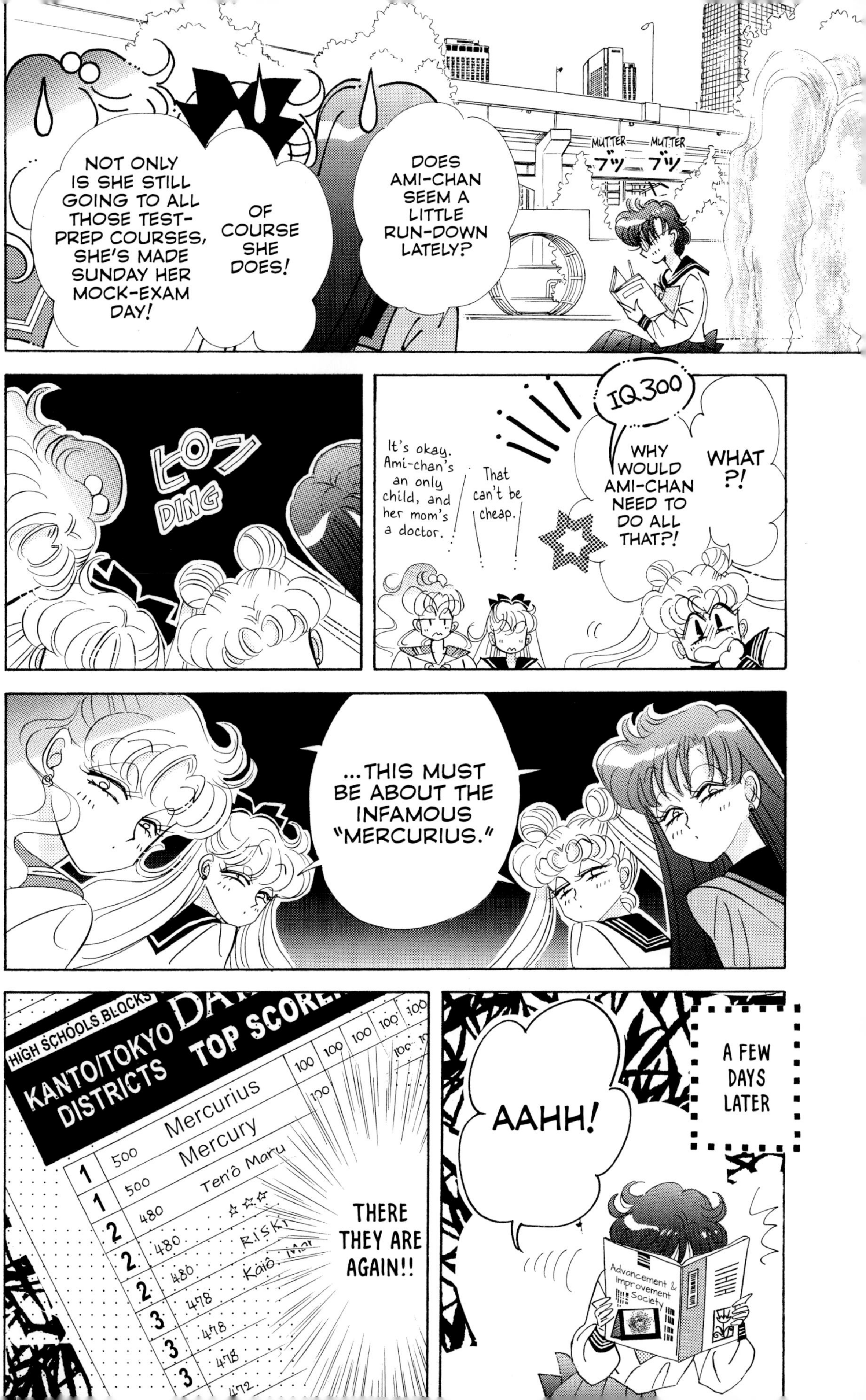
MUTTER MUTTER
ブツ ブツ
DOES AMI-CHAN SEEM A LITTLE RUN-DOWN LATELY?
OF COURSE SHE DOES!
NOT ONLY IS SHE STILL GOING TO ALL THOSE TEST-PREP COURSES, SHE'S MADE SUNDAY HER MOCK-EXAM DAY!
WHAT?!
IQ300
WHY WOULD AMI-CHAN NEED TO DO ALL THAT?!
That can't be cheap.
It's okay. Ami-chan's an only child, and her mom's a doctor.
DING
...THIS MUST BE ABOUT THE INFAMOUS "MERCURIUS."
A FEW DAYS LATER
AAHH!
Advancement & Improvement Society
HIGH SCHOOLS BLOCKS
KANTO/TOKYO DISTRICTS
1 500 Mercurius
1 500 Mercury
2 480 Ten'ô Maru
2 480 ☆☆☆
2 480 R.I.S.K.I
3 478 Kaiô
3 478
3 478
THERE THEY ARE AGAIN!!

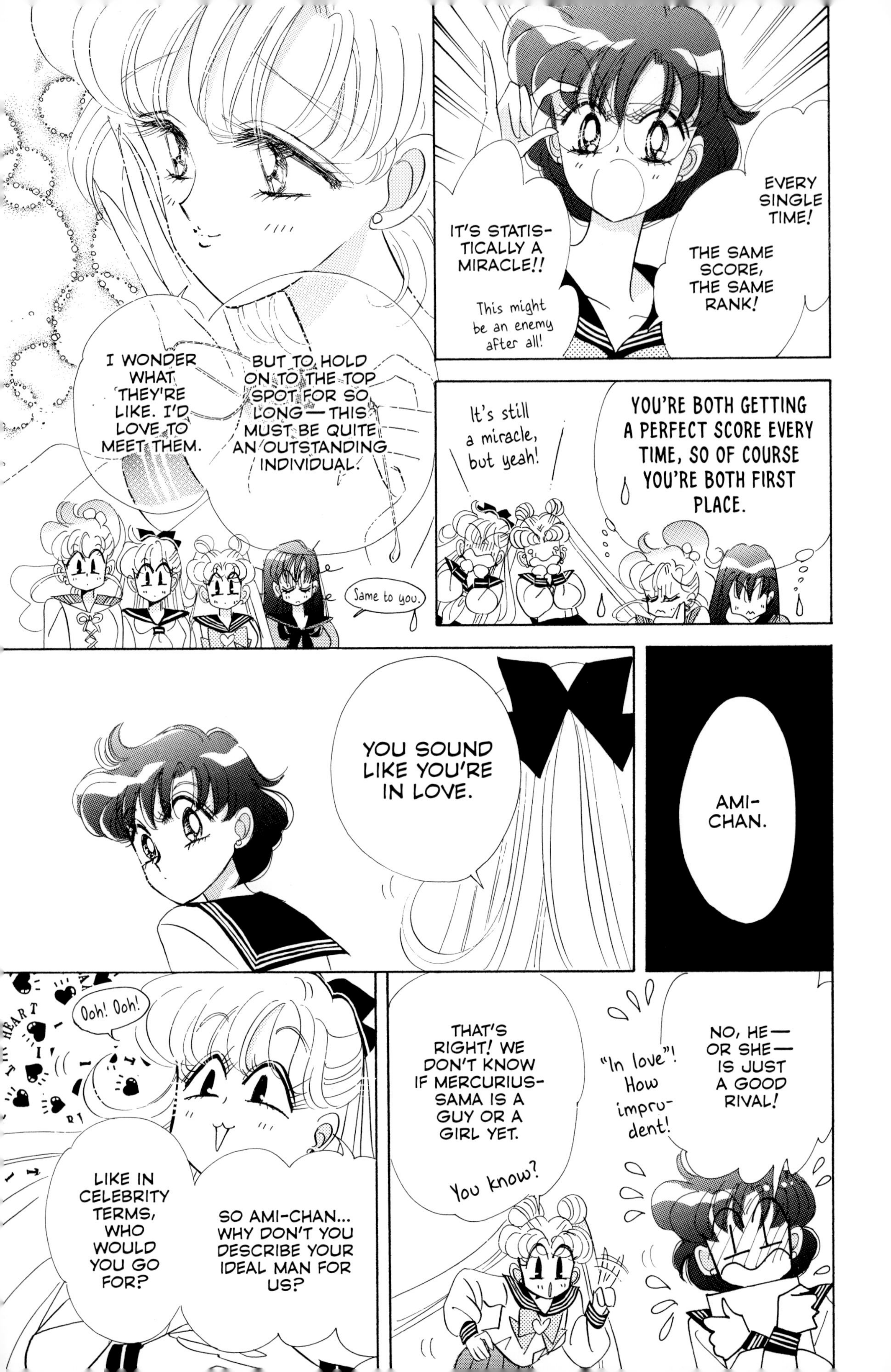
EVERY SINGLE TIME!
THE SAME SCORE, THE SAME RANK!
IT'S STATISTICALLY A MIRACLE!!
This might be an enemy after all!
YOU'RE BOTH GETTING A PERFECT SCORE EVERY TIME, SO OF COURSE YOU'RE BOTH FIRST PLACE.
It's still a miracle, but yeah!
BUT TO HOLD ON TO THE TOP SPOT FOR SO LONG—THIS MUST BE QUITE AN OUTSTANDING INDIVIDUAL.
I WONDER WHAT THEY'RE LIKE. I'D LOVE TO MEET THEM.
Same to you.
AMI-CHAN.
YOU SOUND LIKE YOU'RE IN LOVE.
NO, HE— OR SHE— IS JUST A GOOD RIVAL!
"In love"! How imprudent!
THAT'S RIGHT! WE DON'T KNOW IF MERCURIUS-SAMA IS A GUY OR A GIRL YET.
You know?
Ooh! Ooh!
SO AMI-CHAN... WHY DON'T YOU DESCRIBE YOUR IDEAL MAN FOR US?
LIKE IN CELEBRITY TERMS, WHO WOULD YOU GO FOR?

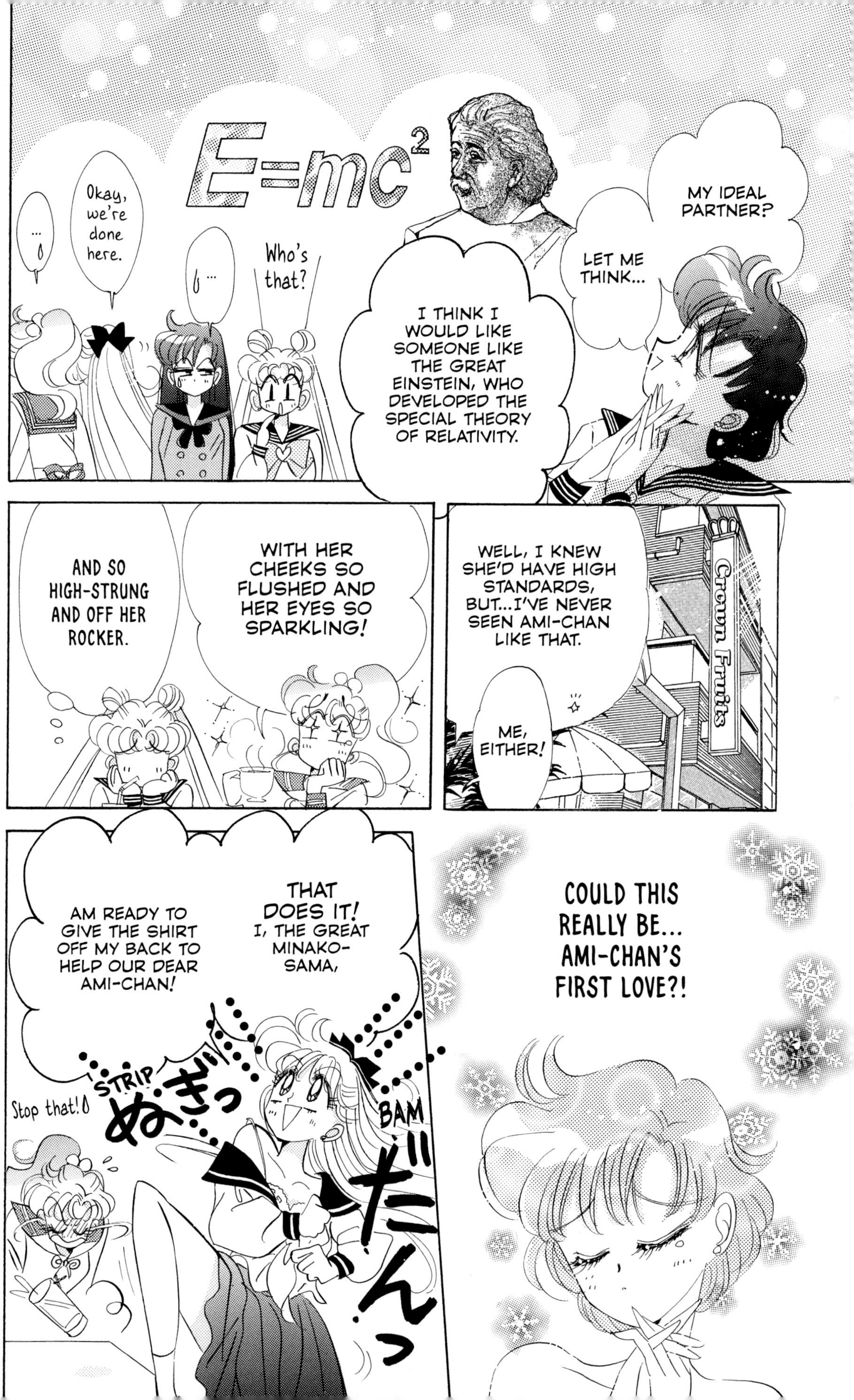
MY IDEAL PARTNER?
LET ME THINK...
I THINK I WOULD LIKE SOMEONE LIKE THE GREAT EINSTEIN, WHO DEVELOPED THE SPECIAL THEORY OF RELATIVITY.
$E=mc^2$
Who's that?
...
Okay, we're done here.
...
WELL, I KNEW SHE'D HAVE HIGH STANDARDS, BUT...I'VE NEVER SEEN AMI-CHAN LIKE THAT.
ME, EITHER!
Crown Fruits
WITH HER CHEEKS SO FLUSHED AND HER EYES SO SPARKLING!
AND SO HIGH-STRUNG AND OFF HER ROCKER.
COULD THIS REALLY BE... AMI-CHAN'S FIRST LOVE?!
THAT DOES IT! I, THE GREAT MINAKO-SAMA,
AM READY TO GIVE THE SHIRT OFF MY BACK TO HELP OUR DEAR AMI-CHAN!
BAM
だんっ
STRIP
ぬぎっ
Stop that!

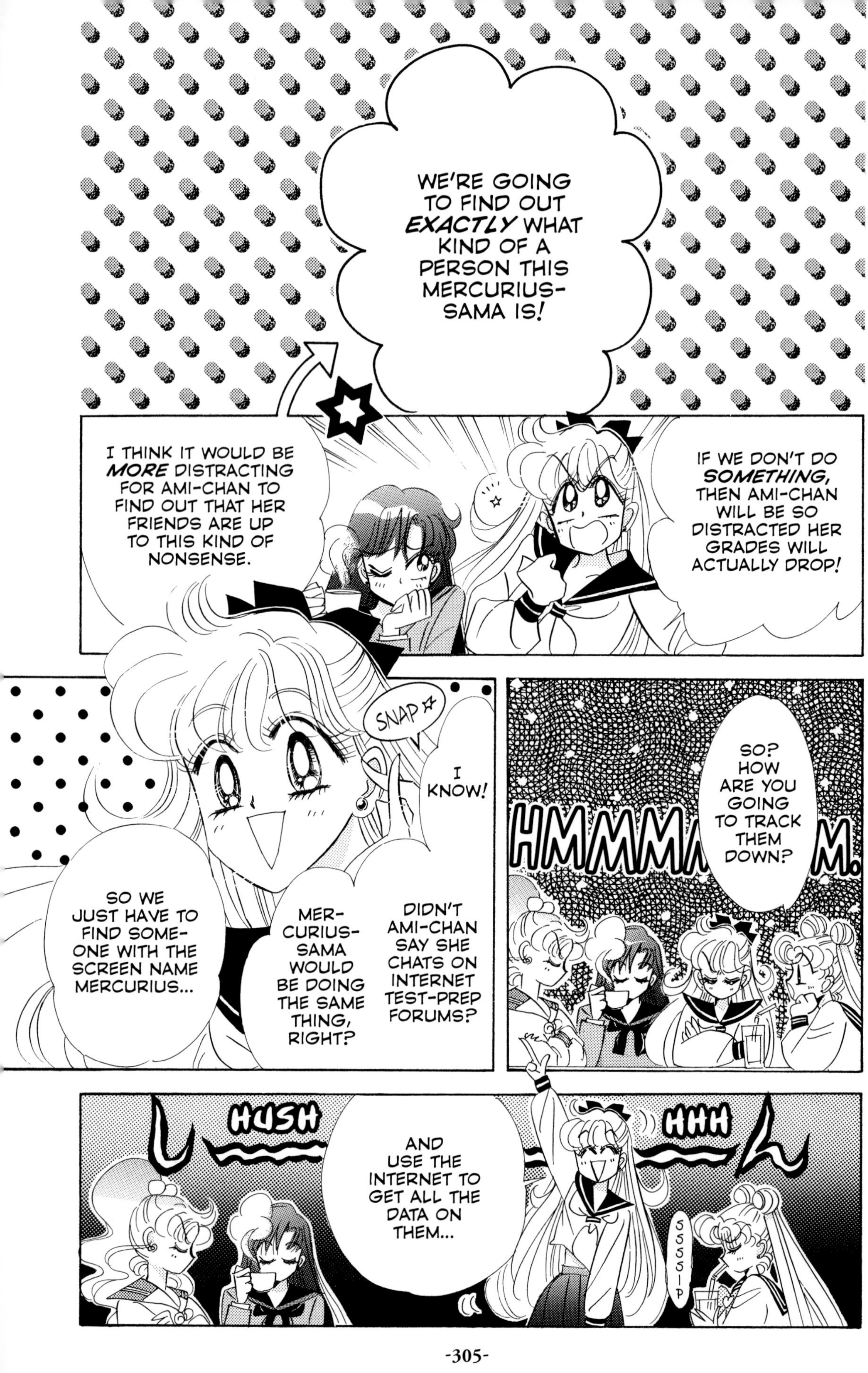
WE'RE GOING TO FIND OUT *EXACTLY* WHAT KIND OF A PERSON THIS MERCURIUS-SAMA IS!
IF WE DON'T DO *SOMETHING,* THEN AMI-CHAN WILL BE SO DISTRACTED HER GRADES WILL ACTUALLY DROP!
I THINK IT WOULD BE *MORE* DISTRACTING FOR AMI-CHAN TO FIND OUT THAT HER FRIENDS ARE UP TO THIS KIND OF NONSENSE.
HMMMM... M.
SO? HOW ARE YOU GOING TO TRACK THEM DOWN?
SNAP
I KNOW!
DIDN'T AMI-CHAN SAY SHE CHATS ON INTERNET TEST-PREP FORUMS?
MER-CURIUS-SAMA WOULD BE DOING THE SAME THING, RIGHT?
SO WE JUST HAVE TO FIND SOME-ONE WITH THE SCREEN NAME MERCURIUS...
HUSH
HHH
AND USE THE INTERNET TO GET ALL THE DATA ON THEM...
SSSSIP

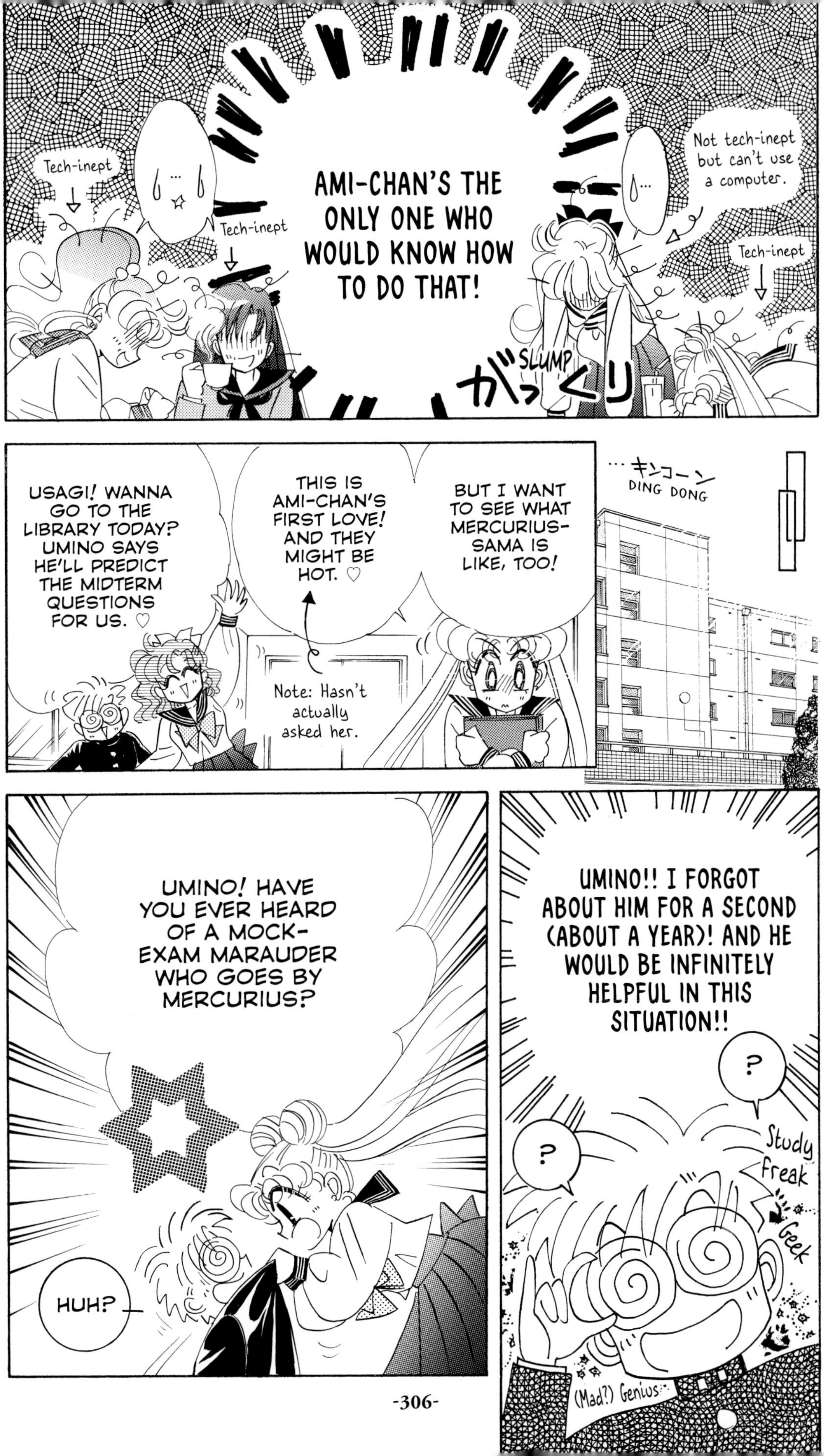

Not tech-inept but can't use a computer.
Tech-inept
...
AMI-CHAN'S THE ONLY ONE WHO WOULD KNOW HOW TO DO THAT!
がっくり
SLUMP
Tech-inept
...
Tech-inept
…キンコーン
DING DONG
BUT I WANT TO SEE WHAT MERCURIUS-SAMA IS LIKE, TOO!
THIS IS AMI-CHAN'S FIRST LOVE! AND THEY MIGHT BE HOT. ♡
Note: Hasn't actually asked her.
USAGI! WANNA GO TO THE LIBRARY TODAY? UMINO SAYS HE'LL PREDICT THE MIDTERM QUESTIONS FOR US. ♡
UMINO!! I FORGOT ABOUT HIM FOR A SECOND (ABOUT A YEAR)! AND HE WOULD BE INFINITELY HELPFUL IN THIS SITUATION!!
?
?
Study Freak
Geek
(Mad?) Genius
UMINO! HAVE YOU EVER HEARD OF A MOCK-EXAM MARAUDER WHO GOES BY MERCURIUS?
HUH?

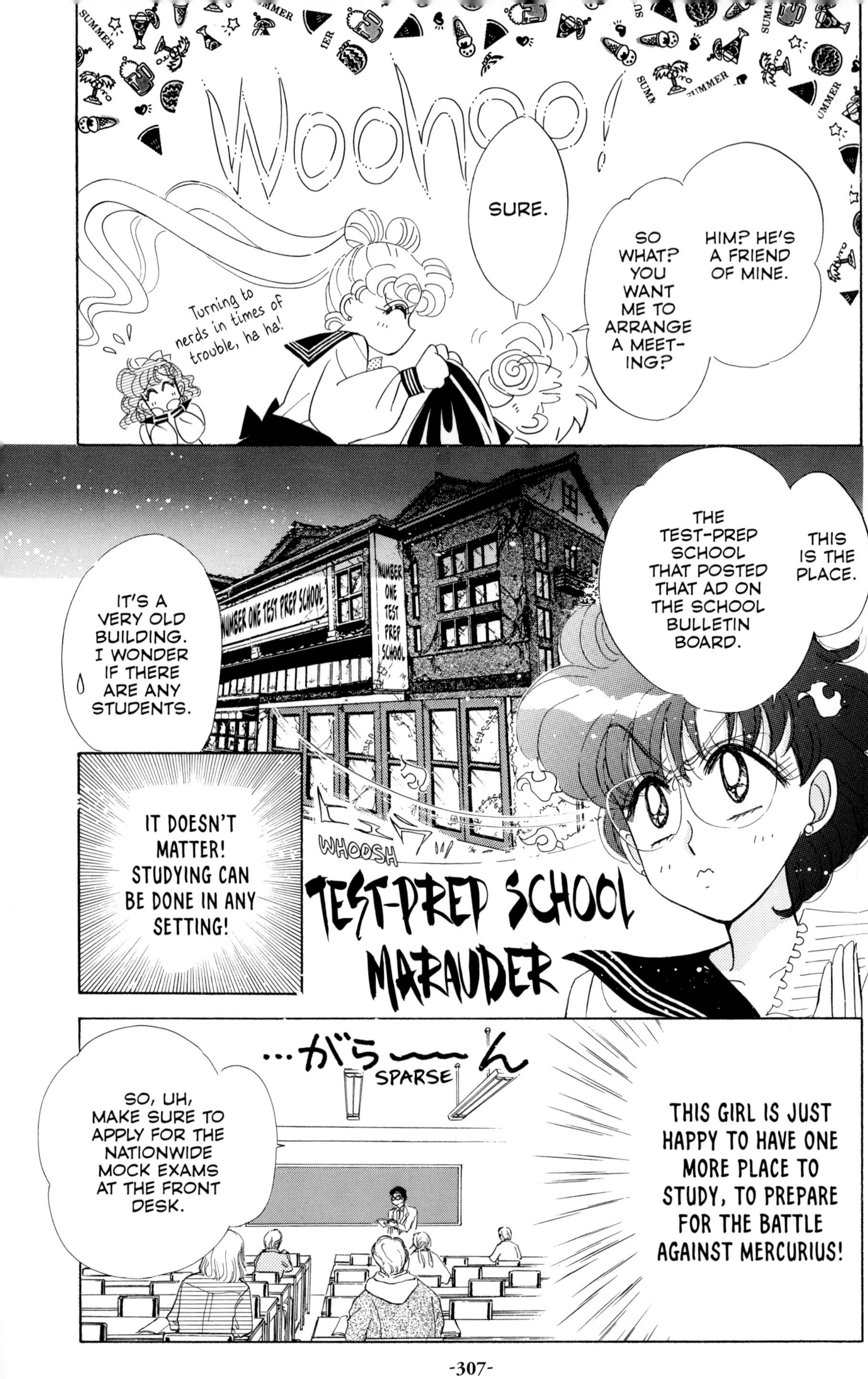
HIM? HE'S A FRIEND OF MINE.
SO WHAT? YOU WANT ME TO ARRANGE A MEET-ING?
SURE.
Woohoo!
Turning to nerds in times of trouble, ha ha!
THIS IS THE PLACE.
THE TEST-PREP SCHOOL THAT POSTED THAT AD ON THE SCHOOL BULLETIN BOARD.
NUMBER ONE TEST PREP SCHOOL
NUMBER ONE TEST PREP SCHOOL
IT'S A VERY OLD BUILDING. I WONDER IF THERE ARE ANY STUDENTS.
WHOOSH
TEST-PREP SCHOOL MARAUDER
IT DOESN'T MATTER! STUDYING CAN BE DONE IN ANY SETTING!
THIS GIRL IS JUST HAPPY TO HAVE ONE MORE PLACE TO STUDY, TO PREPARE FOR THE BATTLE AGAINST MERCURIUS!
…がら〜ん
SPARSE
SO, UH, MAKE SURE TO APPLY FOR THE NATIONWIDE MOCK EXAMS AT THE FRONT DESK.

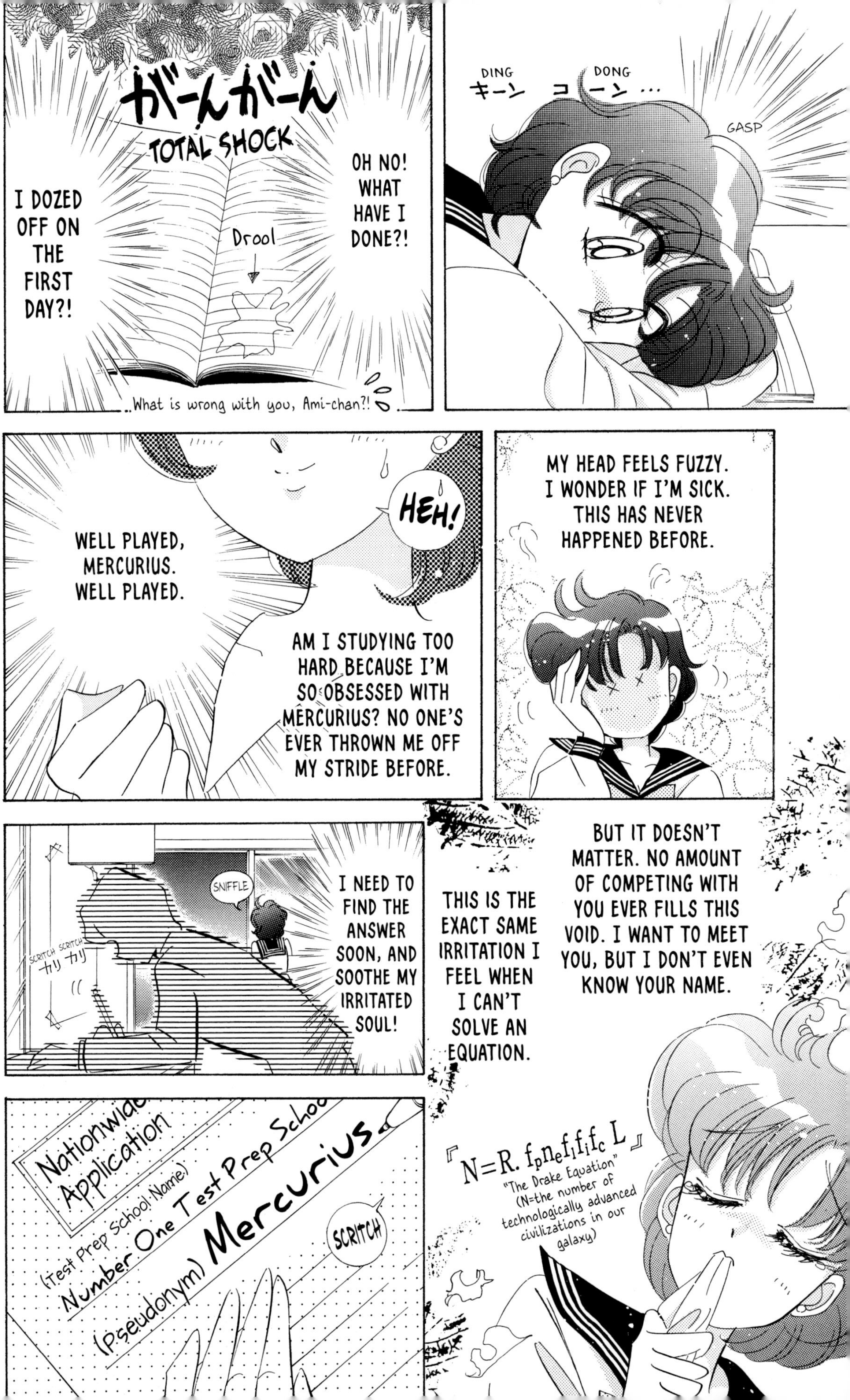
DING
キーン
DONG
コーン…
GASP
がーんがーん
TOTAL SHOCK
OH NO! WHAT HAVE I DONE?!
I DOZED OFF ON THE FIRST DAY?!
Drool
What is wrong with you, Ami-chan?!
MY HEAD FEELS FUZZY. I WONDER IF I'M SICK. THIS HAS NEVER HAPPENED BEFORE.
HEH!
WELL PLAYED, MERCURIUS. WELL PLAYED.
AM I STUDYING TOO HARD BECAUSE I'M SO OBSESSED WITH MERCURIUS? NO ONE'S EVER THROWN ME OFF MY STRIDE BEFORE.
BUT IT DOESN'T MATTER. NO AMOUNT OF COMPETING WITH YOU EVER FILLS THIS VOID. I WANT TO MEET YOU, BUT I DON'T EVEN KNOW YOUR NAME.
THIS IS THE EXACT SAME IRRITATION I FEEL WHEN I CAN'T SOLVE AN EQUATION.
『$N=R.\,f_p n_e f_l f_i f_c\,L$』
"The Drake Equation" (N=the number of technologically advanced civilizations in our galaxy)
I NEED TO FIND THE ANSWER SOON, AND SOOTHE MY IRRITATED SOUL!
SNIFFLE
SCRITCH SCRITCH
カリカリ
Nationwide Application
(Test Prep School Name) Number One Test Prep School
(pseudonym) Mercurius
SCRITCH

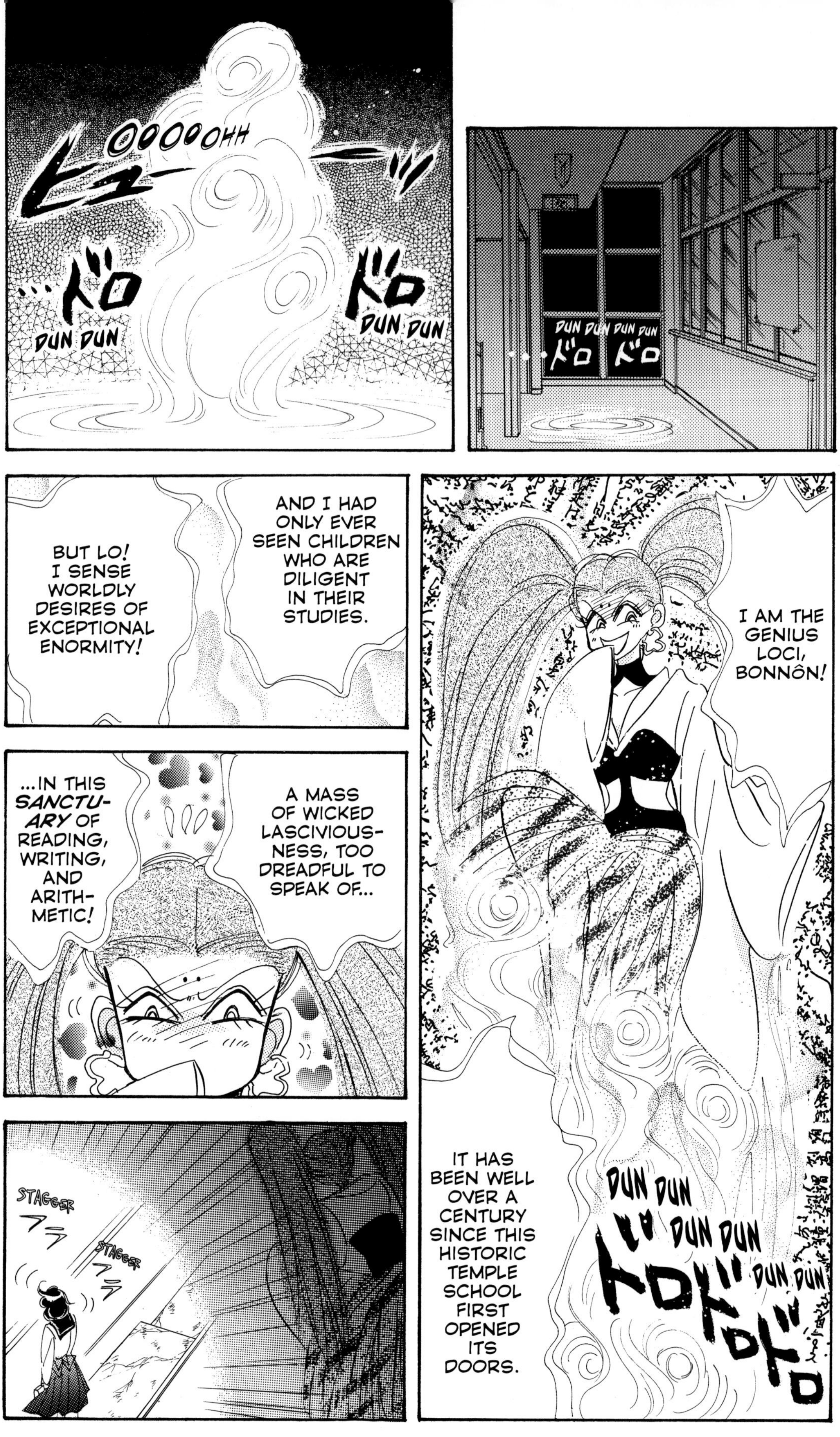
DUN DUN DUN DUN
...ドロ ドロ
OOOOOOHH
ヒュ～ッ
...ドロ
DUN DUN
ドロ
DUN DUN
I AM THE GENIUS LOCI, BONNÔN!
DUN DUN DUN DUN DUN DUN
ドドドドドド
IT HAS BEEN WELL OVER A CENTURY SINCE THIS HISTORIC TEMPLE SCHOOL FIRST OPENED ITS DOORS.
AND I HAD ONLY EVER SEEN CHILDREN WHO ARE DILIGENT IN THEIR STUDIES.
BUT LO! I SENSE WORLDLY DESIRES OF EXCEPTIONAL ENORMITY!
A MASS OF WICKED LASCIVIOUSNESS, TOO DREADFUL TO SPEAK OF...
...IN THIS *SANCTUARY* OF READING, WRITING, AND ARITHMETIC!
STAGGER
フラ
STAGGER
フラ

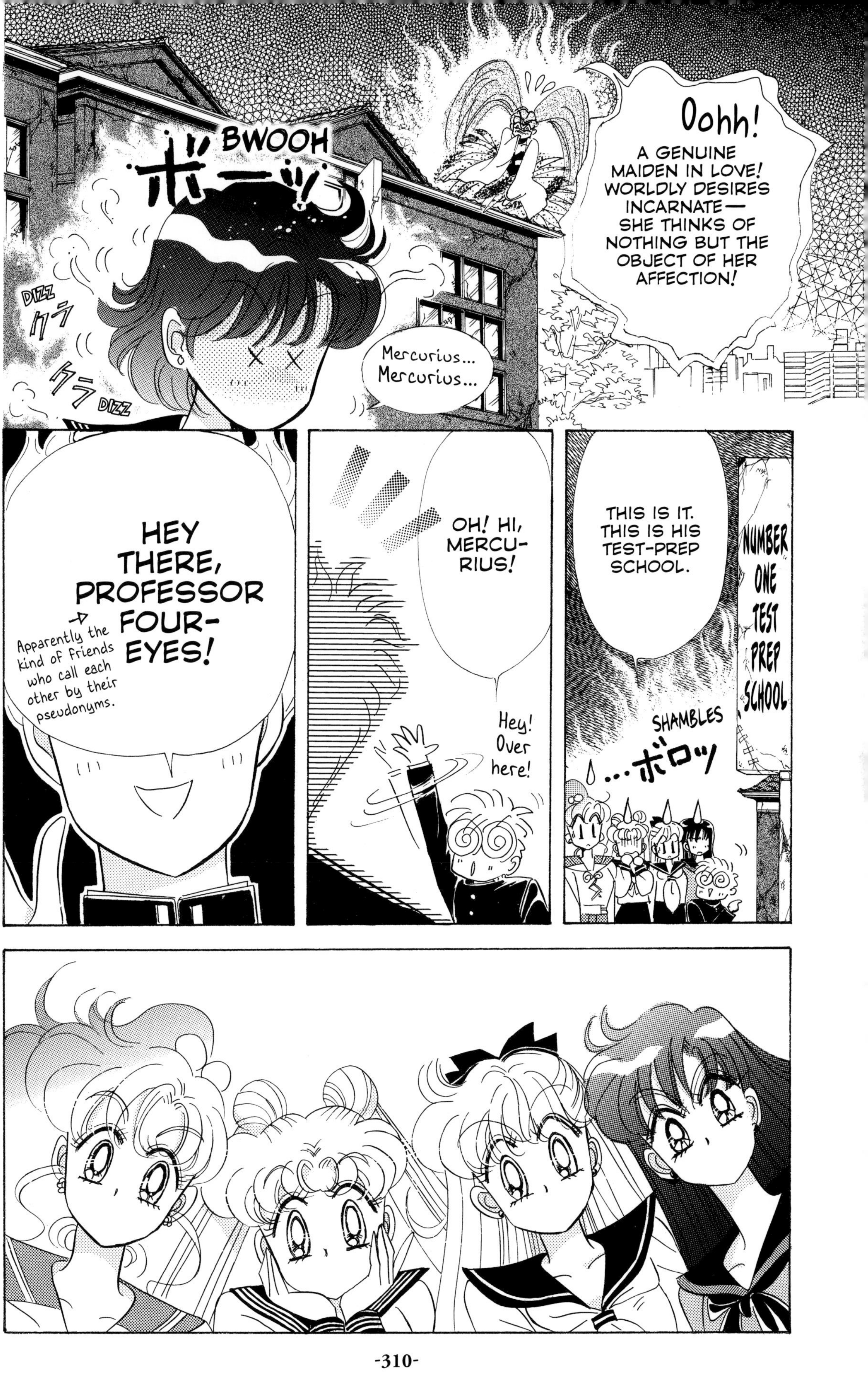

Oohh! A GENUINE MAIDEN IN LOVE! WORLDLY DESIRES INCARNATE— SHE THINKS OF NOTHING BUT THE OBJECT OF HER AFFECTION!
BWOOH
ボーッ!!
Mercurius... Mercurius...
DIZZ
クラ
クラ
DIZZ
THIS IS IT. THIS IS HIS TEST-PREP SCHOOL.
NUMBER ONE TEST PREP SCHOOL
SHAMBLES
...ボロッ
OH! HI, MERCU-RIUS!
Hey! Over here!
HEY THERE, PROFESSOR FOUR-EYES!
Apparently the kind of friends who call each other by their pseudonyms.

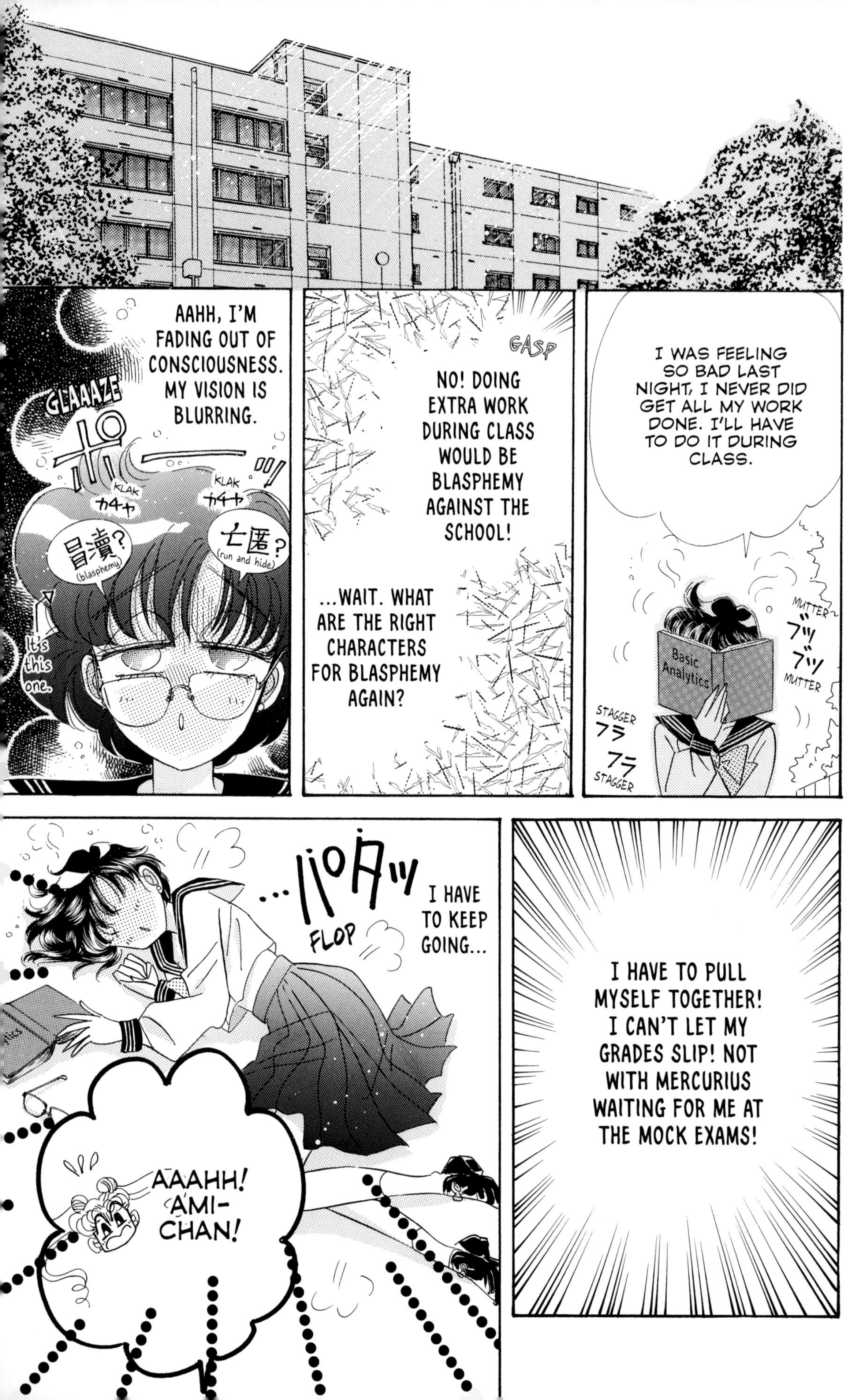
I WAS FEELING SO BAD LAST NIGHT, I NEVER DID GET ALL MY WORK DONE. I'LL HAVE TO DO IT DURING CLASS.
MUTTER
ブツ
ブツ
MUTTER
Basic Analytics
STAGGER
フラ
フラ
STAGGER
GASP
NO! DOING EXTRA WORK DURING CLASS WOULD BE BLASPHEMY AGAINST THE SCHOOL!
...WAIT. WHAT ARE THE RIGHT CHARACTERS FOR BLASPHEMY AGAIN?
AAHH, I'M FADING OUT OF CONSCIOUSNESS. MY VISION IS BLURRING.
GLAAAZE
ポー
KLAK
カチャ
KLAK
カチャ
亡匿?
(run and hide)
冒瀆?
(blasphemy)
It's this one.
I HAVE TO PULL MYSELF TOGETHER! I CAN'T LET MY GRADES SLIP! NOT WITH MERCURIUS WAITING FOR ME AT THE MOCK EXAMS!
...パタッ
FLOP
I HAVE TO KEEP GOING...
AAAHH! AMI-CHAN!

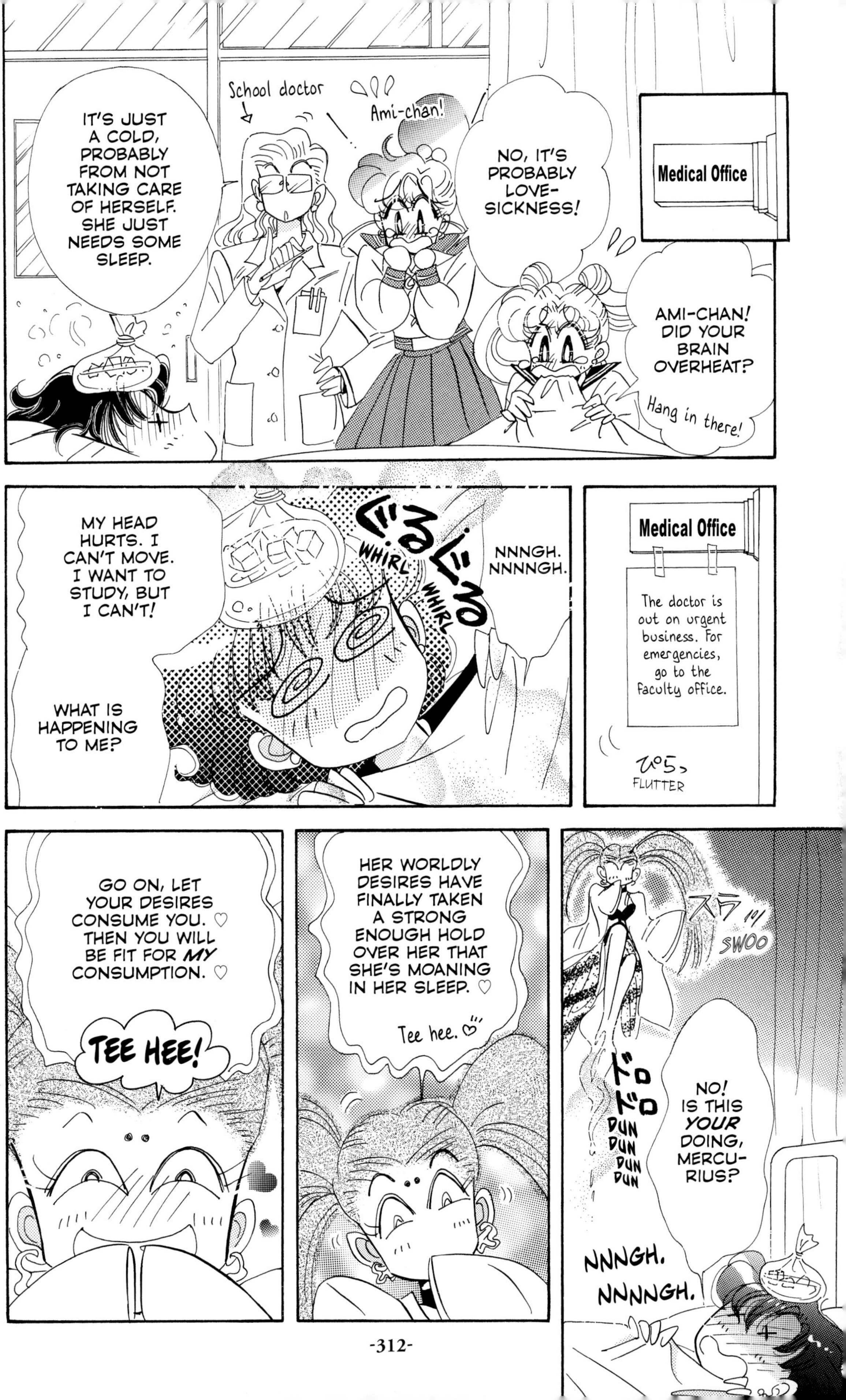

Medical Office
AMI-CHAN! DID YOUR BRAIN OVERHEAT?
Hang in there!
NO, IT'S PROBABLY LOVE-SICKNESS!
Ami-chan!
School doctor
IT'S JUST A COLD, PROBABLY FROM NOT TAKING CARE OF HERSELF. SHE JUST NEEDS SOME SLEEP.
Medical Office
The doctor is out on urgent business. For emergencies, go to the faculty office.
FLUTTER
NNNGH. NNNNGH.
WHIRL
WHIRL
MY HEAD HURTS. I CAN'T MOVE. I WANT TO STUDY, BUT I CAN'T!
WHAT IS HAPPENING TO ME?
SWOO
NO! IS THIS YOUR DOING, MERCURIUS?
ドロドロ
DUN DUN DUN DUN
NNNGH. NNNNGH.
HER WORLDLY DESIRES HAVE FINALLY TAKEN A STRONG ENOUGH HOLD OVER HER THAT SHE'S MOANING IN HER SLEEP. ♡
Tee hee. ♡
GO ON, LET YOUR DESIRES CONSUME YOU. ♡ THEN YOU WILL BE FIT FOR MY CONSUMPTION. ♡
TEE HEE!

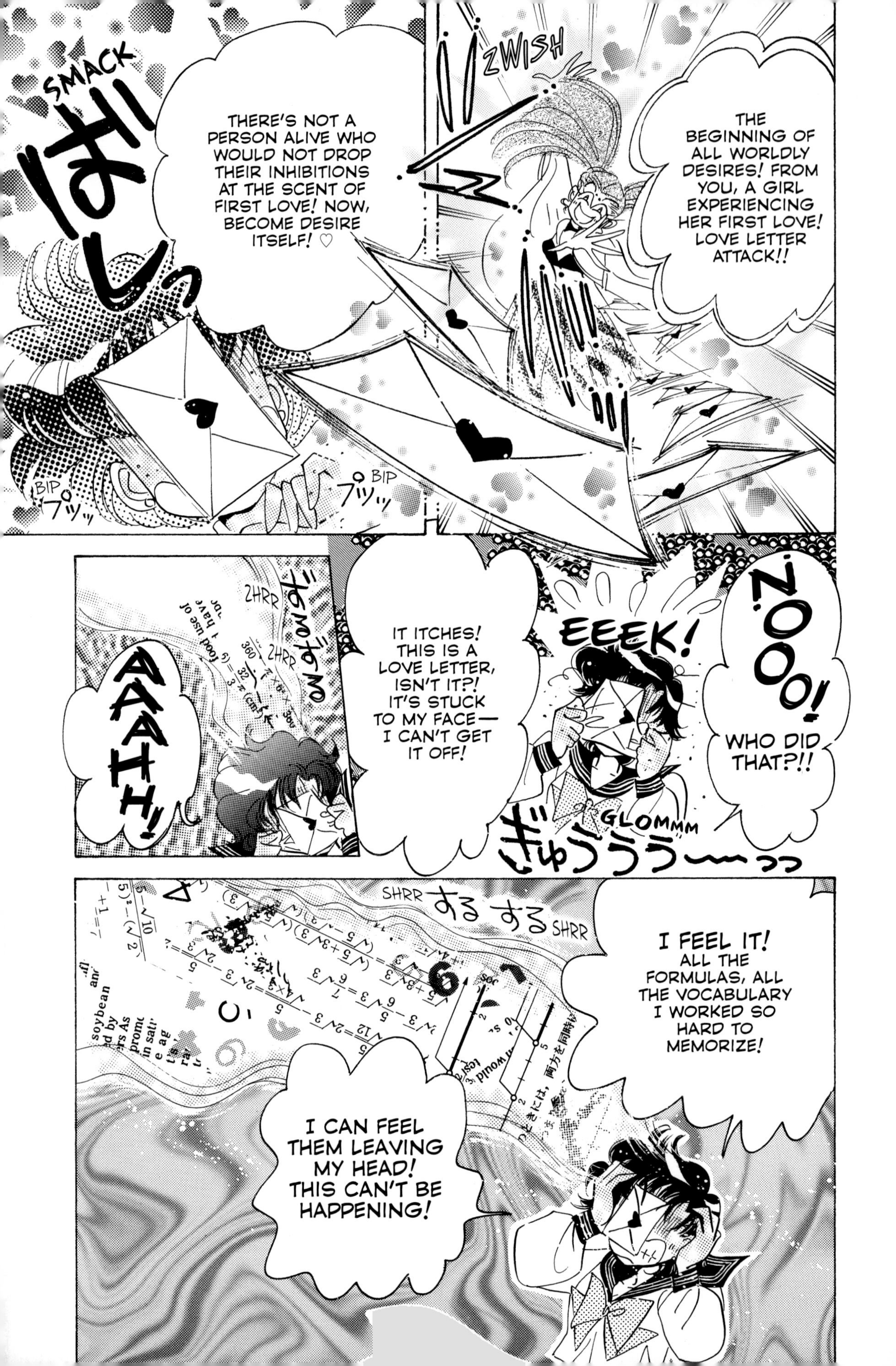

ZWISH
THE BEGINNING OF ALL WORLDLY DESIRES! FROM YOU, A GIRL EXPERIENCING HER FIRST LOVE! LOVE LETTER ATTACK!!
THERE'S NOT A PERSON ALIVE WHO WOULD NOT DROP THEIR INHIBITIONS AT THE SCENT OF FIRST LOVE! NOW, BECOME DESIRE ITSELF! ♡
SMACK
ばしっ
BIP
プツッ
BIP
プツッ
NOOOO!
WHO DID THAT?!!
EEEK!
GLOMMM
ぎゅうううー
IT ITCHES! THIS IS A LOVE LETTER, ISN'T IT?! IT'S STUCK TO MY FACE—I CAN'T GET IT OFF!
ZHRR
ずるずる
ZHRR
AAAHH!
SHRR
するする
SHRR
I FEEL IT! ALL THE FORMULAS, ALL THE VOCABULARY I WORKED SO HARD TO MEMORIZE!
I CAN FEEL THEM LEAVING MY HEAD! THIS CAN'T BE HAPPENING!

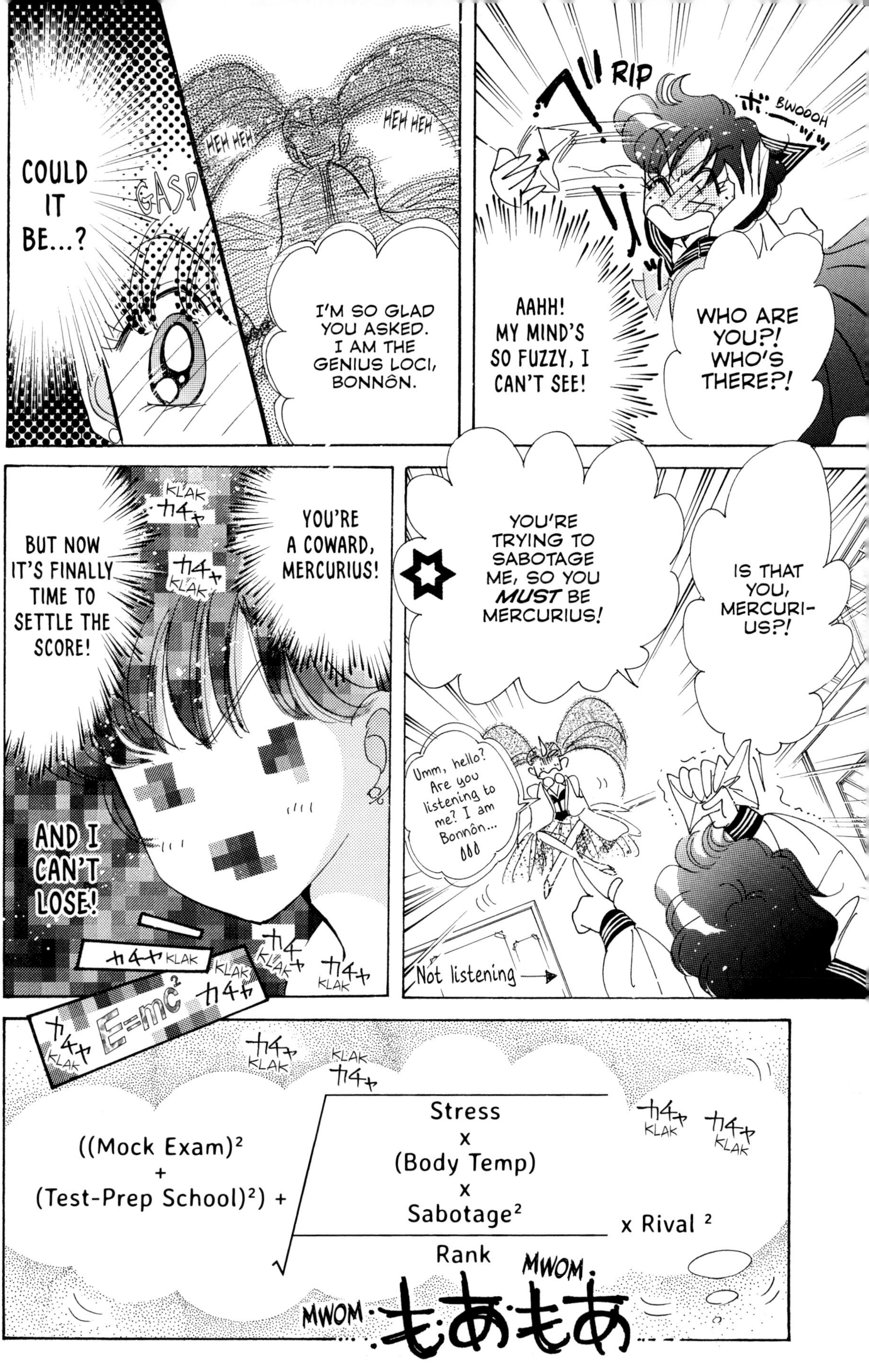
RIP
BWOOOH
WHO ARE YOU?! WHO'S THERE?!
AAHH! MY MIND'S SO FUZZY, I CAN'T SEE!
HEH HEH
HEH HEH
I'M SO GLAD YOU ASKED. I AM THE GENIUS LOCI, BONNÔN.
GASP
COULD IT BE...?
IS THAT YOU, MERCURIUS?!
YOU'RE TRYING TO SABOTAGE ME, SO YOU *MUST* BE MERCURIUS!
Umm, hello? Are you listening to me? I am Bonnôn...
Not listening
YOU'RE A COWARD, MERCURIUS!
KLAK
BUT NOW IT'S FINALLY TIME TO SETTLE THE SCORE!
AND I CAN'T LOSE!
KLAK
E=mc²
KLAK
((Mock Exam)² + (Test-Prep School)²) + √(Stress x (Body Temp) x Sabotage² / Rank) x Rival ²
MWOM
MWOM

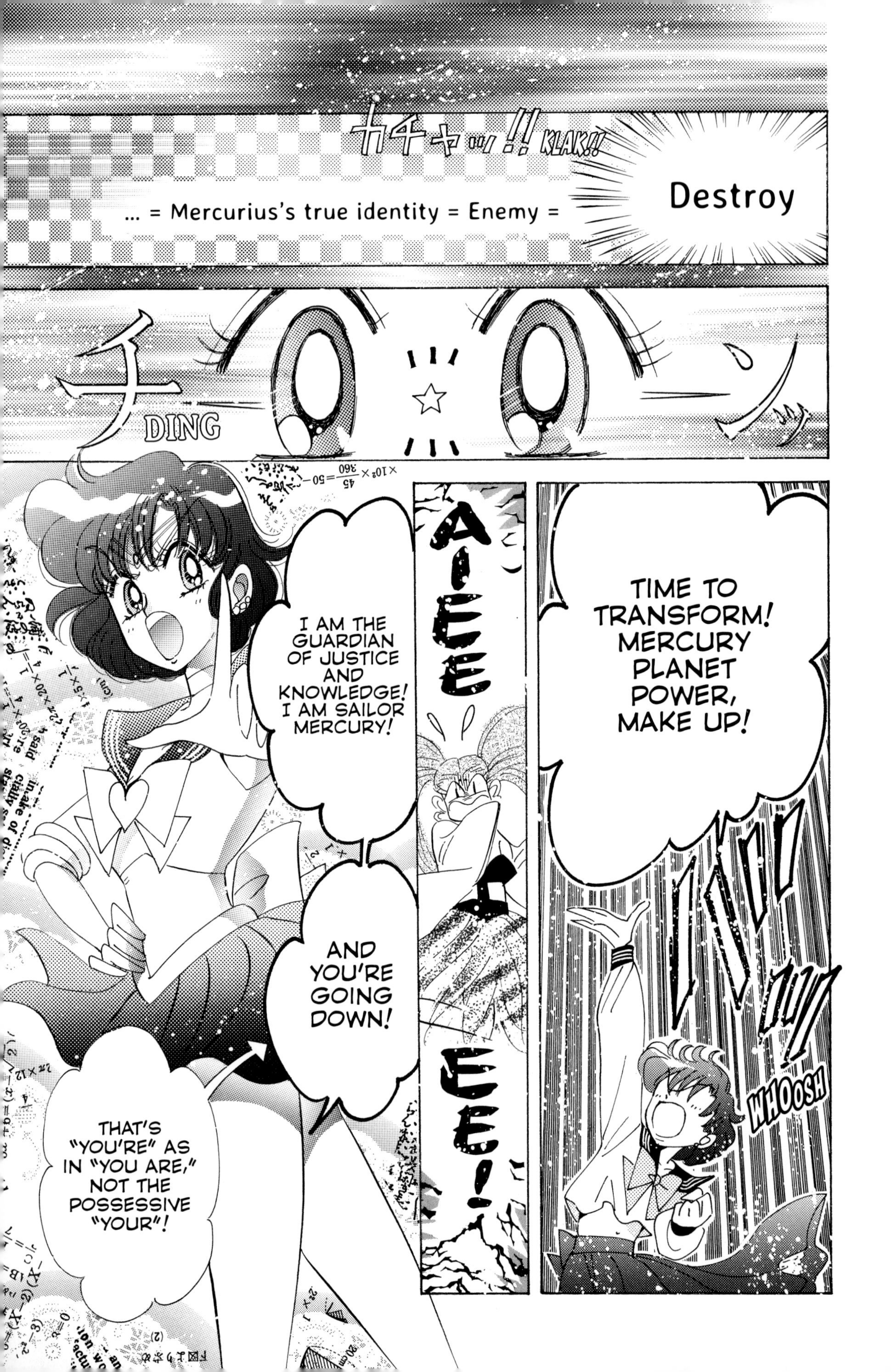

カチャッ!! KLAK!!
... = Mercurius's true identity = Enemy =
Destroy
DING
TIME TO TRANSFORM! MERCURY PLANET POWER, MAKE UP!
WHOOSH
AIEE
EEE!
I AM THE GUARDIAN OF JUSTICE AND KNOWLEDGE! I AM SAILOR MERCURY!
AND YOU'RE GOING DOWN!
THAT'S "YOU'RE" AS IN "YOU ARE," NOT THE POSSESSIVE "YOUR"!

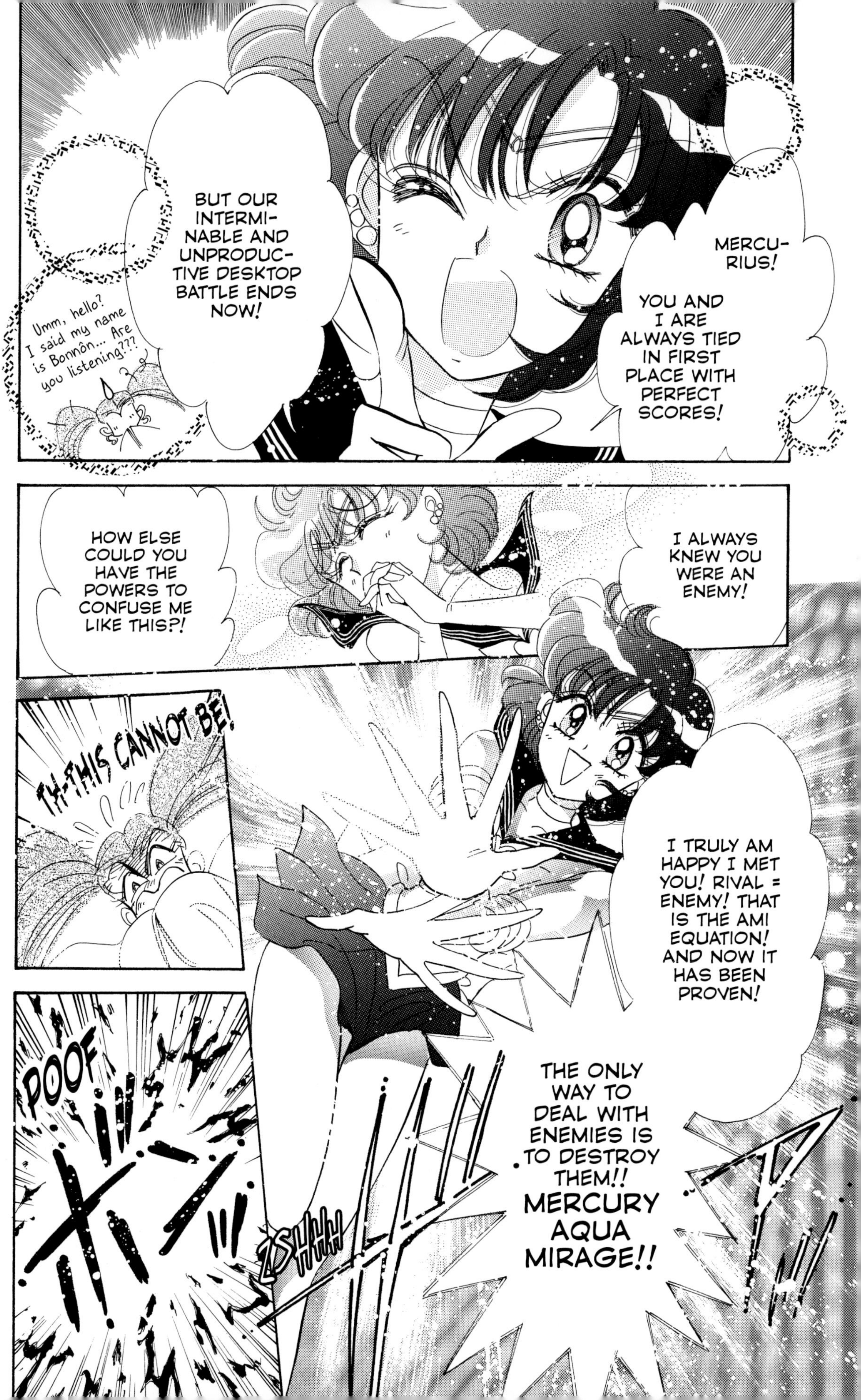
MERCURIUS!
YOU AND I ARE ALWAYS TIED IN FIRST PLACE WITH PERFECT SCORES!
BUT OUR INTERMINABLE AND UNPRODUCTIVE DESKTOP BATTLE ENDS NOW!
Umm, hello? I said my name is Bonnôn... Are you listening???
I ALWAYS KNEW YOU WERE AN ENEMY!
HOW ELSE COULD YOU HAVE THE POWERS TO CONFUSE ME LIKE THIS?!
I TRULY AM HAPPY I MET YOU! RIVAL = ENEMY! THAT IS THE AMI EQUATION! AND NOW IT HAS BEEN PROVEN!
THE ONLY WAY TO DEAL WITH ENEMIES IS TO DESTROY THEM!! MERCURY AQUA MIRAGE!!
ZSHHH
TH-THIS CANNOT BE!
POOF

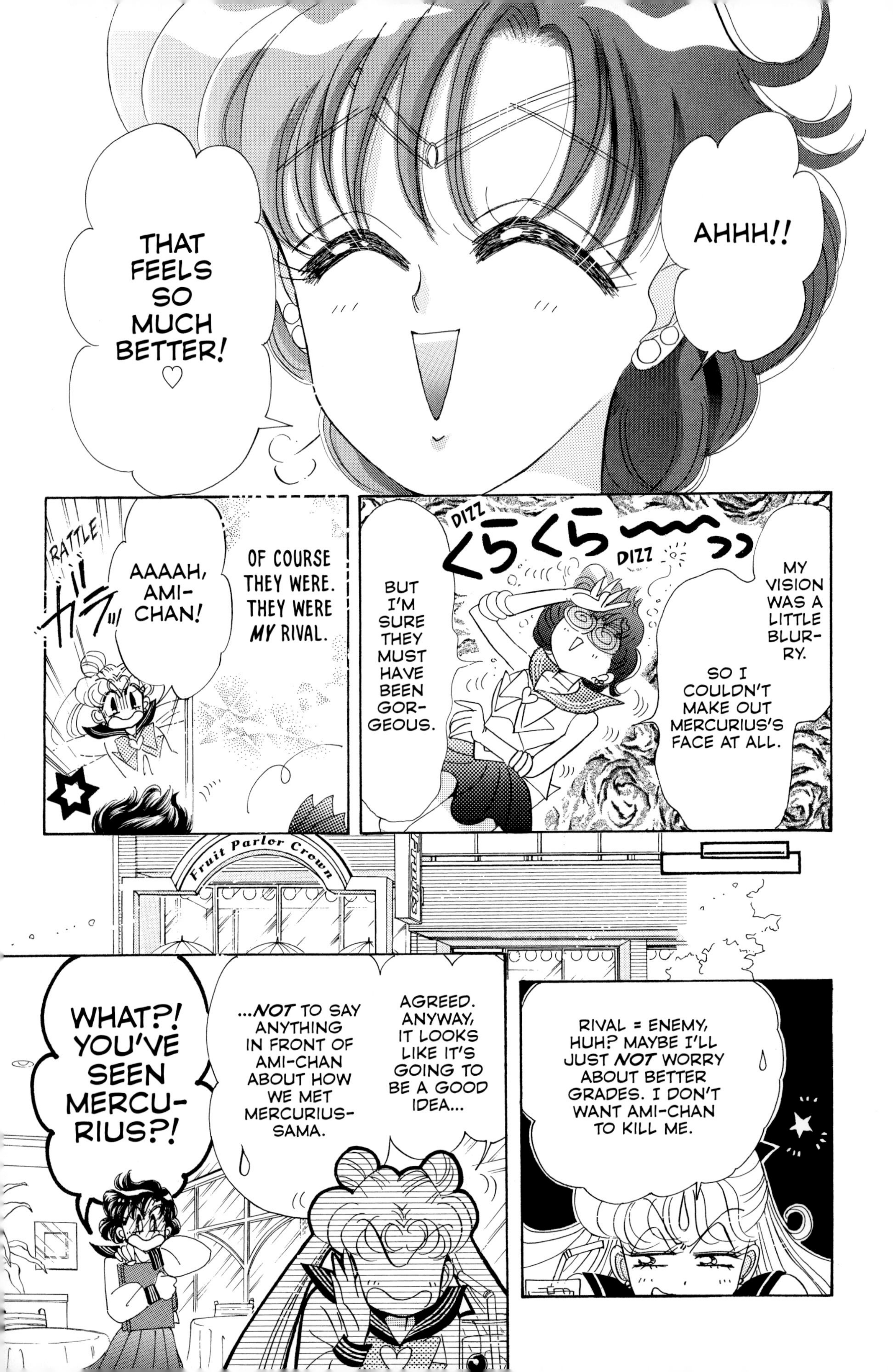

AHHH!!
THAT FEELS SO MUCH BETTER! ♡
MY VISION WAS A LITTLE BLUR-RY.
SO I COULDN'T MAKE OUT MERCURIUS'S FACE AT ALL.
DIZZ
くらくら
DIZZ
BUT I'M SURE THEY MUST HAVE BEEN GOR-GEOUS.
OF COURSE THEY WERE. THEY WERE *MY* RIVAL.
AAAAH, AMI-CHAN!
RATTLE
ガラ
Fruit Parlor Crown
RIVAL = ENEMY, HUH? MAYBE I'LL JUST ***NOT*** WORRY ABOUT BETTER GRADES. I DON'T WANT AMI-CHAN TO KILL ME.
AGREED. ANYWAY, IT LOOKS LIKE IT'S GOING TO BE A GOOD IDEA...
...***NOT*** TO SAY ANYTHING IN FRONT OF AMI-CHAN ABOUT HOW WE MET MERCURIUS-SAMA.
WHAT?! YOU'VE SEEN MERCU-RIUS?!

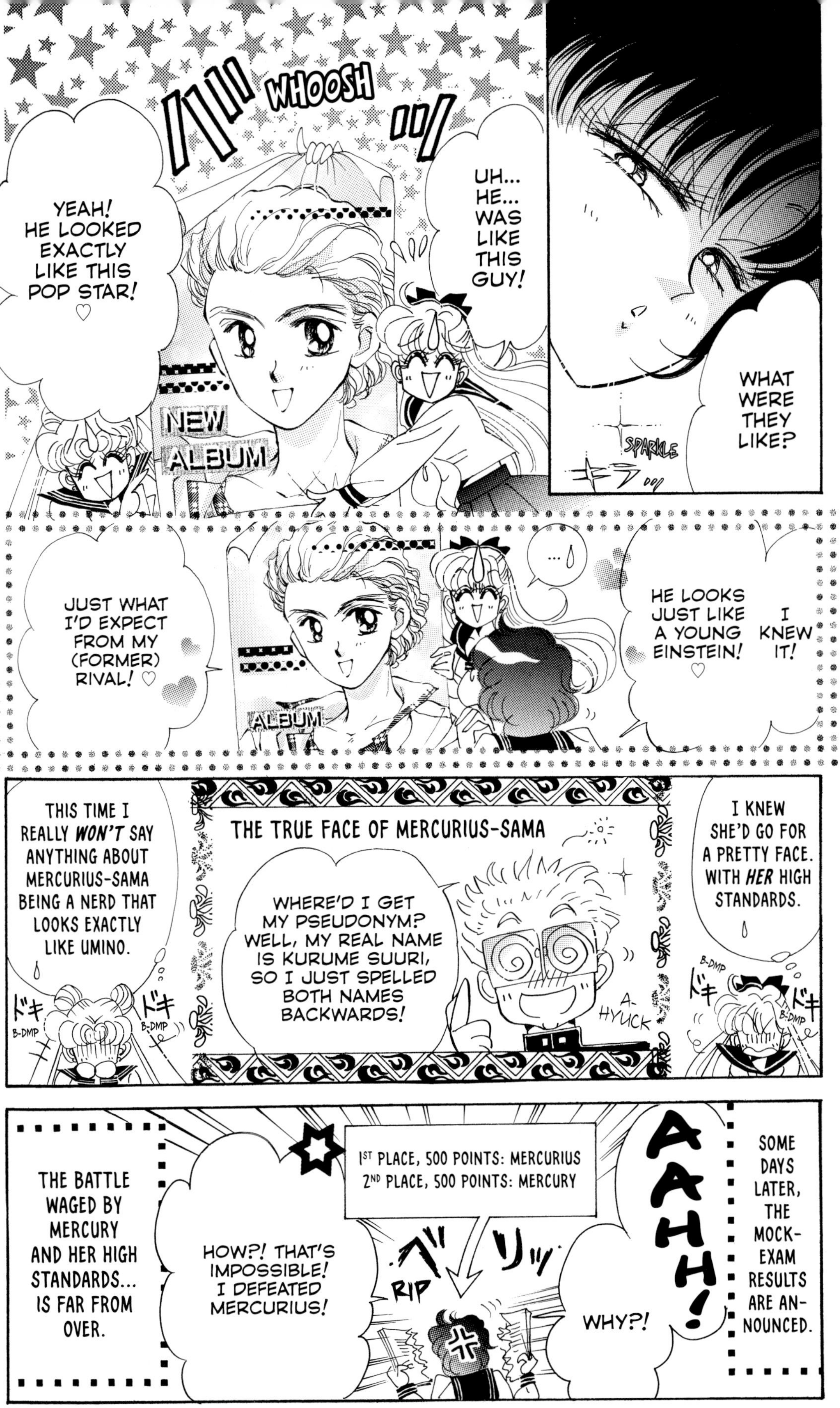
WHAT WERE THEY LIKE?
SPARKLE
キラッ
UH... HE... WAS LIKE THIS GUY!
WHOOSH
YEAH! HE LOOKED EXACTLY LIKE THIS POP STAR! ♡
NEW ALBUM
I KNEW IT!
HE LOOKS JUST LIKE A YOUNG EINSTEIN! ♡
...
ALBUM
JUST WHAT I'D EXPECT FROM MY (FORMER) RIVAL! ♡
I KNEW SHE'D GO FOR A PRETTY FACE. WITH *HER* HIGH STANDARDS.
ドキ B-DMP
ドキ B-DMP
THE TRUE FACE OF MERCURIUS-SAMA
WHERE'D I GET MY PSEUDONYM? WELL, MY REAL NAME IS KURUME SUURI, SO I JUST SPELLED BOTH NAMES BACKWARDS!
A-HYUCK
THIS TIME I REALLY *WON'T* SAY ANYTHING ABOUT MERCURIUS-SAMA BEING A NERD THAT LOOKS EXACTLY LIKE UMINO.
ドキ B-DMP
ドキ B-DMP
SOME DAYS LATER, THE MOCK-EXAM RESULTS ARE ANNOUNCED.
AAHH!
WHY?!
1ST PLACE, 500 POINTS: MERCURIUS
2ND PLACE, 500 POINTS: MERCURY
ベリッ
RIP
HOW?! THAT'S IMPOSSIBLE! I DEFEATED MERCURIUS!
THE BATTLE WAGED BY MERCURY AND HER HIGH STANDARDS... IS FAR FROM OVER.

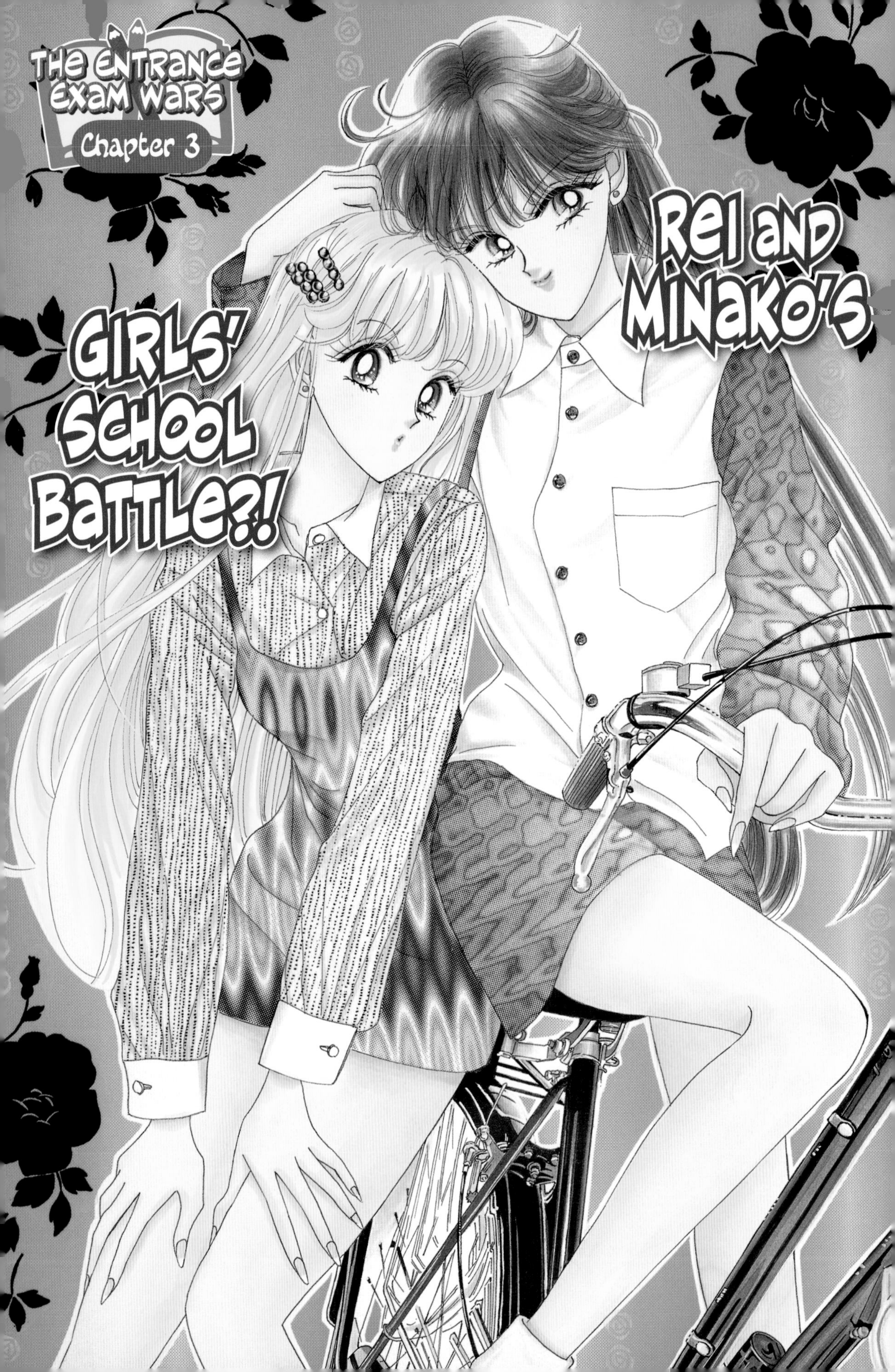
THE ENTRANCE EXAM WARS
Chapter 3
REI AND MINAKO'S
GIRLS' SCHOOL BATTLE?!

Pretty Guardian

Sailor Moon

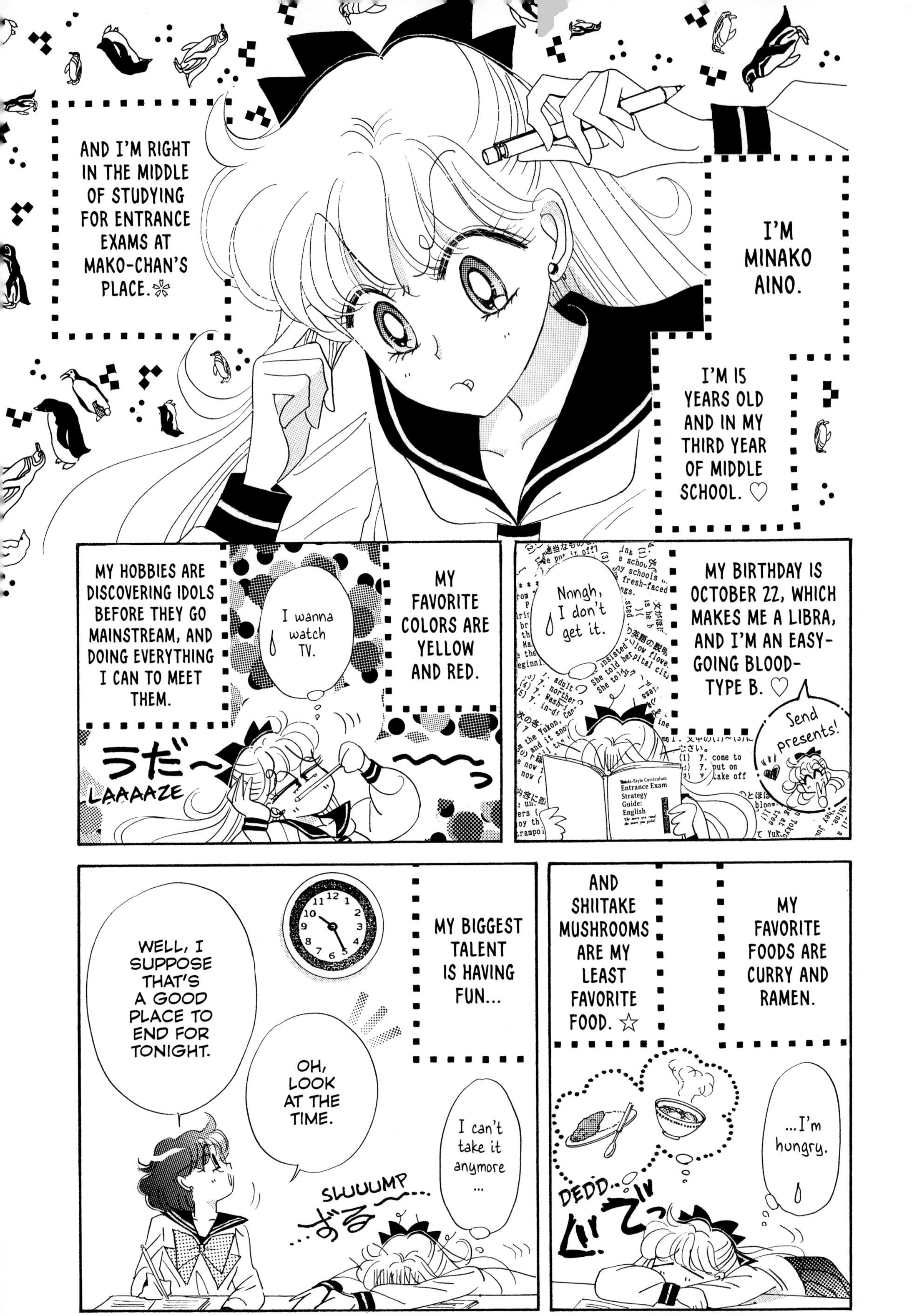
I'M MINAKO AINO.
I'M 15 YEARS OLD AND IN MY THIRD YEAR OF MIDDLE SCHOOL. ♡
AND I'M RIGHT IN THE MIDDLE OF STUDYING FOR ENTRANCE EXAMS AT MAKO-CHAN'S PLACE.
MY BIRTHDAY IS OCTOBER 22, WHICH MAKES ME A LIBRA, AND I'M AN EASY-GOING BLOOD-TYPE B. ♡
Send presents!
Nnngh, I don't get it.
Entrance Exam Strategy Guide: English
MY FAVORITE COLORS ARE YELLOW AND RED.
I wanna watch TV.
MY HOBBIES ARE DISCOVERING IDOLS BEFORE THEY GO MAINSTREAM, AND DOING EVERYTHING I CAN TO MEET THEM.
うだ〜
LAAAAZE
MY FAVORITE FOODS ARE CURRY AND RAMEN.
AND SHIITAKE MUSHROOMS ARE MY LEAST FAVORITE FOOD. ☆
...I'm hungry.
DEDD...
MY BIGGEST TALENT IS HAVING FUN...
I can't take it anymore...
SLUUUMP
...ずる〜
OH, LOOK AT THE TIME.
WELL, I SUPPOSE THAT'S A GOOD PLACE TO END FOR TONIGHT.

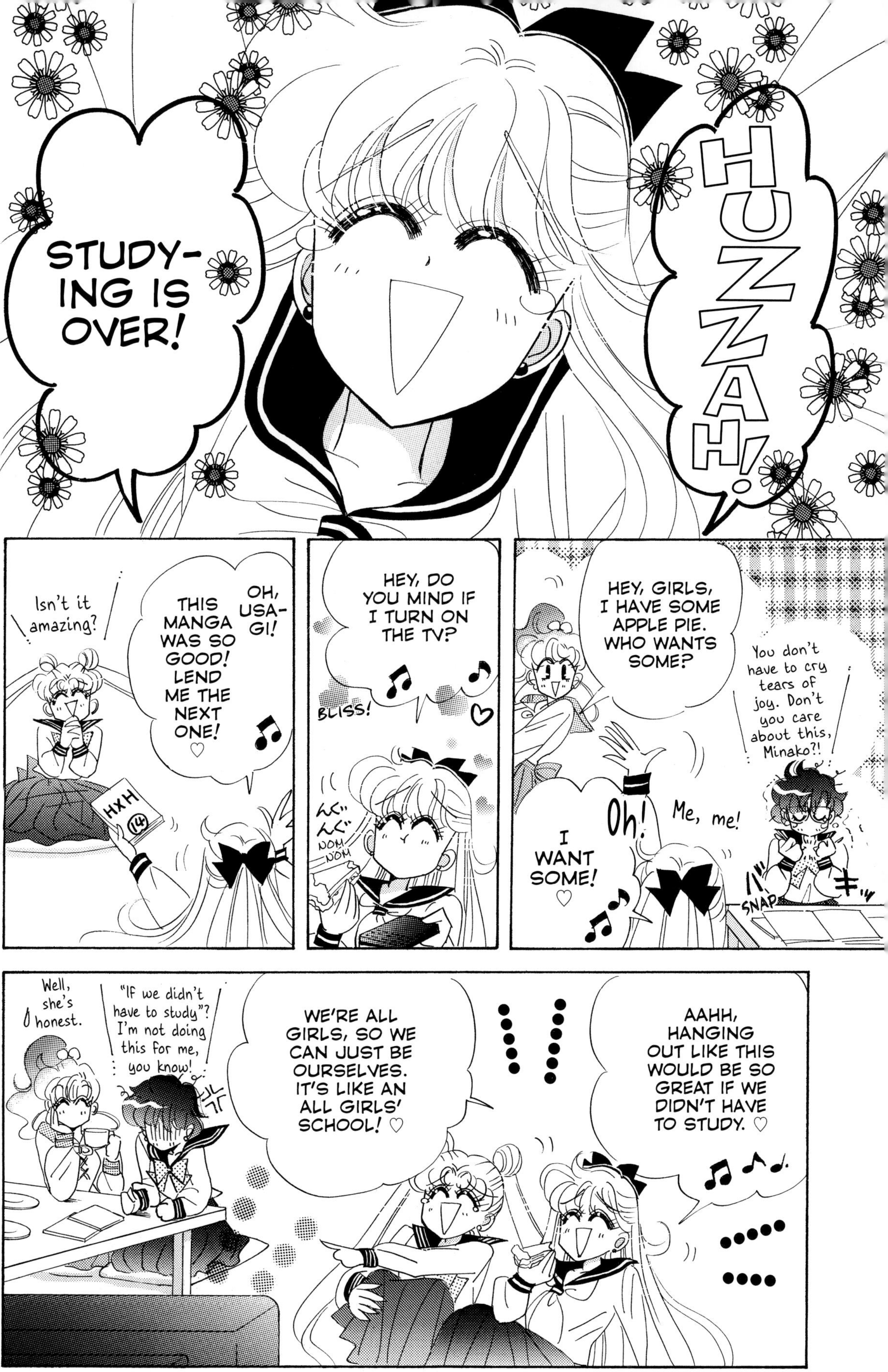
HUZZAH!
STUDYING IS OVER!
HEY, GIRLS, I HAVE SOME APPLE PIE. WHO WANTS SOME?
You don't have to cry tears of joy. Don't you care about this, Minako?!
Oh!
Me, me!
I WANT SOME! ♡
SNAP
HEY, DO YOU MIND IF I TURN ON THE TV?
BLISS!
んぐ んぐ
NOM NOM
OH, USA-GI!
THIS MANGA WAS SO GOOD! LEND ME THE NEXT ONE! ♡
Isn't it amazing?
HxH 14
AAHH, HANGING OUT LIKE THIS WOULD BE SO GREAT IF WE DIDN'T HAVE TO STUDY. ♡
WE'RE ALL GIRLS, SO WE CAN JUST BE OURSELVES. IT'S LIKE AN ALL GIRLS' SCHOOL! ♡
"If we didn't have to study"? I'm not doing this for me, you know!
Well, she's honest.

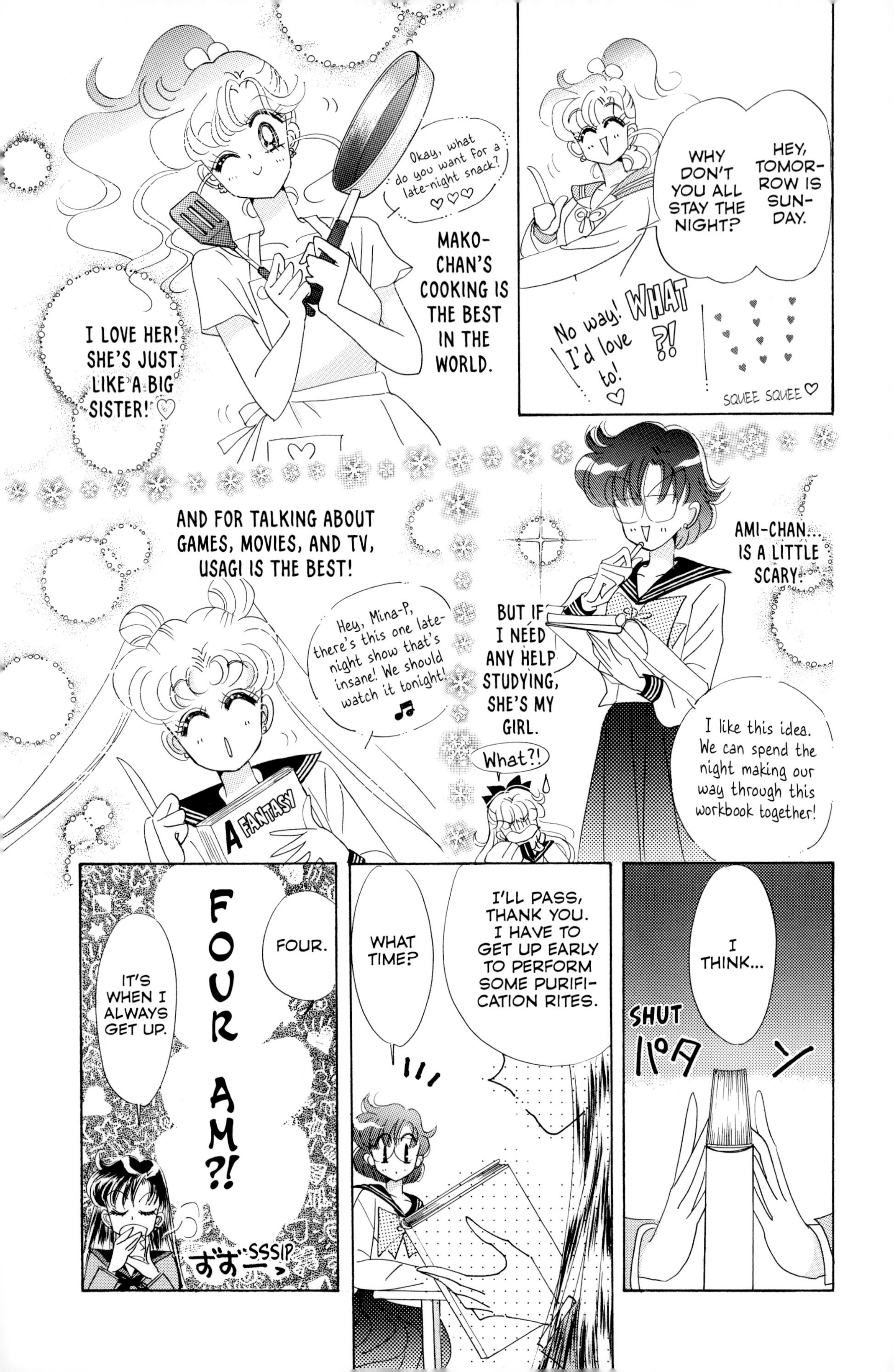
HEY, TOMORROW IS SUNDAY.
WHY DON'T YOU ALL STAY THE NIGHT?
SQUEE SQUEE ♡
WHAT ?!
No way! I'd love to! ♡
Okay, what do you want for a late-night snack? ♡♡♡
MAKO-CHAN'S COOKING IS THE BEST IN THE WORLD.
I LOVE HER! SHE'S JUST LIKE A BIG SISTER! ♡
AMI-CHAN... IS A LITTLE SCARY.
I like this idea. We can spend the night making our way through this workbook together!
BUT IF I NEED ANY HELP STUDYING, SHE'S MY GIRL.
What?!
AND FOR TALKING ABOUT GAMES, MOVIES, AND TV, USAGI IS THE BEST!
Hey, Mina-P, there's this one late-night show that's insane! We should watch it tonight! ♫
A FANTASY
I THINK...
SHUT パタン
I'LL PASS, THANK YOU. I HAVE TO GET UP EARLY TO PERFORM SOME PURIFICATION RITES.
WHAT TIME?
FOUR.
FOUR AM?!
IT'S WHEN I ALWAYS GET UP.
すずー SSSIP

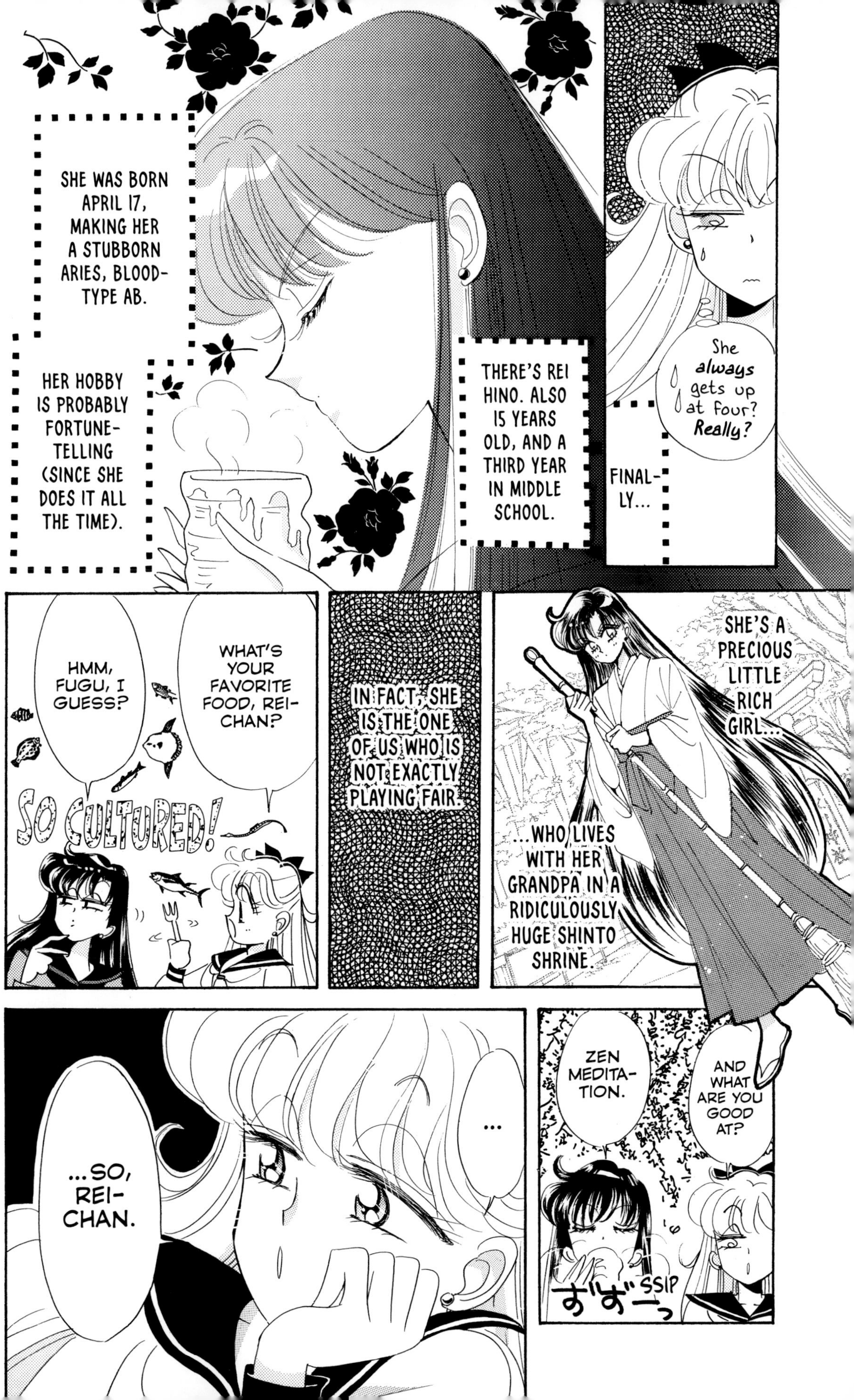
She *always* gets up at four? *Really?*
FINALLY...
THERE'S REI HINO. ALSO 15 YEARS OLD, AND A THIRD YEAR IN MIDDLE SCHOOL.
SHE WAS BORN APRIL 17, MAKING HER A STUBBORN ARIES, BLOOD-TYPE AB.
HER HOBBY IS PROBABLY FORTUNE-TELLING (SINCE SHE DOES IT ALL THE TIME).
SHE'S A PRECIOUS LITTLE RICH GIRL...
...WHO LIVES WITH HER GRANDPA IN A RIDICULOUSLY HUGE SHINTO SHRINE.
IN FACT, SHE IS THE ONE OF US WHO IS NOT EXACTLY PLAYING FAIR.
WHAT'S YOUR FAVORITE FOOD, REI-CHAN?
HMM, FUGU, I GUESS?
SO CULTURED!
AND WHAT ARE YOU GOOD AT?
ZEN MEDITATION.
すずーっ SSIP
...
...SO, REI-CHAN.

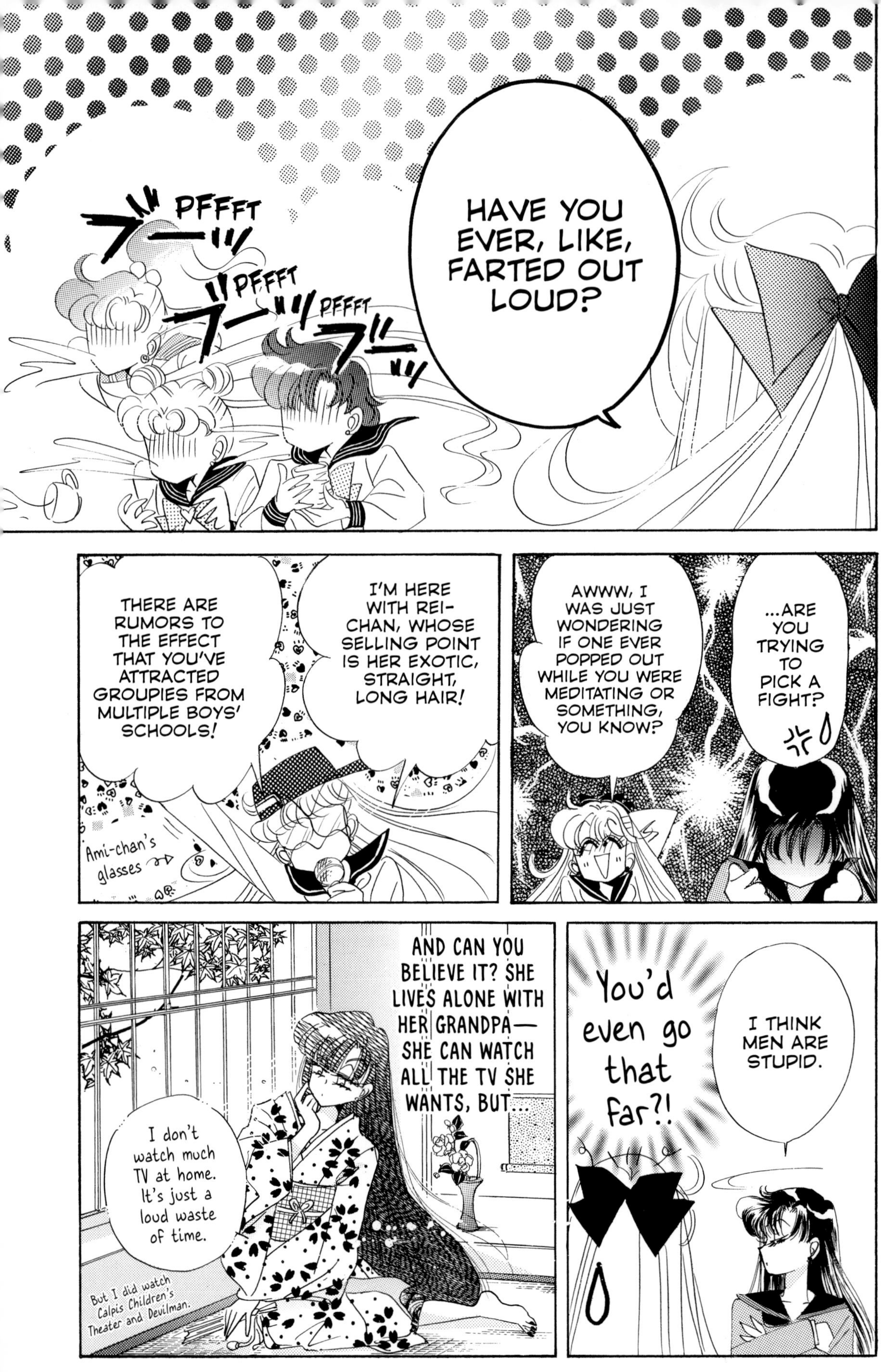
HAVE YOU EVER, LIKE, FARTED OUT LOUD?
PFFFT
PFFFT
PFFFT
...ARE YOU TRYING TO PICK A FIGHT?
AWWW, I WAS JUST WONDERING IF ONE EVER POPPED OUT WHILE YOU WERE MEDITATING OR SOMETHING, YOU KNOW?
I'M HERE WITH REI-CHAN, WHOSE SELLING POINT IS HER EXOTIC, STRAIGHT, LONG HAIR!
THERE ARE RUMORS TO THE EFFECT THAT YOU'VE ATTRACTED GROUPIES FROM MULTIPLE BOYS' SCHOOLS!
Ami-chan's glasses
I THINK MEN ARE STUPID.
You'd even go that far?!
AND CAN YOU BELIEVE IT? SHE LIVES ALONE WITH HER GRANDPA— SHE CAN WATCH ALL THE TV SHE WANTS, BUT...
I don't watch much TV at home. It's just a loud waste of time.
But I did watch Calpis Children's Theater and Devilman.

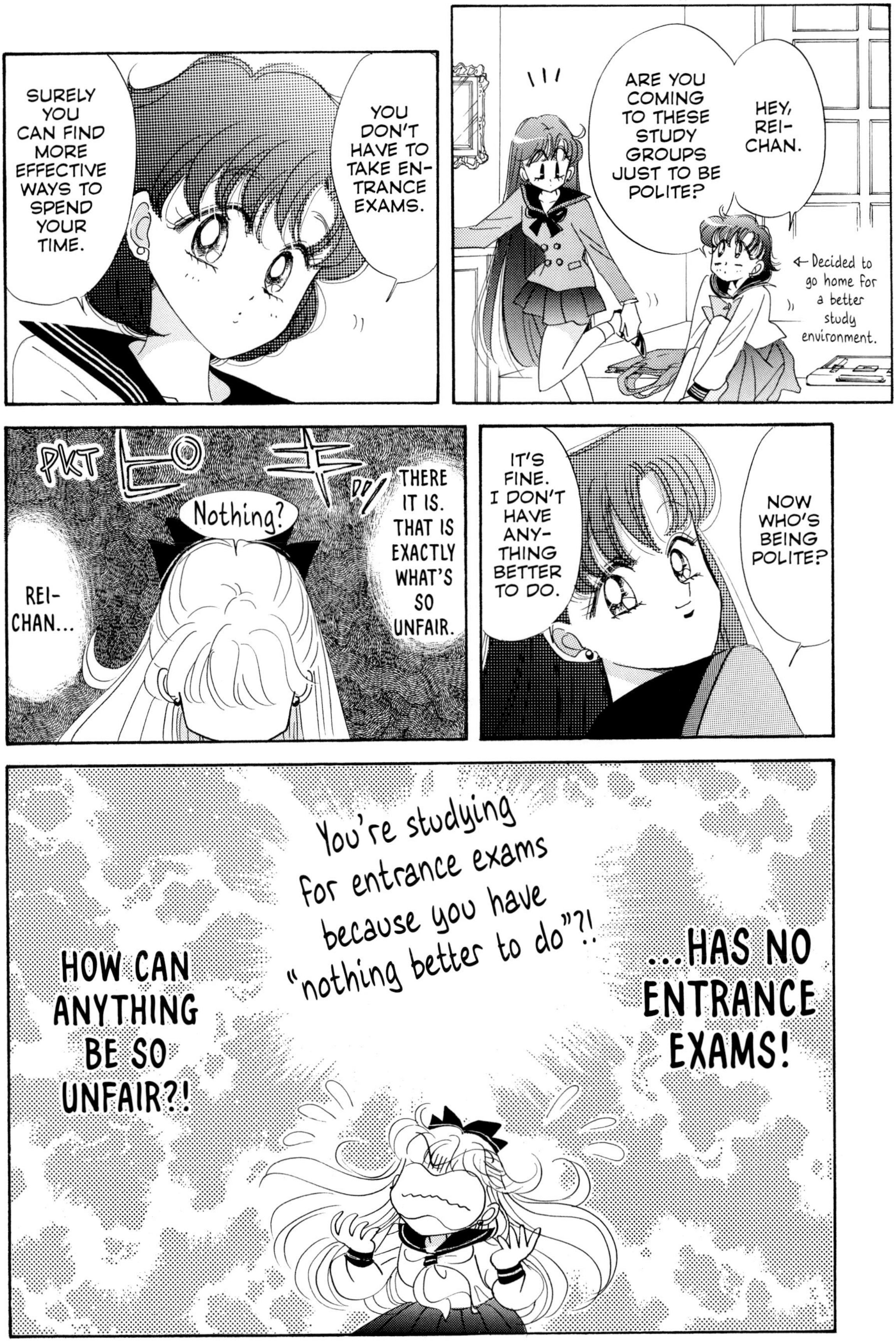
HEY, REI-CHAN.
ARE YOU COMING TO THESE STUDY GROUPS JUST TO BE POLITE?
← Decided to go home for a better study environment.
YOU DON'T HAVE TO TAKE ENTRANCE EXAMS.
SURELY YOU CAN FIND MORE EFFECTIVE WAYS TO SPEND YOUR TIME.
NOW WHO'S BEING POLITE?
IT'S FINE. I DON'T HAVE ANYTHING BETTER TO DO.
THERE IT IS. THAT IS EXACTLY WHAT'S SO UNFAIR.
Nothing?
PKT
REI-CHAN...
You're studying for entrance exams because you have "nothing better to do"?!
...HAS NO ENTRANCE EXAMS!
HOW CAN ANYTHING BE SO UNFAIR?!

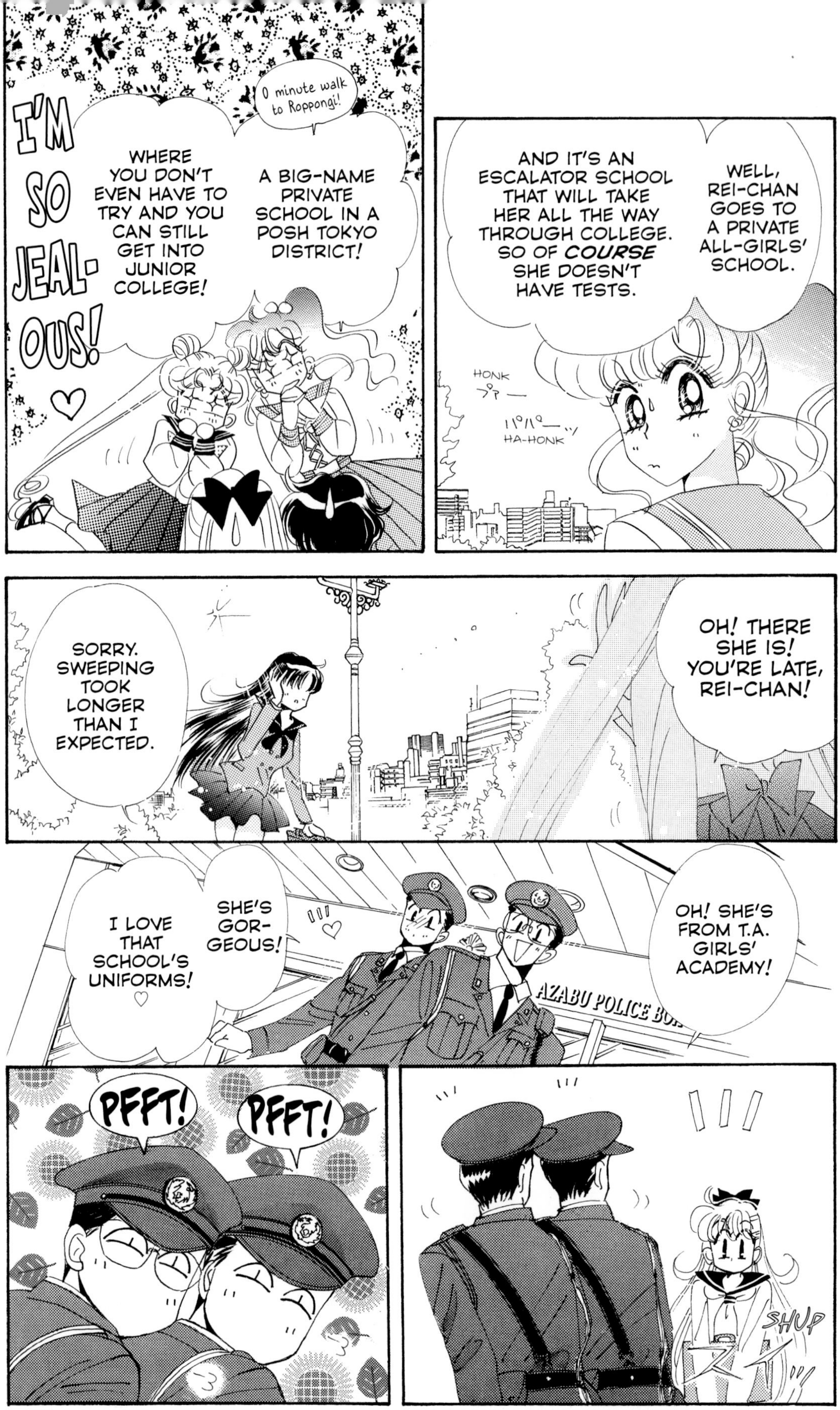
WELL, REI-CHAN GOES TO A PRIVATE ALL-GIRLS' SCHOOL.
AND IT'S AN ESCALATOR SCHOOL THAT WILL TAKE HER ALL THE WAY THROUGH COLLEGE. SO OF *COURSE* SHE DOESN'T HAVE TESTS.
HONK
プァー
パパー ッ
HA-HONK
A BIG-NAME PRIVATE SCHOOL IN A POSH TOKYO DISTRICT!
0 minute walk to Roppongi!
WHERE YOU DON'T EVEN HAVE TO TRY AND YOU CAN STILL GET INTO JUNIOR COLLEGE!
I'M SO JEAL-OUS!
OH! THERE SHE IS! YOU'RE LATE, REI-CHAN!
SORRY. SWEEPING TOOK LONGER THAN I EXPECTED.
OH! SHE'S FROM T.A. GIRLS' ACADEMY!
SHE'S GOR-GEOUS!
I LOVE THAT SCHOOL'S UNIFORMS!
SHUP
スイ
PFFT!
PFFT!

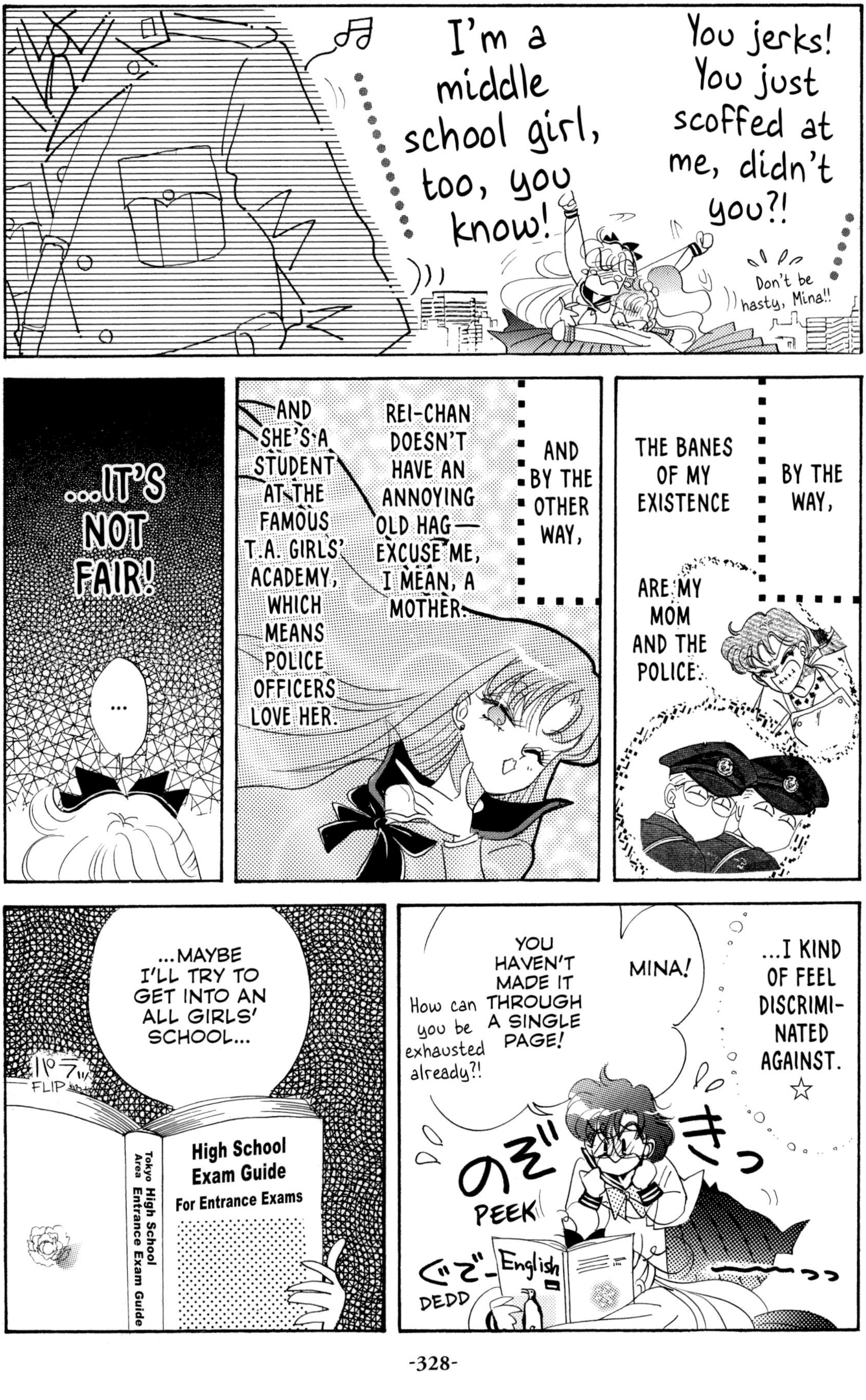
You jerks! You just scoffed at me, didn't you?!
I'm a middle school girl, too, you know!
Don't be hasty, Mina!!
BY THE WAY,
THE BANES OF MY EXISTENCE
ARE MY MOM AND THE POLICE.
AND BY THE OTHER WAY,
REI-CHAN DOESN'T HAVE AN ANNOYING OLD HAG— EXCUSE ME, I MEAN, A MOTHER.
AND SHE'S A STUDENT AT THE FAMOUS T.A. GIRLS' ACADEMY, WHICH MEANS POLICE OFFICERS LOVE HER.
...IT'S NOT FAIR!
...
...I KIND OF FEEL DISCRIMINATED AGAINST. ☆
MINA!
YOU HAVEN'T MADE IT THROUGH A SINGLE PAGE!
How can you be exhausted already?!
きっ
のぞ
PEEK
English
ぐでー
DEDD
...MAYBE I'LL TRY TO GET INTO AN ALL GIRLS' SCHOOL...
パラッ
FLIP
High School Exam Guide
For Entrance Exams
Tokyo Area High School Entrance Exam Guide

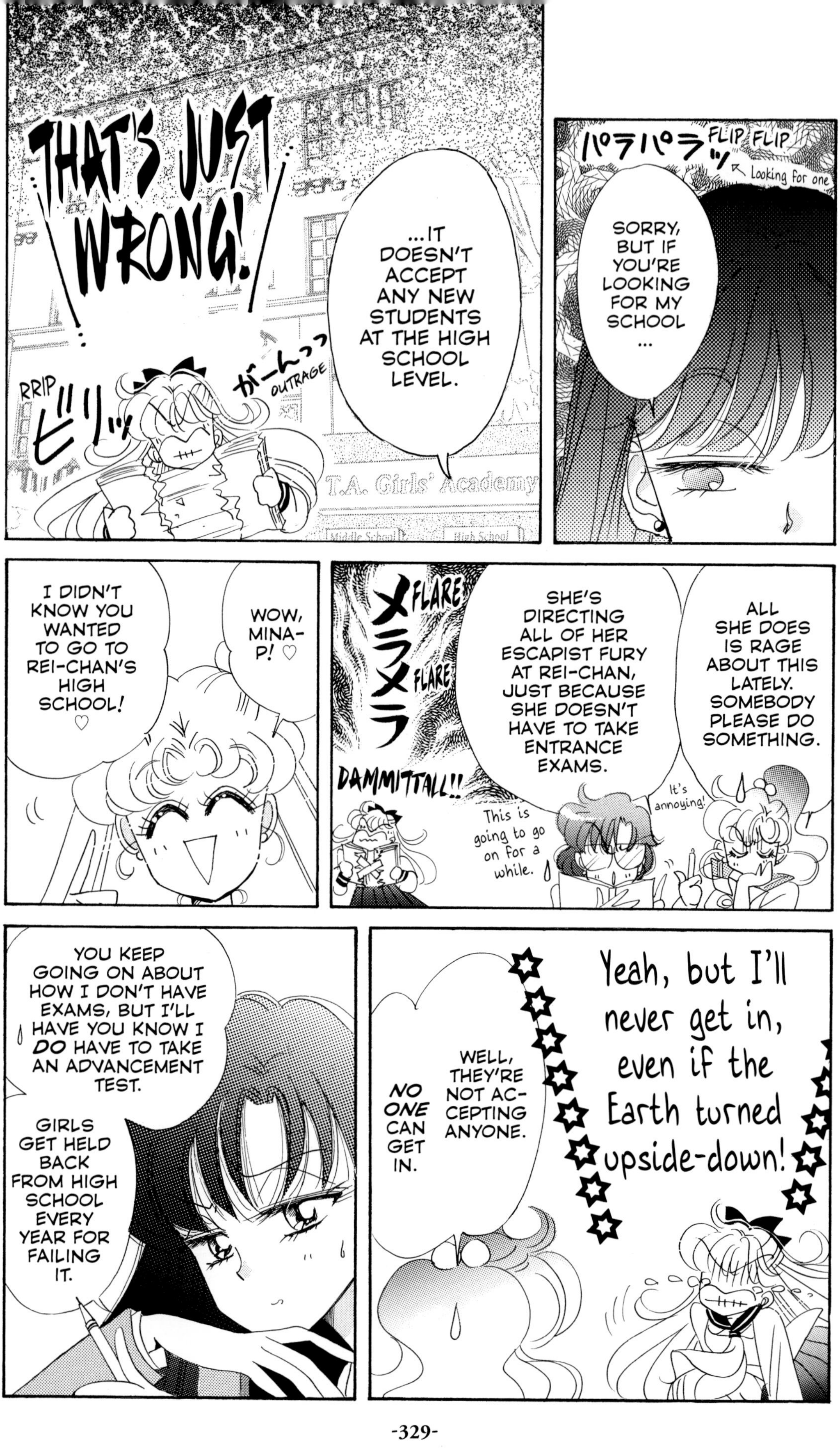
パラパラッ FLIP FLIP
Looking for one
SORRY, BUT IF YOU'RE LOOKING FOR MY SCHOOL ...
...IT DOESN'T ACCEPT ANY NEW STUDENTS AT THE HIGH SCHOOL LEVEL.
THAT'S JUST WRONG!
がーんっっ OUTRAGE
ビリッ RRIP
T.A. Girls' Academy
Middle School
High School
ALL SHE DOES IS RAGE ABOUT THIS LATELY. SOMEBODY PLEASE DO SOMETHING.
SHE'S DIRECTING ALL OF HER ESCAPIST FURY AT REI-CHAN, JUST BECAUSE SHE DOESN'T HAVE TO TAKE ENTRANCE EXAMS.
メラメラ FLARE FLARE
It's annoying!
This is going to go on for a while.
DAMMITTALL!!
WOW, MINA-P! ♡
I DIDN'T KNOW YOU WANTED TO GO TO REI-CHAN'S HIGH SCHOOL! ♡
Yeah, but I'll never get in, even if the Earth turned upside-down!
WELL, THEY'RE NOT AC-CEPTING ANYONE.
NO ONE CAN GET IN.
YOU KEEP GOING ON ABOUT HOW I DON'T HAVE EXAMS, BUT I'LL HAVE YOU KNOW I DO HAVE TO TAKE AN ADVANCEMENT TEST.
GIRLS GET HELD BACK FROM HIGH SCHOOL EVERY YEAR FOR FAILING IT.

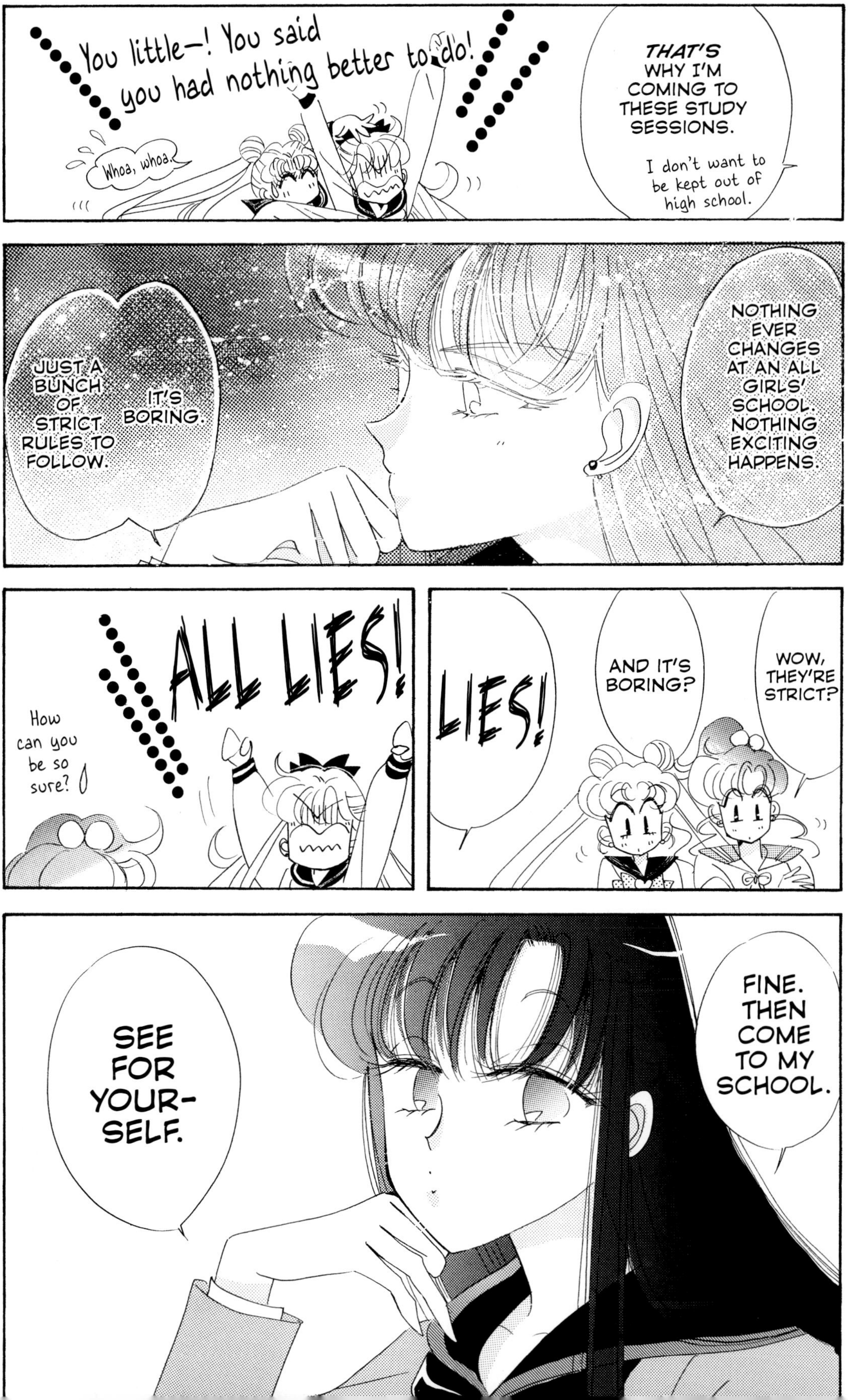
THAT'S WHY I'M COMING TO THESE STUDY SESSIONS.
I don't want to be kept out of high school.
You little—! You said you had nothing better to do!
Whoa, whoa.
NOTHING EVER CHANGES AT AN ALL GIRLS' SCHOOL. NOTHING EXCITING HAPPENS.
JUST A BUNCH OF STRICT RULES TO FOLLOW.
IT'S BORING.
WOW, THEY'RE STRICT?
AND IT'S BORING?
LIES!
ALL LIES!
How can you be so sure?
FINE. THEN COME TO MY SCHOOL.
SEE FOR YOURSELF.

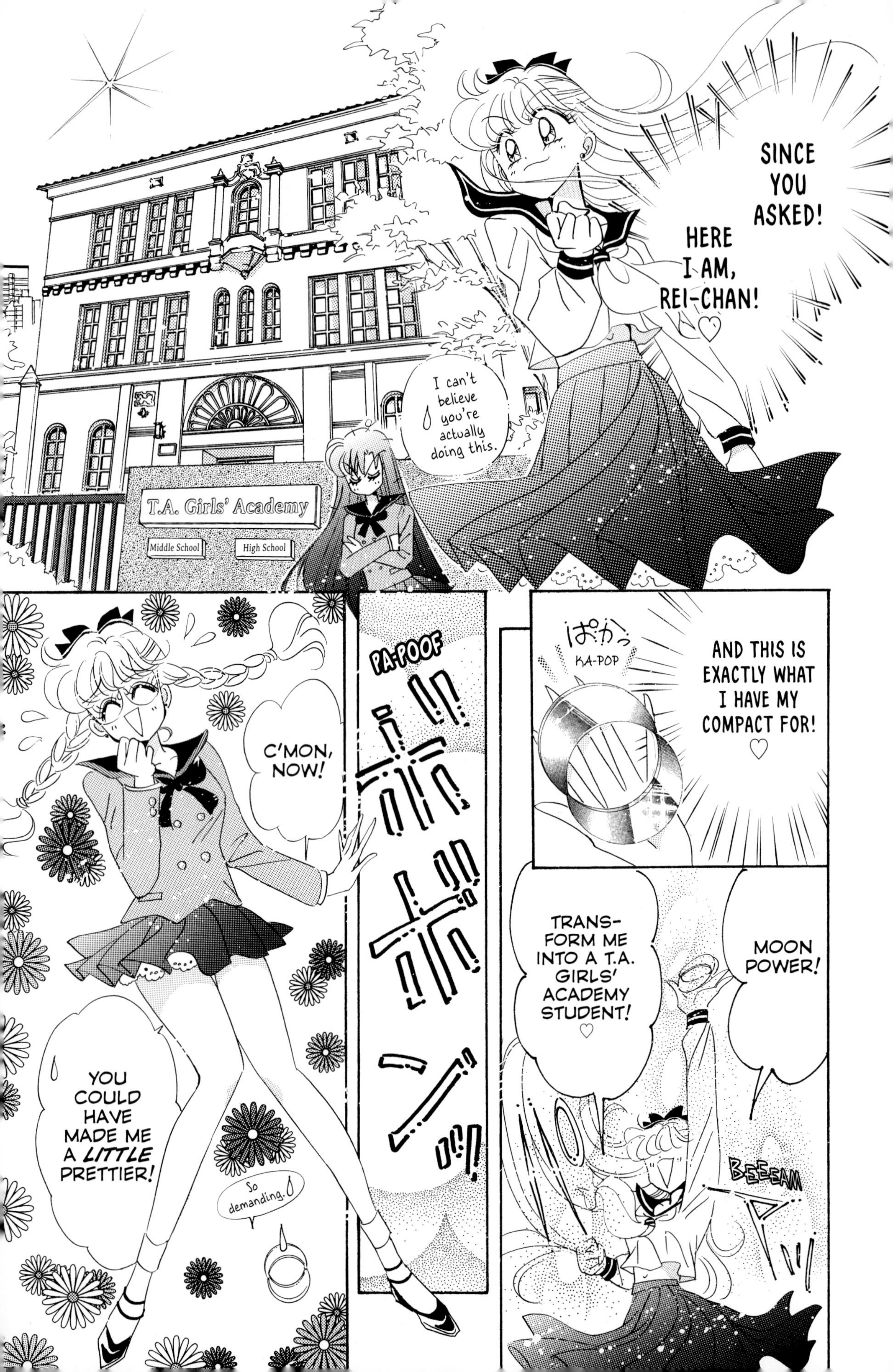
SINCE YOU ASKED!
HERE I AM, REI-CHAN! ♡
I can't believe you're actually doing this.
T.A. Girls' Academy
Middle School
High School
ぱかっ
KA-POP
AND THIS IS EXACTLY WHAT I HAVE MY COMPACT FOR! ♡
MOON POWER!
TRANS-FORM ME INTO A T.A. GIRLS' ACADEMY STUDENT! ♡
BEEEAM
PA-POOF
C'MON, NOW!
YOU COULD HAVE MADE ME A *LITTLE* PRETTIER!
So demanding.

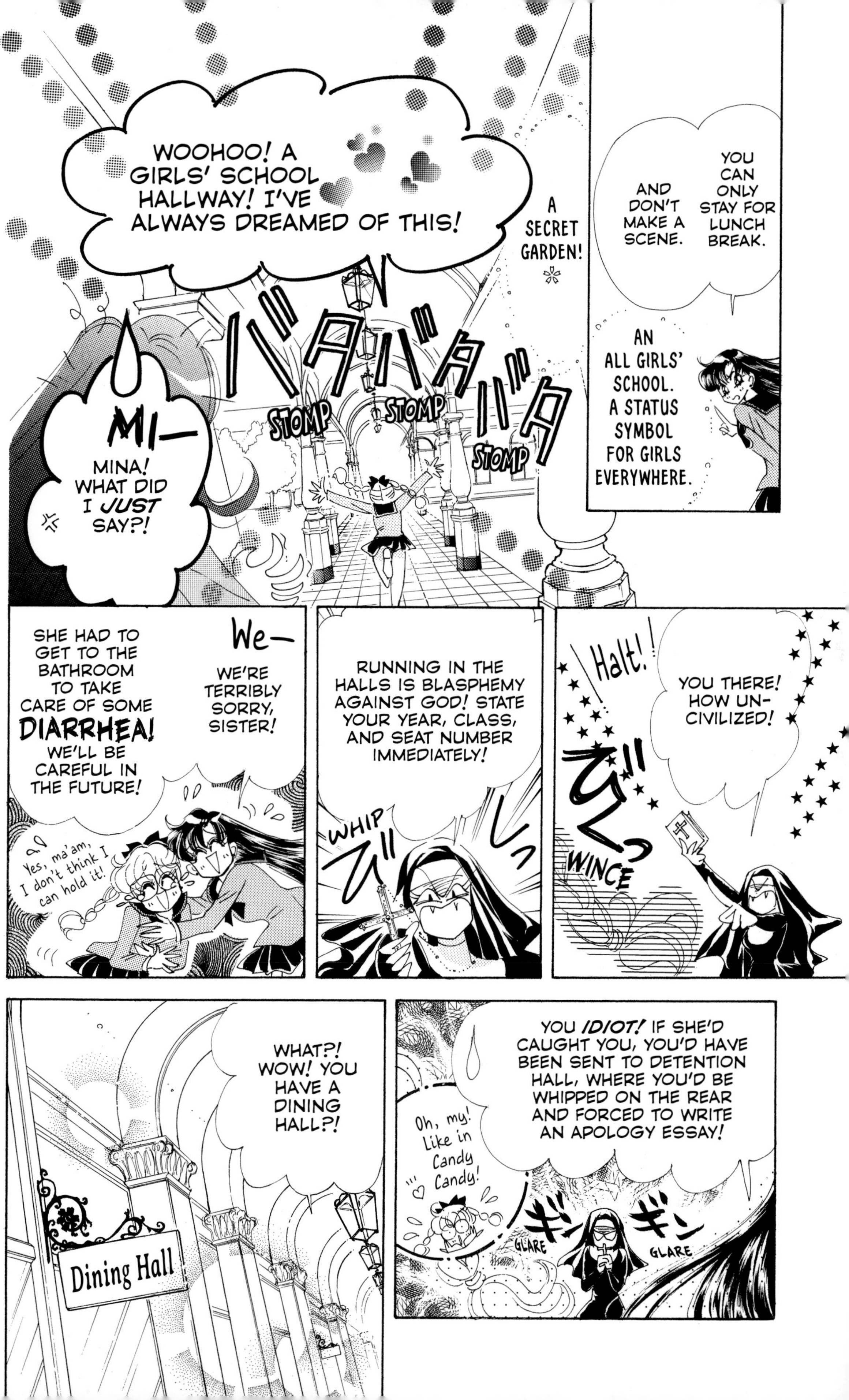

YOU CAN ONLY STAY FOR LUNCH BREAK.
AND DON'T MAKE A SCENE.
AN ALL GIRLS' SCHOOL. A STATUS SYMBOL FOR GIRLS EVERYWHERE.
A SECRET GARDEN!
WOOHOO! A GIRLS' SCHOOL HALLWAY! I'VE ALWAYS DREAMED OF THIS!
STOMP
STOMP
STOMP
MI—
MINA! WHAT DID I JUST SAY?!
Halt!
YOU THERE! HOW UN-CIVILIZED!
WINCE
RUNNING IN THE HALLS IS BLASPHEMY AGAINST GOD! STATE YOUR YEAR, CLASS, AND SEAT NUMBER IMMEDIATELY!
WHIP
We—
WE'RE TERRIBLY SORRY, SISTER!
SHE HAD TO GET TO THE BATHROOM TO TAKE CARE OF SOME DIARRHEA! WE'LL BE CAREFUL IN THE FUTURE!
Yes, ma'am, I don't think I can hold it!
YOU IDIOT! IF SHE'D CAUGHT YOU, YOU'D HAVE BEEN SENT TO DETENTION HALL, WHERE YOU'D BE WHIPPED ON THE REAR AND FORCED TO WRITE AN APOLOGY ESSAY!
Oh, my! Like in Candy Candy!
GLARE
GLARE
WHAT?! WOW! YOU HAVE A DINING HALL?!
Dining Hall

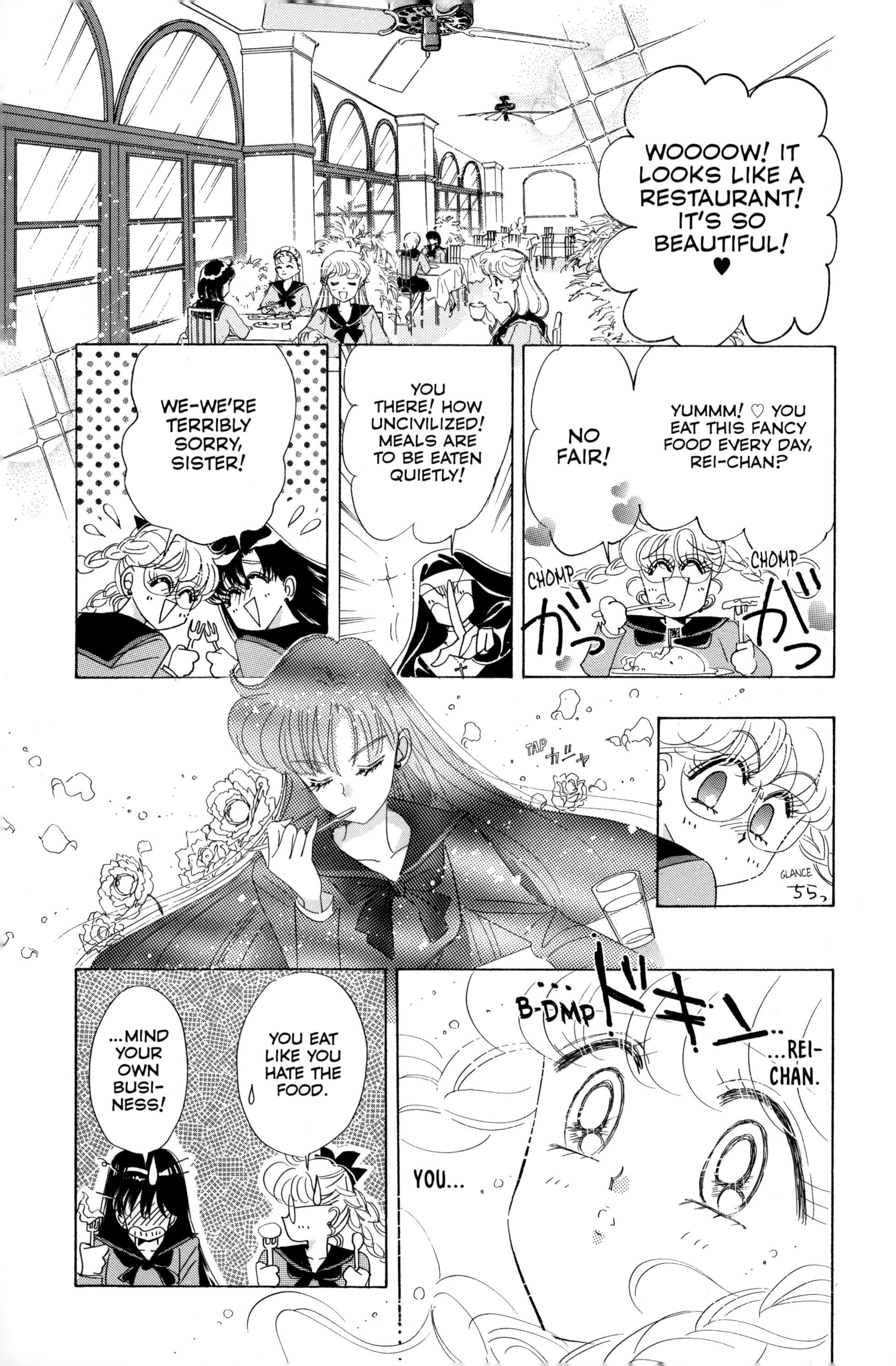
WOOOOW! IT LOOKS LIKE A RESTAURANT! IT'S SO BEAUTIFUL! ♥
YUMMM! ♡ YOU EAT THIS FANCY FOOD EVERY DAY, REI-CHAN?
NO FAIR!
CHOMP がっ
CHOMP がっ
YOU THERE! HOW UNCIVILIZED! MEALS ARE TO BE EATEN QUIETLY!
WE-WE'RE TERRIBLY SORRY, SISTER!
GLANCE ちらっ
TAP カチャ
B-DMP ドキン
...REI-CHAN.
YOU...
YOU EAT LIKE YOU HATE THE FOOD.
...MIND YOUR OWN BUSINESS!

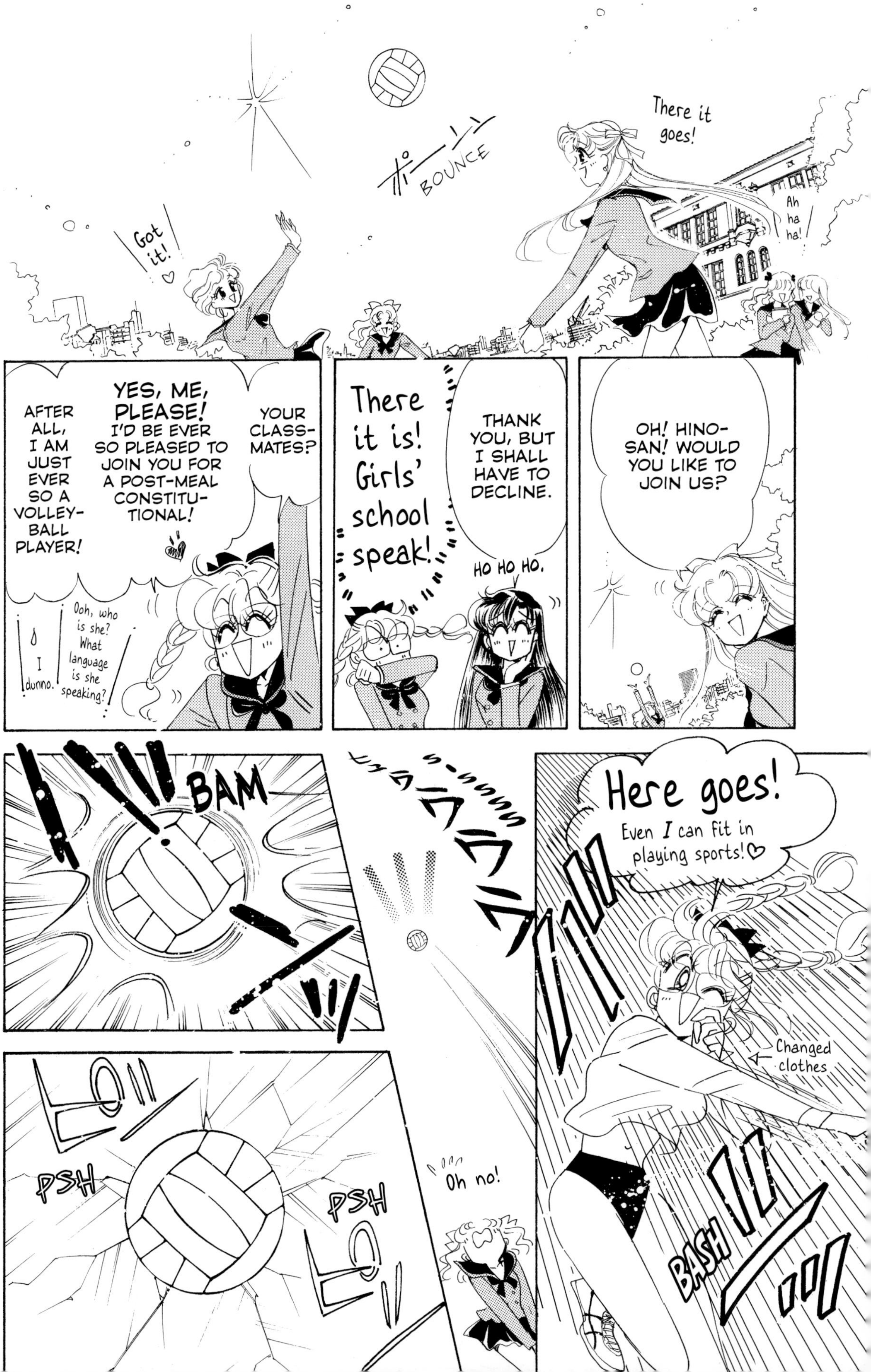
There it goes!
Ah ha ha!
BOUNCE
Got it!
OH! HINO-SAN! WOULD YOU LIKE TO JOIN US?
THANK YOU, BUT I SHALL HAVE TO DECLINE.
HO HO HO.
There it is! Girls' school speak!
YOUR CLASSMATES?
YES, ME, PLEASE! I'D BE EVER SO PLEASED TO JOIN YOU FOR A POST-MEAL CONSTITUTIONAL!
AFTER ALL, I AM JUST EVER SO A VOLLEYBALL PLAYER!
Ooh, who is she? What language is she speaking?
I dunno.
Here goes!
Even I can fit in playing sports!
Changed clothes
BASH
BAM
ssssss-
Oh no!
PSH
PSH

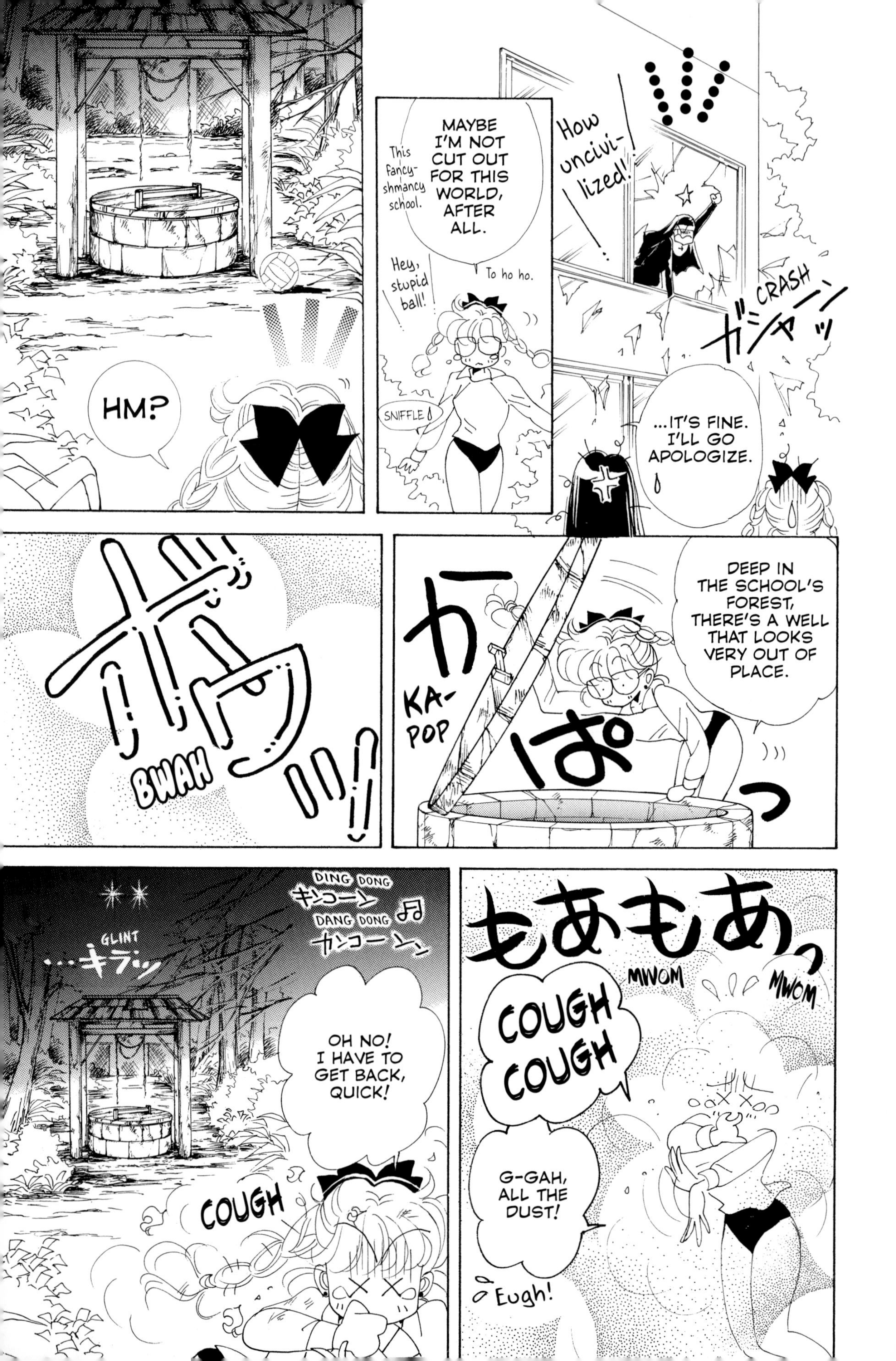
How uncivi-lized!
ガシャーンッ
CRASH
...IT'S FINE. I'LL GO APOLOGIZE.
This fancy-shmancy school.
MAYBE I'M NOT CUT OUT FOR THIS WORLD, AFTER ALL.
To ho ho.
Hey, stupid ball!
SNIFFLE
HM?
DEEP IN THE SCHOOL'S FOREST, THERE'S A WELL THAT LOOKS VERY OUT OF PLACE.
かぽっ
KA-POP
ボワッ
BWAH
もあもあっ
MWOM
MWOM
COUGH COUGH
G-GAH, ALL THE DUST!
Eugh!
キンコーン
DING DONG
カンコーン
DANG DONG
キラッ
GLINT
OH NO! I HAVE TO GET BACK, QUICK!
COUGH

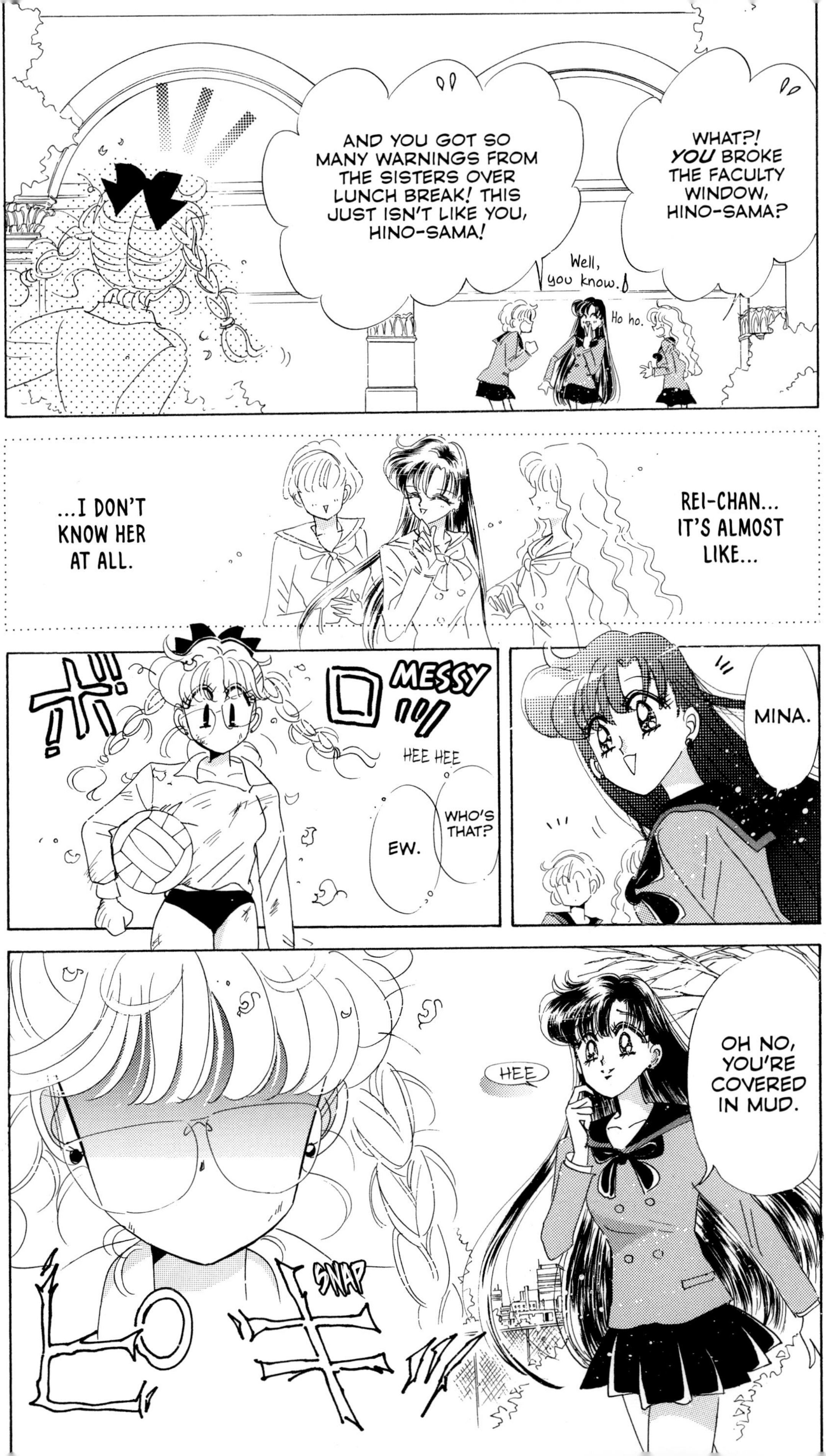
WHAT?! YOU BROKE THE FACULTY WINDOW, HINO-SAMA?
AND YOU GOT SO MANY WARNINGS FROM THE SISTERS OVER LUNCH BREAK! THIS JUST ISN'T LIKE YOU, HINO-SAMA!
Well, you know.
Ho ho.
REI-CHAN... IT'S ALMOST LIKE...
...I DON'T KNOW HER AT ALL.
MINA.
MESSY
HEE HEE
WHO'S THAT?
EW.
OH NO, YOU'RE COVERED IN MUD.
HEE
SNAP

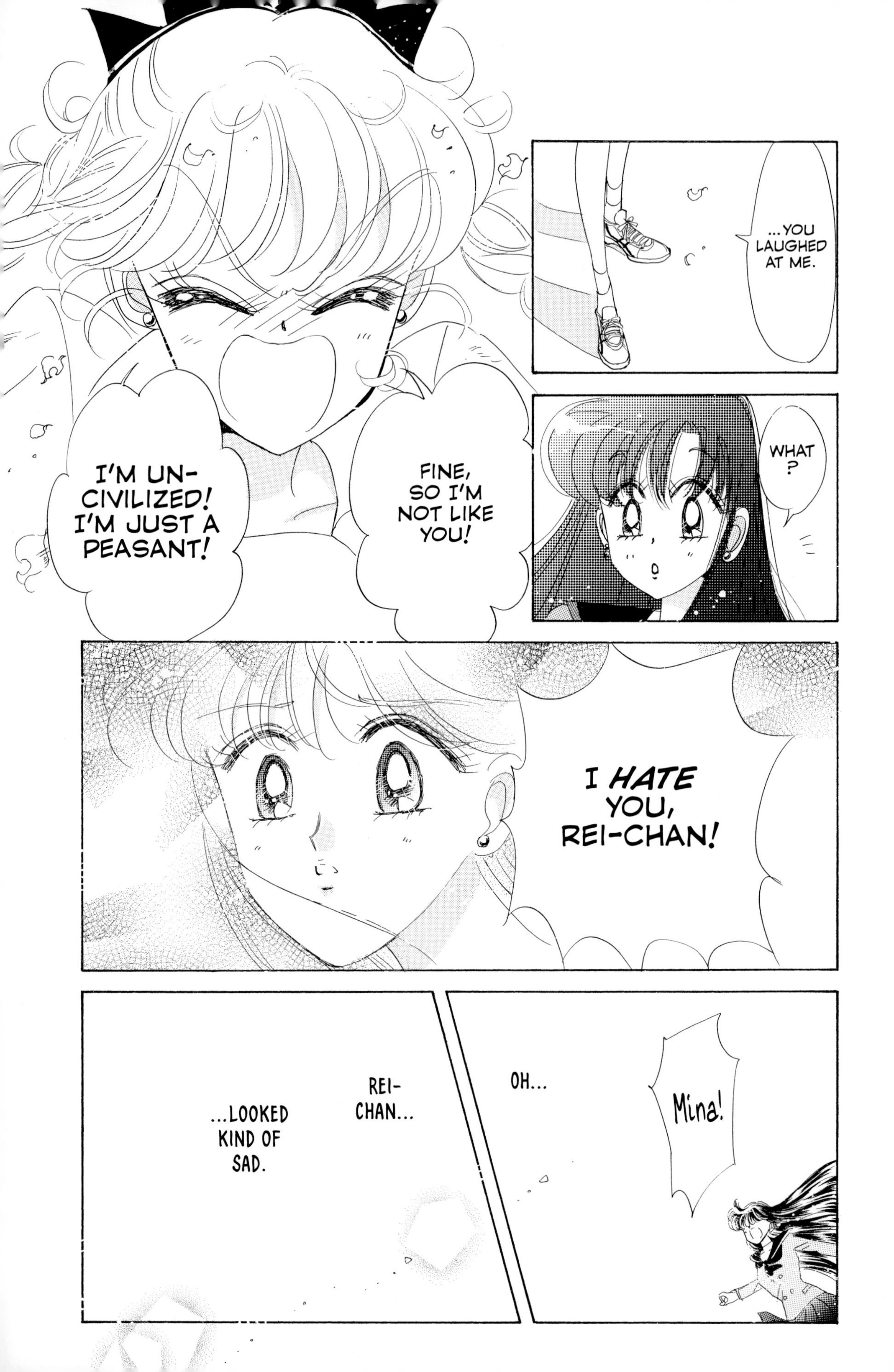
...YOU LAUGHED AT ME.
WHAT?
FINE, SO I'M NOT LIKE YOU!
I'M UN-CIVILIZED! I'M JUST A PEASANT!
I HATE YOU, REI-CHAN!
Mina!
OH...
REI-CHAN...
...LOOKED KIND OF SAD.

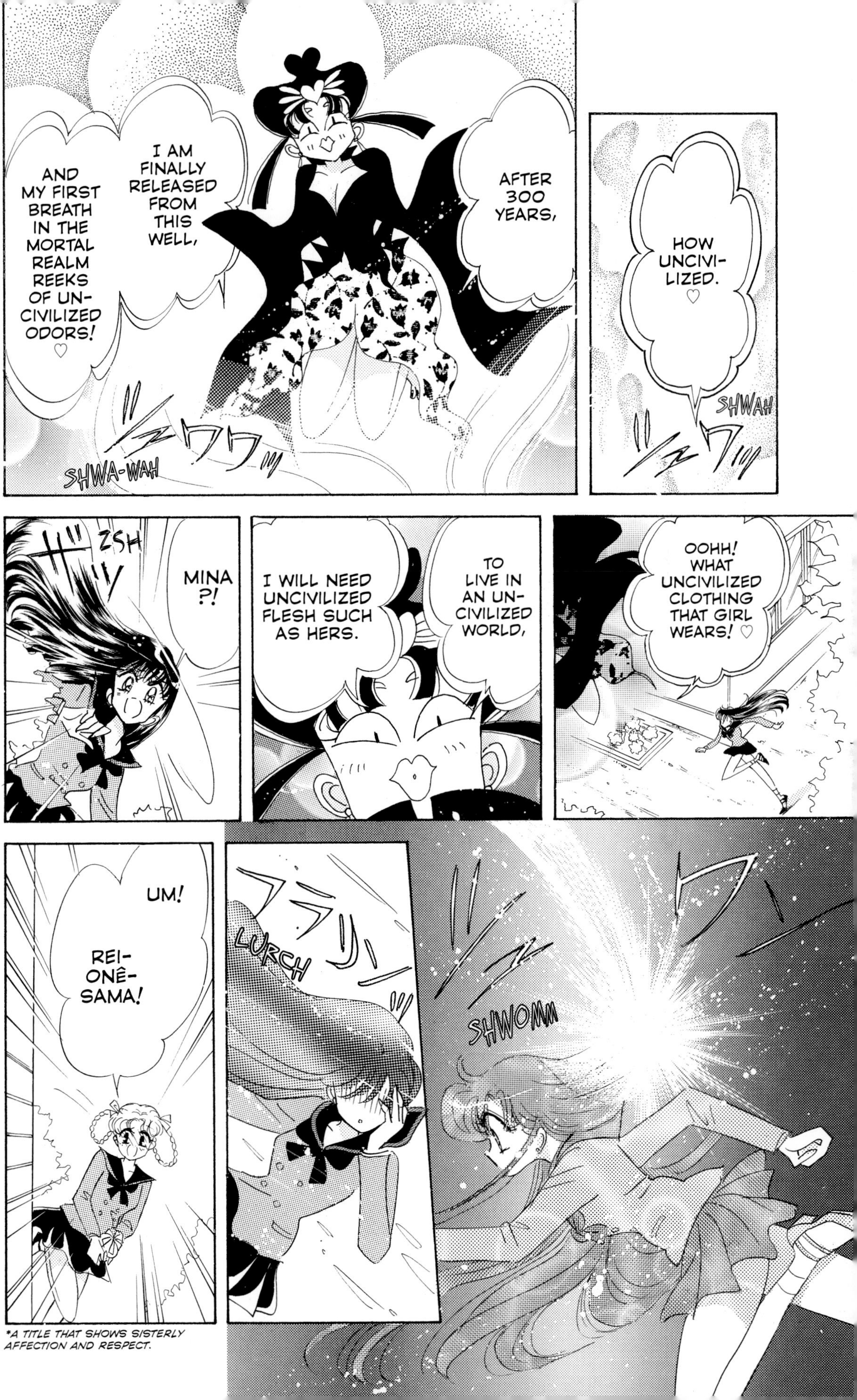
HOW UNCIVILIZED. ♡
SHWAH
AFTER 300 YEARS,
I AM FINALLY RELEASED FROM THIS WELL,
AND MY FIRST BREATH IN THE MORTAL REALM REEKS OF UN-CIVILIZED ODORS! ♡
SHWA-WAH
OOHH! WHAT UNCIVILIZED CLOTHING THAT GIRL WEARS! ♡
TO LIVE IN AN UN-CIVILIZED WORLD,
I WILL NEED UNCIVILIZED FLESH SUCH AS HERS.
ZSH
MINA ?!
SHWOMM
LURCH
UM!
REI-ONÊ-SAMA!

*A TITLE THAT SHOWS SISTERLY AFFECTION AND RESPECT.

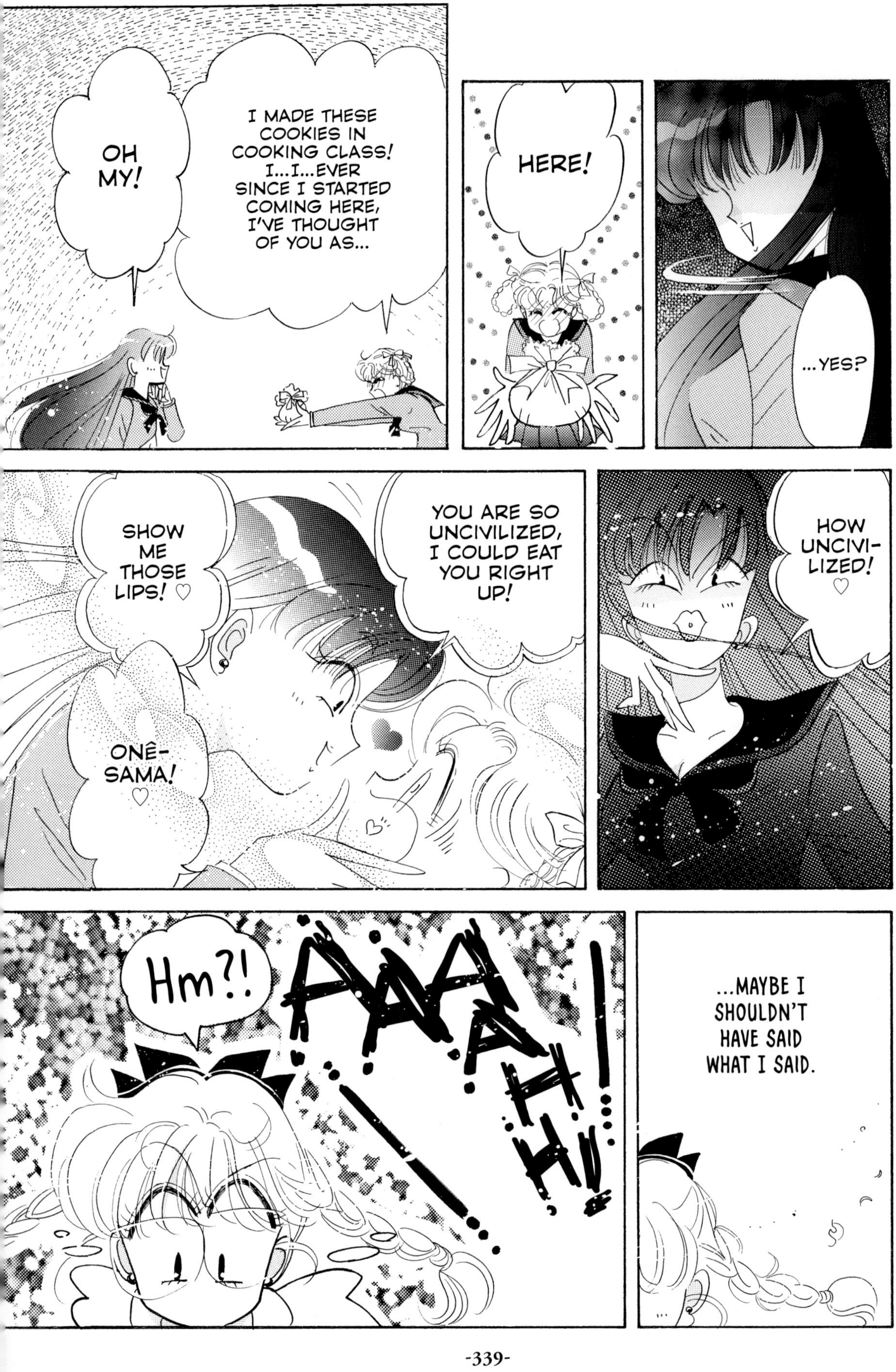
...YES?
HERE!
I MADE THESE COOKIES IN COOKING CLASS! I...I...EVER SINCE I STARTED COMING HERE, I'VE THOUGHT OF YOU AS...
OH MY!
HOW UNCIVI-LIZED! ♡
YOU ARE SO UNCIVILIZED, I COULD EAT YOU RIGHT UP!
SHOW ME THOSE LIPS! ♡
ONÊ-SAMA! ♡
...MAYBE I SHOULDN'T HAVE SAID WHAT I SAID.
Hm?!

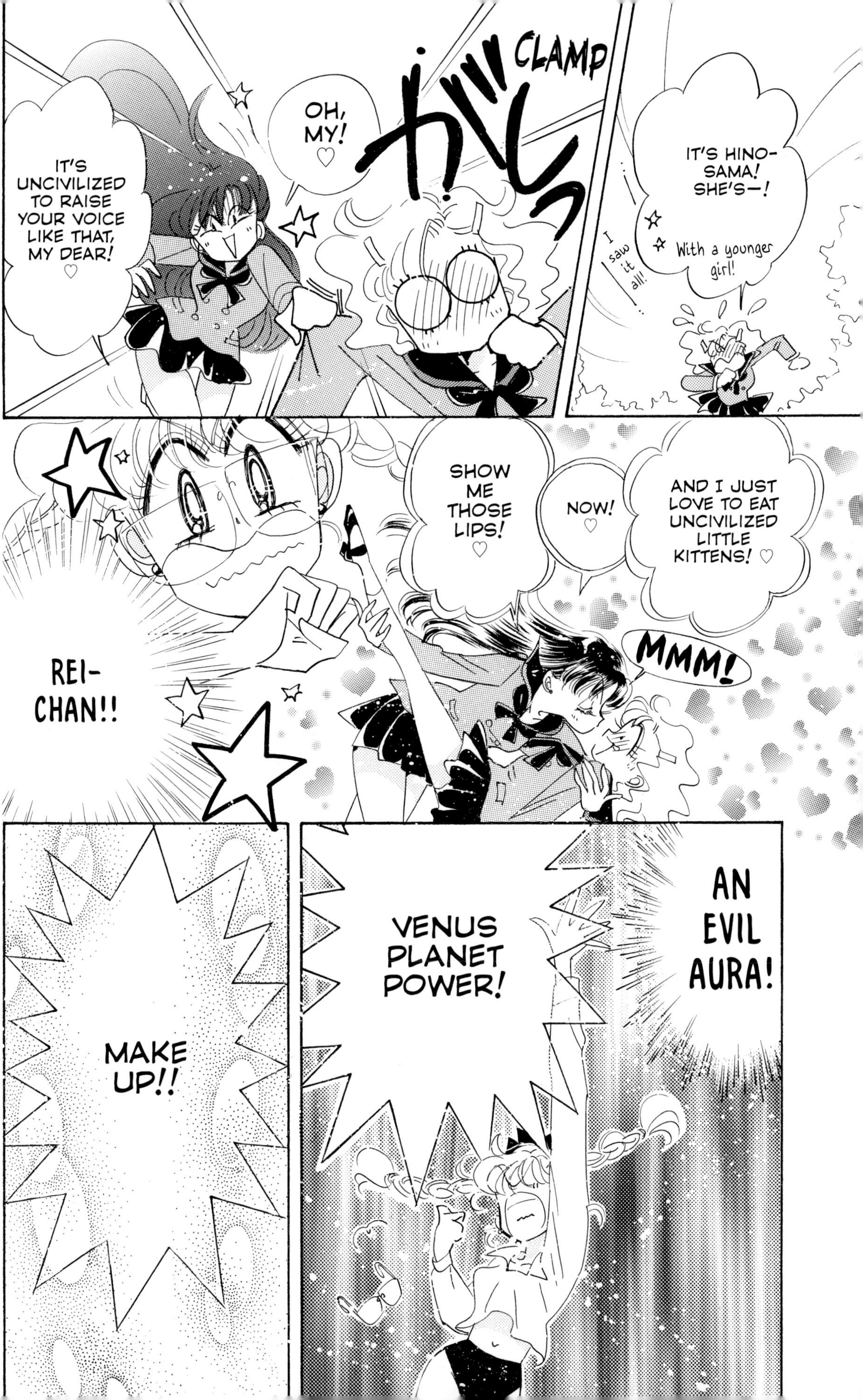
IT'S HINO-SAMA! SHE'S—!
With a younger girl!
I saw it all!
CLAMP
OH, MY! ♡
IT'S UNCIVILIZED TO RAISE YOUR VOICE LIKE THAT, MY DEAR! ♡
AND I JUST LOVE TO EAT UNCIVILIZED LITTLE KITTENS! ♡
NOW! ♡
SHOW ME THOSE LIPS! ♡
MMM!
REI-CHAN!!
AN EVIL AURA!
VENUS PLANET POWER!
MAKE UP!!

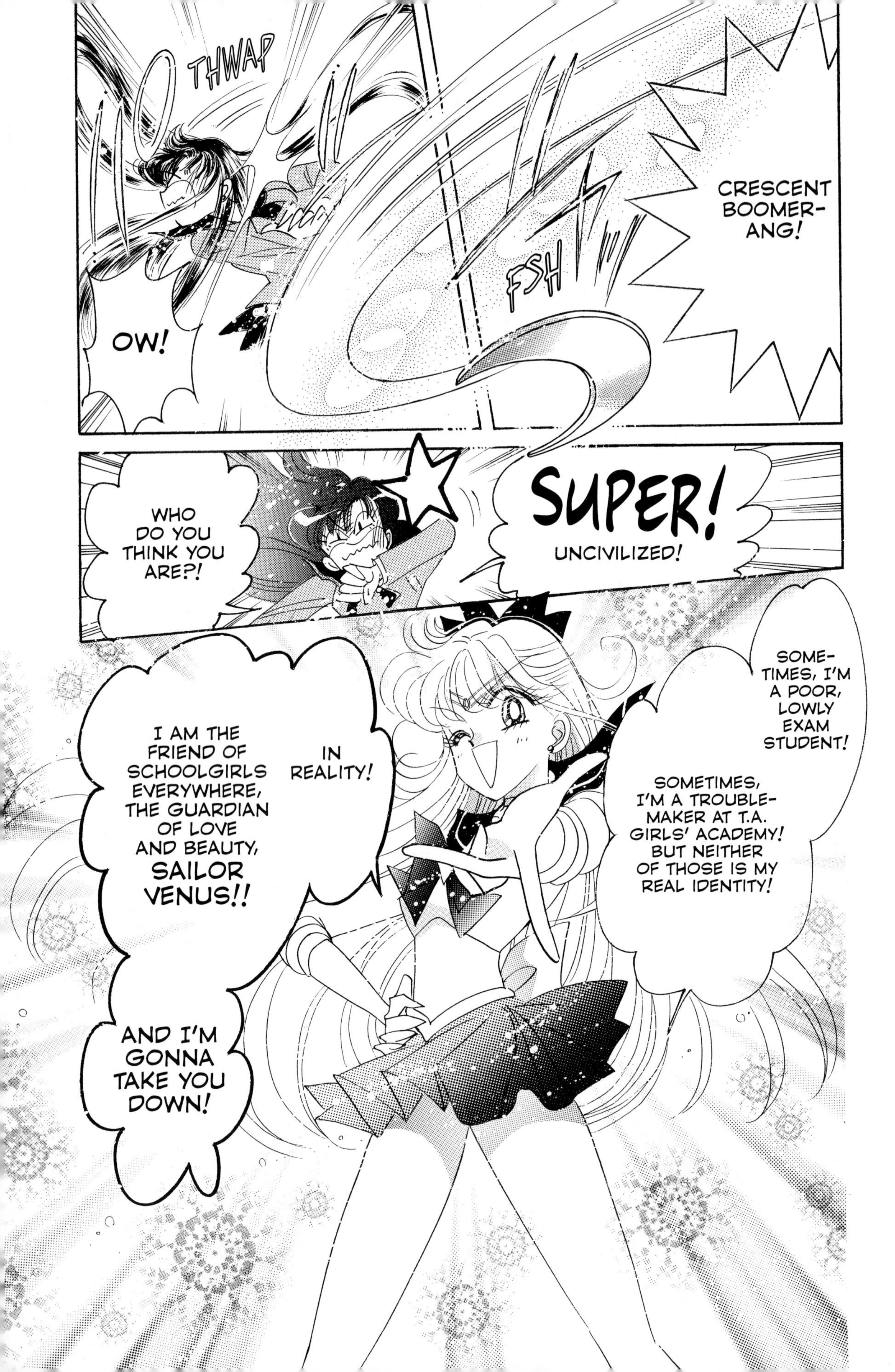
CRESCENT BOOMER-ANG!
FSH
THWAP
OW!
SUPER! UNCIVILIZED!
WHO DO YOU THINK YOU ARE?!
SOME-TIMES, I'M A POOR, LOWLY EXAM STUDENT!
SOMETIMES, I'M A TROUBLE-MAKER AT T.A. GIRLS' ACADEMY! BUT NEITHER OF THOSE IS MY REAL IDENTITY!
IN REALITY!
I AM THE FRIEND OF SCHOOLGIRLS EVERYWHERE, THE GUARDIAN OF LOVE AND BEAUTY, SAILOR VENUS!!
AND I'M GONNA TAKE YOU DOWN!

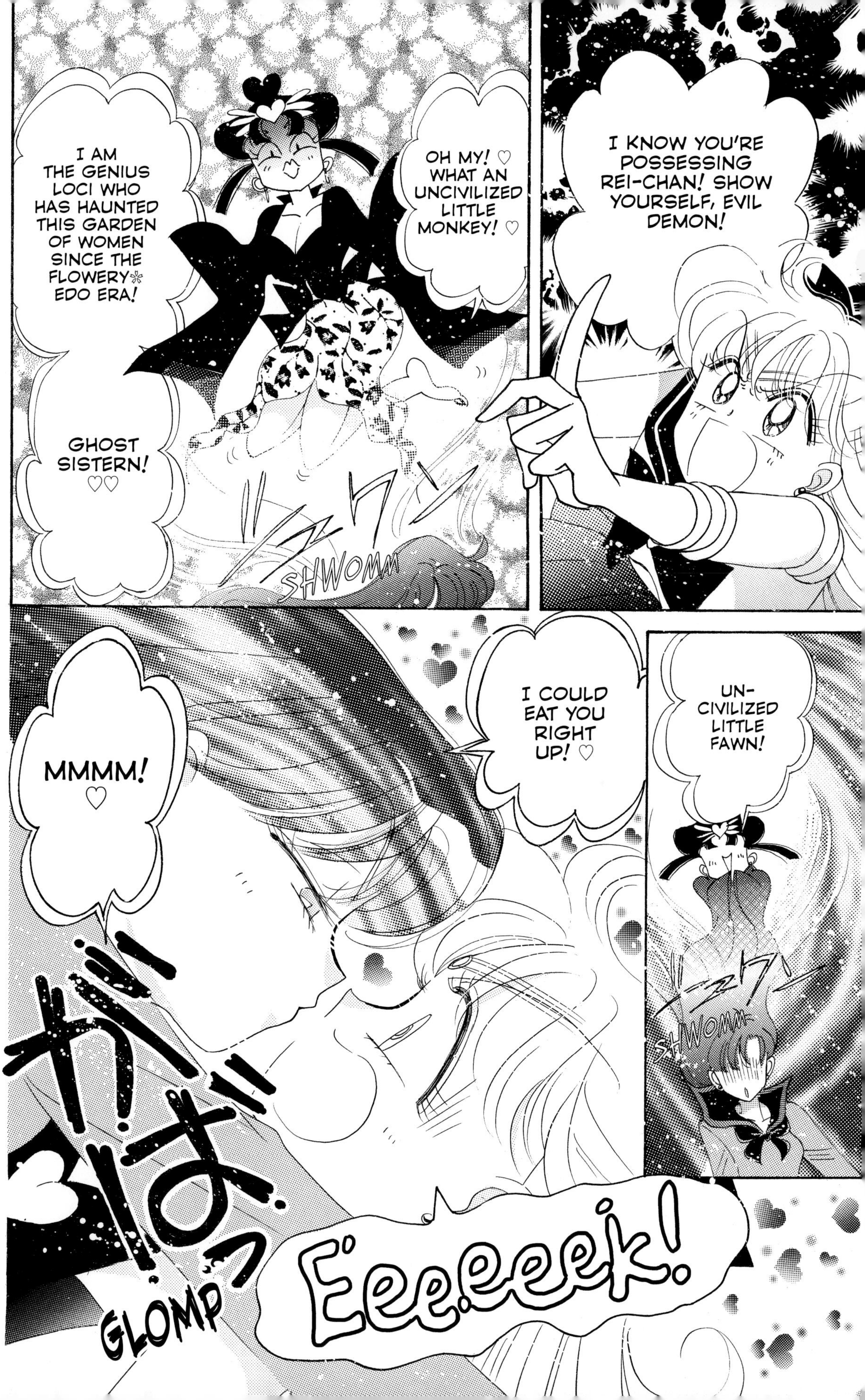
I KNOW YOU'RE POSSESSING REI-CHAN! SHOW YOURSELF, EVIL DEMON!
OH MY! ♡ WHAT AN UNCIVILIZED LITTLE MONKEY! ♡
I AM THE GENIUS LOCI WHO HAS HAUNTED THIS GARDEN OF WOMEN SINCE THE FLOWERY❀ EDO ERA!
GHOST SISTERN! ♡♡
SHWOMM
UN-CIVILIZED LITTLE FAWN!
SHWOMM
I COULD EAT YOU RIGHT UP! ♡
MMMM! ♡
がばっ
GLOMP
Eeeeeek!

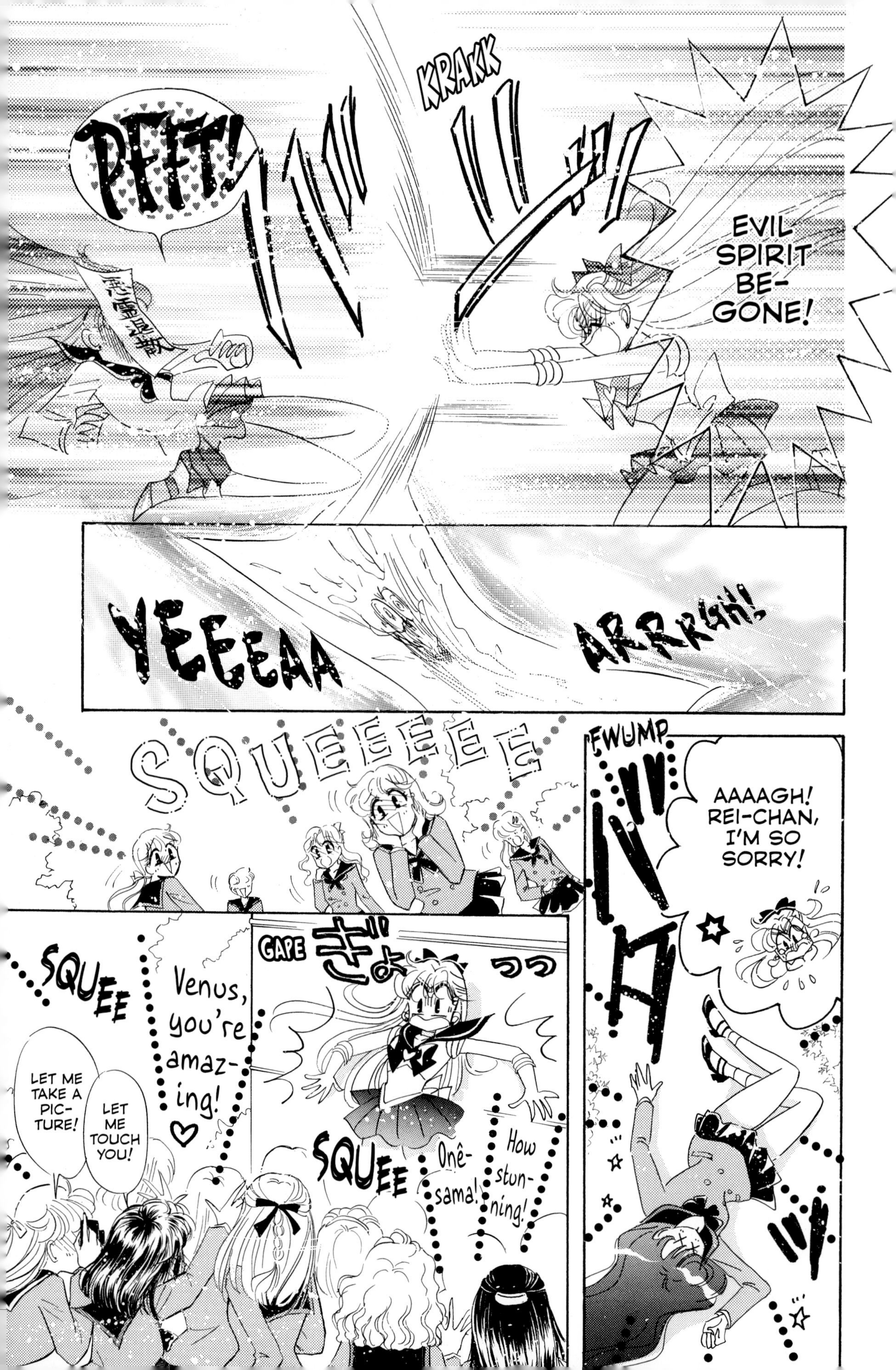
EVIL SPIRIT BE-GONE!
KRAKK
PFFT!
YEEEAA ARRRGH!
FWUMP
AAAAGH! REI-CHAN, I'M SO SORRY!
SQUEEEEEE
GAPE
ぎょ
っっ
How stun-ning!
Onê-sama!
SQUEE
Venus, you're amaz-ing! ♡
LET ME TOUCH YOU!
LET ME TAKE A PIC-TURE!
SQUEE

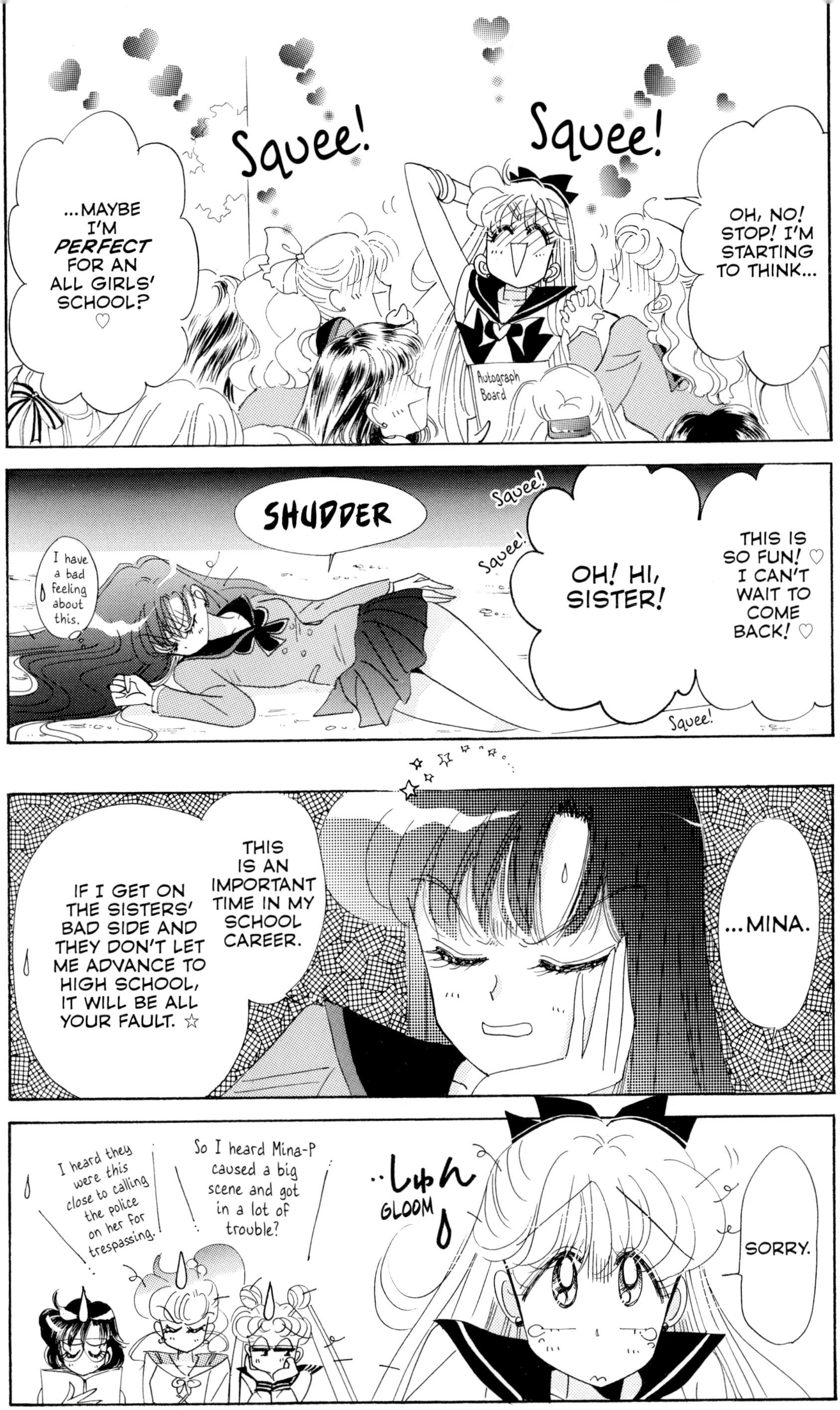
OH, NO! STOP! I'M STARTING TO THINK...
Squee!
Squee!
...MAYBE I'M *PERFECT* FOR AN ALL GIRLS' SCHOOL? ♡
Autograph Board
THIS IS SO FUN! ♡ I CAN'T WAIT TO COME BACK! ♡
OH! HI, SISTER!
Squee!
Squee!
Squee!
SHUDDER
I have a bad feeling about this.
...MINA.
THIS IS AN IMPORTANT TIME IN MY SCHOOL CAREER.
IF I GET ON THE SISTERS' BAD SIDE AND THEY DON'T LET ME ADVANCE TO HIGH SCHOOL, IT WILL BE ALL YOUR FAULT. ☆
SORRY.
..しゅん
GLOOM
So I heard Mina-P caused a big scene and got in a lot of trouble?
I heard they were this close to calling the police on her for trespassing.

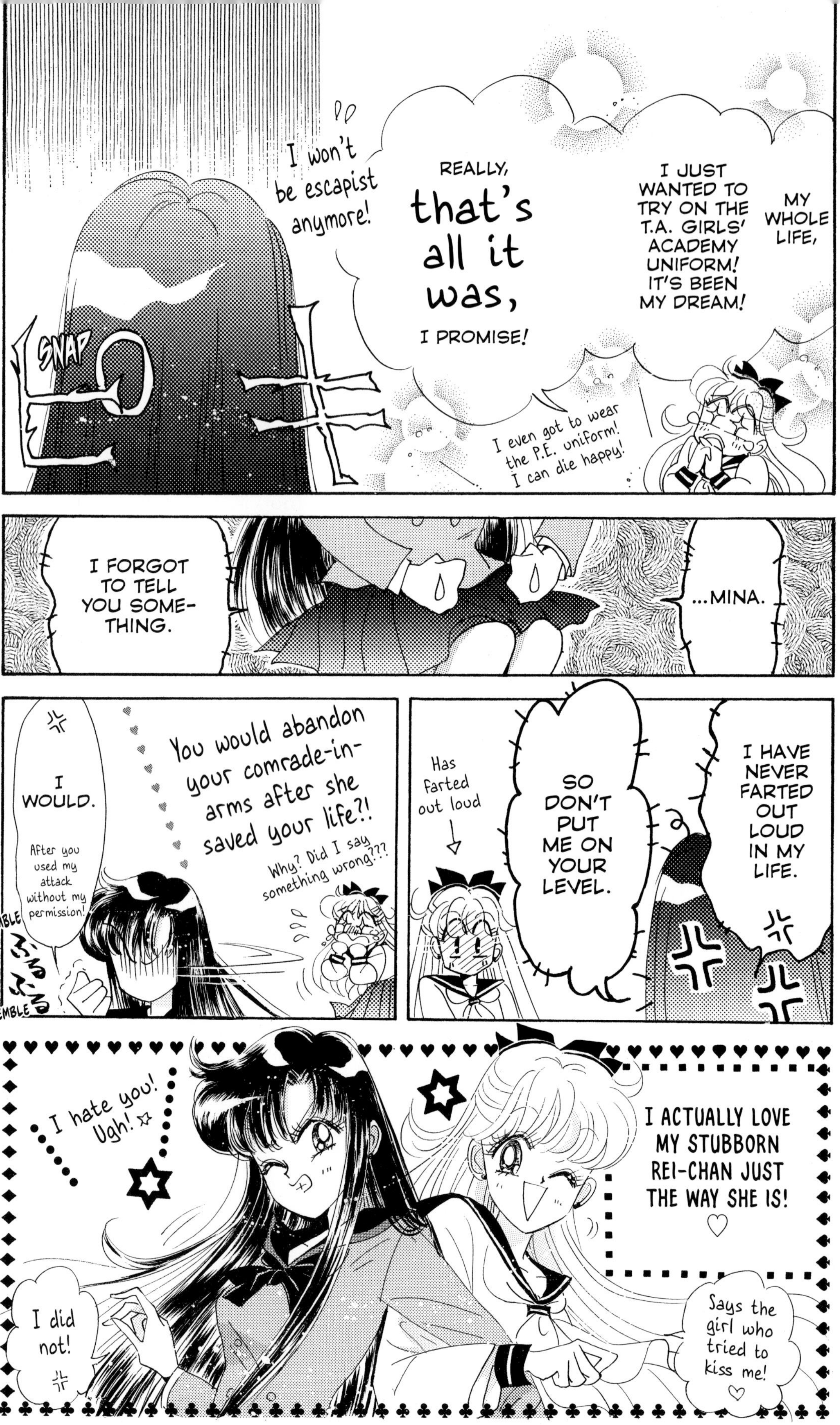
MY WHOLE LIFE,
I JUST WANTED TO TRY ON THE T.A. GIRLS' ACADEMY UNIFORM! IT'S BEEN MY DREAM!
REALLY, that's all it was, I PROMISE!
I even got to wear the P.E. uniform! I can die happy!
I won't be escapist anymore!
SNAP
...MINA.
I FORGOT TO TELL YOU SOMETHING.
I HAVE NEVER FARTED OUT LOUD IN MY LIFE.
SO DON'T PUT ME ON YOUR LEVEL.
Has farted out loud
You would abandon your comrade-in-arms after she saved your life?!
Why? Did I say something wrong???
I WOULD.
After you used my attack without my permission!
TREMBLE
ふるふる
TREMBLE
I ACTUALLY LOVE MY STUBBORN REI-CHAN JUST THE WAY SHE IS! ♡
Says the girl who tried to kiss me! ♡
I hate you! Ugh! ☆
I did not!

Translation Notes

The 50° hell I suffer during my races, page 8
To keep them lighter, and therefore faster, race cars are not equipped with air conditioning systems, so it can get extremely hot in the driver's seat. In fact, Haruka is being modest—in summer races, the inside of the car usually gets up to 60° C (about 140° F), and can be as hot as 70° C (about 160° F). By contrast, highs in the Amazon Rainforest usually get to about 33° C (91° F).

Spherated Steel, page 20
The Japanese name of Ves Ves's attack is *tama-hagane,* where *hagane* means "steel" and *tama,* which means "sphere" when used by the Amazoness Quartet, also means "gem." *Tamahagane* is a specific type of Japanese steel, so named because it is as precious as a gem in value, and is used to make bladed tools like swords and knives. "Spherated" is a play on "serrated," referring to a knife that has more of a saw-like edge than a straight one. Ves Ves's knives may not actually be serrated, but they are a very high quality.

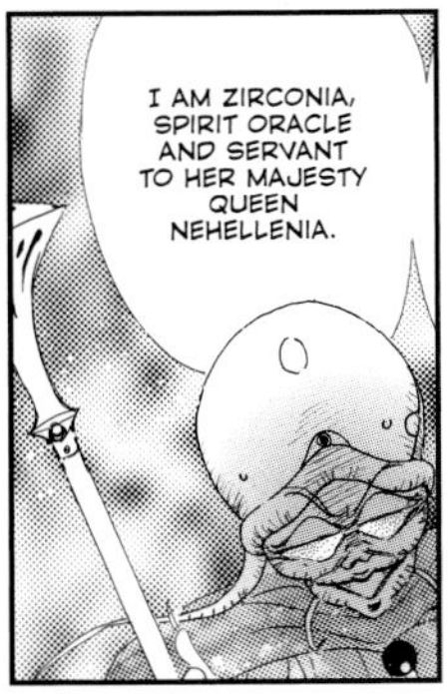
I AM ZIRCONIA, SPIRIT ORACLE AND SERVANT TO HER MAJESTY QUEEN NEHELLENIA.

Spirit oracle, page 35
The title Zirconia gives herself is *reikon dôshi,* where *reikon* means "soul" or "spirit," and *dôshi* gets a little more interesting. By itself, the word *dôshi* refers to a member of Taoist clergy and can be translated as "priest." The word is also used as a Japanese translation of the word "magus," referring a sage or a sorcerer, although it is not the same word used by the Witches 5 when talking about being promoted to Magus (that would be *hijutsushi,* "practitioner of the secret arts"). There is at least one example of *Sailor Moon* merchandise (a trading card) that calls Zirconia a *reikon dôshi* using different *kanji* characters, which would make her a "guide" or "teacher" of spirits. Either way, the impression given is that Zirconia has powers that involve communicating with the spirits of those who sleep, and so the translators have chosen to call her an oracle, someone who speaks with and delivers messages from those in realms beyond.

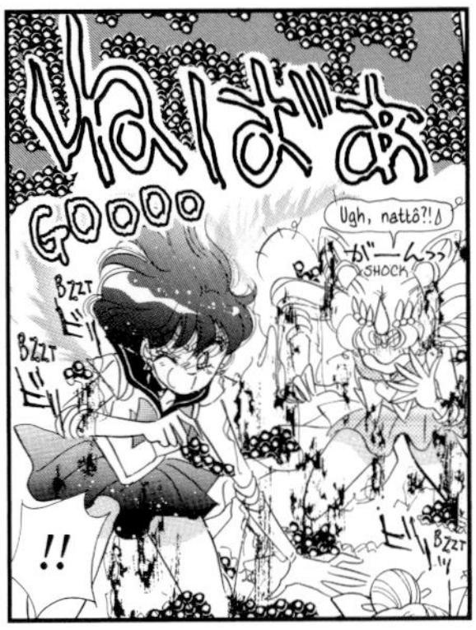
GOOOO
Ugh, nattô?!
SHOCK
BZZT
BZZT
!!
BZZT

Sphere'n'Nattô, page 44
The Japanese name of this spell is *tama-nattô,* referring to a variety of dishes involved eggs (*tamago*) and, more importantly, *nattô. Nattô* is a Japanese dish of fermented soy beans with soy sauce and *karashi* mustard. This food is very sticky, which would make it rather effective in slowing down one's opponents.

Powder and Sphere, page 44
The Japanese name of Jun Jun's attack is *tama-gusuri,* which is an alternate pronunciation of the *kanji* characters making up the word *dan'yaku,* meaning "bullets and gunpowder," or "powder and ball." Technically, the *tama-gusuri* pronunciation refers specifically to gunpowder, but Jun Jun changed the "bullet" character to "sphere" anyway, so it can mean whatever she wants.

Silence Wall, page 45
The *kanji* characters for this attack literally mean "unmovable fortress wall."

Silence Glaive Surprise, page 57
The *kanji* characters for this attack specify that it is a "Silence Glaive surprise **attack.**"

Spheretian Blinds, page 46
The Japanese name of this attack is *tama-sudare,* referring to a type of bamboo screen (*sudare*) that has been used in Japan for centuries to create shade, keep bugs away, block the wind, etc.—similar to shutters or blinds in the West. Since *tama* can mean "jewel," a *tama-sudare* is a bamboo screen that has been decorated with precious gems. "Spheretian Blinds" is a play on "Venetian blinds."

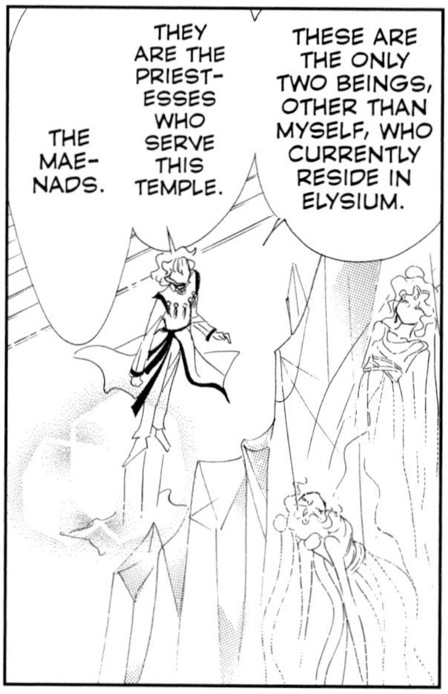
THESE ARE THE ONLY TWO BEINGS, OTHER THAN MYSELF, WHO CURRENTLY RESIDE IN ELYSIUM.
THEY ARE THE PRIEST-ESSES WHO SERVE THIS TEMPLE.
THE MAE-NADS.

Maenads, page 64
There has been some debate as to the origins of the Maenads' title. A straight transliteration of their Japanese name is *menaado,* which reflects the French *Ménade* (Maenad in English), the word for the priestesses of Dionysus, the Greek god of wine and wild partying. However, their name literally means "mad ones," describing their wild, and even violent, natures—natures that don't seem to be shared by these priestesses of Elysium.

The previous edition of this manga offered a theory that these twins were actually named after the Menae—the 50 daughters of Selene and Endymion, representing the individual months in a four-year Olympiad. The connection to the Moon and her lover does lend credence to the theory as it relates to *Sailor Moon.*

The translators of this edition feel a more likely theory is that the priestesses of Elysium were named for the Japanese cosmetic company, Menard. Although the English spelling is different, the company has officially stated that they named themselves after the Greek Maenads (potentially based on the French pronunciation), not because of their drunken revelry, but because they see the Maenads as goddesses of beauty. This seems quite fitting for a series where Guardians transform by calling for their planet's makeup. Furthermore, the cosmetics company runs a resort and spa, which may be considered by some to be a sort of Elysian paradise.

Castles, page 184
Each of the Solar System's princesses has a castle named for a satellite of her mother planet. While Mars's castle is named for both of the planet's moons (it wouldn't be fair to Phobos or Deimos to leave one of them out), most of the castles are named after the planet's largest satellite. Mercury and Venus don't have natural satellites, so their castles share names with NASA probes that were sent to study the planets, presumably long after the castles came into existence.

Eternal Tiare, page 192
A direct transliteration of the name is *etaanaru tiaru*, which most closely resembles the English word "eternal" and the French word *tiare*, meaning "tiara." When the translators discovered this French connection, they reexamined the events of the previous chapter and realized that it was when Super Sailor Moon removed her tiara that she held a shining power in her hands which transformed into the Holy Grail. From that moment on, Sailor Moon wore no tiara, so it is not unthinkable that her tiara—the weapon she had before she ever found the Silver Crystal—has now become the weapon she uses in her most powerful state.

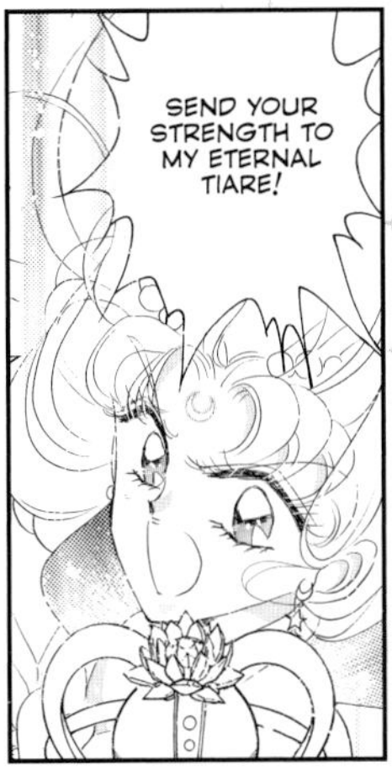
SEND YOUR STRENGTH TO MY ETERNAL TIARE!

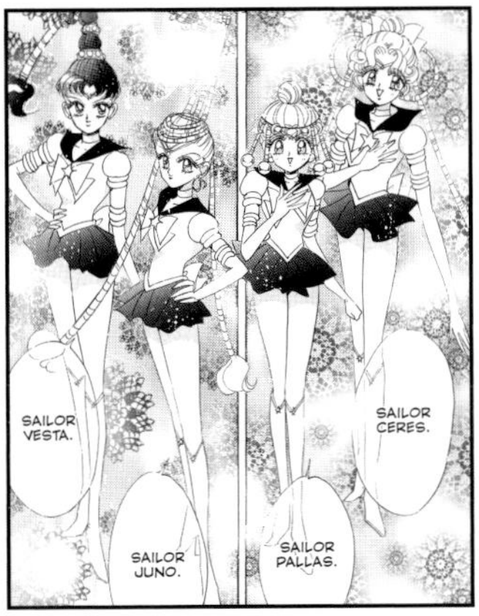
SAILOR CERES.
SAILOR PALLAS.
SAILOR JUNO.
SAILOR VESTA.

Four of the Solar System's asteroids, page 223
The members of the Sailor Quartet take their names from the first four objects discovered in the Solar System's asteroid belt, between Mars and Jupiter. The Japanese word for asteroid is *shôwakusei,* which literally means "little (or perhaps *chibi*) planet."

Steamed chestnut *yôkan,* page 239
The dessert shown here that resembles a brownie is *kuri mushi yôkan,* which means *yôkan* that is made through steaming (*mushi*) and has chestnuts (*kuri*) in it. *Yôkan* is a jellied dessert made from red bean paste and water. Most commonly, it is made into a jelly by using agar—a substance that is something like gelatin, but *mushi yôkan* is made by steaming and requires no agar.

I'm telling Sensei, page 243
It may seem odd to tattle on someone simply for buying food, but in Japan, some schools have rules against buying food on the way to or from school. The rules are old and many people question them today, but in Momoko's time, they were still in full force.

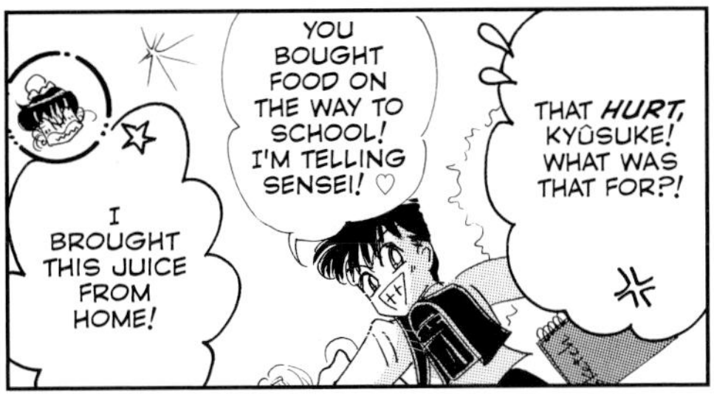
THAT *HURT,* KYÛSUKE! WHAT WAS THAT FOR?!
YOU BOUGHT FOOD ON THE WAY TO SCHOOL! I'M TELLING SENSEI! ♡
I BROUGHT THIS JUICE FROM HOME!

Lord Magistrate, page 246
Here Usagi has assumed the role of a tragic heroine in a historical drama. In many standard good-versus-evil historical dramas, the stock villain is the evil magistrate who has let his power corrupt him absolutely, and is much like the evil landlord in Western melodrama who will force the beautiful heroine to marry him as punishment for failure to pay the rent—or in the case of the evil magistrate, failure to pay the land tax. Of course, she doesn't love him, so she says, "Please, anything but that!"

***Anmitsu,* page 251**
Anmitsu is a Japanese dessert consisting of cubes of agar jelly (jelly made from red algae). It is served with red bean paste, fruit, and other toppings.

Resin the Genius Loci, page 252
Latin for "spirit of a place," the term 'genius loci' is used in modern times to describe the atmosphere or feel of a place, but originally it referred to a spirit who resided in a place as its guardian. In this series, it would seem that the genii locorum (plural for genius loci) are more interested in guarding themselves and their locales than in helping the people inhabiting those places.

This particular Genius Loci is named Resin, after the material dentists use to fill cavities.

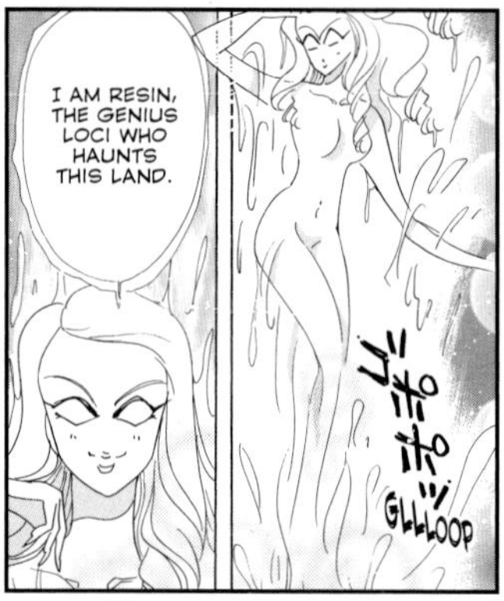
I AM RESIN, THE GENIUS LOCI WHO HAUNTS THIS LAND.
GLLLOOP

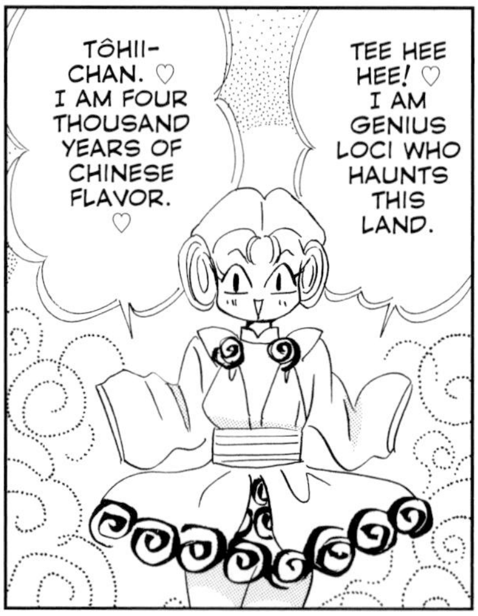
TEE HEE HEE! ♡ I AM GENIUS LOCI WHO HAUNTS THIS LAND.
TÔHII-CHAN. ♡ I AM FOUR THOUSAND YEARS OF CHINESE FLAVOR. ♡

Tôhii-chan, page 285
The name of this Genius Loci has many different puns in it, but the most relevant one to Makoto is that *tôhi* means "escapism," as in escaping the reality of entrance exams in favor of her fantasy world. It can also refer to procrastination. The reading also applies to the Chinese *hinoki* (a type of spruce), which would explain her "Chinese" accent. It's worth noting that the speech pattern manga artists tend to attribute to characters from China is actually the result of a simplified Japanese that was taught to foreigners soon after Japan ended its isolation policies around the middle of the 19th century. The idea behind it was that foreigners didn't need to learn all the complexities of Japanese grammar, but could get their point across with grammatical shortcuts. In modern times, the speech pattern has come to be associated with the Chinese, but in reality it was used by foreigners of all nationalities.

Because Tôhii-chan spells her name with an extra I, her name also sounds like "toffee," a candy made from butter and sugar that would fit right in with the cute, lovely things that Makoto so desperately desires. It is also a fitting name for a spirit that thrives on sugar energy.

As for her line about "four thousand years of Chinese flavor," it's common knowledge in Japan, whether it's true or not, that China has a history of four thousand years. This idea was emphasized back in the 1980s by popular commercials for Myojo Foods' instant ramen, Chûkazanmai, a name which roughly means "full of Chinese flavor." The slogan for this ramen was, "Four thousand years of Chinese flavor."

Sugar energy, page 285
The sugar energy, or *tôki*, that Tôhii-chan uses to attract her prey would be especially tempting to escapists because *tô* can also mean "escape."

Correspondence courses, page 298
More accurately, the system Ami refers to could be translated as "correspondence correction." A student can send in to a mail-order company for a practice test, and after they take the test and send it back, the publisher will grade the test and return it.

Mock-Exam Marauder, page 299
In Japanese, Ami is known as the *moshi arashi,* meaning she goes around wreaking havoc (*arashi*) on mock exams (*moshi*). The translators have chosen the English word "marauder," as it means someone who roams around in quest of plunder—or in this case, mock-exam supremacy.

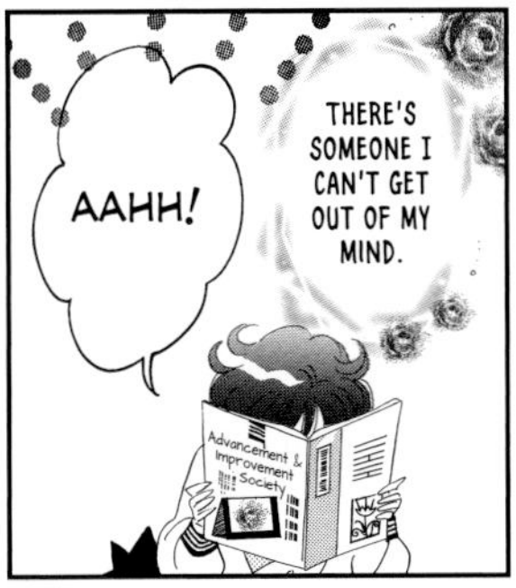

THERE'S SOMEONE I CAN'T GET OUT OF MY MIND.
AAHH!
Advancement & Improvement Society

Advancement & Improvement Society, page 300
The correspondence course publication seems to be a joint venture between Shinken (Advancement) Seminars and Zôshinkai (Improvement Society). In other words, it's the names of two real life publishers of correspondence tests, combined into one fictional one.

Give the shirt off my back, page 304
There is a saying in Japanese used in reference to helping people that translates to "to strip a layer of skin," but of course it's not meant literally. It comes from the days when everyone wore kimono, and the "skin" in question actually refers to the kimono. When helping with physical tasks, the sleeves of the kimono would get in the way, so in order to get more involved, the helper would take his arm out of one sleeve of the kimono, thus bearing his arm and shoulder. In other words, it means the helper is ready to engage in some hard work.

Oooh dun-dun-dun-dun, page 309
Written "hyuu doro doro" in Japanese, this is the sound of ghostly apparitions. It's a sound effect used in Japanese theater (mainly kabuki) when specters appear on stage. The "oooh" is created by a high-pitched flute and sounds like a ghostly wail. The "dun-dun-dun-dun" is the beating of a large drum. This sound effect can be accompanied by pyrotechnic effects, also called "hyuu doro doro," representing ghost fire.

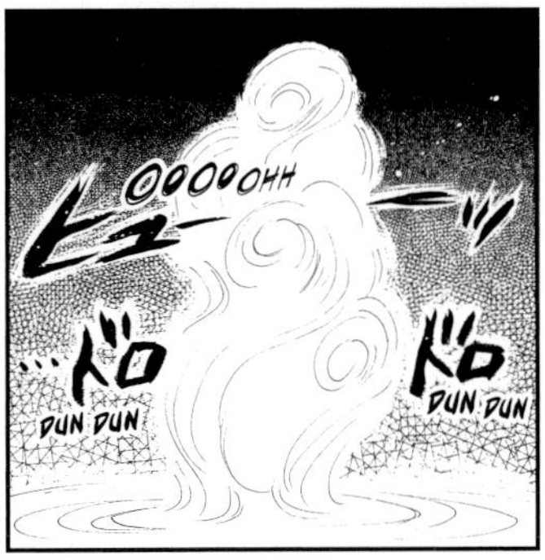

OOOOOHH
DUN DUN
DUN DUN

Bonnôn and the temple school, page 309
A temple school, or *terakoya*, is the Edo Era equivalent of a private school for commoners. Schooling wasn't mandatory at the time, so they would have been attended by students who were truly interested in learning. As the name suggests, these schools were built on Buddhist temple grounds, which would be why Bonnôn takes her name from the Buddhist concept of *bonnô,* often translated as "worldly desires." The word is the Japanese term for *klesha*, and refers to anything that would cloud the mind and prevent someone from obtaining enlightenment and lead to unwholesome actions.

You're going down, page 315

Much to the translators' dismay, immediately after a Sailor Guardian introduces herself, she will almost always say something along the lines of, "And here I am!" In this series, the word used is *sanjô*, which roughly means "coming to call," and has been translated to a variety of different phrases in English. In other hero series, sometimes after the hero introduces him or herself, they will use a different word which means roughly the same thing: *kenzan*. However, the word is actually a misreading of the *kanji* used to write it, and should be pronounced *genzan*. So here, Sailor Mercury says, "Sailor Mercury *genzan!* (Sailor Mercury is here to fight you!)", then takes the opportunity to correct all the superheroes who have been saying it wrong, by reiterating, "Not *kenzan, genzan*." The translators attempted to replicate this effect by using "you're" and "your."

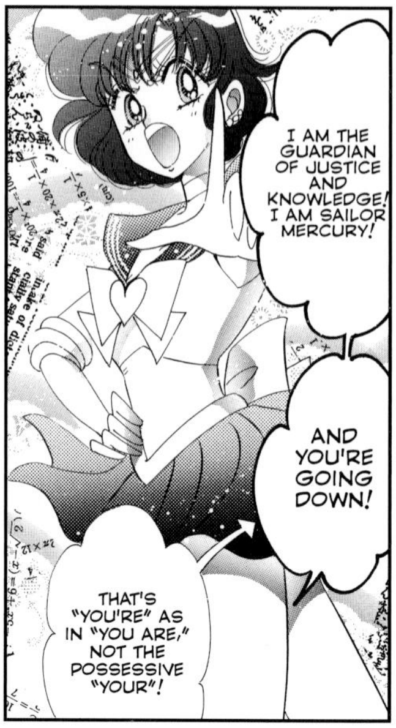

I AM THE GUARDIAN OF JUSTICE AND KNOWLEDGE! I AM SAILOR MERCURY!
AND YOU'RE GOING DOWN!
THAT'S "YOU'RE" AS IN "YOU ARE," NOT THE POSSESSIVE "YOUR"!

Mercurius's true identity, page 318

Mercurius's real name is Kurume Suuri, or Suuri Kurume in Japanese naming order. *Suuri* means "mathematical," and *kurume* means "swirly eyes," referring to near-sighted nerds whose glasses make their eyes look swirly. In other words, he's a math nerd. To get the name Mercurius, he spelled his name backwards, using the Japanese syllabary. So su-u-ri-ku-ru-me becomes me-ru-ku-ri-u-su, which miraculously becomes the Japanese pronunciation of the Latin word for Mercury.

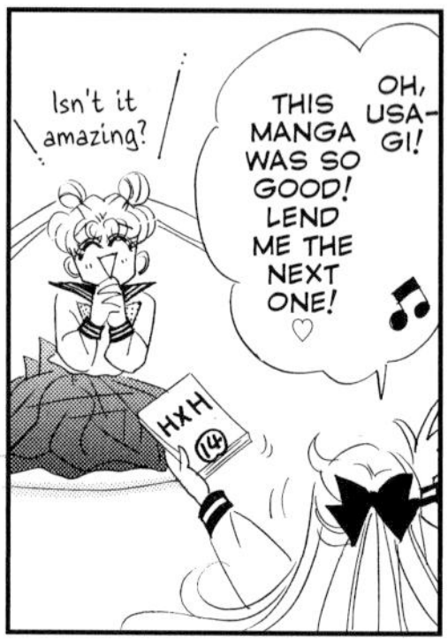

OH, USAGI!
THIS MANGA WAS SO GOOD! LEND ME THE NEXT ONE! ♡
Isn't it amazing?
HxH 14

Usagi's time-traveling manga, page 322

The manga Minako has borrowed from Usagi is *Hunter x Hunter*, volume 14 of which was published six and a half years after the appearance of this story. In fact, when this short story was first published, the title of the manga was *Kakugo no Susume*, published in English as *Apocalypse Zero*, but various tweaks were made to the *Sailor Moon* manga when it was re-released for its tenth anniversary. One of the changes is that this manga became *Hunter x Hunter*, possibly as a tribute to its author, Naoko Takeuchi's manga-artist husband, Yoshihiro Togashi.

***Candy Candy*, page 332**

Candy Candy is a classic anime and manga about an orphan girl in the United States at the start of the 20th century. She eventually went to a boarding school in England, where she fell in with the wrong crowd and was sent to detention hall.

A Kodansha Comics Trade Paperback Original
Sailor Moon Eternal Edition volume 8 copyright © 2014 Naoko Takeuchi
English translation copyright © 2020 Naoko Takeuchi
First published in Japan in 2014 by Kodansha Ltd., Tokyo.

Published in the United States by Kodansha Comics, an imprint of
Kodansha USA Publishing, LLC, New York.

Publication rights for this English edition arranged through
Kodansha Ltd, Tokyo.

ISBN 978-1-63236-595-8

Printed in China.

www.kodanshacomics.com

9 8 7 6 5 4 3 2 1

Translation: Alethea Nibley & Athena Nibley
Lettering: Lys Blakeslee
Additional lettering: James Dashiell
Editing: Lauren Scanlan
Kodansha Comics edition cover design by Phil Balsman